July 8   CH 1   ✓

     15   2   ✓

     22   4   ✓

     29   5-6
              Review for Exam #1 (Red pen)   ✓

Aug   5   Exam #1   ✓
              CH 7
              CH 8

Aug 12   CH 9 + 10   ✓

Aug 19   CH 11 + 13
              Review for Exam #2 (Red pen)   ✓

Aug 26   Exam #2   ✓
              CH 15 + 16

Sept 2   CH 17
              Group Presentations   ☆

Sept 9   CH 18   + Review for Exam
                                     (Red pen)
              Group Presentations

Sept 16   Exam #3

              Exam 1 = CH 1-6
              Exam 2 = CH 7-11 + 13
              Exam 3 = CH 15-18

HUMAN RESOURCES AND PERSONNEL MANAGEMENT

McGraw-Hill Series in Management
Fred Luthans and Keith Davis, Consulting Editors

ARNOLD AND FELDMAN: Organizational Behavior
BARTOL AND MARTIN: Management
BERNARDIN AND RUSSELL: Human Resource Management: An Experiential Approach
BOONE AND BOWEN: Great Writings in Management and Organizational Behavior
BOONE AND KURTZ: Management
BOVEÉ, THILL, WOOD, AND DOVEL: Management
CASCIO: Managing Human Resources: Productivity, Quality of Work Life, Profits
CERTO AND PETER: Selected Cases in Strategic Management
CERTO AND PETER: Strategic Management: A Focus on Process
CERTO AND PETER: Strategic Management: Concepts and Applications
DAUGHTREY AND RICKS: Contemporary Supervision: Managing People and Technology
DAVIDSON AND DE LA TORRE: Managing the Global Corporation: Case Studies in Strategy and Management
DESS AND MILLER: Strategic Management
DILWORTH: Operations Management: Design, Planning, and Control for Manufacturing and Services
DILWORTH: Production and Operations Mangement
DOBLER, BURT, AND LEE: Purchasing and Materials Management: Text and Cases
FELDMAN AND ARNOLD: Managing Individual and Group Behavior in Organizations
FREDERICK, POST, AND DAVIS: Business and Society: Management, Public Policy, Ethics
HODGETTS AND LUTHANS: International Management
HOFFMAN AND MOORE: Business Ethics: Readings and Cases in Corporate Morality
JAUCH AND GLUECK: Business Policy and Strategic Management
JAUCH AND GLUECK: Strategic Management and Business Policy
JAUCH AND TOWNSEND: Cases in Strategic Management and Business Policy
KATZ AND KOCHAN: An Introduction to Collective Bargaining and Industrial Relations
KOONTZ AND WEIHRICH: Essentials of Management
KOPELMAN: Managing Productivity in Organizations: A Practical, People-Oriented Perspective
KURILOFF, HEMPHILL, AND CLOUD: Starting and Managing the Small Business
LEVIN, RUBIN, STINSON, AND GARDNER: Quantitative Approaches to Management

LUTHANS: Organizational Behavior

LUTHANS AND THOMPSON: Contemporary Readings in Organizational Behavior

MILES: Theories of Management: Implications for Organizational Behavior and Development

MILES AND SNOW: Organizational Strategy, Structure, and Process

MILLS. Labor-Management Relations

MITCHELL AND LARSON: People in Organizations: An Introduction to Organizational Behavior

MOLANDER: Responsive Capitalism: Case Studies in Corporate Social Conduct

MONKS: Operations Management: Theory and Problems

NEWSTROM AND DAVIS: Organizational Behavior: Human Behavior at Work

NEWSTROM AND DAVIS: Organizational Behavior: Readings and Exercises

PEARCE AND ROBINSON: Corporate Strategies: Readings from Business Week

PORTER AND MCKIBBIN: Management Education and Development: Drift or Thrust into the 21st Century?

PRASOW AND PETERS: Arbitration and Collective Bargaining: Conflict Resolution in Labor Relations

QUICK AND QUICK: Organizational Stress and Preventive Management

RUE AND HOLLAND: Strategic Management: Concepts and Experiences

RUGMAN, LECRAW, AND BOOTH: International Business: Firm and Environment

SAYLES: Leadership: Managing in Real Organizations

SCHLESINGER, ECCLES, AND GABARRO: Managing Behavior in Organizations: Text, Cases and Readings

SCHROEDER: Operations Management: Decision Making in the Operations Function

STEERS AND PORTER: Motivation and Work Behavior

STEINER: Industry, Society, and Change: A Casebook

STEINER AND STEINER: Business, Government, and Society: A Managerial Perspective, Text and Cases

STEINHOFF AND BURGESS: Small Business Management Fundamentals

SUTERMEISTER: People and Productivity

WALKER: Human Resource Strategy

WEIHRICH: Management Excellence: Productivity through MBO

WEIHRICH AND KOONTZ: Management: A Global Perspective

WERTHER AND DAVIS: Human Resources and Personnel Management

WOFFORD, GERLOFF, AND CUMMINS: Organizational Communications: The Keystone to Managerial Effectiveness

YOFFIE: International Trade and Competition

HUMAN RESOURCES AND PERSONNEL MANAGEMENT

FOURTH EDITION

William B. Werther, Jr., Ph.D.
University of Miami

Keith Davis, Ph.D., Emeritus
Arizona State University

McGRAW-HILL, INC.
New York   St. Louis   San Francisco   Auckland   Bogotá   Caracas
Lisbon   London   Madrid   Mexico   Milan   Montreal   New Delhi
Paris   San Juan   Singapore   Sydney   Tokyo   Toronto

Human Resources and Personnel Management

Copyright © 1993, 1989, 1985, 1981 by McGraw-Hill, Inc. All rights reserved. Printed in the United States of America. Except as permitted under the United States Copyright Act of 1976, no part of this publication may be reproduced or distributed in any form or by any means, or stored in a data base or retrieval system, without the prior written permission of the publisher.

2 3 4 5 6 7 8 9 0 D O C D O C 9 0 9 8 7 6 5 4 3

ISBN 0-07-069551-2

This book was set in New Caledonia by Business Media Resources.
The editors were Lynn Richardson and Dan Alpert; the production supervisor was Friederich W. Schulte. Project supervision was done by Business Media Resources.
R. R. Donnelley & Sons Company was printer and binder.

Library of Congress Cataloging-in-Publication Data

Werther, William B.
    Human resources and personnel management / William B. Werther, Jr. and Keith Davis.—4th ed.
      p. cm.
    Includes index.
    ISBN 0-07-069551-2
      1. Personnel management.   I. Davis, Keith, 1918-   II. Title
HF5549.W439   1993
658.3—dc20
                                                                                            92-10066

ABOUT THE AUTHORS

WILLIAM B. WERTHER, JR. is the Samuel N. Friedland Professor of Executive Management at the University of Miami's School of Business Administration, where he was honored with the school's first endowed professorship. His teaching and research interests include Corporate Strategy and Human Resources.

Dr. Werther is an award-winning author. *Dear Boss* (Meadowbrook, 1989), and *Productivity Through People* (West, 1986) are his most recent books. Besides translations into Spanish, Portuguese, Chinese, Norwegian, and French among his seven books, he also has authored seventy articles for *California Management Review, National Productivity Review,* and other journals. His background includes work as a consulting editor to a dozen publishers and editorial board memberships on several management journals.

Professor Werther stays active as an international corporate and Human Resource Management strategist. His experience includes international teaching assignments in Germany, Portugal, Chile, Mexico, Canada and the Bahamas. He has also worked for the White House Conference on Productivity and the American Productivity and Quality Center. Past or current clients include AT&T, Anheuser-Busch, Bell Canada, Citicorp, Dial, General Motors, Hershey Foods, Hewlett-Packard, IBM, NASA, State Farm Insurance, Sun Bank/Miami, TRW, and scores of others. His organization expertise has been sought by the U.S. House of Representatives, Arizona State Senate, *Fortune, The Wall Street Journal, The Washington Post, U.S. News and World Report, Nation's Business,* the ABC Radio Network, and The Nightly Business Report (PBS). As a result, Werther also is a frequently requested speaker at conventions, conferences, and management meetings, having addressed a wide variety of groups and conducted more than 1,000 management seminars and workshops.

He serves the local community as a labor arbitrator for both the AAA and the FMCS. From 1980 to 1982, he chaired the Public Employment Relations Board for the City of Phoenix. He also works with the legal community as an expert witness involving employee relations, wrongful discharge, and economic worth cases. Additionally, he serves on several boards of directors for non-profit organizations and was a gubernatorial appointee to the International Currency and Barter Exchange Commitee of Florida.

Werther was an N.D.E.A. Title IV Fellow at the University of Florida, where he earned a Ph.D. in Economics and Business Administration (Phi Beta Kappa) in 1971. Prior to joining the faculty at the University of Miami in 1985, he was a Professor of Management at Arizona State University for 14 years.

KEITH DAVIS is professor emeritus of management at Arizona State University, College of Business, and a fellow in both the Academy of Management and the International Academy of Management. He is the author of prominent books on management and the former consulting editor for 135 books in the McGraw-Hill Series in Management. Prior to entering the teaching field, Davis was a personnel specialist in industry and a personnel manager in government.

He received his Ph.D. from Ohio State University and has taught at the University of Texas and at Indiana University. His fields of work are organizational behavior, personnel management, and social issues in management. Davis has been visiting professor at a number of universities, including the University of Western Australia and the University of Central Florida. He also has served as a consultant to a number of business and government organizations, including Mobil Oil Company, Texaco, the U.S. Internal Revenue Service, and the state of Hawaii.

Davis is former president of the Academy of Management, and he received the National Human Relations Award from the Society for Advancement of Management. He has been a national Beta Gamma Sigma distinguished scholar and is an accredited Senior Professional in Human Resources. In 1992 he received the Distinguished Educator Award from the Academy of Management.

Two of Davis's most popular books are (with John W. Newstrom) *Organizational Behavior: Human Behavior at Work* (9th ed., 1993) and (with William C. Frederick and James E. Post) *Business and Society* (7th ed., 1992), both published by McGraw-Hill Book Company. He also has contributed chapters to more than 100 other books and is the author of over 150 articles in journals such as *Harvard Business Review*, *Academy of Management Journal*, *Management International*, and *California Management Review*. Four of his books have been translated into other languages.

*This book is dedicated to
the late Richard E. Werther
and to Sue Davis*

BRIEF CONTENTS

PREFACE xxvii

PART I • FRAMEWORKS AND CHALLENGES

1 / HUMAN RESOURCE MANAGEMENT CHALLENGES, 02
2 / ENVIRONMENTAL CHALLENGES, 35
3 / INTERNATIONAL CHALLENGES, 65
4 / EQUAL EMPLOYMENT CHALLENGES, 86

PART II • PREPARATION AND SELECTION

5 / JOB ANALYSIS AND DESIGN, 120
6 / HUMAN RESOURCE PLANNING, 164
7 / RECRUITMENT, 194
8 / SELECTION, 228

PART III • DEVELOPMENT AND EVALUATION

9 / ORIENTATION AND PLACEMENT, 268
10 / TRAINING AND DEVELOPMENT, 305
11 / PERFORMANCE APPRAISAL, 337
12 / CAREER PLANNING, 375

PART IV • COMPENSATION AND PROTECTION

13 / COMPENSATION MANAGEMENT, 408
14 / INCENTIVES AND GAINSHARING, 440
15 / BENEFITS AND SERVICES, 463
16 / SECURITY, SAFETY, AND HEALTH, 496

PART V • EMPLOYEE RELATIONS AND ASSESSMENT

17 / EMPLOYEE RELATIONS CHALLENGES, 527
18 / UNION-MANAGEMENT RELATIONS, 558
19 / ASSESSING PERFORMANCE AND PROSPECTS, 592

GLOSSARY 623

INDEXES 653

CONTENTS

PREFACE, xxvii

PART I • FRAMEWORKS AND CHALLENGES

1 / Human Resource Management Challenges, 5

THE CENTRAL CHALLENGE, 8
The Response of Human Resource Management, 10
The Objectives of Human Resource Management, 11
Societal objectives, 11
Organizational objectives, 11
Functional objectives, 11
Personal objectives, 11
Human Resource Management Activities, 12
Key human resource activities, 13
Responsibility for human resource activities, 14

THE ORGANIZATION OF A HUMAN RESOURCE DEPARTMENT, 16
Departmental Components, 18
Key Roles in a Human Resource Department, 18
The Service Role of a Human Resource Department, 20

THE HUMAN RESOURCE MANAGEMENT MODEL, 22
A Systems Model, 22
I. Foundations and challenges, 24
II. Preparation and selection, 24
III. Compensation and protection, 25
IV. Employee relations and assessment, 25
An Applied Systems View, 25

PROACTIVE VERSUS REACTIVE HUMAN RESOURCE MANAGEMENT, 27

VIEWPOINTS OF HUMAN RESOURCE MANAGEMENT, 28

SUMMARY, 29

2 / Environmental Challenges, 35

HISTORICAL FOUNDATIONS, 38
Early Causes and Origins, 39
Scientific Management and Human Needs, 39
Modern Influences, 40

EXTERNAL CHALLENGES, 41
Work Force Diversity, 43
Cultural and attitudinal diversity, 44
Diversity through immigration and migration, 45
Diversity and human resource professionals, 46
Technological Challenges, 47
Economic Challenges, 49
Governmental Challenges, 50

ORGANIZATIONAL CHALLENGES, 50
Unions, 50
Information Systems, 51
Organizational Culture and Conflicts, 52

PROFESSIONAL CHALLENGES, 53
Certification, 54
Other Professional Requirements, 55

HUMAN RESOURCE MANAGEMENT IN PERSPECTIVE, 57

SUMMARY, 58

3 / International Challenges, 63

FRAMEWORKS AND INTERNATIONAL CHALLENGES, 67
Assumptions, 68
Departmental Structure, 68
Employee Rights, 69

INTERNATIONAL PREPARATION AND SELECTION, 70
International Recruitment, 71
International Selection, 72

INTERNATIONAL DEVELOPMENT AND EVALUATION, 73
Orientation, 73
Training and Development, 74
Evaluation and Career Development, 74

INTERNATIONAL COMPENSATION AND PROTECTION, 76

INTERNATIONAL EMPLOYEE RELATIONS AND ASSESSMENT, 76

INTERNATIONAL HUMAN RESOURCE MANAGEMENT CHALLENGES, 77
International Human Resource Troubleshooting, 77
International Challenges and Diversity, 77
Cultural Awareness, 79

SUMMARY, 80

4 / Equal Employment Challenges, 86

EQUAL EMPLOYMENT LAWS: AN OVERVIEW, 88

FEDERAL EQUAL EMPLOYMENT LAWS, 90
Title VII, 90
Disparate treatment, 92
Disparate impact, 92
Harassment, 94
Exceptions, 95
Employer retaliation, 97
Enforcement, 97
Remedies, 99
Americans with Disabilities Act, 100
Age Discrimination in Employment, 101
Equal Pay Act, 101
Comparable Worth, 102
Vietnam Era Veterans Readjustment Act, 103

STATE AND LOCAL FAIR EMPLOYMENT PRACTICES, 103

EXECUTIVE ORDERS, 104
Government Agencies, 104
Government Contractors, 105
Executive Orders and Equal Employment Laws, 105

AFFIRMATIVE ACTION, 106
Affirmative Action Issues, 107
Reverse discrimination, 107
Line managers, 107
Development of Affirmative Action Plans, 108

EQUAL OPPORTUNITY IN PERSPECTIVE, 110

SUMMARY, 112

PART II • PREPARATION AND SELECTION

5 / Job Analysis and Design, 123

JOB ANALYSIS INFORMATION: AN OVERVIEW, 126

COLLECTION OF JOB ANALYSIS INFORMATION, 127
Job Identification, 127
Questionnaire Development, 128
Status and identification, 128
Duties and responsibilities, 133
Human characteristics and working conditions, 133
Performance standards, 133
Data Collection, 133
Interviews, 133
Panel of experts, 134
Mail questionnaires, 134
Employee log, 134
Observation, 135
Combinations, 135

APPLICATIONS OF JOB ANALYSIS INFORMATION, 135
Job Descriptions, 135
Job summary and duties, 139
Working conditions, 139
Approvals, 139
Job Specifications, 140
Job Performance Standards, 140

THE HUMAN RESOURCE INFORMATION SYSTEM, 143
Legal Considerations, 144
Organization of the Database, 145

OVERVIEW OF JOB DESIGN, 145
Organizational Elements, 147
Mechanistic approach, 148
Work flow, 148
Ergonomics, 149
Work practices, 149
Environmental Elements, 149
Employee abilities and availability, 150
Social and cultural expectations, 150
Behavioral Elements, 150
Autonomy, 151
Variety, 151

Task identity, 152
Task significance, 152
Feedback, 152

BEHAVIORAL AND EFFICIENCY TRADEOFFS, 152
Graph A: Productivity versus Specialization, 153
Graph B: Satisfaction versus Specialization, 153
Graph C: Learning versus Specialization, 154
Graph D: Turnover versus Specialization, 154

TECHNIQUES OF JOB REDESIGN, 154
Underspecialization, 154
Overspecialization, 155
Job rotation, 155
Job enlargement, 155
Job enrichment, 155
Autonomous work groups, 156

SUMMARY, 157

6 / Human Resource Planning, 164

THE DEMAND FOR HUMAN RESOURCES, 168
Causes of Demand, 168
External challenges, 168
Organizational decisions, 169
Work force factors, 170
Forecasting Techniques, 171
Expert forecasts, 171
Trend projection forecasts, 172
Other forecasting methods, 172
Human Resource Requirements, 174

THE SUPPLY OF HUMAN RESOURCES, 175
Estimates of Internal Supply, 176
Human resource audits, 176
Succession planning, 180
Replacement charts and summaries, 181
Estimates of External Supply, 184
External needs, 184
Labor market analysis, 184
Community attitudes, 185
Demographics, 185

IMPLEMENTATION OF HUMAN RESOURCE PLANS, 186

SUMMARY, 188

7 / Recruitment, 194

CONSTRAINTS ON AND CHALLENGES OF RECRUITMENT, 197
- *Organizational Policies, 198*
  - Promote-from-within policies, 198
  - Compensation policies, 198
  - Employment Status policies, 198
  - International Hiring policies, 199
- *Human Resource Plans, 199*
- *Affirmative Action Plans, 199*
- *Recruiter Habits, 200*
- *Environmental Conditions, 200*
- *Job Requirements, 202*
- *Costs, 203*
- *Incentives, 203*

CHANNELS OF RECRUITMENT, 204
- *Walk-ins and Write-ins, 205*
- *Employee Referrals, 205*
- *Advertising, 206*
- *State Employment Security Agencies, 208*
- *Private Placement Agencies, 209*
- *Professional Search Firms, 209*
- *Educational Institutions, 210*
- *Professional Associations, 210*
- *Labor Organizations, 211*
- *Military Operations, 211*
- *Government Funded and Community Training Programs, 211*
- *Temporary Help Agencies, 212*
- *Leased Employees, 213*
- *Departing Employees, 213*
- *Open House, 214*
- *International Recruiting, 214*

JOB APPLICATION BLANKS, 216
- *Personal Data, 216*
- *Employment Status, 219*
- *Education and Skills, 219*
- *Work History, 219*
- *Military Background, 219*
- *Memberships, Awards, and Hobbies, 220*
- *References, 220*

Signature Line, 220

SUMMARY, 221

8 / Selection, 228
INPUTS AND CHALLENGES TO SELECTION, 230

SELECTION: AN OVERVIEW, 231
Internal Selection, 232
Selection Ratio, 232
Uniform Guidelines on Employee Selection, 233

PRELIMINARY RECEPTION: STEP 1, 235

EMPLOYMENT TESTS: STEP 2, 235
Test Validation, 236
Testing Tools and Cautions, 238

SELECTION INTERVIEW: STEP 3, 241
Types of Interviews, 242
Unstructured interviews, 243
Structured interviews, 243
Mixed interviews, 244
Behavioral interviews, 244
Stress interviews, 244
The Interview Process, 245
Interviewer preparation, 245
Creation of rapport, 246
Information exchange, 247
Termination, 248
Evaluation, 248
Interviewer Errors, 248
Interviewee Errors, 250

REFERENCES AND BACKGROUND CHECKS: STEP 4, 251
Bonding and Security Checks, 252
Immigration and Naturalization Rules, 253

MEDICAL EVALUATION: STEP 5, 253

SUPERVISORY INTERVIEW: STEP 6, 254

REALISTIC JOB PREVIEW: STEP 7, 254

HIRING DECISION: STEP 8, 255

OUTCOMES, PROCESS, AND FEEDBACK, 256

SUMMARY, 257

PART III • DEVELOPMENT AND EVALUATION

9 / Orientation and Placement, 271

PLACEMENT OBSTACLES TO PRODUCTIVITY, 273
Dissonance Reduction, 273
New Employee Turnover, 273

ORIENTATION PROGRAMS, 275
Socialization, 277
Content and Responsibilities for Orientation, 278
Opportunities and Pitfalls, 279
Benefits of Orientation Programs, 280
Orientation Follow-Up, 281
International Implications, 282

EMPLOYEE PLACEMENT, 283
Promotions, 284
Merit-based promotions, 284
Seniority-based promotions, 285
Transfers and Demotions, 285
Job Posting Programs, 286

SEPARATIONS, 287
Attrition, 288
Layoffs, 289
Termination, 291

ISSUES IN PLACEMENT, 292
Effectiveness, 293
Legal Compliance, 293
Prevention of Separations, 294
Voluntary resignations, 294
Retirement, 295
Death, 295
Layoffs, 295
Terminations, 297

SUMMARY, 297

10 / Training and Development, 305
STEPS TO TRAINING AND DEVELOPMENT, 310

Needs Assessment, 310
Training and Development Objectives, 312
Program Content, 313
Learning Principles, 313
   Participation, 314
   Repetition, 314
   Relevance, 314
   Transference, 315
   Feedback, 315

TRAINING AND DEVELOPMENT APPROACHES, 315
Job Instruction Training, 317
Job Rotation, 317
Apprenticeships and Coaching, 318
Lecture and Video Presentations, 318
Vestibule Training, 319
Role Playing and Behavior Modeling, 319
Case Study, 320
Simulation, 321
Self-study and Programmed Learning, 321
Laboratory Training, 322

EVALUATION OF TRAINING AND DEVELOPMENT, 322

DEVELOPMENT OF HUMAN RESOURCES, 324
Employee Obsolescence, 324
International and Domestic Work Force Diversity, 326
Technological Change, 327
Development and Affirmative Action, 327
Employee Turnover, 328

SUMMARY, 329

11 / *Performance Appraisal, 337*

ELEMENTS OF THE PERFORMANCE APPRAISAL SYSTEM, 340
Performance Standards, 342
Performance Measures, 343

PERFORMANCE APPRAISAL CHALLENGES, 344
Legal Constraints, 344
Rater Biases, 345
   The halo effect, 345
   The error of central tendency, 346
   The leniency and strictness bias, 346

Cross-cultural biases, 346
Personal prejudice, 346
The recency effect, 347
Reducing rater bias, 347

PAST-ORIENTED APPRAISAL METHODS, 347

Rating Scales, 348
Checklists, 348
Forced Choice Method, 349
Critical Incident Technique, 350
Behaviorally Anchored Rating Scales, 352
Field Review Method, 353
Performance Tests and Observations, 354
Comparative Evaluation Approaches, 355
Ranking method, 355
Forced distributions, 356
Point allocation method, 357
Paired comparisons, 357

FUTURE-ORIENTED APPRAISALS, 357

Self-Appraisals, 358
Management by Objectives, 359
Psychological Appraisals, 360
Assessment Centers, 360

IMPLICATIONS OF THE APPRAISAL PROCESS, 362

Training Raters and Evaluators, 362
Evaluation Interviews, 364

FEEDBACK FOR THE HUMAN RESOURCE FUNCTION, 366

SUMMARY, 366

12 / Career Planning, 375

CAREER PLANNING AND EMPLOYEE NEEDS, 381

HUMAN RESOURCE DEPARTMENTS AND CAREER PLANNING, 382

Career Education, 384
Information about Career Planning, 386
Career Counseling, 387
Employee self-assessment, 388
Environmental assessment, 388
Career counseling process, 389
Stalled Careers, 390

CAREER DEVELOPMENT, 391

Individual Career Development, 391
Job performance, 391
Exposure, 392
Resignations, 392
Organizational loyalty, 393
Mentors and sponsors, 393
Key subordinates, 394
Growth opportunities, 394
International experience, 395
Human Resource-Supported Career Development, 397
Management support, 398
Feedback, 399

SUMMARY, 400

PART IV • COMPENSATION AND PROTECTION

13 / Compensation Management, 411

OBJECTIVES OF COMPENSATION MANAGEMENT, 414

JOB ANALYSIS, 416

JOB EVALUATIONS, 416

Job Ranking, 416
Job Grading, 417
Factor Comparison Method, 417
Step 1: Determine the compensable factors, 418
Step 2: Determine key jobs, 418
Step 3: Apportion present wages for key jobs, 418
Step 4: Place key jobs on a factor comparison chart, 419
Step 5: Evaluate other jobs, 419
Point System, 421
Step 1: Determine critical factors, 421
Step 2: Determine the levels of factors, 421
Step 3: Allocate points to subfactors, 422
Step 4: Allocate points to levels, 422
Step 5: Develop the point manual, 422
Step 6: Apply the point system, 423

WAGE AND SALARY SURVEYS, 423

Sources of Compensation Data, 424
Survey Procedures, 424

PRICING JOBS, 425
Pay Levels, 425
The Compensation Structure, 426

CHALLENGES AFFECTING COMPENSATION, 428
Prevailing Wage Rates, 428
Union Power, 429
Government Constraints, 429
Comparable Worth and Equal Pay, 430
Wage and Salary Policies and Adjustments, 431
International Compensation Challenges, 431
Productivity and Costs, 432

SUMMARY, 433

14 / Incentives and Gainsharing, 440

INCENTIVES AND GAINSHARING ISSUES, 443
The Purpose of Nontraditional Compensation, 443
Eligibility and Coverage, 444
Payout Standards, 445
Administration, 445

INCENTIVE SYSTEMS, 446
Piecework, 446
Production Bonuses, 446
Commissions, 447
Maturity Curves, 447
Merit Raises, 447
Pay-for-knowledge Compensation, 448
Nonmonetary Incentives, 449
Executive Incentives, 449
International Incentives, 451

GAINSHARING APPROACHES, 452
Employee Ownership, 452
Production-Sharing Plans, 453
Profit-Sharing Plans, 454
Cost Reduction Plans, 454

SUMMARY, 457

15 / Benefits and Services, 463

THE ROLE OF INDIRECT COMPENSATION, 465
Societal Objectives, 465

Organizational Objectives, 465
Employee Objectives, 466

INSURANCE BENEFITS, 467
Health-Related Insurance, 467
Medical insurance, 468
Health maintenance organizations, 469
Vision insurance, 470
Dental insurance, 470
Mental health insurance, 471
Life Insurance, 471
Disability Insurance, 471
Other Related Benefits, 472

EMPLOYEE SECURITY BENEFITS, 472
Employment Income Security, 472
Retirement Security, 474
Developing a Retirement Plan, 474
ERISA, 475
Early retirement, 477
Retirement counseling, 477

TIME-OFF BENEFITS, 478
On-the-Job Breaks, 478
Sick Days and Well Pay, 478
Holidays and Vacations, 479
Leaves of Absence, 480

WORK SCHEDULING BENEFITS, 480
Shorter Workweeks, 480
Flextime, 480
Job Sharing, 481

EMPLOYEE SERVICES, 482
Educational Assistance, 482
Financial Services, 483
Social Services, 483
Child care, 484
Elder care, 485
Relocation programs, 485
Social service leave programs, 485

ADMINISTRATION OF BENEFITS AND SERVICES, 486
Problems in Administration, 486
Traditional Remedies, 487

Cafeteria Benefits: A Proactive Solution, 487

SUMMARY, 489

16 / Security, Safety, and Health, 496

FINANCIAL SECURITY, 499

Social Security, 499
Coverage and administration, 500
Implications for the human resource department, 501
Unemployment Compensation, 502
Coverage and administration, 502
Implications for human resource management, 503
Extended Medical Insurance under COBRA, 504
Coverage and administration, 504
Implications for human resource management, 505
Workers' Compensation, 505
Coverage and administration, 506
Implications for human resource management, 507

PHYSICAL SECURITY, 510

Implications of OSHA for the Workplace, 511
Coverage and administration, 511
Inspections, 513
Standards and appeals, 514
Participation by other governments, 515
Implications of OSHA for Human Resource Management, 517
Compliance, 517
Records, 518
Enforcement, 519
Employee rights, 521

SUMMARY, 521

PART V • EMPLOYEE RELATIONS AND ASSESSMENT

17 / Employee Relations Challenges, 531

THE HUMAN RESOURCE DEPARTMENT'S ROLE, 532

QWL THROUGH EMPLOYEE INVOLVEMENT, 534

QWL AND EI INTERVENTIONS, 536

Quality Circles, 537

Sociotechnical Systems, 538
Codeterminiation, 539
Autonomous Work Groups, 540

EMPLOYEE RELATIONS PRACTICES, 540
Employee Communication, 541
Downward communication systems, 542
Upward communication systems, 543
Employee Counseling, 547
Discipline, 548

EMERGING EMPLOYEE RELATIONS CHALLENGES, 550

SUMMARY, 551

18 / Union-Management Relations, 558

INTERNATIONAL COMPETITION, 560

THE LABOR-MANAGEMENT SYSTEM, 561
Unions and Human Resource Management, 562
Union Structure and Functions, 563
Local unions, 564
National unions, 565
Multiunion associations, 566
Government and Labor Relations Law, 566
National Labor Relations Act, 566
Labor Management Relations Act, 568
Labor-Management Reporting and Disclosure Act, 570

COOPERATION AND DISPUTE RESOLUTION, 570
Collective Bargaining, 572
Dispute Resolution, 574
Types and causes of grievances, 576
Handling grievances, 576
Arbitration, 577

UNION-MANAGEMENT COOPERATION, 578
Union-Management Attitudes, 580
Building Cooperation, 580
Obstacles to cooperation, 580
Cooperative methods, 581

THE CHALLENGES TO HUMAN RESOURCE MANAGEMENT, 584

SUMMARY, 585

19 / Assessing Performance and Prospects, 592

THE SCOPE OF HUMAN RESOURCE AUDITS, 595
Audit of Corporate Strategy, 596
Audit of the Human Resource Function, 597
Audit of Managerial Compliance, 598
Audit of Employee Satisfaction, 599

RESEARCH APPROACHES TO AUDITS, 600

TOOLS OF HUMAN RESOURCE RESEARCH, 602
Interviews, 603
Surveys, 604
Historical Analysis, 606
Safety and health audits, 606
Grievance audits, 606
Compensation audits, 607
Affirmative action audits, 607
Program and policy audits, 607
External Information, 608
Human Resource Research, 608
International Audits, 609

THE AUDIT REPORT, 609

HUMAN RESOURCE PROSPECTS FOR THE FUTURE, 610
Globalization, Diversity, and the Environmental Context, 611
Employee Rights, 613
Employee Performance and Productivity, 613
The Challenging Role of Human Resource Management, 614
Societal challenges, 614
Organizational and functional challenges, 615
Personal challenges, 615

SUMMARY, 615

Glossary, 623
Indexes, 653
Name Index, 653
Subject Index, 658

> *We believe that human resource departments play a pivotal and expanding role in shaping the success of domestic and international organizations.*
> —THE AUTHORS

THE ULTIMATE test of any college textbook is teacher and student acceptance. After three editions and hundreds of adoptions and readoptions, *Human Resources and Personnel Management* has passed the test of the marketplace. Perhaps even more gratifying, large numbers of students have retained their book for their professional libraries after course completion, suggesting that they too found real value in the book.

Adoptions of the book around the world have been led by the Canadian edition (adapted by Professors Hermann F. Schwind and Hari Das of Saint Mary's University), which expanded its role as the leading human resource textbook in Canada. The Spanish, Portuguese, and French translations—along with the international student edition, published in Singapore—gained additional adoptions around the world.

The book's global acceptance is attributed to its balanced coverage of both theory and practice. Students and instructors tell us it is understandably written and pragmatic in orientation. As we wrote in the preface of the first edition in 1981:

Although balanced and thorough coverage is the most important feature of the book, we believe that readers and instructors want more than that. Comments from colleagues and students convinced us that an introductory personnel management text must be readable and teachable. It should:

➤ *Capture the interest of readers*

➤ *Reflect the flavor and challenges of this exciting field*

➤ *Provide instructors with a flexible teaching tool*

In the fourth edition, we continue to stress the application-oriented approach of previous editions by further expanding the use of "real-life" examples, drawn from well known companies around the world. Not only do these examples add interest, but they give authentic insights into this dynamic field. And, given the increased globalization of organizations, this edition expands the discussion of international human resource management throughout the book. At the same time, we have updated the coverage in every chapter and added more extensive citations for those wishing to explore specific topics in greater depth.

Purpose

Our premise is that modern organizations are the most important innovations of our era. Organizations succeed by effectively and efficiently combining resources to implement their strategy. Central to any strategy, to any use of resources are the people employed by the organization. How well an organization obtains, maintains, and retains its human resources determines its success or failure. And the success or failure of our organizations shapes the well-being of every person on earth.

The purpose of this book is to explain the human resource department's role in dealing with employees. It introduces the challenges of human resource management and presents the key concepts, issues, and practices without being encyclopedic. Out focus is practical. We emphasize the applications of theory and practice so that readers will gain a useful understanding of human resource management, whether they seek careers in this field or in other disciplines.

Quality and Acceptance

The guiding principle of this revision was to produce a highly readable book—one that was clear, interesting, and of high quality. A study by George S. Cole of Shippensburg University, published in the *Academy of Management Review*, compared several leading human resource textbooks, including ours.[*] It rated our second edition as the highest-quality personnel textbook. His study also found this book received the most favorable reaction from students and the highest proportion of users saying that they "certainly would" adopt the book again.

[*]George S. Cole, "Managing the Human Resources of Work: A Review of Personnel/Human Resource Management Texts," *Academy of Management Review*, Oct. 1985, pp. 881–888.

We believe this edition improves on its previous editions.

Balanced Coverage and Revision Highlights

The book seeks balanced coverage among traditional topics and emerging challenges to human resource management. Theory and practices are supplemented with "real-life" examples and research summaries, drawn from our experience and the literature. We assume no prior knowledge of the field by the reader.

The fourth edition contains an extensive content revision to reflect the rapid changes in the field. Greater attention has been paid to the department's role as a source of competitive advantage in the on-going internationalization of organizations.

The result has been a new chapter, "International Challenges," added as the third chapter of the book to set the tone and importance of international human resource management for the remainder of the book.

To keep the text at a usable length while adding new materials, the book's nineteen chapters have been reorganized into five parts:

- **PART I**   **FRAMEWORKS AND CHALLENGES**
- **PART II**   **PREPARATION AND SELECTION**
- **PART III**   **DEVELOPMENT AND EVALUATION**
- **PART IV**   **COMPENSATION AND PROTECTION**
- **PART V**   **EMPLOYEE RELATIONS AND ASSESSMENT**

PART I sets the framework for the human resource function, and discusses the internal, external, international, and equal employment challenges that create the framework in which the human resource function must operate. PART II provides the basis of the human resource information system by explaining job analysis and design along with the importance of human resource planning as foundations for the discussions about recruitment and selection. PART III explores the need for orientation, placement, training, development, performance appraisal, and career planning. PART IV examines the roles and practices associated with compensation management, including chapters on incentives and gainsharing; benefits and services; and safety, security, and health. PART V concludes with chapters on employee and labor relations. The last chapter addresses the assessment of human resource management and future challenges.

Besides the addition of a chapter on "International Challenges" in PART I, re-adopters will find that the two chapters covering employee relations practices and quality of work life have been consolidated into a new chapter in PART V, "Employee Relations Challenges." Also in PART V, the two chapters devoted to the union-management framework, bargaining, and contract administration have emerged as a single, new chapter, "Dispute Resolution and Unions." The result, we think, is a better organization of the book with little loss of content.

Besides new chapters, all the other chapters have been updated through new concepts, theories, practices, and examples. The Americans with Disabilities Act is introduced and explained. The Foreign Corrupt Practices Act gains additional exposure in the book, in keeping with the more extensive treatment of international human resource management. Coverage of work force diversity, recent court cases, and future challenges all receive expanded coverage.

Key Features

To make the book both readable and a useful teaching tool, the fourth edition expands upon the key features of previous editions. Among these features users and reviewers report as helpful are:

1. Part-openings. Each of the five parts of the book begins with a brief overview of the following chapters and emphasizes the importance of the topic to readers.

2. Real-life examples. This edition includes more than 200 examples drawn almost exclusively from named companies. Many are new. They demonstrate and reinforce the relevancy of key ideas, while adding to reader interest and retention. To provide greater continuity and integration, the book often uses the same organizations for several examples within a chapter.

3. Two-color figures. Scores of two-color figures are used throughout the book, summarizing key relationships or illustrating concepts. Where appropriate, new figures have been added and previous ones updated.

4. Chapter objectives. Each chapter begins with six learning objectives to highlight key areas of the following chapter. (These objectives are useful review tools, especially from comprehensive and essay examinations.)

5. Opening example. To provide a practical context for the theory and practices discussed in the chapter, the introduction of each chapter contains an opening example, drawn for a major corporation.

6. Chapter quote. Each chapter begins with a quote from a researcher or practitioner. They were selected to stimulate interest in the chapter, underscore the importance of the following content, or offer an interesting counterpoint to conventional wisdom.

7. Chapter summary. A brief summary of each chapter is provided at the end to review the key ideas.

8. Terms for review. The end of each chapter contains a list of the key concepts mentioned in the chapter. Their number has been expanded in this revision, but as in previous editions they are italicized and defined within the chapter. (Definitions of key terms also appear in the glossary at the end of the book.)

9. Review and discussion questions. Each end-of-the-chapter section contains eight review and discussion questions. They are of two kinds: some request a summary of chapter ideas while others focus on the application of concepts.

10. Chapter incidents. Classroom-tested incidents appear at the end of each chapter. They emphasize the application of chapter concepts to specific questions. More than half have been updated for this edition.

11. References. Chapters end with a mixture of classical and current references to allow the reader to explore topics in greater depth and serve as a jumping-off point for course-based assignments. The fourth edition has expanded these references to provide greater detail in documentation.

12. Glossary. Since the book is intended as an introduction to the topic of human resources and personnel management, the extensive glossary of previous editions has been expanded to allow adopters to vary the chapter sequence to suit their personal preferences. (The glossary also serves as a useful review tool for comprehensive examinations.)

SUPPLEMENTARY MATERIALS

A new Study Guide, by Lee Stepina of Florida State University, is designed to augment the learning process by helping students assess their progress as they work through the text. For the instructor, a comprehensive instructor's manual and test bank is available to adopters to augment the balanced coverage and interest-building features of the book. Users of previous editions report that the manual and test bank were two of the most thorough teaching resources available for teaching human resources and personnel management.

Instructor's manual/Test bank

The instructor's manual is set up as a resource book. Section 1 contains a sample course syllabus, alternate course designs, suggested term projects, a film and videotape bibliography with addresses, and other instructional resources. Section 2 offers chapter-by-chapter materials such as lecture notes keyed to chapter outlines, experiential in-class exercises, answers to review and discussion questions, and comments on chapter incidents. Section 3, the test bank contains about 1000 questions, including true-false, multiple-choice, essay, and other formats drawn from the text. It has been extensively revised and expanded to include materials from this edition. Section 4 holds a set of transparency masters selected from the figures in the text. For additional information on prices and availability of these and other supplements for human resource management, contact your local McGraw-Hill representative.

ACKNOWLEDGMENTS

The great laboratory of a free economy combined with the diligent efforts of researchers have created a never ending stream of innovations. The index identifies those who have most contributed to our view of human resource management through their research and writings. To all the others, who have greatly contributed to this field, we believe this book captures the fundamentals of their creative efforts.

Our greatest appreciation goes to those who gave so freely of their time and advice; their good counsel enriched the book in many ways. Where we failed to heed their advice, we remain responsible. In particular, we are most grateful to John W. Newstrom, of the University of Minnesota, Duluth and William E. Reif of Arizona State University. Along with Fred Luthans, of the University of

Nebraska, these scholars played an important role in the initiation of this book in its first edition.

Our sincere appreciation also extends to those who have provided many useful comments and suggestions during the course of this book's development through four editions, especially George Biles, American University; Genie Black, Western Carolina University; George Bohlander, Arizona State University; Alan Browning, Merritt College; Tom Chacko, Iowa State University; Randy L. DeSimone, Rhode Island College; Joseph DiAngelo, Widener University; Robert Gatewood, University of Georgia; Joyce Giglioni, Mississippi State University; Gary L. Gordon, SUNY, Oswego; Ronald E. Guittarr, Northwestern University; Michael M. Harriss, University of Missouri, St. Louis; Stephen Hartman, New York Institute of Technology; Christine L. Hobart, Northeastern University; Wallace Johnson, Virginia Commonwealth University; Thomas Johnston, Nassau County Community College; Paul Keaton, University of Wisconsin, LaCrosse; Linda A Krefting, Texas Tech University; Richard A. Lester, University of North Alabama; Robert McGinty, Eastern Washington University; Carl McKenry, University of Miami; Herff L. Moore, University of Central Arkansas; Gregory Northcraft, University of Arizona; John Overby, University of Tennessee; Richard J. Randolph, Johnson County Community College; Marcus Hart Sandver, Ohio State University; Lee Stepina, Florida State University; George E. Stevens, Oakland University; Arthur Whatley, New Mexico State University; Harold C. White, Arizona State University; and Margarel L. Williams, Purdue University.

William B. Werther, Jr.
Keith Davis

HUMAN RESOURCES AND PERSONNEL MANAGEMENT

I

FRAMEWORKS AND CHALLENGES

1 Human Resource Management Challenges
2 Environmental Challenges
3 International Challenges
4 Equal Employment Challenges

*a*HUMAN RESOURCE department helps people and organizations reach their goals. But it faces many challenges along the way. These challenges arise from the demands of employees, the organization, and their environment. Current domestic and international environments are particularly turbulent because of the growing diversity of the work force and the globalization of businesses. Challenges also come from ever-changing laws, especially those regulating equal employment opportunity. Within this climate, the human resource department must contribute to the organization's bottom line in ways that are ethically and socially responsible.

The first four chapters of this book explore these challenges and lay a foundation upon which the rest of the book is built. Your personal success as a manager of people or a specialist in human resources depends on how these challenges are met. Regardless of your role, you are affected by human resource management because organizations touch your life every day. How well those organizations succeed helps determine your well-being and the well-being of our society.

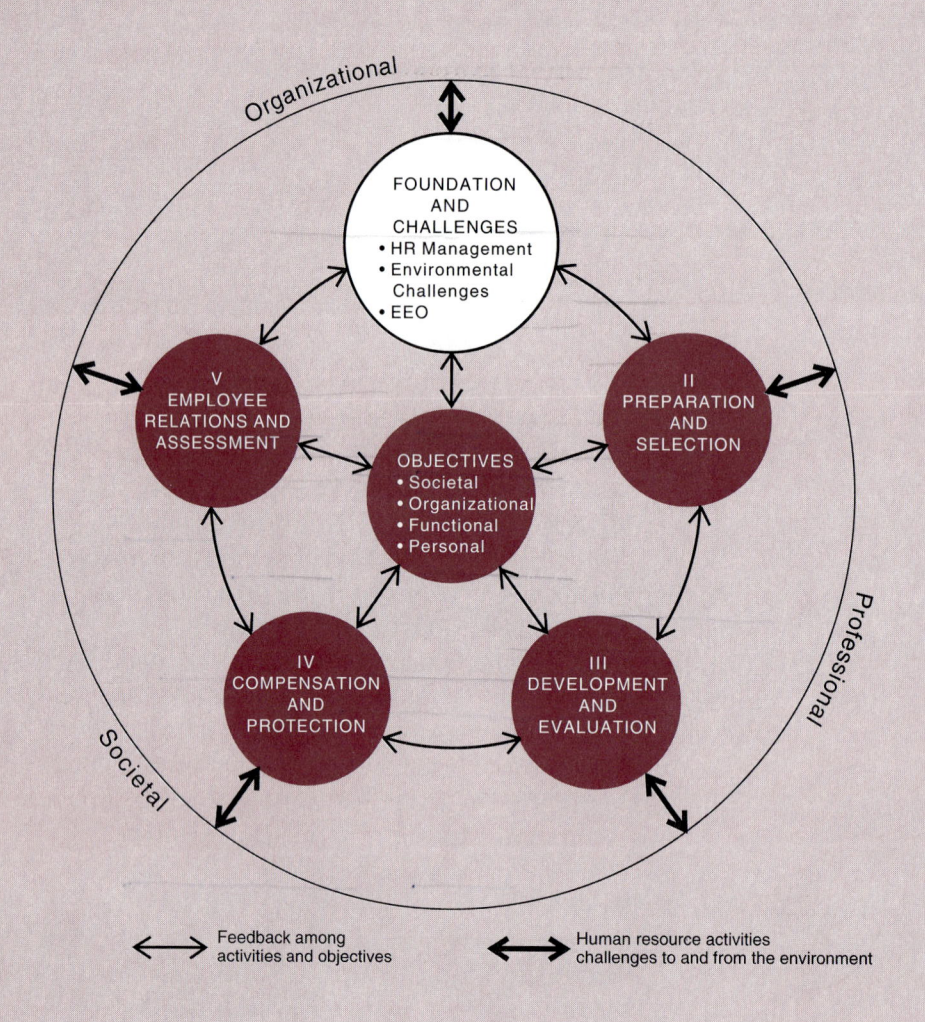

Organizational

FOUNDATION AND CHALLENGES
- HR Management
- Environmental Challenges
- EEO

V EMPLOYEE RELATIONS AND ASSESSMENT

II PREPARATION AND SELECTION

OBJECTIVES
- Societal
- Organizational
- Functional
- Personal

IV COMPENSATION AND PROTECTION

III DEVELOPMENT AND EVALUATION

Societal

Professional

⟷ Feedback among activities and objectives

⟷ Human resource activities challenges to and from the environment

Management...must have the support of all employees. I cannot think of anything more important.
ROBERT CRANDALL[1]

In an information society, human resources is at the cutting edge. And it means that human resource professionals are becoming much, much more important in their organization.
JOHN NAISBITT[2]

HUMAN RESOURCE MANAGEMENT CHALLENGES

/CHAPTER OBJECTIVES

After studying this chapter, you should be able to:

1. DISCUSS the central challenge facing our society.
2. IDENTIFY the challenges arising from the globalization of businesses.
3. EXPLAIN the purpose and objective of human resource management.
4. SUMMARIZE the major activities associated with human resource management.
5. DESCRIBE the human resource responsibilities of all managers.
6. DIAGRAM the relationships among key jobs and basic functions of human resource management.

Global economy

THE SHIPBUILDING, motorcycle, automobile, steel, tire, consumer-electronics, semiconductor, banking, and computer industries of North America were once the envy of the world. In the last few years, however, each of these industries has encountered relentless challenges from international competitors, particularly from those in Japan, South Korea, Taiwan, Germany, and the other nations in the European Common Market. These economic pressures will intensify during the remainder of your career, with even more competition coming from newly emerging competitors in Asia and Eastern Europe. Increasingly, businesses are relying on global strategies in their search for markets, materials, technology, low-cost operations, and people.

How well any country survives in this global economy depends squarely on the performance of its organizations—private and public. Ultimately, every society's wealth and well-being comes from its organizations, which provide the jobs, products, and services needed to sustain a modern industrial or postindustrial nation. By selling more goods and services on international markets, nations are able to earn more wealth for their societies and, in time, increase the standard of living of their citizens.

At the same time, organizations are more than vehicles for international competition. Name the greatest accomplishment of the twentieth century. Biogenetic engineering? Landing on the moon? Computers? The most significant achievement may not even have happened yet, but every major advance of this century shares a common feature: an organization.

Virtually every major advance of this century came from an organization. Biogenetic engineering breakthroughs have come from Stanford University and a company called Genetech, among others. The Apollo missions to the moon were made possible by an organization called the National Aeronautics and Space Administration, or NASA. Likewise, computers were first developed by Sperry Rand and other organizations. Even on a day-to-day basis, organizations play a central role in our lives. The water we drink, the food we eat, the clothes we wear, and the vehicles we drive or the public transportation we take come from organizations. When future historians view our era, they may regard twentieth-century organizations as our greatest accomplishment. Certainly, they will agree with the essayist who observes,

> Organizations are the most inventive social arrangements of our age and of civilization. It is a marvel to know that tens of thousands of people with highly individualized backgrounds, skills, and interests are coordinated in various enterprises to pursue common institutionalized goals.[3]

Common element

People are the common element in every organization. They create the strategies and innovations for which organizations are credited. As a slogan at a Union Carbide plant puts it, "Assets make things possible; people make things happen." It is people who create the strategies that produce a nation's valued products and services. As two writers observe:

I. FRAMEWORKS AND CHALLENGES

Critical to a corporation's growth and prosperity is gaining and retaining competitive advantage. Although corporations may pursue many paths to this end, one that is frequently not recognized is capitalizing on superior human resource management. Currently, many companies recognize the growing importance of their human resources, but few are conceptualizing them in strategic terms—in ways to gain a competitive advantage. As a result, many companies forego the opportunity to seize competitive advantage through human resource practice initiatives.[4]

Bottom-line, ethics, and social responsibility

A human resource department must further its organization's competitive advantage through human resource practices.[5] Members of the department must focus on the economic or bottom-line contributions they make in ways that are ethically and socially responsible. This book examines the practices of specific, real-life companies to show how human resource departments can contribute significantly and responsibly in an increasingly global environment. Consider the first of many examples that highlight the importance of human resource management.

Real-life examples

NUMMI

During the early 1980s, the General Motors (GM) automobile assembly plant in Fremont, California was closed. At that time, the daily absentee rate was approximately 20 percent. Approximately 5,000 outstanding union grievances between the company and its 5,000 employees remained unresolved. Unexpected wildcat strikes interrupted production, then estimated at 240,000 cars per year.

By the mid-1980s, GM formed a joint venture with the Toyota Motor Corporation, called New United Motor Manufacturing, Inc. (NUMMI). GM's primary contribution was the closed Fremont plant. Toyota contributed its management and human resource skills. Within 18 months after NUMMI began production, Fremont had become a different plant.[6]

Adding little new technology, NUMMI's Japanese bosses set up a typical Toyota production system, with a flexible assembly line run by teams of workers in charge of their own jobs. They hired back most of the former United Auto Workers members who wanted to work—even their militant leaders. NUMMI makes a single auto, while GM built several models. But its 2,500 employees can assemble 240,000 cars a year, roughly equal to what it took 5,000 or more people to produce under GM. There are only two grievances outstanding, and absenteeism is running under 2%.[7]

These results were achieved with most of the same people and equipment employed by GM. The main difference was the attention to and treatment of the workers. So compelling were these human-oriented advances at NUMMI, that they shaped the design and operation of GM's newest car division, Saturn.

Although this example was drawn from the automobile industry, the benefits of high-quality human resource management have been demonstrated in other sectors of the economy. Consider an example from the service industry, Delta Air Lines.

Delta Air Lines

C. E. Woolman, long-time president of Delta, stamped his image on the company through his employee relations philosophy. He treated employees as though they were part of a large family. Human resource policies and management actions were designed to take care of Delta's people.

The company went beyond merely promoting from within and offering superior wages and benefits. For example, when other airlines furloughed employees during fuel crises and the air traffic controllers' strike, Delta put surplus pilots and flight attendants to work selling tickets, loading bags, and even washing airplanes. Through these turbulent times, not one full-time Delta employee was laid off. As Delta's senior vice president for administration and personnel observed, "The whole company saw what we did for the pilots and flight attendants...to keep paychecks coming and benefits intact... And I think the company is better off for what we did. Everyone knows we went the extra mile for them, and so today our folks seem to be willing to go the extra mile for us."[8]

A year after these comments were made, Delta gave its employees an eight percent raise while many other airlines were actually cutting wages. The majority of Delta's employees responded by chipping in to buy their employer a $30 million Boeing 767 jet, to facilitate Delta's fleet modernization program.

Although Delta's balance sheet does not list its human assets, those assets are the backbone of the airline that Business Week labeled "the world's most profitable."[9] Its billion-dollar fleet of jets and valuable airport leases in North America, Europe, and Asia would be of little use without its human resources.[10] Delta's management recognizes the importance of its people by "going the extra mile" and ensuring high levels of job security. The point of this example is that people and organizations are mutually dependent. Individual employees rely on Delta for jobs. The airline exists only through the cooperative efforts of its people. And those of us outside the "Delta family" depend on organizations like it to provide transportation. In fact, without modern organizations, society as we know it could not even exist.

Mutual dependency

THE CENTRAL CHALLENGE

Central challenge

Nations and their citizens depend upon organizations, and this dependency is certain to grow.[11] As the challenges shown in Figure 1-1 become more complex, our society will face further demands to compete internationally, feed the hungry, find new energy sources, cure diseases, curb inflation, lower unemployment, and meet other challenges that we cannot imagine. We will respond to

I. FRAMEWORKS AND CHALLENGES

Figure 1-1

The Central Challenge to Organizations

- Global-competitive Challenges
- Unemployment challenges
- Social responsibility challenges
- Medical, food, housing challenges
- Unknown challenges
- Ethical challenges
- Work force diversity challenges
- Population-growth challenges

Central challenge: BETTER ORGANIZATIONS

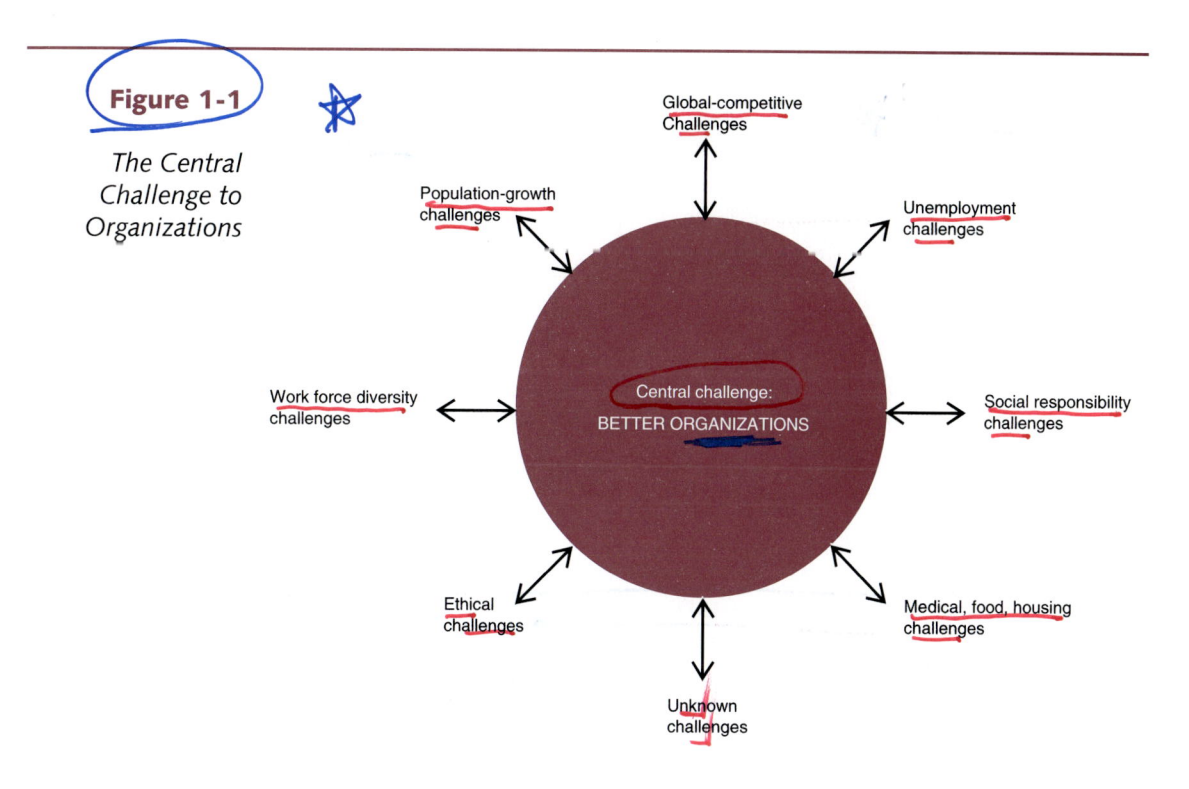

these challenges through our most creative invention: organizations. The better our organizations work, the more easily our society can meet these challenges and opportunities. *Therefore, the central challenge facing our society is the continued improvement of our organizations, both private and public.*

Effective v. efficient

Organizations improve through the more effective and efficient use of their resources. *Effective* means producing the goods and services society deems appropriate. In Delta's case, effective means providing safe and reliable air transportation for people and freight. But Delta must do more than just the *right things*; it must also perform its activities in the *right ways*. Since Delta competes with other carriers, it must be efficient to survive. *Efficient* means using minimum resources needed to produce its goods and services. If Delta's people, for example, can do a better job of scheduling its planes, the company can serve more customers with fewer planes, crews, and fuel. American, United, Air France, Swiss Air, and other airlines must then serve more customers with fewer planes in order to remain competitive. As explained below, the result for society is an improvement in this industry's productivity.

Productivity

As shown in Figure 1-2, *productivity* is the ratio of an organization's outputs (goods and services) to its inputs (people, capital, materials, and energy).[12] Productivity increases as an organization finds new ways to use fewer resources to produce its output. In a business environment, improving productivity is essential

1. HUMAN RESOURCE MANAGEMENT CHALLENGES

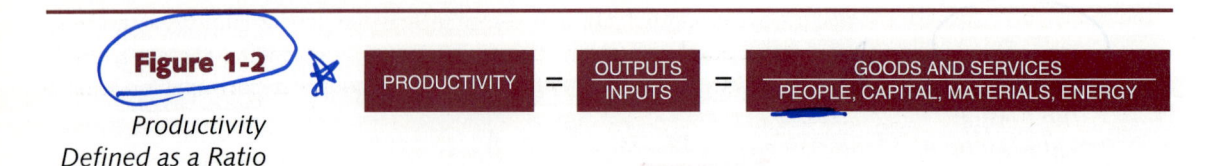

Figure 1-2
Productivity Defined as a Ratio

$$\text{PRODUCTIVITY} = \frac{\text{OUTPUTS}}{\text{INPUTS}} = \frac{\text{GOODS AND SERVICES}}{\text{PEOPLE, CAPITAL, MATERIALS, ENERGY}}$$

for long-term success. Through gains in productivity, managers can reduce costs, save scarce resources, and enhance profits. In turn, improved profits allow an organization to provide better pay, benefits, and working conditions. The result can be a higher quality of work life for employees, who are more likely to be motivated toward further improvements in productivity.

Human resource departments contribute to improved productivity *directly* by finding better and more efficient ways to meet their objectives and *indirectly* by improving the quality of work life for employees.[13] These efforts result in trade-offs between employee satisfaction and economic, or bottom-line, results. Although a high quality of work life alone does not ensure economic success, quality of work life and bottom-line gains must be achieved in ways that are ethical to the parties involved and that are socially responsible in order to benefit the society at large.

This chapter introduces the ways organizations address these tradeoffs through human resource practices. It explains the purpose of human resource departments and how they respond to organizational needs with clear objectives and specific activities to improve the productive contribution of people.

The chapter ends with an overall framework of human resource management in the form of a model. Later chapters expand the model and provide details.

The Response of Human Resource Management

Purpose of HR

The purpose of human resource management is to improve the productive contribution of people to the organization in an ethical and socially responsible way. This purpose guides the study and practice of human resource management, also commonly called personnel management. The study of human resource management describes what human resource managers do and what they should do. In practice, this definition demands actions that enhance the contribution of people to the organization's bottom line.[14]

Improving the contribution of human resources is so ambitious and important that all but the smallest firms create a specialized personnel or human resource department. It is ambitious because although the human resource department does not control many of the factors that shape the employee's contribution, such as the capital, materials, and procedures, it is responsible for managing people in such a way that these factors are most productively used.[15] The department decides neither strategy nor the supervisor's treatment of employees, although it

I. FRAMEWORKS AND CHALLENGES

strongly influences both.[16] Human resource management is important because without gains in employee productivity organizations eventually stagnate and fail. However, to guide its many activities, a human resource department must have objectives.

The Objectives of Human Resource Management

In practice, human resource management achieves its purpose by meeting objectives. *Objectives* are benchmarks against which actions are evaluated. Sometimes these objectives are carefully thought out and expressed in writing. More often, objectives are not formally stated. In either case, objectives guide the human resources function in practice. To do this, objectives must recognize and balance the challenges presented by society, the organization, the human resource function, and the people who are affected. Failure to address these challenges can harm the firm's performance, its profits, and even its survival. These challenges are identified in four objectives that are common to human resource management:

1. **Societal objective.** To be ethically and socially responsible to the needs and challenges of society while minimizing the negative impact of such demands upon the organization. The failure of organizations to use their resources for society's benefit in ethical ways may result in restrictions.[17] For example, society may limit human resource decisions through laws that address discrimination, safety, or other areas of societal concern.

2. **Organizational objective.** To recognize that human resource management exists to contribute to organizational effectiveness. Human resource management is not an end in itself; it is only a means to assist the organization with its primary objectives. Simply stated, the department exists to serve the rest of the organization.

3. **Functional objective.** To maintain the department's contribution at a level appropriate to the organization's needs. Resources are wasted when human resource management is more or less sophisticated than the organization demands. The department's level of service must be tailored to the organization it serves.

4. **Personal objective.** To assist employees in achieving their personal goals, at least insofar as these goals enhance the individual's contribution to the organization. Personal objectives of employees must be met if workers are to be maintained, retained, and motivated. Otherwise, employee performance and satisfaction may decline, and employees may leave the organization.

Consider how one human resource manager contributed to organizational productivity by solving a long-standing employee turnover problem. Notice how this solution helped meet each of the four objectives of human resource management:

Socially responsible solution

> At a Frigidaire plant, the human resource department always sought the best workers it could find. "Best" meant, among other things, the brightest, most intelligent applicants. This strategy created high turnover in one job. This job required the employee only to drill holes in sheets of metal. The employee would pick up the sheet metal, center it on an upright drill press, and drill a hole in it. (The hole was for the intake and discharge tubes of a washing machine.) The average employee quit within three months.
>
> The use of bright employees for this simple job led to boredom and attrition. The problem was solved by filling the job with a mentally handicapped worker who became a productive, long-term employee. The human resource manager contributed to meeting *society's objective*, of finding suitable employment for the handicapped, and was able simultaneously to serve the organization's production needs. The *functional objective*, of assuring the appropriateness of the department's contribution, was met because the organization benefited from the department's revised selection procedures. And the new employee's *personal objective*, of having a decent job, was satisfied as well.

Not every human resource decision meets these four objectives every time. Tradeoffs do occur, but these objectives serve to check and balance decisions. The more these objectives are met by the human resource department's actions, the better its contribution to the organization's bottom line and its response to employees' needs will be. Moreover, by keeping these objectives in mind, the human resource specialist can discern the reasons behind many of a department's activities.

Human Resource Management Activities

To achieve its purpose and objectives, the human resource department obtains, develops, utilizes, evaluates, maintains, and retains the right numbers and types of workers to provide an appropriate work force. As Figure 1-3 shows, these activities meet human resource objectives. When these objectives are met, the purpose of human resource management is achieved through people who contribute to the organization's strategies and overall goals of effectiveness and efficiency.[18] For these reasons, human resource executives are playing an increasingly important role in governing domestic and global companies.[19] Chairman James D. Robinson III of American Express, recognizing the need for strong, entrepreneurial managers among AmEx's fast-growing subsidiaries, such as

HR's role in global companies

Figure 1-3

The Response of Human Resource Management to Societal Needs and Challenges

| HUMAN RESOURCE MANAGEMENT ACTIVITIES | → | HUMAN RESOURCE OBJECTIVES
• Societal
• Organizational
• Functional
• Personal | → | PURPOSE OF HUMAN RESOURCE MANAGEMENT | → | Other resources
HUMAN RESOURCES
Other resources | → | OVERALL ORGANIZATIONAL OBJECTIVES | → | SOCIETAL NEEDS AND CHALLENGES |

Feedback

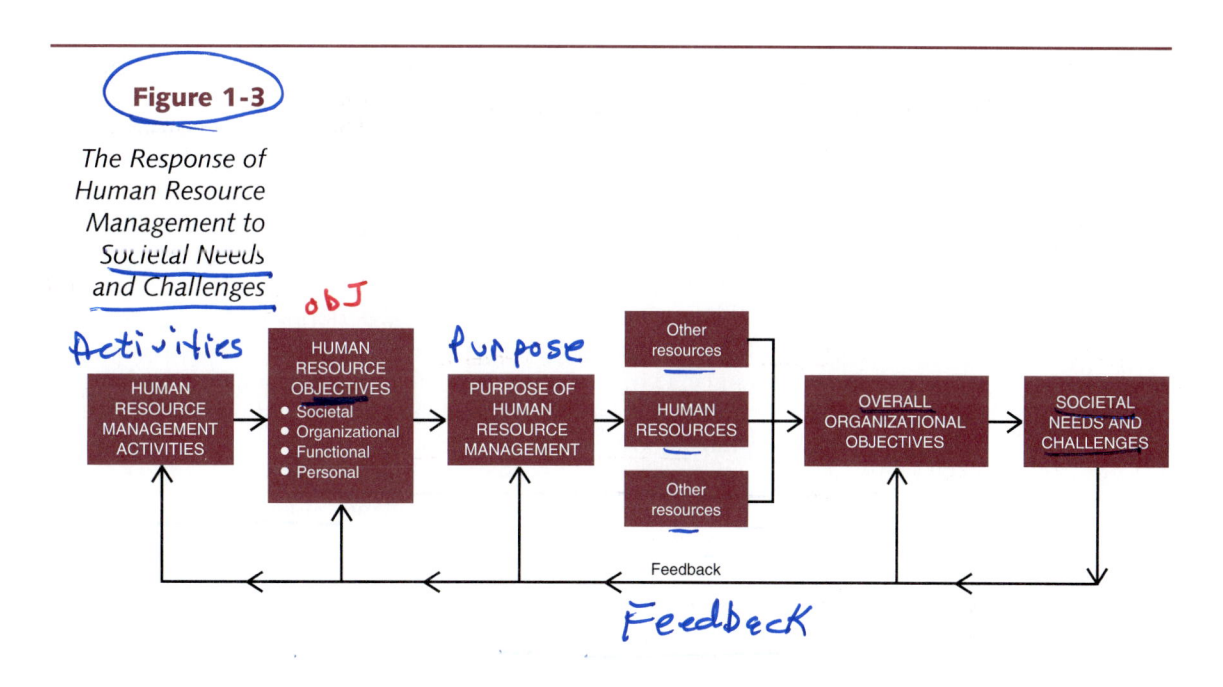

Shearson Lehman Bros., has this to say about human resource strategies and his senior vice president for human resources, Irene (Rennie) C. Roberts:

CEO viewpoint

Chief executives have finally come to realize that people are what give you the competitive edge, and we're telling them how to get the right people.... I look to Rennie Roberts and her staff to be an objective sounding board for an evaluation of people, compensation structures, benefit costs, and work life so that we can attract and hold the people we want.[20]

Key human resource activities. *Human resource activities* are those actions taken to provide and maintain an appropriate work force for the organization. Not every human resource department undertakes every activity discussed in this book. Small ones often lack large enough budgets or staffs to do so. They simply focus upon the activities that are most important to their organization. Large departments are usually "full-service"; they do all the activities shown in Figure 1-3 and described in the following paragraphs.

Full service

Once an organization grows beyond a few employees, attempts are made to estimate the organization's future human resource needs through an activity called *human resource planning*. With an idea of future needs, recruitment seeks to secure job applicants to fill those needs. The result is a pool of applicants who are screened through a *selection process*. This process chooses those people who meet the needs determined by human resource planning.

1. HUMAN RESOURCE MANAGEMENT CHALLENGES   **13**

Since new workers seldom fit the organization's needs exactly, they must be *oriented* and *trained* to perform effectively. As demands change, *placement* activities transfer, promote, demote, lay off, or even terminate workers. Subsequent human resource plans might reveal new staffing needs. These openings are filled by the recruitment of additional workers and by the *development* of present employees. Development gives employees new knowledge, skills, and abilities to ensure their continued usefulness to the organization and to meet their personal desires for advancement.

To check on these various activities, individual performance is *appraised*. Not only does this activity evaluate how well people perform, but it also indicates how well human resource activities have been done. Poor performance might mean that selection, training, or developmental activities should be revised or that there may be a problem with employee relations.

When employees perform, they receive *compensation* in the form of wages, salaries, or incentives, along with a wide variety of employee benefits such as insurance and vacations. Some rewards are *required services* dictated by *legal compliance*, such as social security contributions, safe working conditions, and overtime pay.

To ensure employee retention, satisfaction, and performance, human resource departments become involved with *employee relations*, usually by establishing policies and assisting managers. When employees are dissatisfied, they may band together and take collective action. Management is then confronted with *union-management relations*. To respond to collective demands by employees, human resource specialists may have to negotiate a *labor agreement* and administer it.

Even when human resource activities appear to be going smoothly, modern departments conduct an assessment of their effectiveness to assure their continued success. One means of assessment might be to conduct an evaluation of each activity's effectiveness in meeting company objectives. Traditional budgetary limitations are one form of control.

Figure 1-4 correlates these activities with the four objectives previously discussed. The figure shows that each activity contributes to one or more objectives. For example, appraisal contributes to organizational, functional, and personal objectives. If an activity does not contribute to one or more of the department's objectives, the resources devoted to that activity should be redirected.

Dual responsibility

Responsibility for human resource activities. The responsibility for human resource management activities is shared by *all managers*.[21] When managers throughout the organization do not accept their responsibility, human resource activities are performed only partially or not at all. Even when a human resource department exists within the organization, all operating managers and human resource experts have responsibility for employee performance. Individual managers remain involved in planning, selection, orientation, training, development, evaluation, compensation, and other personnel activities, even though they may be assisted by experts in the human resource department.

I. FRAMEWORKS AND CHALLENGES

Figure 1-4

The Relation of Activities to Objectives in Human Resource Management

MANAGEMENT OBJECTIVES	Supporting Activities
SOCIETAL OBJECTIVE	1. Legal compliance
	2. Benefits
	3. Union-management relations
ORGANIZATIONAL OBJECTIVE	1. Human resource planning
	2. Employee relations
	3. Selection
	4. Training and development
	5. Appraisal
	6. Placement
	7. Assessment
FUNCTIONAL OBJECTIVE	1. Appraisal
	2. Placement
	3. Assessment
PERSONAL OBJECTIVE	1. Training and development
	2. Appraisal
	3. Placement
	4. Compensation
	5. Assessment

When operating managers find that personnel work seriously disrupts their other duties, the work may be reassigned. Personnel activities might be assigned to another worker or to a specialized department that handles human resource matters. This process of getting others to share the work is called *delegation*.[22] Delegation requires the manager to assign duties, grant authority, and create a sense of accountability in those to whom the delegation was given. Duties, authority, and accountability must be explained clearly or the delegation will fail. And even though others may have been asked to handle human resource activities, the manager still remains ultimately responsible for the performance of his or her employees. The action of delegation does not reduce a manager's responsibility; it only shares that responsibility with others who become accountable. For example, a manager may ask a senior worker to train a new employee. If the new employee makes a costly mistake and the experienced worker lets it pass, the manager will be held responsible for the problems that result. As human resource activities become more complex and time-consuming, the need for a separate department may arise.

1. HUMAN RESOURCE MANAGEMENT CHALLENGES

Figure 1-5

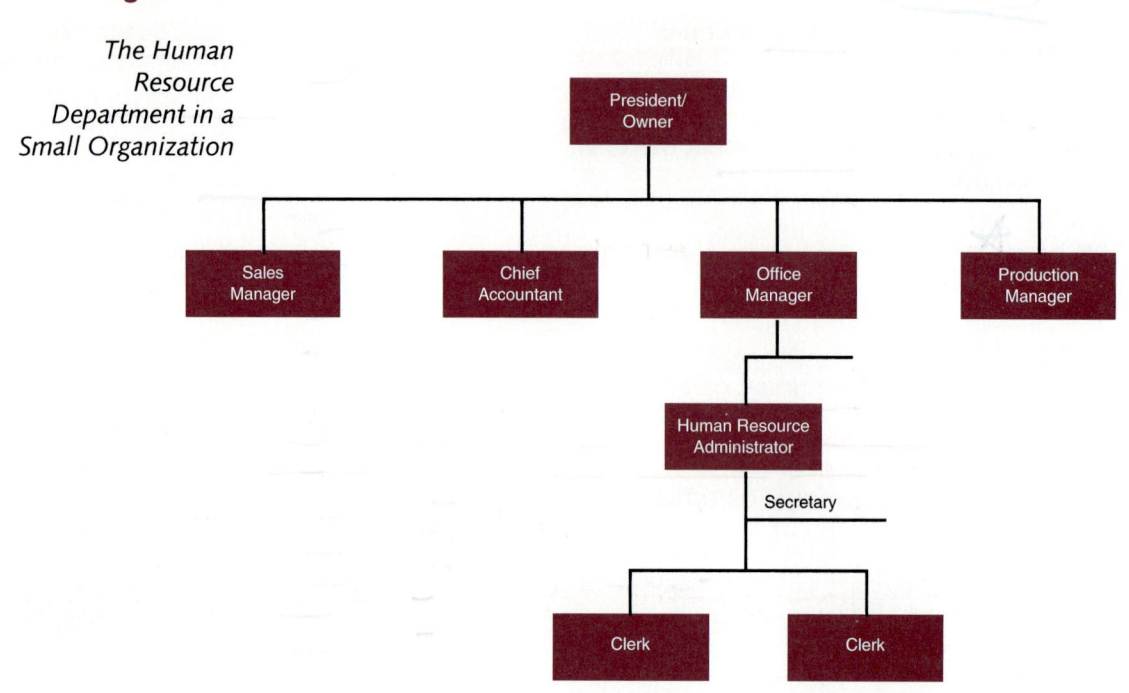

The Human Resource Department in a Small Organization

```
                        President/
                         Owner
        ┌──────────────┬─────┴──────┬──────────────┐
     Sales          Chief         Office        Production
    Manager       Accountant      Manager        Manager
                                     │
                              Human Resource
                               Administrator
                                  Secretary
                          ┌──────────┴──────────┐
                        Clerk                 Clerk
```

THE ORGANIZATION OF A HUMAN RESOURCE DEPARTMENT

HR emergence

A separate department usually emerges when human resource activities become a burden to other departments in the organization. At that point, the expected benefits of a department usually exceed its costs. Until then, managers must handle human resource activities themselves or delegate to subordinates. When a human resources department first emerges, it is typically small and is the responsibility of a middle-level manager. Figure 1-5 illustrates the most common placement of the department at the time it is first formed. Such departments are usually limited to maintaining employee records and helping managers find new recruits. Whether the department performs other activities depends upon the needs of other managers in the firm.

As demands grow, the department becomes more important and more complex. As shown in Figure 1-6, this increased importance is reflected by the human resource department head reporting directly to the chief operating officer, who in this figure is the company president. Increased importance may be signified by changing the title of the human resource manager to vice presi-

I. FRAMEWORKS AND CHALLENGES

staff - advises manager
line - production
functional - expertise in compensation etc

Figure 1-6

The Hierarchy of Jobs within a Large Human Resource Department

I. HEAD OF THE DEPARTMENT — Vice President of Human Resources (under President)

II. MIDDLE OR FIRST-LEVEL MANAGERS — Manager of Employment; Manager of Compensation; Manager of Training and Development; Manager of Safety; Manager of Employee and Labor Relations

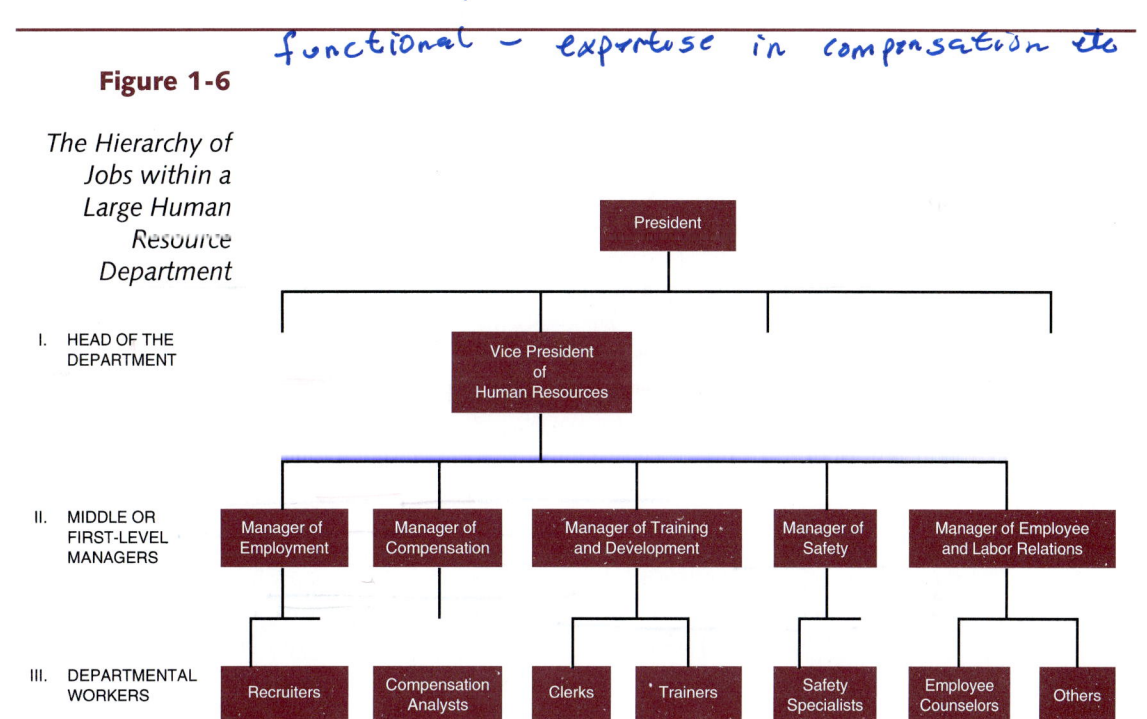

III. DEPARTMENTAL WORKERS — Recruiters; Compensation Analysts; Clerks; Trainers; Safety Specialists; Employee Counselors; Others

dent.[23] In practice, increased complexity also results as the organization grows and new demands are placed on the human resource department. To deal with growth and new demands, jobs in the department become more specialized. Often highly specialized subdepartments emerge to provide a wide range of services, as shown in levels II and III of Figure 1-6.

Size of HR

The size of the department varies widely, depending largely on the size of the organization being supported. One study reported a median ratio of 1.0 human resource staff member per hundred employees in the organization. The average department's budget is one percent of a company's operating expenses.[24] Another study suggests that human resource departments have been spared the layoffs recently experienced by other departments because of their perceived importance to top management.

HR's contribution

The numbers may reflect the more "strategic" role played by these [personnel] divisions today, says Lawrence Schein, director of the Conference Board Survey. . . . Top executives look to them for problem-solving techniques. The survey showed, for example, that 90 percent of executives want their personnel divisions to find ways to improve productivity, which has been woefully low throughout the industrial and service sectors. "Companies are obviously

1. HUMAN RESOURCE MANAGEMENT CHALLENGES   **17**

hoping that personnel management will provide them with a strong competitive edge," he said. [25]

Departmental Components

The subdepartments of a large full-service human resource department approximately correspond with the activities shown in Figure 1-4. For each major activity, a subdepartment may be established to provide the specialized service. The employment subdepartment, for example, involves recruitment and selection. Other divisions in the figure perform the activities their names imply. This specialization allows members of the department to become experts in a limited number of activities.

Activities not shown in Figure 1-4 are shared among the different subdepartments. For example, human resource planning and placement may be shared by employment, training, and development. Performance appraisals are used to determine pay, and so the compensation subdepartment may assist managers with appraising performance. Legally required services fall under the compensation and safety subdepartment. Assessment activities, communications, and counseling are divided among all subdepartments, with the employee and labor relations subdepartment performing most of these tasks. The employee and labor relations subdepartment also provides official union-management coordination, when unions exist. Figure 1-7 shows the organization chart for Delta's personnel division.

Key Roles in a Human Resource Department

The human resource department contains a hierarchy of jobs, as shown in Figure 1-6. The top job varies in importance and title from organization to organization.[26] When the department first is formed, the head of it is often called a personnel or human resource manager, director, or administrator. The title of vice president of personnel or vice president of human resources becomes more likely as the department's size, contribution, sophistication, and responsibility grow.[27] If unions make a major demand on the personnel function, the title of the head of human resources typically becomes director or even vice president of industrial relations.[28]

Human resource departments in large organizations have a variety of positions. The manager of employment helps other managers with recruiting and selection. The compensation manager establishes fair pay systems. The training and development manager provides guidance and programs for those managers who want to improve their human resources. Other activity managers contribute their expertise and usually report directly to the head of human resources. Activity managers may be supported by an assortment of specialists, secretaries, and clerks. It is the specialists in large organizations who actually do the recruiting, training, and other necessary tasks. These specialist positions are often taken by college graduates to start careers in personnel work.[29]

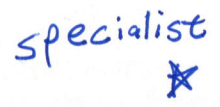

I. FRAMEWORKS AND CHALLENGES

Figure 1-7

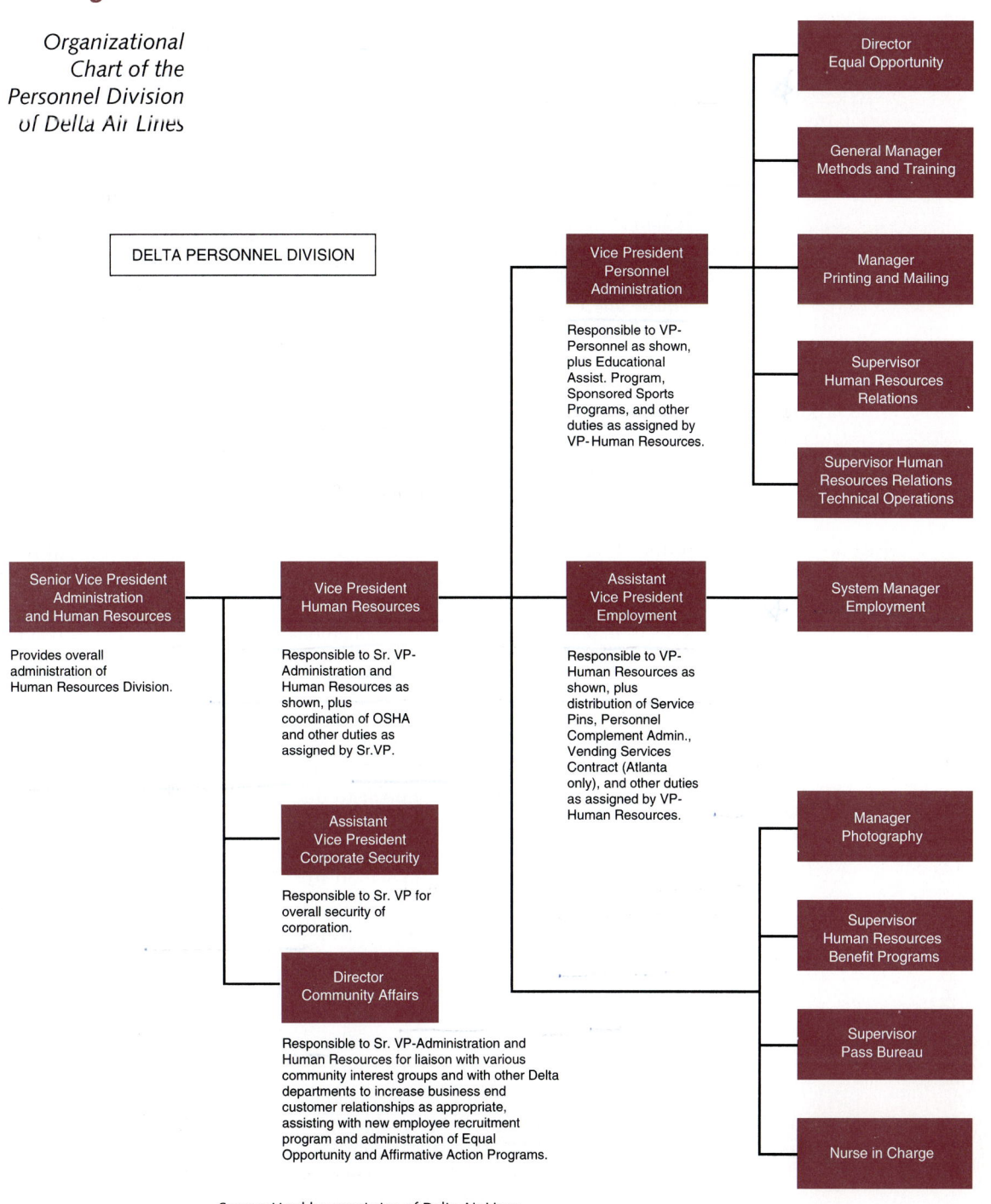

Organizational Chart of the Personnel Division of Delta Air Lines

DELTA PERSONNEL DIVISION

Senior Vice President Administration and Human Resources

Provides overall administration of Human Resources Division.

Vice President Human Resources

Responsible to Sr. VP-Administration and Human Resources as shown, plus coordination of OSHA and other duties as assigned by Sr.VP.

Assistant Vice President Corporate Security

Responsible to Sr. VP for overall security of corporation.

Director Community Affairs

Responsible to Sr. VP-Administration and Human Resources for liaison with various community interest groups and with other Delta departments to increase business end customer relationships as appropriate, assisting with new employee recruitment program and administration of Equal Opportunity and Affirmative Action Programs.

Vice President Personnel Administration

Responsible to VP-Personnel as shown, plus Educational Assist. Program, Sponsored Sports Programs, and other duties as assigned by VP-Human Resources.

- Director Equal Opportunity
- General Manager Methods and Training
- Manager Printing and Mailing
- Supervisor Human Resources Relations
- Supervisor Human Resources Relations Technical Operations

Assistant Vice President Employment

Responsible to VP-Human Resources as shown, plus distribution of Service Pins, Personnel Complement Admin., Vending Services Contract (Atlanta only), and other duties as assigned by VP-Human Resources.

- System Manager Employment
- Manager Photography
- Supervisor Human Resources Benefit Programs
- Supervisor Pass Bureau
- Nurse in Charge

Source: Used by permission of Delta Air Lines.

1. HUMAN RESOURCE MANAGEMENT CHALLENGES

The Service Role and the Human Resource Department's Authority

Human resource departments are service departments. They exist to assist employees, managers, and the organization. Human resource managers and specialists do not have the authority to manage other departments[30]; instead, they have *staff authority*, which is the authority to advise, not direct, other managers. *Line authority* is the authority to direct the operations of those departments that make or distribute the organization's products or service. Those who have line authority are sometimes called line or operating managers. Line managers make the decisions about production, performance, and people. They determine promotions, job assignments, and other people-related decisions, and are ultimately responsible for employee performance. Human resource specialists advise these line managers.

Although advisory, staff authority is powerful. When the human resource manager advises an operating manager about a human resource issue, the line manager may reject the advice. In doing so, however, the operating manager bears the full responsibility for the outcome. If the results cause employee relations problems, the consequences fall on the line manager. To avoid disruptive consequences, managers usually consider the human resource department's advice and follow it. The result is that the department has considerable influence in shaping the actions of operating managers.

In some situations, the cost of not following the department's counsel is so high that top management replaces staff or advisory authority with functional authority over specific issues. *Functional authority* is the authority given to specialists to make the final decision in specified circumstances. In highly technical or routine decisions, functional authority allows the department to make decisions that would otherwise be made by line managers. If, for example, each department manager made separate decisions about employee benefits, which can be technically complex, excessive costs and inequities would result. Therefore, the authority of line managers to determine their employees' benefit package is delegated by top management to the human resource department. If line managers disagree with the department's actions, they can request that top management review or even veto human resource benefit plans. Otherwise, the human resource department is empowered to make decisions about employee benefits to ensure control, uniformity, and the use of their specialized expertise. When a human resource department is given functional authority, it no longer advises. It decides. However, like all organizational decisions, the use of functional authority is subject to review by top management.

The use of line, staff, and functional authority can result in a dual responsibility for human resource management.[31] Both line and human resource managers are responsible for employee productivity and quality of work life. Human resource managers are responsible for creating a productive climate by finding ways to enhance the organization's quality of work life through personnel activities and advice to line managers. At the same time, operating managers are responsible for their employees' day-to-day treatment and for the quality of work life in their departments. Conflicts between line and staff managers occur when their objectives clash. A production manager, for example, may want to reduce costs through layoffs at the first sign of declining sales. The human resource manager, however, may see a temporary layoff of short duration as damaging to the organization's quality of work life. Or a line manager might want to hire someone at a salary above the level recommended by a compensation analyst in the human resource department. Although potentially disruptive to smooth line and staff relations, such conflicts create the benefit of causing managers to review their objectives and methods.

Size and service

The size of the human resource department affects the type of service provided to employees, managers, and the organization. In small departments, the manager handles many of the day-to-day activities related to the organization's human resource needs. Other managers bring their problems directly to the head of the department, and these meetings constantly remind the manager of the contribution that is expected.

When the department grows larger, problems are handled by subordinates. Not only do human resource managers then have less contact with lower-level managers, but other members of the department grow increasingly specialized. At this point, human resource managers and their subordinates may lose sight of the overall contributions that are expected of them or of the limits on their authority. As experts in a complex system, they may become more interested in perfecting their specialties than in asking how they may serve others and further the company's economic interests. Specialists may also assume authority they do not have.[32] For example, consider what happened at a fast-growing minicomputer company:

> For the past five years, Harris Mini-Computers, Inc., had grown at an average rate of 25 percent a year. To keep up with this growth, the human resource department manager, Earl Bates, used budget increases to hire new recruiters. With this strategy, his department was well prepared to find new employees, but recruiting specialists paid little attention to other human resource problems. In one month, three of the company's best computer design engineers quit to go to work for a competitor. Before they left, they were interviewed. They complained that they saw desirable job openings being filled by people recruited from outside the organization. No design engineer had been promoted to supervisor in the past three years, so each of these engineers found jobs where the promotion possibilities looked better.
>
> When Bates reminded these engineers that they lacked experience or training as supervisors, one of them commented that the company should have provided such training. With the next human resource department budget increase, Earl hired a specialist in employee training and development, who designed a supervisory development program.

The human resource manager and the recruiting specialists at Harris Mini-Computers overlooked the variety of activities for which human resource departments are created. They failed to identify both the services that their organization needed from their department and the connections among human resource management activities.

THE HUMAN RESOURCE MANAGEMENT MODEL

Human resource management is a system of many interdependent activities. None of these activities occurs in isolation. Each affects another. Consider, in the following example, what can go wrong when a critical human resource's decision is made in isolation from related considerations.

> In preparing a successful bid for the construction of a football stadium, an estimator miscalculated the human resource requirements. Too many unskilled workers and too few skilled workers were hired. As the expansion of the stadium fell behind schedule, supervisors tried to get work done more quickly. This speedup led to complaints from the union. Finally, the project manager identified the problem. The manager had fired a third of the unskilled workers and replaced them with skilled cement masons and carpenters. This decision led to legal problems over unemployment compensation claims, and with the increase in higher paid, skilled workers, the payroll exceeded estimates. The human resource manager had to intervene. The stadium seats were in place by the first home game, but the contractor lost $385,000 on the job.

As this illustration shows, a poor decision about human resource requirements can lead to problems in employment, placement, legal compliance, union-management relations, and compensation. Only when all human resource activities are involved in the planning process can they serve as an organization's human resource management system.

A Systems Model

HR as a system

When activities are related, a system exists. A system consists of two or more parts (or subsystems) working together as an organized whole with identifiable boundaries.[33] Examples are numerous. A car is a system composed of the subsystems engine, transmission, radio, and the like. A human body is a system composed of respiratory, digestive, circulatory, and other subsystems. Cars, people, and human resource departments have identifiable boundaries.

Human resource activities form an interconnected system with boundaries, as shown in Figure 1-8. This figure demonstrates how each activity (or subsystem) relates directly to every other activity. For example, the challenges faced by the human resource department affect the selection of employees. The selection subsystem influences the department's development and evaluation subsystems. In addition, each subsystem is affected by the department's objectives and

Figure 1-8

Human Resource Management Model and Subsystems

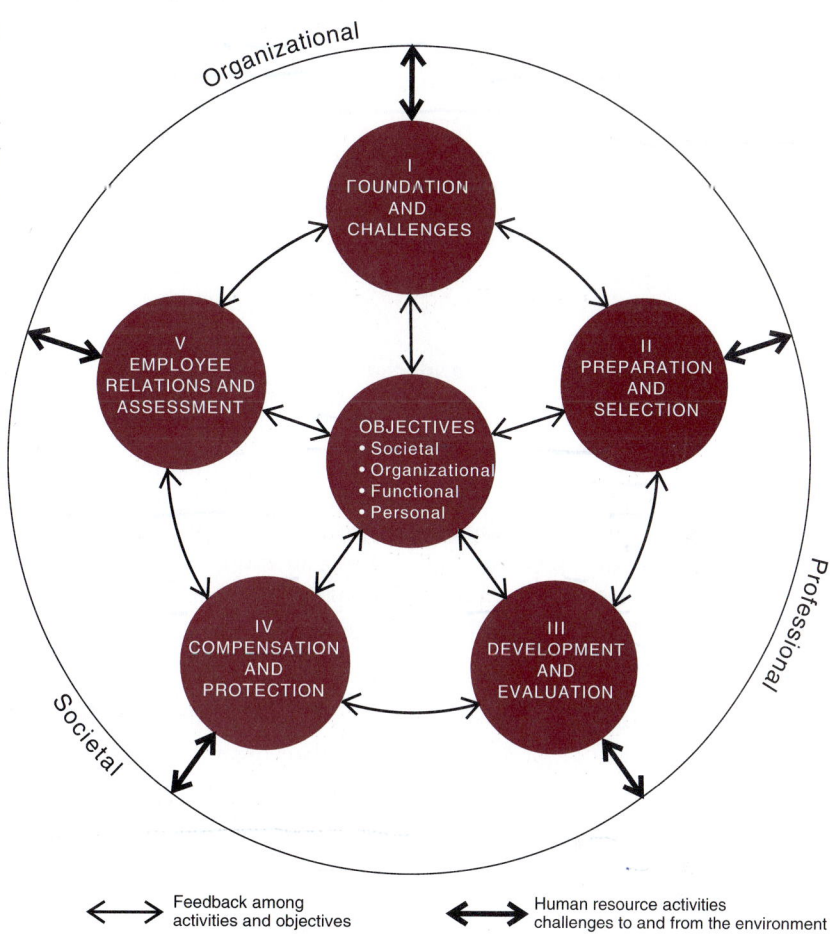

Organizational — Professional — Societal

- I FOUNDATION AND CHALLENGES
- II PREPARATION AND SELECTION
- III DEVELOPMENT AND EVALUATION
- IV COMPENSATION AND PROTECTION
- V EMPLOYEE RELATIONS AND ASSESSMENT

OBJECTIVES
- Societal
- Organizational
- Functional
- Personal

⟷ Feedback among activities and objectives

⟷ Human resource activities challenges to and from the environment

policies and by the external environment in which human resource management takes place.

Thinking in terms of systems is useful because it enables one to recognize the interrelationships among parts. If one adopts a systems view of human resource management, the relationships among activities are less likely to be overlooked. In the preceding example, the stadium cost manager failed to recognize the interdependence between the subparts of the human resource system.

Systems thinking also requires recognition of the system's boundaries, which mark the beginning of a system's external environment. Because most systems are *open systems*, that is, systems that are affected by the environment, the environment is an important consideration. Organizations and people are open systems because they affected by their environments. The human resource department is also an open system, influenced by its external environment. To

1. HUMAN RESOURCE MANAGEMENT CHALLENGES   23

use the preceding example, the stadium contractor's organization is an open system because the society, the organization, and professional human resource practices impact how the department responds. At the same time, systems continually interact with their environments, even influencing their environments, as demonstrated by the impact on the local labor market of the stadium contractor's decision to hire large numbers of skilled workers.

Plan of the book

The following brief discussion of a systems model explains the role of major human resource subsystems. It also serves as a preview of the five parts of this book and their major topics. Each part of the book is identified in the model by a Roman numeral.

I. Foundations and challenges. Human resource management faces many challenges in dealing with people. The central challenge is to assist organizations in improving their effectiveness and efficiency in an ethical and socially responsible way. Meeting this challenge requires that the human resource department be organized in a way that allows it to meet its objectives while serving its organization. As mentioned earlier in this chapter, other challenges arise from the environment in which an organization operates. The changing demands of workers, international and domestic competition, the influence of pressure groups, the need for sustained professional ethics, and compliance with government regulations are only a part of the challenges human resource management must meet. Challenges also spring from within the organization. For example, other departments may compete with the human resource department for larger budgets, for a larger share of their organization's general resources. Perhaps the most pervasive challenges at present are work force diversity, international competition, and the government requirement for equal employment opportunity.[34] Success in advising other managers about these and other forces depends on continued awareness of the demands with which both operating managers and human resource professionals are faced.

II. Preparation and selection. At the heart of human resource management is the need for a sound information base. Without accurate and timely information, departments are seriously limited in their ability to meet the challenges before them. To build a *human resource information system*, data are gathered about each job and about the organization's future human resource needs.[35] From the information, specialists can advise managers about the design of jobs they supervise and even find ways to make those jobs more productive and satisfying. Estimates of future human resource needs allow the department to become proactive in the recruitment and selection of new workers. w aseoutside the firm. The results of the department's efforts should lead to a more effective work force. To evaluate employees, formal performance appraisals are conducted periodically. Appraisals give workers feedback on their performance and can help the department spot its own weaknesses.

24   I. FRAMEWORKS AND CHALLENGES

III. Compensation and protection. One element of retaining and maintaining an effective work force is compensation. Employees must be paid a fair wage or salary relative to their productive contribution. Where appropriate, incentives may be added. When compensation is too low, turnover and other employee relations problems are likely. If pay is too high, the company can lose its competitive position in the marketplace. Modern compensation management, however, goes beyond pay. Benefits are an increasingly important part of any compensation package and must be at a level appropriate to employee productivity if the company is to retain its workers and remain competitive. At the same time, the organization needs to protect its workers from occupational hazards. Through safety and health programs, the department not only assures a safe work environment but also keeps the employer in compliance with the many health and safety laws.

IV. Employee relations and assessment. To maintain an effective work force requires more than just pay, benefits, and safe working conditions. Employees need to be motivated, and the human resource department is partially responsible for ensuring employee satisfaction with the job. Personal and job-related problems may lead to the need for counseling or discipline. Here again, the specialists can provide effective programs or specific advice to line managers. To further employee satisfaction and organizational productivity, communications are used to keep people informed. When employee relations are ineffective, employees may join together and form self-help groups, called unions. When this occurs, human resource departments are usually responsible for dealing with the union. As with any ongoing system, human resource departments need to identify their successes and failures through self-evaluation. Full-service departments regularly conduct audits of their performance and do research to discover more effective ways to serve their organization. Often this research helps uncover future challenges in order to anticipate their impact on the organization and its human resources.

An Applied Systems View

Human resource subsystems affect each other, and specialists must remain aware of this interdependency. Perhaps the most effective way to recognize possible complications is through systems thinking. Figure 1-9 provides a simplified visual model for applying systems thinking.

An applied systems view describes human resource activities as taking *inputs* and *transforming* them into *outputs*. Then the human resource specialist checks on the results to see if they are correct. This checking process produces *feedback*, which is information that helps evaluate success or failure. Consider the situation faced by Carol Torres, the personnel manager at a Veterans Administration hospital:

Figure 1-9

Input-Output Simplification of the Human Resource Management System

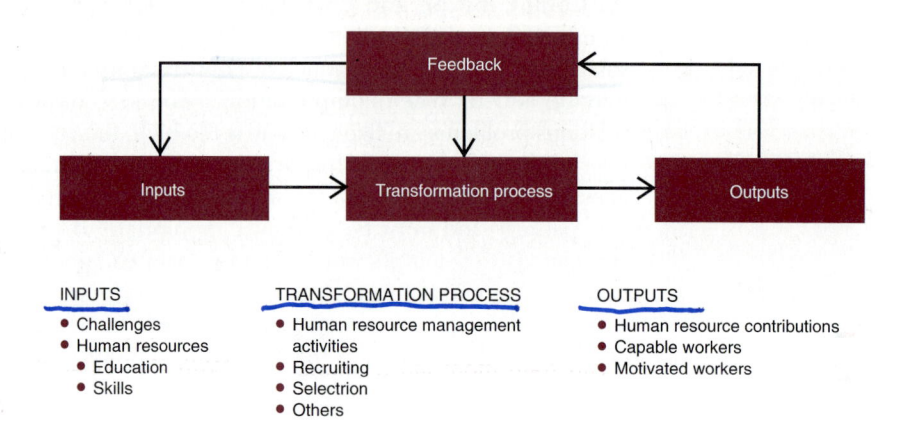

```
                    Feedback
                  ↙         ↖
    Inputs  →  Transformation process  →  Outputs
```

INPUTS
- Challenges
- Human resources
  - Education
  - Skills

TRANSFORMATION PROCESS
- Human resource management activities
- Recruiting
- Selectrion
- Others

OUTPUTS
- Human resource contributions
- Capable workers
- Motivated workers

An anticipated shortage of medical technologists prompted Carol to start an in-house development program to prepare six lab assistants to become licensed medical technologists. After fifteen months, they finished the program and passed the state certification test. Since the program was a success and the shortage had grown worse, eight more lab assistants were recruited for the second program.

The knowledge of a shortage was one input. Another input was the group of lab assistants who signed up for training. The program itself was the transformation process, which created the desired output, a new supply of certified technologists. When all six technologists passed the state certification test, those results gave Carol feedback that the program was a success. In short, the human resource management system transforms inputs into desired outputs. The inputs take the form of challenges, usually in the form of information, and human resources. Through human resource activities, these inputs are transformed into the desired outputs, which become feedback to the human resource management system.

Systems thinking

In practice, applied systems thinking helps identify the key variables. After viewing new information as an input, specialists decide what the desired output is. With input and output variables identified, decision makers draw on their knowledge of human resource activities to transform the inputs into outputs in the most effective way. To verify their success, they acquire feedback about the outcome. Negative feedback means that other inputs (information or people) are needed or that the transformation process (a specific human resource activity) is malfunctioning. Negative feedback demands corrective actions.

PROACTIVE VERSUS REACTIVE HUMAN RESOURCE MANAGEMENT

Human resource departments cannot always wait for feedback before responding. To wait may expose the organization to needless damage from changes in its environment. Reconsider, for example, Carol Torres's predicament when, after learning of the impending shortage of technologists, she discussed the situation with her manager, the assistant hospital administrator:

Carol Torres: "My department budget must be increased by $12,000 so we can train more lab technologists. With the impending shortage of technologists, we will have serious staffing, performance, and employee relations problems if we don't take action now."

Anna Newman: "Hold on! Washington has put a freeze on the budget for six months, and as director of administrative services my hands are tied. Why not wait until we can show Congress complaints from doctors? Then the shortage will be real, and we can get Congress to expand our budget."

Carol Torres: "But then we will probably have to spend $15,000 for training. We will probably have to pay another $30,000 for overtime to the technologists we now have while we train new ones. Besides, with all that overtime, error rates are sure to jump, and so will lawsuits for faulty lab work. All I need is $12,000, but I need it now."

Reactive v. proactive

Anna was suggesting that Carol's department wait until an actual problem occurred and then react. Carol wanted to take action in anticipation of the problem without waiting for feedback in the form of doctors' complaints or lawsuits. Anna's approach was reactive, while Carol's was proactive. Reactive human resource management occurs when decision makers respond to human resource problems. Proactive human resource management occurs when human resource problems are anticipated and corrective action begins before the problem arises.[36]

Effective and efficient human resource departments seek proactive solutions. By applying systems thinking, managers like Carol Torres can take action before serious problems arise. To institutionalize a proactive approach, progressive departments can even assign community, legislative, and other public affairs functions to members of the department as a means of monitoring the environment for proactive opportunities. This proactive approach improves productivity by minimizing the resources needed to respond to changes in the environment. Furthermore, progressive, proactive approaches tend to generate superior financial performance.[37] In short, a proactive approach to the management of human resources is a major step in enhancing organizational productivity.[38]

VIEWPOINTS OF HUMAN RESOURCE MANAGEMENT

Viewpoints and approaches

Throughout this chapter several viewpoints of human resource management have been introduced. These approaches provide complementary themes which we will pursue throughout the book to keep human resource management in perspective. They include:

➤ *Human resource approach.* Human resource management is the management of people. The importance and dignity of human beings should not be ignored for the sake of expediency. Only through careful attention to the needs of employees do successful organizations grow and prosper.

➤ *Management approach.* Human resource management is the responsibility of every manager. The human resource department exists to serve managers and employees through its expertise. In the final analysis, the performance and well-being of each worker is the dual responsibility of that worker's immediate supervisor and the human resource department.

➤ *Systems approach.* Human resource management takes place within a larger system: the organization. Therefore, human resource management must be evaluated with respect to the contribution it makes to the organization's productivity. In practice, experts must recognize that the human resource management model is an open system of interrelated parts. Each part affects the others and is influenced by the external environment.

➤ *Proactive approach.* Human resource management can increase its contribution to employees, managers, and the organization by anticipating challenges before they arise. If efforts are only reactive, problems may be compounded and opportunities may be missed.

Since the practice of human resource management is an open system, it is affected by the environment in which it is practiced. The historical evolution of human resource management and the ongoing cultivation of professional standards in the field help shape that environment. Other influences arise from society and from the organizations that human resource departments serve. These historical, environmental, and professional challenges are the context in which human resource management is practiced. Recognition and understanding of these challenges are fundamental to the proper practice of human resource management. Each of these challenges is explored more fully in Chapter 2. Chapter 3 examines international challenges, and Chapter 4 discusses the challenges of equal employment opportunity.

I. FRAMEWORKS AND CHALLENGES

SUMMARY

THE CENTRAL CHALLENGE facing society is the continued improvement of our organizations, both private and public. The purpose of human resource management is to improve the contribution made by people to organizations.

To carry out its role, human resource departments need to satisfy multiple and sometimes conflicting objectives. Societal, organizational, functional, and personal objectives must be met, and they must be met in a way that is appropriate to the organization being served. These objectives are achieved through a variety of human resource activities, designed to obtain, maintain, utilize, evaluate, and retain an effective work force. These activities are the responsibility of all managers in the organization, even though many of them may be delegated to specialists in the human resource department.

The activities of a department can be viewed as an interrelated system. Each activity directly or indirectly affects other activities. Personnel specialists view information and human resources as the primary inputs. They transform these inputs through various activities to produce results that help the organization meet its goals and further its productivity. Ideally, human resource experts undertake this role proactively.

Terms for Review

Productivity
Purpose of human resource management
Delegation
Staff authority
Human Resource Information System (HRIS)
Line (or operating) authority

Functional authority
Dual responsibility for human resource management
System
Open system
Feedback
Reactive
Proactive

Review and Discussion Questions

1. Explain how the increased globalization of business is making the contribution of human resource departments more important.

2. What is the purpose of human resource management? Identify and explain how its objectives contribute to that purpose.

3. What is productivity and why is it important to organizations?

4. Explain the relationship between societal needs and the activities of a human resource department.

5. Why is a systems approach to human resource management useful?

6. Explain the difference between proactive and reactive approaches to human resource management.

7. Suppose you worked for a maker of automobile parts and the company decided to open a chain of parts stores. Briefly describe what areas of human resource management would concern you if you became the human resource manager for this chain of stores.

8. If a bank opened a branch in a distant city, what activities would the human resource department need to undertake before a fully operational and staffed branch was ready for business?

INCIDENT 1-1
People, Productivity, and Profits at Delta Air Lines

Delta Air Lines was used as an example in this chapter because it represents the type of organization that is successful in a variety of ways. Its treatment of employees, its profitability, and its productivity help set the standards for its industry. As Business Week stated:

> Delta's secret is simple. It combines good planning—15 years ahead for flight equipment and support facilities—with a massive effort to motivate employees. The result: the highest productivity in the trunk airline industry.[39]

To continue its success, Delta's human resource policies are designed to assure good treatment of its employees. So pervasive is the commitment to its people that the organization generates a strong commitment, even zeal, from its employees. Some of Delta's policies include:

➤ Reassignment of employees to avoid layoffs, even at the expense of short-term profits and productivity

➤ Payment of wages that are five to ten cents per hour above the rates paid to unionized workers in other airlines

➤ Fringe benefits for employees that are considered among the most generous in the industry and which provide employees with sound economic security in the event of disability or retirement

➤ Rewards for workers who do an exceptional job of helping passengers in need of assistance

➤ Communications from top management with all employees, in groups of 25 to 30, every year and a half.

Although good planning, modern planes, lean staff, and effective equipment scheduling contribute to Delta's favorable record, the core of its success is the people who do the planning, scheduling, and serving of customers. As Russell Heil, Delta's senior vice president for personnel observed:

> You can spend a fortune on equipment and have the biggest, shiniest and fanciest airplanes in the business, but if you don't have the people, it just won't work. . . .[40]

By creating and maintaining an effective work force, Delta has been able to grow and prosper at a time when other airlines, such as Braniff and Eastern, have declared bankruptcy.

1. Since Delta must pay approximately the same as other airlines for planes, equipment, fuel, and facilities, how can it pay higher wages and fringe benefits while remaining one of the industry's most profitable carriers?

2. From this incident, give examples of how Delta's management uses the human resource, management, systems, and proactive approaches discussed in this chapter.

References

1. Robert Crandall, Chairman, American Airlines, as quoted in Ruth Simon and Graham Button, "What I Learned in the Eighties," *Forbes*, (Jan. 8, 1990), p. 103.

2. John Naisbitt, "What HRM Professionals Can Do to Assume New Leadership Role," *Resource* (March 1986), p. 3.

3. Robert Granford Wright, "Managing Management Resources through Corporate Constitutionalism," *Human Resource Management* (Summer 1973), p. 15.

4. Randall S. Schuler and Ian C. MacMillan, "Gaining Competitive Advantage through Human Resource Management Practices," *Human Resource Management* (Fall 1984), p. 241.

5. William E. Fulmer, "Human Resource Management: The Right Hand of Strategy Implementation," *Human Resource Planning*, vol. 13, no. 1 (1990), pp. 1–11. See also Cynthia A. Lengnick-Hall and Mark L. Lengnick-Hall, "Strategic Human Resources Management: A Review of the Literature and a Proposed Typology," *Academy of Management Review*, vol. 13, no. 3 (1988), pp. 454–470.

6. Aaron Bernstein, Dan Cook, Pete Engardio, and Gregory L. Miles, "The Difference Japanese Management Makes," *Business Week* (July 14, 1986), pp. 47–50.

7. Ibid., p. 50.

8. "Delta: The World's Most Profitable Airline," *Business Week* (Aug. 31, 1981), p. 71.

9. Ibid., pp. 68–72.

10. Bill Leonard, "Making the Message Clear," *Personnel Administrator* (November 1989), pp. 47–49.

11. Karen E. Debats, "The Continuing Personnel Challenge," *Personnel Journal* (May 1982), pp. 332–336, 338, 340, 342, 344.

12. William B. Werther, Jr., William A. Ruch, and Lynne McClure, *Productivity through People* (St. Paul: West Publishing Company, 1986), pp. 3–5.

13. Harold C. White, "Personnel Administration and Organizational Productivity: An Employee View," *Personnel Administrator* (August 1981), pp. 37–42, 44, 46, 48. See also George W. Bohlander and Angelo J. Kinicki, "Where Personnel and Productivity Meet," *Personnel Administrator* (September 1988), pp. 122–130; and, Walter Kiechel III, "Living with Human Resources," *Fortune* (Aug. 18, 1986), pp. 99–100.

14. Joyce D. Ross, "A Definition of Human Resources Management," *Personnel Journal* (October 1982), pp. 781–783.

15. Productivity and the Economy: A Chart Book (Washington, D.C.: U.S. Department of Labor, n.d.), p. i.

16. Dennis R. Briscoe, "Human Resources Management Has Come of Age," *Personnel Administrator* (November 1982), pp. 75–77, 80–83.

17. William C. Frederick, Keith Davis, and James E. Post, *Business and Society*, 6th ed. (New York: McGraw-Hill Book Co., 1988), chap 2.

18. Briscoe, op. cit., p. 77.

19. Laura M. Herren, "The New Game of HR: Playing to Win," *Personnel* (June 1989), pp. 19–22. See also Fulmer, op. cit.

20. John Hoerr, "Human Resources Managers Aren't Corporate Nobodies Anymore," *Business Week* (Dec. 2, 1985), p. 58.

21. Barbara Whitaker Shimko, "All Managers Are HR Managers," *HRMagazine* (January 1990), pp. 67–70.

22. Patrick J. Montana and Deborah F. Nash, "Delegation: The Art of Managing," *Personnel Journal* (October 1981), pp. 784–787.

23. Hoerr, op. cit.

24. "ASPA-BNA Survey No. 53: Personnel Activities, Budgets, and Staffs: 1988–1989" (June 22, 1989), p. 1.

25. "Personnel People," *The New York Times* (May 11, 1986), sec. 3, p. 1.

26. Dennis J. Kravetz, *The Human Resource Revolution: Implementing Progressive Practices for Bottom-Line Success* (San Francisco: Jossey-Bass Inc., Publishers, 1988).

27. Dave Stier, "More Use of Human Resource Titles," *Resource* (October 1989), p. 2.

28. Thomas J. Hutton, "Human Resources or Management Resources," *Personnel Administrator* (April 1987), pp. 66, 68, 70, 72, 74.

29. Duff A. Greenwell, "Not for Students Only," *Personnel Administrator* (September 1981), pp. 16, 19–20.

30. Jac Fitz-enz, "HR Inc.," *Personnel Journal* (April 1986), pp. 34–41.

31. Shimko, op. cit.

32. Joseph A. Litteret, "Pitfalls for 'Professionals,'" *Personnel Journal* (May 1982), pp. 383–385.

33. James Grier Miller and Jessie Louise Miller, "Systems Science: An Emerging Interdisciplinary Field," *The Center Magazine* (September–October 1981), pp. 44–45. For a more detailed discussion of systems theory, see also Daniel L. Katz and Robert L. Kahn, *The Social Psychology of Organizations* (New York: John Wiley & Sons, Inc., 1966), pp. 14–29.

34. Briscoe, op. cit., p. 76.

35. Patricia Teets, "Information Access Comes of Age with Online Data Bases," *Personnel Journal* (January 1987), pp. 112–113. See also Richard B. Frantzreb, "The Microcomputer Based HRIS: A Directory," *Personnel Administrator* (September 1986), pp. 71–100.

36. James G. Goodale and Douglas T. Hall, "Strengthen HR Management: Transcend Its Reactionary Role," *Personnel Journal* (November 1986), pp. 14–18.

37. Kravetz, op. cit.

38. Ilan Meshoulam and Lloyd Baird, "Proactive Human Resource Management," *Human Resource Management* (Winter 1987), pp. 483–502. See also, Goodale and Hall, op. cit.

39. "Delta: The World's Most Profitable Airline," op. cit., p. 68. See also "Delta: Top Brass Listens to Staff," *Dallas Times Herald* (Dec. 27, 1982), pp. b1, b3.

40. Leonard, op. cit, p. 47.

The HR management function has been evolving in most major corporations for decades as new challenges have arisen and as knowledge about HR management has expanded.
EDWARD E. LAWLER III[1]

ENVIRONMENTAL CHALLENGES

CHAPTER OBJECTIVES

After studying this chapter, you should be able to:
1. EXPLAIN the historical challenges that have led to the need for human resource departments.
2. IDENTIFY the external challenges that affect today's human resource practitioner.
3. DISCUSS the impact of cultural diversity on the human resource function.
4. ISOLATE the challenges to human resource management that come from within the organization served.
5. DESCRIBE the challenge of professionalism facing the human resource field.
6. DISCUSS how human resource policies and practices can further the organization's strategy.

ORGANIZATIONS AND their personnel departments are open systems. Both are affected by the environment in which they operate even as they attempt to influence it. Although some challenges to a firm or industry have a narrow impact, many environmental challenges broadly affect human resource departments. For these departments to respond proactively requires an awareness of the external, organizational, and professional environments in which they operate. An example of how one company is responding to international challenges in its environment comes from Motorola.

Motorola's PMP program

Motorola's semiconductor operation is one of the world's leading producers of solid-state electronics, from transistors to state-of-the-art "computer-on-a-chip" technology. Its environment is highly competitive on a worldwide basis. Not only must Motorola compete with domestic rivals—such as Texas Instruments, Intel, and National Semiconductor, but it must also face increasing competition from Japanese manufacturers.

As envisioned by the Japanese Ministry of International Trade and Industry, "Japan's goal for the 1980s is to dominate the computer business, but to do that it must first dominate the semiconductor business."[2] Toward that end, Japanese manufacturers became a major force in the worldwide semiconductor market by the early 1980s. "As the battle for semiconductor supremacy unfolds, the Japanese have a clear advantage because they have an aggressive consumer electronics industry, while U.S. companies have virtually given up on designing and manufacturing such equipment."[3] Japan's large base of consumer-oriented uses for semiconductors gives the nation significant economies of scale which allow for high-volume, low-cost production.

To compete in this environment, Motorola has implemented a variety of business strategies. One of those strategies is called the "participative management program." PMP, as Motorola calls it, began before Japan became a significant force in the semiconductor market. This proactive response to the management of human resources involves employees at Motorola in the decisions that affect their productivity and quality of work life. Through training and subsequent group meetings, employees learn to solve problems and find better ways to make the company's products. The results are not only higher productivity and product quality but also increased employee satisfaction and quality of work life. Through its PMP and other strategies, Motorola does not try to copy the Japanese. Instead, as one senior executive commented, "We plan to be the leaders in technology and people management. We want the Japanese to chase us for worldwide leadership. And we are going to win."[4]

PMP's impact

Whether Motorola will maintain its dominant position in these important markets during the 1990s is too early to tell. What is clear, however, is that the personnel and line managers at Motorola have responded proactively to their environment. They were aware that changes in the external environment meant that the company had to adapt its business and human resource strategies to the new reality of increased foreign competition.

This adaptation process affects nearly every part of the human resource management system shown in Figure 2-1. With a strong foundation in human resource management, Motorola's personnel experts have modified the type of supervisors they seek to hire and develop. More emphasis is placed upon the *development* of employees through PMP *training;* and *performance evaluation* of managers is influenced by how successful their PMP efforts are working. These evaluations, in turn, are reflected in *compensation* decisions that determine incentives and more traditional pay raises. Furthermore, the ideas of employees often lead to improvements in productivity, quality, and *safety*. As the PMP effort enhances the workers' *quality of work life*, employee relations are improved as well. Finally, if the PMP effort continues to improve productivity, favorably influencing the marketplace by contributing high-quality products, the stature of the personnel function at Motorola, which is already high, will grow. In short, the PMP effort enables the personnel department to meet the societal, organizational, functional, and personal objectives discussed in Chapter 1.

Personnel professionals at Motorola, or at any other company, cannot meet the objectives in Figure 2-1 without an awareness and understanding of environmental challenges. Two of the most pervasive environmental challenges faced by human resource departments are international human resource management and governmental regulations.

International experience

Competitive pressures from foreign competitors are reshaping the strategic viewpoints of many companies. Top managements are thinking increasingly globally. Executives at major corporations—such as Procter & Gamble, Ford, Coca-Cola, and others—are increasingly expected to have international experience. For human resource professionals to operate in a global environment, they must be aware of international challenges if they are to make meaningful contributions to the overall success of their organizations' strategies. So important has this challenge of globalism become that the following chapter is devoted to a detailed discussion of it.

Another pervasive challenge is presented by government. Current laws and regulations have such a major impact on contemporary management that Chapter 4 is devoted to one major aspect, equal employment opportunity, and other government challenges, which affect compensation, safety and health, and labor relations, are discussed in subsequent chapters.

This chapter focuses on the nongovernmental challenges that form the environment in which human resource management takes place. In Figure 2-1, these challenges have been added to the model of human resource management first presented in Chapter 1. To explain how present human resource management practices began, this chapter first examines the historical foundations of personnel management. The chapter then explains the challenges that arise from the external, organizational, and professional environments. Throughout the book, we will return to these challenges to see how they affect specific human resource management activities.

2. ENVIRONMENTAL CHALLENGES

Figure 2-1

A Model of the Human Resource Management System and Its Major Environmental Challenges

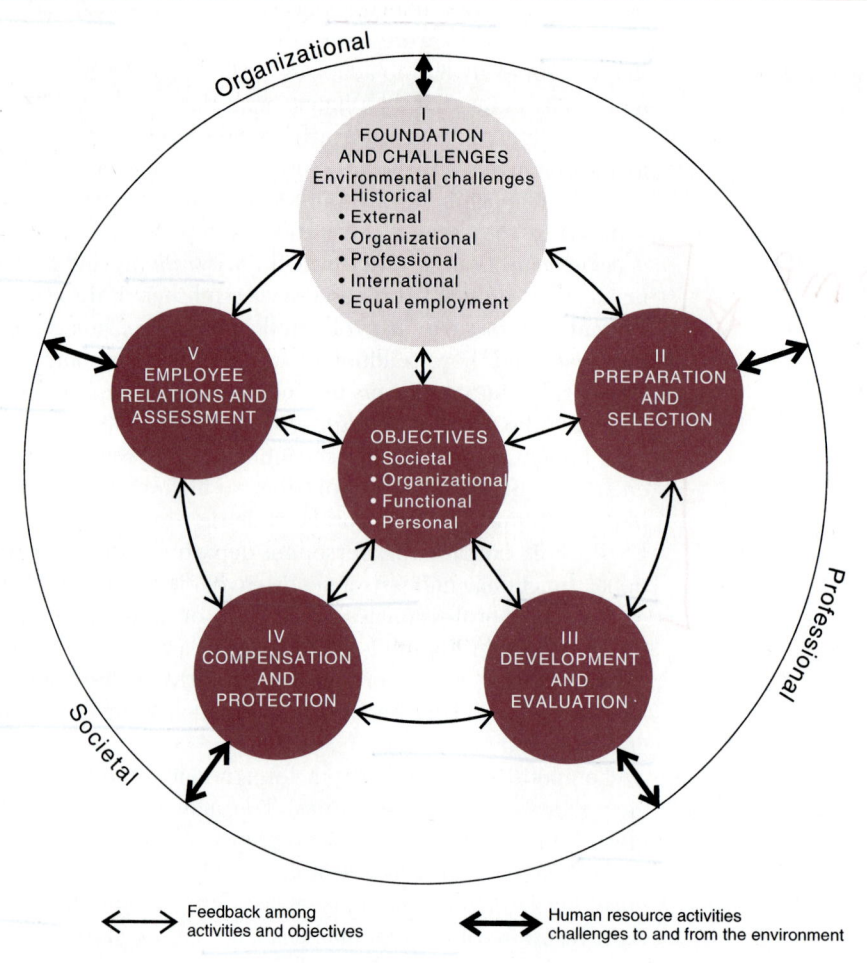

Organizational

I FOUNDATION AND CHALLENGES
Environmental challenges
- Historical
- External
- Organizational
- Professional
- International
- Equal employment

V EMPLOYEE RELATIONS AND ASSESSMENT

OBJECTIVES
- Societal
- Organizational
- Functional
- Personal

II PREPARATION AND SELECTION

IV COMPENSATION AND PROTECTION

III DEVELOPMENT AND EVALUATION

Societal *Professional*

⟷ Feedback among activities and objectives

⟷ Human resource activities challenges to and from the environment

HISTORICAL FOUNDATIONS

HR's evolution

The field of human resource management did not suddenly appear. It evolved into its present form. A review of this evolution shows how the efforts of early pioneers led to today's more sophisticated and more proactive methods.[5] By tracing this evolution, we can also sense the newness and growing importance of the human resource management field. The historical view also demonstrates how the practice of human resource management has been influenced by the changing environment in which it continues to develop.

Early Causes and Origins

Biblical citation

The very earliest origins of personnel management are unknown. The first cave dwellers probably struggled with problems of utilizing human resources. Moses was confronted by one of the earliest recorded human resource challenges when Jethro, his father-in-law, advised, "And thou shalt teach them ordinances and laws, and shalt show them the way wherein they must walk, and the work they must do. Moreover, thou shalt provide out of all the able men . . . rulers." [6]

During the thousands of years between Moses and the industrial revolution, there were few large organizations. Except for religious orders (the Roman Catholic Church, for example) or governments (particularly the military), most work was done in small groups. Whether on the farm, in small shops, or in the home, the primary work unit was the family. There was little need for a formal study of human resource management. However, the industrial revolution changed the nature of work. Big textile mills, foundries, and mines sprang up in England and then in North America. Expensive facilities, steam engines, and other innovations required large numbers of people to work together to attain economies of scale. Collectively, people were still an important resource, but the industrial revolution meant greater mechanization and unpleasant working conditions for many workers.

Welfare secretaries

By the late 1800s, a few employers responded to the human problems caused by industrialization by creating the post of welfare secretary.[7] Welfare secretaries existed to meet worker needs and to prevent workers from forming unions. Social secretaries, as they were sometimes called, helped employees with personal problems such as education, housing, and medical needs. These early forerunners of personnel specialists also sought to improve working conditions. The emergence of welfare secretaries prior to 1900 demonstrates that the personnel activities in large organizations had already become more than some operating managers wanted to handle. Thus, social secretaries marked the birth of specialized human resource management, as distinct from the day-to-day supervision of personnel by operating managers.

Scientific Management and Human Needs

The next noteworthy development was scientific management, as advocated, for example by Frederick Taylor. The scientific management movement showed the world that the systematic, scientific study of work could lead to improved efficiency. The arguments for specialization and improved training which arose from this approach furthered the need for personnel departments.

Stimulated by the developments of scientific management and early unions, the first decades of this century saw primitive personnel departments replace welfare secretaries. These new departments contributed to organizational effectiveness by maintaining wages at proper levels, screening job applicants, and handling grievances. They also assumed the welfare secretary's role of improving working conditions, dealing with unions, and meeting other employee needs. These early departments were not important parts of the organizations they served. They were record depositories with advisory authority only. At that time, production, finance, and marketing problems overshadowed the role of personnel management.

The importance of personnel departments grew slowly as their contributions and responsibilities increased. During World War I, selection tests were developed to match recruits with their roles in the U.S. Army. This advancement led to the industrial use of placement tests, a practice now performed routinely, usually a responsibility of the personnel department.

From the end of World War I until the Great Depression in the 1930s, personnel departments assumed growing roles in handling compensation, testing, union, and employee needs. Recognition of individual needs became even more pronounced as a result of the research studies conducted at Western Electric's Hawthorne plant during this period.[8] These studies showed that scientific efficiency goals had to be balanced by human needs. These elementary observations were eventually to have a profound impact on personnel management. But the Depression and World War II diverted attention to the more urgent matters of organizational and national survival.

Modern Influences

The Depression of the 1930s led citizens to lose faith in the ability of business to meet society's needs. The public turned to government. Government intervened to give workers unemployment compensation, social security, minimum wages, and the federally protected right to join unions. The government's emphasis was on improving employee security and working conditions. The outpouring of legislation in the 1930s helped shape the modern role of personnel departments by assigning to management the responsibility for legal compliance. Organizations now had to consider societal objectives and legal obligations, which elevated the role of personnel departments. In practice, personnel departments were made responsible for discouraging unionization among employees. But with new-found legal protection, unions grew dramatically. These organizing successes startled many organizations into rethinking their *paternalism,* their "management-knows-best" approach to employee welfare. Personnel departments began replacing paternalism with more proactive approaches which encompassed employee desires. When workers did organize, responsibility for dealing with unions also fell to the personnel department, sometimes renamed the industrial relations department to reflect these new duties.

Paternalism fades

Personnel departments continued to increase in importance during the 1940s and 1950s. The recruiting and training demands of World War II lent credibility to personnel departments that successfully met these challenges. After the war, personnel departments grew in importance as they contended with increasingly powerful unions and the expanding need for knowledgeable workers such as engineers and accountants. The explosive growth of employee benefits also contributed to the personnel department's ascendance. At the same time, a widespread understanding of the Hawthorne studies and newer behavioral

Personnel legislation

findings led to concern for improved human relations. These findings helped underscore the importance of sound personnel management practices.

In the 1960s and 1970s, the central influence on personnel was again legislative. Laws were passed to help eliminate discrimination in pay between men and women. Laws intended to end discrimination in employment because of sex, race, religion, national origin, and age were also enacted. Safety and health legislation and pension laws followed in the 1970s. These acts gave human resource departments a still stronger voice—a voice that began to equal those of production, finance, and marketing executives in major corporations.[9]

Figure 2-2 summarizes the key historical developments in the personnel field. As is evident from the figure, many of the historical factors that affected human resource management resulted from external environmental changes. And although these historical events have shaped the role of human resource departments, current challenges from external, organizational, and professional environments mean that more changes in human resource management are likely.

EXTERNAL CHALLENGES

Organizations are surrounded by an external environment filled with challenges that can be viewed as variables over which the organization and its human resource department have little influence. Many of these variables affect the way the organization is operated and, in turn, indirectly affect policies and practices. For example, after scientists at Western Electric developed the transistor, the management at Motorola opened a research facility in Phoenix, Arizona to study this new technology. Western Electric's successes prompted Motorola's management to formulate a corporate strategy centered on high technology.

Corporate strategy and HR

From this strategy and its modest research facility, Motorola's operations in Arizona grew to more than 20,000 employees, all of whom had to be recruited, selected, oriented, trained, compensated, and maintained. As this example illustrates, changes in the external environment, such as a new technology, may impact corporate strategy and planning. Human resource departments then are affected as they respond to these changes and help the organization meet its strategy and objectives.

While some external challenges facing organizations evolve gradually, others occur quickly. Changes in the composition of the work force take place over many years, for example, while new laws or court rulings seemingly occur overnight. Human resource professionals deal with these changes by means of the steps presented in Figure 2-3. Human resource professionals constantly search the environment for changes and evaluate their impact on the organization and on the human resource function. When a noteworthy change is uncovered through reading, continuing education, or studying company strategy, proactive plans are then developed and implemented. As discussed earlier in this chapter, Motorola followed these steps before the Japanese semiconductor industry became a serious threat to its market.

External challenges may arise from many areas. Aside from the international and equal employment challenges discussed in the following two chapters,

Figure 2-2

Key Developments in the Evolution of Personnel Management

YEAR	DEVELOPMENT AND EVENTS
1806	Members of the Philadelphia Cordwainers (shoemakers) are convicted of a criminal conspiracy for striking against their employers.
1842	Merely joining unions is no longer considered illegal, according to the Massachusetts Supreme Court ruling in *Commonwealth v. Hunt*.
1848	Pennsylvania passes child labor laws setting 12 as the minimum working age.
1875	American Express starts a pension plan.
1886	The American Federation of Labor is formed.
1911	F. W. Taylor's book, *The Principles of Scientific Management*, is printed.
1917	World War I selection tests are applied to Army recruits.
1923	American Telephone and Telegraph establishes the position of vice president of personnel relations.
1926	*The Railway Labor Act* sets union-management relations rules in the railroad industry.
1935	Congress passes the *National Labor Relations Act* and the *Social Security Act*.
1938	The *Fair Labor Standards Act* is passed, establishing minimum wages and overtime for hours over forty.
	President Roosevelt orders government agencies to establish personnel departments.
1939	*Management and the Worker*, describing the Hawthorne experiments, is published.
1941	World War II starts, with attendant shortages of human resources and a sudden need to train large numbers of workers.
1947	The *Labor-Management Relations Act* is passed to protect workers and management from union activities.
1955	The American Federation of Labor merges with the Congress of Industrial Organizations to create the AFL-CIO.
1959	The *Labor-Management Reporting and Disclosure Act* provides union members with a "Bill of Rights" in dealing with their union in addition to other labor law change.
1963	The *Equal Pay Act* is passed by Congress, requiring that women be paid the same as men for similar jobs.

YEAR	DEVELOPMENT AND EVENTS
1964	The *Civil Rights Act* is passed by Congress, prohibiting discrimination in employment based on race, color, religion, sex, or national origin.
1967	The *Age Discrimination in Employment Act* is passed by Congress.
1970	The *Occupational Safety and Health Act* is passed by Congress.
1972	The *Equal Employment Opportunity Act* is passed by Congress to amend and strengthen the 1964 Civil Rights Act.
1973	The *Rehabilitation Act* is passed by Congress to aid handicapped workers.
1974	Congress passes *Employee Retirement Income Security Act* to regulate pension plans.
	Congress passes the *Vietnam Era Veterans Readjustment Act*, requiring federal contractors to undertake affirmative action for Vietnam era veterans.
1976	The American Society of Personnel Administrators begins an accreditation program for personnel experts.
1978	The *Pregnancy Discrimination Act* prohibits discrimination against pregnant women.
	The *Comprehensive Education and Training Act* is passed to provide federally funded training programs.
	The *Labor-Management Cooperation Act* authorizes labor-management committees to improve cooperation through government assistance.
1983	The *Job Training Partnership Act* replaces the Comprehensive Education and Training Act, providing for increased consultation with industry about its training needs.
1984	The *Retirement Equity Act* assures retirement benefits to a divorced spouse.
1986	The *Immigration Reform and Control Act* requires all employers to check identities and work authorization papers of all employees while providing amnesty procedures for those living in the United States since before 1982.
	The *Comprehensive Omnibus Budget Reconciliation Act* (COBRA) requires an extension of insurance benefits after specified changes in employment or dependency status. Deferred income annuity and vesting requirements for pension plans also were changed by tax reform.

Figure 2-2

(continued)

The 1967 *Age Discrimination in Employment Act* is amended to remove the age 70 cap on mandatory retirement.

1988 *Polygraph Protection Act* limits employer use of lie detectors in employment-related situations.

Worker Adjustment and Retraining Notification Act requires employers with 100 or more employees to give 60 days notice in plant closings or mass layoffs.

1990 *Americans With Disabilities Act* eliminates discrimination in employment against those with disabilities in the absence of a bona fide occupational qualification.

Older Workers Benefit Protection Act prohibits age discrimination in employee benefits.

Drug-Free Workplace Act requires all organizations receiving federal contracts of $25,000 or more to develop and publish policies that create a drug-free workplace.

1991 Civil Rights Act of 1991 stengthens Title VII of the 1964 Civil Rights Act, granting the opportunity for compensatory damages and clarifying obligations of employers and employees in unintentional discrimination case.

Figure 2-3

Steps in Dealing with Environmental Challenges

1. *Monitor the environment.* Personnel specialists must stay informed about likely changes in the environment by belonging to professional associations, attending seminars, furthering their formal education, and reading widely.
2. *Evaluate the impact.* As new information is acquired, personnel experts ask: "What impact will this information have on the organization today? Tomorrow?" Specialists must diagnose the future meaning of today's events.
3. *Take proactive measures.* Once changes and their impact are evaluated, personnel specialists implement approaches that help the organization reach its goals.
4. *Obtain and analyze feedback.* The results of proactive personnel activities are then evaluated to see if the desired outcomes are reached.

---

common sources of external challenge to the human resource department include work force diversity, technology, economics, and the government, which are discussed in the following sections.

Work Force Diversity

Diversity

The North American work force is the most diverse in the world. It is composed of people born in North America—descending in most cases from immigrants of earlier generations—and newcomers from around the globe. Within this diversity of national origins exists an even wider diversity of cultures, religions, languages and dialects, educational attainments, skills, values, ages, and other variables. Familiarity with this diversity helps human resource professionals develop proactive policies and practices. This knowledge comes from personal

2. ENVIRONMENTAL CHALLENGES

Demographics

observation and, scientifically, from *demography*, the statistical study of population characteristics.

A demographic description of the work force defines its composition in terms of educational levels, race, age, sex, the percentage of the population participating in the work force, and other characteristics. Changes in work force demographics usually occur slowly, are carefully measured, and can be anticipated by demographers. Some companies, such as General Motors, find demographics so important that they hire their own demographers.[10] Although slow-moving, demographic trends can have a significant impact on a human resource department's activities.

Baby boom

The Depression of the 1930s and World War II led to a decline in the U.S. birthrate. This resulted in a drop in the number of people between the ages of 35 and 44 during the late 1960s and the 1970s. Although most mid-level managers come from this age group, reactive personnel departments did little until the shortage became acute. Proactive departments began training and development programs among lower-level managers in the early 1960s in anticipation of the tight supply of middle managers.

Likewise, the post-World War II baby boom which peaked in the late 1950s was followed by a decline in the U.S. birthrate in the 1960s and well into the 1970s. As a result, the growth rate of the work force will be slow in the 1990s. Unless an unanticipatedly large number of immigrants enter North America, human resource departments in businesses that rely heavily on young workers—such as McDonalds, Burger King, and retail stores will encounter an ongoing shortage of new workers throughout the 1990s and into the next century.[11] By the late 1990s, organizations in need of entry-level technical and managerial talent will also continue to face shortages.[12]

Slow growth of work force

Since these demographic trends are expected to continue in coming years, the work force will become even more diverse in the future. During the 1990s, the growth of the U.S. work force is expected to slow to 1.2 percent from about 2.0 percent in the 1980s and nearly 3.0 percent in the 1970s. By the end of the decade, 47 percent of the work force will be women, and 26 percent of all jobs will be held by immigrants and minorities. The traditional, white male majority found in the work force of the early 1980s and before will be reduced to 45 percent of the U.S. work force by the end of this decade.

Cultural and attitudinal diversity. Diversity in the work force is also influenced by cultural values and societal norms. During the 1970s and 1980s, for example, more than half of the growth in the U.S. work force resulted from women seeking employment. Changing values and laws and economic conditions have caused greater participation rates by women in the employment market. The subsequent increase in the diversity of the work force has resulted in a variety of implications for human resource departments and benefits administrators. For example, parental leave and child-care facilities provided by employers have become more common concerns. Motorola, as a case in point, responded to these pressures by selling a piece of land near one of its Phoenix, Arizona plants to a child-care company. In many progressive companies, sick days, paid days off for illness, have been redefined as "personal leave days" to accommodate working parents who must be absent to meet the needs of their children. In response to the increase of dual-career families, more and more human resource departments find themselves helping the spouses of newly hired or transferred employees to find jobs in their local communities.

New attitudes

Changing attitudes and diverse viewpoints have also confronted personnel departments in the form of requests for longer vacations, more holidays, and nontraditional work schedules.[13] Changes in attitudes about work have forced companies such as Motorola, General Motors, and many others to find new ways to motivate employees. Motorola's participative management program discussed earlier in this chapter exemplifies this response to changing attitudes. Changes even in attitudes about honesty are reflected in the growing rate of employee theft with which many human resource departments are forced to contend. Similarly, attitudes about commuting to work are changing as more and more people stay at home and work via computers and telephone lines.[14]

Diverse viewpoints about illegal drug use and sexual freedom also impact human resource departments. In many companies, new hires and even current employees are expected to submit to drug tests. Likewise, employee concerns about working with AIDS-infected (or potentially infected) co-workers often fall to the human resource department to resolve.

It is impossible to identify every changing value in society that may affect human resource management. Nonetheless, as society becomes more diverse in its attitudes, culture, and other dimensions, human resource departments must try to anticipate the impact of these changes and act accordingly.

Guest workers

Diversity through immigration and migration. All advanced economies face some diversity within their work force. This diversity may come from immigration across national borders or migration within a country. Countries such as Germany and Saudi Arabia, for example, have large numbers of guest workers—foreigners who are granted work visas but not citizenship. Other countries, such as Japan, for example, actually discourage guest workers and immigration, leaving Japan with a very homogeneous work force and growing labor shortages—particularly in menial jobs.[15] Regardless of national policies, the greatest work force diversity is most commonly observed in the large cities of advanced economies.

DEC and diversity

Harold Epps, who runs the Digital Equipment Corp. plant that makes computer keyboards, manages the work force of the future. The Boston factory's 350 employees come from 44 countries and speak 19 languages. When the plant issues written announcements, they are printed in English, Chinese, French, Spanish, Portuguese, Vietnamese, and Haitian Creole.[16]

2. ENVIRONMENTAL CHALLENGES 45

Immigration

As the Digital Equipment example suggests, the widening diversity of immigration has reshaped the work force. Historically, the majority of immigrants to North America came from Europe. With growing prosperity there, Europeans now account for only 10 percent of U.S. immigration, while Asia and Latin America each contribute more than 40 percent. Mexico alone provides 15 percent of all new arrivals to the U. S. in a typical year.[17]

Diversity and human resource professionals. Diversity creates new challenges for human resource professionals and their organizations. Consider just three of the many implications suggested by the work force diversity already encountered in the U.S. in the early 1990s.

Baby boom becomes baby bust

The work force is aging at the same time the growth of young workers is slowing. The baby boom that peaked in the late 1950s, declined throughout the 1960s, leading to a baby bust in the 1970s and 1980s, leading to a slower work force growth rate in the 1990s (and presumably beyond). The first challenge of human resource professionals will be to provide advancement opportunities to older workers who are members of the post-World War II baby boom while finding sufficient entry-level workers to meet present and future staffing needs.

Almost two-thirds of all women employed in the U.S. have children under the age of 18, and more than half of these women have children under the age of three. Since women remain the primary caregivers for children, they are confronted with the responsibilities of both a job and child-care arrangements, a situation which often involves unpleasant tradeoffs between career and family. This continuing trend confronts human resource departments with a second challenge—to provide both flexible work schedules (which may be counterproductive in some businesses) and company-sponsored child care facilities (which carry enormous responsibilities and potential liabilities). Yet, as more mothers must work and work force growth slows, the need to obtain, maintain, and retain a skilled work force will force employers to adjust to the growing demands inherent in an increasingly diverse work force.[18]

Participation rates

Labor force participation rates measure the percentage of a given group that participates in the work force. In 1948, for example, 89 percent of all men between the ages of 55 and 64 were in the labor force. By the year 2000, the participation rate for this age group is estimated to be approximately 68 percent. The difference between the 89 and 68 percent participation rates reflects a long-term trend toward earlier (pre-age 65) retirement. In response to this change, human resource departments will face challenges, such as how to retain valued, experienced senior employees at a time when the work force is growing slowly without blocking advancement opportunities for the large number of middle-aged baby boomers who are not yet ready to retire. The challenges presented by different age groups will grow as the diversity within and among these groups grows.[19]

Although these demographic trends complicate the work of human resource professionals and operating managers, such as Mr. Epps at Digital, studies indicate that growing diversity is inevitable. Human resource professionals and operating managers must accept this challenge and use it to benefit both their organization and its people. That is, they must accept and respond to diversity as part of the organization's social responsibility. Organizations that embrace this diversity will find a larger pool of potential applicants from which to hire new employees, and, as the work force growth slows, the acceptance and integration of an ever-widening diversity of employees will be essential to the recruitment plans of growing organizations. Diversity—particularly in managerial, professional, and sales positions—offers North American firms the added competitive advantage of multilingualism and cultural sensitivity in international markets.

Diversity overseas

North American human resource specialists and operating managers, however, must be careful not to presume that their values apply internationally. Long-standing tribal, religious, and ethnic differences may not permit the same degree of work force diversity in overseas operations. For example, in most developing countries, Moslem nations, and even in such advanced economies as Japan, severe limitations may be placed upon women, nonbelievers, or members of specific castes or tribes.[20] Likewise, when transferring foreign nationals to North American assignments, human resource professionals must be sensitive to the potential culture shock these individuals may experience in the work forces of the United States and Canada. Many males from the Near East and the Orient, for example, have never been supervised by a woman.

Technological Challenges

Technology impacts human resource management by changing jobs and skills. One of the greatest potential impacts to jobs since the advent of the industrial revolution may be artificial intelligence. The industrial revolution allowed people to make greater use of mechanical power—from water wheels and steam engines to nuclear power—to amplify human productivity. Artificial intelligence will give a growing number of workers access to expert systems—computerized programs that capture the knowledge and decision-making approaches of experts. One estimate suggests, "As many as 90% of all jobs in American organizations will be candidates for augmentation, replacement, or displacement by expert systems and other forms of artificial intelligence between the year 2000 and 2005."[21] As the capabilities of artificial intelligence give people and machines greater problem-solving powers, jobs and the skills they require will change dramatically, affecting the employment, training, development, compensation, and employee relations activities of the human resource department."[22]

Artificial intelligence

At present, the biggest impact of technology on human resource management derives from how technology alters industries and lifestyles.

The technology of cars and airplanes, for example, modified the transportation industry. Automobile, bus, and aviation companies grew. This growth created a demand for more employees and training. For those already employed within these firms, growth provided promotional opportunities. Railroad companies were affected, adversely, by the same technology; accordingly, their personnel management challenges differed. Revenue lost to cars, trucks, and airplanes limited growth. Advancement opportunities—even employment opportunities—shrank. The human resource departments of railroad companies had to reduce the work force and create early retirement systems.

Automation is another way that technology affects the field of human resource management.

Automation

The introduction of computers into banks changed employment needs. Before computers, personnel specialists recruited large numbers of unskilled and semiskilled clerks to perform routine tabulations. Computers, however, automated these procedures and introduced the need for highly skilled programmers and systems analysts. Also needed were semiskilled employees to process information into computer-usable form. The visible banking systems, that is, those that could be observed by outsiders, changed very little, but the human resource departments of banks dramatically changed their recruiting and training programs.

Robotics

One specific form of automation that is likely to have a significant impact on organizations is robotics. Their increased use seems a certainty since their cost, relative to human resources, is declining.[23] As robots become more common and sophisticated, they will affect organizational productivity and the quality of work life for employees. The good news is that hazardous and boring jobs will be taken over by robots. Dangerous jobs—such as working with toxic chemicals and paints—will be changed by substituting robots for people. Likewise, during the 1990s highly repetitive assembly tasks will be taken over increasingly by robots. Productivity and quality are likely to improve. But at what cost?

The bad news is that human resource professionals may have to contend with increased worker alienation. Job opportunities may shrink, along with opportunities for socialization on the job. Good-paying factory work for unskilled and semiskilled employees may become scarce, leading traditional factory workers to accept lower-paid unskilled jobs in the service sector. To use expensive robots effectively, more and more factories may find it necessary to operate for two or three shifts a day, even on weekends, to fully take advantage of costly robotics. As robots become lighter, faster, stronger, more "intelligent" and cost-efficient, more applications for these marvels will be found in service industries, causing even more widespread dislocations.[24]

I. FRAMEWORKS AND CHALLENGES

Economic Challenges

Worldwide competition is growing as more and more developing nations target specific markets. This increased competition puts pressure on all firms in any industry to be more productive. Robots and other technological advances help boost productivity, but ultimately these technologies are designed, installed, programmed, and maintained by people. To meet the economic pressures that result from increased competition, human resource professionals will need to find more innovative ways to help line managers increase productivity through people.[25]

Business cycles

Domestic economic pressures also affect human resource specialists. As the economy changes from expansion to contraction during the course of a business cycle, organizations must modify their plans. These changes in the business cycle demand that human resource specialists assist their organizations in meeting their new plans. When the economy expands, new employees and training programs are needed. Voluntary departures by employees increase. Pressures for higher wages, better benefits, and improved working conditions also grow. Human resource departments must act cautiously, however. Overstaffing, bloated benefit programs, and higher wages become serious burdens when the business cycle turns down. A recession creates a need to maintain a competent work force and reduce labor costs. Decisions to reduce hours, lay off workers, or accept lower profit margins involve the advice of human resource experts. The more effectively human resource departments monitor the economy, the better they can anticipate the organization's changing needs. Sometimes these departments can even develop proactive policies that anticipate changes in the business cycle. Motorola provides another example.

Motorola

Motorola uses contract labor to fill its human resource needs during periods of peak business activity. Contract labor *consists of people who are hired and often trained by an independent agency that supplies companies with needed human resources for a fee. Although when Motorola finds, for example, that it needs assemblers of electronic components to finish a project, it generally recruits, hires, and trains most of these people through its own human resource department, however some of the workers it uses will be contracted from a temporary help agency which can provide extra staff quickly. These agency workers do not become Motorola employees but work for their agency and are assigned to Motorola to meet the temporary need for more staff. When the project is completed or when the business cycle declines, Motorola informs the agency that it needs fewer of these temporary contract workers. Thus Motorola's human resource department can meet the staffing needs of its divisions while providing a high level of employment security to Motorola's employees. Of course, Motorola has less control over the quality of contract workers, whose loyalty and dedication to Motorola's objectives may be less than that of career Motorolans.*

This policy of using contract labor is another example of how proactive human resource departments seek ways to meet the needs of an organization and its people while remaining sensitive to the firm's economic environment. In Motorola's case, the human resource department did not wait for the economy to go up or down before it reacted. Rather, these practitioners developed policies that allow the organization to adjust smoothly to changes caused by technological, economic, and other challenges.

Governmental Challenges

Government as rule maker

Few challenges encountered by personnel departments are as overwhelming as those presented by government, which, through the enforcement of laws, has a direct and immediate impact on the personnel function. Federal laws regulating the employee-employer relationship challenge the methods personnel departments use. Some, such as the Occupational Safety and Health Act or the Civil Rights Act, make major demands on personnel departments. The impact of these laws has helped elevate the importance of personnel decisions.

Government involvement in the employment relationship seeks to achieve societal objectives—usually the elimination of practices that are considered contrary to public policy. To personnel specialists, government involvement requires compliance and proactive efforts to minimize organizational consequences. Throughout this book, employee-related laws are explained to illustrate the challenges and actions modern personnel departments encounter.

ORGANIZATIONAL CHALLENGES

Besides external demands, personnel departments find current challenges within the organizations they serve. Internal challenges arise because employers pursue multiple objectives. These objectives require tradeoffs between financial, sales, service, production, employee, and other goals. Since personnel objectives are just one set among many in the eyes of top management, personnel managers must confront internal challenges with a balanced concern for other needs. The employer does not exist solely, or even largely, to meet personnel objectives. Instead, personnel departments exist to assist the organization in meeting its other objectives successfully. Personnel departments find several internal challenges in helping the organization achieve its objectives. Included are challenges from unions, informational needs, and organizational character and conflicts.

Unions

Potential and actual challenges

Unions represent an *actual* challenge to unionized companies and a *potential* challenge to nonunionized ones. In companies with unions, the employer and union sign a labor agreement that specifies compensation (wages and benefits),

50   I. FRAMEWORKS AND CHALLENGES

hours, and working conditions. The agreement limits the personnel activities of supervisors and personnel departments. For both, the challenge is to achieve objectives without violating the agreement.

> Karl McPheters wanted to promote Jill Wang to chief switchboard operator because Jill was an excellent employee. But she was only the second most experienced employee; Pam Hale had greater seniority. The labor contract called for promotions to go to the most senior worker, which meant Pam Hale. To promote Jill, Karl found Pam a production job at a higher rate of pay. She took it. This now made Jill the most senior switchboard operator and next in line for the promotion. The contract was honored, and management achieved its objective of promoting the best person, Jill.

Two-tiered wages

A more recent union challenge concerns labor costs and competitiveness, especially when unionized firms compete against nonunion ones. Higher union wage rates have caused some employees to negotiate a *two-tiered wage structure* to avoid outright wage cuts, a practice whereby current union members get their old rate (and maybe a slight raise), but new workers start out at a much lower wage rate. This practice is common, for example, in the airline industry and may result in two workers doing the same work at markedly different rates of pay. Besides the challenges of future contract bargaining—discussed more fully in Chapter 18, the two-tiered wage structure has resulted in challenges of motivation, morale, and employee turnover.[26]

Employers *without* unions are also affected by union challenges. To retain the flexibility of nonunion status, personnel departments implement compensation policies, hours of work, and working conditions similar to those found in unionized operations. Here the personnel challenge is usually determined by top management: try to operate so that unionization is discouraged. For example, major innovative firms in the electronics industry, such as Motorola and Texas Instruments, are mostly nonunion.

Information Systems   HRIS

Human resource departments require large amounts of detailed information. Increasingly, the quality of the personnel department's contribution depends on the quality of its information. Many personnel activities and much effort by personnel professionals are devoted to obtaining and refining the department's information base. The information requirements of a full-service department only begin with such questions as:

Key questions   1-5 questions

▶ What are the duties and responsibilities of *every* job in the organization?

▶ What are the skills possessed by *every* employee?

2. ENVIRONMENTAL CHALLENGES   51

➤What are the organization's future human resource needs?

➤How are external constraints affecting the organization?

➤What are the current trends in compensation of employees?

And this list could be continued for pages!

Clearly, the acquisition, storage, and retrieval of information present a significant challenge.[27] One key part of the challenge is gaining cooperation from others in the organization who provide the department with much of its information. Employee responses to personnel department questionnaires, supervisors' absentee control reports, and most other sources of human resource information come from others. Line managers may see personnel's request for information as far less important than producing or selling the firm's goods and services. To ensure a timely flow of accurate information, personnel specialists must not only communicate the importance of their requests but maintain good working relationships with other managers to earn their cooperation. To store and retrieve information, personnel departments increasingly rely on computer-based information systems—systems that electronically store detailed information about employees, jobs, laws, unions, economic trends, and other internal and external factors. But massive information systems challenge the personnel department's ability to safeguard the privacy of employee records. As a manager at a consulting firm specializing in computer security observed:

Computer privacy and ethics

Computer security is more important in the human resource management field than in any other area where computers might be used.

There is an ethical responsibility to protect the individual. But more importantly and certainly more of a problem is the legal aspect of privacy.

I don't know of any state that doesn't have some sort of privacy legislation on the books regarding the confidentiality of . . . personnel records in general. HRM administrators can be held criminally liable if they do not take adequate measures to protect that data . . .[28]

Organizational Culture and Conflicts

Unique organizations

Every employer is unique. Similarities between organizations can be found among their parts, but each whole organization has a unique culture.[29] *Organization culture* is the product of all the organization's features: its people, its successes, and its failures. Organization culture reflects the past and shapes the future.

The challenge for human resource specialists is to adjust proactively to the culture of the organization. For example, objectives can be achieved in several acceptable ways. This idea, called *equifinality,* means there are usually multiple paths to objectives. The key to success is picking the path that best fits the organization's culture.

Human resource manager, Aaron Chu feared that his request to hire a training assistant would be turned down. Instead of asking for funds to hire someone, Aaron expressed concern that poor supervisory skills were contributing to employee complaints and resignations. He observed at the weekly management meeting that unskilled replacements could lead to rising labor costs.

Knowing that top management was concerned about remaining a low-cost producer, Aaron was not surprised when the plant manager suggested hiring "someone to do training around here." By adjusting to the organization's culture, Aaron got a budget increase for training.

Core values and beliefs

In nearly every organization, a few core values or beliefs shape its culture. Sometimes service is highly valued, as at IBM. Elsewhere, product innovation may be seen as the key to the firm's success, such as at the 3M Company. At Aaron's firm, labor costs were perceived as central. His top management evidently holds the belief that success depends on low labor costs, and it is willing to support actions that promise to keep labor cost low. Effective practitioners identify the values or beliefs of their organizations and strive to further those values.[30]

Depending on the culture of the organization and the attitudes of its people, personnel challenges may arise from conflict among groups. Smoking at work is an example. Should smokers' addiction be treated as a disability and accommodated, or should the rights of nonsmokers be paramount?[31] What obligations, if any, does an employer have to address employee fears of dealing with AIDS-infected coworkers?[32] How do human resource departments help reduce the conflict between stockholders' rights to maximize their financial return and employees' desires for job security, especially during a merger or acquisition?[33] How do employment departments meet the legal requirements to deny employment to undocumented foreign aliens without discriminating against minority citizens under the 1986 Immigration Reform and Control Act?[34] These are not hypothetical conflicts; they occur daily in organizations. And human resource departments are usually responsible for developing and enforcing policies in these areas.

PROFESSIONAL CHALLENGES

HR professionals

Another challenge to human resource experts is professionalism. Human resource management skills are too important to organizations and society to be ignored. External and internal challenges require practitioners who are at least minimally qualified. Since the actual capabilities of experts vary widely, professionalism in the human resource management field became a growing interest.

SHRM

The Society for Human Resource Management (formerly, the American Society

Figure 2-4

Professional Designations Granted by the Society for Human Resource Management

SHRM CERTIFICATION

The Human Resource Certification Institute grants certification after an applicant has:

1. verified current full-time professional exempt experience in the HR field as either a practitioner, educator, researcher or consultant, and . . .
2. passed a comprehensive written examination to demonstrate mastery of the HR Body of Knowledge.

The basic generalist designation
PROFESSIONAL IN HUMAN RESOURCES (PHR)
Four years of professional HR exempt experience

| Two years professional HR exempt experience and a bachelor's degree | **OR** | One year professional HR exempt experience and a graduate degree |

AND

Pass a comprehensive examination

The senior generalist designation
SENIOR PROFESSIONAL IN HUMAN RESOURCES (SPHR)
Eight years of professional HR exempt experience

| Six years professional HR exempt experience and a bachelor's degree | **OR** | Five years professional HR Exempt experience and a graduate decree |

AND

Pass a comprehensive examination

Source: Human Resource Certification Institute (an affiliate of the Society for Human Resource Management)

for Personnel Administration) took an important step toward building the profession of human resource management: certification.

Certification

The Society for Human Resource Management studied the question of certification for a decade.[35] By late 1975, it established standards and credentials for certification. Experienced practitioners and academics were admitted under a "grandfather" clause, which granted them certification based on letters of recommendation and their experience. This provision ended after the first year, and credentials are now earned by testing, which ensures a minimum level of competence among those who receive a professional designation from the Society for Human Resource Management (often referred to by its initials, SHRM).

SHRM created two professional designations, as shown in Figure 2-4. As the figure shows, the designation Professional in Human Resources (PHR) applies to generalists and the designation Senior Professional in Human Resources (SPHR) applies to generalists with more experience. Both designations require that applicants complete a comprehensive test on the following topics:

➤ Compensation and benefits

➤ Employee and labor relations

➤ Selection and placement

➤ Training and development

➤ Health, safety, and security

➤ Management practices.

The test for those seeking the SPHR designation is weighted more heavily in favor of the "Management practices" section. Testing and certification are handled by an affiliate of SHRM called the Human Resource Certification Institute, or HRCI. HRCI also handles recertification, which must take place every three years.

Other Professional Requirements

Certification does not make human resource management a profession. Some argue that the field will never become a profession because there is no common body of knowledge. Human resource management is not a clearly separate discipline like law, medicine, or economics. It draws on a variety of disciplines.

Individual practitioners have little control over their activities, and this limits their professionalism. Unlike self-employed physicians or attorneys who are independent decision makers, or teachers who have some traditionally guaranteed rights under tenure rules, human resource experts are dependent upon the direction of top management and have few rights. And unlike most professions, there are no legal certification or licensing requirements. Most professions have legally sanctioned procedures to establish minimum competency. There are no such requirements in the human resource field. Even SHRM's certification program is voluntary. As a result, there are no widely recognized standard codes of conduct or ethics. Although Figure 2-5 reproduces SHRM's code, neither practitioners nor the public uniformly support it.

Figure 2-5

Code of Ethics of SHRM

SOCIETY FOR
HUMAN
RESOURCE
MANAGEMENT

Code of Ethics

As a member of the Society for Human Resource Management, I pledge myself to:

- Maintain the highest standards of professional and personal conduct.

- Strive for personal growth in the field of human resource management.

- Support the Society's goals and objectives for developing the human resource management profession.

- Encourage my employer to make the fair and equitable treatment of all employees a primary concern.

- Strive to make my employer profitable both in monetary terms and through the support and encouragement of effective employment practices.

- Instill in the employees and the public a sense of confidence about the conduct and intentions of my employer.

- Maintain loyalty to my employer and pursue its objectives in ways that are consistent with the public interest.

  Uphold all laws and regulations relating to my employer's activities.

- Refrain from using my official positions, either regular or volunteer, to secure special privilege, gain or benefit for myself.

- Maintain the confidentiality of privileged information.

- Improve public understanding of the role of human resource management

This Code of Ethics for members of the Society for Human Resource Management has been adopted to promote and maintain the highest standards of personal conduct and professional standards among its members. Adherence to this code is required for membership in the Society and serves to assure public confidence in the integrity and service of human resource management professionals.

Source: Reprinted by Permission of the Society of Human Resource Management, Alexandria, Virginia

Figure 2-6

A Comparison of Personnel Functions as Their Importance Is Perceived by Personnel Directors, Executives, and Managers

	RANKING BY:		
	PERSONNEL DIRECTORS	EXECUTIVES	MANAGERS
Affirmative action/EEO	2	1	1
Recruiting	3	2	2
Wage/salary/administration	1	3	3
Employment selection	27	4	16
Human resource planning	12	5	7
Training/development	23	6	13
Performance appraisal	29	7	12
Orientation	32	8	8
Insurance benefits	5	9	6
Discharges	14	10	14

Source: Adapted from Harold C. White, APD, and Michael N. Wolfe, "The Role Desired for Personnel Administration," *Personnel Administrator*, June 1980, pp. 90–91.

Becoming professional

While debate will continue over whether the field is, or will be recognized as, a profession, the field is *becoming* more professional through the leadership of SHRM, more highly educated practitioners, and more advanced university education in human resource management. The result is a challenge to every practitioner that goes beyond organizational boundaries: Can the field of human resource management become a profession?[36]

HUMAN RESOURCE MANAGEMENT IN PERSPECTIVE

Given the variety of historical, external, internal, and professional challenges that confront the practice of human resource management, its purpose remains the attainment of organizational objectives with maximum effectiveness and efficiency in an ethically and socially responsible way. Human resource management exists to assist others in the organization. It does not direct operations or decide organizational objectives. Its authority is limited. Although research shows that human resource managers perceive themselves as having more authority than they really do,[37] their authority is usually viewed as *advisory* (or staff) *authority*. That is, these managers primarily advise and assist, not decide and direct. In recent years, however, the complexity of the human resource environment and the trend toward greater professionalism has meant that human resource managers are obtaining greater *decision-making* (or line) *authority*. Authority to manage other departments still remains with the managers in those departments, however, as explained in Chapter 1.

Limited authority

In using their authority, human resource experts must recognize different groups within the organization. Research shows that executives and lower-level managers have different expectations about human resource activities.[38] Figure 2-6 illustrates the 10 most important human resource activities as viewed by executives. Note how these perceptions differ from the perceptions of lower-level managers. For example, executives and managers rank selection differently. To be effective, human resource specialists must determine the areas of concern among the different groups they support. Otherwise, their advisory authority will be less effective and more likely ignored.[39]

The most important challenge to human resource professionals is contributing to the success of their employer. Professionals must first be businesspeople and then strive to be experts in human resource management. Although the remainder of this book addresses the challenges and practices that enhance the value of these professionals, their primary role is to help their organizations prosper. When human resources policies and practices hinder organizational success, they must be subordinated to the needs of the organizations.[40] Then, as international competitiveness increases, operating managers will rely more heavily on their "people skills" and human resource professionals. The success of individual managers—whether in staff or operating positions—means the human resource department will face even more demands and challenges.

With limited authority and resources, the personnel department is expected to meet the challenges discussed in this and following chapters. These challenges affect the department's ability to fulfill its purpose of contributing to the organization's effectiveness. If these challenges are not met, then personnel management does not achieve its purpose. Moreover, its challenges are likely to grow in the future, unless personnel specialists can take proactive measures now.

Perhaps the most extensive challenges come from the need to understand the international environment and provide equal employment opportunity. A detailed examination of these challenges in Chapters 3 and 4 reveal how critical the personnel function can be to organizations. Other challenges are reviewed in more depth throughout the book.

SUMMARY

The practice of personnel management is shaped by a variety of environmental challenges. These challenges arise from the historical, external, organizational, and professional demands confronting personnel specialists.

1. The historical challenges began with the industrial revolution, which led to the scientific study of work and workers. As the tools available to managers became more sophisticated, the need for specialists in personnel management and human resources grew. Early in this century, personnel departments emerged to deal with these demands. Today, personnel departments are responsible for meeting the external, organizational, and professional issues that affect employees.

2. The external challenges to human resource management come from several different sources. The major external concerns are created by changing technologies, economic cycles, work force diversity, and government involvement. Each of these factors influences the ways in which personnel departments meet their objectives.

3. Organizational challenges include those elements within the organization that personnel departments cannot ignore if they are to be successful. Unions are one obvious example. They demand that management meet and satisfy its economic objectives within the constraints imposed by organized labor. Nonunionized organizations must be aware of conditions that can cause workers to unionize. A professionally managed personnel department must develop and maintain a sophisticated database in order to be effective. The gathering of information and the successful implementation of human resource activities depends on a solid understanding of the unique aspects of the organization's culture.

The newest challenge to personnel management is professionalism. The important role that personnel departments and their members play in modern organizations requires a professional approach and professionally trained people. The growing importance of this function requires practitioners to strive for high professional standards. The certification program of the Society for Human Resource Management is a major step in that direction.

If human resource departments can successfully meet the environmental challenges discussed in this chapter, they are more likely to contribute effectively to the goals of the organization and its people.

Terms for Review

Paternalism
Contract labor
Demographics
Participation rates
Organization culture
Equifinality
Society for Human Resource Management p 54-57

Certification — p 54-55
Advisory (staff) authority
Decision-making (line) authority
Guest workers
Two-tiered wage rates

Review and Discussion Questions

1. Explain how increased competition—particularly from the Japanese—has made personnel management more important at Motorola's semiconductor group.

2. In what ways did the industrial revolution influence the practice of personnel management?

3. Describe how a proactive personnel department would be affected by the introduction of robotics and other forms of automation into a production department.

4. What are the characteristics of demographic changes? Why should personnel specialists monitor demographic trends? How does work force diversity affect human resource management?

5. How would the increased professionalization of the personnel field benefit personnel practitioners and their employers?

6. What is the purpose of a code of ethics, such as the one developed by SHRM? Can you suggest any additions to SHRM's code?

7. Defend or refute the following statement: Since personnel department budgets usually amount to only one percent of the organization's total budget, top management should not devote more than one percent of its time to personnel management issues.

8. How do economic cycles affect the personnel function? Give an example of a personnel policy that considers variations in the economy.

INCIDENT 2-1
A Possible Technological Scenario

Sometime within the near future, electronic technology will advance to the point where the average home will have:

▶ A computer console and access to several on-line computer systems via satellite communications

▶ A television set (with more than a hundred working channels fed by a cable system) that serves as a visual display for computer outputs and inputs

▶ A photocopy machine connected to the television that permits photocopies of screen information

▶ A two-way video phone.

About the time this all becomes a reality, serious people will ask, "Why do we still follow the primitive ritual of going to work? Why don't we do our jobs at home, since most workers are now white-collar information handlers?" Shortly thereafter, the practice of going to work, which began with the industrial revolution, will end for many workers. People will still work. Some will even have to "go to work." But most people will stay at home, plugged into a worldwide information grid.

Assuming this scenario comes true during your career:

1. What implications does it hold for our culture and our society?

2. What are the implications of these probable changes for personnel management?

INCIDENT 2-2
Government Intervention

Since the 1930s, the federal government has increased its regulation of how employers treat employees. Laws have been passed that permit workers to join unions, require employers to pay minimum wages, ensure safe and healthy work environments, prohibit discrimination, and restrict the freedom of employers to make personnel decisions in other areas.

Some futurists believe the trend of increasing government intervention will continue. To support their argument, these thinkers point to Japan and Europe, where government involvement is far more extensive than in the United States and Canada. These people believe that the federal government will require employers to provide even greater job security against layoffs, develop more extensive training programs for the disadvantaged and handicapped, and follow other regulations that will further limit personnel decisions.

Other experts think that the trend of growing government involvement is beginning to end. Complaints about taxes, deregulation of the airlines and other industries, and the demographic trend toward an older population are the evidence these people cite in support of their position. These people also argue that regulation cannot continue if United States and Canadian firms are to remain competitive in international markets.

1. Which trend do you think will occur and why?

2. If government regulation continues to increase, how will personnel departments be affected?

References

1. Edward E. Lawler III, "Human Resources Management: Meeting the New Challenges," *Personnel* (January 1988), p. 22.

2. *Vision of Industry in the Eighties* (Tokyo: Ministry of International Trade and Industry, 1980).

3. "Japan Inc. Goes International with High Technology," *Business Week* (Dec. 14, 1981), p. 44. See also Bro Uttal, "Here Comes Computer Inc.," *Fortune* (Oct. 4, 1982), pp. 82–90.

4. Ibid., p. 48. See also "Motorola's New Strategy: Adding Computers to Its Base in Electronics," *Business Week* (March 29, 1982), pp. 128–132.

5. Peter F. Drucker, "Management and the World's Work," *Harvard Business Review* (September–October 1988), pp. 65–76.

6. Exodus 18:20–21

7. Peter B. Petersen, "A Pioneer in Personnel," *Personnel Administrator* (June 1988), pp. 60–64.

8. Elton Mayo, *The Human Problems of an Industrial Civilization* (Cambridge: Harvard University Press, 1933). See also F. J. Roethlisberger and W. J. Dickson, *Management and the Worker* (Cambridge: Harvard University Press, 1939).

9. James W. Walker, "Moving Closer to the Top," *Personnel Administrator* (December 1986), pp. 53–57, 117; and "Becoming a Business Partner First," *Personnel Administrator* (December 1986), pp. 61–65, 118.

10. James C. Hyatt, "People Watchers: Demographers Finally Come into Their Own in Firms, Government," *The Wall Street Journal*, Western ed. (July 19, 1978), pp. 1, 31. See also George Odiorne, "The Crystal Ball of HR Strategy," *Personnel Administrator* (December 1986), pp. 103–106.

11. Joan Lindroth, "How to Beat the Coming Labor Shortage," *Personnel Journal* (April 1982), pp. 268–272. See also Kenneth H. Bacon, "The 1990s Economy: Impact of the 'Baby Bust,' " *The Wall Street Journal*, Eastern ed. (April 14, 1986), p. 1.

12. Melinda Beck et al., "The Baby Boomers Come of Age," *Newsweek* (March 30, 1981), pp. 34–37. Valerie Personick, "The Outlook for Industry Output and Employment through 1990," *Monthly Labor Review* (August 1981), pp. 28–41.

13. Jeff Hallett, "New Patterns in Working," *Personnel Administrator* (December 1988), pp. 32–37. See also John P. Robinson, "Time for Work," *American Demographics* (April 1989), p. 68; and M. Ronald Buckley, Donald B. Fedor, and Dianne C. Kicza, "Work Patterns Altered by New Lifestyles," *Personnel Administrator* (December 1988), pp. 40–43.

14. John Scwartz, Dody Tsiantar, and Karen Springen, "Escape from the Office," *Newsweek* (April 24, 1989), pp. 58–60.

15. A survey of 268 companies by Japan's Ministry of Labor found that these firms were unable to recruit even a fourth of the workers they wanted. Louis S. Richman, "The Coming World Labor Shortage," *Fortune* (April 9, 1990), pp. 71–72.

16. Joel Dreyfuss, "Get Ready for the New Work Force," *Fortune* (April 23, 1990), p. 167. See also Philip R. Harris and Robert T. Moran, *Managing Cultural Differences*, 3rd ed. (Houston: Gulf Publishing Co., 1991).

17. "The Mix of People Coming to America," compiled by the staff of *American Demographics* magazine as reported in *The Wall Street Journal* (April 21, 1989), p. b1.

18. Susan Meisinger, "100th Congress Makes Its Mark," *Resource* (October–November 1988), pp. 1, 7.

19. Diane Crispell, "Workers in 2000," *American Demographics* (March 1990), pp. 36–40. See also Leonard H. Chusmir, "A Shift in Values Is Squeezing Older People," *Personnel Journal* (January 1990), pp. 48–52.

20. "How to Turn Workforce Diversity into a Competitive Edge," *BNAC Communicator* (Summer 1990), pp. 1, 5. See also Wayne Wendling, "Response to a Changing Work Force," *Personnel Administrator* (November 1988), pp. 50–54; and Jolie Solomon, "Learning to Accept Cultural Diversity," *The Wall Street Journal*, Western ed. (Sept. 12, 1990), p. b1.

21. Robert W. Goddard, "Work Force 2000," *Personnel Journal* (February 1989), p. 66.

22. Ibid. See also Joseph H. Boyett and Henry P. Conn, *Workplace 2000* (New York: Dutton, 1991).

23. Olga L. Crocker and Richard Guelker, "The Effects of Robotics on the Workplace," *Personnel* (September 1988), pp. 26–36 See also George L. Whaley, "The Impact of Robotics Technology upon Human Resource Management," *Personnel Administrator* (September 1983), p. 70.

24. Russell Mitchell, Richard Brandt, Zachary Schiller, and James E. Ellis, "Boldly Going Where No Robot Has Gone Before," *Business Week* (Dec. 22, 1986), p. 22; Stephen Koepp, "The Boss That Never Blinks," *Time* (July 28, 1986), pp. 38–39; and John Dodd, "Robots: The New 'Steel Collar' Workers," *Personnel Journal* (September 1981), pp. 688–695.

25. William B. Werther, Jr., William A. Ruch, and Lynne McClure, *Productivity through People* (St. Paul.: West Publishing Company, 1986).

26. Daniel J. B. Mitchell, "Compensation: Why Are Wage Concessions So Prevalent?" *Personnel Journal* (August 1986), p. 135.

27. Alfred J. Walker, "The Newest Job in Personnel: Human Resources Data Administrator," *Personnel Journal* (December 1982), pp. 924–928.

28. "Securing Computerized Personnel Records," Resource (November 1982), p. 2; John Rahiya, "Privacy Protection and Personnel Administration: Are New Laws Needed?" *Personnel Administrator* (April 1979), pp. 19–21; and "Employers Sued on Privacy Charges," *Resource* (May 1986), p. 15.

29. William B. Wolf, "Organizational Constructs: An Approach to Understanding Organizations," *Journal of the Academy of Management* (April 1968), pp. 7–15. See also

Robert Granford Wright, *Mosaics of Organizational Character* (New York: Dunellen Publishing Co., Inc., 1975), p. 39.

30. "Putting Excellence into Management," *Business Week* (July 21, 1980), pp. 196–197.

31. "Hospital Finds Smoking Policy Is More Than Signs and Memos," *Resource* (September 1986), p. 3.

32. "Flexibility Called Key to Solving AIDS Problem," *Resource* (May 1986), p. 7.

33. More than one-third of the nation's 100 largest industrial companies now offer change-in-control contracts to their key executives, according to a survey by Towers, Perrin, Forster & Crosby. *Resource* (November 1986), p. 11.

34. Sandra Dibble, "Law Cuts Work Force, Puts Aliens Out of Jobs," *The Miami Herald* (Feb. 1, 1987), pp. 1a, 12a.

35. Ruth E. Thaler, "40 Years of Growth and Service," *Personnel Administrator* (June 1988), pp. 52–58. See also Wiley Beavers, "Accreditation: What Do We Need That For?" *Personnel Administrator* (November 1975), p. 39.

36. George Ritzer, "The Professionals: Will Personnel Occupations Ever Become Professions?" *Personnel Administrator* (May–June 1971), pp. 34–36.

37. Wendell French and Dale Henning, "The Authority-Influence Role of the Functional Specialist in Management," *Academy of Management Journal* (September 1966), p. 203.

38. Harold C. White and Michael N. Wolfe, " The Role Desired for Personnel Administration," *Personnel Administrator* (June 1980), pp. 87–98.

39. "ASPA-BNA Survey No. 52—Personnel Activities, Budgets, and Staffs: 1987-1988," *Bulletin to Management* (September 1, 1988), pp. 1–8.

40. James W. Walker, "Moving Closer to the Top," *Personnel Administrator* (December 1986), pp. 53–57, 117.

The globalization of business is having a significant impact on human resource management.
PETER J. DOWLING AND RANDALL S. SCHULER[1]

The political and economic changes resulting from revolution in Eastern Europe, the 1992 integration of the European Economic Community, and Asian dominance of many industries ensure that major corporations will continue to focus globally.
An obvious corollary . . . is the need to 'globalize' corporate management and human resources.
CALVIN REYNOLDS[2]

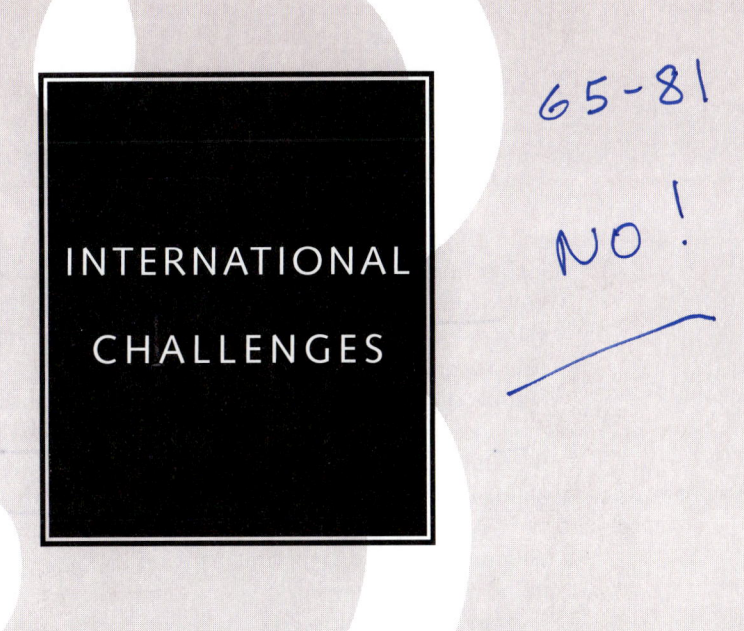

INTERNATIONAL CHALLENGES

CHAPTER OBJECTIVES

After studying this chapter, you should be able to:
1. **IDENTIFY** the major challenges to the human resource function that result from international operations.
2. **RECOGNIZE** how cultural and national assumptions affect human resource management.
3. **EXPLAIN** the challenges that influence the decentralization of international human resource management activities.
4. **DISCUSS** the tradeoffs associated with using home-country versus foreign nationals in international operations.
5. **IDENTIFY** specific human resource actions that assist a company's internationalization efforts.
6. **DISCUSS** International human resource management diversity issues.

CHAPTER 1 stated that "the purpose of human resource management is to improve the productive contribution of people to the organization in an ethical and socially responsible way." As businesses become more international in their outlook, human resource departments face new challenges in supporting the objectives of organizations and their people. Consider the observations of one writer about the international placement of executives:

Overseas failures

There is an alarmingly high failure rate when executives are relocated overseas. This mismatching of executives and foreign subsidiaries is primarily caused by poor or inappropriate selection procedures and inadequate orientation programs. To complicate matters, many executives steer clear of overseas assignments because they feel that their absence from their company's headquarters will hurt their chances for career advancement and that good jobs will not be waiting for them at home when they do repatriate.[3]

International human resource management relies on the objectives, practices, and professionalism discussed in previous chapters. Information must be gathered, for example, job openings filled, and assessments made. But the objectives sought, the practices used, and the challenges faced, all grow in number and complexity. The department is confronted with unfamiliar laws, languages, practices, competitors, attitudes, management styles, work ethics, and more. At the same time, the employee must balance the potential excitement of an international job with the personal, career, and family complexities international jobs can present. Both employees and the organization also are faced with cultural dilemmas, since foreign standards and laws may vary widely from those observed in the home country.

Complexity grows

Many of the inputs and challenges facing human resource management may change, but productive, quality work is still the expected output. To respond, the department must be flexible and proactive. The human resource department at Dow Chemical provides an example of how professional and proactive efforts can meet the needs of the company and its people assigned abroad.

Dow Chemical

Dow Chemical approaches the selection and orientation of employees for international assignment on an individual basis. Each individual, international move is considered unique. Each candidate is given information about the host country and a two-week intensive course in its language and culture. Discussions about the emotional issues likely to be encountered by an international move also take place.

When the decision to relocate has been made, each employee is assigned a "godfather," a high-ranking member in the person's function. The employee and godfather stay in touch, keeping each other informed of activities and career issues. The godfather serves as a mentor and reviews compensation issues. About a year before the employee is to be repatriated, the godfather begins to arrange for the employee's new job at home—a position at the same or a higher level, which was guaranteed before the employee was sent overseas. Small informal support groups at Dow meet to help returning employees readjust.[4]

"There is ample evidence that non-U.S. nationals and those who have had overseas assignments do advance to the top. Consider Dow Chemical: Nearly half of the top management team is non-American and more than three quarters, including Chairman Frank Popoff, have had foreign assignments."[5]

As the Dow example illustrates, international experience is important, and each international move is unique. To encourage employees to accept jobs abroad, most human resource departments in large companies have a variety of programs to assist and inform employees before, during, and after their assignments.

To support the growing internationalization of a business, the human resource department must evolve with the needs of its organization. As a business grows in sophistication and outlook, it moves toward an international perspective, seeking sales or resources abroad. Many international companies still maintain the perspective that the home market is the primary one, international operations being little more than subsidiaries. As the importance of international markets and resources grows, some companies evolve into global ones which operate across international borders in search of business worldwide. National distinctions become less important, as do the location and nationality of employees. As this occurs, the human resource department must adjust its perspective from domestic to global in support of the company's strategies.

The purpose of this chapter is to identify the challenges faced by international human resource management. Paralleling the structure of this book, the chapter begins with an examination of how the human resource management framework (Part I) is impacted by globalization in terms of assumptions, structure, and employee rights. The chapter then discusses international challenges associated with preparation and selection (Part II), development and evaluation (Part III), compensation and protection (Part IV), and employee relations (Part V). The chapter concludes with a look at special challenges facing the department and international employees. Subsequent chapters examine the international challenges associated with managing other specific human resource policies and practices.

FRAMEWORKS AND INTERNATIONAL CHALLENGES

Although the basic human resource functions and activities outlined in Chapter 1 do not change when an organization becomes international, professionals must be aware of their underlying assumptions and how those assumptions affect the structure of the department and employee rights.

Assumptions

Many of the assumptions we make as individuals are embedded in our culture. Individualism itself, for example, is more highly valued by the culture of the United States than by Japanese culture, which stresses the harmony of the group.[6] Operating managers and human resource professionals may find that their nationality, training, and experience have led them to assumptions that must be reexamined in an international context.[7] For example, in many Moslem cultures, developing nations, and even Japan, it is culturally and legally acceptable to discriminate in employment based on a person's sex and other non-performance-related criteria; however, as the next chapter elaborates, it is illegal in the United States to discriminate in employment on the basis of race, sex, age, religion, and national origin. Furthermore, a study of managers at the European Institute of Business Administration (INSEAD) found that more than half of the French, Italian, and Japanese managers considered it important to give precise answers to their subordinate's questions, but only 13 percent of the Americans and Swedes felt it was important.[4] The researcher observes:

> When their responses were analyzed, it appeared that the most powerful determinant of their assumptions was by far their nationality. Overall and across 56 different items of inquiry, it was found that nationality had three times more influence on the shaping of managerial assumptions than any of the respondents' other characteristics such as age, eduction, function, type of company. . . .[9]

Human resource professionals and operating managers must guard against assuming their attitudes and values apply universally. Unfortunately, assumptions reinforced by years of experience in our home culture can often be difficult to recognize, which partially explains why more and more companies expect their senior managers to have gained some international experience.[10]

Departmental Structure

As discussed in Chapter 1, the design of the human resource department is strongly influenced by the objectives and practices expected of it. When organizations become international, the human resource department continues recruitment, selection, placement, compensation, and other traditional activities, but responsibility for these activities may reside in the home-country office or may be decentralized to divisional, regional, national, or facility-based offices. A matrix management approach is often used.[11] With this approach, some responsibilities—such as relocation policy and executive-level replacement planning, are centralized, while other day-to-day activities—such as hiring entry-level workers, skills training, and employee relations, are handled locally. The degree of centralization or decentralization is shaped by the past practices of the department. However, the greater the cultural differences and economic and political risks,

I. FRAMEWORKS AND CHALLENGES

the more important a decentralized approach that allows for rapid and customized responses becomes.[12] Complex local customs and laws also favor a decentralized approach, allowing the local human resource department to adapt policies and practices to local realities.

Employee Rights

USSC and overseas discrimination

Employee rights are a major and complex element in the practice of international human resource management. The dominant laws are those of the country where the employee works. Reinforcing this view, the 1991 session of the U.S. Supreme Court ruled in *Boureslan vs. Aramco Co.* that protection against employment discrimination on the basis of race, sex, religion, age, and national origin does not cover employment abroad.[13] Later in the year, however, the Civil Rights Act of 1991 extended protection to United States citizens when they work in U.S. owned or controlled facilities in foreign lands as long as U.S. laws do not violate the laws of the host country. Although ethical managers and socially responsible employers may wish to apply nondiscrimination standards internationally, local customs or laws may render such standards impractical, even illegal.

Cross-cultural differences can also create challenges in the home country. Japanese managers, for example, are advised not to ask personal questions when interviewing U.S. citizens. This practice is common in Japan. Being asked personal questions in the U.S. may lead applicants, who are not hired, to consider such questions as the basis for a discrimination suit. As a result, many Japanese firms provide handbooks, videotapes, and seminars to their managers who are transferred to the U.S.[14] Likewise, mixing different castes of Hindus or Moslems and Hindus in India may be disruptive to the firm's bottom-line results. To guard against violating local laws, companies may find it advantageous to rely on foreign nationals to staff human resource positions.[15]

Growing European commonality

Although employee rights are unique to each country, similarities exist, particularly among members of common trading blocs, such as the European Economic Community and North America. *Codetermination*, for example, gives employees and their unions the right to participate in board-level decisions. Beginning with the Work Council Act of 1920, Germany has had a long tradition of worker participation in major decisions. Since World War II, codetermination has spread across Europe. Likewise, laws about worker safety and health are common in all industrial nations. Laws and court rulings against wrongful discharge limit employers' abilities to fire or layoff workers in most developed countries. In Europe, termination and layoff laws are far more restrictive than in North America. It has been a post-World-War II tradition in Japan to consider that male workers of large companies typically have "lifetime" employment until they reach retirement age.

Although a discussion of all the work place laws and court rulings in every country would fill volumes, it is important for human resource specialists to understand the rights of employees in each nation where the company does business. This challenge is often met by hiring local professionals and seeking the advice of international law firms that specialize in work-related laws and employee rights, even though the top positions are often reserved for those from the home country.

Burger King

When the British firm Grand Met bought Burger King, for example, it assigned Grand Met's senior manager, financial officer, and human resource officer to Burger King's headquarters in Florida. Grand Met believed it important to fill the senior human resource position with a British employee who is familiar with the company culture, especially since Burger King's operations are global and not limited to the United States. However, the remainder of the department is staffed by U.S. nationals who are familiar with the laws and culture of Burger King's major market, the United States.

INTERNATIONAL PREPARATION AND SELECTION

Reassignment overseas

Planning and staffing organizations overseas is a crucial activity of international human resource management. The slow growth of the work forces in all developed nations makes this activity increasingly important and difficult.[16] Central to the preparation and selection process are the employer's policies about filling openings with foreign nationals or home-country citizens reassigned to the international post. The reassignment of home-country nationals to the foreign openings means the employee is more likely to be familiar with home-country expectations and the company's practices and procedures. A foreign national, of course, will be more familiar with local laws and customs. Although each company adjusts its plans to the specific opening, home-country nationals are more likely to fill the senior position and the chief financial officer's role, as the Burger King example illustrates. When the technologies of products or production processes are complex or unique, home-country experts in design and production are likely to be assigned as senior managers or advisors. As one researcher observes:

Research summary

Complexity, political risk, and cultural distance increase the inherent uncertainty . . . in the foreign country and appear best managed with U.S. nationals acting primarily as sources of information and inobtrusive control. While competition also increases the risk . . . it also increases the importance of local nationals as conduits to the local market. . . . The higher the interdependence between the branch and headquarters, the more U. S. nationals . . . manage the inherent uncertainty. Yet, if the main sources of interdependence are within the nation-state, then . . . local nationals can better manage the uncertainty. . . .[17]

International succession planning

The corporate-level human resource manager plays a particularly important role in international succession planning. From his or her centralized perspective, the head of human resources is often given the responsibility for developing replacement plans. Potential successors are identified for all key positions

I. FRAMEWORKS AND CHALLENGES

throughout the company. Each successor is then evaluated as to deficiencies that can be addressed through training and experience. Working closely with top management, the manager is able to ensure a smooth flow of qualified, internal candidates who are prepared to assume larger responsibilities, domestically and internationally.[18] Recruitment and selection are particularly important human resource activities in this staffing process.

International Recruitment

Global organizations need to identify potential applicants for openings in the home country and abroad. The two sources of candidates are present employees and new hires. The reassignment of present employees offers an opportunity for career development in addition to filling a job opening. Although the glamour of an international assignment often looks attractive to first-time applicants, career, family, language, and cultural considerations may cause more experienced candidates not to apply. The dual-career family, children, and assignments to less developed areas are often significant barriers. For example, the U.S. Department of Labor estimates that by 1995, 81 percent of all marriages will be dual-career partnerships.[19]

Mentors

Even a lack of knowledge about internal openings can be a barrier. One reason some people are reluctant to apply for international jobs is the lack of a mentor. The fear is that the person will lose touch with developments at headquarters and harm their opportunities for career advancement. As a result, many people are forced to rely on their informal networks when the human resource department does not create systematic linkages among people to overcome these concerns. Consider the following example from General Dynamics, a major defense contractor.

General Dynamics

> *William L. Godsey had headed the General Dynamics Corporation's European operations in Brussels . . . when he got a call from Frederick S. Wood, a vice president at St. Louis Headquarters. Mr. Wood thought Mr. Godsey should apply for the newly opened job of vice president for international programs at the company's Pomona, Calif. division.*
>
> *Mr. Godsey did just that. He got the job and a short time later he and his family were winging their way back to the States. "If Fred hadn't called," Mr Godsey said, "I would never have known the job existed."*[20]

To address these and other concerns, companies like Dow, Ciba-Geigy, and Colgate-Palmolive have created mentor programs to help coach employees and serve as a linkage to international company developments.[21] The human resource department may offer incentives and assistance to help overcome barriers to reassignment. The department also may need to consider other sources of recruits. Colgate-Palmolive provides an example:

Colgate-Palmolive

Colgate-Palmolive's senior management noted that the company was having difficulty securing top executive talent for its international operations. Since Colgate's international business is crucial to the company's overall success, management decided to reexamine its recruitment and development practices in this area.

M.B.A.s

As a result, Colgate developed a new strategy of recruiting students from recognized undergraduate and M.B.A. programs whose experience, education, and language skills demonstrated their commitment to an international career.[22]

Recruiting foreign nationals to apply for work in their home country can be more difficult than seeking applicants in the firm's domestic market. In Japan, for example, many people prefer to work for Japanese companies, especially older and longer-term workers who perceive resigning to work for others as a sign of disloyalty. Even in developing nations such as Mexico, recruiting people from local firms is viewed as inappropriate.[23] Working for a foreign company even in one's home country may look unattractive for a variety of other reasons. Some people fear a "glass ceiling," above which promotions are reserved for employees from the company's home country. Differences in cultural expectations can be particularly frustrating for women who may not be considered appropriate to hold senior or professional-level positions by some host-country employers.[24] Although nearly half the senior management at Dow Chemical is non-American, the vice chairman of IBM is Swiss, and the chief executive officer of Coca-Cola is Cuban,[25] companies in Japan and other countries limit the opportunities of non-citizens, making recruitment for key jobs even more difficult.[26]

Glass ceiling

International Selection

As the organization evolves from a domestic to a global company, the initial selection process tends to favor transferring employees from the home country abroad. As the company becomes more international in its scope of operations and outlook, more foreign nationals are hired to staff positions overseas. A more global viewpoint finds the human resource department making fewer distinctions among the nationalities of employees hired to fill openings. As the company matures into a truly global operation, senior managers at headquarters become more diverse in their nationalities, as the mix of executives at Dow Chemical suggests.

The international selection process requires the human resource department to go beyond its traditional assessment of candidates. The determination of who should fill an opening encompasses more than technical or managerial abilities. The candidate's ability to adapt to the company and country cultures is important. Research shows that "maturity and emotional stability" along with "technical knowledge of the business" are two common factors among those selected for international assignment.[27] Whether looking for someone to assign abroad, to bring to the home country, or to work in their country for a foreign employer, the human resource department must pay careful attention to the candidate's

Research-based factors

Family issues

prospective compatibility with the company culture because in international staffing, company-based expectations may differ from the applicant's expectations.

Likewise, family considerations play an important role. Employment opportunities for a spouse[28], education for children, and the family's ability to adapt to new surroundings influence whether the placement will be successful. Although these issues are considered during recruitment, the selection process must determine the candidate's ultimate chances for success. These concerns, however, cannot be used to discriminate against qualified applicants in violation of local laws. Blending legal constraints with the challenges of assimilation makes international selection more complex. Complexity grows when religious, tribal, language, and class or caste standards must be applied as selection criteria.

INTERNATIONAL DEVELOPMENT AND EVALUATION

Once a candidate is selected, he or she needs to be oriented, trained, developed for future responsibilities, and evaluated. Development and placement, as with most other international human resource activities, often involve greater effort from the department.

Orientation

Regardless of how qualified job candidates may be, they generally need an orientation to the company if they are new hires and an orientation to their duties regardless of whether they are new to the company. The orientation touches on the policies, place, procedures, and people to be encountered. Unlike many new employee orientations, which may last only a few hours, an international orientation may begin weeks or months before *and* last for weeks after the assignment is made. Although a predeparture orientation is common and important, an on-site orientation after arrival at the international post further enlightens the new hire or transferee.

Orientation insights

International positions require an extensive orientation to familiarize the employee with the culture, language, and other unique aspects of the assignment. The orientation gives specific insights to local customs and expectations. Social attitudes about time and punctuality, entertaining, cultural taboos, the use of titles, and the degrees of formality expected in various social settings are often included in an international orientation. The employee's spouse may participate in the orientation, as is the case at Dow Chemical, where both the husband and wife are allowed to attend a two-week language and cultural orientation course.[29] Orientation at Dow is also likely to include a visit from another employee or spouse who has served in the location. Besides offering a personal touch, the repatriated employee or spouse is likely to have keen insights about a particular locale.

Training and Development

Training and international experience help develop the employee. Many international firms rely on a series of rotations through different functions in different countries to help develop managers and professionals into potential executives. Exposure to different functions and different cultures produces a broad understanding of the organization and the environments in which it operates. Training and development activities are supplemented with more traditional education and training courses by the human resource department, universities, and private trainers. As more companies expand their international involvements, experience abroad will become an even more important developmental activity.

Global linkages at H-P

Large multinational companies like Hewlett-Packard, for example, use annual conferences on the technical and managerial issues facing company leaders to bring together key managers and professionals from around the world. These meetings result in the development of informal networks which help tie people to the company, regardless of where they are located. Company-wide training programs are also used to develop people and expose them to others in the firm. An additional benefit of bringing people together for these meetings is the development of a shared culture. Perhaps the most striking aspect of visiting an international Hewlett-Packard facility is how similar the corporate culture of any facility is to the culture of the company's headquarters in Palo Alto.

Evaluation and Career Development

Employees in international operations need to be evaluated and need career-planning assistance. Evaluation is particularly difficult if and when the person performing the evaluation is thousands of miles away and unfamiliar with the unique challenges faced by the person being evaluated.

Dow's "godfathers"

At Dow, a senior manager in the same function is assigned the role of "godfather." The employee and his or her godfather (or mentor) are expected to keep each other informed about performance and other matters that affect the employee's career.[30] The godfather helps determine pay raises and locates a job back in the home country when the employee is repatriated.

The unique character of international assignments makes the evaluation and development of those abroad as important as it is difficult. Specific performance expectations not only form the basis for evaluation but also give direction to the expatriate's career development. The development of international managers often relies heavily on job rotation through different jobs within and among different countries. Of particular importance to the international employee and his or her family is compensation, including the expatriation and repatriation benefits which make international assignments a distinctive feature of international human resource management.[31]

INTERNATIONAL COMPENSATION AND PROTECTION

International compensation and protection goes beyond pay and benefits. Pay is expanded to compensate for additional taxes and living expenses. Incentives may be added to pay, especially for assignments in less desirable locations. Supplements may be given to cover the extra costs of educating children, return trips to the home country, and even servants' salaries. Benefits may include a company car, driver, club memberships, housing, or other "perks" normally reserved for top management. Extensive benefits are particularly common in countries with very high tax rates because benefits are typically not subject to taxation. Some companies, like Dow, give explicit job guarantees, assuring the returning employee a comparable or superior job at home. Employment contracts may also specify pay, benefits, termination bonuses, and other terms and conditions of employment.

Emphasis on benefits

Perhaps the most complicated benefit is relocation assistance, which is generally provided to the employee and family, in addition to the employee's training and compensation. This company-paid assistance can range from buying the employee's home at its market value to shipping household goods, cars, and other possessions abroad. Figure 3-1 lists some of the concerns faced by one medium-size company when it places executives internationally.[32] As the figure suggests, the human resource department may also assist in shipping family medical and dental records and in locating housing, schools, or other needed services.[33]

Repatriation

Repatriation of the employee back to the country of origin involves many of the same issues as sending someone abroad. Additionally, there may not be a clear career path for the person upon return. In fact, there may not even be a specific job in the home country. Effective human resource planning by the home office personnel department requires careful consideration of international succession planning to ensure that international assignments and repatriation to the home country result in meaningful jobs and developmental experiences.[34] When planning international placements does not consider eventual repatriation, executives often can end up feeling that their new jobs are less challenging at the same time they are trying to readjust to the home culture. These feelings may lead returning executives to conclude that their overseas experience may be of greater value to another firm, even a competitor. To the extent that expatriates remain in touch with the company through newsletters, return trips, and contacts with mentors and past colleagues, repatriation is more successful.[35] The human resource department can make a significant contribution to the company and its employees by ensuring that international transfers are well planned and facilitated by the department's compensation and benefit plans.

Figure 3-1

Human Resource Department Issues in International Placement

PLACEMENT ISSUES AT FERRO, CORP.

A *few* of the Human Resource Department's concerns at Ferro Corp., when international placement takes place, "include:

➤ Developing an overseas compensation and benefits plan, taking into account cost-of-living differences and any special needs
➤ Giving tax advice and financial counseling
➤ Supervising the sometimes extensive paperwork involved
➤ Assisting with housing and the selection of good schools
➤ Helping the employee set up banking accounts and make cash transfers
➤ Transferring medical, dental, and school records, and assisting with inoculations
➤ Helping with absentee ballots and international driving licenses
➤ Providing language training, through "immersion" courses
➤ Assisting with moves of household furniture and goods abroad
➤ Helping the spouse get work permits and jobs abroad, if possible."

Source: Quoted from Ellen Brandt, "Global HR," *Personnel Journal,* March, 1991, p. 41.

INTERNATIONAL EMPLOYEE RELATIONS AND ASSESSMENT

Perhaps the most complex area of international human resource management is international employee relations. Operating managers, whether they are expatriates or foreign nationals, seek help in dealing with employees from the human resource department. How well relations between managers and employees are handled has a direct impact on the organization's ability to execute its strategies efficiently. Variations in languages, customs, cultures, laws, employee expectations, competition, and other factors prompt all but the smallest international companies to rely on foreign nationals to handle the bulk of international employee relations.

Foreign nationals and HR

The use of foreign nationals, however, does not mean that human resource department headquarters abdicates its role. As discussed earlier, a matrix approach allows the local human resource office to handle the culture-specific tasks of hiring, placement, training, and compensating employees, while the home office sets broad policies and serves an assessment function to ensure that local offices are in compliance with company policies and procedures.

Assessment and prediction of expatriate and foreign national performance encompasses more than the task of individual evaluation. The department must assess its entire placement function, including planning, staffing, development, compensation, and employee relations support systems. Proactive adjustments must be made to ensure effectiveness and efficiency in its international human resource policies and activities. The execution of international human resource management functions offers an important vehicle for the department to contribute to the organization's strategic success and the needs of its people.

INTERNATIONAL HUMAN RESOURCE MANAGEMENT CHALLENGES

Beyond their impact on traditional human resource activities, international challenges affect the organization in less obvious and direct ways. Perspectives change. Outlooks become more global as senior-level managers become more aware of international developments. Those in the organization who lack this perspective (or are unable to develop it) fail to grasp the growing changes in global competition. Strategies and policies become culturally bound and do not benefit from the rich variety of viewpoints found internationally.

International human resource management impacts the company and the personnel department in countless, unforeseen ways. Some of the company-wide concerns raised for the department include the challenges of troubleshooting, work place diversity, and cultural awareness.

International Human Resource Troubleshooting

Worldwide resources

As with domestic operations, human resource problems arise in international operations. Whether a labor shortage, an unexpected resignation, or a union problem, international managers may need assistance with specific human resource issues. It is unrealistic to expect any one person or department to possess the knowledge and skills needed to address the wide array of human resource issues encountered internationally, but the department does need to be able to identify sources of assistance. It must be able to identify people within and outside the company who can provide needed expertise to address issues that may be specific to an individual culture or country. Developing a worldwide list of lawyers, consultants, and other experts may be the only cost-effective way of preparing for the nearly unlimited range of human resource issues that can confront the company.

International Challenges and Diversity

Challenges of work force diversity are amplified by international human resource management. Not only must human resource managers contend with diversity in the domestic work force, but globalization means increased diversity at home and abroad. Diversity increases as foreign nationals are transferred to the home country and as jobs are transferred to other countries. Compounding this diversity will be increasing immigration from a variety of countries, as suggested by the annual pattern of immigration presented in Figure 3-2. Consider these comments:

Figure 3-2

Sources of Immigrants into the United States

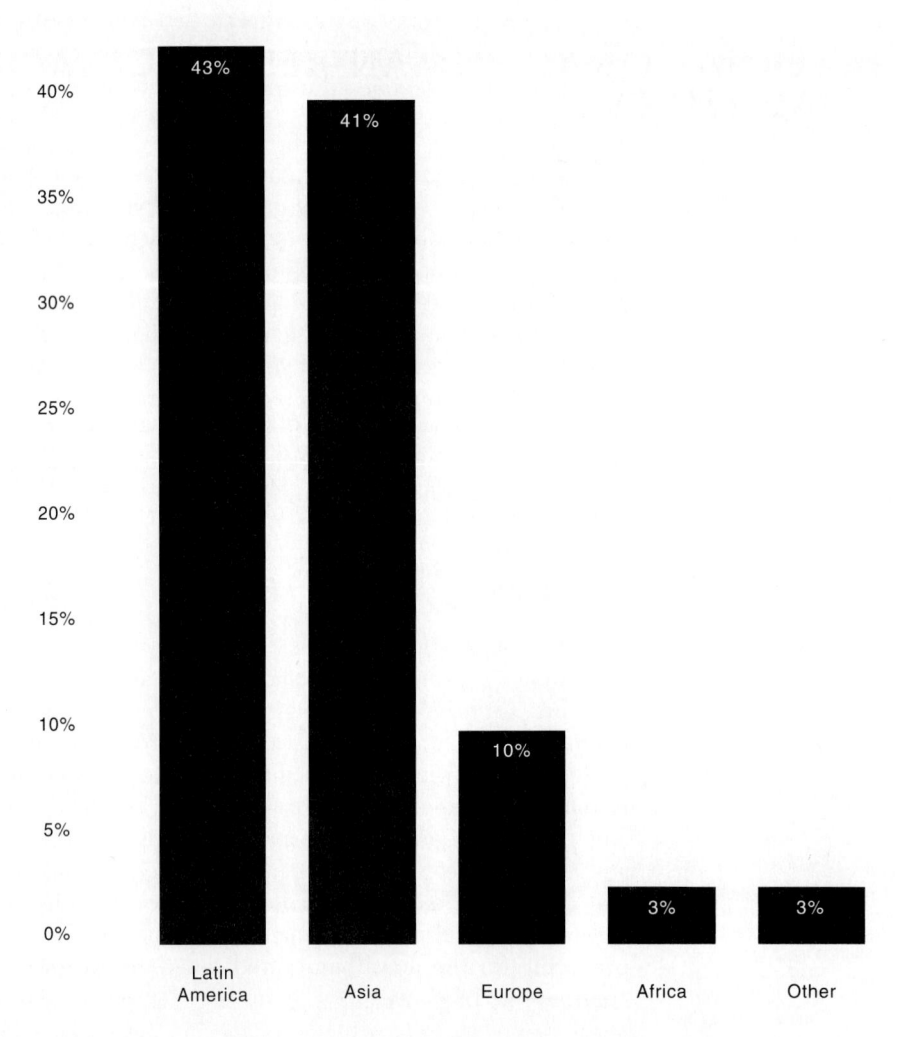

Region	Percentage
Latin America	43%
Asia	41%
Europe	10%
Africa	3%
Other	3%

Source: United States Immigration and Naturalization Service, 1988.

Competition and immigration

Over the next 20 years the working-age population in developing countries will rise by roughly 700 million—just about equal to the *total* current population of North America, Japan, and Western Europe. Says John Sewell, President of the Overseas Development Council, a Washington, D.C., think tank: "The work-hungry multitudes of the Third World will either descend on the developed economies in a flood of immigration, compete with increasing success for the low-skilled and semiskilled jobs that will migrate to them, or most likely, do both."[36]

Worker security in Japan

Whether dealing with immigrants or foreign employees, human resource departments will be facing even more diversity in the work force in coming years.[37] Although some may see this challenge as a threat, it is an opportunity for developed nations to offset the coming labor shortages many may face. In the United States, for example, there will be almost a million fewer new entrants into the work force in each year of the 1990s than in the 1980s.[38] Japan's Ministry of Labor reports that a survey of 268 companies reveals that these firms are already unable to recruit even one-fourth of the new workers they would like.[39] Western Europe's work force is slowing because of low birth rates.[40] Slow labor force growth combined with the growing numbers of retirees in North America, Japan, and Western Europe will demand that human resource departments staff organizations with increasing numbers of foreign nationals at home and abroad.[41]

> In the process of learning about a foreign culture, international managers get a bonus: They become aware of their own cultural values and heritage and may decide to capitalize on or modify some of their accustomed behaviors. Another bonus is the recognition that many cultures coexist in . . . workplaces as well. Changing . . . demographics makes it imperative that these cultural differences be recognized, dealt with, and capitalized on as the work force at home becomes even more richly diverse.[42]

Cultural Awareness

Before cultural differences can be addressed, managers and employees must be aware of these differences and how they can influence their decisions about company plans and operations. The human resource department furthers its contribution to the organization by being informed about cultural differences among the company's international operations. Pilot projects or innovations successfully tried in one country are often duplicated and applied in others. Technically or financially oriented innovations, however, may focus on the technological or financial feasibility, and fail to take into account cultural differences that could reduce their success. The department's role is not to object or block technology transfers or other innovations but to facilitate them. Proactive departments work with operating managers and project leaders to identify solutions to cultural or national differences that may impede company gains.

Women abroad

A specific area where cultural differences commonly impact business plans can be found among the growing cadre of women managers and professionals. In many cultures, women are expected to assume traditional, family-centered roles. Developing countries, Moslem-dominated regions, and, to a lesser extent, Japanese controlled companies have not afforded women equal employment opportunity.[43] In some cultures, for example, women are discouraged from working side-by-side with men; in others, tradition defines what jobs a woman can hold.

Companies that are dedicated to equal employment opportunity must make international assignments available to women if they are to advance to senior-level positions.[44] Awareness of cultural differences can enable succession planning and other departmental efforts to provide equal employment opportunity for women in ways that are most beneficial to the company's objectives and the employee's needs. Equal employment opportunity is so central to the role of human resource departments that the next chapter is devoted to this challenge.

SUMMARY

INTERNATIONAL HUMAN resource management places a wide variety of new pressures on traditional human resource activities. At the same time, the department's ability to meet these challenges provides it opportunities for significant contributions to the company. By helping the best qualified people execute the company's strategy on a global scale, the department can become a source of competitive advantage for the company.

For the department to be a source of competitive advantage, it generally must evolve in support of the organization's transformation from a domestic to an international to a global-oriented company. This evolution requires an awareness of the assumptions and employee rights likely to be encountered in the international arena and a rethinking of the department's structure and activities.

Virtually every human resource department activity is affected directly or indirectly by the internationalization of the firm's business. The need for international succession planning arises, as do policy decisions about the use of foreign nationals and expatriates in assignments abroad. Internal barriers to international assignments need to be identified and reduced, and external sources of needed talent must be located as well. Then, within a wide range of legal constraints, the department must select qualified people who can be assimilated into the company and local cultures.

Orientation, training, and development gain considerable complexity and importance. The success of the foreign national's or expatriate's performance depends heavily upon effective placement and development. Compensation becomes more complex, too. Adjustments, allowances, and incentives, along with unique benefit packages, add considerably to the firm's compensation costs and the human resource department's involvement in customizing individual compensation packages.

The department must assess the effectiveness of its international efforts to improve its processes and to ensure effective employee relations. The department is often called upon to troubleshoot by assisting managers to address employee relations and other human resource issues.

The internationalization of business amplifies the cultural diversity of the organization and requires the department members to become increasingly aware of cultural differences so that other managers can be properly advised.

Terms for Review

- Expatriate
- Foreign national
- Relocation policies
- Repatriation programs
- Succession planning
- Codetermination
- Labor shortages
- Perks
- Mentors
- Glass ceiling
- Lifetime employment

Review and Discussion Questions

1. What explanations can you offer for why some people are reluctant to accept an international job transfer?

2. If you were the senior vice president of human resources at Dow Chemical, what changes would you want to undertake to facilitate the transfer and repatriation of employees in foreign assignments?

3. How do cultural assumptions affect international human resource management? Provide an example of an assumption that differs from those found in developed countries.

4. What factors influence whether a particular human resource activity will be centralized or decentralized in an internationally oriented company?

5. What actions can the human resource department undertake to ensure that international openings are known among present employees?

6. What barriers might a company encounter in hiring foreign nationals to work in their home country for a foreign firm?

7. In relocating an employee overseas, what additional benefits and pay considerations are likely to be involved?

8. Suppose you were asked to design an orientation program to familiarize a foreign national who was being assigned to your country. Excluding the job-related and company-related items, what would you tell him or her about the culture and customs?

INCIDENT 3-1
Bio-medical Instrumentation, Inc.

Bio-medical Instrumentation (BMI) was founded in 1988. During the next five years it grew to a $150 million business, concentrated in the instrumentation segment of the health care field. Quick success with its operating room pumps, artificial skin grafts, and artificial heart valves caused sales to grow rapidly. With some of its products, senior management believed that gaining new market shares in Europe would be easier than expanding against well-entrenched domestic producers. Preliminary market studies supported management's thinking.

A decision was made to open a small sales office in Europe, probably in Frankfurt, Germany, since a new nonstop flight to Frankfurt had just been inaugurated from Ft. Lauderdale, where company headquarters was located. Three people were sent to Germany to identify a possible office site and to learn about European testing procedures and what documentation would be legally required to prove the safety and effectiveness of the company's medical instruments. All three people were selected because they were fluent in German.

If the reports on Germany are favorable, the company expects to have 30 to 40 people working in Europe within one year. Assuming you were Bio-medical's vice president of human resources:

1. What additional information would you want these three employees to find out?

2. Outline the major issues you would consider in developing an orientation program for the people who are to be permanently transferred to Europe.

3. What human resource policies are likely to be needed within the year before the transfers to Europe begin?

References

1. Peter J. Dowling and Randall S. Schuler, *International Dimensions of Human Resource Management* (Boston: PWS-Kent Publishing Company), 1990, p. vii.

2. Calvin Reynolds, "HR Must Influence Global Staff Strategy," *HRNews* (March 1991), p. c1.

3. Paul L. Blocklyn, "Developing the International Executive," *Personnel* (March 1989), pp. 44.

4. Ibid, pp. 44–47.

5. Reynolds, op cit.

6. Susan Moffat, "Should You Work for the Japanese?" *Fortune* (Dec. 3, 1990), pp. 107–120. See also Deborah L. Jacobs, "Japanese-American Culture Clash," *The New York Times* (Sept. 9, 1990), sec. 3, part 2, p. 23.

7. Andre Laurent, "The Cross-Cultural Puzzle of International Human Resource Management," *Human Resource Management* (Spring 1986), pp. 91–102. See also Eduard Gaugler, "HR Management: An International Comparison," *Personnel* (August 1988), pp. 24–30.

8. Ibid.

9. Ibid, p. 93.

10. Simcha Ronen and Oded Shenkar, "Using Employee Attitudes to Establish MNC Regional Divisions," *Personnel* (August 1988), pp. 32–39.

11. Rae Sedel, "Europe 1992: HR Implications of The European Unification," *Personnel* (Oct. 1989), p. 20.

12. Nakiye Boyacigiller, "The Role of Expatriates in the Management of Interdependence, Complexity and Risk in Multinational Corporations," *The Journal of International Business* (Third Quarter 1990), p. 373. See also Jay R. Galbraith and Robert K. Kazanjian, "Organizing to Implement Strategies of Diversity and Globalization: The Role of Matrix Designs," *Human Resource Management* (Spring 1986), pp. 37–54.

13. Linda Thornburg, "Supreme Court Rules on ARAMCO Title VII Case," *HRNews* (May 1991), p. 13.

14. Jacobs, op. cit.

15. Boyacigiller, op. cit.

16. Louis S. Richman, "The Coming World Labor Shortage," *Fortune* (April 9, 1990), pp. 70–77. See also Alan Riding, "Now, the Graying of Europa," The *International Herald Tribune* (Frankfurt, Germany, July 23, 1990), p. 1; and Wayne Wendling, "Responses to a Changing Work Force," *Personnel Administrator* (Nov. 1988), pp. 50–54.

17. Boyacigiller, op. cit.

18. James E. McElwain, "Succession Plans Designed to Manage Change," *HRMagazine* (Feb. 1991), pp. 67–71.

19. Calvin Reynolds and Rita Bennett, "The Career Couple Challenge," *Personnel Journal* (March 1991), pp. 46–48. See also Linda L. Ball, "Overseas Dual-Career Family, an HR Challenge," *HRNews* (March 1991), p. c8; and Richard Souders, "HR Exec Best to Design, Manage Compensation," *HRNews* (March 1991), p. c5; and Cecil G. Howard, "How Relocation Abroad Affects Expatriates' Family Life," *Personnel Administrator* (Nov. 1980), pp. 71–78.

20. Claudia H. Deutsch, "Getting the Brightest To Go Abroad," *The New York Times*, national ed. (June 17, 1990), sec. 3, part 2, p. 25.

21. Blocklyn, op. cit.

22. Ibid., p. 45.

23. Brian O'Reilly, "Doing Business on Mexico's Volcano," *Fortune* (August 29, 1988), pp. 72–74.

24. Banu Golesorkhi, "Why Not a Woman in Overseas Assignments?" *HRNews* (March 1991), p. c4.

25. Reynolds, op. cit.

26. Moffat, op. cit.

27. Rosalie L. Tung, "Selection and Training of Personnel for Overseas Assignments," *Columbia Journal of World Business*, vol. 16, no. 1 (1981), pp. 68–78. See also Fortunat F. Mueller-Maerki, "Help Wanted: Adam Marx or Karl Smith: A New Breed of Executive for Eastern Europe," *Corporate Issues Monitor*, vol. 6, no. 1 (1991, pp. 1–4.

28. Ball, op. cit. See also William Q. Kirk and Robert C. Maddox, "International Management: The New Frontier for Women," *Personnel* (March 1988), pp. 46–49.

29. Blocklyn, op. cit., p. 46. See also J. Steward Black and Mark Mendenhall, "Cross-Cultural Training Effectiveness: A Review and a Theoretical Framework for Future Research," *Academy of Management Review*, vol. 15, no. 1 (1990), pp. 113–136.

30. Blocklyn, op cit.

31. Rosalie L. Tung, "Career Issues in International Assignments," *The Academy of Management Executive*, vol. 2, no. 3 (1988), pp. 241–244.

32. Ellen Brandt, "Global HR," *Personnel Journal* (March 1991), p. 41.

33. Richard S. Savich and Waymond Rodgers, "Assignment Overseas: Easing the Transition Before and After," *Personnel* (August 1988), pp. 44–48. See also Souders, op. cit.

34. McElwain, op. cit.

35. Michael C. Harvey, "The Other Side of Foreign Assignments: Dealing with the Repatriation Dilemma," *Columbia Journal of World Business* (Spring 1982), pp. 53–59.

36. Richman, op. cit., p. 71.

37. Jolie Solomon, "Learning to Accept Cultural Diversity," *The Wall Street Journal*, Eastern ed. (Sept. 12, 1990), p. b1.

38. Wendling, op. cit., p. 51.

39. Richman, op. cit., p. 70.

40. Riding, op. cit.

41. William B. Johnston, "Global Work Force 2000: The New World Labor Market," *Harvard Business Review* (March–April 1991), pp. 115–127.

42. Victoria J. Marsick, Ernie Turner, and Lars Cederholm, "International Managers as Team Leaders," *Management Review* (March 1989), p. 47.

43. Ball, op. cit.

44. Thornburg, op. cit.

> half the U.S. work force now consists of minorities, immigrants, and women, so white, males, though undoubtedly still dominant, are themselves a statistical minority.
> R. ROOSEVELT THOMAS, JR.[1]

EQUAL EMPLOYMENT CHALLENGES

CHAPTER OBJECTIVES

After studying this chapter, you should be able to:
1. DISCUSS the impact of work force diversity on equal employment and affirmative action.
2. LIST the major equal employment laws and their main provisions.
3. DISCUSS the leading court cases that interpret equal employment laws.
4. MATCH major equal employment laws with the remedies for violations.
5. EXPLAIN the effect of equal employment laws on the role of human resource specialists.
6. OUTLINE the key elements of an affirmative action program.

FEW OF the challenges discussed in this book affect organizations as much as government. It acts with the force of law. Organizations must comply or face potential lawsuits and penalties. Human resource departments become involved when laws deal with the employment relationship.

Changing employment patterns

Governmental attention to human resource issues reflects changes in our society undreamed of 150 years ago, when laws covering the employment relationship were virtually nonexistent. Most jobs were then found on the farm, in skilled trades, or with small proprietorships. Most people worked for themselves or for the owner-manager of a small business. However, a society of farmers, ranchers, skilled craft workers, and proprietors in the 1800s became a nation mostly of wage earners in the 1900s. As the well-being of society came to depend increasingly on employment relationships, Congress and state legislatures passed laws and established agencies to administer them. Historical work force diversity has made equal employment opportunity in the U. S. particularly important. Human resource specialists became involved as these laws and regulations began to impact employees and the employer. Ultimately, compliance with employment laws is an obvious standard that socially responsible employers try to meet.

EEO challenges

Equal employment opportunity (EEO) laws create an extensive legal challenge for human resource departments to provide equal employment opportunity without regard to race, religion, sex, disability, pregnancy, national origin, or age. Unlike other employment laws, equal employment is not limited to one or two personnel activities. It affects nearly every human resource function, including human resource planning, recruitment, selection, placement, training, compensation, and employee relations. Perhaps no other single development rivals the impact of equal employment laws on the management of human resources. To illustrate the scope of these laws, consider how equal employment laws affected the American Telephone and Telegraph Company (AT&T).

Classic EEO case: AT&T

In the 1970s, the American Telephone and Telegraph Company asked the Federal Communication Commission for approval to increase long-distance telephone rates. The Equal Employment Opportunity Commission (EEOC, the federal agency that is largely responsible for policing equal employment laws) filed a petition to stop the rate increases. The EEOC argued that "approval of the rate increase would be both unconstitutional and contrary to the public interest because AT&T had engaged . . . in extensive violations of Federal, State and constitutional prohibitions against job discrimination."[2] This case "was the first government effort to attack all significant patterns and practices of discrimination of a major national employer."[3]

After more than two years of hearings and negotiations—and hundreds of thousands of pages of exhibits, testimony, and statistical data—AT&T negotiated a settlement. It outlined a series of actions that AT&T would take to remedy the alleged patterns and practices of discrimination. As the federal district court judge who signed the consent decree commented, it was "the largest and most impressive civil rights settlement in the history of the nation."[4]

The consent decree required AT&T to pay some $45 million to affected employees during the first year. Officially, the EEOC estimates that AT&T spent $100 million in back pay and incentive awards.[5] *Not only was money paid to nearly 50,000 AT&T employees who had been financially affected by past practices, but AT&T was required to become more aggressive in recruiting, hiring, developing, and promoting women and minorities. Labor relations problems also resulted as AT&T's unions filed suits to protect the seniority rights of those employees who did not benefit from the back pay and accelerated training opportunities.*

These issues were not resolved quickly. AT&T remained under the consent decree for six years before the EEOC agreed that the company had met most of its equal employment objectives. By 1991, as a result of the ongoing efforts of AT&T's human resource department and senior management, minorities counted for 21 percent of AT&T's work force and 17 percent of its managers.[6]

As the AT&T example illustrates, virtually every aspect of human resource management in Figure 4-1 is affected by EEO law. Preparation, selection, development, evaluation, and compensation must all be done without discrimination. If past actions have had a discriminatory result, the government can require that corrective action be taken, including affirmative actions by the employer to remedy past discrimination. Although equal employment is only one of the challenges listed in Figure 4-1, its impact on human resource management may be the most pervasive.

Since regulation of the employment relationship concerns human resource practitioners, they have three responsibilities. First, they must stay abreast of new laws, agency decisions, and court rulings. Otherwise, these experts soon find their knowledge outdated and useless to the organization. Second, they must develop and administer programs that ensure their organization's compliance with the laws. Failure to do so may lead to discrimination, loss of government contracts, poor public relations, and suits by government agencies or affected individuals, as occurred at AT&T. Third, they must pursue their traditional roles of obtaining, maintaining, and retaining an optimal work force. No organization benefits from compliance with EEO laws at the expense of poorly qualified workers.

Since EEO laws are a major challenge to human management, they are fully examined in this chapter. The implications of these laws will then be discussed throughout the book.

EQUAL EMPLOYMENT LAWS: AN OVERVIEW

EEO objectives

EEO laws have the common objective of outlawing discrimination in employment based on race, color, religion, sex, disability, pregnancy, national origin, or

I. FRAMEWORKS AND CHALLENGES

Figure 4-1

A Model of the Personnel Management System and Its Major Environmental Challenges

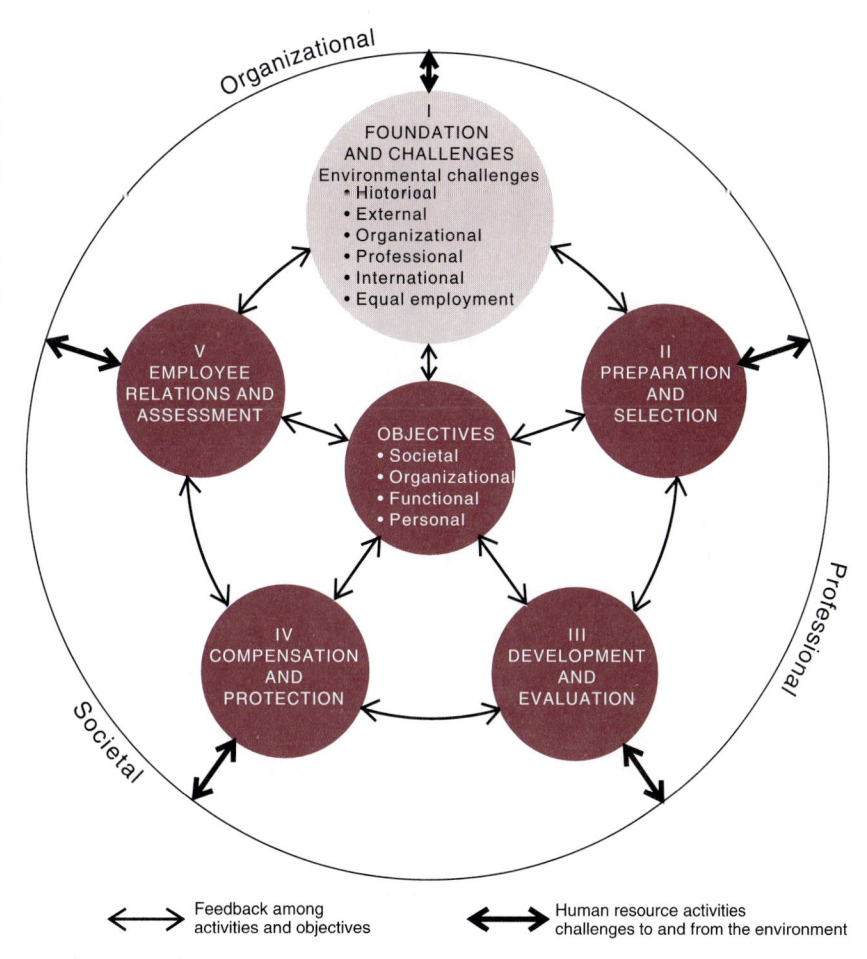

I FOUNDATION AND CHALLENGES
Environmental challenges
- Historical
- External
- Organizational
- Professional
- International
- Equal employment

II PREPARATION AND SELECTION

III DEVELOPMENT AND EVALUATION

IV COMPENSATION AND PROTECTION

V EMPLOYEE RELATIONS AND ASSESSMENT

OBJECTIVES
- Societal
- Organizational
- Functional
- Personal

Organizational · Professional · Societal

⟷ Feedback among activities and objectives

⟷ Human resource activities challenges to and from the environment

---

age (over 40). Vietnam era veterans are also covered under specific conditions discussed later in the chapter.

Equal employment constraints emerged during the 1960s and 1970s from three sources: federal acts, state and local legislation, and executive orders of the president. Each source sought similar—and sometimes overlapping—objectives and jurisdictions.[7] Figure 4-2 summarizes the three sources of employment law. As the figure implies, coverage overlaps because federal jurisdiction includes only those employers whose operations affect interstate commerce, some government agencies, and federal government contractors. Employers who do not fall into these categories might discriminate if state and local legislative bodies did not pass fair employment practice laws to fill this void. Executive orders are presidential decrees that affect federal agencies and contractors. To comply with

State and local laws

4. EQUAL EMPLOYMENT CHALLENGES   89

Figure 4-2

Types, Sources, Objectives, and Jurisdiction of Equal Employment Laws

TYPES	SOURCE	OBJECTIVES AND JURISDICTION
FEDERAL ACTS	Passed by Congress and enforced by the executive branch.	To ensure equal employment opportunities with employers involved in interstate commerce, with government agencies, and with most government contractors.
STATE AND LOCAL LAWS (Sometimes called fair employment practices)	Enacted by state legislatures or local lawmakers and enforced by state or local executive branches.	To ensure equal employment opportunities within the state or local community.
EXECUTIVE ORDERS	Decreed by the president and enforced by the executive branch.	To ensure equal employment opportunities with federal agencies and with certain government contractors.

equal employment laws or to remedy past discrimination, human resource specialists develop affirmative action plans. These programs set forth the employer's plan and timetable for ensuring compliance with the equal opportunity laws.

Before affirmative action programs are examined, the three layers of equal employment law will be discussed. We will look at the purpose, prohibitions, enforcement, implications, and major court decisions of these laws.

FEDERAL EQUAL EMPLOYMENT LAWS

To a human resource specialist, the federal equal employment acts are an important group of laws. They form the basis for nearly all attempts to provide equal employment opportunity. Most state and local fair employment practices are modeled after the federal acts in Figure 4-3. When conflicts arise between federal and other laws, the most demanding—usually a federal law—dominates. And among federal laws, none is as encompassing as Title VII of the 1964 *Civil Rights Act,* as amended several times since.

Title VII

CRA of 1964

Title VII of the Civil Rights Act of 1964 attempts to ensure equal employment opportunity by prohibiting discrimination in hiring, promotion, compensation, and other conditions of employment. As a result, discrimination in employment based upon race, color, religion, sex, pregnancy, or national origin is illegal. Sections 703(a) and (d) are presented in Figure 4-4 and discussed below.

As sections 703(a) and (d) indicate, the intent of Title VII is to cover all

Figure 4-3

Major Federal Equal Employment Opportunity Laws

EQUAL EMPLOYMENT ACTS	MAJOR PROHIBITIONS	JURISDICTION
TITLE VII OF THE CIVIL RIGHTS ACT OF 1964 As amended in 1972, amended again in 1978 (by the Pregnancy Discrimination Act) and 1991	Outlaws discrimination in employment based on race, color, religion, sex, pregnancy, or national origin.	Employers with fifteen or more employees; unions with fifteen or more members; employment agencies; union hiring halls; institutions of higher education, federal, state, and local governments.
AGE DISCRIMINATION IN EMPLOYMENT ACT OF 1967	Outlaws discrimination against those who are 40 and above.	Employers with twenty or more employees; unions with twenty-five or more members; employment agencies; federal, state, and local governments.
EQUAL PAY ACT OF 1963	Outlaws discrimination in pay based on the sex of the worker.	Employers engaged in interstate of commerce and most employees of federal, state, and local governments.
VIETNAM ERA VETERANS READJUSTMENT ACT OF 1974	Outlaws discrimination against Vietnam era veterans.	Employers with federal contracts of $10,000 or more.

aspects of the employment relationship. Included are all actions by an employer that adversely affect an individual's status or opportunities because of that person's membership in a particular group or class. The range of protected classes is specified in Title VII, as it has been amended since 1964. Discrimination on the basis of a person's sex, race, or color is the most common violation. However, discrimination because of one's national origin or the national origin of one's parents is also a violation.[8] Laws and amendments passed since 1964 also outlaw discrimination against a disabled person[9] or a pregnant women,[10] provided the person can perform the job. Likewise, an employer cannot discriminate because of a person's religion.[11] In fact, an employer must accommodate an employee's religious observances or practices, as long as they do not impose an undue hardship on the employer.

Advisable discrimination

Discrimination among workers because of their effort, performance, or other work-related criteria remains both *permissible* and *advisable*. EEO laws *do* permit employers to reward outstanding performers and penalize unacceptable productivity. These laws only require that the basis for rewards and punishment be work-related—not based on unrelated issues such as a person's sex, race, or religion. Not only do these laws prohibit intentional discrimination, arising from evil intent or motive, but they also prohibit disparate treatment and disparate impact even when such discrimination is unintentional.

Figure 4-4

Excerpts of Title VII, the Civil Rights Act of 1964, as Amended

---

TITLE VII OF THE CIVIL RIGHTS ACT OF 1964 AS AMENDED

Section 703. (a) It shall be an unlawful employment practice for an employer—

(1) to fail or refuse to hire or to discharge any individual or otherwise to discriminate against any individual with respect to his compensation, terms, conditions, or privileges of employment, because of such individual's race, color, religion, sex, or national origin; or

(2) to limit, segregate, or classify his employees or applicants for employment in any way which would deprive or tend to deprive any individual of employment opportunities or otherwise adversely affect his status as an employee, because of such individual's race, color, religion, sex, or national origin.

(d) It shall be an unlawful employment practice of any employer . . . controlling . . . training programs to discriminate against any individual because of his race, color, religion, sex, or national origin in admission to, or employment in, any program established to provide apprenticeship or other training.

Unequal treatment

Disparate treatment. *Disparate treatment* occurs when members of a protected class receive unequal treatment. If AT&T regularly hired female applicants as telephone operators without letting them apply for the higher-paying and more skilled craft jobs, the result would be unequal or disparate treatment. Unequal treatment also occurs when different standards are applied to different groups.[12] For example, an employer who refuses to hire women with small children because those children may cause her to miss work but hires men with young children is applying a different standard.

Unequal impact

Disparate impact. *Disparate impact* occurs when the results of an employer's actions have a different impact on one or more protected classes. Even when an employer develops a uniform standard and applies it equally to all classes, the results may be discriminatory.[13] Consider the comments of Gerald H. Trautman, former chairman of the board for the Greyhound Corporation, when he observed that the federal government:

Greyhound

. . . went after us in San Francisco to eliminate our safety rule which required any applicant, male or female, for the driver's position to be five foot seven. They took us to court and wanted us to give up the rule. But we finally decided it just wasn't worth the fight. . . . The first four people who were under five foot seven . . . flunked the test. They weren't able to handle the bus. But we don't have that rule any more.[14]

When standards discriminate against one or more protected groups, the burden has historically been on the employer to prove the standard is necessary. In the Greyhound example, management thought the standard was reasonable. However, the impact of a height standard was to discriminate against women and

I. FRAMEWORKS AND CHALLENGES

males of Asian descent, since these groups tend to be shorter than males of European or African heritage. Treatment was equal, but the impact was discriminatory. In *Griggs v. Duke Power Company*,[15] a similar outcome was ruled upon by the U.S. Supreme Court.

Duke Power

> *The Duke Power Company had a long standing policy of requiring a high school degree for all jobs except those in the labor pool. As a result, the labor pool consisted mostly of black men who were denied an opportunity for better jobs at the utility because they did not have a high school degree. The requirements of a high school diploma and general intelligence test were challenged in court. Duke Power Company could not show that a high school diploma was necessary to perform many jobs or that the test bore any relationship to on-the-job performance.*

Case law

Regardless of the company's intent, the result of its actions was ruled as discriminatory because the degree requirement and tests tended to have an unequal impact on one protected class: blacks. The test and degree requirements were disallowed even though they were applied equally to black and white workers. In *Griggs* and the Greyhound example, the burden of proof was placed on the employer. In 1990, however, the Supreme Court weakened these standards in its *Wards Cove v. Antonio* finding.[16] Congress reacted with the *Civil Rights Act of 1991*, which amended the 1964 *Civil Rights Act* and overruled *Wards Cove*, keeping the burden of proof on the employer.

Discrimination tests

When a disparate impact results—even when business reasons justify the result—the human resource department should find other methods that do not have a disparate impact. In *Albemarle Paper Company v. Moody*,[17] the employer had business reasons for its actions. However, the U.S. Supreme Court found that discrimination resulted because Albemarle relied on employment tests that were discriminatory and the company could not satisfactorily prove that the tests were related to the jobs for which people were being hired. The implication for human resource specialists is that all actions must be related to a business purpose and not be discriminatory in intent or result. If job-related actions discriminate against a protected class, those actions should be discontinued in favor of nondiscriminatory approaches.

Even if the overall impact on a protected class is nondiscriminatory, this standard may not be an effective defense against charges of discrimination. In *Connecticut v. Teal*, the Supreme Court ruled that every individual employee is protected against discriminatory treatment and practices.

Pregnancy

Even though pregnancy affects one protected group, the U.S. Supreme Court ruled in *General Electric v. Gilbert*[18] that the denial of pregnancy-related benefits *did not* violate Title VII. Congress subsequently amended Title VII with the *Pregnancy Discrimination Act* of 1978, and employers could no longer require women to take leaves of absence or resign because of pregnancy. As long as the woman was still capable of doing her job, the employer could not discriminate in

Figure 4-5

Guidelines for Pregnancy Leave

The *Pregnancy Discrimination Act* of 1978 amended Title VII of the 1964 *Civil Rights Act*. As a result, covered employers may not:

▶ Treat disabilities related to pregnancy or childbirth differently from other types of disabilities or medical conditions.

▶ Use any employment practice that discriminates against applicants or employees because of pregnancy, childbirth, abortion, or a planned adoption.

▶ Apply leave standards for childcare that differ from those for other nonmedical leaves.

▶ Withhold any fringe benefits to a woman because of an abortion or planned abortion, except that employer-provided health insurance need not cover the expense of an abortion unless performed to protect the mother's life.

---

benefits or other conditions of employment.[19] The implications for pregnancy-related leaves are listed in Figure 4-5.[20]

Harassment. Perhaps the most difficult form of discrimination to deal with is *harassment*. Whether it occurs because of someone's race or sex, it is prohibited. Although racial harassment may exist as open racism or subtle comments, it creates a discriminatory environment which violates Title VII. The *Civil Rights Act of 1991* further clarifies that racial harassment or intentional discrimination are prohibited in all facets of employment decisions, including hiring, promotion, access to training and other employment related opportunities. Open or subtle sexual harassment also violates the law. Sexual harassment is defined by the Federal Government as:

Sexual harassment defined

Unwelcome sexual advances, requests for sexual favors, and other verbal or physical conduct of a sexual nature constitute sexual harassment when (1) submission to such conduct is made either explicitly or implicitly a term or condition of an individual's employment, (2) submission to or rejection of such conduct by an individual is used as the basis for employment decisions affecting such individual, or (3) such conduct has the purpose or effect of unreasonably interfering with an individual's work performance or creating an intimidating, hostile, or offensive working environment.

Although one experienced mediator made the following statement about sexual harassment, these comments and the ones that follow could well apply to any form of prohibited harassment.

The most serious aspect of almost all reported cases is the power relationship between the alleged offender and the offended person.... reports of harass-

I. FRAMEWORKS AND CHALLENGES

ment usually involve fear of retribution because of the supposed power of a... supervisor. In fact, most reported cases do involve a supervisor-subordinate relationship; hence, productivity is threatened.[21]

Ease of violation

One difficulty with allegations of racial or sexual harassment is proof.[22] These allegations often become one person's word against another's. As a result, it is believed that most offenses go unreported to company officials or government agencies.[23] Another concern is the ease with which harassment can occur, especially when the wrongdoer believes his or her actions are made playfully or in jest. Even those in nonsupervisory positions should realize that sexual or racial comments may be the basis for legal action, regardless of the actual intent.

HR policy

Human resource departments usually develop and communicate a strongly worded policy about harassment. The policy clearly states that racial or sexual harassment violates company rules. Those who use their position in the company to harass other employees can expect harsh discipline, often termination of their employment. Finally, the policy directive usually indicates what actions an offended party should take.[24] Strong action is needed by the human resource department because of the unfair nature of harassment and the U.S. Supreme Court's view that the employer can be held liable, as it ruled in *Meritor Savings Bank v. Vinson*.[25]

Exceptions. Although sexual or racial harassment is never permitted, Title VII and the courts do permit some exceptions to equal employment opportunity. These exceptions include bona fide occupational qualifications, seniority systems, preferential quota systems, illegal aliens, international employment, and religious organizations as employers.

BFOQ

A *bona fide occupational qualification* (BFOQ) exists when discrimination against a protected group is reasonably necessary to the normal operation of the organization. A preference by the employer or personnel specialist or a long-standing tradition is insufficient. There must be a "justified business reason." For example, in *Diaz v. Pan American World Airways, Inc.*, Pan Am argued that hiring only female flight attendants was a BFOQ. The courts found no reason why male flight attendants could not perform the same functions and ruled against Pan Am.

Sex seldom a BFOQ

Seniority

In labor agreements negotiated between employers and their unions, *seniority clauses* are common. These provisions usually require that promotions, pay, and other conditions of employment are preferentially affected by how long the worker has been employed. When the senior workers are predominantly of one race or sex, the application of seniority may lead to a disparate impact on those in protected classes. However, Title VII anticipates this issue with the following section:

Section 703(h). Notwithstanding any other provision of this title, it shall not be an unlawful employment practice for an employer to apply different standards

4. EQUAL EMPLOYMENT CHALLENGES

of compensation, or different terms, conditions, or privileges of employment-pursuant to a bona fide seniority or merit system. . . .

In *International Brotherhood of Teamsters v. United States*,[26] the U.S. Supreme Court upheld this section of Title VII, provided that the seniority system was not created to discriminate against some protected class. Furthermore, the seniority system must apply equally to all people covered by it. When a seniority systems intentionally discriminates against someone, the *Civil Rights Act of 1991* allows it to be challenged. Furthermore, this legal challenge can be undertaken when the system is adopted, when the person becomes subject to it, or when harm occurs.

Quotas

A third exception is *preferential quota systems*. These approaches reserve a proportion of job openings, promotions, or other employment opportunities for members of protected classes who may have been discriminated against previously. When an employer recognizes that members of a protected class have unequal representation in a particular job classification, the employer may develop a plan to correct this imbalance. Kaiser Aluminum & Chemical Corporation's Gramercy, Louisiana, plant provides a landmark example.

Kaiser Aluminum & Chemical

> Kaiser's work force at the plant was 14.8 percent black, and the labor force in the area was 39 percent black. In the skilled (and better paying) craft jobs, less than 2 percent of the workers were black. Kaiser's management entered into a nationwide collective bargaining agreement with the United Steelworkers. An on-the-job training program for craft jobs was established. It was decided that the entry ratio into the program would be one white to one black until minority representation at Kaiser equaled minority representation in the area's general civilian labor force.
>
> Eventually this preferential quota system was challenged in the courts by Brian F. Weber, an employee of the plant, who believed the one-to-one ratio discriminated against him. The U.S. Supreme Court ruled in *United Steelworkers of America and Kaiser Aluminum & Chemical Corporation v. Weber* that preferential systems would help undo the effects of past discrimination.[27] Although not every preferential quota approach is sure to be legal, such an approach may offer a defense against allegations of discrimination when its purpose is to remedy past discrimination.

Immigration reform

Another exception comes from the *Immigration Reform and Control Act* of 1986. This federal law imposes civil and criminal penalties on employers who knowingly hire illegal aliens. Thus, even though the *Civil Rights Act* prohibits discrimination on the basis of national origin, the law does not protect illegal aliens. To comply with the Immigration Reform and Control Act, human resource departments need to verify citizenship or review a work permit from the Immigration and Naturalization Service.

> Under a little-known but sweeping provision . . ., every employer in the United States will become an unofficial branch of the Immigration and Naturalization Service. . . .
> . . . regulations . . . require every person in the United States . . . to fill out an immigration form and prove he or she is a U.S. citizen or has federal permission to work in the country. Everyone.[28]

USSC rules

Human resource professionals need to be concerned about employment laws when dealing with international employees. Not only do most developed nations have detailed employment laws that cover employees working in their country, but the company's ability to attract top international talent is shaped by the treatment it provides employees. And foreign companies doing business in the United States must comply with U.S. laws, regardless of their home-country practices.[30]

Religious discrimination is permitted by churches and other religious organizations for their religion-related employment needs. For example, a Catholic school could discriminate against non-Catholics when hiring instructors to teach religion classes.

Intentional discrimination and practices that lead to disparate treatment or impact are prohibited. When they occur, human resource professionals further their functional, organizational, and societal objectives by ending these forms of discrimination. The only exceptions are bona fide occupational qualifications, valid seniority systems, appropriate preferential quota systems, illegal aliens, international employment, and religious organizations as employers.

Exceptions

Retaliation

Employer retaliation. As with most employment laws, it is a separate violation to retaliate *in any way* against those who exercise their Title VII rights. Those who file charges, testify, or otherwise participate in any Title VII action are protected by the law. If a supervisor tries to "get even" with an employee who filed charges, the act is violated.[31] The usual remedies are reinstatement (if a discharge is involved) and back pay to cover lost wages.

EEOC

Enforcement. The five-member *Equal Employment Opportunity Commission* (EEOC) enforces Title VII through offices in major cities. The EEOC was created to enforce Title VII, but its powers initially were limited. Congress expanded the authority of the commission by passing the *Equal Employment Opportunity Act* of 1972. Under the 1972 act, the EEOC is empowered to initiate court action against noncomplying businesses.[32]

Figure 4-6 summarizes the EEOC's enforcement procedures. Enforcement begins when a charge is filed. It may be filed by the aggrieved person, someone acting on behalf of the aggrieved person, or one of the EEOC commissioners. In states with fair employment laws, charges can be filed with the state agency. If charges are filed with EEOC, it defers jurisdiction to qualified state or local agencies for sixty days. These jurisdictions are known as *deferral jurisdictions*.

Charges are filed directly with the EEOC in *nondeferral jurisdictions*—jurisdictions without qualified agencies. The accused parties are notified within ten

4. EQUAL EMPLOYMENT CHALLENGES **97**

Figure 4-6

EEOC Enforcement Procedure

INITIATION	Charge filed by appropriate party.
DEFERRAL	Qualified state agency ← In deferral state ← EEOC
NOTIFICATION INVESTIGATION	EEOC notifies accused and investigates.
JUSTIFICATION	No ← EEOC finds reasonable cause. → No
CONCILIATION	Conciliation efforts work. → Yes
LITIGATION	No ← Suit brought against... Private employer / Public employer; by EEOC / by Attorney General
	Right-to-sue letter
	Individual suit
DISPOSITION	U.S. district court / EEOC closes case.
APPEAL	U.S. court of appeals

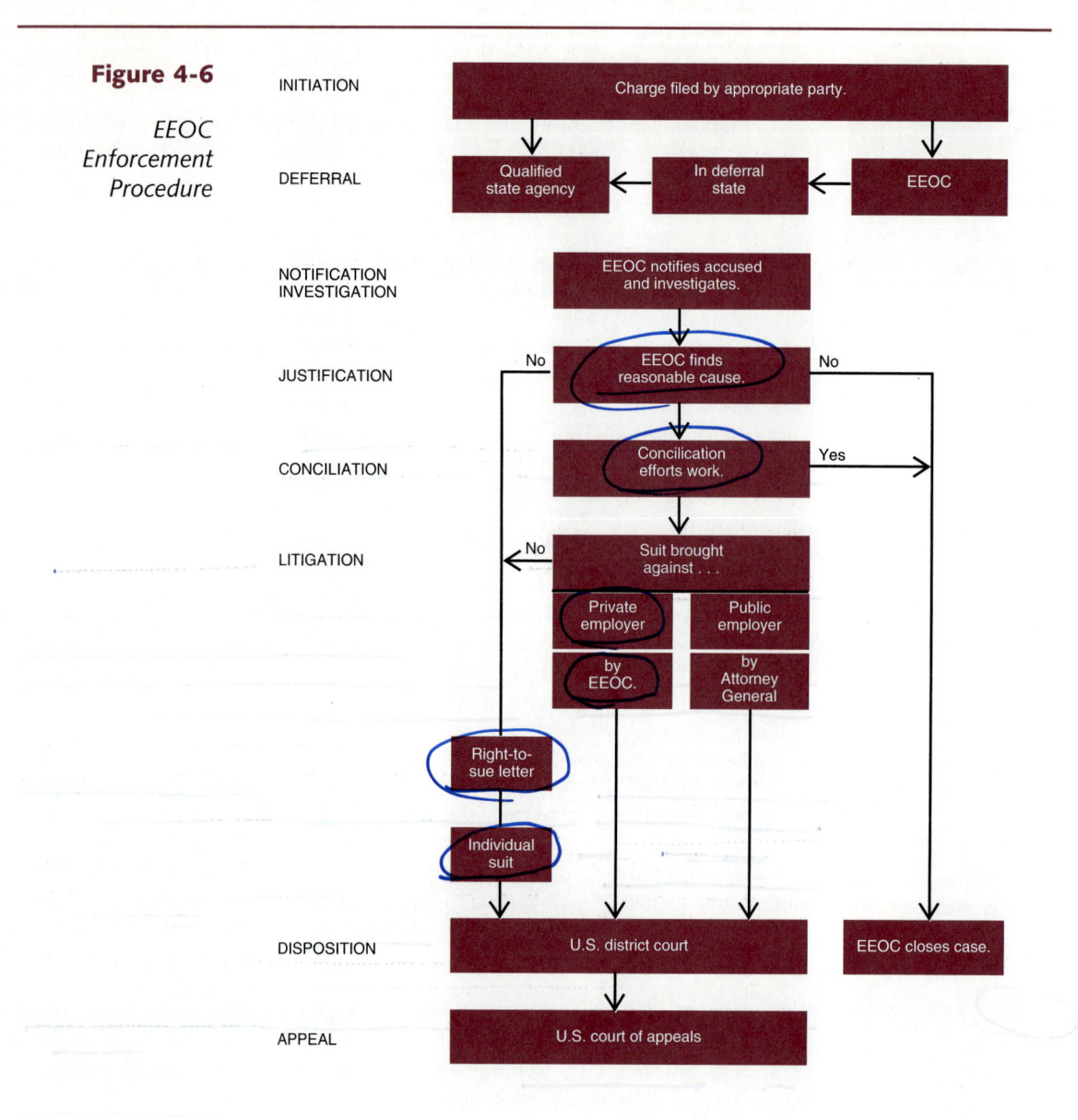

Conciliation

days by the EEOC once charges are filed. The EEOC then conducts an investigation and decides whether the charges are a violation. If there is reason to believe a violation has occurred, the EEOC seeks a *conciliation agreement*. This agreement is a negotiated settlement acceptable to the EEOC and all parties involved. Its acceptance closes the case.

If conciliation fails, court action may result. A suit can be brought by the

98   I. FRAMEWORKS AND CHALLENGES

EEOC when the wrongdoer is a private employer or by the U.S. attorney general when the charges are against a public employer. Even individuals may file suit within 90 days once a *right-to-sue letter* has been issued by the EEOC. A right-to-sue letter is granted when:

1. ➤ The EEOC dismisses the charges.

2. ➤ No suit is brought after the EEOC fails to obtain a conciliation agreement.

Remedies. Title VII clearly acknowledges that remedies can include a wide range of penalties.

> *Section 203(g).* If the court finds that the respondent has intentionally engaged in or is intentionally engaging in an unlawful employment practice charged in the complaint, the court may enjoin the respondent from engaging in such unlawful employment practice, and order such affirmative action as may be appropriate, which may include, but is not limited to, reinstatement or hiring of employees, with or without back pay (payable by the employer, employment agency, or labor organization, as the case may be, responsible for the unlawful employment practice), or any other equitable relief as the court deems appropriate.

Perhaps the most controversial changes in the Equal Employment remedies came from the *Civil Rights Act of 1991*. This Act allows those who are victims of intentional discrimination to ask for a jury trial where they can sue for compensatory and punitive damages. Punitive damages are intended to punish the wrongdoer, but only when the discrimination was with malice or reckless indifference. Punitive damages are limited to a range of $50,000 for employers with less than 100 employees to $300,000 for employers with more than 500 employees.

AT&T remedies

Whether compliance results from a conciliation agreement or a court order, remedies have similar characteristics when punitive and compensatory are not present. Reconsider the AT&T example described earlier in this chapter. AT&T agreed to:

1. ➤ Cease and desist from practices that caused disparate treatment or impact

2. ➤ Hire, train, and promote those in protected classes that are allegedly discriminated against

3. ➤ Make financial payments to compensate for past discrimination in order to "make whole" those affected.

4. EQUAL EMPLOYMENT CHALLENGES

As the AT&T example points out, remedies typically include an agreement by the company to cease and desist from discriminatory practices. Past patterns and practices of discrimination against entire groups (for example, women and minorities at AT&T) may have to be corrected with affirmative action plans that include special hiring, training, and promoting quotas and programs. If there has been any financially measurable harm done to those in protected classes, the employer often must pay financial restitution to "make whole" those who were affected. This requirement means making up losses suffered because of the discriminatory actions. Reinstatement with no loss of seniority and full payment of back wages are common *make-whole remedies* in illegal discharge cases, for example. Even when no discharges are involved, monetary adjustments may be required to compensate those who were discriminated against. When funds are paid to those affected, the company receives little benefit. Therefore, most human resource professionals try to have financial penalties made payable in the form of dollars to be spent on training those who were discriminated against. This way the company captures some value for its often huge outlays.

Americans with Disabilities Act

Handicapped employees

In 1990, Congress passed and the president signed the *Americans with Disabilities Act* (ADA). It prohibits employers from discriminating against the disabled in employment decisions. A disabled person is defined as someone who has a physical or mental impairment that substantially limits that person in a major life activity. The definition also includes those who have a record of such impairment. For example, a person who has recovered from a heart attack but is discriminated against would be considered to have a *record* of an impairment. Employers are required to undertake "reasonable accommodations" to adjust the work environment to meet the special needs of the disabled.[33] Installing a ramp for a wheelchair-bound person is an example.

The law does not require employers to hire every handicapped person, only those who are qualified to perform the work. If accommodations would impose an undue hardship on the employer, whether by the difficulty of the accommoda-

Exclusions

tion or expense, the employer may reject the person. Likewise, the law specifically excludes from coverage current illegal drug users, homosexuals, people with sexual disorders, and compulsive gamblers (though local or state laws may offer protection). AIDS- and HIV-infected individuals are covered as long as they do not pose a direct health or safety threat to others.

Differently abled

Simply put, a "differently abled" person cannot be discriminated against in employment if he or she can perform the essential job duties when "reasonably accommodated" by the employer. When discrimination does occur, the enforcement provisions of Title VII of the *Civil Rights Act* will be applied by the EEOC.[35]

I. FRAMEWORKS AND CHALLENGES

Age Discrimination in Employment

Equal opportunity is sometimes denied because of age. To prevent this form of discrimination, the U.S. Congress passed the *Age Discrimination in Employment Act* of 1967. As amended over the years, it now prohibits discrimination against those age 40 and above, when the person's age is a factor in employment-related decisions. Violations can be time-consuming, costly, and difficult to separate from legitimate business decisions.[36]

The 1986 amendments to the Act eliminate the mandatory retirement age for all workers, except that there is a seven-year exemption for police officers, firefighters, and college faculty members. This exemption (from 1987 to 1994) was provided to give these employers an adjustment period during which to adapt to the end of mandatory retirement.[37] As with Title VII, bona fide occupational qualifications are permitted, but they are extremely limited. For example, a casting director can discriminate against older actors when hiring for children's roles.

Enforcement is handled by the EEOC and follows the procedures outlined for Title VII violations. However, federal law requires that the government attempt to achieve voluntary compliance before legal action is taken. If voluntary compliance efforts fail, a suit can be filed in federal court. Since courts have wide latitude in deciding remedies, human resource departments often find voluntary compliance less costly.[38]

Equal Pay Act

The growing number of households headed by women and the obvious discrimination behind paying men more than women led Congress to pass the *Equal Pay Act* in 1963. The act requires employers to pay equal wages for equal work.[39] Jobs are considered equal when both sexes work at the same place and the job demands substantially the same skill, effort, responsibility, and working conditions. When one of these factors differs, the employer is justified in paying different wages. As Figure 4-7 lightheartedly illustrates, the greater effort of Santa justifies a higher wage rate than that paid to the Easter Bunny. Had male Santas been paid more than female Santas, a violation would have existed. The figure also shows that equal work is determined by an examination of the job duties, not simply job titles.

The Equal Pay Act does permit employers to reward workers for individual merit or performance. Even seniority can be rewarded with higher pay. As long as seniority and merit pay differentials are not based on the sex of the worker, they are legal. Likewise, companies can pay employees according to their productivity, paying for each unit produced. As with other employment laws, those who exercise their rights under the Equal Pay Act are protected against employer retaliation.

The Equal Pay Act of 1963 may be enforced by either the federal government or state agencies. In the absence of state laws and agencies, the EEOC handles equal pay violations. Its enforcement procedures are the same as those applied to age discrimination cases, except the Equal Pay Act does not require that the

Figure 4-7

Sad News for the Easter Bunny

The Easter Bunny lost its sex discrimination dispute with Santa Claus yesterday.

Because Santa works harder, keeps longer hours and sees more children each year, he's worth 90 cents more an hour than department store bunnies, a California deputy labor commission ruled.

... After a two-hour hearing in San Jose conducted by Commissioner Andrew Evans of the state's Division of Labor Standards, ... he found no evidence of discrimination.

"There are some basic differences in the job," Evans noted. "Santa works harder."

He found that Santa sees more children and is twice as successful as the Easter Bunny in the business of selling parents snapshots of their children on his lap.

However, Evans said, he found that a man or a woman who suits up as Santa earns the same wage; and a male and female Easter Bunny earn equal pay, even though it's less than Santa's.

Source: *San Francisco Chronicle*, Feb. 25, 1976, p. 5. Used by permission.

---

government pursue voluntary conciliation before a suit is brought against the employer. Since courts have wide discretion under this act, they have granted back-pay awards in some cases to thousands of workers.

Wheaton Glass fined

A federal court found Wheaton Glass Company had violated the Equal Pay Act. The court ordered Wheaton to pay $900,000 in back pay and interest to 2000 female employees.[40]

Comparable Worth

The Equal Pay Act has been law since 1963. However, women still earn less than 70 percent of the income that men earn. This disparity has many origins, ranging from career choices and child responsibilities to discrimination.[41] Some advocates of income equality between the sexes doubt equality will occur through the Equal Pay Act, which only seeks to assure equal pay for equal work. Instead, some suggest that equality depends on the comparable worth doctrine becoming law.

Beyond "equal" pay

The concept of *comparable worth* requires that jobs equal in value to the organization be equal in pay.[42] For example, if an electrician and a nurse are of equal value to a hospital, they would be paid the same under the comparable worth doctrine. The compensation methods used by virtually all organizations differ from the comparable worth approach. Compensation specialists compute a job's pay based on the job's content, responsibilities, and going wage rate in the labor market. If electricians are better compensated than nurses in the labor market, the hospital must pay more to obtain and retain electricians. Should Congress modify the law or the courts interpret present laws to include comparable worth, new methods of determining pay levels would have to be devised.

I. FRAMEWORKS AND CHALLENGES

How much value a nurse brings to a hospital compared with how much value an electrician brings to the hospital, for example, is difficult to judge. Without a comparable worth law, women as a group are likely to earn substantially less than men until the patterns of traditional male and female occupations disappear. Enactment of comparable worth legislation probably would mean increases in labor costs and inflation in addition to the need for new compensation procedures.[43]

Vietnam Era Veterans Readjustment Act

The *Vietnam Era Veterans Readjustment Act* of 1974 is more limited in scope than other federal laws. Its major provisions were summarized in Figure 4-3 and are discussed below. As Vietnam era veterans were discharged from military service, many found it difficult to obtain employment. To assist their integration into the private economy, Congress passed the Vietnam Era Veterans Readjustment Act of 1974. The act requires government contractors with contracts of $10,000 or more to provide equal employment opportunity to Vietnam era veterans. Violations can lead to the loss of government contracts. Human resource departments help ensure compliance by actively seeking applications from veterans through contacts at local military bases and through work with veterans' affairs offices at most large universities.

Honeywell

Honeywell, Inc.'s efforts go even further than the law requires. As a proactive move, the company appointed a "Vietnam veterans program coordinator" to help workers who are veterans deal with psychological problems and advance their careers. The coordinator works to get vets hired, organizes family counseling sessions, and publishes a company newsletter for them.[44]

STATE AND LOCAL FAIR EMPLOYMENT PRACTICES

State and local laws, which are often called *fair employment practices*, are the second major source of EEO laws. They are limited to employers within the jurisdiction of state or local governments. Although important to companies that are covered, fair employment practices are too numerous and too varied to be discussed here in detail. In general, however, they seek the same objective as federal acts: providing equal opportunity. They provide equal opportunity in two ways. One is to extend state or local protection to groups exempted from federal laws. For example, some jurisdictions prohibit discrimination on the basis of marital status or sexual preference. The other way is by sharing jurisdiction with the federal government in deferral jurisdictions. Except in circumstances where fair employment standards cover omissions in federal laws or federal agencies have agreed to defer to state agencies, federal law is supreme when conflicts exist.

Besides this shared objective, enforcement and remedies under state and local

4. EQUAL EMPLOYMENT CHALLENGES   **103**

Figure 4-8

Executive Orders Designed to Ensure Equal Employment Opportunity

EXECUTIVE ORDERS	MAJOR PROHIBITIONS	JURISDICTION
E.O. 11246	Outlaws discrimination in employment based on race, color, religion, or national origin.	Government contractors
E.O. 11375	Revises E.O. 11246 to prohibit sex discrimination.	Government contractors
E.O. 11478	Outlaws discrimination in employment based on race, color, religion, national origin, sex, political affiliation, marital status, or physical handicap.	Government agencies and the Postal Service
E.O. 11141	Outlaws discrimination in employment based on age.	Government agencies Government contractors

laws parallel federal procedures. Administration of these practices is typically the responsibility of state or local fair employment practices commissions. These commissions can normally be found in the executive branch of state or local government. In nearly all situations, compliance with the federal laws results in compliance with state and local fair employment practices. Nevertheless, experienced human resource practitioners also stay informed of state and local laws.

EXECUTIVE ORDERS

Presidential orders

The executive branch of the federal government is the single largest employer and consumer in the United States. By applying equal employment opportunity standards to itself, it sets an example for other employers; by requiring its contractors to follow equal employment rules, government can influence many employment relationships. Toward these ends, various presidents have issued *executive orders,* described in Figure 4-8. The purpose and content of these executive orders parallel the federal equal employment laws already discussed. But, like the Vietnam Era Veterans Readjustment Act, executive orders have a narrow jurisdiction. These presidential orders are aimed solely at federal government agencies and contractors.

Government Agencies

Federal agencies are required to provide equal employment opportunity, which means they are prohibited from discriminating on the basis of race, color, religion, national origin, sex, political affiliation, marital status, and physical handicap under Executive Order 11478. Likewise, these agencies are prohibited from discrimination on the basis of age under Executive Order 11141. Under both orders, those who think they have been mistreated may file complaints and have the discrimination ended by the offending agency.

Government Contractors

Human resource specialists are affected by executive orders when their employer is a government contractor. Government contractors must abide by all equal employment laws: Title VII of the Civil Rights Act, Americans with Disabilities Act, the Age Discrimination in Employment Act, the Equal Pay Act, and the Vietnam Era Veterans Readjustment Act. In addition, they must comply with Executive Order 11246, as revised (by Executive Order 11375), which duplicates Title VII. It outlaws discrimination based on race, color, religion, national origin, and sex. Age discrimination by these employers also is illegal according to Executive Order 11141.

Extra standards

Government contractors are significantly affected by Executive Order 11246. This presidential decree applies to an entire company even if only one plant or division sells to the federal government. The order requires that government contractors take affirmative action—systematic steps to ensure that past discrimination is remedied and that further discrimination does not occur. To enforce this affirmative requirement, government contractors must file affirmative action plans with the Office of Federal Contract Compliance Programs (OFCCP), which is located in the U.S. Department of Labor. The OFCCP devotes most of its efforts to reviewing contractors' affirmative action plans and visiting sites to interview managerial and nonmanagerial employees. Violation of OFCCP rules and regulations can lead to the loss of government contracts, although this penalty is seldom used.

Executive Orders and Equal Employment Laws

Executive orders overlap federal and state acts. This duplication exists for two reasons. First, some federal equal employment acts specifically exempt agencies of the federal government, and state laws do not apply to federal employees. To assure federal employees of equal employment opportunities, executive orders were passed to fill the void. Second, since government agencies and contractors spend public funds, they are subject to close examination.

Enforcement among government agencies is policed by the Office of Personnel Management; employer violations are reviewed by OFCCP or the EEOC. Enforcement procedures under federal and state laws are largely reactive. Investigations normally do not start until a complaint is made against the employer. But under executive orders, the federal government can demand compliance whether a charge is filed or not. Compliance prior to charges often requires government contractors to submit affirmative action programs.

AFFIRMATIVE ACTION

AAPs defined

Employers develop affirmative action programs to qualify as government contractors, to remedy past discrimination, or to prevent discrimination in the future. Human resource departments of most large employers develop these plans whether their organization is a government contractor or not. *Affirmative action programs* are written, systematic plans that outline goals in hiring, training, promoting, and compensating those groups protected by federal EEO laws, fair employment practices, and executive orders.[45] These programs exist for several reasons. From a practical standpoint, employers seldom benefit by excluding people who belong to some particular group. Excluding an entire class of workers, such as women or minorities, limits the labor pool from which the employer can draw; moreover, with the growing diversity of the work force, the majority of all applicants in the 1990s will come from protected classes. Open discrimination can also lead to negative public relations, boycotts by consumers, and government intervention. To ensure that such discrimination does not occur, employers often develop affirmative action programs voluntarily.

Voluntary compliance is also a practical way to correct past discrimination because compliance can avoid costly and time-consuming legal battles. As the *United Steelworkers of America and Kaiser Aluminum & Chemical Corporation v. Weber* case illustrated, voluntary affirmative action programs are a legal way to remedy past discrimination. Moreover, the ruling in the Weber case suggests that voluntary plans may be a defense against "reverse discrimination" suits, when based on self-analyses that identify and seek to rectify racial imbalances.

Sometimes compliance is the best course, even when the company thinks its past actions were legal, because time, legal costs, and adverse publicity can be minimized. At other times compliance results from a *consent decree,* which is a legally binding agreement to undertake specific actions. AT&T's massive affirmative action plan began with the consent decree it signed with the EEOC, Department of Justice, and the Department of Labor.[46]

AT&T

AT&T was in a delicate position. As the largest private employer in the United States at the time of the suit, it made an attractive target for the government. The EEOC's victory put large and small employers on notice that the government was serious about enforcement. AT&T recognized that its ability to get rate increases on long-distance calls might have been delayed for years if it had fought the EEOC all the way through court appeals.

Since every employer with fifteen or more employees is covered under Title VII of the 1964 Civil Rights Act, as amended, virtually all companies should have some form of affirmative action. These activities are usually the responsibility of the human resource department, which develops a plan to achieve the organization's affirmative action goals in the least disruptive manner.

I. FRAMEWORKS AND CHALLENGES

Affirmative Action Issues

The design and implementation of an affirmative action plan may lead the human resource department to take action that employees and line managers do not like. For example, an aggressive plan may cause the human resource department to hire and promote qualifiable workers, rather than qualified ones. A *qualifiable worker* is one who does not currently possess all the required knowledge, skills, or abilities to do a job but through additional training and experience will become qualified. Other employees may well resent being passed over by a qualifiable worker, especially if those employees believe themselves to be qualified already. Likewise, line managers may resent the loss of their authority to make final hiring, firing, or other employment decisions. The issues of reverse discrimination and the impact on line management merit further discussion.

Reverse discrimination. The use of affirmative action plans has led to charges of reverse discrimination against employers. These charges usually arise when an employer seeks to hire or promote a member of a protected class over an equally (or better) qualified candidate who is not a member of the protected class. For example, if an employer has an affirmative action program that gives preference to women over men when promotions occur, a qualified male may sue the employer and claim he was discriminated against because of his sex. Since equal employment laws prohibit discrimination on the basis of sex, courts have entertained such suits in the past.

Charges of reverse discrimination put human resource departments in a difficult position. On one hand, the department is responsible for eliminating discrimination. On the other, giving preference to members of a protected class (such as women) raises questions about whether the department is fair.[47] Although preferential treatment will always raise questions of fairness, the U.S. Supreme Court has ruled in *United Steelworkers of America and Kaiser Aluminum & Chemical Corporation v. Weber* that such treatment is not discriminatory when used to meet the objectives of a bona fide affirmative action program. Even when such programs are voluntary and not required by law or courts, preferential treatment to meet affirmative action goals is permissible and not in violation of Title VII of the 1964 Civil Rights Act.

Line managers. The implementation of an affirmative action program may cause line managers to feel a loss of authority. Operating managers may lose the right to make final hiring and promotion decisions. To achieve the objectives of the plan, the human resource department may overrule line managers. In time, supervisors may believe that members of protected classes are getting different treatment. If workers also sense an element of reverse discrimination, conflicts may arise and lessen the effectiveness of the work group.

To overcome the potentially damaging side effects of affirmative action plans, human resource specialists must educate line managers—particularly first-line supervisors. Training programs, seminars, and explanations of human resource

4. EQUAL EMPLOYMENT CHALLENGES   **107**

decisions affecting protected classes must be given to managers. Otherwise, their support and understanding of affirmative action are likely to be low; and, in turn, the perceived quality of the work environment may decline.

Development of Affirmative Action Plans

Affirmative action plans are situational. Their design depends on the specific discriminatory practices that are involved. For example, when an employer has a high number of protected class members doing a particular job, concentration exists. *Concentration* occurs when the proportion of protected class members holding a particular job is greater than the proportion of the labor market that class represents. When AT&T signed its consent decree, for example, women represented less than half of the labor market but held more than 98 percent of all telephone operator jobs. *Underutilization* is just the opposite. It occurs when protected class members are underrepresented in particular jobs compared with the availability of such members in the work force. The scarcity of women in middle-level management positions at AT&T at the time of the consent decree is an example of underutilization. Thus the affirmative action strategy used by an organization must consider the extent of concentration or underutilization.

Over- and under-representation

The nature of the program also depends on the organization's growth rate. A slow-growing employer uses affirmative action strategies that are different from those of a fast-growing company with greater opportunities for promotions. Likewise, the reasons for the affirmative action plan influence its final form. For example, a large government contractor's program must meet every agency regulation, whereas a totally voluntary program need only meet the employer's objectives.

Regardless of these situational variables, human resource departments are likely to encounter resistance to the plan by those who fear reverse discrimination and by managers who believe their authority may be diminished. To gain acceptance, some authorities recommend using an educational strategy before the plan is developed.[48] Preplan development may begin with the creation of an affirmative action advisory committee that includes line managers, workers, and staff members from the human resource department. If well chosen, the committee can be used to reflect the concerns of others in the organization. The committee may even conduct a survey to learn about the perceptions held by others. As they help design the plan, committee members not only increase their understanding of affirmative action but also are likely to educate their peers as to the scope, goals, and need for the plan. Goals set participatively are more likely to be accepted. Certainly, resistance from those on the committee is apt to be lower.

Beyond the internal strategies used to educate and win support for affirmative action, human resource departments usually follow common steps in developing these plans. The major steps are summarized in Figure 4-9.

Stereotypes and perceptions

A key aspect of affirmative action planning is overcoming past perceptions. For example, a major problem faced by AT&T was overcoming perceptions that telephone operator jobs were for women and outside repair jobs were for men.

108   I. FRAMEWORKS AND CHALLENGES

Figure 4-9

Major Steps in Affirmative Action Programs

1. *Exhibit* strong employer commitment.
2. *Appoint* a high-ranking director.
3. *Publicize* commitment internally and externally.
4. *Survey* the work force for underutilization and concentration.
5. *Develop* goals and timetables.
6. *Design* remedial and preventive programs.
7. *Establish* control systems and reporting procedures.

To break down these perceptions, AT&T had to exhibit a strong commitment to affirmative action. Managers were evaluated on how well they met their affirmative action plans, and the company appointed a high-ranking director to manage affirmative action. The company also publicized its commitment by declaring in its internal and external communications that it was an "equal opportunity employer."

The company also followed the other steps in Figure 4-9. It surveyed its work force to find areas of concentration and underutilization. Then it developed goals and timetables to systematically correct these situations. AT&T also designed remedial and preventive programs. For example, some equipment used in training and in the field was redesigned to accommodate members of protected classes so that more would successfully complete training and be promoted. Beyond the required reports for the Equal Employment Opportunity Commission, AT&T developed its own internal reporting and control systems to ensure that affirmative action would become an ongoing way of life and would receive proper visibility within the company.

SHRM

In reviewing a recent series of U.S. Supreme Court decisions about affirmative action, a monthly newsletter by the Society for Human Resource Management concludes:

> It appears that courts may order, and employers may voluntarily establish, affirmative action plans, including numerical standards, to address problems of underutilization. Further, these plans need not be directed solely to identified victims of discrimination but may include general class-wide relief for all members of the included class. While the courts will almost never approve a plan that would result in whites *losing* their jobs through layoffs, the court has apparently sanctioned plans that would impose limited burdens on whites in hiring and promotions.[49]

Merely developing an affirmative action plan may not be enough. Proactive employers not only seek to eliminate concentration and underutilization but also aim to remove the less obvious attitudes and barriers to equal opportunity that may exist within the organization. Consider the efforts of the PQ Corporation of Valley Forge, Pennsylvania:

PQ Corporation

Human resource professionals realized that demographic trends all but assured increased competition for highly qualified professional women and minorities. They also realized that stereotypical, negative attitudes among some in the firm served as barriers to the proper advancement of those in protected groups. Although emphasizing demographic trends and legal repercussions of discrimination helps change attitudes, the department also knew that an important step in changing attitudes was "to provide qualified and experienced women and minority candidates."[50]

To eliminate discriminatory attitudes, incidents, and other barriers in staffing decisions by managers, a detailed hiring procedure was developed. This staffing procedure requires an evaluation of the job requirements for each job opening. Then, as part of the selection process, the manager has to complete a two-part checklist. The first part asks fourteen questions about each aspect of the selection process, from internal posting requirements to whether qualified minority candidates were available and interviewed.

The second part of the checklist evaluates the relationship between job criteria and candidate attributes. These questions force the focus of the selection process to be on a match of job requirements and applicant abilities, rather than on nonmeritorious elements or stereotypical attitudes.

"Any program such as this one has inherent risks,"[51] two members of PQ's personnel department observed. Not only may such an elaborate effort be resisted by operating managers, but an EEO audit of the company's selection process would uncover detailed documentation of any discriminatory incidents that did exist. However, this program forces operating managers to consider skills, not stereotypes. If the human resource department can provide qualified candidates, the presence of competent women and minorities assures, perhaps best of all, the fading away of discriminatory and stereotypical attitudes.

EQUAL OPPORTUNITY IN PERSPECTIVE

Equal employment laws have a broad impact on the practice of human resource management. Professionally, the challenge of equal employment has given human resource professionals more visibility and power within their organizations. Threats of suits and government investigations, and even the remote possibility of losing a government contract, have caused top management to lend more support to activities that further equal employment opportunity. At the same time, some human resource departments have found that their relationships with other managers in the organization can suffer. When line managers believe that the human resource department's rules prevent them from hiring the best candidates or require them to spend valuable hours completing reports, these managers question whether the department is truly furthering organizational objectives. At the extreme, the department can be viewed as a hindrance. When this happens, many of the other services provided by the department are too often overlooked. The result can be that operating managers may not seek the assistance they need to improve their operation's productivity and their workers' quality of work life.

As mentioned in Chapter 1, the human resource department is a service department. It may be required to carry out societal and even organizational objectives that line managers do not appreciate and may even dislike. Nevertheless, activities such as assuring equal employment are critical to human resource management. What professionals must do, however, is to meet their organizational, societal, functional, and personal objectives simultaneously. As illustrated in the model shown in Figure 4-1, these objectives are at the center of all human resource activities. They must be pursued. But care must be taken so that the human resource department's pursuit of these objectives causes the least disruption to the organization's performance. One way to minimize the disruption caused by equal employment opportunity is to consider its impact on the other human resource activities:

Critical HR activity

1. ➤ *Human resource plans* must reflect the organization's affirmative action goals.

2. ➤ *Job descriptions* must not contain unneeded requirements that exclude members of protected classes.

3. ➤ *Recruitment* must ensure that all types of applicants are sought without discrimination.

4. ➤ *Selection* of applicants must use screening devices that are valid and nondiscriminatory.

5. ➤ *Training and development* opportunities must be available to workers without regard to factors that discriminate.

6. ➤ *Performance appraisals* must be free of biases that discriminate.

7. ➤ *Compensation programs* must be based on skills, performance, and/or seniority and cannot discriminate against jobholders because of their membership in a protected class.

Virtually every human resource activity is affected by equal employment and affirmative action plans.[52] If equal employment implications are weighed when other activities are undertaken, the need for remedial programs will decline as organizations move closer to complete equal employment opportunity.

Part II of this book addresses the actions that human resource departments undertake to assure a timely flow of qualified applicants. As the chapters in Part II reveal, equal employment must be addressed in all phases of the staffing process—especially during the human resource planning process discussed in Chapter 6 and the selection process discussed in Chapter 8.

SUMMARY

SINCE GOVERNMENT acts with the force of law, it presents a major challenge to the practice of human resource management. Its influence is through laws aimed at the employment relationship. Although most laws are limited in scope, EEO laws affect virtually every human resource department activity.

The three main sources of EEO laws are federal acts, state and local fair employment practices, and executive orders. The most significant law is Title VII of the 1964 Civil Rights Act, as amended. Along with the Americans with Disabilities Act and the Age Discrimination in Employment Act, it defines the major protected classes. Other federal equal employment laws include the Equal Pay Act and the Vietnam Era Veterans Readjustment Act.

Title VII seeks to eliminate both intentional discrimination in employment and employment practices that cause disparate treatment or impact. It also prohibits racial and sexual harassment.

To eliminate past discrimination and ensure future compliance, most organizations have developed affirmative action programs, designed to identify areas of past and present discrimination, develop affirmative goals, and implement corrective programs. Many government contractors develop affirmative action plans to comply with the OFCCP in the Department of Labor.

Terms for Review

- Protected groups
- Civil Rights Act
- Disparate treatment
- Disparate impact
- Harassment
- Bona fide occupational qualification (BFOQ)
- Equal Employment Opportunity Commission
- Deferral and nondeferral jurisdictions
- Comparable worth
- Employer retaliation p 97
- Equal Pay Act
- Conciliation agreement
- "Make-whole" remedies
- Americans with Disabilities Act
- Age Discrimination in Employment Act
- Qualified handicapped
- Qualifiable worker
- Executive orders
- Fair Employment Practices
- Affirmative action programs

I. FRAMEWORKS AND CHALLENGES

✓ Concentration
✓ Reverse discrimination
✓ Underutilization
✓ Vietnam Era Veterans Readjustment Act

Review and Discussion Questions

1. The growing diversity and the slower growth of the work force during the remainder of the 1990s seem virtually certain. How do you think these social trends will impact employer efforts at providing equal employment?

2. Suppose during your first job interview after graduation you were asked, "Why should a company have an affirmative action plan?" How would you respond?

3. If you were a supervisor in the production department of a textile mill and an employee were to demand to be allowed to miss work on Fridays for religious reasons, what would you do? Under what circumstances would you be required to let the employee have time off? Under what circumstances could you require attendance?

4. List the major equal employment laws and their primary prohibitions.

5. Since Title VII of the Civil Rights Act does not cover U.S. citizens working overseas, international human resource specialists need not be concerned about equal employment overseas. Do you agree or disagree? Why?

6. Suppose you were told that your first duty as a human resource specialist would be to construct an affirmative action plan. What would you do? What types of information would you seek?

7. What conditions would have to be met before you could bring suit against an employer who discriminated against you because of your sex?

8. Under what circumstances would a disabled veteran have special legal protections?

INCIDENT 4-1
Casinos Unlimited and Affirmative Action

Casinos Unlimited is a small casino by Las Vegas standards. It has been in operation since 1962 and employs nearly 100 workers in a variety of job classifications. Although its total employment is equally divided between men and women, the dealers are all men. Women are concentrated in waitressing jobs in the bar and small restaurant. The food and beverage manager, casino operations manager, head chef, chief cashier, and head of security are also all men.

When a suit was brought against the casino by two women, they alleged that the employment and hiring practices at the casino were discriminatory because of the concentration of women in the lower paying jobs and the underutilization of women in management positions. The general manager, a man, argued that since employment at the casino was equally balanced between men and women, the government had no right to tell him who should be in which jobs. Besides, he argued, we are not a government contractor.

The case was eventually settled through voluntary compliance with the EEOC. Compliance required back pay and additional training for women to become dealers and members of management. Furthermore, the manager agreed to develop an affirmative action plan that would promote two women to each three openings for dealers or managers.

The need for the first supervisory promotion occurred in the casino operations department. The need was for a shift supervisor. The new assistant general manager was the only woman manager in the casino. Nevertheless, she argued that Bob Rillo should become supervisor since he was best qualified. Bob had spent two years as a shift supervisor in a larger casino. The assistant director of operations agreed that Bob should get the promotion. The director of casino operations argued that Julie Newell should get the promotion because promoting her would be in compliance with the affirmative action program and because she had more seniority with the casino than Bob. In addition, Julie had been taking the supervisory courses offered by the casino as part of the affirmative action plan. They decided that the human resource director should make the final decision.

1. What weight would you give to (*a*) Julie's seniority and training, (*b*) Bob's superior experience, (*c*) the recommendations of the managers, and (*d*) the new affirmative action program?

2. What are the implications for the affirmative action program if Bob gets the job? What are the implications for the employees presently taking job-related courses if Julie gets the promotion?

3. What decision would you make if you were the personnel manager?

4. Once the decision is made, what employee relations problems might occur? What actions would you take to address employee concerns?

References

1. R. Roosevelt Thomas, Jr., "From Affirmative Action to Affirming Diversity," *Harvard Business Review* (March–April 1990), pp. 107–117.

2. *Equal Employment Opportunity Commission Eighth Annual Report (Fiscal Year 1973)* (Washington, D.C.: 1975), p. 25.

3. Ibid.

4. "U.S. Government Finds AT&T in Compliance," *U.S. Equal Employment Opportunity Commission News Release* (Government Printing Office, Washington, D.C., 1979), p. 3.

5. *Equal Employment Opportunity Commission Tenth Annual Report (Fiscal Year 1975)*, (Government Printing Office, Washington, D.C., 1977), p. 5.

6. Howard Gleckman et al., "Race in the Work Place: Is Affirmative Action Working?" *Business Week* (July 8, 1991), pp. 56, 58.

7. David P. Twomey, *A Concise Guide to Employment Law: EEO & OSHA* (Cincinnati: South-Western Publishing Co., 1986), p. iii. See also Roger B. Jacobs, "Employment Discrimination and Continuing Violations: An Update of *Ricks* and Recent Decisions," *Labor Law Journal* (October 1982), pp. 684–689; Charles F. Schanie and William L. Holley, "An Interpretive Review of the Federal Uniform Guidelines on Employee Selection Procedures," *Personnel Administrator* (June 1980), pp. 44–48. Also, the enforcement agencies provide many free or low-cost pamphlets on nearly every aspect of equal employment.

8. Paul S. Greenlaw and John P. Kohl, "National Origin Discrimination and the New EEOC Guidelines," *Personnel Journal* (August 1981), pp. 634–636.

9. "What ADA Means to You," *Recruitment Today* (Summer 1990), pp. 6–10.

10. David Gold and Beth Unger, "Better Pregnancy Benefit Not Discriminating," *HR News* (Jan. 1990), p. 7. See also David Gold and Nancy Russell, "What Laws Cover Pregnant Workers?" *Resource* (June 1988), p.3.

11. James G. Frierson, "Religion in the Workplace," *Personnel Journal* (July 1988), pp. 60–67.

12. Robert H. Faley, Lawrence S. Kleinman, and Mark L. Lengnick-Hall, "Age Discrimination and Personnel Psychology: A Review and Synthesis of the Legal Literature with Implications for Future Research," *Personnel Psychology*, vol. 37 (1984), pp. 327–350.

13. Ibid.

14. Gerald H. Trautman, "Greyhound Ain't No Dog," *Arizona* (June 12, 1977), p. 10. According to Charlotte M. Cloninger, director of women's affairs for the Greyhound Corporation, the height rule required applicants to be "more than five-feet, six inches tall."

15. *Griggs v. Duke Power Company*, 401 U.S. 424 (1971).

16. Judith A. Winston and Claudia A. Withers, "A Turn to the Right: Civil Rights in the Supreme Court, the 1988–90 Term," *Legal Report* (Fall 1989), pp. 1–5.

17. *Albemarle Paper Company v. Moody*, 422 U.S. 405 (1975).

18. *General Electric v. Gilbert*, 429 U.S. 125 (1976).

19. Richard Trotter, Susan Rawson Zacur, and Wallace Gatewood, "The Pregnancy Disability Amendment: What the Law Provides," *Personnel Administrator* (Feb.1982), pp. 47–48, 50–54. See also Betty Southard Murphy, Wayne E. Barlow, and D. Diane Hatch, "U.S. Supreme Court Approves Preferential Treatment for Pregnancy," *Personnel Journal* (March 1987), p. 18.

20. "What Are Regulations for Pregnancy Leave?" *Resource* (July 1986), p. 3.

21. Mary P. Rowe, "Dealing with Sexual Harassment," *Harvard Business Review* (May–June 1981), p. 42; and *Harassment and Pay Discrimination in the Workplace* (Chicago: Commerce Clearing House, 1986).

22. Michele Galen, Zachary Schiller, Joan O'C. Hamilton, and Keith H. Hammonds, "Ending Sexual Harassment: Business Is Getting the Message," *Business Week* (March 18, 1991), pp. 98–100.

23. Eliza G.C. Collins and Timothy B. Blodgett, "Sexual Harassment . . . Some See It . . . Some Won't," *Harvard Business Review* (March–April 1981), pp. 77–95.

24. Donald J. Petersen and Douglas Massengill, "Sexual Harassment: A Growing Problem in the Workplace," *Personnel Administrator* (Oct. 1982), pp. 79–89. See also Patricia Linenberger and Timothy J. Keaveny, "Sexual Harassment in Employment," *Human Resource Management* (Spring 1981), pp. 11–17; and George E. Biles, "A Program Guide for Preventing Sexual Harassment in the Workplace," *Personnel Administrator* (June 1981), pp. 49–54, 56.

25. "High Court Rules on Harassment," *Resource* (July 1986), p. 2. The U.S. Supreme Court ruling appeared in *Meritor Savings Bank v. Vinson* (1986). See also "Training Can Help Prevent Harassment," *Resource* (July 1986), p. 12; and Dawn Bennett-Alexander, "Sexual Harassment in the Office," *Personnel Administrator* (June 1988), pp. 174–188.

26. *International Brotherhood of Teamsters v. United States*, 431 U.S. 324 (1977).

27. *United Steelworkers of America and Kaiser Aluminum & Chemical Corp. v. Weber*, 443 U.S. 193.

28. Martin Merzer, "New Immigration Law Reaches Beyond Aliens," *The Miami Herald* (May 10, 1987), p. 12a. See also Sandra Dibble, "Law Cuts Work Force, Puts Aliens Out of Jobs," *The Miami Herald* (Feb. 1, 1987), pp. 1a, 12a. See also David S. Bradshaw, "Immigration Reform: This One's for You," *Personnel Administrator* (April 1987), pp. 37, 40.

29. Betty Southard Murphy, Wayne Barlow, and D. Diane Hatch, "Title VII Doesn't Cover Americans Working Abroad," *Personnel Journal* (Jan. 1989), pp. 19–20.

30. Faye Rice, Should You Work for a Foreigner?" *Fortune*, Aug. 1, 1988, pp. 123–134.

31. Bette Bardeen Durling, "Retaliation: A Misunderstood Form of Employment Discrimination," *Personnel Journal* (July 1981), pp. 555–558.

32. Robert H. Sheahan, "Responding to Employment Discrimination Charges," *Personnel Journal* (March 1981), pp. 216–220.

33. "What ADA Means to You," op. cit.

34. J. Freedly Hunsicker, Jr., "Ready or Not: The ADA," *Personnel Journal* (Aug. 1990), pp. 81–83.

35. Ibid.

36. Gary Dessler, "Age in the Work Place Is No Joke: A Boss Can Be Sued for Harassment," *The Miami Herald*, Business Monday (April 20, 1987), p. 47.

37. Morton C. Paulson, "How to Protect Your Job If the Boss Says You're Too Old," *National Observer* (July 4, 1977), p. 1. See also Carl E.B. McKenry, "Enforcement of Age Discrimination in Employment Legislation," *Hasting's Law Journal* (May 1981), pp. 1157–1193.

38. Joan L. Kelly, "Employers Must Recognize that Older People Want to Work," *Personnel Journal* (Jan. 1990), pp. 44–47. See also "Retirement Age Law to Keep 200,000 on Job," *Resource* (Nov. 1986), p. 3.

39. Elizabeth A. Cooper and Gerald V. Barrett, "Equal Pay and Gender: Implications of Court Cases for Personnel Practices," *Academy of Management Review*, vol. 9, no. 1 (1984), pp. 84–94. See also *Harassment and Pay Discrimination in the Workplace*, op. cit.; and Paul S. Greenlaw and John P. Kohl, "The EEOC's New Equal Pay Act Guidelines," *Personnel Journal* (July 1982), pp. 517–521.

40. *Schultz v. Wheaton Glass Company*, 421 F. 2d 259.

41. Robert Buchele and Mark Aldrich, "How Much Difference Would Comparable Worth Make?" *Industrial Relations* (Spring 1985), pp. 222–233.

42. Thomas A. Mahoney, "Approaches to the Definition of Comparable Worth," *Academy of Management Review* (Jan. 1983), pp. 14–22. See also John R. Schnebly, "Comparable Worth: A Legal Overview," *Personnel Administrator* (April 1982), pp. 43–48; George L. Whaley, "Controversy Swirls Over Comparable Worth Issue," *Personnel Administrator* (April 1982), pp. 51–56, 58–61.

43. Buchele and Aldrich, op. cit.

44. "Veterans' Advocate: A Firm Makes Special Efforts to Solve Vets' Problems," *The Wall Street Journal*, Western ed. (Dec. 28, 1982), p. 1.

45. The U.S. Equal Employment Opportunity Commission has published a useful pair of booklets related to affirmative action: *Affirmative Action and Equal Employment: A Guidebook for Employees*, vols. 1 and 2 (Jan. 1974). See also Daniel Seligman, "Affirmative Action Is Here to Stay," *Fortune* (April 19, 1982), pp. 143–144, 148, 152, 156, 160, 162.

46. The U.S. Supreme Court has held that a consent decree does not violate Title VII even if the employer agrees to do more through affirmative action than a federal court could require. This holding comes from *Local 93, Firefighters, AFL-CIO v. the City of Cleveland*, Docket Number 84-1999 (July 2, 1986). See also Lawrence S. Kleiman and Robert H. Faley, "Voluntary Affirmative Action and Preferential Treatment: Legal and Research Implications," *Personnel Psychology*, vol. 41 (1988), pp. 481–496.

47. Ibid.

48. Benson Rosen, Thomas H. Jerdee, and John Huonker, "Are Older Workers Hurt by Affirmative Action?" *Business Horizons* (Sept.–Oct. 1982), pp. 67–70.

49. "High Court Shifts Direction in Affirmative Action Ruling," *Resource* (Aug. 1986), p. 6.

50. Jeanne C. Poole and E. Theodore Kautz, "An EEO/AA Program That Exceeds Quotas: It Targets Biases," *Personnel Journal* (Jan. 1987), p. 104. See also Dorothy P. Moore and Marsha Hass, "When Affirmative Action Cloaks Management Bias in Selection and Promotion Decisions," *Academy of Management Executive*, vol. 4, no. 1 (1990), pp. 84–90.

51. Ibid., p. 105.

52. Horace E. Johns and H. Ronald Moser, "Where Has EEO Taken Personnel Policies?" *Personnel* (Sept. 1989), pp. 63–66.

II

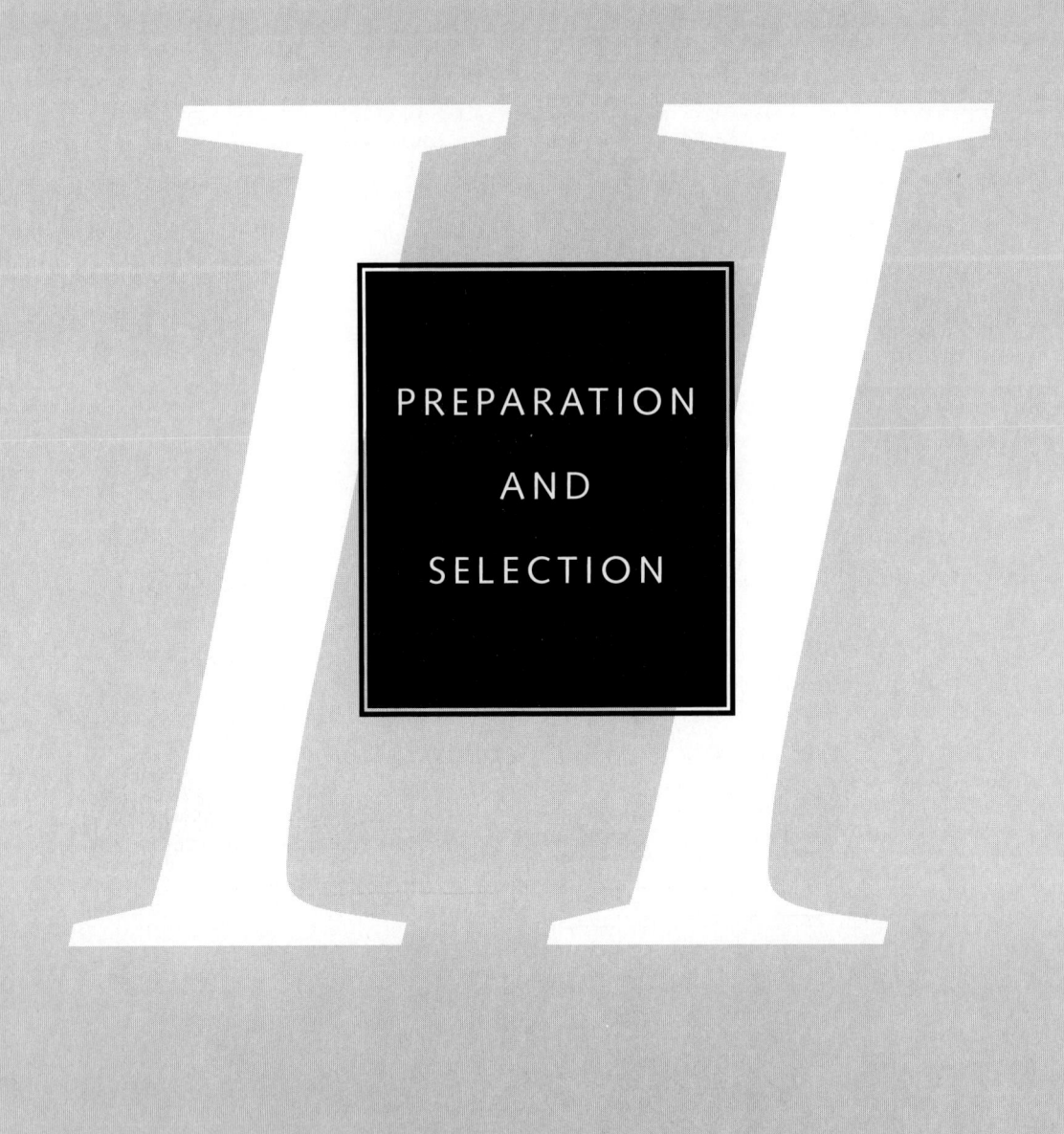

PREPARATION AND SELECTION

5 Job Analysis and Design
6 Human Resource Planning
7 Recruitment
8 Selection

THE HUMAN resource department hires people to help the organization meet objectives. To staff the organization effectively, the department studies the organization's jobs and the future human resource needs to fill them. Then it recruits and selects people to fill job openings. Preparation and selection are crucial because an organization can be no better than the people it hires.

The next four chapters discuss the activities used to select employees. You are affected as either a human resource specialist or a manager because your success depends on the people you hire. Good selection decisions help assure good performance. You also are involved in the selection process each time you look for a job.

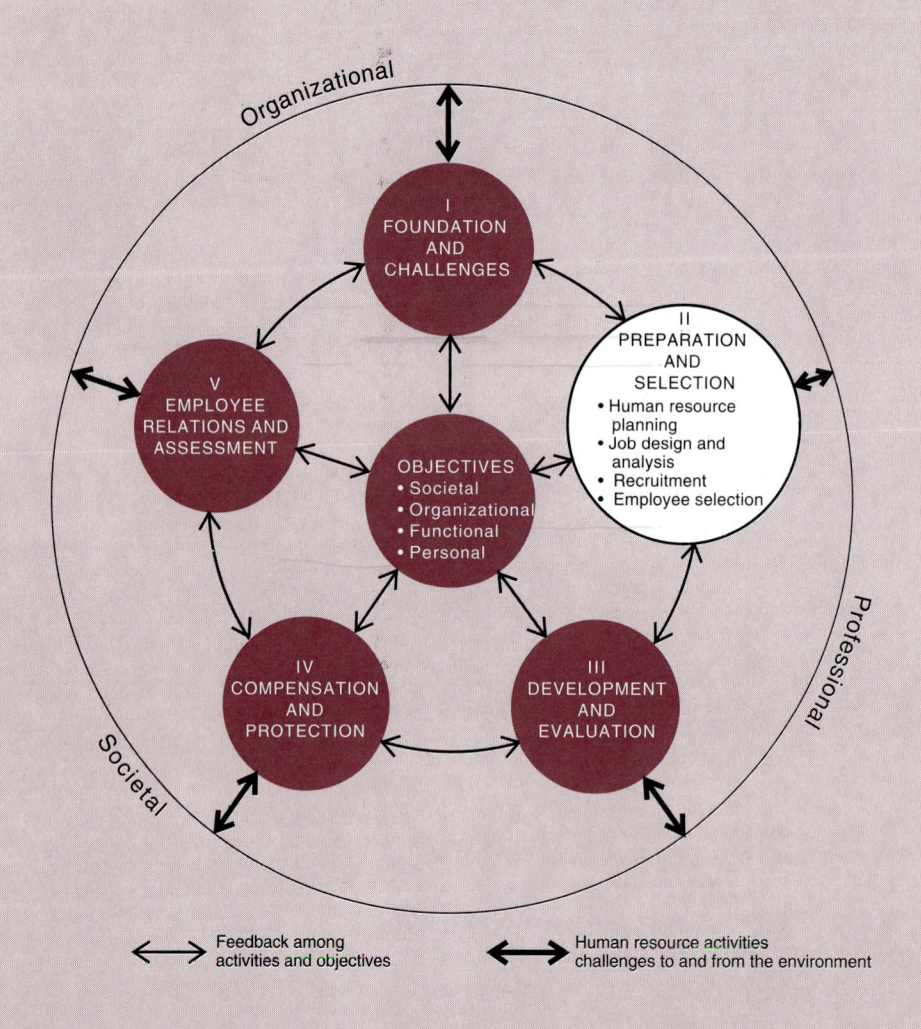

A Model of Human Resource Management

Environmental boundary: Organizational · Professional · Societal

I. Foundation and Challenges

II. Preparation and Selection
- Human resource planning
- Job design and analysis
- Recruitment
- Employee selection

III. Development and Evaluation

IV. Compensation and Protection

V. Employee Relations and Assessment

Objectives
- Societal
- Organizational
- Functional
- Personal

⟷ Feedback among activities and objectives

⟷ Human resource activities challenges to and from the environment

The data generated by job analyses have significant use in nearly every phase of human resources administration: designing jobs and reward systems; staffing and training; performance control and more.

PHILIP C. GRANT[1]

JOB ANALYSIS AND DESIGN

CHAPTER OBJECTIVES

After studying this chapter, you should be able to:
1. DISCUSS the foundations of a human resource information system.
2. EXPLAIN why human resource departments must have job analysis information.
3. LIST the major methods of collecting job analysis information.
4. DESCRIBE the content and uses of a job description.
5. IDENTIFY the efficiency and behavioral considerations in the design of jobs.
6. DISCUSS the different job-redesign techniques used to improve the quality of work life.

Research study

THE ENVIRONMENTAL, international, and legal challenges discussed in previous chapters should be part of each human resource professional's knowledge base. Experience, reading, and seminars continually add to this storehouse of information. But for professionals to act in a proactive manner, they must have access to an in-house, human resource information system (HRIS). In small operations, needed information may be handled by a reliance on paper files. As the organization's complexity grows, information about jobs, applicants, compensation, and related personnel matters is typically computerized. One study of 568 firms found that 74 percent use computers to track job applicants.[2] Thus, those seeking a career in human resource management find that computerized, data management skills are of growing importance.[3]

Jobs and HRIS

The cornerstone of a department's HRIS is information about jobs, as shown in Figure 5-1.[4] Jobs are at the core of every organization's productivity. If they are designed well and done right, the organization makes progress toward its objectives. Otherwise, productivity suffers; profits fall; and the organization is less able to meet the demands of society, customers, employees, and others with a stake in its success. For the human resource department to assist with the organization of jobs, it must have an HRIS that captures knowledge about jobs and an understanding of job design principles. The importance and implications of well-designed jobs are, perhaps, best illustrated by an example.

Shenandoah Life

Shenandoah Life Insurance Company of Roanoke, Virginia spent $2 million to computerize its claims processing operations. The results? A typical application for a policy conversion still took 27 working days, 32 clerks, and three departments to process.

The technology worked. But jobs had to be reorganized before the benefits of automation became apparent. The human resource department had to study clerks' jobs and add that information to its HRIS. Then, by applying its job design knowledge, jobs were regrouped and responsibilities were expanded. As a result, case-handling time fell to two days and complaints practically vanished. By the last half of the 1980s, Shenandoah Life was using 10 percent fewer workers and processing 50 percent more applications.[5]

An HRIS that detailed the nature of the clerks' jobs combined with an understanding of job design produced an improvement in performance. Not all attempts to restructure jobs succeed as well as this example from Shenandoah Life. However, improvements in productivity, quality, and cost often begin with the job employees do. For a human resource department to be effective, its members must have a clear understanding of the jobs found throughout organizations. But with hundreds or even thousands of jobs, it is nearly impossible for specialists to know the details of every job. The solution is an effective human resource information system that contains detailed information about every job in the organization. With this written or electronically stored information, specialists

124 II. PREPARATION AND SELECTION

Figure 5-1

The Cornerstones of a Human Resource Information System

- Environmental challenges
- Equal employment opportunity
- International challenges
- Jobs

(HUMAN / RESOURCE / INFORMATION / SYSTEM)

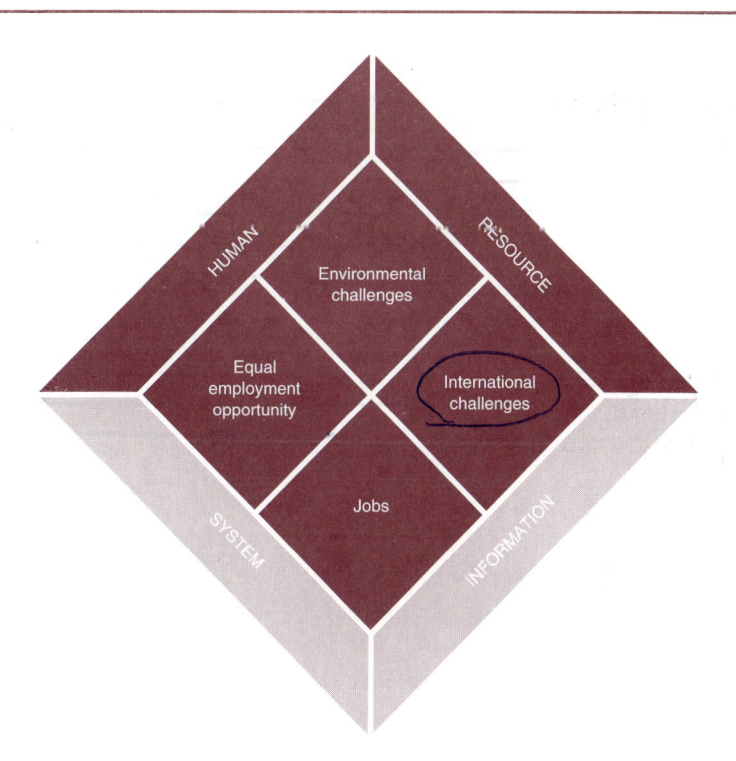

can quickly learn the details of any job. This knowledge is crucial to the success of a human resource department—especially in a large corporation like Shenandoah Life—because it enables specialists to be more proactive in their efforts to assist the organization. If they lack this information base, they will be less able to redesign jobs, recruit new employees, train present employees, determine appropriate compensation, and perform many other human resource functions.

This chapter describes three closely related topics: job analysis information, human resource information systems, and job design. It shows how human resource professionals expand their department's information base through job analysis. Then the chapter addresses the HRIS and its implications. The chapter concludes by showing how specialists use job analysis stored in the department's HRIS to help design and redesign jobs. Subsequent chapters detail other applications of job analysis information and expand on the information captured in an HRIS.

5. JOB ANALYSIS AND DESIGN   125

JOB ANALYSIS INFORMATION: AN OVERVIEW

Before a human resource department is created, line managers handle all personnel matters. Since operating managers are familiar with all the jobs they supervise, they seldom need recorded job information. They already know the characteristics, standards, and human abilities required of the jobs they supervise. As human resource activities grow in scope and complexity, many duties—such as recruiting and compensating—are delegated to the human resource department. But the people in the department seldom have much knowledge about the jobs in other departments. Knowledge about jobs and their requirements must be collected through job analysis. *Job analysis* systematically collects, evaluates, and organizes information about jobs. These actions are usually done by specialists, called *job analysts*, who gather data about each job but not about every person.

Job analysis defined

Shenandoah Life

For example, suppose Shenandoah had 50 accounts payable clerks in its central accounts payable department. Each job is the same since each clerk does the same work—process incoming invoices so they can be paid. Job analysts do not need to study all 50 clerks. Instead, the analyst only needs to review a random sample of these 50 positions. Data collection on a sample of accounts payable clerk positions generates an accurate information base for all fifty positions. Simply stated, a job analyst can understand the accounts payable clerk's job without studying the tasks of each clerk.

Applications

Recorded job information plays a crucial role because it influences most human resource activities.[6] Some of the affected areas are listed in Figure 5-2. For example, without job analysis information, analysts would find it difficult to evaluate how environmental challenges or specific job requirements affect workers' productivity or quality of work life. To match job applicants to openings and applicants, human resource specialists must know what each job requires.

Requirements must be specific enough to enable specialists to recruit those with the needed knowledge, skills, and abilities. When human resource functions are applied across international borders, for example, knowledge about cultural, language, and other unique attributes must be captured through job analysis information and made part of the human resource information system. Yet unneeded or marginal requirements may cause the department to screen out qualified minority or handicapped applicants.[7] Likewise, compensation analysts cannot determine a fair wage or salary without detailed knowledge about jobs. Although operating managers and supervisors may know the details of every job they manage, the human resource department must formalize the collection, evaluation, and organization of job analysis information.

II. PREPARATION AND SELECTION

Figure 5-2

Major Human Resource Management Actions That Rely on Job Analysis Information

1. *Evaluate* how environmental challenges affect individual jobs.
2. *Eliminate* unneeded job requirements that can cause discrimination in employment.
3. *Discover* job elements that help or hinder the quality of work life.
4. *Plan* for future human resource requirements.
5. *Match* job applicants and job openings.
6. *Determine* training needs for new and experienced employees.
7. *Create* plans to develop employee potential.
8. *Set* realistic performance standards.
9. *Place* employees in jobs that use their skills effectively.
10. *Compensate* jobholders fairly.

COLLECTION OF JOB ANALYSIS INFORMATION

Job analysts gather information about jobs and jobholder characteristics. Before collecting the information about specific jobs, the analyst should be familiar with the external environment and the organization—its purpose, strategies, design, inputs (people, materials, and procedures), and outputs (products and services). Familiarity with company, industry, and government reports about the work to be analyzed further equips the analyst to develop more useful job analysis information. Armed with a general understanding of the environment, organization, work, and workers to be studied,[8] analysts:

Steps to job analysis

▶ Identify the jobs to be analyzed.

▶ Develop a job analysis questionnaire.

▶ Collect job analysis information.

Job Identification

Analysts identify the various jobs in the organization before they collect job information. The process of job identification is simple in small organizations because there are few jobs. In large companies, analysts may have to construct lists of jobs from payroll records, organization charts, or discussions with workers and supervisors. If job analysis has been done previously, analysts may be able to use prior records to identify many of the jobs in the firm.[9]

5. JOB ANALYSIS AND DESIGN **127**

Questionnaire Development

Other approaches

To study jobs, analysts usually develop checklists or questionnaires, which help ensure that the information is collected in a consistent manner for all jobs. Analysts may elect to use standardized forms, such as the *Position Analysis Questionnaire*[10] (PAQ) or the *Job Element Inventory*.[11] Regardless of what they are called, these forms seek to collect job information uniformly. The questionnaire reveals the duties, responsibilities, human abilities, and performance standards of the jobs investigated. It is important to use the same questionnaire on similar jobs. Analysts want differences in job information to reflect differences in the jobs investigated, not differences in the questions asked. Uniformity is especially hard to maintain in large organizations. When analysts study similar jobs in different departments, only a uniform questionnaire is likely to result in usable data.

> *After two appliance producers merged, each initially retained its separate personnel department and separate job analysis schedule. As a result, all the production supervisors evaluated by one form had their jobs and pay substantially upgraded. The supervisors in the other plant had identical jobs, but they received only modest pay raises.*

As this example points out, similar jobs should be studied with identical checklists. This does *not* mean that the personnel department is limited to one questionnaire. Job analysts often find that technical, clerical, and managerial jobs require different checklists. Different checklists, however, should never be applied to similar jobs.

What are the questions asked in a job analysis questionnaire? Figure 5-3 offers an abbreviated sample form. The major parts of a standard questionnaire are described in the following paragraphs.

Status and identification. The first two headings in the figure indicate how current the information is and identify the job being described. Without these entries, users of job analysis data may rely on out-of-date information or apply it to the wrong job. Since most jobs change over time, outdated information may misdirect other personnel activities.

Brevard General Hospital

> *Job analysis information about the position of billing clerk at Brevard General Hospital had not been collected for two years. This outdated information indicated that bookkeeping experience was the major skill needed. But since the hospital's entire billing system recently had been computerized, bookkeeping skills actually were unimportant. Instead, new billing clerks needed skills to process billing information into the computer.*

128   II. PREPARATION AND SELECTION

Figure 5-3

A Job Analysis Questionaire

> *Status + Identification*
> *reveal duties + respon*
> *human abil*
> *perf stand of jobs.*
>
> *Don't always keep track*

BREVARD GENERAL HOSPITAL

Job Analysis Questionnaire

(Form 110-JAQ)

A. Job Analysis Status

    1. Job analysis form revised on _____

    2. Previous revisions on _____

    3. Date of job analysis for specified job _____

    4. Previous analysis on _____

    5. Job analysis is conducted by _____

    6. Verified by _____

B. Job Identification

    1. Job title _____

    2. Other titles _____

    3. Division(s) _____

    4. Department(s) _____

    5. Supervisor(s) title _____

C. Job Summary

Briefly describe purpose of job, what is done, and how. _____

_____

_____

D. Duties

    1. The primary duties of this job are best classified as:

        _____ Medical   _____ Technical   _____ Managerial

        _____ Clerical   _____ Professional

2. List *major* duties and the proportion of time each involves:

   a. _____, _____ %

   b. _____, _____ %

   c. _____, _____ %

3. List other duties and the proportion of time each involves:

   a. _____, _____ %

   b. _____, _____ %

   c. _____, _____ %

4. What constitutes successful performance of these duties? _____
   _____

5. To perform these duties, how much training is needed for normal performance?
   _____
   _____

E. Responsibility

   1. What are the responsibilities found in this job and how significant are these responsibilities?

      Significance of Responsibility

Responsibility for:	Minor	Major
a. Equipment operation	_____	_____
b. Use of tools	_____	_____
c. Materials usage	_____	_____
d. Protection of equipment	_____	_____
e. Protection of tools	_____	_____
f. Protection of materials	_____	_____
g. Personal safety	_____	_____
h. Safety of others	_____	_____
i. Other's work performance	_____	_____
j. Other (Specify _____)	_____	_____

F. Human Characteristics/Job Specifications

   1. What physical attributes are necessary to perform the job? _____
   _____

2. Of the following characteristics, which ones are needed and how important are they?

Characteristic	Unneeded	Helpful	Essential
1. Vision	_____	_____	_____
2. Hearing	_____	_____	_____
3. Talking			_____
4. Sense of smell	_____	_____	_____
5. Sense of touch	_____	_____	_____
6. Sense of taste	_____	_____	_____
7. Hand-eye coordination	_____	_____	_____
8. Overall coordination	_____	_____	_____
9. Strength	_____	_____	_____
10. Height	_____	_____	_____
11. Health	_____	_____	_____
12. Initiative	_____	_____	_____
13. Ingenuity	_____	_____	_____
14. Judgment	_____	_____	_____
15. Attention	_____	_____	_____
16. Reading	_____	_____	_____
17. Arithmetic	_____	_____	_____
18. Writing	_____	_____	_____
19. Education (Level ____)	_____	_____	_____
20. Other (Specify ____)	_____	_____	_____

3. Experience for this job:

    _____ a. Unimportant

    _____ b. Includes _____ (months) as (job title) _____

4. Can training be substituted for experience?

    _____ Yes   How: _____

    _____ No   Why: _____

G. Working Conditions

1. Describe the physical conditions under which this job is performed. _____

_____

2. Are there unusual psychological demands connected with this job? _____
_____

3. Describe any conditions under which the job is performed that make it unique.
_____
_____

H. Health or Safety Features

1. Describe fully any health or safety hazards associated with this job. _____
_____
_____

2. Is any safety training or equipment required? _____
_____

I. Performance Standards

1. How is the performance of this job measured? _____
_____

2. What identifiable factors contribute most to the successful performance of this job?
_____

J. Miscellaneous Comments

Are there any aspects of this job that should be noted? _____
_____
_____

_____   _____
Job Analyst's Signature   Date Completed

Matching people to jobs

2. **Duties and responsibilities.** Many forms briefly explain what the purpose of the job is, what duties are performed, and how the duties are performed. This summary provides a quick overview of the job. The specific duties and responsibilities are listed to provide more detailed insight into the position. Questions about responsibility are expanded significantly when the checklist is applied to management jobs. Additional questions map areas of responsibility for decision-making, controlling, organizing, planning, and other managerial functions.

3. **Human characteristics and working conditions.** Besides information about the job, analysts need data about the qualifications required to perform the job. This section of the checklist reveals the particular knowledge, skills, abilities, training, education, experience, and other characteristics that jobholders should possess. These facts are invaluable when filling job openings or advising workers about new job assignments or career planning. Information about the job environment also improves the understanding of the job. Working conditions may explain the need for particular skills, training, knowledge, or even a particular job design. Knowledge of hazards allows the human resource department to redesign the job or protect workers through the use of training and safety equipment. Unique working conditions influence hiring, placement, and compensation decisions.

> *One airplane manufacturer had problems installing fuel tanks inside the wings of the bombers it was building. The crawl space was extremely narrow and cramped. These tight conditions caused considerable production delays. When the personnel department learned about this situation, it recruited welders who were less than 5 feet tall and weighed under 100 pounds.*

4. **Performance standards.** The job analysis questionnaire also seeks information about job standards which are used to evaluate performance. This information is collected on jobs with obvious and objective standards of performance. When standards are not readily apparent, job analysts may ask supervisors or industrial engineers to develop reasonable standards of performance.

Data Collection

There is no best way to collect all the information found on the job analysis questionnaire. Analysts must evaluate the trade-offs between time, cost, and accuracy associated with the use of interviews, juries of experts, questionnaires, employee logbooks, observations, or some combination of these techniques.[12]

Interviews. Face-to-face interviews are an effective way to collect job information. The analyst has the job checklist as a guide but can add other questions

Approaches to data collection

where needed. Although the process is slow and expensive, it allows the interviewer to explain unclear questions and probe into uncertain answers. Both jobholders and supervisors are usually interviewed. The analyst often talks with a limited number of workers first. Then interviews with supervisors are conducted to verify the information. This pattern ensures a high level of accuracy.

Panel of experts. Another expensive and time-consuming method is to use a panel or jury of experts. The panel consists of senior job incumbents and immediate supervisors. Together the group embodies considerable knowledge and experience about the job. To get the job analysis information, the analyst conducts an interview with the group. The interaction of the members during the interview can add insight and detail that the analyst might not get from individual interviews. A side benefit of this process can be a clarification of expected job duties among workers and supervisors who are on the jury.[13]

Mail questionnaires. A fast and less costly option is a mail questionnaire developed from the job analysis checklist. This approach allows many jobs to be studied at once and at little cost. However, there is less accuracy because of misunderstood questions, incomplete responses, and unreturned questionnaires. Supervisors can also be given mail questionnaires to verify employee responses.

Employee log. An employee log or diary is another option. Workers periodically summarize their tasks and activities in the log. If entries are made over the entire job cycle, the diary can prove quite accurate. It may even be the only feasible way to collect job information, when interviews, experts, and questionnaires are unlikely to capture a complex job.

Public relations jobs

A New York public relations firm has three-dozen account executives. Each handles a bewildering array of activities for clients. Since interviews and questionnaires often overlooked major parts of the job, the personnel department suggested a logbook. Most account executives initially resisted, but eventually they agreed to a one-month trial. The personnel department obtained the information it wanted, and account executives learned how they actually spent their days.

Logs are not a popular technique. They are time-consuming for both jobholders and personnel specialists. This makes them costly. Managers and workers often see them as a nuisance and resist their introduction. And after the novelty wears off, accuracy may decline as entries become infrequent.

Observation. Another approach is direct observation. It is slow, costly, and potentially less accurate than other methods. Accuracy may be low because the analysts may miss irregularly occurring activities. But observation is the preferred method in some situations. When analysts question data from other techniques, observation may confirm or remove doubts. Language barriers may occasion the use of observation, especially among workers for whom English is a second language.

Combinations. Since each method has faults, analysts often rely on combinations. That is, two or more techniques are used concurrently.

Typical application

A lumber company has six facilities scattered throughout the United States and Canada. To interview a few workers and supervisors at each facility was considered prohibitively expensive; to rely only on questionnaire data was thought to be too inaccurate. So the personnel department interviewed selected employees at the home office and sent questionnaires to other facilities.

Human resource departments often use multiple approaches even when all employees are at the same location. When international operations are involved, intercultural differences are more likely to go unnoticed unless analysts use varying methods to collect job analysis information. Moreover, a combination of approaches can ensure higher accuracy at minimum costs, as the lumber company example implies. Regardless of the technique used, job analysis information is of little value until it is put into more usable forms.

APPLICATIONS OF JOB ANALYSIS INFORMATION

Outcomes of job analysis

The relationship between preparation, collection, and application of job analysis information is shown in Figure 5-4. Through the preparation and collection phases of job analysis, human resource departments obtain information about jobs. The immediate application of this information transforms it into job descriptions, job specifications, and job standards. Together, these applications of job analysis information become key elements in the department's human resource information system, allowing the department to undertake the tasks outlined earlier in this chapter in Figure 5-2.

Job Descriptions

A *job description* is a written statement that explains the duties, working conditions, and other aspects of a specified job.[14] Within a firm, all the job descriptions should follow the same format, although between companies form and content may vary. One approach is to write a narrative description in a few

5. JOB ANALYSIS AND DESIGN **135**

Figure 5-4

The Three Phases of Job Analysis Information

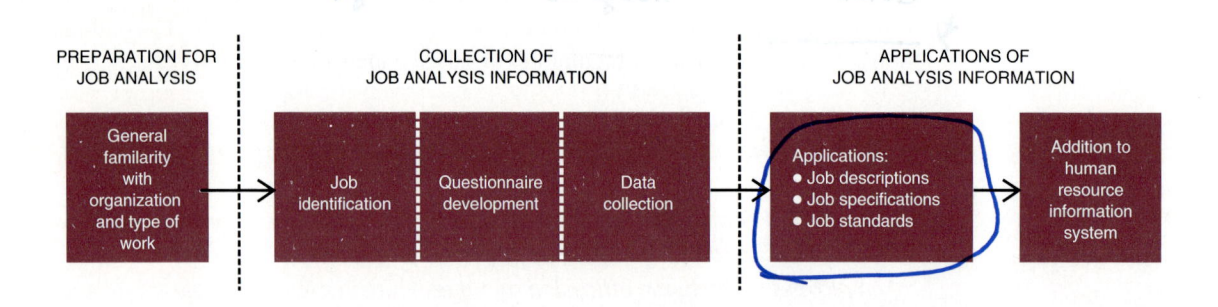

PREPARATION FOR JOB ANALYSIS	COLLECTION OF JOB ANALYSIS INFORMATION	APPLICATIONS OF JOB ANALYSIS INFORMATION
General familiarity with organization and type of work	Job identification → Questionnaire development → Data collection	Applications: • Job descriptions • Job specifications • Job standards → Addition to human resource information system

paragraphs. Another way is to break down the description into several subparts, illustrated in Figure 5-5.[15] This figure shows a job description that parallels the job analysis checklist which originally generated the data.

In a job description, the job identification section may include a *job code*. Job codes use numbers, letters, or both to provide a quick summary of the job. These codes are useful for comparing jobs. Figure 5-6 explains the code used in the *Dictionary of Occupational Titles* (DOT). It is an all-numeric code that helps arrange jobs into occupational groups. Once grouped, codes can be compared to see what relationships exist between different jobs. The code also identifies relationships among data, people, and things.[16]

Job codes

The job identification section of the job description (Figure 5-5) contains other useful information:

▶*Date.* The date is essential. It tells subsequent users how old the description is. The older the description, the less likely it is to reflect the current job.

▶*Author.* The writer of the description is identified so that questions or errors can be brought to the attention of the author.

▶*Job location.* The department (or departments) where the job is performed helps identify the job for future reference. Location references may include division, plant, or other organization breakdowns.

Figure 5-5

A Job Description

BREVARD GENERAL HOSPITAL

Job Description

Job Title:	Job Analyst	Job Code:	166.088
Date:	January 3, 1993	Author:	John Doakes
Job Location:	Personnel Department	Job Grade:	
Supervisor:	Harold Grantinni	Status:	Exempt

Job Summary: Collects and develops job analysis information through interviews, questionnaires, observation, or other means. Provides other personnel specialists with needed information.

Job Duties: Designs job analysis schedules and questionnaires. Collects job information.

Interacts with workers, supervisors, and peers.

Writes job descriptions and job specifications.

Reports safety hazards to area manager and safety department.

Verifies all information through two sources.

Performs other duties as assigned by supervisors.

Working Conditions: Works most of the time in well-ventilated modern office. Data collection often requires on-site work under every working condition found in company. Works standard 8 a.m. to 5 p.m., except to collect second-shift data and when traveling (one to three days per month).

The above information is correct as approved by:

(Signed)	(Signed)
Job Analyst	Department Manager

Figure 5-6

Explanation of Job Codes in the Dictionary of Occupational Titles

Each job in the *Dictionary of Occupational Titles* has a six-digit code. The first digit divides all jobs into nine occupational categories.

0.
1. Professional, technical, or managerial occupations
2. Clerical and sales occupations
3. Service occupations
4. Farming, fishery, forestry, and related occupations
5. Processing occupations
6. Machine trades occupations
7. Bench work occupations
8. Structural work occupations
9. Miscellaneous occupations

The second and third digits narrow the occupation to one of 603 occupational groups. For example, a job analyst's code is 166.088. The 1 indicates a job analyst is a "professional, technical, or managerial occupation." The first two digits (16) indicate "occupations in administrative specializations." The addition of the third digit (166) classifies the job as being in "personnel and training administration occupations." Thus, from the DOT code, the 166 means a professional, technical, or managerial administrative specialization in personnel or training administration.

The last three digits explain the jobs relationship to data (fourth digit), people (fifth digit), and things (sixth digit). The job analyst code of 166.088 means that the analyst synthesizes data but has no significant relationship with people or things.

DATA (FOURTH DIGIT)	PEOPLE (FIFTH DIGIT)	THINGS (SIXTH DIGIT)
0. Synthesizing	0. Mentoring	0. Setting up
1. Coordinating	1. Negotiating	1. Precision working
2. Analyzing	2. Instructing	2. Operating-Controlling
3. Compiling	3. Supervising	3. Driving-Operating
4. Computing	4. Diverting	4. Manipulating
5. Copying	5. Persuading	5. Tending
6. Comparing	6. Speaking-Signaling	6. Feeding-Offbearing
7. No significant relationship	7. Serving	7. Handling
	8. No significant relationship	8. No significant relationship

For those familiar with the DOT code, just the six digits of the job analyst's code indicates "a professional, technical, or managerial administrative specialization in personnel or training administration that synthesizes data but bears no significant relationship to people or things." (Compare this explanation with the more verbal explanation in Figure 5-4.)

Source: *Dictionary of Occupational Titles* (vol. 1), U.S. Department of Labor, 1978, p. xvi.

➤ *Job grade.* Job descriptions may have a blank for adding the job grade or level. This information helps rank the job's importance for pay purposes.

➤ *Supervisor.* The supervisor's title may be listed to help identify the job and its relative importance.

➤ *Status.* Analysts may identify the job as exempt or nonexempt from overtime laws.

Job summary and duties. After the job identification section, the next part of the job description is the job summary. It is a written narrative that concisely summarizes the job in a few sentences. It tells what the job is, how it is done, and why. Most authorities recommend that job summaries specify the primary actions involved. Then in a simple, action-oriented style, the job description lists the job duties. Figure 5-5 provides an example of this style.

Emphasize performance

This section is important to personnel specialists. It explains what the job requires. Since the effectiveness of other personnel actions depends upon an understanding of the job, each major duty is described in terms of the actions expected. Tasks and activities are identified. Performance is emphasized. Even responsibilities are implied or stated within the job duties. If employees are in a union, the union may want to narrow the duties associated with specific jobs to prevent real or imagined abuses by supervisors.

Before the union organized, the employee job descriptions contained the phrase "or other work as assigned." The union believed supervisors abused this clause by assigning idle workers to do unrelated jobs. With the threat of a strike, management removed the phrase, and supervisors lost much of their flexibility in assigning work.

Working conditions. A job description also explains working conditions. It may go beyond descriptions of the physical environment. Hours of work, safety and health hazards, travel requirements, and other features of the job expand the meaning of this section.

Approvals. [*Sign it*] Since job descriptions affect most human resource decisions, their accuracy should be reviewed by selected jobholders and their supervisors. Once a job description is acceptable, supervisors are asked to approve it. This approval serves as a further test of the job description and a further check on the collection of job analysis information. Neither personnel specialists nor managers should consider approval lightly. If the description is in error, the human resource department will become a source of problems rather than assistance.

5. JOB ANALYSIS AND DESIGN

In explaining the job of foundry attendant to new employees, recruiters relied on an inaccurate job description. Many new employees quit the job during the first two weeks. When asked why, most said the duties were less challenging than they were led to believe. When analysts checked, they found that the job description had never been verified by the supervisors. A more proactive approach of reviewing and revising this information would have prevented this turnover problem before it occurred.

Job Specifications

The difference between a job description and a job specification is one of perspective. A job description defines what the job is; it is a profile of the job. A *job specification* describes what the job demands of the employee who does it and the human skills that are required.[17] It is a profile of the human characteristics needed by the person performing the job. These requirements include experience, training, education, and physical and mental characteristics. When the position crosses national boundaries, language, legal, and cultural familiarity may become important additions to the specifications.

Since the job description and specification both focus on the job, they are often combined into one document, commonly called a job description. Whether part of a job description or a separate document, the job specification includes the information illustrated in Figure 5-7. The information needed to compile the job specification also comes from the job analysis collection process.

The job specification, if it is a separate document, contains a job identification section. The job specification form lists the skills and effort required by each job—which may include the use of specific tools, performance of specific actions, and experience, education, and training requirements which help clarify what is needed for successful job performance. Job specifications also describe the physical effort in terms of the actions demanded by the job. Specifics are preferred to generalizations. For example, "lifts 100-pound bags" is better than "lifts heavy weights."[18] Specifications of mental effort help personnel experts determine the intellectual abilities that are needed. Figure 5-7 contains several examples of the physical and mental efforts required by jobs in a hospital.

Do the working conditions make any unusual demands on jobholders? The working conditions found in job descriptions may be translated by job specifications into demands faced by workers. Figure 5-8 provides examples for the job of hospital orderly. It shows that a simple statement of working conditions found in the job description can hold significant implications for jobholders. For example, compare points 2 and 3 in the job description column to points 2 and 3 of the job specification.

Job Performance Standards

Job analysis has a third application, *job performance standards*. These standards serve two functions. First, they become targets for employee efforts.

New employee should sign Job description

Figure 5-7

A Job Specifications Sheet

BREVARD GENERAL HOSPITAL

Job Description

Job Title:	Job Analyst	Job Code:	166.088
Date:	January 3, 1993	Author:	John Doakes
Job Location:	Personnel Department	Job Grade:	
Supervisor:	Harold Grantinni	Status:	Exempt

Skill Factors

    Education: College degree required.

    Experience: At least one year as job analyst trainee, recruiter, or other professional assignment in personnel area.

    Communication: Oral and written skills should evidence ability to capsulize job data succinctly. Must be able to communicate effectively with diverse workforce, including foreign-born employees.

Effort Factors

    Physical demands: Limited to those normally associated with clerical jobs: sitting, standing, and walking.

    Mental demands: Extended visual attention is needed to observe jobs. Initiative and ingenuity are mandatory since job receives only general supervision. Judgment must be exercised on job features to be emphasized, jobs to be studied, and methods used to collect job data. Decision-making discretion is frequent. Analyzes and synthesizes large amounts of abstract information into job descriptions, job specifications, and job standards.

Working Conditions

Travels to hospital clinics in county from one to three days per month. Travels around each work site collecting job information. Works mostly in an office setting.

Success criteria and feedback

The challenge or pride of meeting objectives may serve to motivate employees. Once standards are met, workers may feel accomplishment and achievement. This outcome contributes to employee satisfaction. Without standards, employee performance may suffer.

5. JOB ANALYSIS AND DESIGN

Figure 5-8

Translation of Working Conditions Job Description to Job Specifications

HOSPITAL ORDERLY

JOB DESCRIPTION STATEMENT ON WORKING CONDITIONS	JOB SPECIFICATIONS INTERPRETATION OF WORKING CONDITIONS
1. Works in physically comfortable surroundings.	1. Must be willing to work inside.
2. Deals with physically ill and diseased patients.	2. Exposed to unpleasant situations and communicable diseases.
3. Deals with mentally ill patients.	3. Exposed to verbal and physical abuse.

2. Second, standards are criteria against which job success is measured. They are indispensable to managers or personnel specialists who attempt to control work performance. Without standards, no control system can evaluate job performance.

All control systems have four features: standards, measures, correction, and feedback. The relationship between these four factors is illustrated in Figure 5-9. Job performance standards are developed from job analysis information, and actual employee performance is then measured. When measured performance strays from the job standard, personnel experts or line managers intervene and corrective action is taken. The action serves as feedback about the standards and the employee's actual performance. This feedback leads to changes in either the standards (if they were inappropriate) or actual job performance.

Job analysis may cause other changes

At a regional Veterans Administration (VA) office, each loan supervisor was expected to review a standard of 16 VA mortgage applications per day. Actual output averaged 12. After new job analysis information was collected, analysts discovered that Congress, the VA, and area banks had added new duties since the standard was first set. Corrective action involved new job designs, revised job descriptions, and lower standards.

Job standards are a key part of any control system. When the standards are wrong, as in the VA example, they alert managers and personnel specialists to problems that need correction. The VA example also underscores the need for keeping job analysis information current.

Figure 5-9

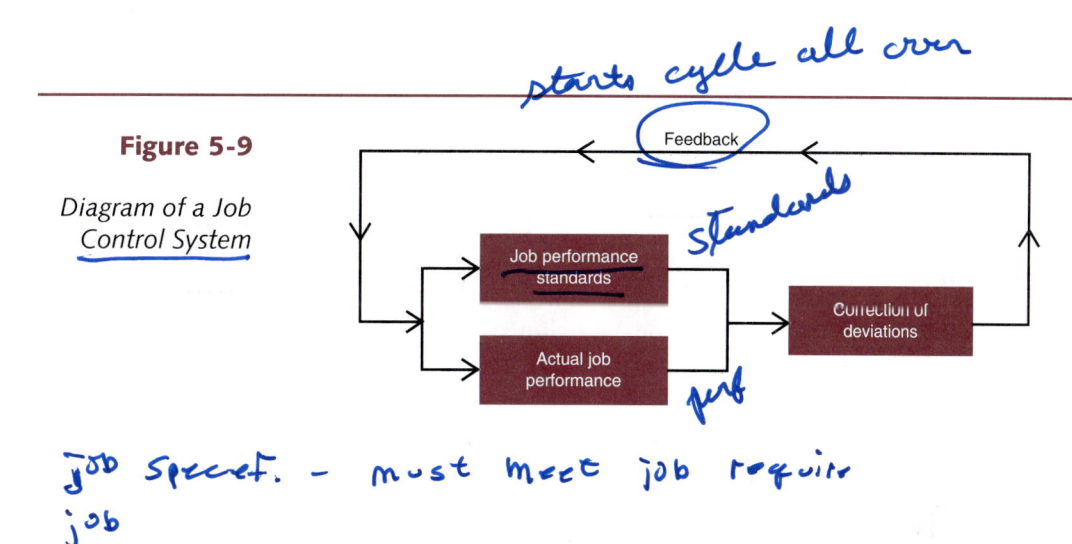

Diagram of a Job Control System

THE HUMAN RESOURCE INFORMATION SYSTEM

Job descriptions, job specifications, and performance standards are important additions to the human resource information system (HRIS). Together they explain each job, allowing human resource specialists to make informed, proactive decisions. To this storehouse of information, human resource plans, applicant information, performance results, compensation figures, and many other types of data are added. The result often is an overload of data, with little of it in the form of usable information.

HRIS at TRW

TRW, an aerospace and automotive conglomerate based in Ohio with operations in 27 countries around the world, faced the problem of data overload in its HRIS. Besides job analysis information, the TRW human resource department manages other employee-related databases, such as applicant, employee, and benefit information. Valdis Krebs, a manager at TRW's Electronics and Defense sector in Redondo Beach, California, developed an interactive network of Apple Macintoshes that allows human resource specialists to access these databases in both text and graphic formats. It includes in one information system, plant locations, organization charts, photos, benefits information, and other data that can be quickly accessed through menu-driven choices.[19]

The TRW HRIS is more sophisticated than most human resource information systems presently in use. Most systems do not yet allow this wide range of text and graphic information integration. However, the trends toward computer-based support systems for decision makers, combined with the growing use of computers and the need to reduce staff costs, are leading an increasing number of departments to create on-line systems. Although many of these systems may initially only support one function—such as job analysis information or applicant

5. JOB ANALYSIS AND DESIGN

tracking[20]—the trend in the 1990s is to interconnect various HRIS subsystems, leading to a truly integrated HRIS through which human resource professionals and line managers can access human resource information.

The need to document the acquisition and preparation of data will, of course, remain[21]; but more and more of the department's information needs will be computerized into an integrated system, such as TRW's. Perhaps the biggest current barrier to creating and maintaining a sophisticated HRIS is gaining top management support for the transition and maintenance costs associated with a fully interconnected system[22].

Two other concerns about human resource information systems warrant attention: legal considerations and organization.

Legal Considerations

For the most part, job analysis information is an internal matter which is little affected by external challenges. Job analysis information can be brought to bear, however, on such legal considerations as equal employment opportunity.[23] As discussed more fully in Chapter 4, *Griggs v. Duke Power Company* provides a classic example of how unneeded job requirements can lead to a violation of equal employment laws.

Key CASP law

> In *Griggs v. Duke Power Company,* the employer required a high school degree for nearly all jobs within the company, except those in the labor pool. When the need for a high school diploma was challenged in court, the employer could not show that this job specification was absolutely necessary to perform many of the jobs for which it was required. Although this requirement was applied equally to all applicants, it had an unequal impact on minority job applicants. As a result, many blacks were offered jobs only in the labor pool.

Unneeded demands may violate EEO

As the Duke Power Company case illustrates, it is important for personnel specialists to include in job descriptions and specifications only those items that are job-related.[24] Otherwise, charges of discrimination may result from the unequal impact of needless job requirements. Even if legal considerations are ignored, needless job requirements exclude potentially qualified individuals from consideration, and this exclusion can reduce the effectiveness of other personnel activities, such as human resource planning, recruitment, selection, and training. Moreover, excluding otherwise qualified candidates is not socially responsible and may violate equal employment laws discussed in the previous chapter.

Organization of the Database

Whether job information is compiled on printed forms or in computer memory, it is organized around individual jobs.[25] Human resource departments also need job information that is organized around job families. *Job families* are groups of jobs that are closely related in terms of duties, responsibilities, skills, or other job elements. For example, the jobs of clerk, typist, clerk-typist, word processor operator, and secretary constitute a job family. Job families allow personnel departments to facilitate permanent job transfers, training, career counseling, compensation, and other personnel decisions.

Job families can be constructed in several ways. One way is to carefully study job analysis information. By matching the data in job descriptions, the human resource department can identify jobs with similar requirements. A second method is to use the codes in the *Dictionary of Occupational Titles*. Similarities in the job codes indicate similarities in jobs. A third approach uses the *position analysis questionnaire*. The position analysis questionnaire (also called the PAQ) is a standardized, preprinted form used to collect specific information about job tasks and worker traits. Through statistical analysis of PAQ responses, job analysts can group related jobs into job families.[26]

The ability to review job information, human resource plans, and affirmative action requirements prepares personnel professionals to undertake a variety of activities, particularly to generate reports about employment costs and trends. This information also assists with career counseling, recruitment, and job design.

OVERVIEW OF JOB DESIGN

Mere knowledge of job analysis information and the organization's HRIS—important as that knowledge is—does not give a complete understanding of jobs. Jobs are more than a collection of tasks recorded on a job analysis schedule and summarized in a job description. Jobs are the foundation of organizational productivity and employee satisfaction—or lack thereof. How well jobs are designed will play an increasingly important role in the success, even survival, of many organizations during the 1990s. As the number of new workers coming into the labor market slows and international competition increases, well designed jobs will become even more important in attracting and retaining a motivated work force which is capable of producing quality products and services.

GM's job redesigns at Saturn

Recognizing Japanese superiority at producing small high-quality cars, General Motors created the Saturn Corporation as a wholly owned subsidiary. Saturn was created on the premise of using the best manufacturing approaches in the world to produce a small car with world-class standards. Although new designs and technologies were employed in making the Saturn, perhaps the most radical change introduced by the Saturn Corporation was the recomposition of jobs. In the traditional North American automobile factory, workers are employed in a variety of narrowly defined jobs, often doing the same tasks

5. JOB ANALYSIS AND DESIGN 145

over and over, with little influence on work practices, inventory procedures, or the scheduling of activities.

"At Saturn, there is only one production classification for unskilled workers and three for specific skilled employees. While there is still an assembly line, employees do not perform repetitive, mundane tasks.

Instead, groups of 6 to 15 workers decide how to do all necessary tasks, what inventory needs are, how to manage leave and vacation schedules of fellow team members, and other functions usually associated with front-line supervision."[27]

Although the initial reports of car quality from the plant are favorable, it may be years before an accurate assessment of GM's approach at the Saturn plant can be made. Nevertheless, how well people perform is determined, at least in part, by the characteristics of their jobs.[28] Job design affects both productivity and quality of work life. Jobs are the central link between employees and the organization. Job openings are why organizations need human resources. If human resource departments are going to help the organization obtain and maintain a desired work force, human resource specialists must have a thorough understanding of job design.

Demands on job design

Figure 5-10 illustrates a systems view of job design. The design of a job reflects the organizational, environmental, and behavioral demands placed on it. Job designers take these elements into consideration and try to create jobs that are both productive and satisfying. Tradeoffs among these elements of job design mean, however, that some jobs are more or less satisfying than others. Employee productivity and satisfaction provide feedback on how well a job is designed. Poorly designed jobs may lead to lower productivity, employee turnover, absenteeism, complaints, sabotage, unionization, resignations, and other problems. Returning to the Shenandoah example introduced earlier in the chapter, consider the impact that job redesign had.

Shenandoah Life

Before the redesign of the jobs at Shenandoah Life, each clerk had narrowly defined responsibilities. Each clerk did a specific function and moved the paperwork on to someone else. One result was that no one clerk had responsibility for handling an application for a policy conversion. In fact, no single department had responsibility because conversion activities were spread over three departments.

The job redesign grouped the clerks into teams of five to seven employees. Each team was trained to perform the functions of all three departments. Members learned new skills, job satisfaction went up, and pay improved since each team member now had greater skills and responsibilities.[29]

As suggested by Figure 5-10, organizational, environmental, and behavioral elements are all considered in such job design decisions. Customers in

II. PREPARATION AND SELECTION

Figure 5-10

The Job-Design Input-Output Framework

```
                                    Feedback
                                       ↑
         ┌──→ Organizational ──┐
         │      elements       │
         │                     ↓
    ─────┼──→ Environmental ──→ Job ──→ Productive and
         │      elements       design    satisfying job
         │                     ↑
         │                     │
         └──→  Behavioral  ────┘
                elements

         INPUTS │ TRANSFORMATION │ DESIRED
                │    PROCESS     │ OUTPUTS
```

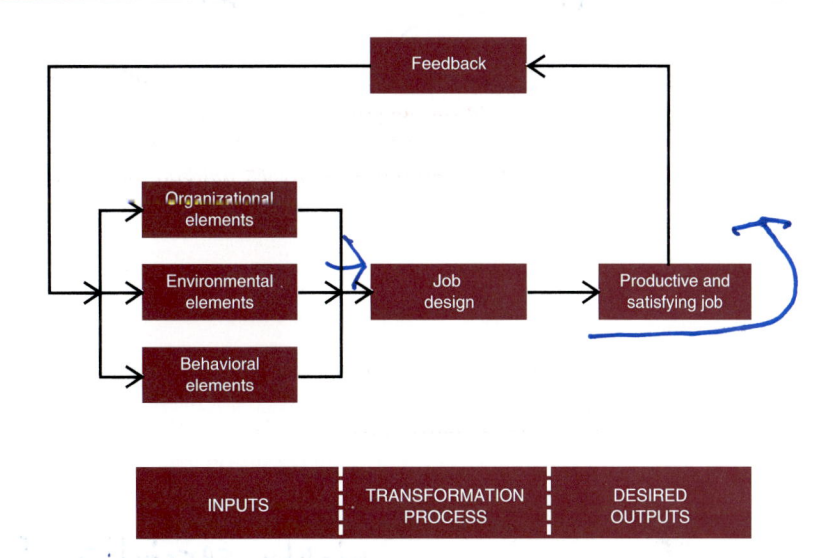

Shenandoah's sales environment received better service, the organization gained better productivity, and the behavioral elements of Figure 5-11 were injected into the jobs.

Job redesign does have some tradeoffs. Under the new structure at Shenandoah Life, each clerk must now have knowledge of several activities. More training for these clerks is necessary. And as these clerks become more qualified, Shenandoah pays them a higher salary. To explore these tradeoffs more fully, a review of the organizational, environmental, and behavioral elements of job design follows. The chapter concludes with a discussion of job redesign techniques.

Organizational Elements

Organizational elements of job design are concerned with efficiency. Efficiently designed jobs allow a highly motivated and capable worker to achieve maximum output. This concern for efficiency was formalized by Fredrick Taylor and other management scientists around the turn of the century. They devoted much of their research to finding the best ways to design efficient jobs. Their success with stopwatches and motion pictures even gave rise to a new discipline, industrial engineering. They also contributed to the formal study of management as a separate discipline. From their efforts, we have learned that specialization is a key element in the design of jobs. When workers are limited to a few repetitive tasks, output is usually higher. The findings of these early researchers are still

Efficiency in design

5. JOB ANALYSIS AND DESIGN

147

Figure 5-11
Elements of Job Design

ORGANIZATIONAL ELEMENTS	ENVIRONMENTAL ELEMENTS	BEHAVIORAL ELEMENTS
➤ Mechanistic approach	➤ Employee abilities and availability	➤ Autonomy
➤ Work flow	➤ Social and cultural expectations	➤ Variety
➤ Work practices		➤ Task identity
➤ Ergonomics		➤ Task significance
		➤ Feedback

applicable today. They can be summarized under the heading of the mechanistic approach.

Mechanistic approach. The mechanistic approach seeks to identify every task in a job so that tasks can be arranged to minimize the time and effort of workers. Once task identification is complete, a limited number of tasks are grouped into a job. The result is *specialization*. Specialized jobs lead to short *job cycles*, the time allotted to complete every task in the job. For example:

> An assembly-line worker in Detroit might pick up a headlight, plug it in, twist the adjustment screws, and pick up the next headlight within thirty seconds. Completing these tasks in thirty seconds means this worker's job cycle takes one-half a minute. The job cycle begins when the next headlight is picked up.

Headlight installation is a specialized job. It is so specialized that training takes only a few minutes. And the short job cycle means that the assembler gains much experience in a short time. Said another way, short job cycles require small investments in training and allow the worker to learn the job quickly. Training costs remain low because the worker only needs to master one job.

This mechanistic approach stresses efficiency in effort, time, labor costs, training, and employee learning time. Today, this technique is still widely used in assembly operations. It is especially effective when dealing with poorly educated workers or workers who have little industrial experience. But the efficient design of jobs also considers such organizational elements as work flow, ergonomics, and work practices.

Work flow. The flow of work in an organization is strongly influenced by the nature of the product or service. The product or service usually suggests the sequence of and balance between jobs if the work is to be done efficiently. For example, the frame of a car must be built before the fenders and doors can be added. After the sequence of jobs is determined, the balance between jobs is established.

Human interfaces

Suppose it takes one person thirty seconds to install each headlight. In two minutes, an assembler can put on four headlights. If, however, it takes four minutes to install each of the two sets of headlight receptacles, then the job designer must balance these two interrelated jobs by assigning two people to install the receptacles. Otherwise, a production bottleneck results. Since the work flow demands two receptacle installers for each headlight installer, one worker specializes on the right-side receptacles and another specializes on the left side.

Ergonomics. Optimal productivity requires that the physical relationship between the worker and the work be considered in designing jobs. *Ergonomics* is the study of how human beings physically interface with their work. Although the nature of job tasks may not vary when ergonomics are considered, the location of tools, switches, and the work product itself are evaluated and placed in position for ease of use. On an automobile assembly line, for example, a car frame may actually be elevated at a workstation so that the worker does not become fatigued from stooping. Similarly, the locations of dashboard instruments in a car are ergonomically engineered to make driving easier.[30]

Work practices. Work practices are set ways of performing work. These methods may arise from tradition or the collective wishes of employees. Either way, the human resource department's flexibility to design jobs is limited, especially when such practices are part of a union-management relationship. Failure to consider work practices can have undesired outcomes.

General Motors

General Motors decided to increase productivity at its Lordstown, Ohio, plant by eliminating some jobs and adding new tasks to others. These design changes caused workers to stage a strike for several weeks because traditional practices at the plant had required a slower rate of production and less work by the employees. The additional demands on their jobs by management were seen as an attempt by the company to disregard past work practices.[31]

Environmental Elements

A second aspect of job design concerns environmental elements. As with most human resource activities, job designers cannot ignore the influence of the external environment. In designing jobs, specialists and managers should consider the ability and availability of potential employees. At the same time, social expectations also have to be weighed.

Employee abilities and availability. Efficiency considerations must be balanced against the abilities and availability of the people who are to do the work. When Henry Ford made use of the assembly line, for example, he was aware that most potential workers lacked any automobile-making experience. So jobs were designed to be simple and require little training. Thought must be given to who will actually do the work. An extreme example clarifies this point.

Buying progress

Governments of less developed countries often think they can "buy" progress. To be "up to date," they seek the most advanced equipment they can find. Leaders of one country ordered a computerized oil refinery. This decision dictated a level of technology that exceeded the abilities of the country's available work force. As a result, these government leaders have hired Europeans to operate the refinery.

Social and cultural expectations. The acceptability of job design is also influenced by social and cultural expectations. With the growing diversity of the North American work force, these expectations will play an increasingly important role in designing jobs. For example, many uneducated immigrants who moved to North America during the early days of the railroad and automobile industries readily accepted highly specialized jobs that demanded long hours and hard physical labor. Often they had fled countries where jobs were unavailable; this made a job—any job—acceptable to them. Today, industrial workers are much better educated and have higher expectations about the quality of work life. Although work flow and work practices may suggest a particular job design, the job must meet the expectations of workers. When designing jobs for international operations, uniform designs are almost certain to neglect national and cultural differences. Hours of work, holidays, vacations, rest breaks, religious beliefs, management styles, and worker sophistication and attitudes are just some of the predictable differences that can and do affect the design of jobs across international borders. Failure to consider these social expectations can create dissatisfaction, low motivation, hard-to-fill job openings, and a low quality of work life—especially when foreign nationals are involved in the home country or overseas.

Foreign considerations

Behavioral Elements

Jobs cannot be designed by using only those elements that aid efficiency. To do so ignores the human needs of the people who are to perform the work. Instead, job designers draw heavily on behavioral research to provide a work environment that helps satisfy individual needs. Higher-level needs are of particular importance. One pair of researchers provides a useful framework:

> People with a strong desire to satisfy higher-order needs perform their best when placed on jobs that are high on certain dimensions. These are:
>
> *Autonomy:* responsibility for work
>
> *Variety:* use of different skills and abilities
>
> *Task identity:* doing the whole piece of work
>
> *Feedback:* information on performance.[32]

Task significance should be added to the list because people like to feel that their work has meaning to others inside and outside the organization.

Freedom on the job

Autonomy. Autonomy is having responsibility for what one does. It is freedom to control one's response to the environment. Jobs that give workers authority to make decisions provide added responsibilities which tend to increase the employee's sense of recognition and self-esteem. The absence of autonomy, on the other hand, can cause employee apathy or poor performance.[33]

> A common problem in many production operations is that employees develop an "I don't care attitude" because they believe they have no control over their jobs. On the bottling line of a small brewery, teams of workers were allowed to speed up or slow down the rate of the bottling line as long as they met daily production goals. Although total output per shift did not change, there were fewer cases of capping machines jamming or breaking down for other reasons. When asked about this unexpected development, the supervisor concluded, "Employees pride themselves on meeting the shift quota. So they are more careful to check for defective bottle caps before they load the machine."

Boredom

Variety. A lack of variety may cause boredom. Boredom in turn leads to fatigue, and fatigue causes mistakes. By injecting variety into jobs, personnel specialists can reduce fatigue-caused errors. Being able to control the speed of the bottling line in the brewery example added variety to the pace of work and probably reduced both boredom and fatigue.

5. JOB ANALYSIS AND DESIGN

One research study found that diversity of work was partially responsible for effective performance.[34] And another study found that autonomy and variety were major contributors to employee satisfaction.[35]

Task identity. One problem with some jobs is that they lack any *task identity*. Workers cannot point to any complete piece of work. They have little sense of responsibility and may lack pride in the results. After completing their jobs, they may have little sense of accomplishment. When tasks are grouped so that employees feel they are making an identifiable contribution, job satisfaction may be increased significantly.[36] Again, returning to the Shenandoah Life example, we saw that productivity and satisfaction increased when employees became responsible for an identifiable and sensible group of tasks.

Task significance. Closely related to task identity is *task significance*. Doing an identifiable piece of work makes the job more satisfying. Task significance, knowing that the work is important to others in the organization or outside it, makes the job even more meaningful for incumbents. Their personal sense of self-importance is enhanced because they know that others are depending on what they do. Pride, commitment, motivation, satisfaction, and better performance are likely to result.

Feedback. When jobs do not give the workers any feedback on how well they are doing, there is little guidance or motivation to perform better. For example, by letting employees know how they are doing relative to the daily production quota, the brewery gives workers feedback that allows them to adjust their efforts. Overseas work may demand managers show great sensitivity to how feedback is provided. In some countries, such as Japan, for example, care must be exercised in providing negative feedback so those responsible can "save face" and not be unduly embarrassed. Feedback leads to improved motivation.[37]

BEHAVIORAL AND EFFICIENCY TRADEOFFS

Behavioral elements of job design instruct job design specialists to include autonomy, variety, task identity, task significance, and feedback. But efficiency elements point to greater specialization, less variety, and minimum autonomy. Thus, to make jobs more efficient may cause them to be less satisfying. Conversely, satisfying jobs may prove to be inefficient. What should specialists do? There is no simple solution. Instead, experts often make tradeoffs between efficiency and behavioral elements. Figure 5-12 depicts the most significant tradeoffs faced by job designers.

Figure 5-12

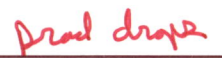

Efficiency versus Behavioral Trade-offs in Job Design

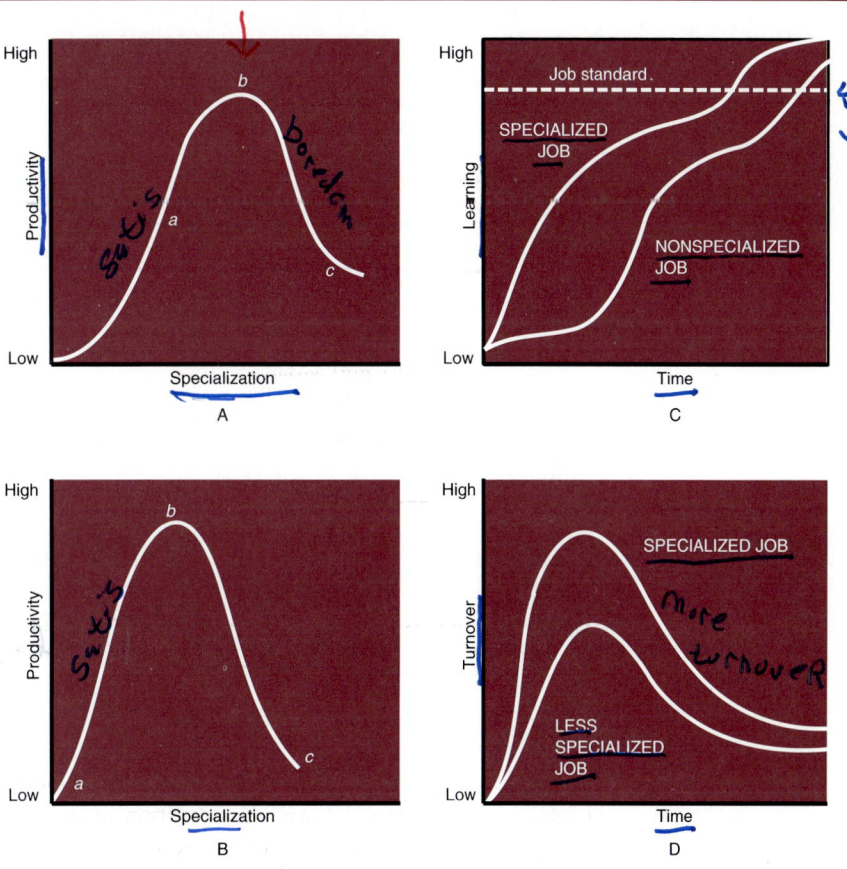

A. Productivity vs. Specialization — productivity rises to point *b* then falls to *c* (satisfaction, boredom noted).

B. Satisfaction vs. Specialization — similar inverted-U curve from *a* through *b* to *c*.

C. Learning vs. Time — Specialized Job reaches Job standard faster; Nonspecialized Job lags.

D. Turnover vs. Time — Specialized Job shows more turnover; Less Specialized Job shows less.

Graph A: Productivity versus Specialization

As jobs are made more specialized, productivity climbs until behavioral elements such as boredom offset the advantages of further specialization. In Figure 5-12A, additional specialization beyond point *b* causes productivity to drop. In fact, in jobs that are between *b* and *c*, productivity can be *increased* by reducing the degree of specialization.

Graph B: Satisfaction versus Specialization

Satisfaction first goes up with specialization, and then additional specialization causes satisfaction to drop quickly. Jobs without any specialization take too long to learn; frustration is decreased and feedback increased by adding some specialization. However, when specialization is carried past point *b* in Figure 5-12B,

5. JOB ANALYSIS AND DESIGN

satisfaction drops because of a lack of autonomy, variety, and task identification. Notice that even while satisfaction is falling in Graph B, productivity may still increase in Graph A, from a to b. Productivity continues to go up only if the advantages of specialization outweigh the disadvantages of dissatisfaction.

Graph C: Learning versus Specialization

It takes less time to learn a specialized job than a nonspecialized one. Graphically, this means that the rate of learning reaches an acceptable standard (shown as a dashed line) more quickly.

Graph D: Turnover versus Specialization

Although overspecialized jobs are learned more quickly, the lower levels of satisfaction generally associated with them can lead to higher turnover rates. When turnover rates are high, redesigning the job with more attention to behavioral elements may reduce this quit rate.

TECHNIQUES OF JOB REDESIGN

The central question often facing job designers is whether a particular job should have more or less specialization. As can be seen in Graph A in Figure 5-12, the answer depends on whether the job is near point a, b, or c. Jobs near point a may need more specialization to become more effective. Analysis and experimentation are the only sure ways to determine where a particular job is located on the graph.

Underspecialization

When job designers believe jobs are not specialized enough, they engage in *work simplification*. That is, the job is simplified. The tasks of one job may be assigned to two jobs. Unneeded tasks are identified and eliminated. What remains are jobs that contain fewer tasks.

When the Allyndale Weekly Newspaper operated with its old press, Guy Parsons could catch the newspapers as they came off the press, stack them, and wrap them. But when a new high-speed press was added, he could not keep up with the output. The circulation manager simplified Guy's job by making him responsible only for stacking the newspapers. Two part-time high school students took turns catching and wrapping.

The risk of work simplification is that jobs may be so specialized that boredom causes errors or resignations. This potential problem is more common in advanced industrial countries that have a highly educated work force. In less developed countries, highly specialized factory jobs may be acceptable and even appealing because they provide jobs for workers with limited skills.

Overspecialization

In advanced industrial societies, routine jobs that are very specialized, such as assembly-line positions, hold limited appeal. These jobs seldom offer opportunities for accomplishment, recognition, psychological growth, or other sources of satisfaction. To increase the quality of work life for those who hold such jobs, job designers can use a variety of methods to improve jobs. The most widely practiced techniques include job rotation, job enlargement, and job enrichment.

Job rotation. *Job rotation* moves employees from job to job. Jobs themselves are not actually changed; only the workers are rotated. Rotation breaks the monotony of highly specialized work by calling on different skills and abilities. The organization benefits because workers become competent in several jobs rather than only one. Knowing a variety of jobs improves the worker's self-image, provides personal growth, and makes the worker more valuable to the organization.

Human resource experts should caution those who desire to use job rotation. It does not improve the jobs themselves; the relationships between tasks, activities, and objectives remain unchanged. It may even postpone the use of more effective techniques while adding to training costs. Job rotation should be implemented only after other techniques have been considered.

Job enlargement. *Job enlargement*, also known as *horizontal loading*, expands the number of related tasks in the job. Enlargement adds similar duties to provide greater variety and reduces monotony by expanding the job cycle and drawing on a wider range of employee skills. According to an IBM summary of job design research:

> IBM reported job enlargement led to higher wages and more inspection equipment, but improved quality and worker satisfaction offset these costs.
>
> Maytag Company claimed that production quality was improved, labor costs declined, worker satisfaction and overall efficiency were increased, and production schedules became more flexible.[38]

Job enrichment. *Job enrichment* adds new sources of satisfaction to jobs. It increases responsibility, autonomy, and control. Adding these elements to jobs is sometimes called *vertical loading*. The job enrichment approach breaks a job into

5. JOB ANALYSIS AND DESIGN 155

three areas of responsibility: plan, do, and control.³⁹ Job enlargement, or horizontal loading, adds more tasks to *do*. Enrichment, or vertical loading, adds more *planning* and *control* responsibilities. These additions to the job, coupled with rethinking the job itself, can lead to increased motivation and other improvements, as was seen in the Shenandoah Life example. A similar example comes from one of the former members of AT&T's Bell System.

Ohio Bell

> The Ohio Bell Telephone Company reported that the work force needed to compile directories in one office declined from 120 to 74 as the result of job enrichment and other changes.⁴⁰
>
> Directory compilation improvements resulted from assigning individual clerks broad responsibility for entire small rural directories or identifiable sections of large metropolitan directories. Prior to the change, each clerk's activities were narrowly defined with close controls, little task identity, and limited autonomy. Vertical and horizontal loading lengthened job cycles, added task identity and autonomy, reduced turnover, increased productivity, and lowered labor costs.

Job enrichment, however, is not a cure-all. If it were, this book could end here. Instead, job enrichment techniques are merely tools. They are not applied universally. When the diagnosis indicates that jobs are unrewarding and unchallenging and that they limit the motivation and satisfaction of employees, personnel departments *may* find job enrichment the most appropriate strategy. Even then, job enrichment can produce problems. One author has identified 22 reasons against job enrichment.⁴¹ The most compelling problems are union resistance, the costs of design and implementation, and limited research on the long-term effects of enrichment. Another criticism of job enrichment is that it does not go far enough. To enrich the job and ignore other variables that contribute to the quality of work life may simply increase dissatisfaction with the unimproved aspects of the job environment.⁴²

Autonomous work groups. *Autonomous work groups* (also called *self-directed* or *leaderless* work teams) are groups of workers with such widely defined jobs that their responsibilities often include duties normally reserved for supervisors or managers. Work teams usually consist of three to fifteen members who are extensively cross-trained in each other's jobs. Team members are given production or service objectives to be met by their team. Then they decide collectively among themselves how they will achieve the needed level of performance. Work assignments are made within the team, often with members informally trading-off to relieve boredom and fatigue. Peer pressure helps ensure that everyone contributes, especially since group members often vote on new hires, the acceptance of probationary employees, and even pay raises and vacation schedules. The Saturn Corporation discussed earlier in this chapter is an example of the use

Jobs at Saturn

of autonomous teams. Other examples abound in companies such as TRW, Texas Instruments, Procter & Gamble, Digital Equipment, General Mills, and Federal Express.[43]

Self-directed work teams have been created for many reasons.[44] Some companies see this approach as the best way to achieve high productivity and quality while at the same time improving the quality of work life for employees. Other organizations appreciate the reduction in supervisory overhead, although this alone is seldom a motivating force in the creation of autonomous teams. General Electric's Columbia, Maryland facility reports that its self-directed work force has saved $1.5 million dollars in workers' compensation claims over three years.[45] In Sweden (and other advanced industrial countries with extensive, government-provided services), companies such as Volvo have used various forms of leaderless work teams to improve the quality of work life. Citizens of Sweden and other northwestern European countries receive such extensive unemployment benefits, health care, and other social services from their governments that employers who offer unattractive jobs find it difficult to attract and retain workers. As a result, job design among European firms has proved essential to their competitive position. With the declining growth rate of the North American work force, job design is likely to grow in importance on this side of the Atlantic as well.

Sweden

Bottom-line and social responsibility

Ultimately, however, human resource departments must balance the need for high-quality work life with the bottom line, the economic results of the firm. The goal is not to produce "happy workers." The human resource department must enhance the economic viability of the organization in an ethical, socially responsible way, improving quality of work life within the constraints of competition, technology, cultural diversity, and economic efficiency.

SUMMARY

JOB ANALYSIS information provides the foundation of an organization's human resource information system. Job analysts seek to gain a general understanding of the organization and the work it performs. Then they design job analysis questionnaires to collect specific data about jobs, jobholder characteristics, and job performance standards.

Job analysis information can be collected through interviews, juries of experts, mail questionnaires, employee logs, direct observation, or some combination of these techniques. Once collected, the data are converted into such useful applications as job descriptions, job specifications, and job standards.

Job analysis information is important because it tells personnel specialists what duties and responsibilities are associated with each job. This information is then used when personnel specialists undertake other personnel management activities, such as job design, recruitment, and selection. Jobs are the link between organizations and their human resources. The combined accomplishments of all jobs allow the organization to meet its objectives. Similarly, jobs represent both a source of income to workers and a means of fulfilling their other needs. For the

5. JOB ANALYSIS AND DESIGN 157

organization and its employees to receive these mutual benefits, jobs must provide a high quality of work life.

Achieving a high quality of work life requires that jobs are well designed. Effective job design seeks a tradeoff between efficiency and behavioral elements. Efficiency elements stress productivity. Behavioral elements focus on employee needs. The role of personnel specialists is to achieve a balance of these elements. When jobs are underspecialized, job designers may simplify them by reducing the number of tasks. If jobs are overspecialized, they must be expanded or enriched.

Terms for Review

- Job analysis
- Job description
- Job code
- *Dictionary of Occupational Titles* (DOT)
- Job specification
- Job performance standards
- Job families
- Position analysis questionnaire
- Specialization
- Job cycles
- Ergonomics
- Autonomy
- Autonomous work teams
- Task identity
- Task significance
- Work simplification
- Job rotation
- Job enlargement
- Job enrichment

Review and Discussion Questions

1. What types of raw data do the questions on a job analysis checklist seek to obtain? Are there other data you should seek for management jobs?

2. What are the different methods of collecting job analysis information, and what are the advantages and disadvantages of each technique?

3. In collecting job analysis information for jobs located in different countries, what additional considerations should analysts consider?

4. Suppose you were assigned to write job descriptions in a shirt factory in Tucson, Arizona that employed mostly Mexican immigrants who spoke little English. What methods would you use to collect job analysis data?

5. If a manager in the shirt factory refused to complete a job analysis questionnaire, what reasons would you use to persuade this reluctant manager?

6. What are some of the problems you would anticipate in an organization that had carefully designed its jobs for maximum efficiency without careful consideration of employee needs?

7. How would your answer to question 6 change if the organization were located in a developing nation with low educational levels and a work force that had no prior industrial experience?

8. Suppose you were assigned to re-design the jobs of "ticket clerks" for an intrastate airline. How would you handle the following tradeoffs?

    a. Would you design a few highly specialized jobs to minimize training or one broad job with all clerks cross-trained to handle multiple tasks? Why?

    b. Would you change your answer if you knew that employees tended to quit the job of ticket clerk within the first six months? Why or why not?

9. Assume you were asked to evaluate a group of jobs in a boat-building business. After studying each job for a considerable amount of time, you identify the following activities associated with each job. What job redesign techniques would you recommend for these jobs, if any?

    a. Sailmaker. Cuts and sews material with very little variety in the type of work from day to day. Job is highly skilled and takes years to learn.

    b. Sander. Sands rough wood and fiberglass edges almost continuously. Little skill is required in this job.

    c. Sales representative. Talks to customers, answers phone inquiries, suggests customized additions to special-order boats.

    d. Boat preparer. Cleans up completed boats, waxes fittings, and generally makes the boat ready for customer delivery. Few skills are required for this job.

INCIDENT 5-1
The Brazilian Subsidiary

A large, well-known Canadian company had fully depreciated the equipment used to make specialized automobile components for North American automobile producers. Although the equipment had been well maintained and worked well, it required considerable hands-on labor to use. The result was high labor costs that made the company's brake assemblies, axle mounts, and related products unprofitable. A decision was made to replace the equipment with more highly automated, numerically controlled machine tools. Since the economic value of the old equipment exceeded its value as scrap, the company shipped the equipment to its Brazilian facility, where labor costs were considerably lower.

Shortly after the equipment had been set up in the new facility, the company received numerous orders from Brazil's rapidly growing automobile industry. Though the labor hours per product remained about the same, lower Brazilian labor rates made the new facility profitable. Soon a second shift was added, and problems began. The equipment experienced increasing "down-time" because of machine failures. Quality—particularly quality on part dimensions—declined dramatically.

At a staff meeting, the Brazilian plant manager met with his staff, including several industrial engineers who had been trained in Canada and the United States. The engineers argued that the problems were almost certainly caused by poor maintenance since the machinery had worked well in Canada and initially in Brazil. The human resource director agreed that maintenance of the old machinery was probably involved but also noted that many of the instructions printed on machines and in maintenance manuals had not been translated into Portuguese. He also observed that the problems began after the second shift was hired.

1. From the discussion of job analysis information and job design addressed in the chapter, what actions would you recommend to the human resource department?

2. Given that the problems seem to be associated with the second shift, what differences would you look for between first and second shift workers?

3. Since the Canadian workers had considerable experience with the equipment and the workers (particularly on the second shift) in Brazil had little, what implications do you see for job design?

EXERCISE 5-1

Preparation of a Job Description

As discussed in this chapter, there are several ways to collect job analysis information. One way is through observation. Using the form in Figure 5-3, complete parts C through J for the job of professor. After you have completed those sections of the job analysis questionnaire, use the format in Figure 5-5 and write a job description for the job of professor. When finished, look up the definition of professor provided in the *Dictionary of Occupational Titles*.

1. How does the description in the *Dictionary of Occupational Titles* vary in format and content from the one you wrote?

2. What parts of the professor's job are the most important in your opinion?

References

1. Philip C. Grant, "What Use is a Job Description?" *Personnel Journal* (Feb. 1988), p. 50.

2. Margaret Magnus and Morton E. Grossman, "Using Computers is Catching On," *Recruitment Today* (Summer 1990), p. 17.

3. Valdis E. Krebs, "Planning for Information Effectiveness," *Personnel Administrator* (Sept. 1988), pp. 34–42.

4. Edward S. Goldmacher, "HRIS Project Management and Ownership," *Personnel Administrator* (Jan. 1986), pp. 28, 30–32. See also Jo Ann Verdin, "The HRIS and Management Performance," *Personnel Administrator* (Oct. 1986), pp. 24, 26, 28.

5. John Hoerr, Michael A. Pollock, and David E. Whiteside, "Management Discovers the Human Side of Automation," *Business Week* (Sept. 29, 1986), pp. 70–75. See also Tody D. Wall, Nigel Kemp, Paul R. Jackson, and Chris W. Clegg, "Outcomes of Autonomous Workgroups: A Long-Term Field Experiment," *Academy of Management Journal*, vol. 29, no. 2, pp. 280–304.

6. Nancy Howe, "Documentation Takes Form," *Personnel Journal* (Dec. 1988), pp. 66–73.

7. Susan R. Meisinger, *Legal Report—The Americans with Disabilities Act of 1990: A New Challenge for Human Resource Managers* (Alexandria, Va.: Society for Human Resource Management, 1990), p. 4.

8. Patrick R. Conley and Paul R. Sackett, "Effects of Using High- Versus Low-Performing Job Incumbents as Sources of Job-Analysis Information," *Journal of Applied Psychology*, vol. 72, no. 83 (1987), pp. 434–437. See also Yitzhak Fried and Gerald R. Ferris, "The Validity of the Job Characteristics Model: A Review and Meta-Analysis," *Personnel Psychology*, vol. 40 (1987), pp. 287–322; and Wayman C. Mullins and Wilson W. Kimbrough, "Group Composition as a Determinant of Job Analysis Outcomes," *Journal of Applied Psychology*, vol. 73, no. 4 (1988), pp. 657–664.

9. J.D. Dunn and Frank M. Rachel, *Wage and Salary Administration: Total Compensation Systems* (New York: McGraw-Hill Book Company, 1971), pp. 139–141.

10. P.R. Jeanneret, *A Study of the Job Dimensions of "Worker-Oriented" Job Variables and of Their Attribute Profiles* (doctoral dissertation) (West Lafayette, In.: Purdue University, 1969). See also E.J. McCormick, P.R. Jeanneret, and R.C. Mecham, "A Study of Job Characteristics and Job Dimensions as Based on the Position Analysis Questionnaire (PAQ)," *Journal of Applied Psychology*, vol. 56, no. 2 (1971), pp. 347–368.

11. Robert J. Harvey, Lee Friedman, Milton D. Hakel, and Edwin T. Cornelius III, "Dimensionality of the Job Element Inventory, a Simplified Worker-Oriented Job Analysis Questionnaire," *Journal of Applied Psychology*, vol. 73, no. 4 (1988), pp. 639–646.

12. Ibid., p. 143.

13. Jerrold Markowitz, "Four Methods of Job Analysis," *Training and Development Journal*, (Sept. 1981), pp. 115–117.

14. Judith A. DeLapa, "Job Descriptions that Work," *Personnel Journal* (June 1989), pp. 156–158, 160. See also Michael A. Campion and Paul W. Thayer, "How Do You Design a Job?" *Personnel Journal* (Jan. 1989), pp. 43–44, 46.

15. Grant, op. cit. See also Mark A. Jones, "Job Descriptions Made Easy," *Personnel Journal* (May 1984), pp. 31–34.

16. Michael A. Campion, "Ability Requirement Implications of Job Design: An Interdisciplinary Perspective," *Personnel Psychology*, vol. 42, no. 1 (1989), pp. 1–24. See also U.S. Department of Labor, *Dictionary of Occupational Titles* (Washington, D.C.: U.S. Superintendent

of Publications, 1965), vol. I, p. xvi. For a criticism of this approach, see Edwin T. Cornelius III and William Sanders, "A Scalogram Analysis of the Worker Function Hierarchies," unpublished paper presented at the Academy of Management Meetings (New York, August 1982).

17. Allan N. Nash and Stephen J. Carroll, Jr., *The Management of Compensation* (Monterey: Brooks/Cole Publishers, 1975, pp. 116–117.

18. Paul Sheibar, "A Simple Selection System Called 'Job Match,' " *Personnel Journal* (Jan. 1979), p. 26.

19. Valdis E. Krebs, "TRW Makes the Move to Macintoshes," *Personnel Journal* (Dec. 1989), pp. 58–63.

20. Magnus and Grossman, op. cit.

21. Maureen MacAdam, "HRIS: Document What You're Doing," *Personnel Journal* (Feb. 1990), pp. 57–63.

22. John E. Sprig, "Selling the HRIS to Top Management," *Personnel* (Oct. 1988), pp. 26–32, 34.

23. George R. Wendt, "Should Courts Write Your Job Descriptions?" *Personnel Journal* (Sept. 1976), pp. 442–445, 450. See also Frederick S. Hills, "Job Relatedness vs. Adverse Impact in Personnel Decision Making," *Personnel Journal* (March 1980), pp. 211–215, 229.

24. Mary Green Miner and John B. Miner, *Employee Selection within the Law* (Washington, D.C.: Bureau of National Affairs, 1978), pp. 329–331.

25. Michael N. Wolfe, "Computerization—It Can Bring Sophistication into Personnel," *Personnel Journal* (June 1978), pp. 325ff. See also Patricia Teets, "Information Access Comes of Age with Online Data Bases," *Personnel Journal* (Jan. 1987), pp. 112–113.

26. Edwin T. Cornelius III, Angelo S. Denisi, and Allyn G. Blencoe, "Expert and Naive Raters Using the PAQ: Does It Matter?" *Personnel Psychology* (1984), pp. 453–467.

27. Hank Guzda, "Saturn: The Sky's the Limit," *Labor Relations Today* (March/April 1990), p. 2. John Morrell & Co. received a $1.25 million fine because ". . . it exposed workers to 'serious and sometimes disabling' injuries caused by repetitive job motions. . . ." according to Christopher Drew, "Morrell to pay $1.25 Million in Safety Case," *Chicago Tribune* (March 21, 1990), sec. 3, p. 3.

28. Loretta D. Foxman and Walter L. Polsky," Job Design v. Job Evaluation," *Personnel Journal* (March 1988), pp. 35–36. See also William H. Glick, G. Douglas Jenkins, Jr., and Nina Gupta, "Method versus Substance: How Strong Are Underlying Relationships between Job Characteristics and Attitudinal Outcomes?" *Academy of Management Journal*, vol. 29, no. 3 (1985), pp. 441–464. See also Daniel A. Ondrack and Martin Evans, "Job Enrichment and Job Satisfaction in Quality of Working Life and Nonquality of Working Life Work Sites," *Human Relations*, vol. 39, no. 9 (1986), pp. 871–889.

29. Hoerr, Pollock, and Whiteside, op. cit.

30. "Dole Announces That Ford Motor Has Agreed to Corporate-wide Ergonomic Improvements in Historic Settlement," *U.S. Department of Labor News Release* (July 23, 1990), pp. 1–3.

31. Barbara Garson, "Luddites in Lordstown," *Harpers* (June 1972), pp. 68–73.

32. J.R. Hackman and E.E. Lawler III, "Employee Reactions to Job Characteristics," in W.E. Scott and L.L. Cummings, eds., *Readings in Organizational Behavior and Human Performance* (Homewood, Ill.: Richard D. Irwin, Inc., 1973), p. 231. For a detailed summary of research on job design see C.L. Hulin and M.R. Blood, "Job Enlargement, Individual Differences, and Worker Responses," *Psychological Bulletin* (1968), pp. 41–55. For a more recent summarization see Jon L. Pierce and Randall B. Dunham, "Task Design: A Literature Review," *The Academy of Management Review* (Oct. 1976), pp. 83–97. Also see Ricky W. Griffin, Ann Welsh, and Gregory Moorhead, "Perceived Task Characteristics and Employee Performance: A Literature Review," *Academy of Management Review* (Oct. 1981), pp. 644–664.

33. Frederick Herzberg, Bernard Mausner, and Barbara Snyderman, *The Motivation to Work* (New York: John Wiley & Sons Inc., 1959). See also E.F. Stone and L.W. Porter, "Job Characteristics and Job Attitudes: A Multivariate Study," *Journal of Applied Psychology* (1975), pp. 57–64.

34. G.E. Farris, "Organizational Factors and Individual Performance: A Longitudinal Study," *Journal of Applied Psychology* (1969), pp. 87–92.

35. Stone and Porter, op. cit.

36. Hackman and Lawler, op. cit.

37. Edward E. Lawler III, "Job Attitudes and Employee Motivation: Theory, Research, and Practice," *Personnel Psychology* (Summer 1970), p. 234.

38. Richard W. Woodman and John J. Sherwood, "A Comprehensive Look at Job Design," *Personnel Journal* (August 1977), p. 386.

39. J. Barton Cunningham and Ted Eberle, "A Guide to Job Enrichment and Redesign," *Personnel* (Feb. 1990), pp. 56–61. See also M. Scott Myers, *Every Employee and Manager* (New York: McGraw-Hill Book Company, 1970).

40. Robert N. Ford, "Job Enrichment Lessons from AT&T," *Harvard Business Review* (Jan.–Feb. 1973), p. 105.

41. Robert H. Schappe, "Twenty-two Arguments Against Job Enrichment," *Personnel Journal* (Feb. 1974), pp. 116–123.

42. William B. Werther, Jr., "Beyond Job Enrichment to Employment Enrichment," *Personnel Journal* (August 1975), pp. 438–442.

43. Brian Dumaine, "Who Needs a Boss?" *Fortune* (May 7, 1990), pp. 52–60.

44. Ibid.

45. John Jenkins, "Self-directed Work Force Promotes Safety," *HRMagazine* (Feb. 1990), pp. 54–56.

46. Larry Eichel, "Model Welfare State Succumbs to Chill of Economics," *The Miami Herald* (Nov. 2, 1990), p. 19a.

When asked, managers generally express a favorable view toward HRP.
PETER BAMBERGER, LEE DYER, SAMUEL B. BACHARACH[1]

Through human resource planning, management prepares to have the right people at the right places at the right times to fulfill both organizational and individual objectives.
JAMES W. WALKER[2]

HUMAN RESOURCE PLANNING

CHAPTER OBJECTIVES

After studying this chapter, you should be able to:
1. EXPLAIN why large organizations use human resource planning more than small ones do.
2. DISCUSS the relationship between strategic planning and human resource planning.
3. IDENTIFY the factors that shape an organization's demand for human resources.
4. DESCRIBE the shortcomings of methods used to forecast the demand for human resources.
5. EXPLAIN the role of skills inventories in developing succession plans.
6. RECOMMEND solutions to staffing shortages or surpluses.

forecasting for future demand

hUMAN RESOURCE planning (HRP) systematically forecasts an organization's future demand for, and supply of, employees.³ By estimating the number and types of employees that will be needed, the human resource department can better plan its recruitment, selection, training, career planning, and other activities. Human resource planning—or employment planning, as it is also called—allows the department to staff the organization at the right time with the right people. Not only can it help companies like AT&T meet their affirmative action goals, but effective HRP improves a department's ability to respond proactively and in a socially responsible manner to the challenges it faces.

Short- and long-range business plans are carried out by people. If the organization is not properly staffed with the right number and types of people, corporate plans may fail. Production, financial, and marketing plans also are, of course, important cornerstones of a company's strategic plans. More and more executives are realizing, however, that well-conceived human resource plans are a key cornerstone because qualified people make plans of any sort easier to accomplish.⁴ For example, the decisions of high-technology firms like Motorola and IBM to develop new products and enter new markets often depend on the availability of qualified technical and support people. Without sufficient engineering talent, market opportunities can be lost to more appropriately staffed competitors.

improve utilization

At IBM, strategic business planning begins with "top-down" revenue and profit targets established by the company's policy committee. Then, executives of the different business areas develop the strategies, product thrusts, and sales volumes needed to reach the policy committee's goals. From here, national and international divisions of IBM create functional strategies for development, manufacturing, marketing, and service. Line managers are responsible for folding the functional plans into divisional ones.

The human resource department's role is to review all divisional plans before they are sent to the corporate division. Although line managers have wide latitude in addressing human resource issues, concerns about human resources are injected into the business plans by proactive specialists who work closely with divisional managers. These managers are encouraged to involve personnel specialists because the business plan will be reviewed for human resource considerations before it is finalized.⁵ In addition, IBM improves the effectiveness of its planning by holding planners responsible for their estimates.

As *Business Week* observes:

> Each year IBM's personnel department . . . develops a five-year strategic plan in the spring and a two-year tactical plan in the fall. No major business

HRP defined

HRP

People constraints

IBM

6. HUMAN RESOURCE PLANNING

165

decision goes to a top management committee for final approval without . . . concurrence.⁶

Through their involvement in the strategic business planning process, IBM's human resource planners are better able to develop their corporate and functional human resource plans.⁷ And these plans are likely to have a better fit with the company's short- and long-range plans.

International strategies

International expansion strategies depend upon human resource planning, too. The department's ability to fill key jobs with foreign nationals and the reassignment of home-country employees across national borders is a major challenge facing international businesses, particularly large, global companies like IBM.⁸ With the growing trend toward global operation, the need for human resource planning will grow, as will the need to more closely integrate human resource planning into the organization's strategic plans.⁹ Human resource planning will grow increasingly important as the process of preparing for staffing needs across foreign borders and the attendant cultural, language, and development considerations grow increasingly complex.¹⁰ Without effective human resource planning and the subsequent attention to employee recruitment, selection, placement, development, and career planning (discussed in the following chapters), the growing competition for international executives may lead to expensive and strategically disruptive turnover among key decision makers.

Ideally, all organizations should identify their short-range and long-range employee needs through human resource planning. Short-range plans point out job openings that must be filled in the coming year. Long-range plans estimate the human resource situation for two, five, or, occasionally, ten years into the future. There is no one right approach to human resource planning. Each organization must find a blend of practices that work within the company culture and the realities of business necessity.¹¹ This view is summarized by John W. Boroski of the Eastman Kodak Company, a worldwide producer of film, cameras, chemicals, and industrial equipment.

Kodak's view

Like many large companies, Eastman Kodak has experimented with various approaches to human resource (HR) planning over the years. At the corporate level, HR planning was thought of as a means for ensuring that the right number and the right kinds of people were at the right places at the right times.

. . . HR planning has no universally accepted definition. Our evolving thinking has been . . . influenced by . . . academics, consultants, and practitioners. In effect, we have borrowed, adapted, discovered, and created our way to an approach to HR planning that is congruent with our current business circumstances and responsive to change.¹²

The advantages of human resource planning to large organizations like Eastman Kodak include the abilities to:

➤ Improve the utilization of human resources

➤ Efficiently match personnel activities and future organizational objectives

➤ Achieve economies in hiring new workers

➤ Expand the human resource management information base to assist other personnel activities and other organizational units

➤ Make major and successful demands on local labor markets

➤ Coordinate different human resource management programs such as affirmative action plans and hiring needs.

A small organization can expect similar advantages, but gains in effectiveness are often considerably smaller because its situation is less complex. In fact, the benefits of human resource planning in small firms may not justify the time and costs. Consider the different situations faced by a small- and large-city government.

Two government views

Rural City employs 20 workers and is growing 10 percent a year. For Rural City, that means adding 2 new employees each year. Metropolis has 8,000 employees and is growing by 5 percent a year. For Metropolis, that means 400 new employees plus replacements for those who leave each year. If it costs $1,000 to find and hire a typical employee, Rural City will spend $2,000 to hire two new workers and Metropolis will spend $400,000 to add the new employees it will need. If employment planning saves 25 percent, Rural City's manager cannot justify detailed planning efforts for $500. But for $100,000, Metropolis can afford a specialist and still save thousands of dollars after planning expenses are deducted.

Nevertheless, human resource planning is useful to personnel specialists in both small and large organizations. It shows small employers the human resource considerations they face if they should expand rapidly. (For example, if Rural City attracted several large factories to its area, expansion of city services would depend partly on the city's human resource planning.) Large organizations can benefit from planning because it reveals ways to make the personnel function more effective, especially at a company like IBM, which strives to avoid layoffs.

This chapter examines the two dimensions of human resource planning. It begins with an explanation of how the human resource department estimates future job openings. It ends by showing the methods used by personnel experts to identify potential sources of employees to fill those vacancies.

economy booming more resign.

Figure 6-1

Cause of Demand for Human Resources in the Future

EXTERNAL	ORGANIZATIONAL	WORK FORCE
► Economics	► Strategic plans	► Retirement *no age cap*
► Social-political-legal	► Budgets	► Resignations
► Technology	► Sales and production forecasts	► Terminations
► Competitors	► New ventures	► Deaths
	► Organization and job designs	► Leaves of absence

Family Leave act.

THE DEMAND FOR HUMAN RESOURCES

An organization's future demand for people is central to human resource planning. Most firms predict their future employment needs (at least informally) even if they do not estimate their sources of supply. One study found that employers are two times more likely to estimate human resource demand than to estimate supply.[13] The challenges that determine this demand and the methods of forecasting it merit brief review.

Causes of Demand

Shaping HR demand

Although many challenges influence the demand for human resources, changes in the environment, organization, and work force usually are involved.[14] These factors are common to short-range and long-range employment plans. The causes of these changes are summarized in Figure 6-1. Some of these causes are within the organization's control, and others are not.

External challenges. Developments in the organization's environment are difficult for personnel specialists to predict in the short run and sometimes impossible to estimate in the long run. Reconsider the example of the small-city government. City planners are seldom aware of major factory relocations until shortly before construction begins. Other *economic* developments have a noticeable effect but are difficult to estimate. Examples include inflation, unemployment, and interest rates that curtail construction and the need for construction workers.

Social, political, and *legal* challenges are easier to predict, but their implications are seldom clear. The impact on human resource planning of the civil rights laws passed in the 1960s was unclear until the 1970s. Now most large firms have affirmative action programs and compliance officers, as discussed in Chapter 4. Likewise, the implications of abolishing the mandatory retirement age in 1986 may be unknown until a generation has lived without the "65 and out" tradition.[15]

WARN Act

The *Worker Adjustment and Retraining Notification Act* of 1988 restricted the employers' ability to make adjustments in the size of their work force through layoffs by requiring a 60-day advance notification under some circumstances.[16] In quite another way, the Gulf War with Iraq in 1991 upset many human resource plans as thousands of military reservists were called to active duty.

Technology changes the way business is done, is difficult to predict, and is difficult to assess. Many thought the computer would cause mass unemployment, for example. Today, the computer industry directly or indirectly employs millions of people. Technology complicates human resource planning because it tends to reduce employment in one department (bookkeeping, for example) while increasing employment in another (such as computer operations). The growing use of computers—especially networks of interconnected personal computers—even allows companies to reorganize and "downsize," further complicating the human resource planning process. The use of robotics and other forms of computerized automation will undoubtedly complicate future employment planning even more.

Competitors are another external challenge that affects the demand for human resources. Growing foreign competition has forced many firms in North America and around the world to reduce their work force in order to remain economically viable. The search for lower labor costs has led some firms to relocate facilities or to consolidate operations in such industries as automobiles, electronics, data processing, and even research and development.

Organizational decisions. Major organizational decisions affect the demand for human resources. The organization's *strategic plan* is the most influential decision.[17] It commits the firm to long-range objectives—such as growth rates and new products, markets, or services. These objectives dictate the number and types of employees needed in the future. If long-term objectives are to be met, personnel specialists must develop long-range human resource plans that accommodate the strategic plan. In the short run, planners find that strategic plans become operational in the form of *budgets*. Budget increases or cuts are the most significant short-run influences on human resource needs.

Sales and production forecasts are less exact than budgets but may provide even quicker notice of short-run changes in human resource demand.

The human resource manager for a nationwide chain of furniture outlets observed a sharp decline in sales brought on by a recession. The manager quickly discarded the short-range human resource plan and imposed an employment freeze on all outlets' hiring plans.

Failure to adjust to a reduced employment demand may require a reduction in forces or a layoff.

New ventures also mean changing human resource demands. When a new venture is begun internally from scratch, the lead time may allow planners to develop short-range and long-range employment plans. But a new venture begun by an acquisition or merger causes an immediate revision of human resource

6. HUMAN RESOURCE PLANNING 169

demands and can lead to reorganization and new job designs. Reorganization, especially after a merger or an acquisition, can radically alter human resource needs. Likewise, the redesign of jobs changes the skill levels required of future workers.[18] At a time when companies are constantly acquiring, merging, spinning off divisions, entering new businesses, and getting out of old ones, management must base strategic decisions more than ever on HR considerations—matching skills with jobs, keeping key personnel after mergers, and solving the human problems that arise from such changes as new technology or plant closures.[19]

> *For example, to ensure that the people side of mergers and acquisitions was given full consideration, CSX, a major U.S. railroad, merged its human resource group with its corporate planning staff.[20]*

Turnover

Work-force factors. The demand for human resources is modified by such employee actions as retirements, resignations, terminations, deaths, and leaves of absence. When large numbers of employees are involved, past experience usually serves as a reasonably accurate guide. However, reliance on past experience means that personnel specialists must be sensitive to changes that upset past trends.

> *Jim Santino used to keep close track of employees nearing retirement so that his human resource plan remained accurate. But in 1986 Congress prohibited employers from requiring mandatory retirement at any age. This meant that all employees of Universal Book Publishers could continue to work as long as they desired. As a result, Jim can no longer use past experience as a guide to when older workers will retire. This change has caused Jim to seek other ways to forecast his short-range human resource needs.*

AIDS

Although heart disease and cancer take more lives each year than AIDS (Acquired Immune Deficiency Syndrome), the role of AIDS on the demand for human resources is less well understood. The limited experience of planners in dealing with a growing epidemic makes the impact on the demand for future employees difficult to predict. The affects of the disease also happen to be uneven, hitting the poor and unemployed disproportionally, particularly in large cities. Some industries—especially the fashion industry—have been impacted more forcefully than others. However, the Center for Disease Control in Atlanta estimates that by 1993, more than 315,000 Americans have died from the disease, with more than 1,000,000 others infected. With more Americans dead from AIDS than died in World War II and the Vietnam War combined, the spreading epidemic will significantly affect more and more organizations and their human resource plans.[21]

Figure 6-2

Forecasting Techniques for Estimating Future Human Resource Needs

EXPERT	TREND	OTHER
▸ Informal and instant decisions	▸ Extrapolation	▸ Budget and planning analysis
▸ Formal expert survey	▸ Indexation	▸ New-venture analysis
▸ Nominal group technique	▸ Statistical analysis	▸ Computer models
▸ Delphi technique		

Forecasting Techniques

Predicting HR needs

Human resource forecasts are attempts to predict an organization's future demand for employees.[22] As Figure 6-2 shows, forecasting techniques range from the informal to the sophisticated. Even the most sophisticated methods are not perfectly accurate; instead, they are best viewed as approximations. Most firms make only casual estimates about the immediate future. As they gain experience in forecasting human resource needs, they may use more sophisticated techniques (especially if they can afford the specialized staff). Each of the forecasting methods in Figure 6-2 is explained below.

Expert forecasts. *Expert forecasts* are based on the judgments of those who are knowledgeable about future human resource needs. Since most employment decisions are made by line managers, human resource planners must devise methods to learn about these managers' staffing needs. In small organizations, the director of operations or the personnel manager may have all the needed knowledge. In larger organizations, the simplest method is to *survey* these managers, who are the ultimate experts about future staffing needs of their departments.

NGT

The survey may be an informal poll, a written questionnaire, or a focused discussion using the *nominal group technique* (NGT). The NGT presents a group of five to 15 managers with a problem statement, such as "What will cause our staffing needs to change over the next year?" Then each participant writes down as many answers as he or she can imagine. After five to ten minutes, these ideas are shared in round-robin fashion until all written ideas and any new ones that they have stimulated have been recorded. The group's ideas are then discussed and ranked by having each member vote for the three to five most important ones.[23]

Delphi technique

If the experts cannot be brought together with the nominal group technique, additional sophistication can be brought to the survey approach with the *Delphi technique.*[24] It solicits estimates of future human resource needs from a group of experts, usually managers. Then personnel department planners act as intermediaries, summarize the various responses, and report the findings to the experts.

The experts are surveyed again after they get this feedback. Summaries and surveys are repeated until the experts' opinions begin to agree. (Usually four or five surveys are enough.) For example, the personnel department may survey all production supervisors and managers until an agreement is reached on the number of replacements that will be needed during the next year.

Trend projection forecasts. Perhaps the quickest forecasting technique is to project past trends. The two simplest methods are extrapolation and indexation. *Extrapolation* involves extending past rates of change into the future. For example, if an average of 20 production workers were hired each month for the past two years, extrapolating that trend into the future would forecast that 240 production workers will be added during the upcoming year.

Indexation is a method of estimating future employment needs by measuring employment growth against a particular index. A common example is the ratio of production employees to sales. For example, planners may discover that for each million-dollar increase in sales, the production department requires ten new assemblers.

Extrapolation and indexation are crude approximations in the short run because they assume that the causes of demand—external, organizational, and work force factors—will remain constant, which is seldom the case. These methods are very inaccurate for long-range human resource projections. More sophisticated *statistical analyses* make allowances for changes in the underlying causes of demand.[25]

Other forecasting methods. There are several other ways planners can estimate the future demand for human resources. One approach is through *budget and planning analysis*. Organizations that need human resource planning generally have detailed budgets and long-range plans. A study of department budgets reveals the financial authorizations for more employees. These data plus extrapolations of work force changes (resignation, terminations, and the like) can provide short-range estimates of human resource needs. Long-range estimates can be made from each department or division's long-range plans.

When new ventures complicate employment planning, planners can use new-venture analysis. *New-venture analysis* requires planners to estimate human resource needs by comparison with firms that already perform similar operations. For example, a petroleum company that plans to open a coal mine can estimate its future employment needs by determining employment levels of other coal mines.

The most sophisticated forecasting approaches involve computers. *Computer models* are a series of mathematical formulas that simultaneously use extrapolation, indexation, survey results, and estimates of work force changes to compute future human resource needs. Through time, actual changes in human resource demand are used to refine the computer's formulas.

There are four levels of complexity in human resource forecasting.[26] These stages of forecasting sophistication are summarized in Figure 6-3. As can be seen, they range from informal discussions to highly complex computerized forecasting

Figure 6-3

Stages of Complexity and Sophistication in Human Resource Forecasting

STAGE 1	STAGE 2	STAGE 3	STAGE 4
➤ Managers discuss goals, plans, and thus types and numbers of people needed in the short term. ➤ Highly informal and subjective.	➤ Annual planning and budgeting process includes human resource needs. ➤ Specify quantity and quality of talent needs as far as possible. ➤ Identify problems requiring action: individual or general.	➤ Using computer-generated analyses, examine causes of problems and future trends regarding the flow of talent. ➤ Use computer to relieve managers of routine forecasting tasks (such as vacancies or turnover).	➤ On-line modeling and computer simulation of talent needs, flows, and costs to aid in a continuing process of updating and projecting needs, staffing plans, career opportunities, and thus program plans. ➤ Provide best possible current information for managerial decisions. ➤ Exchange data with other companies and with government (such as economic, employment, and social data).

Source: James W. Walker, "Evaluating the Practical Effectiveness of Human Resource Planning Applications," *Human Resource Management,* Spring 1974, p. 21.

systems. The more sophisticated techniques are found among large organizations that have had years of experience in human resource planning. Small firms or those just beginning to forecast human resource needs are more likely to start with stage 1 and progress to other stages as planners seek greater accuracy.

These forecasting techniques must be applied with great sensitivity when used in the foreign arena. Differences in culture may lead to radically different constraints. For example, in some Arabic nations, women are excluded from some jobs and work settings. Work force projections based on the roles or participation rates of women in North America would be inaccurate. In countries such as India, caste systems limit what type of work a person may do. Although country-specific constraints may seem inappropriate, they are often deeply embedded in a nation's culture and religion. Human resource plans that do not incorporate these variations are likely to be useless, if not disruptive.

Figure 6-4

Components of the Future Demand for Human Resources

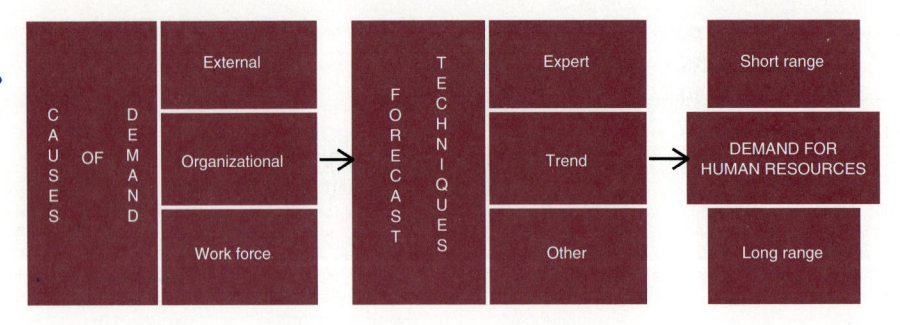

CAUSES OF DEMAND: External, Organizational, Work force → FORECAST TECHNIQUES: Expert, Trend, Other → DEMAND FOR HUMAN RESOURCES: Short range, Long range

Human Resource Requirements

Figure 6-4 provides an overview of the key considerations involved in estimating the demand for human resources. It shows that forecasts translate the causes of demand into short-range and long-range statements of needs. The resulting long-range plans are, of necessity, general statements of *probable* needs. Specific numbers are either estimated or omitted entirely because initially they have a low level of accuracy. But as planners become more familiar with the causes of demand and the forecasting techniques, their estimates of human resource demand become more accurate.

Staffing table

Short-range plans are more specific and may be reported as a staffing table, as shown in Figure 6-5. A *staffing table* lists the future employment needs for each type of job. The listing may be of specific jobs or of approximate ranges of needs, depending on the accuracy of the underlying data. Staffing tables (also called manning tables) are neither complete nor wholly accurate. They are only approximations. But these estimates allow personnel specialists to match short-range demand and supply. They help operating departments run more smoothly and can enhance the image of the human resource department.

With specific estimates of future human resource needs, personnel specialists can become more proactive and systematic. For example, a review of Figure 6-5 shows that the city's human resource department must hire 32 police academy recruits every three months. This knowledge allows recruiters in the human resource department to plan their recruiting campaign so that it peaks about six weeks before the beginning of the next police academy class. The advanced planning allows the human resource department to screen applicants and notify them at least three weeks before the class begins. Recruiters can inform applicants who cannot be ready that quickly when later classes will begin. If the recruiters waited for the police department to notify them, notification might

Figure 6-5

A Partial Staffing Table for a City Government

staffing table

METROPOLIS
CITY GOVERNMENT
STAFFING TABLE

Date Compiled: _____

Budget Code Number	Job Title	Using Department(s)	Total	1	2	3	4	5	6	7	8	9	10	11	12
100-32	Police Academy Recruit	Police	128	32			32			32			32		
100-33	Police Dispatcher	Police	3	2					1						
100-84	Meter Reader	Police	24	2	2	2	2	2	2	2	2	2	2	2	2
100-85	Traffic Supervisor	Police	5	2			1			1			1		
100-86	Team Supervisor –Police (Sergeant)	Police	5	2			1			1			1		
100-97	Duty Supervisor –Police (Lieut.)	Police	2	1					1						
100-99	Shift Officer –Police (Captain)	Police	1	1											
200-01	Car Washer	Motor Pool	4	1			1			1			1		
200-12	Mechanic's Asst.	Motor Pool	3				1			1			1		
200-13	Mechanic III	Motor Pool	2	1									1		
200-14	Mechanic II	Motor Pool	1						1						
200-15	Mechanic I (Working Supervisor)	Motor Pool	1	1											
300-01	Clerk IV	Administration	27	10			5			6			6		

---

come too late to allow a systematic recruiting and screening process. Staffing tables enable recruiters to be proactive and to plan their activities better.

THE SUPPLY OF HUMAN RESOURCES

Once the department projects the future demand for human resources, its next major concern is filling projected openings.[27] There are two sources of supply: internal and external. The internal supply consists of present employees who can be promoted, transferred, or demoted to fill expected openings. For example, some of the previously mentioned openings at the police academy might be filled by other city employees who want to transfer from their present jobs into police work. Those people represent the internal supply. The external

Figure 6-6

Factors That Determine the Future Supply of Human Resources

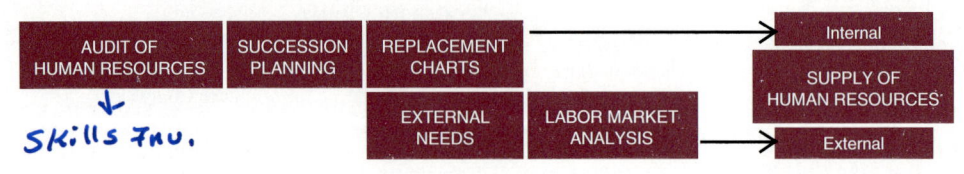

AUDIT OF HUMAN RESOURCES	SUCCESSION PLANNING	REPLACEMENT CHARTS	→	Internal
		EXTERNAL NEEDS	LABOR MARKET ANALYSIS	SUPPLY OF HUMAN RESOURCES
			→	External

supply consists of people who do not work for the city, such as employees of other organizations and the unemployed.

Estimates of Internal Supply

Estimates of the internal supply involve more than merely counting the number of employees. As Figure 6-6 implies, planners audit the present work force to learn about the capabilities of workers. This information allows planners to estimate tentatively which openings can be filled by present employees. These tentative assignments usually are recorded on a replacement chart. Considering present employees for future job openings is important if workers are to have lifelong careers with their employer rather than dead-end jobs.[28]

Audits and replacement charts also are important additions to the personnel department's information base. With greater knowledge of employees, the department can plan recruiting, training, and career planning activities more effectively. This knowledge can even help personnel meet its affirmative action plan by identifying internal minority candidates for job openings. Since audits and replacement charts are important to proactive personnel work, they are explained more fully below.

Audits and inventories

Human resource audits. *Human resource audits* summarize each employee's skills and abilities. The audits of nonmanagers are called *skills inventories;* the audits of managers are called *management inventories*. Whatever name is used, an inventory catalogs each employee's skills and abilities. This summary gives planners a comprehensive understanding of the capabilities found in the organization's work force.

An example of a skills inventory form is shown in Figure 6-7. It is divided into four parts. Part I can be completed by the personnel department from employee

II. PREPARATION AND SELECTION

Figure 6-7

A Skills Inventory Form

METROPOLIS
CITY GOVERNMENT
SKILLS INVENTORY

Date: _____

PART I (To be completed by human resource department)

1. Name _____   2. Employee Number _____

3. Job Title _____   4. Experience _____ Years

5. Age _____   6. Years with City _____

7. Other Jobs Held:

    With City: Title _____ From _____ to _____

                      Title _____ From _____ to _____

    Elsewhere: Title _____ From _____ to _____

                      Title _____ From _____ to _____

PART II (To be completed by employee)

8. Special Skills. List below any skills you possess even if they are not used on your present job. Include types and names of machines or tools with which you are experienced.

    Skills: _____

    Languages: _____ Fluency: Speak _____ Read _____ Write _____

    Machines: _____

    Tools: _____

9. Duties. Briefly describe your present duties. _____

_____

10. Responsibilities. Briefly describe your responsibilities for:

    City Equipment: _____

    City Funds: _____

    Employee Safety: _____

    Employee Supervision: _____

(continued)

always need to update

Figure 6-7
(continued)

11. Education. Briefly describe your education and training background:

    Academic: (Circle highest grade)   6 7 8 9 10 11 12 Fr So Jr Sr Gr

    Job Training: _____

    Special Courses: _____

    Military Training: _____

PART III (To be completed by human resource department with supervisory inputs)

12. Overall Evaluation of Performance _____
_____

13. Overall Readiness for Promotion _____

    To What Job(s): _____

    Comments: _____

14. Current Deficiencies _____
_____

15. Supervisor's Signature _____ Date:: _____

PART IV (To be completed by Human Resource department representative)

16. Are the two most recent performance evaluations attached? _____ Yes _____ No

17. Prepared by _____ Date: _____

---

records. It identifies the employee's job title, experience, age, and previous jobs. Part II seeks information about the skills, duties, responsibilities, and education of the worker. From these questions, planners learn about the mix of employee abilities. The personnel department may collect these data by telephone or face-to-face interviews, or the questions may be sent periodically to the employee through the company mail. The employee's future potential is briefly summarized by the immediate superior in Part III. Performance, readiness for promotion, and any deficiencies are noted here. The supervisor's signature helps ensure that the form is reviewed by someone who knows the employee better than the personnel specialists do. Part IV is added as a final check for completeness and for the addition of recent employee evaluations, which give more insight into past performance.

USAF and GE use computer matches

Inventories of human resources are often computerized to match talent with openings and are updated periodically.[29] Large organizations, such as General Electric and the U.S. Air Force, use computer-based systems to quickly match jobs with skilled personnel. Computerized records also facilitate updating, which should be done at least every two years if employees are encouraged to report

178   II. PREPARATION AND SELECTION

major changes to the personnel department when they occur. Major changes include new skills, degree completions, changed job duties, and the like. Failure to update skills inventories can lead to present employees being overlooked for job openings within the organization.

Moonlighting

> *After working hours, Rafael Corda "moonlighted" by helping his brother do maintenance work at a large paint factory. Rafael became interested in maintenance work and completed several courses in air-conditioning and plumbing. Since his full-time employer seldom updated its skills inventory on employees, the personnel manager at the First National Bank was unaware of Rafael's diverse skills. After several weeks of searching, the personnel manager hired a maintenance worker from outside the bank's present work force. The bank spent $1,000 to find this new maintenance worker. When Rafael found out, he was understandably upset.*

Management inventories should be updated periodically since they are also used for key personnel decisions. In fact, some employers use the same form for managers and nonmanagers. When the forms differ, the management inventory requests information about management activities. Common topics include:

➤ Number of employees supervised

➤ Total budget managed

➤ Duties of subordinates

➤ Types of employees supervised

➤ Management training received

➤ Previous management duties.

Diversity

The growing work force diversity discussed in Chapter 2 must be considered by many firms as they conduct human resource audits. Even in a city government, skills and management audits should solicit information about language abilities. Supervisors and employees who have customer contact may be more ideally suited for some job openings if they are bilingual. Of course, such skills should be bona fide occupational qualifications or they may be the basis for Equal Employment discrimination charges. Global companies also seek information about language skills and many ask about international travel as inputs for possible international placement.

6. HUMAN RESOURCE PLANNING   179

Succession plans

Succession planning. Human resource audit information is used by planners to make judgments about possible promotions and transfers. *Succession planning* is the process human resource planners and operating managers use to convert information about current employees into decisions about future internal job placements. Since potential promotions and other placement decisions are usually the responsibility of operating managers, the human resource department serves in a confidential advisory role. Given the complexities and time demands of developing these plans, succession planning is usually limited to key employees and those identified as having long-term potential.

Exxon

> Exxon is so far ahead in the succession planning game that it has already hired its CEO for the year 2010. Although it is not public knowledge who that person is, he or she is already being challenged, assessed, and groomed for the top spot. The primary purpose of Exxon's succession planning program . . . is to provide a systematic succession of first-rate managers throughout the company. To date, virtually the entire senior management staff . . . is a product of the . . . system.[30]

By identifying successors to key jobs and high-potential employees, corporations like Exxon, IBM, Eastman Kodak, and others help assure a steady flow of internal talent to fill important openings. Not only does succession planning encourage hiring from within and create an environment in which employees have careers, not merely jobs, it identifies human resource shortages and skill deficiencies before openings occur. Then through special assignments, job rotation, training, and other forms of human resource development, candidates can be prepared to accept the greater responsibilities of future job openings. The result for the organization is greater continuity of operations and better qualified incumbents.

Another result of effective succession planning can be a more unified corporate culture. State Farm Insurance Companies use succession planning to identify potential candidates to fill openings in their regional offices and headquarters. By moving top managers through regional and headquarter offices, a more uniform company culture results while creating dedication to the company, not simply individual operations. In a similar manner, Sara Lee Corporation uses succession planning to better integrate its subsidiaries. Since it has acquired more than 40 companies in recent years, its succession planning process mandates that two of every five candidates for managerial promotions come from another subsidiary.[31]

Global issues

Global companies use succession planning for the same purposes as domestic firms. In addition, international succession planning and the resulting transfers serve to develop managers and executives with a more global perspective. Assignments in different countries and exposure to different cultures challenge the international executive's assumptions about business practices and ways of dealing with people. And, of course, international succession planning allows the organization to draw on a larger pool of talent, increasing the possibilities of having the best people in the right jobs. However, the job of planning career moves across international boundaries is more complex than domestic planning. The need to consider language, family, cultural differences, relocation complications, return travel, and related considerations make this newly emerging area of human resource management particularly important and difficult.[32]

Replacement charts and summaries To consolidate the results of human resource audits and succession planning, the human resource department may develop replacement charts, such as Figure 6-8, or more detailed replacement summaries, as seen in Figure 6-9.

Replacement charts

Replacement charts are a visual representation of who will replace whom in the event of a job opening. The information for constructing the chart comes from the human resource audit. Figure 6-8, a typical replacement chart, shows the replacement status of only a few jobs in the administration of a large city.

Although different firms may seek to summarize different information in their replacement charts, the figure illustrates the minimum information usually included. The chart, much like an organizational chart, depicts the various jobs in the organization and shows the status of likely candidates. Replacement status consists of two variables: present performance and promotability. Present performance is determined largely from supervisory evaluations. Opinions of other managers, peers, and subordinates may contribute to the appraisal of present performance. Future promotability is based primarily on present performance and on the estimates by immediate superiors of future success in a new job. The Human Resource department may contribute to these estimates through the use of psychological tests, interviews, and other methods of assessment. Replacement charts showing the candidates' ages could lead to allegations of age discrimination. As a result, this information is now deleted on many replacement charts.

Human Resource and management decision makers find that these charts provide a quick reference. Their shortcoming is that they contain very limited information.[33] To supplement the chart, and, increasingly, to supplant it, personnel specialists develop replacement summaries. *Replacement summaries* list likely replacements for each job and indicate their relative strengths and weaknesses. As Figure 6-9 shows, a summary provides considerably more data than a replacement chart. This additional data allows decision makers to make more informed decisions.

Most companies that are sophisticated enough to engage in detailed human resource planning typically computerize their personnel records, including human resource inventories. Then planners can update and compile replacement summaries when needed. These summaries also indicate which positions lack human resource backups.

7-Eleven fast trackers

> For example, Southland Corp., the Dallas-based parent of the 7-Eleven convenience store chain, has computerized its search for fast-trackers—those who are making exceptionally quick career progress. Twice yearly, Southland managers file reports about the promotability of their subordinates. By consol-

6. HUMAN RESOURCE PLANNING 181

Figure 6-8

A Partial Replacement Chart for City Government

```
                          CITY MANAGER
                          H. Jarvis (63)
                    A/1   C. Smythe (58)
                    B/1   L. Katz (52)

                        ASSISTANT
                        CITY MANAGER
                        C. SYMTHE (58)
                    A/1   L. Katz (52)
                    B/2   A. CAROL (43)
```

A. Ready for promotion
B. Needs more experience
C. Not suitable for job

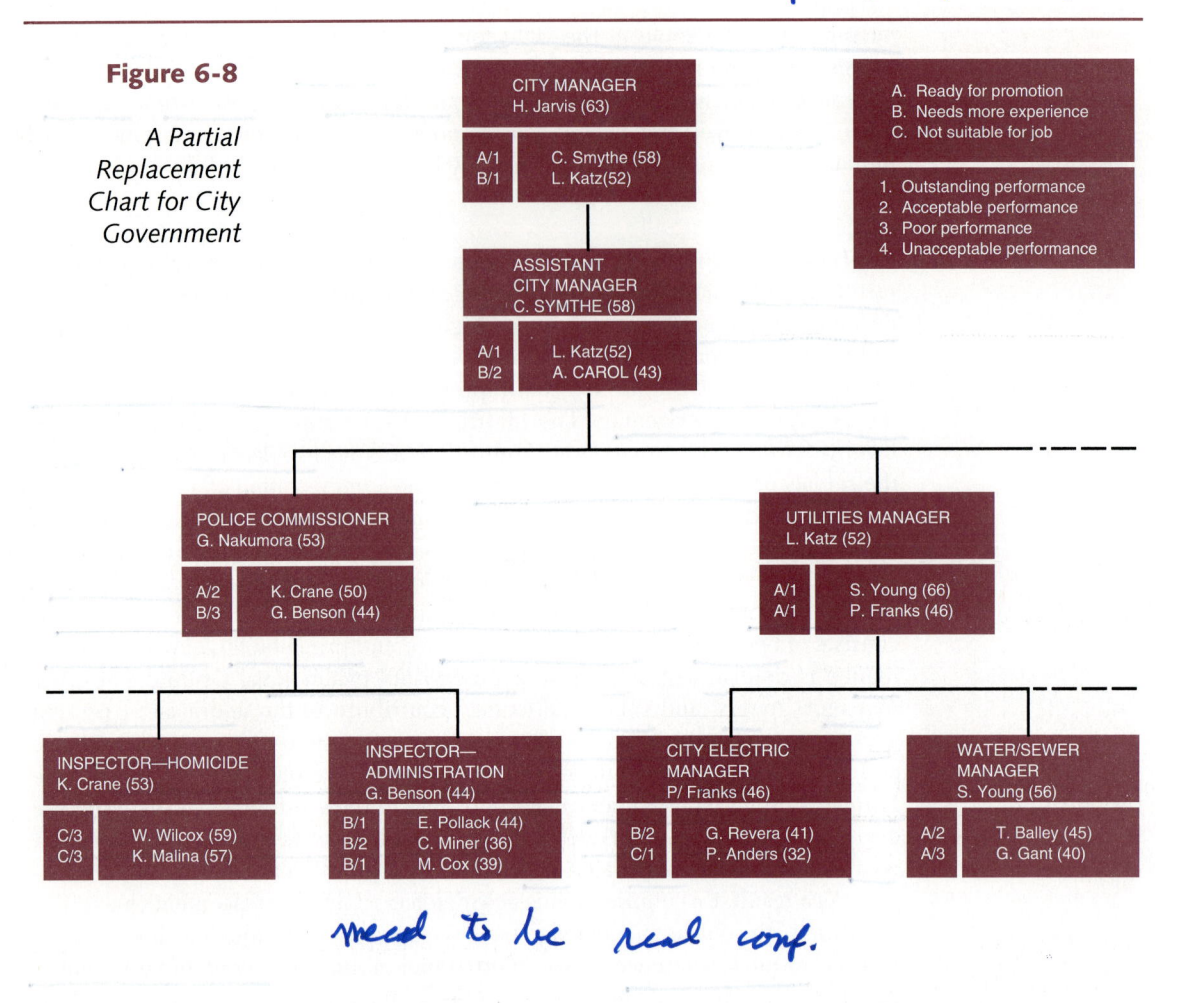

1. Outstanding performance
2. Acceptable performance
3. Poor performance
4. Unacceptable performance

```
        POLICE COMMISSIONER                 UTILITIES MANAGER
        G. Nakumora (53)                    L. Katz (52)
   A/2   K. Crane (50)                 A/1   S. Young (66)
   B/3   G. Benson (44)                A/1   P. Franks (46)

INSPECTOR—HOMICIDE    INSPECTOR—          CITY ELECTRIC       WATER/SEWER
K. Crane (53)         ADMINISTRATION      MANAGER             MANAGER
                      G. Benson (44)      P/ Franks (46)      S. Young (56)
C/3  W. Wilcox (59)   B/1  E. Pollack (44) B/2  G. Revera (41) A/2  T. Balley (45)
C/3  K. Malina (57)   B/2  C. Miner (36)   C/1  P. Anders (32) A/3  G. Gant (40)
                      B/1  M. Cox (39)
```

idating the reports on a computer, "We find out whether there will be a deficit of people coming up through the ranks," says Blake Frank, Southland's manager of personnel research. A separate program helps produce career-development plans, pinpointing weaknesses and suggesting solutions—university courses, in-house training, a different job, or a special assignment.[34]

In the long run, the Human Resource department can encourage employees to upgrade their capabilities and prepare for future vacancies. In the short run, an opening without a suitable replacement requires someone to be hired from the external labor market. Whether replacement charts or summaries are used, this information is normally kept confidential. Confidentiality not only guards the privacy of employees but prevents dissatisfaction among those who are not immediately promotable.[35]

Figure 6-9

A Replacement Summary for the Position of City Manager

[handwritten: More detailed confidential]

Replacement Summary for the Position of City Manager

Present Office Holder Harold Jarvis   Age 63

Probable Opening In two years   Reason Retirement

Salary Grade 99 ($78,500 yearly)   Experience 8 years

Candidate 1 Clyde Smythe   Age 58

Current Position Assistant City Manager   Experience 4 years

Current Performance Outstanding   Explanation Clyde's performance evaluations by the City Manager are always the highest possible.

Promotability Ready now for promotion.   Explanation During an extended illness of the City Manager, Clyde assumed all duties successfully including major policy decisions and negotiations with city unions.

Training Needs None

Candidate 2 Larry Katz   Age 52

Current Position Utilities Manager   Experience 5 years

Current Performance Outstanding   Explanation Larry's performance has kept costs of utilities to citizens 10 to 15 percent below that of comparable city utilities through careful planning.

Promotability Needs more experience.   Explanation Larry's experience is limited to utilities management. Although successful, he needs more broad administrative experience in other areas. (He is ready for promotion to Assistant City Manager at this time.)

Training Needs Training in budget preparation and public relations would be desirable before promotion to City Manager.

Estimates of External Supply

Entry-level jobs

Not every future opening can be filled with present employees. Some jobs simply lack replacements. Other jobs are entry-level positions. That is, they are beginning jobs that are filled with people who do not presently work for the organization. When there are no replacements or when the opening is for an entry-level job, there is a need for external supplies of human resources.

External needs. Employer growth and the effectiveness of the personnel department largely determine the need for external supplies of human resources. Growth is primarily responsible for the number of entry-level job openings, especially if the company promotes from within to fill job vacancies. The number of non-entry-level openings depends in part on how well the personnel department assists employees to develop their capabilities. If workers are not encouraged to expand their capabilities, they may not be ready to fill future vacancies. The lack of promotable replacements creates job openings that need to be filled externally.

Labor market analysis. Success in finding new employees depends on the labor market and on the skills of the employment specialists in the human resource department. The relevant labor market depends on the skill levels being sought. For highly skilled jobs, the relevant labor market may be the entire country. The labor market for unskilled jobs is generally the local community. Whether employment rates are high or low, many needed skills are difficult to find.[36] Even during a severe recession, for example, a look at newspaper classified advertisements shows that many job openings go unfilled week after week. In the short run, the national unemployment rate serves as an approximate measure of how difficult it is to acquire new employees; however, personnel specialists realize that this rate varies among different groups as well as from region to region and from city to city. These regional differences parallel international imbalances in human resource availability. One such imbalance has caused some countries, such as Germany, to import guest workers from developing countries during periods of extremely low unemployment.

Unemployment rates

Some researchers suggest that there may be a shortage of managerial talent, which is partly related to attitudes held by those in the work force. If potential managers are not oriented toward work in hierarchical organizational structures, shortages of managerial talent may result whether overall unemployment is high or low.[37]

Regardless of the unemployment rate, external needs may be met by attracting employees who work for others. In the long run, local developments and demographic trends have the most significant impact on labor markets.[38] Local developments include community growth rates and attitudes. For example, the population of many Midwestern farm towns is in decline. When these towns attempt to attract new business, employers fear declining population may mean future shortages in the local labor market. So new businesses often locate elsewhere. The lack of jobs results in still more people leaving the local labor market. Conversely, cities in the Sun Belt are attractive to employers because these growing centers promise even larger labor markets in the future.

Community attitudes. Community attitudes also affect the nature of the labor market. Antibusiness or no-growth attitudes may cause employers to locate elsewhere. Fewer jobs mean a loss of middle-class workers. The shrinking work force discourages new businesses, and the cycle is complete.

Community limitations

The people of Santa Barbara, California limited growth in their community by restricting the number of permits available for connecting to the city water system. Construction slowed. In time, housing prices increased dramatically. Young families that could not afford housing left the Santa Barbara labor market. New employers found the situation discouraging. Established employers found it difficult to attract new workers, especially the low-paid workers required for one of the town's major industries, tourism. Regardless of the unemployment rate, personnel departments in Santa Barbara faced a difficult task when they had to rely on the external supply of workers.

Demographics. Demographic trends are another long-term development that affects the availability of external supply. Fortunately for planners, these trends are known years in advance of their impact.[39]

Demographics

The low birthrates of the 1930s and early 1940s were followed by a baby boom during the late 1940s and 1950s. When the post-World War II babies started to go to college in the 1960s, the low birthrates of the 1930s led to a shortage of college teachers. These demographic trends were already in motion by 1950. Long-range human resource planning, which was sensitive to demographic developments, could have predicted the shortage soon enough for proactive colleges to take corrective action. Today, there is a decline in the number of 18- to 24-year-olds, a demographic trend which affects military and college enrollments.

Useful publications

As for the specific shortages that affect a particular industry or occupation in the long run, ample information is readily available. The National Commission for Manpower Policy issues reports on major developments in the labor force. The U.S. Department of Labor publishes the *Occupational Outlook Handbook* and quarterly reports in the *Occupational Outlook Quarterly*. These publications discuss the expected developments in various occupational groupings. Similarly, the department publishes the population estimates of the Census Bureau; projections of the total labor force; the percentage of the population that will be in the work force; and projected changes in the work force by sex, age, race, marital status, and other criteria.[40]

Although exceptions exist, many postindustrial nations are experiencing a slowing of their population growth, especially among their more educated classes. As a result, shortages among skilled workers may exist even though overall population growth suggests an expanding work force. This may be especially true in Japan, for example. In the United States and Canada, immigration policies may offset slower growth rates. How European Economic Community countries will be affected by immigration is uncertain, given the increased unification of member nations and the on-going changes in Eastern Europe.

IMPLEMENTATION OF HUMAN RESOURCE PLANS

Figure 6-10 summarizes the key concepts discussed throughout this chapter. The left side of the figure identifies the major causes of human resource demand—which are external, organizational, and work force factors. These causes of demand are forecast by experts, trend data, and other methods to determine the short- and long-range demand for human resources.[41] This demand is fulfilled either internally, by present employees, or externally, by newcomers. The internal supply is shown in replacement charts, which are based on audits of the organization's human resources. External sources are identified by analysis of the relevant labor market. The results include short- and long-range human resource plans that are fulfilled by internal and external staffing processes.

Once the supply and demand of human resources are estimated, adjustments may be needed. When the internal supply of workers exceeds the firm's demand, a *human resource surplus* exists. Most employers respond to a surplus with a hiring freeze. This freeze stops the personnel department from filling openings with external supplies of workers. Instead, present employees are reassigned. Voluntary departures, called *attrition,* slowly reduce the surplus.[42] If it persists, leaves of absence are encouraged. After the summer tourist peak, for example, TWA and other airlines often grant leaves of absence to employees who request them. These leaves help reduce the total work force during the slack fall and winter months.

Layoffs are a temporary loss of employment to workers; layoffs are used in cases of short-range surplus. If the surplus is expected to persist into the foreseeable future, employers often encourage early retirement on a *voluntary* basis. (Forced early retirement could violate the Age Discrimination in Employment Act.) Should the surplus still persist, employees are discharged. The blow of discharge may be softened through formal *outplacement* procedures, which help present employees find new jobs with other firms. These efforts may include office space, secretarial services, use of photocopying machines, long-distance phone calls, counseling, instruction in how to look for work, and even invitations to competitors to meet with employees.[43]

If the internal supply cannot fulfill the organization's needs, a human resource *shortage* exists. Planners have little flexibility in the short run and must rely on

Figure 6-10

Supply and Demand Considerations in Human Resource Planning

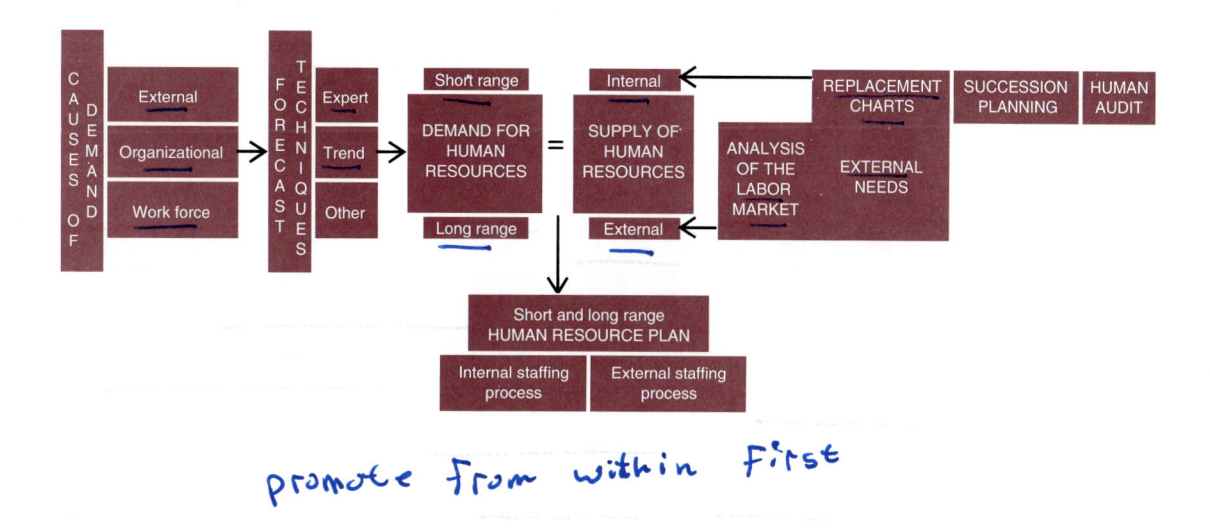

```
CAUSES OF DEMAND: External, Organizational, Work force
→ FORECAST TECHNIQUES: Expert, Trend, Other
→ DEMAND FOR HUMAN RESOURCES (Short range, Long range)
= SUPPLY OF HUMAN RESOURCES (Internal, External)
    Internal ← REPLACEMENT CHARTS, SUCCESSION PLANNING, HUMAN AUDIT
    External ← ANALYSIS OF THE LABOR MARKET, EXTERNAL NEEDS
→ Short and long range HUMAN RESOURCE PLAN
    → Internal staffing process
    → External staffing process
```

promote from within first

the external staffing process to find new employees. In the long run, responses can be more flexible. Planners can use the internal staffing process; that is, they can redouble efforts to have employees develop the necessary knowledge, skills, and attitudes to fill these jobs.

Whether staffing needs are met internally or externally, planners must consider their employer's affirmative action plan. That plan, as discussed in Chapter 4, contains the company's strategy for undoing past discrimination and ensuring that future discrimination does not occur. As internal and external candidates are selected to fill job openings, human resource decisions must match the goals and timetables found in the affirmative action plan. The human resource plan indicates whether the employer's affirmative action goals will be met. For example, even modest goals of increasing minority representation in a company are unlikely if the human resource plan indicates that no new hires are planned and the company intends to reduce overall employment through attrition.

The human resource plan does more than serve as a check on the likelihood of the affirmative action plan's success. It is an important part of the organization's *human resource information system*. The information contained in the human resource plan serves as a guide to recruiters, trainers, career planners, and other human resource specialists. With the knowledge of the firm's internal and external employment needs, personnel specialists, operating managers, and individual

HRIS

employees can direct their efforts toward the organization's future staffing needs. Managers can groom their employees through specific training and development efforts. Even individual employees can prepare themselves for future openings through education and other self-help efforts.

From the perspective of the personnel department, however, the human resource plan is only one part of the department's information system. Another important part of the system is information about the people who are hired from outside the organization. Meeting staffing needs externally is the focus of the next two chapters.

SUMMARY

Human resource planning requires considerable time, staff, and financial resources. The return for this investment may not justify the expenditure for small firms. Increasingly, however, large organizations use human resource planning as a means of achieving greater effectiveness. This planning is an attempt by the human resource department to estimate the organization's future needs and supplies of staff. The data collected in the course of this planning is becoming increasingly necessary as companies go global.

Given some level of anticipated demand, planners try to estimate the availability of current workers to meet that demand. Such estimates begin with an audit of present employees. Then possible replacements are identified. Internal shortages are resolved by seeking new employees in external labor markets. Surpluses are reduced by normal attrition, leaves of absence, layoffs, or terminations.

As Figure 6-10 illustrates, both external and internal staffing processes are used to fulfill human resource plans. The result is short- and long-range plans that outline future demands and the likely sources of supply. This information becomes an important addition to the department's human resource information system.

Terms for Review

- Strategic plan
- Human resource forecasts
- Human resource audits
- Delphi technique
- Extrapolation
- Indexation
- Nominal Group Techniques
- Staffing table
- Skills inventories
- Replacement charts
- Replacement summaries
- Succession planning
- Labor market analysis
- Attrition
- Outplacement

Review and Discussion Questions

1. Why is human resource planning more common among large organizations than among small ones? What are the advantages of human resource planning for large organizations?

2. List and briefly describe the factors that change an organization's demand for human resources.

3. As the work force in postindustrial societies becomes more diverse, what impact will this have on human resource planning?

4. What is the purpose of a human resource audit? Specifically, what information acquired from a human resource audit is needed to construct a replacement chart or replacement summary?

5. Suppose human resource planners estimated that because of several technological innovations your firm will need 25 percent fewer employees in three years. What actions would you take today?

6. Suppose you manage a restaurant in a winter resort area. During the summer it is profitable to keep the business open, but you need only half the cooks, table servers, and bartenders. What actions would you take at the beginning of the peak tourist season?

7. Explain why replacement charts and replacement summaries must be treated confidentially.

8. As organizations become more global, human resource planning becomes more important and complex. Explain.

INCIDENT 6-1
Church College's Human Resource Needs

For years, Church College had operated at a deficit. Since the school was supported by a national religious organization, this loss was made up from the general fund of the national organization. Because of inflation and recession, the drain on the general fund budget had tripled to $21 million by 1991.

Several members of the Church College Board of Directors had heard that college enrollments were going to decline during the 1990s. A decline in enrollment would lead to overstaffing and even larger deficits. The president of the college hired Bill Barker to develop a long-range human resource plan for the college. An excerpt of his report stated:

The declining birthrates of the 1960s and 1970s mean that there will be a decline in college-age students at least into the mid-1990s. If the college is to avoid soaring deficits, it must institute an employment freeze now. Furthermore, a committee should be formed to develop new curricula that appeal to those segments of the work force that are going to experience rapid growth between now and the year 2000.

The president of the college argued,

An employment freeze would cut the college off from hiring new faculty members who have the latest training in new areas. Besides, our enrollments have grown by two to four percent every year since 1970. I see no reason to doubt that trend will continue.

1. Assuming you are a member of the board of directors, would you recommend that the college implement an employment freeze?

2. If Bill Barker used national birthrate information, what other population information could the president use to support his argument that college enrollment will keep growing?

3. What strategies, if any, would you recommend to allow the college to hire newly trained faculty yet avoid serious budget deficits in the 1990s if enrollments drop?

References

1. Peter Bamberger, Lee Dyer, Samuel B. Bacarach, "Human Resource Planning in High Technology Entrepreneurial Startups," *Human Resource Planning* (Jan. 1990), p. 37.

2. James W. Walker, "Linking Human Resources Planning and Strategic Planning," *Human Resource Planning* (Spring 1978), p. 2.

3. George T. Milkovich and Thomas A. Mahoney, "Human Resource Planning Models: A Perspective," in James W. Walker, ed., *The Challenge of Human Resource Planning: Selected Readings* (New York: Human Resource Planning Society, 1979), pp. 73–84.

4. Eddie C. Smith, "Strategic Business Planning and Human Resources: Part I," *Personnel Journal* (August 1982), pp. 606–610. (Part II appears in *Personnel Journal* (Sept. 1982), pp. 680–682.). See also Stella M. Nkomo, "The Theory and Practice of HR Planning: The Gap Still Remains," *Personnel Administrator* (August 1986), p. 71; Matt Hennecke, "The 'People' Side of Strategic Planning," *Training* (Nov. 1984), pp.

25–32; and Anil K. Gupta, "Matching Managers to Strategies: Points and Counterpoint," *Human Resource Management*, vol. 25, no. 2 (Summer 1986), pp. 215–234.

5. Lee Dyer, "Human Resource Planning at IBM," *Human Resource Planning* (Spring 1984), pp. 111–125.

6. John Hoerr, "Human Resource Managers Aren't Corporate Nobodies Anymore," *Business Week* (Dec. 2, 1985), p. 58.

7. Gerald L. McManis and Michael S. Leibman, "Integrating Human Resource and Business Planning," *Personnel Administrator* (Feb. 1989), pp. 32, 34, 36, 38.

8. Allen L. Hixon, "Why Corporations Make Haphazard Overseas Staffing Decisions," *Personnel Administrator* (March 1986), pp. 91–94.

9. Rosalie L. Tung, "Human Resource Planning in Japanese Multinationals: A Model for U.S. Firms?" *Journal of International Business Studies* (Fall 1984), pp. 139–149.

10. Faneuil Adams, Jr., "Developing an International Workforce," *Columbia Journal of World Business* (Jan. 1989), pp. 23–25.

11. John W. Boroski, "Putting it Together: HR Planning in '3D' at Eastman Kodak," *Human Resource Planning* (Jan. 1990), pp. 45–57.

12. Ibid.

13. Herbert Heneman and G. Seltzer, *Employer Manpower Planning and Forecasting* (Manpower Research Monograph no. 19) (Washington, D.C.: U.S. Department of Labor, 1970), p. 42.

14. Raymond E. Miles and Charles C. Snow, "Designing Strategic Human Resources Systems," *Organizational Dynamics* (Summer 1984), pp. 36–52.

15. Eugene H. Seibert and Joanne Seibert, "Retirement: Crisis or Opportunity," *Personnel Administrator* (August 1986), pp. 43–49.

16. Mark A. de Bernardo, "The New Federal 'Plant Closings' Law: What Employers Should Know," *Congressional Action* (Special Reports 2–4) (August 30, 1988), pp. 1–4.

17. Harold L. Angle, Charles C. Manz, and Andres H. Van de Ven, "Integrating Human Resource Management and Corporate Strategy: A Preview of the 3M Story," *Human Resource Management* (Spring 1985), pp. 51–68.

18. Gregory Moorhead, "Qualitative Factors of Corporate Fit in Mergers and Acquisitions," *The Merger/Acquisition Consultant* (Dallas: Pritchard and Associates, 1982).

19. John Hoerr, op. cit.

20. Phil Farish, "Novel Link," *Personnel Administrator* (Feb. 1989), p. 22. See also Gary Szakmary, "How HRD Can Contribute to Company Expansion," *Personnel Journal* (August 1988), pp. 39–40.

21. "U.S. Death Toll from AIDS passes 100,000," *The Miami Herald* (Jan. 25, 1991), p. 12a.

22. Thomas H. Stone and Jack Fiorito, "A Perceived Uncertainty Model of Human Resource Forecasting Technique Use," *Academy of Management Review*, vol. 11, no. 3, 1986, pp. 635–642. See also John D. Gridley, "Who Will Be Where When? Forecast the Easy Way," *Personnel Journal* (May 1986), pp. 51–58.

23. A.L. Delbecq, A.H. Van de Ven, and D.H. Gustafson, *Group Techniques for Progress Planning: A Guide to Nominal and Delphi Processes* (Glenview, Ill.: Scott, Foresman & Co., 1975); J.M. Bartunek and J.K. Muringhan, "The Nominal Group Technique: Expanding the Basic Procedure and Underlying Assumptions," *Group and Organization Studies*, vol. 9 (1984), pp. 417–432.

24. James W. Walker, *Human Resource Planning* (New York: McGraw-Hill Book Company, 1980), pp. 105.

25. Don Bryant, "Manpower Planning Models and Techniques," *Business Horizons* (April 1973), pp. 69–73. See also David J. Bartholomew, "Statistics in Human Resource Planning," *Human Resource Planning* (Nov. 1978), pp. 67–77.

26. James W. Walker, "Evaluating the Practical Effectiveness of Human Resource Planning Applications," *Human Resource Management* (Spring 1974), p. 21; and Paul Pakchan, "Effective Manpower Planning," *Personnel Journal* (Oct. 1983), pp. 826–830.

27. Douglas B. Gehrman, "Objective-Based Human Resources Planning," *Personnel Journal* (Dec. 1981), pp. 942–946.

28. Jeffrey Pfeffer and Yinon Cohen, "Determinants of Internal Labor Markets in Organizations," *Administrative Science Quarterly* (1984), pp. 550–572. See also Douglas R. Wholey, "Determinants of Firm Internal Labor Markets in Large Law Firms," *Administrative Science Quarterly* (1985), pp. 318–335.

29. William M. Bulkeley, "The Fast Track: Computers Help Firms Decide Whom to Promote," *The Wall Street Journal*, Eastern ed. (Sept. 18, 1985), p. 33.

30. Gerald L. McManis and Michael S. Leibman, "Succession Planners," *Personnel Administrator* (March 1989), p. 24.

31. Ibid.

32. Bamberger, Dyer, and Bacharach, op. cit. See also Hixon, op. cit.

33. George S. Odiorne, "For Successful Succession Planning . . . Match Organizational Requirements to Corporate Human Potential," *Management Review* (Nov. 1982), pp. 49–54.

34. Bulkeley, op. cit.

35. Joe Pasqualetto, "Staffing, Privacy and Security Measures," *Personnel Journal* (Sept. 1988), pp. 84, 86–89.

36. Joan Lindroth, "How to Beat the Coming Labor Shortage," *Personnel Journal* (April 1982), pp. 268–272.

37. John N. Pearson and Jeffrey S. Bracker, "The Coming Shortage of Managerial Talent, *Management Education and Development*, vol. 17, no. 3 (1986), pp. 243–251.

38. George S. Odiorne, "The Crystal Ball of HR Strategy," *Personnel Administrator* (Dec. 1986), pp. 103–106. See also John A. Byrne and Alison Leigh Cowan, "Should Companies Groom New Leaders or Buy Them?" *Business Week* (Sept. 22, 1986), pp. 94–96.

39. Alan L. Otten, "Decision Makers Often Fail to Spot Key Changes behind the Statistics," *The Wall Street Journal* (Dec. 6, 1986), p. 33.

40. See the annual *Employment and Training Report of the President* (Washington, D.C.: U.S. Government Printing Office).

41. R. J. Stalcup, "Avoiding Short-term HR Planning," *Personnel Administrator* (Sept. 1986), pp. 35–39.

42. Kendrith M. Rowland and Scott L. Summers, "Human Resource Planning: A Second Look," *Personnel Administrator* (Dec. 1981), pp. 73–80. See also William H. Hoffman and L.L. Wyatt, "Human Resource Planning," *Personnel Administrator* (Jan. 1977), pp. 19–23.

43. For one example of a well-managed outplacement effort, see "A Happy Ending in Connecticut," *Resource* (August 1985), pp. 2, 6.

Labor shortages, which are predicted to last into the next century, are expected to increase the importance of applicant attraction for organizations.
SARA L. RYNES AND ALISON E. BARBER[1]

RECRUITMENT

CHAPTER OBJECTIVES

After studying this chapter, you should be able to:
1. DESCRIBE how recruiters use affirmative action plans, job analysis information, and human resource plans to plan recruitment strategies.
2. EXPLAIN the crucial role recruiters play in meeting their organization's affirmative action goals.
3. DISCUSS the constraints under which the recruitment process takes place.
4. MATCH appropriate recruiting methods to different types of needed recruits.
5. DISCUSS the role of placement firms, state unemployment offices, and other outside organizations that assist recruiters.
6. DEVELOP an appropriate application blank.

ECRUITMENT IS the process of finding and attracting capable applicants for employment. The process begins when new recruits are sought and ends when their applications are submitted. The result is a pool of applicants from which new employees are selected. (The process of selecting from among these applicants is the topic of Chapter 8.) Responsibility for recruitment usually belongs to the personnel department. This responsibility is important because the quality of an organization's human resources depends on the quality of its recruits. Since large organizations recruit almost continuously, their personnel departments use specialists in the recruiting process, called *recruiters*.

Recruiters work to find and attract capable applicants. Their methods depend on the situation since there is no best recruiting technique. However, the job descriptions and specifications described in Chapter 5, "Job Analysis and Design," are essential tools, especially for recruiters in large organizations. With hundreds of jobs to recruit for, it is impossible for recruiters to know the duties and employee requirements of every job. Job descriptions and specifications provide the needed information upon which the recruitment process rests.

Normally, recruiters follow several steps. As Figure 7-1 illustrates, recruiters identify job openings through human resource planning or requests by managers. The human resource plan can be especially helpful because it shows the recruiter both present openings and those expected in the future. As mentioned in Chapter 6, "Human Resource Planning," advanced knowledge of job openings allows the recruiter to be proactive. After identifying openings, the recruiter learns what each job requires by reviewing the job analysis information, particularly the job descriptions and job specifications. This information tells the recruiter the characteristics of both the jobs and the people who will fill them. When the job analysis information appears outdated or seems superficial, recruiters can learn more about a job's requirements from the requesting manager. The potential importance of recruitment to the organization is shown by an example from John Hancock Financial Services when it was encountering a tight labor market during the late 1980s:

> *John Hancock Financial Services is the eighth-largest life insurance company in the United States. Headquartered in Boston, Massachusetts, it faced many of the recruiting issues confronting employers throughout North America, Europe, and Japan, including a diverse work force, tight labor markets, insufficiently educated workers, and a realization that traditional approaches to recruiting were not always successful. Simply put, Hancock was unable to fill the approximately 1,000 full-time, part-time, and temporary jobs that came open each year in its headquarters operations.*
>
> *Adopting a "customer service" orientation to meet the needs of operating managers who faced staffing shortages, Lyn Rosenstein began a variety of efforts to expand the potential pool of recruits available to her company. As personnel director, she expanded community outreach programs to attract more applicants. Recruiters were told to view themselves as public relations*

Figure 7-1

An Overview of the Recruitment Process

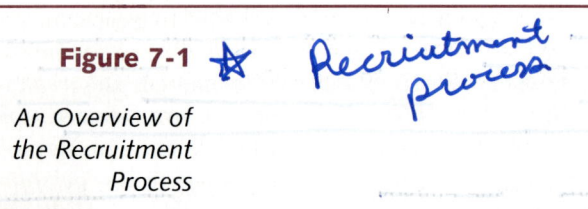

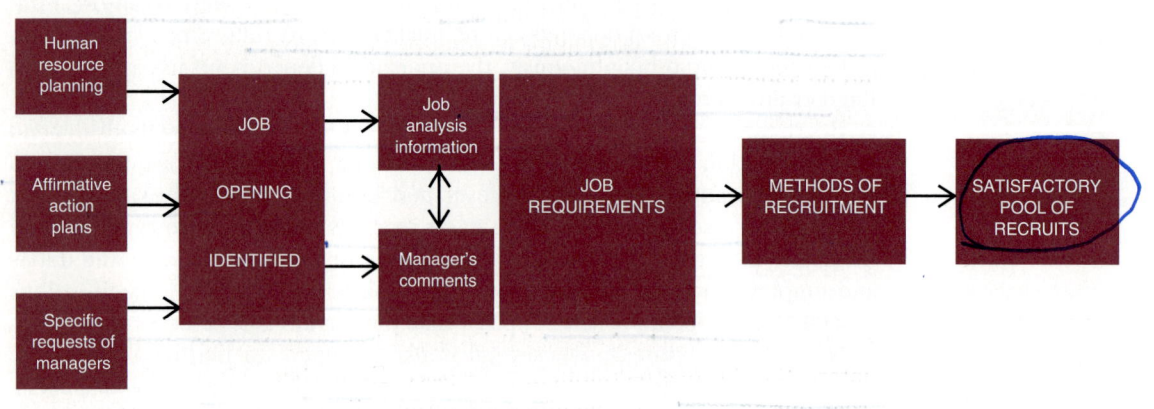

```
Human resource planning ─┐
                         │
Affirmative action plans ─┼─→  JOB OPENING IDENTIFIED  ⇄  Job analysis information
                         │                              ⇅
Specific requests of     ─┘                             Manager's comments
managers
```

JOB OPENING IDENTIFIED → JOB REQUIREMENTS → METHODS OF RECRUITMENT → SATISFACTORY POOL OF RECRUITS

---

representatives of the company and she then sent them out to recruit at local schools and community training agencies for the disadvantaged. Besides these proactive measures, Lyn joined with other Boston-area companies to lobby for increased aid to Boston's schools to enhance business education.

Given that many applicants were poorly trained, Lyn relied on the company's extensive in-house training programs, which allowed her to hire "qualifiable" candidates—that is, people who were not able to do the jobs for which they were hired without extensive training.[2]

This John Hancock example illustrates several issues related to recruitment. First, recruiters face growing constraints and challenges in attracting applicants.[3] Second, traditional sources, or channels, of recruits are unlikely to be sufficient as the growth in the labor force slows during the 1990s. Third, human resource departments must continue to meet the needs of their "customers"—the operating managers who have jobs that need to be filled. Finally, the growing competition for scarce human resources will mean that many applicants will have to be given more extensive, post-hire training and development.

Compounding an already difficult recruitment environment will be the added complexity of international recruitment. As more firms spread their operations across international boundaries, finding and attracting foreign managers to work for domestic firms and finding domestic workers to join foreign organizations will place additional demands on recruiters.

The hunt for global managers

The hunt for the global manager is on. From Amsterdam to Yokohama, recruiters are looking for a new breed of multilingual, multifaceted executive who can map strategy for the whole world. The action is especially heavy in Europe.[5]

Even in Japan, where lifetime employment focuses recruiters' attention on hiring recent school graduates almost exclusively, recruiters are facing the need to attract candidates from other employers, especially as non-Japanese firms set-up operations in Japan and begin looking for qualified, experienced talent.[6] For example:

KFC in Japan

... managers of Japan's Kentucky Fried Chicken franchises developed a unique strategy for attracting qualified help, offering new hires a trip to Hawaii.[7]

It is against this backdrop of tightening labor markets, both domestically and internationally, that recruitment takes place. Even when unemployment numbers soar during recessions, qualified applicants often remain difficult to find and retain. To explain the recruitment process requires an examination of the constraints, challenges, and channels of recruitment that result in prospective employees completing an application for employment.

CONSTRAINTS ON AND CHALLENGES OF RECRUITMENT

Recruiters must be sensitive to the constraints on the recruitment process. These limits arise from the organization, the recruiter, and the external environment. Although the emphasis may vary from situation to situation, the following list includes the most common constraints and challenges faced by recruiters:

➤ Organizational policies

➤ Human resource plans

➤ Affirmative action plans

➤ Recruiter habits

➤ Environmental conditions

➤ Job requirements

7. RECRUITMENT

197

➤ Costs

➤ Incentives.

Organizational Policies

Organizational policies seek to achieve uniformity, economies, public relations benefits, or other objectives that are sometimes unrelated to recruiting. At times, policies can be a potent source of constraints. Those policies that may affect recruitment are highlighted below.

Promote-from-within policies. Promote-from-within policies are intended to give present employees the first opportunity for job openings. These policies help assure that each employee has a career, not just a job. These policies also aid employee morale, attract recruits looking for jobs with a future, and help retain present employees. When such policies have an unequal impact, the EEOC may sue the employer. Although these policies reduce the flow of new people and ideas into various levels of the organization, the alternative is to pass over employees in favor of outsiders. Bypassing current employees can lead to employee dissatisfaction and turnover. Of course, promoting-from-within is made easier and more effective when a computer-based skills inventory already exists.

Compensation policies. A common constraint faced by recruiters is pay policies. Organizations with human resource departments usually establish pay ranges for different jobs to ensure equitable wages and salaries. If the recruiter finds a promising candidate, the pay range will influence the job seeker's desire to become a serious applicant. Recruiters seldom have the authority to exceed stated pay ranges. Of course, pay ranges must be adjusted for special cases such as international openings. To apply domestic compensation rates overseas often means to overpay or underpay foreign nationals compared with what they would normally earn. At the same time, employees who are reassigned overseas often need and expect an increase to handle extraordinary living expenses.

Employment status policies. Some companies have policies about hiring part-time and temporary employees. Although there is growing interest in hiring these types of workers, policies can cause recruiters to reject all but those seeking full-time work. Limitations against part-time and temporary employees reduce the pool of potential applicants, especially since this segment of the work force is a fast-growing one. In fact, one study of 484 firms found a one-third increase in the use of part-timers during the early 1980s.[8]

International hiring policies. Policies also may require foreign job openings to be staffed with local citizens. The use of foreign nationals reduces relocation expenses, lessens the likelihood of nationalization (as when a government confiscates property owned by others) and—if top jobs are held by local citizens—minimizes charges of economic exploitation. Unlike relocated employees, foreign nationals are more apt to be involved in the local community and to understand local customs and business practices. The problem is that finding local citizens for certain jobs can be very difficult. For example, recruiters for Western firms in Japan find it difficult to attract many Japanese managers because ". . . most are unwilling to give up the stability and job security they receive in Japan. Most large Japanese companies, after all, offer cradle-to-grave employment."[9] To complicate matters further, it can sometimes be equally difficult to find home-country employees who are willing to relocate. Many jobs in Saudi Arabia are hard to fill because many Western women and men are reluctant to move there because of the societal restraints placed on women, often preventing them from enjoying a Western lifestyle.

Human Resource Plans

In companies sophisticated enough to have human resource plans, recruiters use the plan to design recruitment strategies, especially when promote-from-within-policies are followed. The human resource plan outlines which jobs should be filled by recruiting outside the firm and which are to be filled internally. Foresight by the recruiter can lead to considerable economies for the company. Internal placements are much less costly and time-consuming than external recruitment, although internal placements do limit the pool of talent from which to recruit. When external recruiting must take place, grouping together similar jobs for college recruitment trips or advertisements can also be a cost-effective move. In short, the human resource plan enables recruiters to view the organization's overall hiring needs so that individual job openings can be placed in perspective with other employment needs.

Affirmative Action Plans

Before recruiting for any position, the recruiter would want to review the firm's affirmative action plan for guidance. Affirmative action plans (discussed in Chapter 4) may alert a recruiter to the need to recruit more minority or female candidates. When affirmative action needs suggest a greater balance in the mix of employees, recruiters must adjust their plans accordingly. In one case, *United States v. Georgia Power Company*, the Fifth Circuit Court of Appeals ruled that recruitment only at particular scholastic institutions can exclude members of protected classes. Although recruiting at any one school is not wrong, the effect of such a limited recruitment policy can be to exclude members of protected classes. When that result occurs, the employer may be guilty of discrimination because its recruiting policies have an unequal impact on protected classes.[10]

Although bona fide occupational qualifications can be applied, special care is needed to avoid charges of discrimination.

Recruiter Habits

A recruiter's past success can lead to unexamined and unproductive habits. Admittedly, habits can eliminate time-consuming decisions that reach the same answers. However, habits may also continue past mistakes or avoid more effective alternatives.[11] Even though recruiters need positive and negative feedback, they must guard against self-imposed constraints in the form of habits, especially since more than 40 percent of recruiters never receive training from their company.[12]

Environmental Conditions

External conditions strongly influence recruitment. Changes in the relevant labor market and the challenges mentioned in Chapter 2 affect recruiting. The unemployment rate, the pace of the company, spot shortages in specific skills, projections of the labor force by the Department of Labor, labor laws, and the recruiting activities of other employers each impact the recruiter's efforts. Although these factors are considered in human resource planning, the economic environment can change quickly after the plan is finalized. To be sure that the plan's economic assumptions remain valid, recruiters can check three fast-changing measures:

Indicators

1. ▶*Leading economic indicators.* Each month the U.S. Department of Commerce announces the direction of the leading indicators. These economic indexes suggest the future course of the national economy. If these indexes signal a sudden downturn in the economy, recruiting plans may have to be modified.

2. ▶*Predicted versus actual volume of business.* Since human resource plans are partially based upon the firm's predicted volume of business, usually sales, variations between actual and predicted sales may indicate that these plans are inaccurate. Recruiting efforts may need to be changed accordingly.

3. ▶*Want-ads index.* The Conference Board monitors the volume of want ads in major metropolitan newspapers. An upward trend in this index indicates increased competition for engineers and managers who are recruited on a nationwide basis. For clerical and production workers, who are usually recruited on a local basis, the personnel department may want to create its own index to monitor local changes in want ads.

As the economy, sales, and want ads change, recruiters must adjust their efforts accordingly. Tighter competition for applicants may require more vigor-

200 II. PREPARATION AND SELECTION

ous recruiting efforts. When business conditions decline, an opposite approach is called for, as the following example illustrates.

> As a major amusement park was opening in central Florida, the leading economic indicators dropped. Although the human resource plan called for recruiting 100 workers a week for the first month, the employment manager set a revised target of 75. Lower recruiting and employment levels helped establish a profitable operation even though first-year admissions fell below the projections used in the original human resource plan.

FLSA

Laws are another environmental constraint that cannot be overlooked. Besides the equal opportunity prohibitions that exclude discrimination on the basis of race, sex, age, creed, national origin, pregnancy, veteran status, and disabilities, other limitations exist. The *Fair Labor Standards Act* prescribes minimum wage requirements and child labor limitations that must be honored in recruiting. Likewise, the *National Labor Relations Act*, as amended, prohibits discrimination against someone who is, was, or wants to be a member of a labor union. These important legal constraints are pervasive and are widely understood by personnel professionals and managers.

Immigration issues

A more recent legal constraint comes from the *Immigration Reform and Control Act of 1986*.[13] The act seeks to limit illegal immigration by imposing sanctions on employers who hire undocumented aliens. Employers can face fines from $250 to $10,000 for *each* illegal alien hired. For employers that have relied on undocumented aliens, to perform, for example, seasonal agricultural work, recruitment holds new constraints. Employers in south Florida, New York, Chicago, California, Arizona, New Mexico, and Texas are most affected, since those areas have high concentrations of U.S. citizens who are recent and legal immigrants. A major challenge to personnel—especially in these areas—will be to comply with the act without discriminating against U.S. citizens because of their national origins.[14]

Even the courts have imposed legal constraints. Promises made in recruiting can be enforceable in court:

Exxon

> Exxon Corporation lost a $10.1 million breach-of-contract judgment when "a jury upheld Ian Dowie's claim that Exxon never intended to keep promises made to him when he was hired as marketing vice president of Qyx, Inc., Exxon's ill-fated office-systems venture."[15]

ADA

Another legal constraint concerns recruiting the handicapped. Under the 1990 *Americans with Disabilities Act* (ADA), recruiters cannot discriminate against those with disabilities, unless the disability would prevent the person from doing the job after reasonable accommodations by the employer.[16] Proactive employers,

7. RECRUITMENT

201

such as Pizza Hut, for example, began innovative recruitment programs among the disabled even before the ADA became law.

Pizza Hut

> *Pizza Hut realized that there were 8 million disabled Americans who want to work but are without jobs. Viewing its need for entry-level workers and seeing a large pool of potential recruits, Pizza Hut began a successful program in Orange County, California, to hire the handicapped, including the mentally retarded.*[17]

Job Requirements

Research summary

Within the legal and other environmental constraints, recruiters must not lose focus on the job to be filled. What does the job require? A study by the Committee for Economic Development surveyed 438 large businesses and 6,000 small ones to identify what contributes to job success. The study found that specific vocational skills are less crucial than a high level of literacy. In addition, responsible attitudes toward work, the ability to communicate in English, and the capacity to learn were all found to be important.[18]

For specific openings in a specific organization, recruiters learn how demanding a job is from job analysis information and from conversations with the requesting manager as shown in Figure 7-1 earlier in the chapter. Knowledge of a job's requirements allows the recruiter to choose the best way to find recruits, given all the other constraints under which the recruiter must operate.

"Find the best" fallacy

"Find the best and most experienced applicant you can" is often a constraint that is imposed on recruiters as though it were a job requirement. At first, this demand by a requesting manager seems reasonable. All managers want to have the best and most experienced people working for them. However, several potential problems exist with this seemingly innocent request. One obvious problem is the recruiter's ability to locate good candidates, especially since the average recruiter maintains 36 open requisitions at the same time.[19] Another problem in seeking out the best and most experienced applicants is cost. People with greater experience usually require a higher salary than less experienced people. If a high level of experience is not truly necessary, the recruit may become bored shortly after being hired. Moreover, if the personnel department cannot show that a high degree of experience is needed, then experience may be an artificial job requirement that discriminates against applicants who are members of protected classes. Another point about experience is worth remembering: For some people in some jobs, ten years of experience is another way of saying one year of experience repeated ten times. Someone with ten years of experience may not be any better than an applicant who has only one year of experience.

II. PREPARATION AND SELECTION

Costs

Recruiters must operate within budgets. Thus, the cost of identifying and attracting recruits is an ever-present limitation. Consider the observations of one analyst who has studied the issue of recruiting costs.

New-hire costs

> The cost-of-employment figures I have seen suggest that the average is over $7,000 per new hire. Even college recruiting can cost as much as $6,000 per hire. . . . At the higher levels of management, the numbers become staggering. Fees plus expenses paid to recruiting firms undertaking a search to fill a $100,000-a-year position can easily top $30,000. These fees are large in and of themselves; if the recruiting process takes several months or if the final candidate fails to remain with the organization, the costs accumulate to a truly respectable total.[20]

Careful human resource planning and forethought by recruiters can minimize these expenses. One cost-saving measure, for instance, is recruiting for multiple job openings simultaneously. The best solution is to use proactive personnel practices to reduce employee turnover, thus minimizing the need for recruiting. Evaluating the quantity, quality, and costs of recruitment helps ensure that it is efficient and cost-effective.

Incentives

As with any marketing effort, incentives may be necessary to stimulate a potential recruit's interest. Inducements can also be a constraint, as when other employers are using them. Inducements may be a response designed to overcome other limitations facing the recruiter. Some examples of inducements include:

Burger King

▶ Fast-food chains usually have high turnover. To encourage recruits (and retain present employees longer), Burger King introduced an educational assistance program that allows employees to accrue up to $2,000 worth of tuition credits over two years. Turnover among participants is 22 percent versus 97 percent for nonparticipants.[21]

American Bankers

▶ American Bankers Insurance Group uses on-premises day care to attract (and retain) working mothers who are a significant proportion of the company's work force.

▶ State Mutual Life Assurance Company of America offers employees and their children a training program to help families adjust to having a mother work outside the home.[22]

Northrop

▶ As with Burger King, the U.S. military services offer tuition assistance. Preenlistment training options are another inducement.

▶ Northrop's Defense Systems Division used an emotional appeal. They produced a pamphlet that highlights the advantages of living in the Chicago area and directed it to those who once lived in that area. The brochure was designed around the theme, "Northrop DSD has one great reason to come home."[23]

Shrinking pool of new entrants

The number of new entrants in the work force between the ages of 18 and 24 will actually be less in the 1990s than in the 1980s. Not until the year 2000 will the number of people in this age group be at the same level as 1988. The impact will be a scarcity of entry-level workers, military recruits, and college applicants. In addition to some of the creative approaches taken by Burger King, American Bankers, and others, the basics still apply. For example, one study found that among college seniors the most sought after benefits are health and life insurance.[24] Aside from sophisticated studies, common sense dictates that employers will have to become more proactive, as the John Hancock example earlier in the chapter suggests. Recruiters also will have to develop a more "customer-service" attitude in dealing with recruits. They will have to keep applicants better informed, schedule interviews at the applicant's convenience, and minimize the number of return interviews.[25] Higher pay and benefits will be important, too.

TRW

TRW's Space and Defense Sector faces a particularly difficult recruiting challenge: hiring highly trained technical employees and managers. Company analysts estimate that the cost of recruiting a new engineer and bringing him or her up the learning curve is $180,000. The figure jumps to $320,000 for managers. To meet this challenge, TRW strives to become the preferred employer among applicants. It seeks to create a work environment that is compatible with personal and family needs. Benefits programs are customized to individual needs, and ongoing career counseling is provided.[26]

CHANNELS OF RECRUITMENT

The ways of finding recruits are sometimes referred to as *channels*. Recruiters and applicants historically use a limited number of channels through which they pursue one another. No single approach works best. In reviewing the most common channels, recruiters must be aware of the constraints in each approach, and the need for creativity if the recruiting effort is to be effective and efficient. The channels most widely used by applicants and recruiters are discussed below.

1. Walk-ins and Write-ins

Unsolicited recruits

Walk-ins are job seekers who arrive at the personnel department in search of a job. *Write-ins* are those who send written inquiries. Both groups normally are asked to complete application forms to list their abilities and interests. Usable applications are kept in an active file until suitable openings occur or until the applications are too old to be considered valid, usually a period of six months.

2. Employee Referrals

Employees may refer job seekers to the personnel department. Employee referrals have several distinctive advantages. First, employees with hard-to-find job skills may know others who do the same work. For example, a shortage of welders on the Alaskan pipeline was partially solved by having welders ask their friends in the "lower 48 states" to apply for the many unfilled openings. TRW and McDonald's even pay employees a referral bonus when qualified candidates are recommended at some locations.[27] Second, new recruits already will have learned something about the organization from the employees who refer them. Thus, referred applicants may be more strongly attracted to the organization than are casual walk-ins. Third, employees tend to refer their friends, who are likely to have similar work habits and work attitudes. Even if work values are different, these candidates may have a strong desire to work hard so that they do not let down the person who recommended them.

Referral bonuses at McDonald's

Employee referrals are an excellent and legal recruitment technique. However, recruiters must be careful that this method does not intentionally or unintentionally discriminate. The major problem with this recruiting method is that it tends to maintain the status quo of the work force in terms of race, religion, sex, and other features. Those results can be viewed as discriminatory. For example, in the Georgia Power Company case, the company not only limited its recruitment to a few scholastic institutions but also made extensive use of employee referrals. One civil rights expert noted:

Key case

> In *United States v. Georgia Power Company,* the Fifth Circuit Court of Appeals ruled that the respondent's form of recruitment by referrals from present workers had the effect of excluding blacks because it perpetuated the generally all-white composition of its work force. The court stated:
>
> > "Word-of-mouth hiring and interviewing for recruitment only at particular scholastic institutions are practices that are neutral on their face. However, under the facts of the instant case, each operates as a 'built-in-headwind' to blacks and neither is justified by business necessity."[28]

7. RECRUITMENT

3. Advertising

Advertising is another effective method of seeking recruits. Since ads can reach a wider audience than employee referrals or unsolicited walk-ins, many recruiters use them as a key part of their efforts.

Want ads

Want ads describe the job and the benefits, identify the employer, and tell those who are interested how to apply. They are the most familiar form of employment advertising. For highly specialized recruits, ads may be placed in professional journals or out-of-town newspapers located in areas with high concentrations of the desired skills. For example, recruiters in the aerospace industry often advertise in Los Angeles, St. Louis, Dallas-Ft. Worth, and Seattle newspapers because these cities are major aerospace centers.

Want ads have some severe limitations. They may invite thousands of job seekers for one popular job opening and only a few for less attractive jobs. For example, few people apply for door-to-door sales jobs if they know the product is encyclopedias. Furthermore, ideal recruits are probably already employed and are not reading want ads. Finally, advertising for a recruit to replace an incumbent cannot be done secretly with traditional want ads. These limitations are avoided with *blind ads*.

Blind ads

A blind ad is a want ad that does not identify the employer. Interested applicants are asked to send their résumés to a mailbox number at the post office or to the newspaper. The *résumé*, which is a brief summary of the applicant's background, is then forwarded to the employer. These ads allow the opening to remain confidential, prevent countless telephone inquiries, and avoid the public relations problem of disappointed recruits.

The wording of advertisements has a significant impact on the pool of applicants. An advertisement that is written too narrowly may limit the pool of applicants; one written too broadly may attract too many unqualified applicants.

As one writer observed, "Recruitment advertising should be written from the viewpoint of the applicant and his or her motivations rather than exclusively from the point of view of the company."[29] Since the cost of most classified advertising is determined by the size of the advertisement, short blurbs are the norm. These ads usually describe the job duties, outline minimum job qualifications, and tell interested readers how to apply. Short telegraphic phrases and sentences, sometimes written in the second person, are the usual format. Figure 7-2 provides an example. However, some experts doubt that traditional approaches will remain sufficient, particularly when recruiting people with hard-to-find skills or whenever labor markets are tight. As one researcher suggests, employment ads:

Researcher recommendations

... must contain not only information about the job but also information presented in a way that effectively portrays a message about the job and the company. This can't be done if the ad contains information that explains only what responsibilities the job includes, who can be qualified, where it is located, and how and when to apply.[30]

Figure 7-2

A Sample Want Ad

ENGINEERING GRADUATES

Blakely Electronics seeks junior mechanical and electrical engineering trainees for our growing team of engineering professionals. You will work with senior engineers in designing state-of-the-art electronic equipment for home and industry. Qualified applicants will be engineers graduating by the end of this term and wanting immediate employment. Send your résumé and transcripts to: Chuck Norris, Employment Office, Blakely Electronics, P.O. Box 473, Salt Lake City, Utah 84199. Do it today for an exciting career tomorrow.

Blakely Electronics is an equal opportunity employer of minority, female, and handicapped workers.

More important, in today's labor market, where increasing demands are being made for job relevance, quality of work life, and other job satisfaction factors . . . the need for more descriptive job information and information concerning working environment, supervisory style, and organizational climate are necessary.[31]

Another authority suggests:

> Ad layout, design and copy should reflect an accurate image of the company and department represented. It should reflect whether the company is:
>
> ➤ Conservative v. progressive
>
> ➤ Small, medium, or large
>
> ➤ Dynamic v. static
>
> ➤ Expanding v. stabilizing
>
> ➤ Centralized v. decentralized
>
> When evaluating the image and layout of an ad, ask yourself whether it commands attention—both by itself and in comparison with other recruitment advertisements.
> Remember, you're trying to convince qualified applicants to apply. . . . Be sure to emphasize the benefits of the package while being specific enough about requirements and job responsibilities to screen out candidates who are not right. . . .[32]

Placement of advertisements depends on whether you expect potential recruits to be searching for a job or you expect to have to search for applicants. For many common jobs—clerical jobs, for example—want ads are an effective choice. For unusual jobs or ones that are hard to staff, advertisements have to go where the likely applicants are. For engineers, for example, advertisements in professional and trade journals might be appropriate. Advertisements for recruits through other media—billboards, television, and radio, for example—are seldom used because the results seldom justify the expense. However, these approaches may be useful when unemployment is low and the target recruits are not likely to be reading want ads.[33]

Ad design and media selection can be evaluated by monitoring the quality and quantity of responses, using the insights gained to upgrade future employment ads.[34]

4. State Employment Security Agencies

Government unemployment offices

Every state government has a *state employment security agency*. Often called the unemployment office or the employment service, these state agencies match job seekers with job openings. These agencies have resulted from a federal and state partnership which was established in 1933. At the federal level, the U.S. Employment Service sets national guidelines. Within these uniform regulations, state agencies operate more than 2,400 local offices that help more than one-fifth of all unemployed workers to find jobs.

To match candidates with job openings, the employment service in virtually every state uses a statewide *job bank*. It works as follows. When an employer has a job opening, the personnel department voluntarily notifies the employment service of the job and its requirements. Job openings then are computerized and reduced to a printout each workday morning. This updated information helps employment service counselors identify appropriate openings. Data about job seekers are also increasingly computerized so that the matching process can be done electronically.

Two useful spin-offs of job banks are the job information service and *Job-flo*. Both are aimed at matching recruiters and recruits. The *job information service* provides self-service stations within local unemployment offices. Job seekers who know the jobs they want can quickly review the job bank listing without waiting to speak with a counselor. Then they can contact the employer that has the desired opening. *Job-flo* is a monthly report on frequently listed openings from job banks throughout the country. Issued by the U.S. Department of Labor, *Job-flo* is designed to give nationwide exposure to hard-to-fill job openings. It lists pay, duration of unfilled openings, location, and job qualifications. These listings encourage geographic mobility among job hunters, which helps balance supply and demand in the labor market. For example, if a construction boom in the West creates a shortage of carpenters, *Job-flo* reports alert employment offices in the East to advise unemployed carpenters of employment possibilities.

For many years state employment service offices suffered from a poor image. Recruiters often viewed these agencies as a source of unskilled or poorly quali-

EEO legislation

fied workers. Such self-fulfilling attitudes encouraged many skilled workers to use other channels to find employment. However, politicians increasingly see the employment service as an important weapon against unemployment. As a result, new programs such as *Job-flo* have been initiated and funded.[35] These changes and equal employment legislation have encouraged many personnel departments to list all their openings with state agencies to ensure wide exposure. Today, government run employment services are becoming an important source of recruits and services for personnel departments, especially since these services are free to both employers and applicants and listing openings with state unemployment offices helps assure wide exposure for affirmative action efforts.[36]

5. Private Placement Agencies

Private placement firms

Private placement agencies were developed in the vacuum created by the poor image of the public employment service. These for-profit companies—which exist in every major metropolitan area—arose to help employers find capable applicants. Private placement firms take employers' requests for recruits and then solicit job seekers, usually through advertising or among walk-ins. Candidates are matched with employer requests and then told to report to the employer's personnel department for an interview. The matching process conducted by private agencies varies widely. Some placement services carefully prescreen applicants for the personnel department. Other firms simply provide a stream of applicants and let the personnel department do most of the screening.

Users of private placement agencies should realize that payment is handled in one of two ways: either the employer or the applicant pays the placement firm a fee. It commonly equals 10 percent of the first year's salary or one month's wages. *Fee-paid* positions are those openings that the employer agrees to pay. Other positions require the recruits to pay once they are offered a job or begin employment.

Users of private placement agencies should be advised to review carefully any contracts that the agency asks to be signed. Some agencies will provide minimum assistance, being more interested in placement than in the appropriateness of the match between applicant and employer. Even an unsatisfactory placement may therefore lead to a financial obligation on the part of the recruit or recruiter.

6. Professional Search Firms

Professional search firms are much more specialized than placement agencies. *Search firms* usually recruit only specific types of human resources for a fee paid by the employer. For example, some search firms specialize in executive talent, while others use their expertise to find technical and scientific personnel. Perhaps the most significant difference between search firms and placement agencies is their approach. Placement agencies hope to attract applicants through advertising, but search firms actively seek out recruits among the employees of

7. RECRUITMENT

other companies. Although they may advertise, search firms use the telephone as their primary tool to locate and attract prospective recruits.³⁷

> The Nelson Radar Company needed a quality control manager for its assembly line. After several weeks of unsuccessful recruiting effort, the personnel manager hired a search firm. The search firm reviewed the in-house phone directories of competing firms and telephoned the assistant quality control manager at one of Nelson's competitors. The phone call was used to encourage this assistant manager to apply for the position at the Nelson Company.

Headhunters

This brief example illustrates several important points. First, search firms may have in-depth experience with specific types of applicants. Second, search firms are often willing to undertake actions that an employer would not do, such as calling a competitor. Third, some personnel professionals consider search firms unethical because these firms engage in "stealing," "raiding," or "pirating" among their client's competitors. This last point shows why search firms sometimes are called "headhunters."³⁸

7. Educational Institutions

Schools

Schools are another common source of recruits. Many universities, colleges, and vocational schools offer placement assistance to their current students and alumni. This assistance helps employers and graduates to meet and discuss employment opportunities and the applicants' qualifications. Work/study education programs, counselors, and vocational teachers may also provide recruiters with leads to desirable candidates in local high schools.³⁹

Although some applicants sought through educational institutions are experienced, many are not. New entrants are more likely to be swayed by the recruiter's manner and behavior in the interview than by the attributes of the job, the latter being the deciding factor for experienced workers. The success of recruiters at educational institutions and other sources of new entrants may depend very heavily on the recruiter's style.⁴⁰ Educational institutions also offer an excellent source of hiring foreign nationals. Foreign students in domestic schools offer the advantage of being bilingual and bicultural. Some foreign students actually desire jobs with domestic firms to gain experience in addition to their degrees or to secure citizenship.

8. Professional Associations

Professional associations are another source of recruits. Professional groups of engineers, accountants, trainers, and others often maintain placement rosters and job fairs, especially at annual conventions. Some even publish journals that accept classified ads which reach their memberships. A growing number of associations are willing to sell mailing lists classified by geographic area and zip code, a practice that makes direct-mail appeals possible. What makes these associations particularly appealing to recruiters is that members of professional associations are more likely to remain informed of the latest developments in their field, thus, arguably leading to higher-quality applicants from these sources. Another advantage of these sources is that recruiters can zero in on specific specialties, especially in hard-to-fill technical areas.[41]

9. Labor Organizations

Unions

Many people with trade skills—such as carpenters, plumbers, electricians, and others in the construction trades—use the local union as a source of job referrals. In the construction industry, many contractors work on a project basis, sometimes many miles from their home labor market. As a result, the union hiring hall often presents the most efficient way to find qualified tradespeople.

10. Military Operations

Discharged military

Many communities are located near military bases, from which trained people having completed military service leave every day. Mechanics, welders, pilots, heavy equipment operators, and a wide range of other skilled workers can be found through this recruitment channel.[42]

11. Government-funded and Community Training Programs

Many people lack the skills to compete for meaningful jobs. Some are the victims of poor education; others have been displaced by down-sizing, mergers, and bankruptcies resulting from domestic and international competition. In an attempt to reduce unemployment among these groups and provide employers with better qualified workers, government and community organizations have created a variety of training and retraining programs. Some are aimed at specific groups, such as the hard-core unemployed who have experienced long-term underemployment or unemployment. Other programs seek to ease the transition of displaced workers as businesses or entire industries undergo major reductions in employment.[43]

Structural unemployment

Government concern stems from the belief that *some* unemployment is structural in nature. *Structural unemployment* occurs when people are ready, willing, and able to work, but their skills do not match the jobs available. For example, an unemployed coal miner in the Appalachian region of the United States is of little use to an electronics firm that seeks trained assemblers and technicians. Through government-sponsored training and retraining programs, unemployed workers are given skills to make them employable in today's labor markets.

7. RECRUITMENT

One of the problems with these programs has been that the training sometimes prepared people for jobs that were unneeded. For example, trucking deregulation and recession combined to create a surplus of truck drivers in the early 1980s; yet some of the government-sponsored training centers kept graduating truck drivers. Likewise, some training centers have focused on such low-paying jobs that trainees found it economically advantageous to remain on government welfare and assistance programs. For example, some entry-level jobs for which training has been provided—in banks, restaurants, hotels, and motels—proved to pay less than welfare. Nevertheless, whenever unemployment is high, the federal government usually funds training and retraining for the unemployed.

JTPA

One example of this type of legislation is the *Job Training Partnership Act* of 1983. This law provides federal funds to authorized training contractors, often city or state government agencies. These moneys are used to train people in new, employable skills. The Job Training Partnership Act differs from previous government-sponsored training laws because it mandates greater consultation between industry and the government contractors that do the training. As a result of this consultation, it is hoped that graduates will meet the needs of employers. A better match between job openings and training will mean that more of these graduates can leave the welfare and unemployment rolls in favor of meaningful and productive jobs.

Human resource departments that have an ongoing demand for skilled or semiskilled entry-level employees should work closely with their local training centers. These centers can prove to be a low-cost source of recruits who are trained in the specific areas of interest to the company. And since many of the centers are operated by minority groups and often seek trainees from protected classes, their graduates may help the firm meet its affirmative action plans. At the same time, the personnel department can help fulfill societal goals of turning the unemployed into productive, taxpaying citizens.

Temporary Help Agencies

Temps

Most large cities have temporary help agencies that can respond quickly to an employer's need for help. These agencies do not provide recruits. Instead, they are a source of supplemental workers. Temporary help actually work for the agency and are "on loan" to the requesting employer. For temporary jobs—during vacations, flu epidemics, or peak seasons—these agencies can be a better alternative than recruiting new workers for short periods of employment. Some companies—such as Motorola, TRW, Merrill Lynch, Control Data, and IBM—actually rely on temporary workers to fill a part of the company's staffing needs. They use "temps" as a buffer of people who can be terminated quickly without laying off the company's full-time, career-oriented employees when sales fall short of expectations. Besides handling the recruiting and bookkeeping tasks associated with hiring new employees, temporary help agencies often can provide clerical and secretarial talent on short notice—sometimes in less than a day.[44] And when the temporary shortage is over, the company need not lay off surplus workers because temporaries work for the agency, not the company. Temporary workers can be put on layoff without creating unemployment claims against the employer and good temporary workers often can be quickly reassigned by their agencies to other companies. Of course, for jobs that require a detailed understanding of company procedures, the needed training may not be justified for short-duration employment, thus reducing the effectiveness of temps for many jobs. Occasionally, temporary workers are recruited to become permanent employees. However, many of the people who work for temporary help agencies do so because they do not seek long-term, full-time careers. College students, retirees, and others who do not want a long-term job are the bulk of the temporary work force.[45]

Some companies have even established their own job banks of retirees to meet temporary needs. Organizations such as Travelers, Grumman, Wells Fargo, Hewlett-Packard, and others find that retirees have knowledge of company procedures and often a strong work ethic. The Travelers program has more than 700 retirees on its rolls and Wells Fargo draws from among its 6,300 retirees to create an active roster of 650 temporary employees.[46]

13. Leased Employees

"Renting" employees

Similar to for-profit temporary agencies, a slightly different variation actually leases employees to employers as long-term employees. Instead of having to recruit, hire, pay, train, and perform other traditional human resource functions, some companies simply lease some or all of their work force from other organizations. Small businesses, for example, often find the complexities of modern human resource management, with its complex laws, mandated payroll taxes, and other requirements, worth avoiding.

> When Dale Voss bought Noel Ice Co. . . . the first thing he did was fire all the employees.
>
> But the cube-making didn't melt down for a minute. Those same employees were back at the freezers of the Nashville-based company the next day, although another company was signing the paychecks.
>
> Noel joined the growing number of businesses leasing some or all their employees, a strategy that can cut costs and eliminate management headaches ranging from payroll deductions to employer-sponsored health insurance.[47]

14. Departing Employees

An often overlooked source of recruits can be found among departing employees. Many workers leave because they can no longer work the traditional 40-hour workweek. School, child-care needs, and other commitments are the common reasons. Many employees might gladly stay if they could rearrange their hours of work or responsibilities, and a transfer to a part-time job would retain their valuable skills and training.[48] Even if part-time work is not a solution, a temporary

7. RECRUITMENT   213

Buy-backs

leave of absence may satisfy the employee and some future recruiting need of the employer.

Buy-backs are a channel worthy of mention, although personnel specialists and workers tend to avoid them. A *buy-back* occurs when an employee resigns to take another job, and the original employer outbids the new job offer. Even when the authority to enter into a bidding war exists, the manager may discover that other workers expect similar raises. Employees may reject a buy-back attempt because of the ethical issue raised by not reporting to a job that has already been accepted. Besides, what is to prevent the manager from using a blind ad to find a replacement?

15. Open House

A relatively unusual technique of recruiting involves holding an open house. People in the adjacent community are invited to see the company facilities, have refreshments, and maybe view a film about the company. This method has proved successful in recruiting clerical workers when people with office skills are in short supply.[49] G.D. Searle & Co., in Skokie, Illinois, used this method when it had problems recruiting enough clerical help. From the 75 people who attended the open house, the company expected to hire 20 secretaries and clerks.[50]

G.D. Searle

16. International Recruiting

Different standards

Recruitment in foreign countries presents recruiters with special challenges. In advanced industrial nations, recruiters will find many of the same channels that exist in North America. Additional help can sometimes be obtained from the embassy or consulate offices. The use of consultants or other professionals may be necessary for higher-level positions that require social acceptance, school ties, and other appropriate hallmarks of success which may be considered more important than past experience or other more traditional criteria used in the home country.

In developing nations, private or public support services may be less common or less developed. Beyond employee referrals and embassy assistance, recruiters may find that they have to develop their own network of contacts, ranging from newspaper reporters to government officials in the host country. Of particular importance are cultural conflicts, if any. Historical animosities may exist between different factions within the country, whether these be different native tribes, elements of a formal caste systems, or rivals by virtue of long-standing tradition.

International recruitment has many similarities with domestic efforts; unfortunately, the problems encountered by recruiters are often more difficult to resolve. Members of two-career families may be reluctant to apply for overseas jobs. Immigration barriers, employment laws, and other roadblocks may prevent a promising recruit from becoming a bona fide applicant because of concerns about the spouse's employment possibilities. Costs are another problem. Cost-of-living differentials, moving expenses, education for children, income tax require-

Figure 7-3

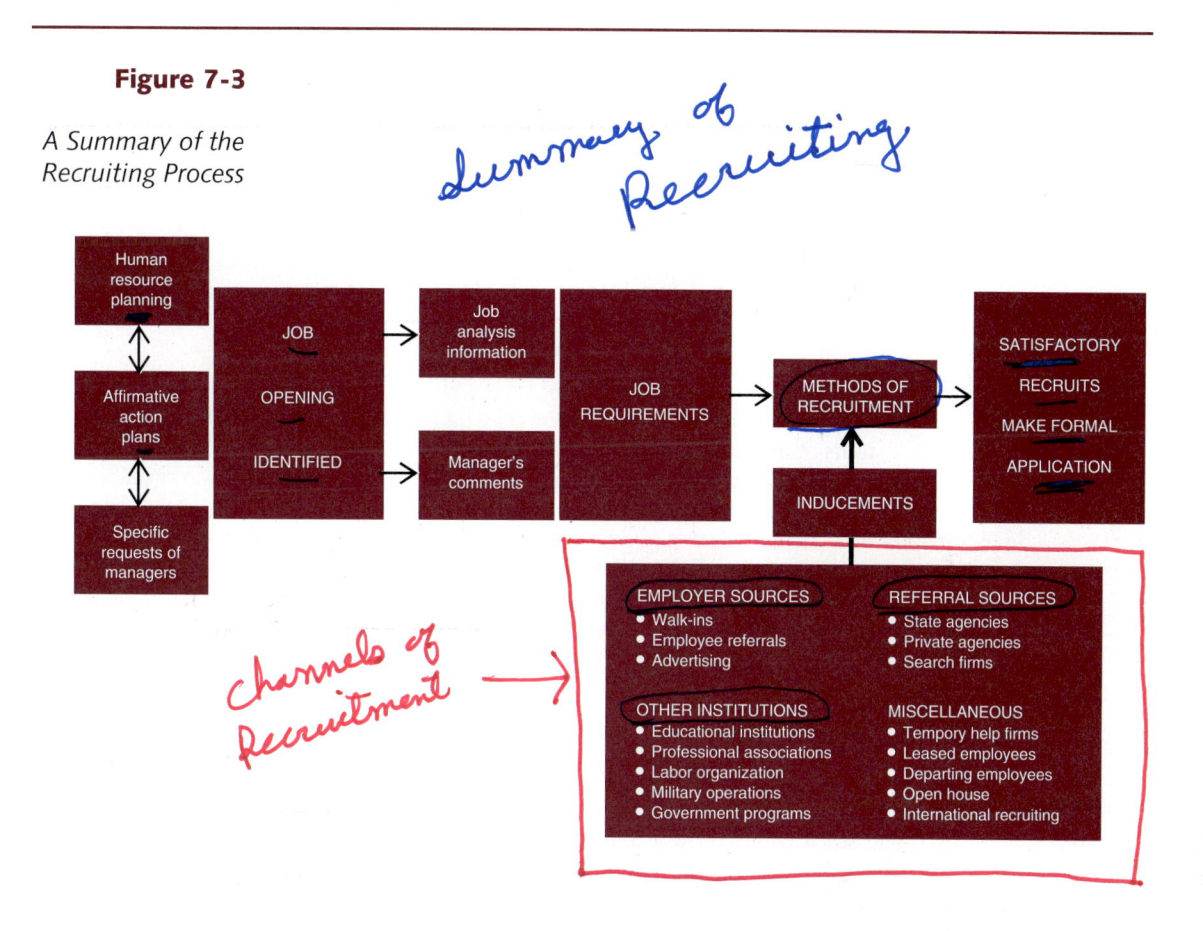

A Summary of the Recruiting Process

Summary of Recruiting

```
Human resource planning ⇄ Affirmative action plans ⇄ Specific requests of managers
   ↓
JOB OPENING IDENTIFIED → Job analysis information / Manager's comments → JOB REQUIREMENTS → METHODS OF RECRUITMENT → SATISFACTORY RECRUITS MAKE FORMAL APPLICATION
                                                                              ↑
                                                                         INDUCEMENTS
```

channels of Recruitment →

EMPLOYER SOURCES
- Walk-ins
- Employee referrals
- Advertising

REFERRAL SOURCES
- State agencies
- Private agencies
- Search firms

OTHER INSTITUTIONS
- Educational institutions
- Professional associations
- Labor organization
- Military operations
- Government programs

MISCELLANEOUS
- Tempory help firms
- Leased employees
- Departing employees
- Open house
- International recruiting

ments of the home and foreign location, and housing costs are common issues. These complexities apply whether the recruiter is trying to fill an overseas position with a domestic employee or is trying to recruit a foreign national into the home country.[51]

When recruiting internationally, recruiters should become familiar with the employment practices in the foreign country. Not only are employment contracts different, but cultural expectations may lead to unforeseen problems. For example, some Japanese regard working for foreign firms as less prestigious than staying with a Japanese-owned company. In Mexico, recruiting from competitors is seldom done, so the common practice of hiring from competitors as a way to ensure a fast startup may have to be rethought by recruiters interested in staffing jobs there.[52]

Figure 7-3 summarizes the recruiting process and identifies each of the commonly used channels of recruitment. As the figure indicates, the recruitment process ends when a recruit makes formal application, usually by completing an application blank.

Raiding in Mexico

7. RECRUITMENT 215

JOB APPLICATION BLANKS

Job application blanks

The *job application blank* collects information about recruits in a uniform manner. Even when recruits volunteer detailed information about themselves, applications are often required so that the information gathered is comparable. Each personnel department generally designs its own application blank. Nevertheless, common features exist. Figure 7-4 provides an example of an application blank and its major divisions. Although the application blank is a fairly typical one, it may contain questions that are illegal under some state jurisdictions. As one writer observed:

> While the majority of employers may be aware of . . . relevant federal regulations, many aren't aware that equal opportunity laws in some states are more stringent than federal requirements. For example, while federal regulations require the employer to be able to justify preemployment inquiries as bona fide occupational qualifications (BFOQs) upon request, Ohio law says inquiries into inappropriate areas (i.e., sex, race, etc.) must be certified by the Ohio Civil Rights Commission prior to their use.
> In states where local laws are more stringent than federal law, job application forms are an even more critical concern. . . .[53]

Research observation

It is not enough to be in compliance with just the federal laws. State laws are important, too. When the two levels of law conflict, usually the most stringent one must be followed. And ignorance of the state laws is no defense in court. In one study of application blanks, two researchers reported that 73 percent of the forms had one or more inappropriate preemployment inquiries.[54] The remainder of this chapter discusses the various parts of the application blank shown in Figure 7-4.

Personal Data

Most application blanks begin with a request for personal data. Requests for name, address, and telephone number are nearly universal. But requests for some personal data, such as place of birth, sex, race, religion, or national origin, may lead to charges of discrimination. Since it is illegal to discriminate against applicants who are members of a protected class, an unsuccessful applicant may conclude that rejection was motivated by discrimination when discriminatory questions are asked. The personnel department must be able to show that these questions are job-related.

ADA

Applications may solicit information about health, height, weight, handicaps that relate to the job, major illnesses, and claims for injuries. Here again, there may be legal problems, since employers may not discriminate against the handicapped under the *Americans with Disabilities Act*. The burden of proof to show the job-relatedness of such questions falls on the employer. Information about marital status, dependents, and whom to contact in a medical emergency is also

216   II. PREPARATION AND SELECTION

Figure 7-4

A Typical Application Blank

BLAKELY ELECTRONICS, INC.
"An Equal Opportunity Employer"

Application for Employment

Personal Data

1. Name _____

2. Address _____ 3. Phone number _____

_____

Employment Status

4. Type of employment sought _____ Full-time _____ Part-time

_____ Permanent _____ Temporary

5. Job or position sought _____

6. Date of availability, if hired _____

7. Are you willing to accept other employment if the position you seek is unavailable?

_____ Yes _____ No

8. Approximate wages/salary desired $_____ per month.

Education and Skills

9. Circle the highest grade completed:

    8 9 10 11 12   13 14 15 16   Graduate School

    High School   College

10. Please provide the following information about your education. (Include high school, trade or vocational schools, and colleges.)

    a. School name _____ Degree(s) or diploma _____

        School address _____

    b. School name _____ Degree(s) or diploma _____

        School address _____

11. Please describe your work skills. (Include machines, tools, equipment, and other abilities you possess.) _____

_____

Work History

Beginning with your most recent or current employer, please provide the following information about each employer. (If additional space is needed, please use an additional sheet.)

12. a. Employer _____ Dates of employment _____

    Employer's address _____

    Job title _____ Supervisor's name _____

    Job duties _____

    Starting pay _____ Ending pay _____

7. RECRUITMENT

Figure 7-4

(continued)

b. Employer _____ Dates of employment _____
Employer's address _____
Job title _____ Supervisor's name _____
Job duties _____
Starting pay _____ Ending pay _____

Military Background
If you were ever a member of the Armed Services, please complete the following:

13. Branch of service _____ Rank at discharge _____
    Dates of service _____ to _____
    Responsibilities _____

Memberships, Awards, and Hobbies
14. What are your hobbies? _____
15. List civic/professional organizations to which you have belonged. _____

_____

16. List any awards you have received. _____

_____

References
In the space provided, list three references who are not members of your family:

17. a. Name _____ Address _____
    b. Name _____ Address _____
    c. Name _____ Address _____

18. Please feel free to add any other information you think should be considered in evaluating your application.

_____

_____

_____

By my signature on this application, I:
a. Authorize the verification of the above information and any other necessary inquiries that may be needed to determine my suitability for employment.
b. Affirm that the above information is true to the best of my knowledge.
c. Realize that falsification may be grounds for dismissal.

_____ Date _____
Applicant's Signature

commonly sought. Here again, this information cannot be used to discriminate against members of a protected class.

Employment Status

Some questions concern the applicant's employment objective and availability. Included here are questions about the position sought, willingness to accept other positions, date available for work, salary or wages desired, and acceptability of part-time and full-time work schedules. This information helps a recruiter match the applicant's objective and the organization's needs. Broad or uncertain responses can prevent the application from being considered.

Education and Skills

Skills

The education and skills section of the application blank is designed to uncover the job seeker's abilities. Traditionally, education has been a major criterion in evaluating job seekers, but its importance has been diminished by the requirement that personnel departments show how education is job-related. Educational attainment does imply certain abilities and, therefore, is a common request on virtually all applications. Questions about specific skills are also used to judge prospective employees. More than any other part of the application blank, the skills section reveals the suitability of a candidate for a particular job.

Work History

Experience

Job seekers must frequently list their past jobs. From this information, a recruiter can tell whether the applicant is one who hops from job to job or is someone likely to be a long-service employee. A quick review of the stated job title, duties, and responsibilities also shows whether the candidate is a potentially capable applicant. If this information does not coincide with what an experienced recruiter expects to see, it may be that the candidate exaggerated job title, duties, or responsibilities.

Military Background

Many applications request information on military experience. Questions usually include date of discharge, branch of service, and rank at discharge. This information helps explain the applicant's background and ability to function in a structured environment, and it suggests specialized training. Increasingly, applications omit this information to avoid questions of discrimination against veterans.

Memberships, Awards, and Hobbies

Recruits are more than potential workers. They are also representatives of the employer in the community. For managerial and professional positions, off-the-job activities may make one candidate preferable to another. Memberships in civic, social, and professional organizations that are related to the job indicate the recruit's concern about community and career. Awards show recognition for noteworthy achievements. Hobbies may reinforce important job skills and indicate outlets for stress and frustration, or opportunities for further service to the company. Some companies have dropped questions in this area since such activities are often unclearly related to the job requirements.

Related insights

> When handed a pile of completed applications for manager of the car- and truck-leasing department, Frank Simmons (the personnel manager for a New Orleans Ford dealership) sorted the completed applications into two piles. When asked what criteria were being used to sort the applicants, he said, "I'm looking for golfers. Many of our largest car and truck accounts are sold on Saturday afternoons at the golf course."

References

Besides the traditional references from friends or previous employers, applications may ask for other "referencelike" information. Questions may explore the job seeker's criminal record, credit history, friends and relatives who work for the employer, or previous employment with the organization. Criminal record, credit history, and friends or relatives who work for the company may be important considerations if the job involves sensitive information, cash, or other valuables. Job-relatedness must be substantiated if these criteria discriminate against some protected group. Previous employment with the organization means that there are records of the applicant's performance.

Signature Line

Candidates usually are required to sign and date their applications. Adjacent to the signature line, a blanket authorization commonly appears. This authorization allows the employer to check references, verify medical, criminal, or financial records, and undertake any other necessary investigations. Some employers include an "at will" statement where the employee acknowledges that his or her employment is at the will of the employer—only for so long as the employer wishes to retain the employee. Another common provision of the signature line is a statement that the applicant affirms the information in the application to be true and accurate as far as is known. Although many people give this clause little thought, falsification of an application blank is grounds for discharge in most organizations.

"At will" statements

II. PREPARATION AND SELECTION

When the application is completed and signed, the recruitment process is finished. Its unanswered questions and implications continue to affect human resource management. In fact, the end of the recruitment process marks the beginning of the selection process, which is discussed in the next chapter.

SUMMARY

RECRUITMENT IS the process of finding and attracting capable applicants to apply for employment. Although line managers are often involved, much of the recruitment process is the responsibility of professionals in the human resource department, called recruiters. Recruiters should be aware of the constraints and challenges surrounding the recruitment process before they undertake to find suitable applicants. At a minimum, recruiters should be familiar with the organization's policies, human resource and affirmative action plans, environmental conditions, job requirements, costs, possible incentives that can be used to induce recruits to become applicants, and the recruiter's own habits.

Recruiters pursue applicants through a variety of channels. Although walk-ins and write-ins are common sources, the growing diversity in the work force and changing demographics often require recruiters to be more proactive. Employee referrals and advertisements are other channels. To help recruiters, a variety of public and private organizations exist, such as state unemployment offices, private placement agencies, and search firms. Many institutions—schools, labor organizations, professional associations, military facilities, and government and community training programs—also offer placement assistance which recruiters can access. Temporary, leased, and departing employees are other sources of potential recruits.

International recruitment involves many of the same issues as domestic staffing, except the issues are often far more complex, regardless of whether the recruiter seeks to bring someone to the home country or to send someone overseas. Of particular importance, recruiters must be aware of national differences in recruitment practices and employee expectations.

Completed application blanks from ready, willing, and able applicants mark the end of the recruitment process and the beginning of the selection process, discussed in the next chapter.

Terms for Review

- ✓ Recruitment
- ✓ Walk-ins
- ✓ Write-ins
- ✓ Blind ads
- ✓ Résumé
- ✓ State employment security agency
- ✓ Job bank
- ✓ Job information service
- ✓ Job-flo
- ✓ Search firms
- ✓ Structural unemployment
- ✓ Job Training Partnership Act
- ✓ Buy-back

Review and Discussion Questions

1. What background information should a recruiter know before beginning to recruit job seekers?

2. Under what circumstances would a blind ad be a useful recruiting technique?

3. Suppose that after months of insufficient recognition (and two years without a raise), you were to accept an offer from another firm for $2,500 a year more than your present salary. When you told your boss that you were resigning, you were told how crucial you were to the business and were offered a raise of $4,250 a year. What would you do? Why? What problems might arise if you were to accept the buy-back?

4. Suppose you were a manager who just accepted the resignation of a crucial employee. After you send your request for a replacement to the personnel department, how could you help the recruiter do a more effective job?

5. If your company's regular college recruiter became ill and you were assigned to recruit at six universities in two weeks, what information would you need before leaving on the trip?

6. In small businesses, managers usually handle their own recruiting. What methods would you use for the following situations? Why?

 a. The regular janitor is going on vacation for three weeks.

 b. Your secretary has the flu.

 c. Two more salespeople are needed: one to help local customers and one to open a sales office in Puerto Rico.

 d. Your only chemist is retiring and must be replaced with a highly skilled individual.

7. "If a job application omits important questions, needed information about recruits will not be available. But if a needless question is asked, the information can be ignored by the recruiter without any other complications." Do you agree or disagree? Why?

8. When recruiting a worker to potentially fill a job in another country, what issues are likely to arise that complicate the international move but would likely not arise in a domestic opening?

INCIDENT 7-1
The International Nurse Connection

Several hospitals and large nursing homes in New York faced an ongoing shortage of nurses. Although the problem was not new, the high occupancy (called a high census in the health care field) of the hospitals forced them to use an excessive amount of overtime to cover all shifts and weekends. The nurses were complaining, and many had resigned. Many other nurses were specializing to achieve higher pay levels or were looking for positions in administration, away from hands-on nursing. Although the shortage of nurses affected all nursing classifications, it was most acute among general-duty nurses who attended to patients while they recovered in the hospital or were assigned to nursing homes.

The shortage had become so critical that even the temporary nursing services were unable to fill all the requests, prompting still more nurses to leave the area's hospitals and nursing homes in favor of higher-paying jobs offered through temporary work by visiting nurse services.

Several New York area hospital human resource directors met to explore the possibility of recruiting degreed nurses from overseas. Given the high proportion of Spanish-speaking patients, the human resource group decided to recruit nurses from the Philippines, Spain, and Latin American countries. A Spanish-speaking recruiter from one of the hospitals was selected by the group to explore the possibilities of recruiting nurses overseas for New York area hospitals.

Assume you were given the responsibility for developing a recruitment strategy for this consortium of health care organizations:

1. Identify the major roadblocks you might encounter in actually recruiting these nurses.

2. What recruitment channels would you use to find and attract qualified applicants? Why?

References

1. Sara L. Rynes and Alison E. Barber, "Applicant Application Strategies: An Organizational Perspective," *Academy of Management Review*, vol. 15, no. 2 (1990), p. 286.

2. Jill Andresky Fraser, "The Making of a Work Force," *Business Month* (Sept. 1989), p. 58–62.

3. Joshua Hyatt, "Hire Employees," *Inc.* (March 1990), pp. 106–108.

4. Brian Bremmer, "Among Restaurateurs, It's Dog Eat Dog," *Business Week* (Jan. 9, 1989), p. 86.

5. Shawn Tully, "The Hunt for the Global Manager," *Fortune* (May 21, 1990), p. 140.

6. Ibid., p. 144.

7. C.S. Manegold, Bill Powell, and Yuriko Hoshiai, "Hang Up the Help-Wanted Sign," *Newsweek* (July 16, 1990), p. 39.

8. "More Firms Offer Benefits to Part-timers, Survey Shows," *Resource* (Nov. 1985), p. 105.

9. Stephanie Strom, "The Art of Luring Japanese Executives to American Firms," *The New York Times*, National ed. (March 25, 1990), p. 12.

10. Jeanne C. Poole and E. Theodore Kantz, "An EEO/AA Program That Exceeds Quotas—It Targets Biases," *Personnel Journal* (Jan. 1987), p. 104. See also Mary Green Miner and John B. Miner, *Employee Selection within the Law* (Washington, D.C.: Bureau of National Affairs, 1978), pp. 25–26.

11. Laura M. Graves and Gary N. Powell, "An Investigation of Sex Discrimination in Recruiters' Evaluations of Actual Applicants," *Journal of Applied Psychology*, vol. 73, no. 1 (1988), pp. 20–29. See also Jean Powell Kirnan, John A. Farley, and Kurt F. Geisinger, "The Relationship between Recruiting Source, Applicant Quality, and Hire Performance: An Analysis by Sex, Ethnicity, and Age," *Personnel Psychology*, vol. 42 (1989), pp. 293–308.

12. B. Posner, "Comparing Recruiter, Student, and Faculty Perceptions of Important Applicant and Job Characteristics," *Personnel Psychology*, vol. 33, pp. 329–339.

13. Maria E. Recio and Robert Neff, "The Immigration Bill: Business Joins the Border Patrol," *Business Week* (Oct. 27, 1986), pp. 41–42.

14. Bruno Lopez, "Mexican Leaders, Scholars Differ on Effects of U.S. Immigration Bill," *The Miami Herald* (Nov. 2, 1986), pp. a10–a11.

15. Selwyn Feinstein, "Recruiting Promises Take on New Substance with Court Decision," *The Wall Street Journal*, Midwest ed. (Sept. 30, 1986), p. 1.

16. "What the ADA Means to You," *Recruitment Today* (Summer 1990), pp. 6, 8, 10. See also Susan R. Meisinger, *Legal Report—The Americans with Disabilities Act of 1990: A New Challenge for Human Resource Managers* (Alexandria, Va.: Society for Human Resource Management, 1990), pp. 1–16.

17. "Disabled Win at Pizza Hut," *Business Month* (Sept. 1989), p. 16.

18. Owen B. Butler, "Why Johnny Can't Get a Job," *Fortune* (Oct. 28, 1985), pp. 163–168.

19. "HRM Update: Recruiter Work Loads," *Personnel Administrator* (Sept. 1986), p. 16.

20. Jeffrey J. Hallett, "Why Does Recruitment Cost So Much?" *Personnel Administrator* (Nov. 1986), p. 22.

21. Sal D. Rinella and Robert J. Kopecky, "Burger King Hooks Employees with Educational Incentives," *Personnel Journal* (Oct. 1989), pp. 90–99. See also Rynes and Barber, op. cit., pp. 286–310; and Liz Amante, "Help Wanted: Creative Recruitment Tactics," *Personnel* (Oct. 1989), pp. 32–36.

22. Allan Halcrow, "Child Care: The Latchkey Option," *Personnel Journal* (July 1986), p. 12.

23. "HRM Update: Magnetic Appeal," *Personnel Administrator* (Oct. 1986), p. 14.

24. "Benefits Preferences of New Hires," *Small Business Reports* (Jan. 1989), p. 78.

25. Mary Ann Von Glinow, "Reward Strategies for Attracting, Evaluating, and Retaining Professionals," *Human Resource Management*, vol. 24, no. 2 (Summer 1985), pp. 191–206. See also Linda B. Robin, "Troubleshoot Recruitment Problems," *Personnel Journal* (Sept. 1988), pp. 94–96.

26. Chris Chen, "TRW S&D Strives to be the Preferred Employer," *Personnel Journal* (July 1990), pp. 70–73.

27. Allan Halcrow, "Employees Are Your Best Recruiters," *Personnel Journal* (Nov. 1988), pp. 42–48. See also Jennifer J. Laabs, "The Pizza Party Incentive: New Life for TJ Max's Referral Program," *Recruitment Today* (Summer 1990), pp. 48–49.

28. Richard Peres, *Dealing with Employment Discrimination* (New York: McGraw-Hill Book Company, 1978), p. 20.

29. Van M. Evans, "Recruitment Advertising in the '80's," *Personnel Administrator* (March 1978), p. 20. See also Jennifer Koch, "Ads with Flair," *Personnel Journal* (Oct. 1989), pp. 46–55.

30. James W. Schreier, "Deciphering Messages in Recruitment Ads," *Personnel Administrator* (March 1983), p. 35. See also Nancy A. Mason and John A. Belt, "Effectiveness of Specificity in Recruitment Advertising," *Journal of Management*, vol. 12, no. 3 (Fall 1986), pp. 425–432.

31. Schreier, op. cit., p. 39.

32. Cathy Edwards, "Aggressive Recruitment: The Lessons of High-Tech Hiring," *Personnel Journal* (Jan. 1986), pp. 41–48. See also Margaret Magnus, "Is Your Recruitment All It Can Be?" *Personnel Journal* (Feb. 1987), pp. 54–63.

33. Margaret Magnus, "TV Channel's Recruitment Effort," *Recruitment Today* (August 1988), pp. 86–88. See also Jennifer Koch, "Applicants Tune in Radio," *Recruitment Today* (Fall 1989), pp. 7–8, 10–12.

34. Edwards, op. cit.

35. Neale Baxter, "Job-Flo: How to Learn If There's a Job in Dallas When You're Jobless in Des Moines," *Occupational Outlook Quarterly* (Summer 1976), p. 2. See also James M. Carter, "The Role of the Job Bank in the Placement Process," *Monthly Labor Review* (Dec. 1972), pp. 28–29.

36. "Cooperation Called Key in Recruitment," *Resource* (August 1988), pp. 1, 6–7.

37. Kenneth J. Cole, *The Headhunter Strategy: How to Make it Work for You* (New York: John Wiley & Sons Inc., 1985).

38. Ibid. See also John Byrne, "The New Headhunters," *Business Week* (Feb. 6, 1990), pp. 63–71. See also Claudia H. Deutsch, "Inviting the Headhunters Inside," *The New York Times*, National ed. (August 5, 1990), sec. 3, part 2, p. 25.

39. Patrick C. Ross, "How to Find the Perfect Intern," Recruitment Today (Spring 1990), pp. 40–42. See also "Precruitment," *Personnel Administrator* (Nov. 1988), p. 21; and Kermit R. Davis, William F. Giles, and Hubert S. Field, "Opting for Benefits," *Personnel Administrator* (August 1988), pp. 62–66.

40. Gary N. Powell, "Effects of Job Attributes and Recruiting Practices on Applicant Decisions: A Comparison," *Personnel Psychology*, vol. 37 (1984), pp. 721–732.

41. Gloria Glickstein and Donald C.Z. Ramer, "The Alternative Employment Marketplace," *Personnel Administrator* (Feb. 1988), pp. 100–104.

42. Patrick Townsend, "A Practical Guide for Hiring a Retired Military Officer," *Personnel Administrator* (June 1984), pp. 67–68, 70, 72–73. See also Holly Rawlinson, "Turn to the Military for Talent," *Recruitment Today* (August 1988), pp. 23–24.

43. "Cooperation Called Key in Recruitment," op. cit.

44. William Smith, "They Serve Two Masters," *Personnel Administrator* (April 1988), pp. 112–114, 116.

45. Harold E. Johnson, "Older Workers Help Meet Employment Needs," *Personnel Journal* (May 1988), pp. 100–105.

46. "Retiree Job Banks Growing in Popularity," Working Age (Jan.–Feb. 1990), pp. 1–2.

47. Mariann Caprino, "Leased Employees Save Money for Most Firms," *The Miami Herald* (April 16, 1989), p. cl. See also Suzanne Woolley, "Give Your Employees a Break—By Leasing Them," *Business Week* (August 14, 1989), p. 135.

48. William B. Werther, Jr., "Part-timers: Overlooked and Undervalued," *Business Horizons* (Feb. 1975), pp. 13–20.

49. Roberta M. Kenney, "The Open House Complements Recruiting Strategies," *Personnel Administrator* (March 1982), pp. 27–32.

50. "Open House: It's a New Technique for Employers to Find the Workers They Want," *The Wall Street Journal*, Western ed. (May 23, 1978), p. 1.

51. Carole Gould, "A Checklist for Accepting a Job Abroad," *The New York Times*, National ed. (July 17, 1988), p. 33. See also Faye Rice, "Should You Work for a Foreigner?" *Fortune* (August 1, 1988), pp. 123, 126, 130, 134.

52. Brian O'Reilly, "Doing Business on Mexico's Volcano," *Fortune* (August 29, 1988), pp. 72–74.

53. Carl Camden and Bill Wallace, "Job Application Forms: A Hazardous Employment Practice," *Personnel Administrator* (March 1983), p. 31.

54. Ibid.

Organizations have always been concerned with attracting and selecting the right types of employees.
SARA L. RYNES AND ALISON E. BARBER[1]

One of the most perplexing problems that face personnel administrators today is . . . the communication of misleading and/or fraudulent information by job applicants on their resumes, applications and during employment interviews.
RICHARD D. BROUSSARD AND DALTON E. BRANNEN[2]

SELECTION

CHAPTER OBJECTIVES

After studying this chapter, you should be able to:
1. EXPLAIN the dependency of human resource activities on the selection process.
2. DESCRIBE the standards found in the EEOC's Uniform Guidelines on Employee Selection.
3. DISCUSS the importance of using a differential approach with multiple measures in selecting a diverse workforce.
4. EXPLAIN the importance of validity and reliability in employee selection.
5. CONDUCT an employment interview and avoid the major pitfalls.
6. DESCRIBE the supervisor's role in the selection process and in realistic job previews.

p 229-258

RECRUITMENT SEEKS to create a pool of suitable applicants. Once that pool has been assembled, the selection process begins. Although in many cases the final hiring decision may be made by the immediate supervisor or manager, the human resource department's role is to validate applicants as to their potential suitability. This process involves a series of steps with multiple evaluation points which add time and complexity to the hiring process. The time and complexity involved can lead to frustration among applicants who need jobs and operating managers who need their job openings filled. However, making valid hiring decisions requires several important steps that cannot be overlooked. By way of introduction, consider an overview of the hiring process at Merrill Lynch, Pierce, Fenner & Smith Inc., the largest securities firm in the United States.

Merrill Lynch

Applicants for the position of account executive at Merrill Lynch complete an application, take a written test, and undergo an interview. But none of these steps prepares them for the account-executive simulation test. As described by a reporter for The Wall Street Journal, *the test can be unnerving.*

"Welcome to the Merrill Lynch account-executive simulation exercise, or, as dubbed by some, the Merrill Lynch stress test. It's a nail-biting three hours . . . that leaves many longing for the good old days of calculus finals.

The stakes are high, too. Those taking part in the simulation . . . are applicants for the job of account executive, or stockbroker. . . . The simulation exercise is designed to gauge how they will perform under conditions similar to those that a real stockbroker faces."[3]

The test works by telling each applicant that he or she is replacing a stockbroker who has gone to another office. The stockbroker left the client book, which describes the accounts of each client. In addition, the applicants are given a variety of unanswered memos, letters, and telephone messages that they must sort through and take action on. In the background, recorded sounds of a brokerage office are played to add an air of confusing noises, shouts, telephone rings, and other unexpected distractions. During the three hours, fictitious clients call, and other messages and reports are dropped on the applicant's "desk." As one applicant commented an hour after the simulation was over, "I just can't calm down. It was a real high."[4]

The point of this illustration is simply that the simulation exercise is only one part of Merrill Lynch's selection process. Other steps precede and follow it. Although most employers do not use a screening device that is this elaborate, all employers put applicants through a selection process. The *selection process* is a series of specific steps used to decide which recruits should be hired. The process begins when recruits apply for employment and ends with the hiring decision. In the steps in between, the department and the hiring manager match the employment needs of the applicant and the organization.

8. SELECTION

229

In many human resource departments, recruiting and selection are combined and called the *employment function*. In large departments, the employment function is the responsibility of the employment manager. In smaller departments, personnel managers handle these duties.[5] Employment is often the primary reason for the department's existence, since the selection process is central to the human resource function. Improper selection causes the department to fail at the objectives set forth in Chapter 1 and the challenges discussed throughout this book. Therefore, it is not an exaggeration to say that selection is central to the success of the department and even the organization.

To underscore how crucial selection can be, consider the increased use of litigation against employers who are finding that they may become liable for the criminal acts of those they hire.[6] When employers are negligent in hiring or retaining employees who are likely to be harmful to others, those injured may sue and win, as suggested by the following examples:

Negligent hiring

> A judgment was rendered against the Fort Worth Cab and Baggage Company for nearly $5 million after one of its drivers raped a passenger in his cab. An Illinois court ordered the Apollo Detective Agency to pay $25,000 to the victim of a sexual assault by one of its security guards in the building the guard was assigned to protect. A Maryland landlord reportedly settled a similar suit for $375,000.[7]

Attention to the employment process may be the most important aspect of human resource management, and it may be one of the most important actions taken by a line manager. An organization cannot perform better than the quality of the people it hires. And when the selection process discussed in this chapter does not weed out unacceptable or dangerous applicants, legal and financial risks result.[8]

INPUTS AND CHALLENGES TO SELECTION

As Figure 8-1 suggests, the selection process relies on three helpful inputs. Job analysis information provides the description of the jobs, the human specifications, and the performance standards each job requires. Human resource plans identify likely job openings and allow selection to proceed in a logical and effective manner. Finally, recruits form a pool of applicants from which employees are selected. At the same time, other challenges to the selection process limit the actions of human resource specialists and line managers. Policies against discrimination reinforce external prohibitions, for example, and internal decrees may create additional restrictions. For example, policies that prohibit layoffs further societal objectives but may restrict the available pool of applicants.

HRP plans

Tradeoffs

Internally generated challenges include the following tradeoff: Operating managers want to fill job vacancies promptly with the most reasonably qualified people available. Line managers frequently wait until a staffing need is apparent before sending a requisition to the human resource department. Normal internal

230   II. PREPARATION AND SELECTION

Figure 8-1

Dependency of Personnel Management Activities on the Selection Process

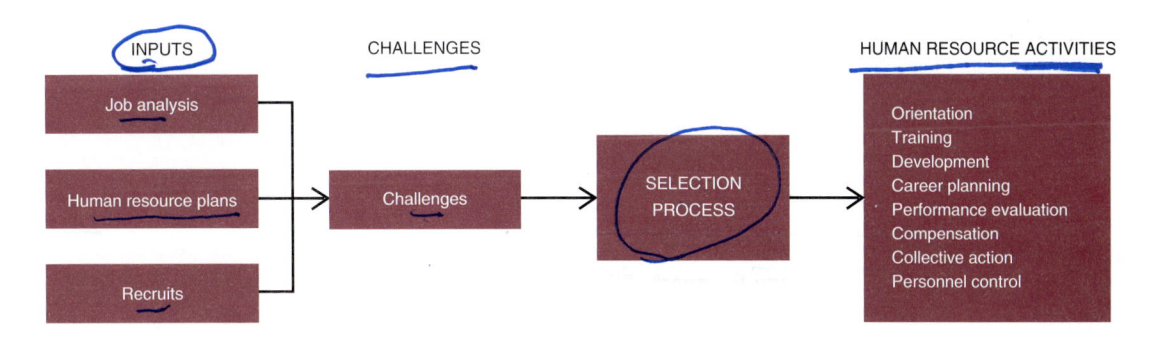

INPUTS	CHALLENGES		HUMAN RESOURCE ACTIVITIES
Job analysis			Orientation
Human resource plans	Challenges	SELECTION PROCESS	Training / Development / Career planning / Performance evaluation / Compensation / Collective action / Personnel control
Recruits			

posting requirements may give present employees a week or longer to apply for the opening. Days, even weeks, may be required to evaluate these internal applicants. If an acceptable candidate is selected, weeks or months may pass before that person can be released from his or her present job to fill the new opening. When no internal applicants are suitable, the external recruiting and selection process adds more weeks or even months before the opening is filled. Although using computerized tracking as part of the human resource information system can speed up the department's processing,⁹ line managers see days slip into weeks or months and then pressure employment managers for action. On the other hand, quick action may mean qualified applicants are few or nonexistent. Whichever tradeoff—quickness or quality—employment specialists make, criticism is likely to result.

Computerized HRIS tracking

To succeed, employment managers must overcome a variety of challenges that affect the selection process. Otherwise, the human resource activities summarized in Figure 8-1 (discussed later in the book) lose much of their effectiveness, and the organization must contend with improperly selected workers.

SELECTION: AN OVERVIEW

Not one sequence

The selection process is a series of steps through which applicants pass. A typical set of steps is suggested in Figure 8-2. Although the sequence of steps may vary from firm to firm—with some steps even taking place simultaneously—

ideally, the process determines the candidates who are likely to be successful and eliminates those likely to fail.[10] Within each step, multiple approaches help distinguish between performance-related and non-performance-related issues, which may arise, for example, from the cultural and ethnic diversity of those in the applicant pool.[11] Ultimately, the selection decisions must focus on performance-related issues if the selection process is to contribute to the firm's success. At the same time, selection is strongly influenced by whether candidates are being picked from within or outside the firm, the availability of applicants, and equal employment opportunity challenges. These issues will be discussed before examining each step in the selection process.

Internal Selection

Succession planning (discussed in Chapter 6, "Human Resource Planning") identifies potential internal candidates. With this information stored in the HRIS, internal selection can be accelerated greatly.

Citibank

At Citibank in New York City, the selection process has been simplified and computerized in order to match present employees with internal openings. The "Job Match" selection system rests upon matching a profile of candidates for a nonprofessional job with the requirements of the job. The specific tasks required of the job are programmed into the computer along with the specific abilities of employees. Those employees with the highest match for a given opening are then considered for the job. One shortcoming of the Job Match system is that it does not consider nontask factors, such as whether the employee actually wants the job.[12]

With internal applicants, some steps in Figure 8-2 can be scaled down or eliminated. For example, there is seldom a need to provide a preliminary reception of applicants, verify references, or do medical evaluations. But when external applicants are being considered, the steps in Figure 8-2 are common.

Selection Ratio

Toyota's flood of applicants

Some jobs are so hard to fill that there are few applicants. Low-paying jobs or openings for extremely specialized work are examples of positions with small selection ratios. A *selection ratio* is the relationship between the number of applicants hired and the total number of applicants available. A ratio of one hiree to 25 applicants, or 1:25, is an example of a large ratio; a small selection ratio is 1:2. Attractive jobs with attractive employers can have very large selection ratios, as Toyota experienced when it had 120,000 applicants for 1700 jobs in its Kentucky plant,[13] or a selection ration of about 1:70. A small selection ratio means there are

Figure 8-2

Steps in the Selection Process

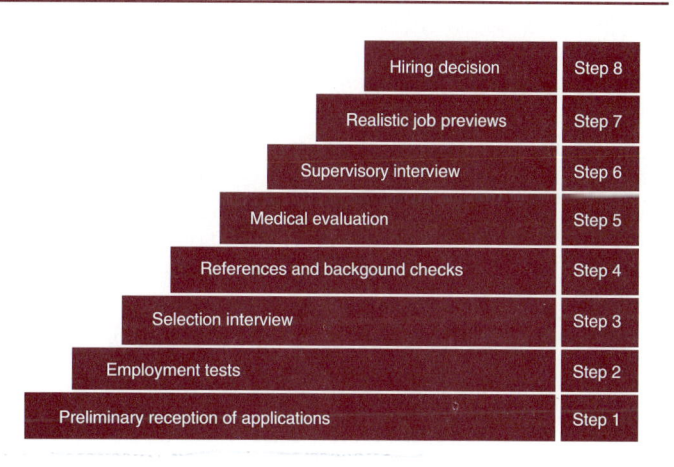

Hiring decision	Step 8
Realistic job previews	Step 7
Supervisory interview	Step 6
Medical evaluation	Step 5
References and backgound checks	Step 4
Selection interview	Step 3
Employment tests	Step 2
Preliminary reception of applications	Step 1

few applicants from which to select. In many instances a small selection ratio also means a low quality of recruits. The ratio is computed as follows:

$$\frac{\text{Number of applicants hired}}{\text{Total number of applicants}} = \text{selection ratio}$$

Uniform Guidelines on Employee Selection

An ongoing challenge to all phases of human resource work is equal employment opportunity. However, the importance and high visibility of the selection process demand that all steps in the process are free from discriminatory bias. Those involved in the selection process must eliminate even unintentional bias, if the firm is to be socially responsible and in legal compliance.[14]

In an attempt to reduce discrimination in selection, the Equal Employment Opportunity Commission has created the *Uniform Guidelines on Employee Selection*. These guidelines establish certain standards that employers must meet. A primary goal of the guidelines is to prevent disparate or unequal impact. As described in Chapter 4, disparate impact results when an employer's actions have a disproportionate effect on members of protected groups. One quick test for disparate impact suggested by the guidelines is the *four-fifths rule*. Generally, disparate impact is assumed to exist when the *proportion* of protected class applicants that are actually hired is less than 80 percent (or four-fifths) of the *proportion* of majority applicants selected. The four-fifths rule addresses the proportions of people hired, *not* the total number of people hired. For example, assume an employer has 100 white male applicants for an entry-level job and hires one-half of them, resulting in a selection ratio of 1:2, or 50 percent ($^{50}/_{100}$). The four-

8. SELECTION

4/5 rule

fifths rule *does not* mean that the employer must hire from protected classes four-fifths of the total number of white applicants hired, or 40 protected-class members. Instead, the four-fifths rule means that the employer's selection ratio of protected-class applicants should be at least four-fifths of the majority group selection ratio. Assume that during the same time period the employer had 100 majority applicants and hired 50 of them, the employer had 50 protected-class applicants. In order to conform to the four-fifths rule the employer would have to hire 80 percent of 50 percent—or 40 percent—of the protected class applicants. Since 40 percent of 50 applicants is 20 applicants, the employer would hire 20 protected-class applicants.

But suppose the company only hires 10 of them. Thus, the selection ratio for majority applicants is 1:2 (50/100, or 50 percent), and it is 1:5 (10/50, or 20 percent) for protected-class members. The result is that the *proportion* of protected-class new hires to the *proportion* of majority-class hires is only 40 percent (20/50 percent equals 40 percent). This ratio employed in this example can be calculated as follows[15]:

$$\frac{S(PCM)}{A(PCM)} \text{ divided by } \frac{S(MAJ)}{A(MAJ)} \text{ or } \frac{10}{50} \text{ divided by } \frac{50}{100} \text{ equals } \frac{2}{5} \text{ equals } 40\%$$

where
- S(PCM) = number of applicants selected from protected class members
- A(PCM) = number of applicants from protected class
- S(MAJ) = number of applicants selected from the majority group
- A(MAJ) = number of applicants from the majority group

Since the ratio of protected class members hired (10/50) to the ratio of the majority hired (50/100) is 2/5, protected class members in this example were hired at a selection rate less than the required 4/5. As a result, it is reasonable to assume that the employer's selection procedures would have a disparate impact on members of the protected class. The company's employment specialists may have been very careful not to discriminate at any stage of the selection process. However, the overall result is a disproportionate impact on members of a protected class. Not only will the department have to revise its selection procedures, but if it has used these procedures for long, it probably has an imbalanced work force that will require an affirmative action plan to correct. (See Chapter 4 for a more detailed explanation of disparate impact and affirmative action plans.)

Historically, when an employer's overall selection process met the four-fifths rule (or *bottom-line test,* as it is called in the guidelines), the EEOC allowed some steps within a firm's selection process to have a disparate impact as long as the overall selection process did not. However, the U.S. Supreme Court ruled in *Connecticut v. Teal* that the courts would ignore the four-fifths rule if disparate impact occurred in any step of the selection process. The implication for professionals is obvious: When one step in the selection process has an adverse impact, it should be reviewed and improved.[16]

Key case

The rest of this chapter examines the challenges and different approaches[17] associated with each step in the selection process shown in Figure 8-2. It should be noted, however, that even following each of these steps is no guarantee of perfect hiring decisions. In some cases, the process eliminates people who would have performed well (as a result of what are called false negative errors); at other times, people will be hired who fail (as a result of what are called false positive errors). Selection is not an exact science. Nevertheless, the human resource department can materially benefit the company and its bottom line by improving its ability to hire correctly. Beyond the bottom line, human resource professionals have an ethical responsibility to the employer and other employees to get the best people possible. Likewise, socially responsible employers have an obligation to ensure equal opportunity.

PRELIMINARY RECEPTION: STEP 1

Applicants also select employers

The selection process is a two-way street. The organization selects employees, and *applicants select employers.* Selection starts with a visit to the human resource office or with a written request for an application. On the basis of how this initial reception is handled, the applicant begins to form an opinion of the employer. And two researchers suggest that applicants' perceptions of an organization influence their intentions to sign up for interviews and request further information.[18] As the growth rate of the work force slows in the 1990s and beyond, the perceptions of applicants will become increasingly important in ensuring an acceptable pool of applicants.

When the applicant appears in person, a preliminary interview may be granted as a courtesy. This "courtesy interview," as it is often called, is simply a matter of good public relations.[19] It also helps the department screen out obvious misfits and get application information on these drop-in applicants. Later steps in the selection process verify this application information if the courtesy interview suggests a fit between the applicant and the employer's needs.

EMPLOYMENT TESTS: STEP 2

Testing

Employment tests are devices that assess the probable match between applicants and job requirements. Some are paper-and-pencil tests; others are exercises that simulate working conditions. A math test for a bookkeeper is an example of a paper-and-pencil test, and the account executive test at Merrill Lynch is an example of a simulation. Tests are used more frequently for candidates for hourly-paid jobs than for management openings because jobs paid hourly usually have a limited number of skills that are more easily tested.[20] A survey by the Society for Human Resource Management found that 84 percent of employers "include testing in their employment decision-making procedures."[21] Management and professional jobs are often too complex to be tested fairly and economically. When tests are used for these positions, however, they often are a simulation of real-life situations that are evaluated by several raters, as is the case at Merrill Lynch. Besides testing for specific skills and abilities, tests may have other screening benefits. In another study of 390 firms by the Society for Human Resource Management (SHRM), for example, 17 percent of employers used drug screening tests on applicants, and 12 percent applied these tests to current workers; only 13 percent of applicants and 9 percent of employees were screened for alcoholism. What is even more telling, perhaps, is that over two-thirds (68 percent) of the companies had increased the use of testing or were considering increases.[22]

Considerable care must be used in regard to testing foreign nationals, whether they are applying for jobs in their country or in the home country of the company. First and most obvious, the test may have cultural biases, including slang terms that are unfamiliar. Second, laws in other countries may prevent some types of testing. Third, because of social standing or political connections, some candidates may regard taking a test as an insult.[23]

Test Validation

Testing became popular on a large scale during World War I when intelligence tests were given to army recruits.[24] During the following years, tests were developed for a wide range of employment uses, but many of these tests were assumed to be valid without sufficient proof. *Validity* means that the test scores significantly relate to job performance or to some other relevant criterion. The stronger the relationship between test results and performance, the more effective the test is as a selection tool.[25] When scores and performance are unrelated, the test is invalid and should not be used for selection.

> *A Miami, Florida trucking company gave all applicants an extensive reading test. One-third of its applicants were Cuban immigrants, but no Cuban drivers were hired. Since the drivers received their instructions orally and were shown on a map where to go, the reading test had no relationship to job performance. It was invalid. The test did not distinguish good drivers from bad ones. It only distinguished among those who could read English well.*[26]

When an invalid test eliminates people of a particular race, sex, religion, or national origin, it violates the 1964 Civil Rights Act. The U.S. Supreme Court has ruled that any test (or any other selection method) that has a disparate impact on a protected class and is not job-related violates the act.[27] This ruling in the *Griggs v. Duke Power* case means that testing specialists should be especially cautious when a test disproportionately excludes some identifiable group. In *Griggs*, and later in *Albemarle Paper Co. v. Moody*, the U.S. Supreme Court recognized the EEOC Uniform Guidelines on Employee Selection, which outline how tests should be evaluated to determine if they are valid.[28] Ensuring that tests are valid requires validation studies. These studies compare test results with performance or traits needed to perform the job. Figure 8-3 summarizes the most common

Figure 8-3

An Explanation of Common Approaches to Test Validation

EMPIRICAL APPROACHES

Empirical approaches to test validation attempt to relate test scores with a job-related criterion, usually performance. If the test actually measures a job-related criterion, the test and the criterion exhibit a positive correlation between 0 and 1.0. The higher the correlation, the better the match.

➤ *Predictive validity* is determined by giving a test to a group of applicants. After these applicants have been hired and mastered the job reasonably well, their performance is measured. This measurement and the test score are then correlated.

➤ *Concurrent validity* allows the personnel department to test present employees and correlate these scores with measures of their performance. This approach does not require the delay between hiring and mastery of the job.

RATIONAL APPROACHES

When the number of subjects is too low to have a reasonable sample of people to test, rational approaches are used. These approaches are considered inferior to empirical techniques, but are acceptable validation strategies when empirical approaches are not feasible.

➤ *Content validity* is assumed to exist when the test includes reasonable samples of the skills needed to successfully perform the job. A typing test for an applicant that is being hired simply to do typing is an example of a test with content validity.

➤ *Construct validity* seeks to establish a relationship between performance and other characteristics that are assumed to be necessary for successful job performance. Tests of intelligence and scientific terms would be considered to have construct validity if they were used to hire researchers for a chemical company.

---

approaches to validation, which often demand statistical analysis of test scores and performance.

Validation approaches

Empirical validation approaches rely on predictive or concurrent validity. Both methods attempt to relate test scores to some criterion, usually performance. The higher the correlation between test scores and the criterion, the more effective the test is. Courts and the EEOC guidelines generally prefer empirical approaches because they are less subjective than rational methods.

Rational validation approaches include content and construct validity. These techniques are used when empirical validation is not feasible because the small number of subjects does not permit a reasonable sample upon which to conduct the validation study.

Regardless of which approach is used, testing experts advise separate validation studies for different subgroups, such as women and minorities.[29] The use of separate studies for different subgroups is called *differential validity*. Without differential validity, a test may be valid for a large group (white male applicants) but not for subgroups of minorities or women. Even when tests are validated, courts may examine how effective such validation attempts are. Invalid procedures, no matter how well-intentioned, cannot be relied on to prove a test's validity.

Key law case

The Albemarle Paper Company gave several black workers a battery of tests that had not been validated. The workers sued Albemarle, and the company then implemented a validation study. The study had several weaknesses, and the court ruled the tests invalid and discriminatory.

The problem faced by Albemarle was that:

▶ *The company used tests that had been validated for advanced jobs, not for the entry-level positions to which the tests were being applied. Validation on advanced jobs does not prove that the tests are valid for entry-level positions. Tests must be validated on those jobs to which they are being applied.*

▶ *The company validated the test on one group (white workers) and then applied the test to another group (black workers). Tests must be validated for all the groups to whom they are applied.*[30]

Reliability

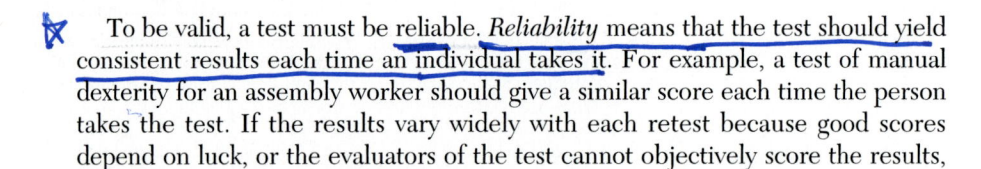

To be valid, a test must be reliable. *Reliability* means that the test should yield consistent results each time an individual takes it. For example, a test of manual dexterity for an assembly worker should give a similar score each time the person takes the test. If the results vary widely with each retest because good scores depend on luck, or the evaluators of the test cannot objectively score the results, the test is not reliable, and, therefore not valid.

Although validity and reliability are most closely associated with testing, other steps in the selection process must be both valid and reliable if the human resource department is to do an effective job of selection.

Testing Tools and Cautions

Test validation studies

There are a wide variety of employment tests, but each type of test has only limited usefulness. The exact purpose of a test, its design, the directions for its administration, and its applications are recorded in the test manual, which should be reviewed before a test is used. The manual also reports the test's reliability and the results of validation efforts by the test designer. Today, many tests have been validated on large populations. But testing specialists should conduct their own studies to make sure a particular test is valid for its planned use.[31] Each type of test has a different purpose.[32] Figure 8-4 lists examples and gives a brief explanation of several different types of tests.

Psychological tests are those that measure personality or temperament. They are among the least reliable. Validity suffers because the relationship between personality and performance is often vague or nonexistent.[33]

Knowledge tests are more reliable because they determine information or knowledge. A math test for an accountant and a weather test for a pilot are both

Figure 8-4

Some Applications of Employment-Related Tests

NAME	APPLICATION
PSYCHOLOGICAL TESTS	
► Minnesota Multiphasic Personality Inventory	Measures personality or temperament (executives, nuclear power, security)
► California Psychological Inventory	Measures personality or temperament (executives, managers, supervisors)
► Guilford-Zimmerman Temperament Survey	Measures personality or temperament (sales personnel)
► Watson-Glaser Critical Thinking Appraisal	Measures logic and reasoning ability (executives, managers, supervisors)
► Owens Creativity Test	Measures creativity and judgment ability (engineers)
► Myers-Briggs Type Indicator	Measures personality components
KNOWLEDGE TESTS	
► Leadership opinion questionnaire	Measures knowledge of leadership practices (managers and supervisors)
► General aptitude test battery	Measures verbal, spatial, numeric, and other aptitudes and dexterity (job seekers at unemployment offices)
PERFORMANCE TESTS	
► Stromberg Dexterity Test	Measures physical coordination (shop workers)
► Revised Minnesota Paper Form Board Test	Measures spatial visualization (draftsmen and draftswomen)
► Minnesota Clerical Test	Measures ability to work with numbers and names (clerks)
► Job simulation tests	Measures a sample of "on-the-job" demands (managers, professionals)
GRAPHIC RESPONSE TEST	
► Polygraph (Lie Detector)	Measures physiological responses to questions (police, retail store workers)
ATTITUDE TESTS	
► Honesty Test	Measures attitudes about theft and related subjects (retail workers, securities employees, banks)
► Work opinion questionnaire	Measures attitudes about work and values (entry-level, low-income workers)
MEDICAL TESTS	
► Drug tests	Measures the presence of illegal or performance-affecting drugs (athletes, government employees, equipment operators)
► Genetic screening	Identifies genetic predispositions to specific medical problems
► Medical screening	Measures and monitors exposure to hazardous chemicals (miners, factory workers, researchers)

8. SELECTION

knowledge tests. But specialists must be able to demonstrate that the knowledge is needed to perform the job. The Miami trucking company example is a case where the tested knowledge (reading at an advanced level) was unneeded.

Performance tests measure ability of applicants to do some parts of the work for which they are to be hired—for example, a typing test for typists. Validity is often assumed when the test includes a representative sample of the work the applicant is to do upon being hired. However, if the test discriminates against some protected group, the test must be backed by detailed validation studies. Merrill Lynch's test is likely to be considered valid in content and construct when subjected to rational validation because it includes samples of the work an account representative would be expected to do.

Attitude and honesty tests are being used in some circumstances to learn about the attitudes of applicants and employees on a variety of job-related subjects. Since *The Employee Polygraph Protection Act* (1988), polygraph (lie detector) tests have been effectively banned in employment situations.[34] In their place, attitude tests are being used to assess attitudes about honesty and, presumably, on-the-job behaviors.[35] Attitude tests also reveal employee attitudes and values about work. The *Work Opinion Questionnaire,* for example, has been effectively used in predicting the job performance of entry-level, low-income workers.[36]

Medical tests in recent years have grown in popularity. Through analysis of urine, hair, or blood samples, laboratories are able to screen for the presence of drugs. Concern about employee drug abuse has spurred IBM, American Airlines, Storer Communications, and many others to require all job applicants to pass a urinalysis test for marijuana and cocaine.[37]

As technology has improved, testing for genetic defects or predispositions has become technically and financially feasible. Genetic screening may alert employers to those with higher chances of developing specific diseases.[38] Likewise, medical monitoring of diseases such as acquired immune deficiency syndrome (AIDS) or the buildup of toxic chemicals such as lead or mercury poisoning among workers may alert employers to high-risk employees or shortcomings in health standards in the workplace.

When an unfavorable test result does occur, employers may give more sophisticated retests or use other methods of verification to assure fairness in selection. If tests discriminate against members of a protected class disproportionately, EEO violations may occur. And since the 1990 *Americans with Disabilities Act* became effective in 1992, medical or other tests that discriminate against those who are "differently abled" also risk an EEO violation.[39] And to many applicants and employees these tests are an invasion of their privacy.[40]

Besides heeding specific cautions associated with individual tests and potential controversies, personnel specialists should realize that testing is not always feasible. Even when tests can be developed or bought, the cost may not be justified for jobs that have low selection ratios or that are seldom filled. Examples include technical, professional, and managerial jobs.

Even when feasible, the use of tests must be flexible. They need not always be the first or last step in the selection process. Instead, experts use tests during the selection process at the point they deem appropriate. Consider the comments of an experienced manager for a chain of grocery stores.

> Many human resource managers in other industries use testing only after other steps in the selection process. In the grocery business you must test first. Why waste time interviewing a grocery clerk who doesn't know that three for 88 cents is 30 cents a piece? Besides, when we take applications on Tuesdays, we may have 300 of them. Interviews would take 75 hours a week, and my staff consists of a clerk and myself. But through testing, we can test the entire group in an hour. Then we interview only those who score well.

Finally, the employment test is only one of several techniques in the selection process because its use is limited to factors that can be easily tested and validated.[41] Other items, not measurable through testing, may be equally important, such as enthusiasm and motivation.

SELECTION INTERVIEW: STEP 3

Most widely used

The *selection interview* is a formal, in-depth conversation conducted to evaluate the applicant's acceptability. The interviewer seeks to answer three broad questions: Can the applicant do the job? Will the applicant do the job? How does the applicant compare with others who are being considered for the job?

Selection interviews are the most widely used selection technique.[42] One study reports that 90 percent of all companies surveyed had more confidence in interviews than in any other source of selection information.[43] Their popularity stems from their flexibility. They can be adapted to unskilled, skilled, managerial, and professional employees. They also allow a two-way exchange of information: interviewers learn about the applicant, and the applicant learns about the employer.[44]

Interviews do have shortcomings. Their most noticeable flaws are in the areas of reliability and validity.[45] Good reliability means that the interpretation of the interview results should not vary from interviewer to interviewer. But it is common for different interviewers to form different opinions. Reliability is improved when identical questions are asked, especially if interviewers are trained to record responses systematically.[46]

American Bankers

For example, American Bankers Insurance Group uses a computer-driven interview process, where clerical applicants are asked standardized questions via computer. The computer measures the time to answer individual questions and indicates areas where the applicant hesitated to suggest follow-up questions in the subsequent face-to-face interview.[47]

8. SELECTION

Figure 8-5

Different Combinations of Interviewer and Applicants

	NUMBER OF INTERVIEWERS	NUMBER OF APPLICANTS
INDIVIDUAL INTERVIEW	1	1
GROUP INTERVIEWS	2 or more	1
	1	2 or more
	2 or more	2 or more

Variables affecting interviews

The validity of interviews is often questionable because few departments use standardized questions upon which validation studies can be conducted. However, proactive departments are beginning to realize this problem and are comparing interview results with actual performance or other criteria, such as stability of employment.[48] More validation of interviews is needed because they may relate more to the personal characteristics of candidates than to the candidates' potential performance. For example, one study reported that two of the most important variables that influence an interview are fluency of speech and composure.[49] If these findings are applicable to most employment interviews, the results of the interviews may correlate with fluency and composure, instead of potential performance. Whether validated or not, face-to-face interviews persist because of their adaptability and perceived effectiveness.[50]

Types of Interviews

Interviews are commonly conducted between the interviewer and the applicants, on a one-to-one basis. Group interviews, however, are sometimes used. Variations of group interviews appear in Figure 8-5.

Group interviews

One form of group interview is to have applicants meet simultaneously with two or more interviewers.[51] This allows all interviewers to evaluate the individual on the same questions and answers. Another major variation reflected in Figure 8-5 is to have two or more applicants interviewed together, by one or more interviewers. Park workers at Disneyland, for example, meet in groups of three with an interviewer for 45 minutes to allow the interviewer to observe how potential workers will interact with others.[52] This saves time and permits the answers and interactions of different applicants to be compared immediately.

Whether in a group or individual interview, various interview formats can be used. Questions can be structured, unstructured, mixed, problem-solving, or stress-producing. Figure 8-6 compares these different formats. The mixed format

Types of interviews

Figure 8-6

Different Question Formats in Interviews

INTERVIEW FORMAT	TYPES OF QUESTIONS	USEFUL APPLICATIONS
UNSTRUCTURED	Few if any planned questions. Questions are made up during the interview.	Useful when trying to help interviewees solve personal problems or understand why they are not right for a job.
STRUCTURED	A predetermined checklist of questions, usually asked of all applicants.	Useful for valid results, especially when dealing with large numbers of applicants.
MIXED	A combination of structured and unstructured questions, which resembles what is usually done in practice.	Realistic approach that yields comparable answers plus in-depth insights.
BEHAVIORAL	Questions limited to hypothetical situations. Evaluation is on the solution and the approach of the applicant.	Useful to understand applicant's reasoning and analytical abilities under modest stress.
STRESS	A series of harsh, rapid-fire questions intended to upset the applicant.	Useful for stressful jobs, such as handling complaints.

is most common in practice, although each of the formats plays an appropriate role.[53]

1. **Unstructured interviews.** As the summary in Figure 8-6 indicates, the *unstructured* interview allows employment specialists to develop questions as the interview proceeds. The interviewer goes into topic areas as they arise, trying to simulate a friendly conversation. In Japan, for example, where EEOC guidelines obviously do not apply, managers prefer the wide-ranging, unstructured interview as a means to get to know an applicant and his or her personal life. Unfortunately, this unstructured method, which is also called *nondirective* interviewing, lacks the reliability of a structured interview because each applicant is asked a different series of questions. Even worse, this approach may overlook key areas of the applicant's skills or background.

    Nondirective interviewing

2. **Structured interviews.** *Structured*, or *directive*, interviews rely on a predetermined set of questions.[54] The questions are developed before the interview begins and are asked of every applicant, as with American Bankers' computerized

8. SELECTION

approach. Structured questions improve the reliability of the interview process, but they do not allow the interviewer to follow up interesting or unusual responses. Here the process seems quite mechanical to all concerned. The rigid format may even convey disinterest to applicants who are used to more flexible interviews.

3. **Mixed interviews.** In practice, interviewers typically use a blend of structured and unstructured questions. The structured questions provide a base of information that allows comparisons between candidates. But the unstructured questions make the interview more conversational and permit greater insights into the unique differences between applicants. College recruiters, for example, use mixed interviews most of the time.[55]

4. **Behavioral interviews.** *Behavioral* interviewing focuses on a problem or a hypothetical situation that the applicant is expected to solve. Often these are hypothetical situations, and the applicant is asked what should be done. Both the answer and the approach are evaluated. This interview technique has a very narrow scope. It primarily reveals the applicant's ability to solve the types of problems presented.[56] Validity is more likely if the hypothetical situations match those found on the job. The interview might consist of situations similar to the following:

Hypothetical scenarios

> *Suppose you had to decide between two candidates for a promotion. Candidate A is loyal, cooperative, punctual, and hard-working. Candidate B is a complainer and is tardy and discourteous, but is the best producer in your department. Whom would you recommend for promotion to supervisor? Why?*

The way the applicant reacts to the questions is noted. The question also produces modest amounts of stress and suggests how the applicant may function under moderately stressful situations.

5. **Stress interviews.** When the job involves much stress, *stress* interviews attempt to learn how the applicant will respond to the pressure. Originally developed during World War II to see how selected recruits might react under stress behind enemy lines, these interviews have useful applications in civilian employment. For example, applicants for police work are sometimes put through a stress interview to see how they might react to problems they encounter in the streets. The interview itself consists of a series of harsh questions asked in rapid-fire succession and in an unfriendly manner. Since stressful situations are usually only part of the job, this technique should be used in connection with other interview formats. Even then, negative public relations are likely among those who are not

Harsh questioning

The Interview Process

Figure 8-7

Stages in the Typical Employment Interview

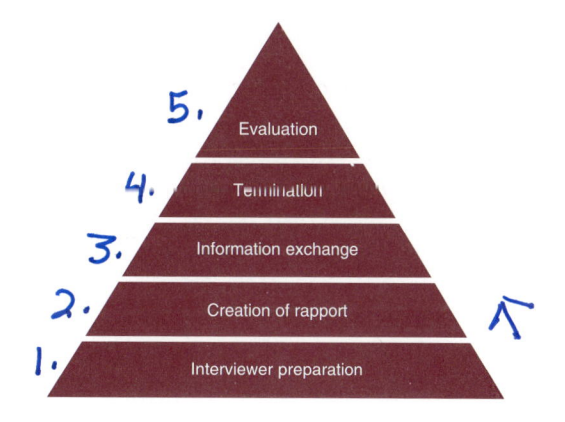

5. Evaluation
4. Termination
3. Information exchange
2. Creation of rapport
1. Interviewer preparation

hired. Reliability and validity are hard to demonstrate since job stress may differ from the stress posed in the interview.

The Interview Process

Beyond the different types of interviews, the interview process has sequential steps, shown in Figure 8-7. These stages are interviewer preparation, creation of rapport, information exchange, termination, and evaluation. They are discussed to illustrate how the actual interview process occurs.[57]

Getting ready

Interviewer preparation. Before beginning the interview, the interviewer needs to review the application and job description information to prepare specific questions. Answers to these questions decide the applicant's suitability. At the same time, the interviewer must consider what questions the applicant is likely to ask. Since interviews help persuade top applicants to accept subsequent job offers, interviewers need to be able to explain job duties, performance standards, pay, benefits, and other areas of interest.

A list of typical questions asked by college recruiters and other interviewers appears in Figure 8-8. These questions are intended to give the interviewer insights into the applicant's interests, attitudes, and background. Specific or technical questions are added to the list according to the job opening. A review of the job description and position specifications helps the interviewer prepare specific questions. In preparing those questions, the interviewers must be especially careful not to ask any that could be interpreted as discriminatory. As one researcher concluded, "the employment interview has increasingly come under judicial scrutiny as a result of charges that . . . questions are biased or unfair toward racial, religious and ethnic minorities, females, the handicapped,

8. SELECTION   245

Figure 8-8

Sample Questions in Employment Interviews

1. How do you spend your spare time? What are your hobbies?
2. What community or school activities have you been involved in?
3. Describe your ideal job. In what type of work are you interested?
4. Why do you want to work for our company?
5. What were your favorite classes? Why?
6. Do you have any geographic preferences?
7. Why did you select your college major?
8. What do you know about our company's products or services?
9. Describe the ideal boss.
10. How often do you expect to be promoted?
11. What is your major weakness? Strength?
12. Why do you think your friends like you?
13. Do you plan to take additional college courses? Which ones?
14. What jobs have you had that you liked most? Least?
15. Describe your least favorite boss or teacher.
16. What are your career goals?
17. If you could go back five years, what would you do the same? Different?
18. Why should you be hired by our company?
19. Describe your last job.
20. How many hours do you think you will have to work at your job?
21. What job skills do you have?

and elderly persons."[58] Questions asked of a protected group but not of members of the majority are usually the ones that cause violations. An example is asking women about child-care arrangements but not asking men the same question.[59] Likewise, questions about sex, age, national origin, handicaps, or religion are likely to be considered discriminatorily motivated, unless they concern a bona fide occupational qualification.[60] (See Chapter 4 for a discussion of BFOQs.)

Research shows that the quality of the interviewer's decision is significantly better when the completed application blank is present at the time of the interview.[61] With or without the application blank, interviewers seem to take about the same length of time to reach a conclusion, from four to ten minutes.[62] The longer the interview is scheduled to last and the better the quality of the applicant, the longer it takes the interviewer to reach a decision.[63]

Rapport

2. **Creation of rapport.** The burden of establishing rapport falls on the interviewer, although applicants can improve their prospects by sharing this responsibility. One writer addresses the interviewer's role as follows:

> Comes the appointed hour, you will act the perfect host or hostess, greeting the candidate with a warm smile, showing him into your office, making small

talk in the hope of putting him at ease. Of course he's nervous, acting stiff, withdrawn, or cocky as a result. Your challenge—it being your show, and you so self-assured from all the preparation you have done—is to reduce that nervousness; the closer the interview comes to a friendly conversation, the more you will learn about the real him or her.[64]

Another commentator reaches similar conclusions:

Heart of the interview

The heart of the interview process is rapport. Only in a relationship of mutual trust and comfort—a relationship largely free of anxiety—will a candidate talk freely.... No interview is without stress, however. The candidate is anxious about making a favorable impression.... In view of this mutual anxiety, every effort should be made to allay the normal fears of both parties. This can be done by ... projecting an image of confidence, competence and concern, especially in the early stages of the interview.[65]

Rapport is aided by beginning the interview on time and starting with nonthreatening questions such as, "Did you have any parking problems?" At the same time, the interviewer may use body language to help relax the applicant. A smile, a handshake, a relaxed posture, and the moving aside of paperwork—all communicate without words. This rapport is maintained through such nonverbal communications as nodding one's head, smiling, and relaxing one's posture during the session.[66]

Purposeful conversation

3. **Information exchange.** The interview process is a conversation that exchanges information. To help establish rapport while learning about the candidate, some interviewers begin by asking the interviewee if he or she has any questions. This establishes two-way communication and allows the interviewer to begin to judge the recruit by the type of questions asked. Consider these responses to the interviewer's opening statement, "Let's start with any questions you may have." Which gives the most favorable impression?

Applicant 1:   I don't have any questions.
Applicant 2:   I have several questions. How much does the job pay? Will I get a two-week vacation at the end of the first year?
Applicant 3:   What will my responsibilities be? I am hoping to find a job that offers me challenges now and career potential down the road.

Each response creates a different impression on the interviewer. But only the third applicant appears concerned about the job. The other two applicants are either unconcerned or interested only in the benefits they will receive.

In general, an interviewer will ask questions in a way that yields as much information as possible. Questions that begin with how, what, why, compare, describe, expand, or "could you tell me more about . . . " are more likely to get an open response. Questions that can be answered with a simple "yes" or "no" do not give the interviewer much insight. For example, an interviewer is likely to get narrow, limited answers by asking questions that begin "Are you . . . " or "Did you . . . " These questions often result in very abbreviated answers.[67] Specific questions and areas of interest to an interviewer are suggested in Figure 8-8. Besides knowing the answers to those questions, the interviewer may want more specific information about the applicant's background, skills, and interests.

4. **Termination.** As the list of questions dwindles or available time ends, the interviewer must draw the session to a close. Once again, nonverbal communication is useful. Sitting erect, turning toward the door, glancing at a watch or clock—all clue the applicant that the end is near. Some interviewers terminate the interview by asking, "Do you have any final questions?" At this point, the interviewer notifies the applicant of the next step in the interview process, which may be to wait for a call or letter. Regardless of the interviewer's opinions, the applicant should not be given an indication of his or her prospects for getting the job. Not only may a subsequent candidate look better, but subsequent steps in the selection process may cause the final selection decision to be much different than it might appear at the end of the interview.

5. **Evaluation.** Immediately after the interview ends, the interviewer should record specific answers and general impressions about the candidate. Figure 8-9 shows a typical checklist used to record the interviewer's impressions. Use of a checklist like the one in the figure can improve the reliability of the interview as a selection technique.[68] As the checklist shows, the interviewer is able to obtain a large amount of information even from a short interview.

Interviewer Errors

Regardless of the steps an interviewer follows, mistakes or errors occur. To the extent that the cautions in Figure 8-10 are not followed, the effectiveness—particularly the validity and reliability—of the interview is lessened. When the applicant is judged according to the halo effect, or personal biases, results are misinterpreted. Applicants are accepted or rejected for reasons that may bear no relationship to their potential performance, harming the validity of the interview. Likewise, leading questions and domination do not allow the interviewer to learn of the applicant's potential. The evaluation of the applicant is then based on guesswork, with little or no substantiation. No matter which pitfall is involved, it reduces the reliability and validity of the interview. When biases are presented, the interview only wastes both organizational resources and the applicant's time.

When evaluating foreign nationals for jobs, many interviewers tend to expect similar body language, expressions, and behaviors.[69] For example, if an applicant does not look the interviewer directly in the eyes, the subtle message sent by this

248   II. PREPARATION AND SELECTION

Figure 8-9

A Postinterview Checklist

EMPIRE INC.

"An equal opportunity employer"

Postinterview Checklist

Applicant's Name _____ Date _____

Position under Consideration _____ Interviewer _____

Interviewer's Comments

A. Rate the applicant on the following (1 = low; 10 = high):

_____	Appearance	_____	Ability to perform job
_____	Apparent interest	_____	Education/training
_____	Experience/background	_____	Timely availability
_____	Reasonable expectations	_____	Past employment stability

B. List specific comments that reveal the candidate's strengths and weaknesses for the job being considered:

1. Attitude toward previous job _____

2. Attitude toward previous boss _____

3. Expectations about job duties _____

4. Career or occupational expectations _____

5. Other specific comments about applicant _____

Follow-up Actions Required

_____	None	_____	Follow-up interview with personnel
_____	Testing	_____	Applicant unacceptable (file)
_____	Supervisory interview	_____	Notify applicant of rejection

_____ Applicant unacceptable for job under consideration. Reconsider for job as _____

---

behavior may be interpreted as a lack of self-confidence or even that the candidate is hiding something. However, in some cultures, direct eye contact from someone in a subservient position (such as an interviewee) may be seen as highly

Figure 8-10

A Summary of Typical Interviewer Errors

HALO EFFECT

Interviewers who use limited information about an applicant to bias their evaluation of that person's other characteristics are subject to the halo effect.

Examples:
- An applicant who has a pleasant smile and firm handshake is considered a leading candidate before the interview begins.
- An applicant who wears blue jeans to the interview is rejected mentally.

LEADING QUESTIONS

Interviewers who "telegraph" the desired answer by the way they frame their questions are using leading questions.

Examples:
- "Do you think you'll like this work?"
- "Do you agree that profits are necessary?"

PERSONAL BIASES

Interviewers who harbor prejudice against specific groups are exhibiting a personal bias.

Examples:
- "I prefer sales personnel who are tall."
- "Some jobs are for men and others for women."

INTERVIEWER DOMINATION

Interviewers who use the interview to oversell the applicant, brag about their successes, or carry on a social conversation instead of an interview are guilty of interviewer domination.

Examples:
- Spending the entire interview telling the applicant about company plans or benefits.
- Using the interview to tell the applicant how important the interviewer's job is.

---

inappropriate. Similar comments can be made about physical appearance, dress, and even hygiene. To allow these cultural or behavioral differences to interfere with the interviewer's judgment may cause an otherwise good candidate to be excluded from further consideration, again harming the validity of the process.

Interviewee Errors

Interviewees make errors, too. Some may be to cover up job-related weaknesses. Others may emerge from simple nervousness. While interviewers—especially those in the human resource department—may conduct hundreds of job interviews in a year, most applicants never experience that many in a lifetime. The National Association of Corporate and Professional Recruiters asked execu-

Interview mistakes

tive headhunters and human resource specialists to identify common interviewing mistakes made by job candidates. The top five mistakes were playing games, talking too much, boasting, not listening, and being unprepared.

Playing games, such as acting nonchalant, is often taken at face value: The candidate is not interested. Although the candidate may be excited or nervous, talking too much, especially about irrelevant topics such as sports or weather, may entertain the interviewer but is not appropriate. Instead, applicants should stick to the subject at hand. Likewise, boasting is a common mistake. Sure applicants need to "sell themselves." But distorting credentials—even if just "embellishing"—about responsibilities and accomplishments or simply bragging can turn off the interviewer's interest. Failure to listen may result from anxiety about the interview. Unfortunately, it usually means missing the interviewer's questions and failing to maintain rapport. And, of course, being unprepared means asking poorly thought-out questions and even conveying disinterest, neither of which is likely to land the job being sought.[70]

REFERENCES AND BACKGROUND CHECKS: STEP 4

What type of person is the applicant? Is the applicant a good, reliable worker? Are the job accomplishments, titles, educational background, and other facts on the resume or application true? And most importantly, what information is relevant to matching the applicant and a job? To answer these questions, employment specialists use reference and background checks.[71] They may even supplement the application blank with a biographical information blank that goes beyond that found in the application blank.[72]

Credential distortion

Credential distortion by applicants suggests that reference and background checks are increasingly important, especially when customers or coworkers may be harmed by poor performance or illegal behavior.[73] Research suggests that credential distortion occurs frequently.

Jeremiah McAward, president of a New York City credential verification agency, states, "Of the thousands of resumes we investigate, there are outright lies on 22 percent."[74]

According to the National Credential Verification Service, approximately one-third of the résumés it examines misrepresent academic degrees, the distortion ranging from mild embellishment to absolute fabrication.[75]

In a survey of 501 executives by Ward Howell International Inc., an executive search firm, 17 percent of the executives said their new hires had misrepresented job qualifications and 9 percent of their applicants had inflated their salaries.[76]

Limited credential checks

Failure to verify credentials can result in public relations, financial, or other problems for the employer.

8. SELECTION

251

Unethical behavior

Janet Cooke, a journalist for the Washington Post, confessed to having fabricated her Pulitzer Prize-winning story about an eight-year-old heroin addict living in Washington, D.C. slums. Upon closer scrutiny of her credentials, "irregularities" surfaced in her educational background. She had claimed to be a magna cum laude graduate of Vassar and to have earned a master's degree from the University of Toledo; actually she only attended Vassar during her freshman year and held a bachelor's degree from the University of Toledo.[77]

Imagine the personal and professional embarrassment among those in the human resource department of the *Washington Post* when the distorted credentials were uncovered. In this example, the selection processes lacked a thorough evaluation of credentials.

Personal versus employment references

Many professionals have a very skeptical attitude toward references. *Personal references*—those that attest to the applicant's sound character—are usually provided by friends or family. Their objectivity and candor are certainly questionable. When writing a reference, the author usually emphasizes only positive points. Thus personal references are less commonly used. *Employment references* differ from personal references because they discuss the applicant's work history. As privacy legislation continues to expand,[78] many supervisors and human resource departments are growing less willing to provide employment references because they fear potential lawsuits for libel and slander. Even though supervisors or personnel specialists may be protected under what the law calls "qualified privilege," that protection may end if there are any doubts about the truth of the recommendation, whether the recommendation is made with malice, or whether the information goes into issues not covered by privilege—such as personal information not related to employment. As a result, many human resource departments have policies that limit providing reference information to little more than verifying that the person actually worked for company.[79] Some personnel departments will not even do that much.

Candor

This lack of candor has caused some employers to omit this step entirely from the selection process. Other companies have substituted telephone inquiries for written references,[80] although these are also subject to the legal complications and restrictive policies. Besides a faster response, often at lower cost, voice inflections or hesitancy to blunt questions may tip off underlying problems. In practice, less than 22 percent of all reference checks seek negative information, according to one study.[81] That same study revealed that 48 percent of reference checks are used to verify application information and 30 percent are used to gather additional data.

Bonding and Security Checks

When an applicant is going to have access to money, valuables, or classified information—as an account executive at Merrill Lynch would have—a background search may be conducted that goes significantly beyond letters of reference. Bonding companies may want far more detail than appears in the application blank. The department may want to check criminal records and credit ratings. If national defense security is involved, a detailed background check may be needed before the employee can receive the necessary clearances to work on classified materials. For some highly secret jobs with government contractors, these clearances may take up to six months or longer and often involve checks on family members and the applicant's past.[82]

Immigration and Naturalization Rules

Illegal aliens

The *Immigration Reform and Control Act* of 1986 adds a complicating twist to background checks. While the EEO laws and regulations preclude discrimination on the basis of national origin, the Immigration Reform and Control Act demands that employers not hire undocumented aliens, sometimes referred to as "illegal aliens."

Employers who knowingly recruit, hire, or refer foreign aliens for employment are subject to civil or criminal penalties. However, personnel specialists who vigorously seek to comply with the Immigration Act might discriminate or at least appear to discriminate against those of specific national or ethnic origins.[83] The challenge for employment specialists is to verify that applicants are not undocumented aliens without discriminating against U.S. citizens or properly documented foreign aliens.

MEDICAL EVALUATION: STEP 5

Health checklists

The selection process may include a medical evaluation of the applicant before the hiring decision is made. Normally, the evaluation is a health checklist that asks the applicant to indicate health and accident information. The questionnaire is sometimes supplemented with a physical examination by a company nurse or physician. The medical evaluation may:

▶ Entitle the employer to lower health or life insurance rates for company-paid insurance

▶ Be required by state or local health officials—particularly in food-handling operations where communicable diseases are a danger

▶ Be useful to evaluate whether the applicant can handle the physical or mental stress of a job.

ADA

Many employers have done away with this step because of *The Americans with Disabilities Act* makes the qualified disabled a protected class under the equal employment opportunity laws. To conduct a medical evaluation may uncover disabilities or potential disabilities.[84] Then, if the applicant is not hired, charges of discrimination may be brought under the Act. A preexisting health condition may be considered a disability, and failure to hire may be seen as discrimination against the qualified handicapped. To avoid such pitfalls, if the employer wants a medical evaluation, it may be scheduled after the hiring decision has been made.

Drug testing

One noteworthy exception to the trend of performing fewer medical evaluations is drug testing. A growing number of corporations and governments include drug screening as part of their employment process, either before or immediately after the hiring decision. These organizations seek to avoid the economic and legal risks associated with drug users. Increases in mortality rates, accidents, theft, and poor performance, which are often associated with drug use, affect the employer's economic performance. And if the drug user's performance carries negative consequences for customers or fellow employees, lawsuits are likely.[85]

SUPERVISORY INTERVIEW: STEP 6

Technical evaluation

Since immediate supervisors are ultimately responsible for newly hired workers, they should have input into the hiring decision. The supervisor is often able to better evaluate the applicant's technical abilities. Likewise, the immediate supervisor can often answer the interviewee's specific job-related questions with greater precision and often has the authority to make the hiring decision.

When supervisors make the final decision, the employment function is to provide the supervisor with the best prescreened applicants available. From these two or three applicants, the supervisor decides whom to hire. Some employers leave the final hiring decision to the human resource department, especially when applicants are hired into a training program instead of a specific job. If supervisors reject particular groups, such as minorities or women, the department may be given final hiring authority to avoid future charges of discrimination.

Supervisor commitment

Regardless of who has the final hiring authority, the commitment of supervisors is generally higher if they participate in the selection process. When the supervisor recommends hiring someone, it creates on the supervisor's part a psychological commitment to ensure the employee's success. If the candidate turns out to be unsatisfactory, the supervisor is more likely to accept some of the responsibility for failure.

REALISTIC JOB PREVIEW: STEP 7

RJPs

Often the supervisory interview is supplemented with a realistic job preview. A *realistic job preview* (RJP) shows the employee the job and the job setting before the hiring decision is made.[86] Often this involves showing the candidate the type of work, equipment, and working conditions involved. In some cases, an RJP is provided as part of the recruiting process to help weed out inappropriate candidates.

Unmet expectations about a job can contribute to initial job dissatisfaction. The realistic job preview attempts to reduce the initial surprise of a new job—and potential job dissatisfaction—by giving the newcomer an insight into the job.[87] Recently hired employees who have had a realistic job preview are less likely to be shocked by the job or by the job setting on the first day they report to work. Two writers conclude that:

> The RJP functions very much like a medical vaccination. The typical medical vaccination injects one with a small, weakened dose of germs, so that one's body can develop a natural resistance to that disease. The RJP functions similarly by presenting job candidates with a small dose of "organizational reality." And, like the medical vaccination, the RJP is probably much less effective after a person has already entered a new organization.[88]

RJPs and turnover

Research on the effectiveness of realistic job previews shows that employee turnover was lower when the job previews are used. The average turnover rate in nine out of ten studies was 28.8 percent higher without RJPs.[89] Although research findings vary, realistic job previews may help to reduce turnover.[90] RJPs are most appropriate when the applicant is not familiar with the job and least appropriate when job expectations are known. As two researchers conclude:

> Telling prospective employees about unpleasant working conditions may improve the probability that they will remain on the job in comparison to those who are not told about the conditions. However . . . those who are told about less pleasant conditions will be no more satisfied with them once they are experienced than will those who are not told. To improve satisfaction and the quality of work, ultimately some changes must be made in those aspects of the work environment with which employees are dissatisfied.[91]

HIRING DECISION: STEP 8

Whether made by the supervisor or by the human resource department, the final hiring decision marks the end of the selection process, assuming the candidate accepts the job offer. To maintain good public relations, employers should notify applicants who were not selected. Employment specialists may want to consider rejected applicants for other openings since these recruits already have gone through various stages of the selection process. Even if no openings are available, the applications of unsuccessful candidates should be kept on file for future openings. Retaining these applications can be useful in defending against charges of employment discrimination.

Personnel file

The applications of those hired should also be retained. The application blank begins the employee's personnel file and contains useful information for studies that the human resource department may conduct to learn about the source of its

8. SELECTION

applicants—such as which recruiting channels work best. If some recruits prove unsatisfactory after they are hired, for example, the employment managers may be able to reconstruct the selection process beginning with the application. In their reconstruction, they may uncover invalid tests, improperly conducted interviews, or other flaws in the selection process.

OUTCOMES, PROCESS, AND FEEDBACK

The final outcome of the selection process is the people who are hired. If the preselection inputs are considered carefully and the major steps of the selection process are valid, then new employees are likely to be productive. And productive employees are the best evidence of an effective selection process. Mismatches or employees who soon leave are expensive and time-consuming. As a result, many employees are considered probationary and not eligible for all the firm's benefits until 30, 60, or 90 days have passed. One manager who prefers to hire temporary employees before making them permanent does so because of the many costs involved with putting an employee on the payroll.

Post-hiring paperwork

The paperwork does not stop after the initial job application, interview, and reference checking. There are recordkeeping responsibilities for pay, Social Security, unemployment insurance, workers' compensation, Consolidated Omnibus Budget Reconciliation Act (COBRA), federal and state income tax, and disability insurance, all mandated by law for each worker. These records must be continued for at least six years regardless of the employee's length of service or date of discharge.[92]

To succeed, employment managers must overcome a variety of other challenges that impact the selection process. Otherwise, improper selection can crush individual hopes and violate equal employment laws along organizational practices. Challenges discussed throughout this chapter and identified in Figure 8-1T include the slow growth in labor markets, credential distortion, Immigration and Naturalization Services rules, and other legal constraints.

Ethics

Another challenge facing human resource professionals is the ethics of controlling the selection process. Since employment specialists strongly influence the hiring decision, that decision is shaped by their ethics. The temptation of hiring an unqualified friend, accepting gifts from a placement agency, or accepting bribes (a problem more often presented abroad) all challenge the employment specialists' ethical standards. If those standards are low, new employees may not be properly selected.

Feedback is another crucial element of an effective selection process. Learning about successful placements can sometimes be difficult because supervisors claim responsibility for them. Feedback on failures, however, is ample. It can include legal suits, displeased supervisors, growing employee turnover and absenteeism, poor performance, low employee satisfaction, and even union activity.[93]

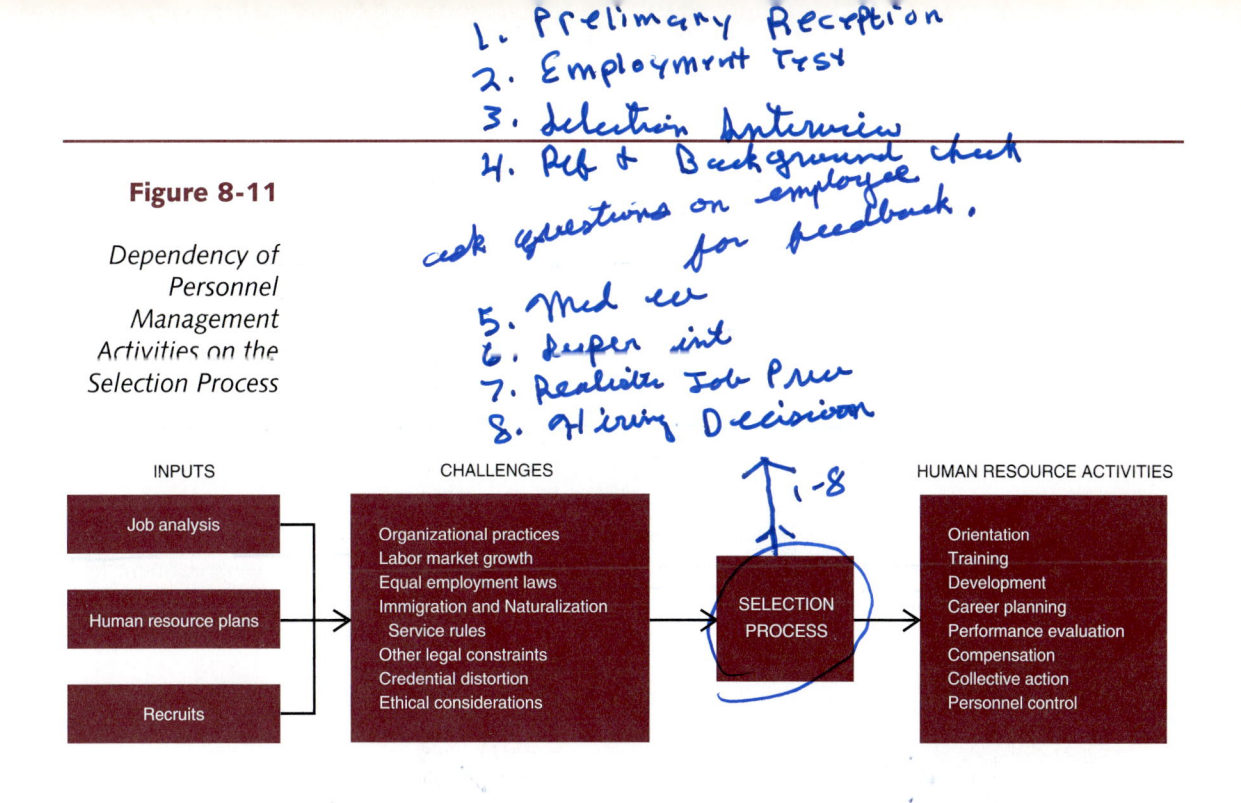

Figure 8-11

Dependency of Personnel Management Activities on the Selection Process

INPUTS	CHALLENGES		HUMAN RESOURCE ACTIVITIES
Job analysis	Organizational practices		Orientation
	Labor market growth		Training
	Equal employment laws		Development
Human resource plans	Immigration and Naturalization Service rules	SELECTION PROCESS	Career planning
			Performance evaluation
	Other legal constraints		Compensation
	Credential distortion		Collective action
Recruits	Ethical considerations		Personnel control

More constructive feedback is obtained through specific questions. How well does the new employee adapt to the organization? To the job? To the career of which the job is a part? And finally, how well does the employee perform? Answers to each of these questions provide feedback about the employee and the selection process. The chapters in Part III of this book examine each of these questions in depth.

SUMMARY

The SELECTION process depends heavily upon inputs such as job analysis, human resource plans, and recruitment, as Figure 8-11 shows. These inputs are used within the context of challenges posed by organizational policies, equal employment laws, Immigration and Naturalization Service rules, a slow-growing supply of labor, credential distortion, and other legal concerns faced by the organization.

The key challenge that underlies the entire selection process is to ensure that the steps in the process are valid. In all phases of the selection process, human resource professionals also must be concerned about the potential for adverse impact. Even when the overall selection process does not show a disparate impact upon members of protected classes, evidence of a discriminatory impact at any step in the process should be investigated and the discrimination eliminated where found.

8. SELECTION

With these inputs and challenges, the selection process takes recruits and puts them through a series of steps to evaluate their potential. These steps vary from organization to organization and from one job opening to another. In general, the selection procedure relies on testing for many hourly-paid jobs and on interviews for virtually every opening that is to be filled. Verifying references and performing medical evaluations are common steps found in the selection process of many employers, although both are used somewhat less frequently today as a result of legal constraints.

The supervisor's role should include participation in the selection process, usually through an interview with job candidates. As a result of this participation, the supervisor is more likely to be committed to the new worker's success. Growing research also supports the use of realistic job previews.

Once the hiring decision is made, the HRIS should be updated with detailed information about the new hire. Assuming the human resource department uses valid procedures and ethical behaviors, its selection process can make a substantial contribution to the success of the employer and, therefore, to its bottom line.

Terms for Review

- Selection process
- Employment function
- Selection ratio
- Four-fifths rule
- Validity
- Differential validity
- Reliability
- Selection interviews
- Structured interviews
- Stress interviews
- Behavioral interviews
- Supervisory interviews
- Realistic job previews

Review and Discussion Questions

1. Suppose you are an employment specialist. Would you expect to have a large or small selection ratio for each of the following job openings?

   a. Janitor

   b. Nuclear engineer with five years of experience designing naval nuclear reactors

   c. Clerk-typist

   d. Supervisor

   e. Elementary school teacher in northern Alaska? In southern Florida?

2. List and briefly describe each of the steps in the selection process.

3. If the employment manager asked you to develop a selection process for identifying and selecting internal candidates for job openings, how would you change the steps for selecting external candidates?

4. In selecting candidates for international openings, what considerations should be kept in mind?

5. Why should tests be validated?

6. As you begin interviewing a job applicant, you notice the candidate is very nervous. Your evaluation of the application blank indicates that this person is a highly qualified applicant. What would you do to put this person at ease in order to establish rapport?

7. Some people believe that the human resource department should have the authority to decide who is hired because the department contains the experts on hiring. Others say that the immediate supervisor is responsible for employee performance and should have the final authority. Support one argument or the other and explain your reasoning.

8. Explain why realistic job previews help reduce turnover among recently hired employees.

INCIDENT 8-1
National Food Brokers Selection Process

National Food Brokers buys carload orders of nonperishable food products for resale to food wholesalers. Phone-sales personnel take orders from major food wholesalers, write up the orders, and send them to the appropriate food producers. Nearly 90 of National's 130 employees work in the phone-sales department. Since the job requires long hours on the phone to different accounts, the work is not very pleasant and turnover is high.

The manager of the phone-sales department, Carol Decinni, told the following observations to the personnel manager, Craig Reems:

Most of the people that work in the department fall into two groups. There are those who have been here for two or more years. They seem reasonably content and are the top sellers we have. The other group consists of people who have been here for less than two years. Most of our turnover comes from this group. In fact, we lose one of every three new employees during the first two months. When I talk with the people who are quitting, most of them tell me that they have no idea how much time they had to spend on the phone. I am generally pleased with the quality of recruits the personnel department provides. But we cannot continue with this high turnover. My supervisors are spending most of their time training new workers. Is there anything the personnel department can do to hire more stable workers?

Suppose you are asked by the personnel manager to suggest some strategies for improving the selection process in order to hire more stable workers.

1. What suggestions do you have for

   a. preemployment testing

   b. reference checks?

2. Do you believe an interview with a supervisor in the department would help applicants understand the work better?

3. What do you think the supervisors should do to give the applicants a realistic understanding of the job before they are hired?

EXERCISE 8-1
Uniform Guidelines: The Four-fifths Rule versus the Bottom-line Test

During the last three years a company had 600 applicants, 400 whites and 200 blacks. Of this group, 100 whites and 20 blacks passed the company's standardized preemployment test. Of the 100 whites who passed the test, 80 were rated by interviewers as usable candidates; and of the 80, 60 passed the company's detailed background check. Of the 20 blacks who passed the test, 18 received acceptable evaluations from the interviewers, and 9 passed the detailed background check. The end result was that the company hired 60 white and 9 black workers during the past three years.

1. Would this company pass the bottom-line test specified by the EEOC in its uniform guidelines?

2. Which of the selection steps above, if any, fail the four-fifths rule?

3. What recommendations would you make to this company?

References

1. Sara L. Rynes and Alison E. Barber, "Applicant Attraction Strategies: An Organizational Perspective," *Academy of Management Review*, vol. 15, no. 2 (1990), pp. 286–310.

2. Richard D. Broussard and Dalton E. Brannen, "Credential Distortions: Personnel Practitioners Give Their Views," *Personnel Administrator* (June 1986), p. 129.

3. Lawrence Rout, "Going for Broker: Our Man Takes Part in Stock-selling Test," *The Wall Street Journal*, Eastern ed. (April 4, 1979), p. 1.

4. Ibid.

5. American Society of Personnel Administrators, *The Personnel Executive's Job* (Englewood Cliffs, N.J.: Prentice-Hall International Inc., 1977).

6. Tim Chauran, "The Nightmare of Negligent Hiring," *Recruitment Today* (Feb./March 1989), pp. 33–37.

7. R. Craig Scott, "Negligent Hiring: Guilt by Association," *Personnel Administrator* (July 1987), p. 32.

8. Suzanne H. Cook, "How to Avoid Liability for Negligent Hiring," *Personnel* (Nov. 1988), pp. 32–36.

9. Elliott Witkin, "Information, Not Paperwork," *Recruitment Today* (Nov./Dec. 1988), pp. 29–41.

10. For a concise review of the recent research on employment selection see Edwin A. Fleishman, "Some New Frontiers in Personnel Selection Research," *Personnel Psychology*, vol. 41 (1988), pp. 679–701. See also Michael M. Harris, "Reconsidering the Employment Interview: A Review of Recent Literature and Suggestions for Future Research," *Personnel Psychology*, vol. 42 (1989), pp. 691–726.

11. Jonathan S. Leonard, "The Changing Face of Employees and Employment Regulation," *California Management Review* (Winter 1989), pp. 29–38.

12. Paul Sheibar, "A Simple Selection System Called 'Job Match,' " *Personnel Journal* (Jan. 1979), pp. 26–29, 53. See also Robert P. Delamontagne and James B. Weitzul, "Performance Alignment: The Fine Art of the Perfect Fit," *Personnel Journal* (February 1980), pp. 115–117, 131.

13. Blayne Cutler, "My Old Kentucky Tatami," *American Demographics* (June 1989), p. 46.

14. Richard Peres, Dealing with Employment Discrimination, (New York: McGraw-Hill Book Company, 1978), pp. 18–37. See also Richard R. Reilly and Georgia T. Chao, "Validity and Fairness of Some Alternative Employee Selection Procedures," *Personnel Psychology*, vol. 35, no. 1 (Spring 1982), pp. 1–61.

15. James Ledvinka, *Federal Regulation of Personnel and Human Resource Management* (Belmont, Calif: Wadsworth Publishing Co., 1982), pp. 101–110.

16. Ibid.

17. Reilly and Chao, op. cit.

18. Thomas A. Loenko and M. Susan Taylor, "Organizational Image: Dimensionality and Relationships to Job Search Attitudes & Behaviors," *Wisconsin Working Paper* (8-82-36) (August 1982). Additional research suggests that the final acceptance or rejection of a job offer appears most influenced by job attributes. See Gary N. Powell, "Effects of Job Attributes and Recruiting Practices on Applicant Decisions: A Comparison," *Personnel Psychologist*, vol. 37, no. 4 (Winter 1984), pp. 721–732.

19. Vincent Loretto, "Recruitment: Effective Interviewing Is Based on More Than Intuition," *Personnel Journal* (Dec. 1986), p. 101.

20. James D. Walls, "Testing Has Survived Time and Trial," *Recruitment Today* (Jan./Feb. 1990), pp. 14–16.

21. "Most Employers Test New Job Candidates, ASPA Survey Shows," *Resource* (June 1988), p. 2.

22. Ibid.

23. Shawn Tully, "The Hunt for the Global Manager," *Fortune* (May 21, 1990), pp. 140–144.

24. Fleishman, op. cit.

25. Barry R. Nathan and Ralph W. Alexander, "A Comparison of Criteria for Test Validation: A Meta-analytic Investigation," *Personnel Psychology*, vol. 41 (1988), pp. 517–535. See also Michael A. McDaniel, Frank L. Schmidt, and John E. Hunter, "A Meta-analysis of the Validity of Methods for Rating Training and Experience in Personnel Selection," *Personnel Psychology*, vol. 41 (1988), pp. 283–314.

26. Fritz Drasgow, "Study of the Measurement Bias of Two Standardized Psychological Tests," *Journal of Applied Psychology*, vol. 72, no. 1 (1987), pp. 19–29.

27. *Willie S. Griggs et al. v. Duke Power Company*, 401 U.S. 424.

28. In *Griggs v. Duke Power Company* the U.S. Supreme Court said that the EEOC's uniform guidelines were "entitled to great deference." *Albemarle Paper Company v. Moody*, 422 U.S. 405 (1975). See also Douglas D. Baker and David E. Terpstra, "Employee Selection: Must Every Job Test Be Validated?" *Personnel Journal* (August 1982), pp. 602–604; James M. Norborg, "A Warning Regarding the Simplified Approach to the Evaluation of Test Fairness in Employee Selection Procedures," *Personnel Psychology*, vol. 37, no. 2 (Summer 1984), pp. 483–486.

29. Moshe Zeidner, "Test of the Cultural Bias Hypothesis: Some Israeli Findings," *Journal of Applied Psychology*, vol. 72, no. 1 (1987), pp. 38–48.

30. James Ledvinka and Lyle F. Schoenfeldt, "Legal Developments in Employment Testing: Albemarle and Beyond," *Personnel Psychology* (Spring 1978), pp. 1–3.

31. K. Dow Scott, Robert M. Madigan, and Diana L. Deadrick, "Selecting the Right Employee," *Personnel Administrator* (Dec. 1988), pp. 86–89.

32. Garry L. Hughes and Erich P. Prien, "Evaluation of Task and Job Skill Linkage Judgments Used to Develop Test Specifications," *Personnel Psychology*, vol. 42 (1989), pp. 283–342.

33. Robin Inwald, "How to Evaluate Psychological/Honesty Tests," *Personnel Journal* (May 1988), pp. 40–46.

34. Michael J. Lotito, "The Employee Polygraph Protection Act: Striking a Balance between Employer and Employee Rights," *Legal Report* (Winter 1988), pp. 1–8. See also John W. Jones and William Terris, "After the Polygraph Ban," *Recruitment Today* (May/June 1989), pp. 25–31.

35. Elizabeth M. Cosin, "Tests to Spot the Pinocchios May Fail the Honest Abes," *Insight* (July 30, 1990), pp. 42–43. See also Claudia H. Deutsch, "Pen-and-Pencil Integrity Tests," *The New York Times* (Feb. 11, 1990), sec. 3, part 2, p. 29. See also Ed Bean, "More Firms Use 'Attitude Tests' to Keep Thieves Off the Payroll," *The Wall Street Journal* (Feb. 17, 1987), p. 33; and Robert M. Madigan, K. Dow Scott, Diana L. Deadrick, and J.A. Stoddard, "Employment Testing: The U.S. Job Service Is Spearheading a Revolution," *Personnel Administrator* (Sept. 1986), pp. 102–112.

36. Charles D. Johnson, Lawrence A. Messe, and William D. Crano, "Predicting Job Performance of Low Income Workers: The Work Opinion Questionnaire," *Personnel Psychology*, vol. 37, no. 2 (Summer 1984), pp. 291–299.

37. Fern Schumer Chapman, "The Ruckus over Medical Testing," *Fortune* (August 19, 1985), p. 73.

38. Judy D. Olian, "Genetic Screening for Employment Purposes," *Personnel Psychology*, vol. 37, no. 2 (Summer 1984), pp. 423–438.

39. Gopal C. Pati and Guy Stubblefield, "The Disabled Are Able to Work," *Personnel Journal* (Dec. 1990), pp. 30–34.

40. "Meese Speech Raises Employee Privacy Rights Debate," *Resource* (Dec. 1986), p. 5. See also Michael Waldholz, "Drug Testing in the Workplace: Whose Rights Take Precedence?" *The Wall Street Journal*, Eastern ed. (Nov. 11, 1986), p. 39.

41. Paul L. Blocklyn, "Preemployment Testing," *Personnel* (Feb. 1988), pp. 66–68.

42. For a review of research on interviewing, see Harris, op. cit. See also Richard D. Arvey and James E. Campion, "The Employment Interview: A Summary and Review of Recent Research," *Personnel Psychology*, vol. 35 (1982), pp. 281–323.

43. Bureau of National Affairs, *Personnel Policies Forum*, Survey no. 114 (September 1976).

44. Walter Kiechel III, "How to Pick Talent," *Fortune* (Dec. 8, 1986), pp. 201, 203.

45. Ronald J. Karren and Stella M. Nkomo, "So, You Want to Work for Us . . .," *Personnel Administrator* (April 1988), pp. 88–92. See also Angelo Kinicki and Chris A. Lockwood, "The Interview Process: An Examination of Factors Recruiters Use in Evaluating Job Applicants," *Journal of Vocational Behavior*, vol. 26 (1985), p. 117.

46. Robert N. McMurray, "Validating the Patterned Interview," *Personnel* (Jan. 1947), pp. 263–272. See also Eugene Mayfield, "The Selection Interview—A Reevaluation of Published Research," *Personnel Psychology* (Autumn 1964), pp. 239–260; Edward C. Andler, "Preplanned Question Areas for Efficient Interviewing," *Personnel Journal* (Jan. 1976), pp. 8–10; and Frederick S. Hills, "Job Relatedness v. Adverse Impact in Personnel," *Personnel Journal* (March 1980), pp. 211–215, 229.

47. Christopher L. Martin and Dennis H. Nagao, "Some Effects of Computerized Interviewing on Job Applicant Responses," *Journal of Applied Psychology*, vol. 74, no. 1 (1989), pp. 72–80.

48. McMurray, op. cit.

49. James G. Hollandsworth, Jr., and others, "Relative Contributions of Verbal, Articulative, and Nonverbal Communication to Employment Decisions in the Job Interview Setting," *Personnel Psychology* (Summer 1979), pp. 359–367. See also Kinicki and Lockwood, op. cit., pp. 117–125.

50. Brooks Mitchell, "Face-to-Interface," *Personnel* (Jan. 1990), pp. 23–25.

51. David J. Weston and Dennis L. Warmke, "Dispelling the Myths about Panel Interview," *Personnel Administrator* (May 1988), pp. 109–111.

52. Charlene Marmer Solomon, "How Does Disney Do It?" *Personnel Journal* (Dec. 1989), pp. 50–57.

53. Avery and Champion, op. cit. See also Tracy McDonald and Milton D. Hakel, "Effects of Applicant Race, Sex, Suitability, and Answers on Interviewer's Questioning Strategy and Ratings," *Personnel Psychology*, vol. 38, no. 1 (Spring 1985), pp. 321–334.

54. Michael A. Campion, Elliott D. Pursell, and Barbara K. Brown, "Structured Interviewing: Raising the Psychometric Properties of the Employment Interview," *Personnel Psychology*, vol. 41 (1988), pp. 25–42.

55. Avery and Champion, op. cit.

56. John Byrne, "All the Right Moves for Interviewers," *Business Week* (Sept. 17, 1990), p. 156. See also "How to Conduct a Behavioral Interview," *Impact* (August 9, 1989), p. 4.

57. Kiechel, op. cit.

58. F.M. Jablin, "Use of Discriminatory Questions in Screening Interviews," *Personnel Administrator* (March 1982), p. 44.

59. John F. Binning, Mel A. Goldstein, Mario F. Garcia, and Julie H. Scattaregia, "Effects of Preinterview Impressions on Questioning Strategies in Same- and Opposite-Sex Employment Interview," *Journal of Applied Psychology*, vol. 73, no. 1 (1988), pp. 30–37.

60. Jablin, op. cit.

61. William L. Tullar, Terry W. Mullins, and Sharon A. Caldwell, "Effects on Interview Length and Applicant Quality on Interview Decision Time," *Journal of Applied Psychology*, vol. 64, no. 6 (1979), pp. 669–674.

62. D.H. Tucker and P.M. Rowe, "Consulting the Application Form Prior to the Interview: An Essential Step in the Selection Process," *Journal of Applied Psychology*, vol. 62, no. 5 (1977), pp. 558–664.

63. Tullar, Mullins, and Caldwell, op. cit.

64. Kiechel, op. cit.

65. John W. Cogger, "Are You a Skilled Interviewer?" *Personnel Journal* (Nov. 1982), pp. 840–843.

66. Richard G. Nehrbass, "Psychological Barriers to Effective Employment Interviewing," *Personnel Journal* (Dec. 1976), pp. 598–600. See also S. Trevor Michaels, "Seven Questions That Will Improve Your Managerial Hiring Decisions," *Personnel Journal* (March 1980), pp. 199–200, 224; and Kiechel, op. cit.

67. Michael H. Frisch, *Coaching and Counseling Handbook* (New York: Resource Dynamics, 1981).

68. Avery and Champion, op. cit. See also Kenneth A. Kovach, "Subconscious Stereotyping in Personnel Decisions," *Business Horizons* (Sept.–Oct. 1983), pp. 60–66; McDonald and Hakel, op. cit.; and Kinicki and Lockwood, op. cit.

69. Sondra Thiederman, "Overcoming Cultural and Language Barriers," *Personnel Journal* (Dec. 1988), pp. 34–40.

70. John A. Byrne, "Interviews: The Best Face Is Your Own," *Business Week* (Feb. 1987), p. 122.

71. Richard C. Long, "What's Missing from Most Background Checks," *Recruitment Today* (August 1988), pp. 40–48.

72. Edson G. Hammer and Lawrence S. Kleiman, "Getting to Know You," *Personnel Administrator* (May 1988), pp. 86–88.

73. Dianna L. Stone and Eugene F. Stone, "Effects of Missing Application-Blank Information on Personnel Selection Decisions: Do Privacy Protection Strategies Bias the Outcome?" *Journal of Applied Psychology*, vol. 72, no. 3 (1987), pp. 452–456.

74. Broussard and Brannen, op. cit.

75. Ibid., p. 131.

76. Winifred Yu, "Firms Tighten Resume Checks of Applicants," *The Wall Street Journal*, Western ed. (August 20, 1985), p. 27.

77. Broussard and Brannen, op. cit.

78. Virginia E. Schein, "Privacy and Personnel: A Time for Action," *Personnel Journal* (Dec. 1976), pp. 604–607, 615. See also John Rahiya, "Privacy Protection and Personnel Administration: Are New Laws Needed?" *Personnel Administrator* (April 1979), pp. 19–21, 28; and Lawrence E. Dube, Jr., "Labor Relations: Employment References and the Law," *Personnel Journal* (Feb. 1986), pp. 87–91.

79. Gerard P. Panaro, "Minimize the Danger of Giving References," *Personnel Journal* (August 1988), pp. 93–96. See also David Stier, "Many Ask, but Don't Give References," *HR News* (Feb. 1990), p. a2.

80. Erwin S. Stanton, "Fast-and-Easy Reference Checking by Telephone," *Personnel Journal* (Nov. 1988), pp. 123–130.

81. George M. Beason and John A. Belt, "Verifying Applicants' Backgrounds," *Personnel Journal* (July 1976), p. 345. See also Jeremiah Bogert, "Learning the Applicant's Background through Confidential Investigations," *Personnel Journal* (May 1981), pp. 376–377; Bruce D. Wonder and Kenneth S. Keleman, "Increasing the Value of Reference Information," *Personnel Administrator* (March 1984), pp. 98–103; and Broussard and Brannen, op. cit.

82. Carole Sewell, "Preemployment Investigations: The Key to Security in Hiring," *Personnel Journal* (May 1981), pp. 376–377. See also Wonder and Keleman, op. cit.; and Broussard and Brannen, op. cit.

83. Maria E. Recio and Robert Neff, "The Immigration Bill: Business Joins the Border Patrol," *Business Week* (Oct. 27, 1986), pp. 41–42. See also David Israel, "INS Issues 'Advice' for Employers," *Resource* (March 1987), pp. 1, 6; and Bruno Lopez, "Mexican Leaders, Scholars Differ on Effects of U.S. Immigration Bill," *Arizona Republic* (Nov. 2, 1986), pp. a10–11. See also Roger Skrenny, "Employer Sanctions: 25 Questions," *Personnel Journal* (Oct. 1987), pp. 60–63.

84. Rosemary M. Collyer, "Preemployment Medical Testing: An Overview," *Legal Report* (Summer 1989), pp. 1–8.

85. Chapman, op. cit.

86. Bruce M. Meglino, Angelo S. DeNisi, Stuart A. Youngblood, and Kevin J. Williams, "Effect of Realistic Job Previews: A Comparison Using Enhancement and Reduction Preview," *Journal of Applied Psychology*, vol. 73, no. 2 (1988), pp. 259–266.

87. Lyman Porter and Richard Steers, "Organizational, Work, and Personal Factors in Employee Turnover and Absenteeism," *Psychological Bulletin*, vol. 80 (1973), pp. 151–176.

88. Paula Popovich and John P. Wanous, "The Realistic Job Preview as a Persuasive Communication," *Academy of Management Review* (Oct. 1982), p. 571.

89. Ibid., p. 572.

90. John P. Wanous, "Realistic Job Previews: Can a Procedure to Reduce Turnover Also Influence the Relationship between Abilities and Performance?" *Personnel Psychology* (Summer 1978), pp. 249–258. See also Powell, op. cit.

91. Bernard L. Dugoni and Daniel R. Ilgen, "Realistic Job Preview and the Adjustment of New Employees," *Academy of Management Journal* (Sept. 1981), p. 590. See also James A. Breaugh, "Realistic Job Previews: A Critical Appraisal and Future Research Directions," *The Academy of Management Review* (Oct. 1983), pp. 612–619.

92. Kevin M. Kelly, "Employment by Trial," *Personnel Journal* (March 1989), pp. 40–43.

93. Jean Powell Kirnan, John A. Farley, and Kurt F. Geisinger, "The Relationship between Recruiting Source, Applicant Quality, and Hire Performance: An Analysis by Sex, Ethnicity, and Age," *Personnel Psychology*, vol. 42 (1989), pp. 293–308.

III

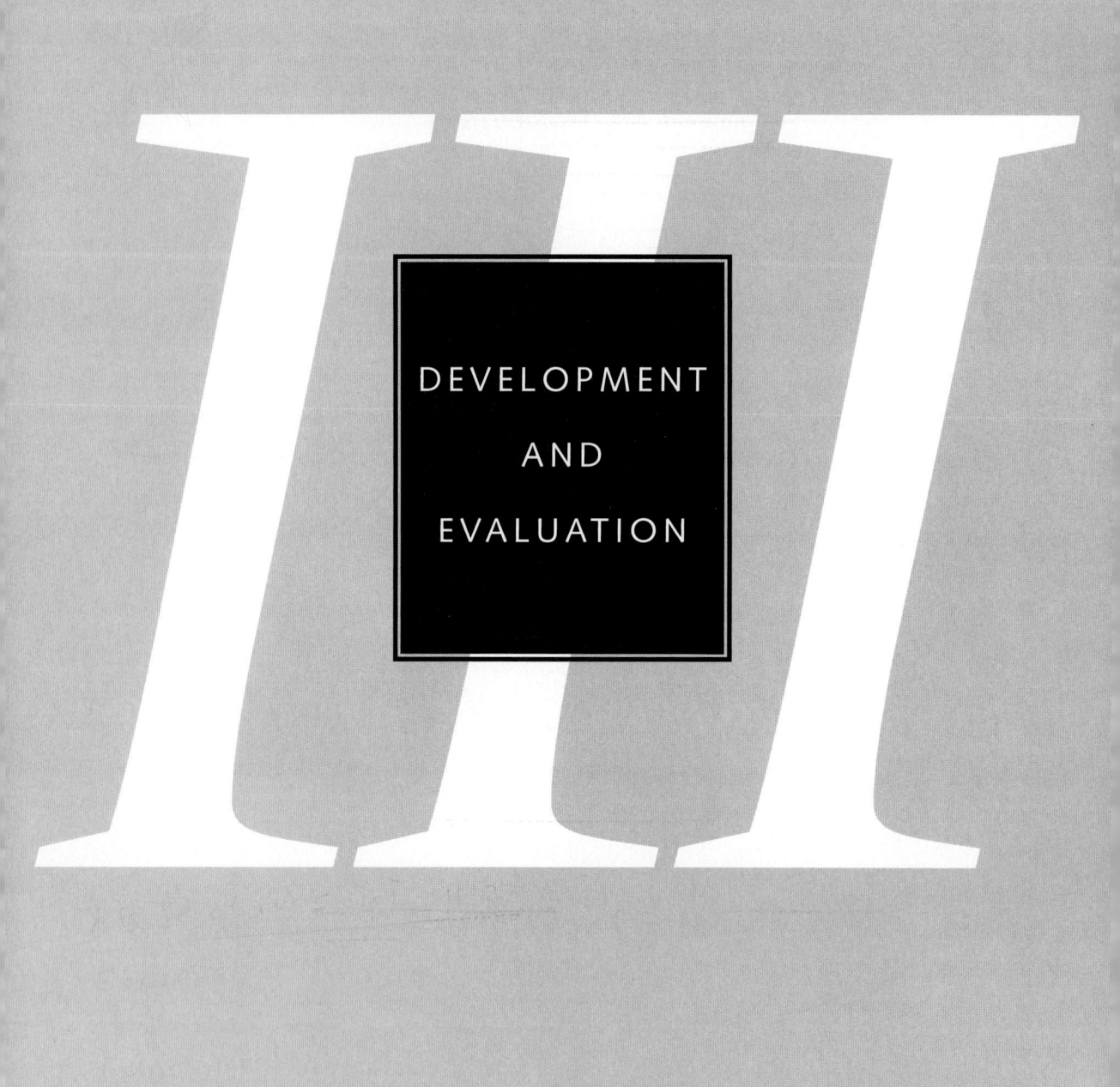

DEVELOPMENT AND EVALUATION

9 Orientation and Placement
10 Training and Development
11 Performance Appraisal
12 Career Planning

*W*HEN A new employee is hired or a present employee is reassigned, orientation should follow. New jobholders need to be trained to do their present jobs and developed to handle future responsibilities. The success of the individual and of the human resource department depends on receiving feedback about performance. Through performance appraisal, the employee and the human resource department learn how successful their efforts have been. Some employers even offer career planning assistance to further encourage the development of employees.

The next four chapters are about employee development and evaluation. The human resource department's role in these activities affects you whether you work in a human resource department or elsewhere in an organization. Knowledge of these activities allows you to be a better employee and a more effective manager.

Organizational

I
FOUNDATION
AND
CHALLENGES

V
EMPLOYEE
RELATIONS AND
ASSESSMENT

II
PREPARATION
AND
SELECTION

OBJECTIVES
- Societal
- Organizational
- Functional
- Personal

IV
COMPENSATION
AND
PROTECTION

III
DEVELOPMENT
AND
EVALUATION
- Orientation and placement
- Training and development
- Career planning
- Performance appraisal

Professional

Societal

↔ Feedback among activities and objectives

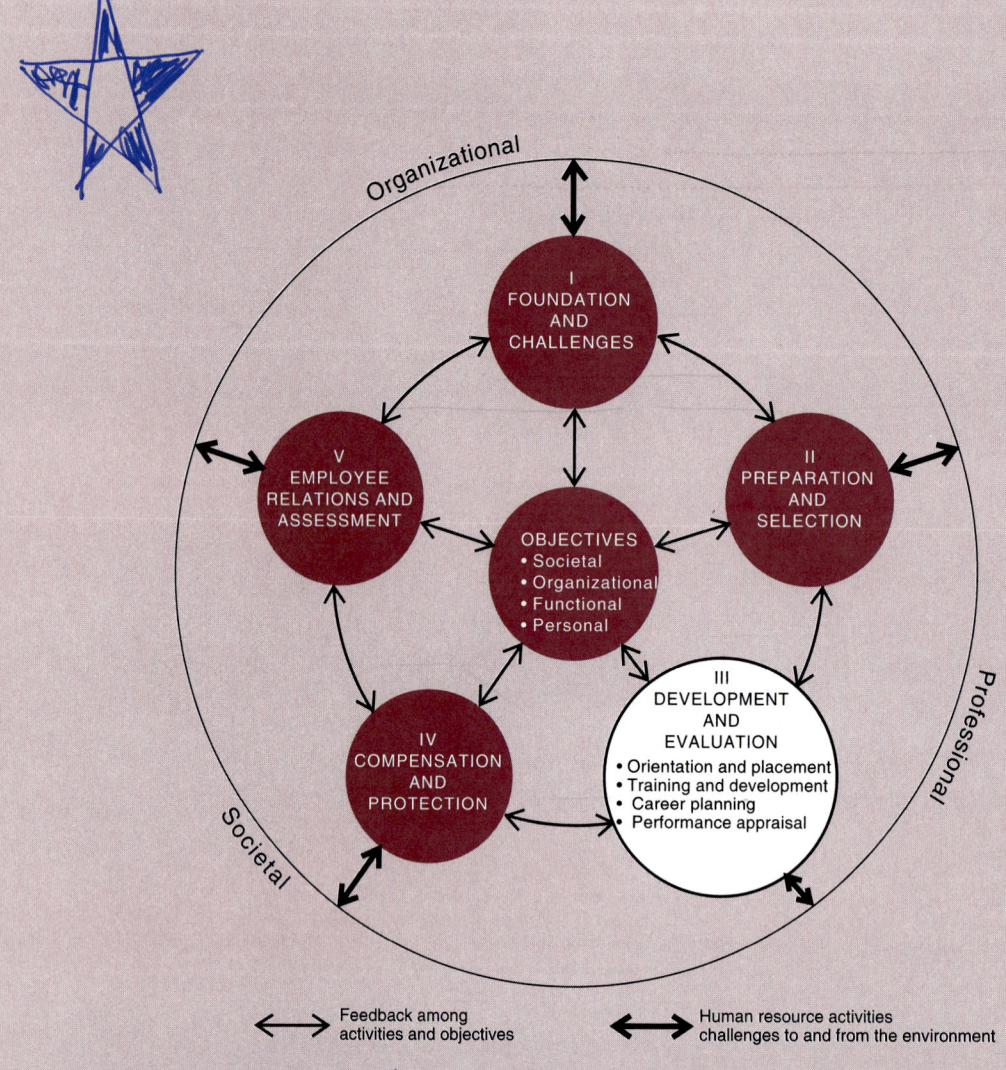

↔ Human resource activities challenges to and from the environment

Objectives of H.R

1. Societal
2. Org.
3. Functional
4. Personal

How employees are hired, trained, developed, and moved among jobs is likely to determine employees', and therefore the firm's, ability to adapt.
KAREN N. GAERTNER[1]

Effective socialization means an internal commitment to the organization, rather than just compliance with organization practices.
JOHN P. WANOUS[2]

ORIENTATION AND PLACEMENT

CHAPTER OBJECTIVES

After studying this chapter, you should be able to:
1. TELL why orientation is needed for new employees and employees in new jobs.
2. EXPLAIN how a new-employe orientation affects turnover and learning.
3. IDENTIFY the human resource department's and the supervisor's role in employee orientation.
4. EXPLAIN how placement decisions affect the human resource department.
5. DISCUSS the human resource department's role in separations.
6. IDENTIFY strategies used to ensure greater job security.

p272-298

h

Newcomer concerns

UMAN RESOURCE management is much more than just hiring people. Once hired, proactive human resource departments help the new hire become a productive and satisfied employee. This help also extends to current employees who are reassigned to new jobs through promotions, transfers, and demotions.

As the last two chapters about recruiting and selection have shown, organizations devote considerable time and resources to hiring people. By the first day, the employer already has an investment in the worker. And there is a job—or at least a potential job—that needs to be done. At the same time, the newcomer has needs that may hinder the transition from recruit to productive employee. Often these needs are stimulated by anxieties such as "Will I be able to do the job?" or "Will I fit in around here?" or "Will the boss like me?" These "first-day jitters" may be natural, but they reduce both the employee's satisfaction and his or her ability to learn. Psychologists tell us that initial impressions are strong and lasting because newcomers have little else by which to judge. To help the employee become a satisfied and productive member, the human resource department must make those initial impressions favorable.

Met Life

Metropolitan Life (Met Life) is a major life insurance company based in New York City. When the human resource department set out to redevelop the company's orientation program, it began by determining who is responsible for employee orientation. The answer was those who stood to gain or lose from the program: new employees and their managers. So, fifty managers from different lines of business were interviewed to learn what was important in an orientation and how it should be addressed.

The Met Life training and development department involved customers to reinforce the importance of customer service while describing this large and complex business to those being oriented. The content of the orientation is suggested by the program's name, "Quality from the Start." It addressed "quality and customer focus," along with "accountability of results" and "teamwork." Emphasis also was place on Met Life's mission and the importance of individual contributions to the success of the company.

The resulting program was done in modules. It included a core module, covering general company information. Other modules addressed more specific concerns of individual lines of business. These modules also reflected the suggestions of more than 1,000 employees who were surveyed about what content they thought would be appropriate to speed the newcomers' integration into the organization. The core module was designed to have multiple uses for dealing with the general public, current, and prospective employees.

Managers were involved not only in the design of the program, but they also received an employee orientation checklist. Surveys were sent to employ-

272   III. DEVELOPMENT AND EVALUATION

*ees and their managers following the orientation to further evaluate the "Quality from the Start" program. The survey sought to find out what modules of the orientation were actually used, their effectiveness, and the need for changes.*³

This Met Life example illustrates a proactive approach to creating an effective orientation program. The "Quality from the Start" program illustrates several important dimensions. First, orientation efforts must involve the employee's manager. Not only does supervisory involvement start their relationship, it also gives the employee specific details about his or her job and job setting. Second, tapping the suggestions of other employees ensures that the content of the program is relevant. Third, from a systems viewpoint, the follow-up survey provides the department with a feedback loop to further refine the program. And, fourth, modules enable the relevant parts to be used with employees who change jobs.

PLACEMENT OBSTACLES TO PRODUCTIVITY

One obstacle to a productive and satisfied work force is that employees are more likely to quit during their first few months than at any other time in their employment. This initial turnover is common. Some of it may even be beneficial if it is among those new hires who sense that the organization or the job is not right for them.⁴

Dissonance Reduction

Dissatisfaction

As discussed at the end of Chapter 8, "Selection," realistic job previews close the psychological gap between what newcomers expected and what they find. This difference between what one expects and what one finds is called *cognitive dissonance*.⁵ If dissonance is too high, people take action. For new employees, that action may mean quitting.

Other potential causes of dissonance exist besides the job itself. New employees may not like work-related policies, coworkers, supervision, or other aspects of their employment relationship. And until the newcomer reports to work, neither the employee nor the personnel department can tell which areas will be of concern.

New Employee Turnover

When the Human Resource department helps employees meet their personal objectives, employee satisfaction tends to improve, which may benefit the organization through lower turnover costs.⁶ Turnover is expensive. The expenses not only of recruiting and selection but also of creating new employee records in the

Figure 9-1 EMPLOYEE ORIENTATION NEEDS OF METROPOLITAN LIFE MANAGERS

Goals of Metropolitan Life Managers for Company Orientation Program

▶ *Fosters* pride in belonging to a quality company.
▶ *Creates* an awareness of the scope of the company's business and its impact as a major financial institution.
▶ *Emphasizes* that customer focus and service are a competitive advantage.
▶ *Decreases* the concerns associated with a new job.
▶ *Helps* speed the development of a contributing team member.
▶ *Clarifies* the standards of quality by which performance is measured.
▶ *Establishes* that the responsibility for personal growth and development is shared by the employee and management.

Source: Susan Berger and Karen Huchendorf, "Ongoing Orientation at Metropolitan Life," *Personnel Journal*, December, 1989, p. 34.

Turnover costs

human resource department, establishing payroll records in accounting, giving new employees training, and providing them with necessary safety equipment are lost when employees leave. These costs never appear on the profit and loss statement as "turnover expenses," although if they did, top management might pay closer attention to turnover. Instead, the costs of turnover are reflected in the budgets of the personnel, accounting, training, and safety departments. The exact cost per employee probably can never be determined accurately. For entry-level, unskilled workers who quit in the first day or so, the expense is likely to be a few hundred dollars. For newly hired salaried managers and professionals—particularly if the employer had to pay a search firm fee—the cost of turnover can be many thousands of dollars.

IBM

To a large firm, a few thousand dollars may seem inconsequential. But if thousands of employees leave each year, the costs of turnover can quickly escalate into millions of dollars. At IBM, for example, turnover averages three percent of its 242,000 domestic work force, or more than 7,000 employees, annually.[7] And when experienced, long-service employees quit, the loss may be incalculable because of the training, knowledge, and skills that these workers take with them.[8] In general, the human resource department can reduce turnover by meeting the personal objectives of employees. When that happens, both the employee and the organization can benefit.

The remainder of this book discusses what human resource departments can do to maintain and retain a productive work force. This chapter shows how the department can ease an employee's transition into a new job. As Figure 9-1 suggests, a new employee's capabilities are seldom enough to meet the demands of the job. Those capabilities need to be supplemented with orientation and training. This chapter discusses how orientation facilitates the placement of employees into productive roles within the organization. The following section outlines the content, responsibilities, and benefits of orientation programs. The last section of the chapter identifies other issues in the placement of human resources within the organization.

ORIENTATION PROGRAMS

One widespread method for reducing turnover among newly hired employees is an orientation program that familiarizes new employees with their roles, the organization, its policies, and other employees. For example, consider the situation faced some years ago by one department at Texas Instruments, a worldwide producer of microelectronics and electronic equipment.[9]

Texas Instruments

At Texas Instruments—or TI, as it is called by the employees—the orientation program was superficial at best. New employees went to a large room where they were quickly told about the company and its fringe benefits. They completed forms about benefits and other job-related matters and then were sent to their supervisors to report for work.

Most supervisors took a few minutes to introduce the newcomer to the other assemblers. The supervisor often assigned the new employee to a work station with instructions for nearby workers to show the newcomer what to do. After being put through a superficial orientation program and quickly introduced to coworkers, the employee found himself or herself (most of the employees were female) sitting between two other employees trying to learn the job of assembling electronic components.

As many groups of workers do, the experienced assemblers had developed a little ritual for newcomers to endure. It was mild hazing, which is nearly impossible for a human resource department to stop by prohibiting it. The trainees were told that Texas Instruments treated employees unfairly and that their present supervisor was one of the worst in the company. The newcomers' anxieties were greatly increased, to say the least. Their ability to learn and do the job suffered and some of the new employees would even go on a break or go to lunch and never return—not even to pick up their one-half day paycheck.

The human resource department reacted by recruiting an even larger number of new employees to offset the high initial turnover. After an internal investigation into the causes of this turnover, the department revamped its entire orientation process. New employees were given an extended orientation. The session, which lasted nearly all morning, explored the background and personnel policies of the company. Some forms were completed at the session, but the thrust of the orientation was to create a more positive attitude about TI among the recently hired recruits. Newcomers also were told that they had a high probability of success. Shortly before lunch, the new employees were taken to a roped-off section of the cafeteria where they had lunch with their future supervisors.

9. ORIENTATION AND PLACEMENT

Figure 9-2

The Impact of Thorough Orientation on Employee Turnover and Employee Learning

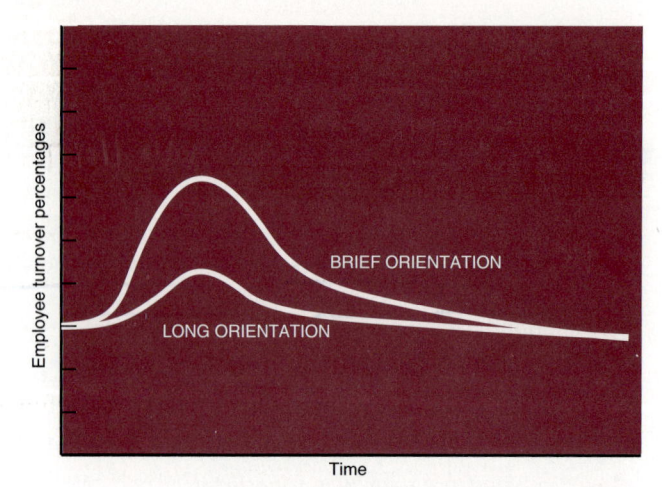

A.

Employee turnover percentages

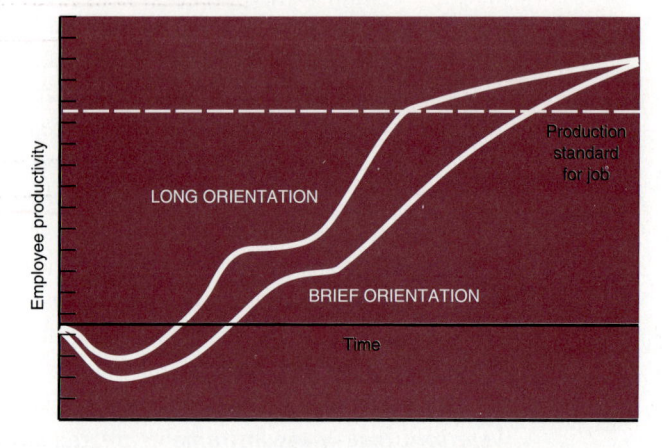

BRIEF ORIENTATION

LONG ORIENTATION

Time

B.

Employee productivity

LONG ORIENTATION

Production standard for job

BRIEF ORIENTATION

Time

Following lunch, the supervisor would take the new employee back to the department and provide introductions to the other assemblers. Although the hazing went on for some time, the new employees had a more wholesome understanding of the company and were apparently better able to recognize the hazing for what it was, a ritualized introduction to the work group.

Benefits at TI

The newly revised orientation approach led to some significant changes at TI. The two major developments are illustrated in Figure 9-2. Turnover among recently hired employees dropped, as seen in Figure 9-2A. A higher percentage of employees stayed on the job. The turnover lines merge after a short time

276 III. DEVELOPMENT AND EVALUATION

because orientation programs have little measurable impact on workers' intentions to remain after they have been with the company for a year or more. Other factors such as supervision, policies, and pay seem to have more impact on turnover among long-service employees. Both turnover curves in the figure start at the same point because an orientation program cannot have any impact on the turnover that occurs before the first day of work. For example, if a human resource department hires twenty people and asks them to report for orientation in two weeks, it is likely that some of the twenty will find even better jobs in the interim and not show up at all.

Orientation and learning

The orientation program had another interesting impact, which is diagrammed in Figure 9-2B. Recipients of the new orientation program learned their jobs more quickly. That is, the more fully oriented employees mastered their jobs at an acceptable level of productivity more quickly than those employees who had the short orientation. This outcome was unexpected, since the workers in the new program were off the job for four hours while the workers in the shorter program missed only an hour or so of work. It would have seemed, particularly since this job was not very skilled, that a short orientation would get newcomers on the job quicker so they might learn their jobs faster. But the more fully oriented employees probably had fewer anxieties. They probably felt more at ease and more motivated to stay with the organization, which seems to explain why they mastered their jobs sooner than those with the shorter and more superficial orientation. Quick mastery of the job also may help lower turnover even further because research suggests that good performers are more likely to stay with an organization.[10]

Socialization

"Fitting in"

The department's efforts help integrate the newcomer into the organization and enable socialization to take place. *Socialization* is the ongoing process through which an employee begins to understand and accept the values, norms, and beliefs held by others in the organization.[11] The socialization process helps the organization meet its needs for productive employees while enabling the new employee to meet his or her needs. As described in Chapter 1, an important objective of human resource management is to assist employees in achieving their personal goals, at least insofar as these goals enhance the individual's contribution to the organization.

The revised TI orientation program succeeded because it accelerated the socialization of new employees. Figure 9-3 depicts the socialization process as the meeting of the organization's culture and the individual's personality. Through formal methods such as orientation programs and informal ones such as hazing in the TI example, the values of the organization are transmitted to newcomers.

Orientation programs are particularly effective socialization tools because they are used among new employees. Since most newcomers have a strong desire to be accepted, they attempt to internalize "the way things are done in the organization" and make it "their way," too. Training (discussed in Chapter 10) furthers

9. ORIENTATION AND PLACEMENT **277**

Figure 9-3

The Socialization Process

Organization's culture and values → SOCIALIZATION PROCESS ← Individual's personality

the socialization process by having the employee actually learn and perform the desired behavior.

As a person is exposed to orientation, training, and the peer group, the organizational values, beliefs, and traditions are slowly absorbed.[12] Eventually, the newcomer becomes more fully integrated into the organization. Acceptable levels of satisfaction, productivity, and stability of employment are then more likely. The orientation process is an effective way to speed up socialization so that employees can become more productive contributors to the organization sooner.

Content and Responsibility for Orientation

Formal orientation programs usually rely on the human resource department and on the supervisor.[13] This *two-tiered orientation program* is common because the issues covered in an orientation fall into two broad categories: general topics of interest to most new employees and specific, job-related issues of concern only to specific jobholders. Figure 9-4 shows the common topics in an orientation program. Those labeled "organizational issues" and "employee benefits" are general concerns to virtually every new employee, so they are explained by representatives from the human resource department. The coverage of organizational issues and fringe benefits often is supplemented with an *employee handbook* that describes company policies, rules, regulations, benefits, and other items. Sophisticated orientation programs—such as Met Life's or TI's—may include films or videotapes about the company's history as well as videotaped greetings from key executives. However, the bulk of the information comes from the personnel department representative.[14]

Employee handbook

Supervisory role

In addition to the department's presentation, the orientation is continued by the employee's supervisor. The supervisor handles the job-related introductions. This tier of the orientation program should include introducing new employees to their coworkers. Sometimes newcomers also need to meet others who work in different departments. Inspectors, supervisors, accountants, and even peers in other departments may be part of the social network to which the employee becomes attached. Equally important are job duties and related issues. These items are normally explained by the supervisor, too. The supervisory-level orientation reviews the job and its objectives. The session covers specific information about tasks, safety requirements, job location, the relationship of the job to other

[handwritten top: to be successful orgs go with two-tier approach]

Figure 9-4

Topics Often Covered in Employee Orientation Programs

[handwritten: Drawing EAP]

ORGANIZATIONAL ISSUES

- History of employer
- Organization of employer
- Names and titles of key executives
- Employee's title and department
- Layout of physical facilities
- Probationary period
- Product line or services provided
- Overview of production process
- Company policies and rules
- Disciplinary regulations
- Employee handbook
- Safety procedures and enforcement

EMPLOYEE BENEFITS

- Pay scales and paydays
- Vacations and holidays
- Rest breaks
- Training and education benefits
- Counseling
- Insurance benefits
- Retirement program
- Employer-provided services to employees
- Rehabilitation programs

INTRODUCTIONS

- To supervisor
- To trainers
- To coworkers
- To employee counselor

JOB DUTIES

- Job location
- Job tasks
- Job safety requirements
- Overview of job
- Job objectives
- Relationship to other jobs

[handwritten: supervisor weakest part – too busy. use buddy system]

jobs, and other issues in Figure 9-4. To be truly effective, employees need a two-tiered orientation using both the personnel department and the supervisor. One study reported that 9.8 percent of orientations lasted one hour, while 51 percent took a day or longer. More than two-thirds of the firms conducted the orientation immediately after the employee reported to work.[15]

Opportunities and Pitfalls

The weakest part of most orientation programs is at the supervisory level. Even when the human resource department has designed an effective orientation program and trained supervisors to conduct their part of it, orientation still may not be effective. In their defense, it is only fair to say that supervisors may have more pressing problems or that everything seems so familiar to them that nothing really stands out as important for the newcomer to learn. Supervisors are often more interested in immediate production issues and may see orientation as far less important than other problems they face. To help ensure a systematic orientation, the supervisor may be given a checklist of topics to cover, as is done at Met Life, for example. The supervisor's checklist focuses on the introductions and job duties in Figure 9-4.

Buddy system

One helpful supplement to the job-related orientation is the assignment of the newcomer to a buddy. Under the *buddy system* of orientation, an experienced employee is asked to show the new worker around, conduct the introductions for the supervisor, and answer the newcomer's questions. One advantage of this approach is the candid insights the newcomer is likely to gain. Moreover, the "buddy" will probably bring the new employee along to lunch and maybe to after-work activities. These social interactions give the newcomer an introduction to people in a relaxed setting and can help accelerate his or her feelings of acceptance within the work group.[16]

The buddy system is a *supplement* to the supervisor's orientation efforts. If the buddy system is *substituted* for the supervisory orientation, the supervisor loses an excellent opportunity to establish open communications with new employees. Very soon, newcomers may find it more comfortable to ask coworkers, rather than the supervisor, about job-related issues. Supervisors who pass up the opportunity to spend some time with new employees miss a chance to create a favorable relationship before the employee becomes influenced by what other people think about the supervisor and the organization.

Besides the ever-present potential for a weak supervisory orientation, other common pitfalls exist that the personnel department and supervisor should consider. Both the personnel department and the supervisor are responsible for seeing that the employee is not:

➤ *Overwhelmed* with too much information to absorb in a short time

➤ *Overloaded* with forms to complete

➤ *Given* only menial tasks that discourage job interest and company loyalty

➤ *Asked* to perform tasks where there is a high chance for failure that could needlessly discourage the employee

➤ *Pushed* into the job with a sketchy orientation under the mistaken belief that "trial by fire" is the best orientation

➤*Forced* to fill in the gaps between a broad orientation by the human resource department and a narrow orientation at the department level.

Benefits of Orientation Programs

Although research about orientation programs is limited, several benefits are commonly reported.[17] Most benefits revolve around reducing the employees' anxieties. With less anxiety, newcomers can better learn their duties. Hazing by peers or criticism by supervisors can be kept in perspective since properly oriented workers have more realistic job expectations. As a result, well-oriented newcomers need less attention from coworkers and supervisors, perform better, and are less likely to quit.[18] Reconsider the Texas Instruments example earlier in this chapter.

Texas Instruments

At Texas Instruments, one group of employees received an extended orientation program. The special program focused on the social adaptation problems usually encountered by employees at TI. They were told that they had a high probability of success, that other employees might kid or haze them, that their supervisors were helpful people, and that as new employees they should initiate communications with supervisors if there were any questions.

The results of the specially oriented group showed that material waste was reduced by 80 percent; training costs dropped by two-thirds; product costs were 15 percent lower; and training time, absenteeism, and tardiness were cut in half.[19]

These types of benefits occur because the orientation program helps an individual understand the social, technical, and cultural aspects of the workplace. As new employees are accepted, they become a part of the social fabric of the organization. Orientation programs help speed up that socialization process and benefit both the employee and the organization.

Orientation Follow-up

Successful orientation programs include built-in follow-up procedures, such as those at Met Life. Follow-up is needed because new employees often are reluctant to admit that they do not recall everything they were told in the initial orientation sessions. Without follow-up, their questions might go unanswered. The personnel department often uses a prescheduled meeting or a simple checklist that asks the employee to critique the weaknesses of the orientation program. Weaknesses, presumably, are topics about which an employer needs more information. The checklist also serves as feedback to help the personnel department identify those parts of the program that are strong. Although the checklist can be effective, face-to-face meetings between the employee and the supervisor are the most important type of orientation follow-up.

Face-to-face follow-up

Many supervisors believe they follow up with the new hire frequently, but many new employees often do not perceive their supervisor's actions as true follow-ups. One problem may be the supervisor's body language, for example. A supervisor may ask, "Is everything okay? Let me know if you have any questions." But if this is stated as the supervisor continues to walk past the employee, the body language received by the employee is, "My supervisor really doesn't want to stop and talk." Instead of raising questions, the employee responds with some affirmative indication that all is okay. Or the supervisor appears and disappears so quickly that even an assertive employee may not think of appropriate questions before the supervisor is gone.

Sometimes the supervisor cannot answer an employee's question and must refer it to someone else. Even though a referral may be the best answer, the employee may feel that the supervisor does not really care about the problem. An even worse situation occurs when the supervisor says "I'll find out" and never gets back to the employee with the correct answer. That *is* indifference. Consider how Exxon attacked this problem of weak follow-up by supervisors at its Research and Engineering Company in Florham Park, New Jersey.

Exxon

At Exxon Research and Engineering Company, 50 to 150 engineers have been hired each year for several years. In recognition of the need for a smooth entry into the organization, Exxon had an action guide and reference manual developed for supervisors to help them do a better job with newcomers. The manual outlines actions the supervisor should take before the employee arrives, such as arranging for workspace, telephones, office supplies, and the like. It also describes the actions a supervisor should take after the new employee arrives.

The particularly innovative parts of the program are the follow-up meetings that supervisors are supposed to have with their new engineers. These sessions are called "How's It Going" meetings. They are intended to open up communications between the newcomer and the supervisor. Information is shared, concern is shown, and matters of interest are discussed. To make these sessions as effective as possible, they are held separately from meetings that give work assignments or review performance. Supervisors also are trained to conduct these meetings. The objectives of the training are to increase the supervisor's awareness of the new employee's needs, introduce the supervisors to the company's socialization procedures, and improve the supervisor's skills at communicating with new employees.

Internal company research showed that after the training, supervisors were 40 percent more likely to hold initial orientation discussions with newcomers and were 20 percent more likely to hold follow-up sessions at the end of three months.[20]

International Implications

When new hires or employees are moved across international borders, orientation becomes more important and complicated.[21] The traditional use of a company orientation, usually done by the human resource department, and a supervisory orientation remain valid. The employee still needs to be briefed about the company—its organizational and employee benefit issues and the specific job to be done. The need for introductions and a "buddy" system, along

III. DEVELOPMENT AND EVALUATION

with follow-up, also remain valid. What makes orientation of people moved across international borders different is the need for additional background orientation.²²

Cultural practices, language, and even differences in business laws should be included in orientations that involve moves across borders. For United States nationals going overseas or foreign nationals working for United States-based firms, for example, it is particularly important that they be briefed about the *Foreign Corrupt Practices Act*. This U.S. law restricts—with potentially severe penalties—the use of bribes (sometimes thinly disguised as "commissions"). Even though "commissions" or "kickbacks" may be a culturally accepted method of conducting business overseas, they violate this U.S. law.

Foreign Corrupt Practices Act

Even before the employee arrives in the foreign country, extra assistance may be needed with local customs, housing, shopping, or schooling.²³ The human resource department may even be called upon to assist with finding employment for the employee's spouse. International orientation should include additional follow-up. Merely being able to find traditional foods of expected quality can be a source of problems. In some cases, an otherwise good placement may fail when the family-related pressures of a foreign assignment lead to a request to return to the home country or a resignation.²⁴ These concerns apply equally whether people are being transferred from or to the headquarter country.²⁵ Good follow-up by the department can be crucial to a successful international placement.

EMPLOYEE PLACEMENT

As discussed in Chapter 6, "Human Resource Planning," staffing needs are met in two ways: new employees are hired from outside the firm or present employees are reassigned. New employees must be recruited, selected, oriented, and trained. Similar to newcomers, present employees must be internally recruited, selected, and oriented before they can be reassigned. Taking over a different job in the same department may mean a relatively quick orientation about new duties. Movement between departments demands a progressively more complete orientation, as do promotions and demotions. However, these activities are seldom as elaborate as for new hires.

The allocation of people to jobs is called *placement*. Placement is the assignment or reassignment of an employee to a new or different job. It includes the initial assignment of new employees and the promotion, transfer, or demotion of present employees. The placement of present workers is less elaborate because the human resource department maintains employee records that contain the internal candidate's original application, skills inventory, and work history. With this information, recruitment of internal candidates is easier, particularly if employee career paths have been recorded and computerized. Likewise, selection goes more quickly because the past performance and abilities of employees are better known than those of external recruits. Time and effort also are saved in orientation. When present employees are assigned to a new job, for example, they seldom need both tiers of the orientation program. The department's part usually can be skipped, although the supervisory orientation still is needed to speed up the socialization within the new work group.

Most placement decisions are made by line managers. The employee's supervisor in consultation with higher levels of line management usually decides the future placement of each employee. When the placement decision involves the employee going to work in a different part of the organization, placement decisions usually are made by the employee's prospective supervisor. The department's role is to advise these line managers about the company's policies and to provide counseling to the employee.

Types of placement

Within these constraints, the three major classes of placement decisions are: promotions, transfers, and demotions. Each of these decisions should be coupled with an orientation and follow-up, regardless of whether the placement is caused by down-sizing, merger, acquisition, or some other change in internal staffing needs. The following sections review these three placement decisions.

Promotions

A *promotion* occurs when an employee is moved from one job to another that is higher in pay, responsibility, and/or organizational level. It is one of the more pleasant events that happen to people in an organization. Generally, it is given as a recognition of a person's past performance and future promise. Promotions usually are based on merit and/or seniority.[26]

Merit-based promotions. *Merit-based promotions* occur when an employee is promoted because of superior performance in the present job. In cases where promotion is mostly a "reward" for past efforts and successes, two problems may be encountered.

One problem is whether decision makers can objectively distinguish the strong performers from the weak ones. When merit-based promotions are being used, it is important that the decision reflect the individual's performance and not the selection biases discussed in the previous chapter on selection.[27] An example occurs when the best performer is a member of a protected class and the decision maker is prejudiced. The decision maker should not allow personal prejudices to affect promotions. Decisions that are swayed by personal feelings are more common when job performance is not measured objectively. When promotion decisions result from personal biases, the organization ends up with a less competent person in a higher, more important position. And the resulting resentment among those not promoted is likely to harm their motivation and satisfaction.

Peter Principle

A second problem with merit-based promotions is the *Peter Principle*.[28] It states that in a hierarchy, people tend to rise to their level of *incompetence*. Although not universally true, the "principle" suggests that good performance in one job is no guarantee of good performance in another. For example, if one of the new engineers hired at Exxon's Research and Engineering Company consistently made major cost-saving design changes in a refinery, that would be an

III. DEVELOPMENT AND EVALUATION

example of superior performance. However, suppose the engineer were promoted to supervisor. The skills needed to be an effective supervisor are very different from those needed to be a top engineer. As a result of such a promotion, Exxon might gain an ineffective supervisor and lose a superior engineer.

Seniority

Seniority-based promotions. In some situations, the most senior employee gets the promotion. "Senior" in this case means the employee who has the longest length of service with the employer. The advantage of this approach is that it is objective. All one needs to do is compare the seniority records of the candidates to determine who should be promoted.

Part of the rationale for this approach is to eliminate biased promotions and to require management to develop its senior employees since they will eventually be promoted. *Seniority-based promotions* usually are limited to hourly employees. For example, a promotion from mechanic second class to mechanic first class may occur automatically by seniority whenever an opening for mechanic first class occurs. Labor organizations often seek this type of promotion to prevent employers from discriminating among union members.

Most personnel experts express concern about the competency of those promoted solely because of seniority since not all workers are equally capable. Sometimes the person who is the best mechanic, for example, is not the most senior one. Under seniority-based promotions, the best person is denied the job unless the individual happens to be the most senior worker as well. This approach to promotion causes human resource departments to focus their efforts on training senior workers to ensure that they are prepared to handle future promotions.[28] In addition, the department must be concerned with maintaining an accurate seniority list. Where promotions are not based solely on seniority, both *merit* and seniority are guiding factors.

Transfers and Demotions

Transfers and demotions are the other two major placement actions available to the organization. *Transfers* occur when an employee is moved from one job to another that is relatively *equal* in pay, responsibility, and/or organizational level. *Demotions* occur when an employee is moved from one job to another that is *lower* in pay, responsibility, and/or organizational level.

Flexibility is often one key to organizational success. Decision makers must be able to reallocate their human resources to meet internal and external challenges. One common tool is the employee transfer.[29] By moving people into jobs that are neither a promotion nor a demotion, managers may be able to improve the utilization of their human resources. Transfers may even be beneficial to jobholders. The broadening experience of a transfer may provide a person with new skills and a different perspective that makes him or her a better candidate for future promotion. A transfer may even improve an individual's motivation and satisfaction, especially when a person finds little challenge in the old job. The new position, although not a promotion, may offer new technical and interpersonal

Dual-career families

challenges. In turn, these challenges may prove to be a growth opportunity for the transferee. Even when the challenges are minimal, the transfer at least offers some variety, which may enhance feelings of job satisfaction.

Transfers that involve geographic moves increasingly affect *dual-career families*, families in which both husband and wife are pursuing careers. Whether by a promotion, demotion, or a lateral move, a placement decision that transfers the employee out of the local community involves more than the employee; the spouse is affected, too. Human resource departments can ease the transition in several ways. Human resource professionals are often part of a network of other professionals in local chapters of the Society for Human Resource Management. These contacts can be used to find leads for spouses. Some departments may recommend using—even paying—local placement professionals to help the spouse. In extreme cases, especially in international transfers, the company may recommend a higher salary to help offset the spouse's lower income.

Demotions seldom hold positive outcomes for the individual. Usually they are associated with discipline; the individual is demoted for poor job performance or for inappropriate behavior such as excessive absenteeism. One problem with demotions is that the demoted employee may become "demotivated" or, worse, openly antagonistic toward those responsible for the demotion decision. Besides being a negative influence on the morale of others, this person is likely to be a poor producer. And lawsuits over demotions grow more likely.[30]

Sometimes demotions are intended to be a kindly alternative to firing an employee who cannot do his or her present job. Rather than sever the employment relationship, a decision is made to retain the employee but at a lower level of responsibility. If the reasons for the demotion are beyond the employee's control—such as poor health—the wage or salary may even be left unchanged, although future raises are unlikely.

Bumping

When employees are members of a union, they may be "bumped" into a lower job. Bumping occurs when a worker with seniority is told that his or her job is being eliminated. That worker can either become unemployed or take a lower-level job for which the union member is qualified. In other words, the more senior employee can "bump" another employee out of a job. In turn, the newly bumped employee can displace a still less senior worker in a similar or lower-level job, which sets off another round of bumping and demotions. These "bumping" rights give senior workers greater job security.

Job-Posting Programs

Job-posting programs inform employees about unfilled job openings and qualifications. The announcement of the opening invites qualified employees to apply. The notices usually are posted on company bulletin boards or placed in the company newspaper. The posted qualifications and other facts typically are drawn from job analysis information (discussed in Chapter 5). Then through *self-nominations* or the recommendations of supervisors, employees who are interested in the posted opening report to the personnel department and apply.

The purpose of job posting is to encourage employees to seek promotions and transfers that help the personnel department fill internal openings and meet employees' personal objectives. Not all job openings are posted. Senior management and top staff positions may be filled by merit promotions or, like entry-level positions, by external recruiting. Job posting is most common among lower-level clerical, technical, and supervisory positions.[31] When lower-level jobs are filled without posting them, employees may believe that they should have been allowed to apply through the posting program. Therefore, it is important for the personnel department to make the rules of the job-posting program known and to follow them consistently.

A trend toward posting even higher-level management jobs may be suggested by some firms' responses to affirmative action:

Consolidated Edison

> The Ralph Parsons Company, a construction firm based in California, began posting jobs to give qualified minorities knowledge of job openings. Likewise, the Consolidated Edison Company of New York posts 40 percent of its management openings, partly for reasons of affirmative action. CBS, Inc., in New York and Bendix in Michigan also post jobs, including some in management.[32]

Although most job bidders seek promotions, some self-nominations are likely from those who seek a transfer to broaden their skills or for personal reasons. Even self-nominated demotions are possible if the person is frustrated in his or her present job or if the person sees the demotion as a means to a job with more favorable promotion possibilities. For example, a typesetter at a newspaper might seek a "demotion" to a junior reporter because the long-term career options as a reporter may be more favorable.

Self-nominations

Self-nominations may also be used by management trainees. Many organizations hire recent college graduates for management training programs. Many of these programs are little more than an extended job rotation throughout each of several departments. After this rotation is completed, the company may allow the trainees to nominate themselves to fill posted job openings.

SEPARATIONS

A *separation* is a decision for the individual and the organization to part. It may be motivated by disciplinary, economic, business, or personal reasons. Regardless of the reasons behind the decision, the personnel department's role is to find the most satisfactory method of conducting the separation in a way that minimizes the harm to the organization and to the individual. Separations can take several forms, such as attrition, layoff, and termination.[33]

Attrition

Attrition is the normal separation of people from an organization as a result of resignation, retirement, or death. It is initiated by the individual worker and not by the company. In most organizations, the key component of attrition is resignation, which is a voluntary separation.

Although attrition is a slow way to reduce the employment base in an organization, it presents the fewest problems. Voluntary departures simply create a vacancy that is not filled, and the staffing level declines without anyone being forced out of a job. Human resource planning enables organizations to rely more heavily on attrition than on layoffs because this planning process attempts to project future employment needs, as explained in Chapter 6. When those projections indicate that a surplus of employees is likely, the personnel department can recommend an *employment freeze*, which curtails future hiring. The employment level then begins to decline as people voluntarily leave the organization. When there is sufficient lead time, attrition can reduce or even eliminate the projected surplus.

Bank of America

The effect of attrition can be significant even in a short time period. In a five-year span, Bank of America (B of A) added 14,500 people and reached a total of 87,500 employees. However, as an article in Forbes *observed, "The expansion did nothing for profitability—Citicorp netted about $9,000 for each of its 58,000 employees . . . compared with B of A's $5,000 per employee. However, B of A's employee count is dropping as the California division alone reduced its rolls 4.5% . . . all by attrition."*[34] *And this decrease in staff size took place during a one-year period.*

Age Discrimination caution

A special form of attrition is *early retirement*. It is one form of separation that the human resource department can actively control. It is used to reduce staffing levels and to create internal job openings. Early retirement plans are designed to encourage long-service workers to retire before the traditional retirement age of 65. Since people who retire before age 65 are going to draw benefits longer, their monthly retirement benefits may be reduced proportionately. Of course, an employer must take care not to discriminate against those who wish to stay past age 65, since they are protected under the *Age Discrimination in Employment Act*, as amended. If the employer is anxious to reduce the number of senior workers, the early retirement provisions may be supplemented so that there is no reduction in retirement benefits. The advantage of this form of separation is that it can start a chain reaction of promotions for several layers of junior workers. Moreover, senior workers tend to be the highest paid employees; when they retire, the employer's labor costs may decline.[35] Of course, encouraging early retirements can be financially expensive. It also may result in many employees leaving, especially key ones.

The advantages of early retirement to the organization combined with a concern for long-service employees have led proactive departments to offer pre-

288 III. DEVELOPMENT AND EVALUATION

and post-retirement counseling. By preparing employees for the financial and emotional considerations of retirement, the department eases the transition. The program almost always consists of seminars for retirees (and often their spouses) along with financial planning information. Some organizations permit employees to work part-time as a transition to full retirement. Others retain an affiliation with the employee by creating pools of retirees from which temporary openings are filled. Regional phone companies and other organizations even support clubs for retirees.

Layoffs

Layoffs are the separation of employees from the organization for economic or business reasons. The separation may last only a few weeks if, for example, its purpose is to adjust inventory levels or to allow a factory to retool for a new product. If caused by a business cycle, the layoff may last many months or years. However, if the layoff occurs because of restructuring, such as down-sizing or mergers and acquisitions, the "temporary" layoff may become permanent.[36]

When placement decisions are driven by a need to reduce costs, or to absorb a recent merger or acquisition, the department's role is much more involved.[37] Consider, for example, the human resource activities undertaken to reduce IBM's costs and make it more responsive to its markets.

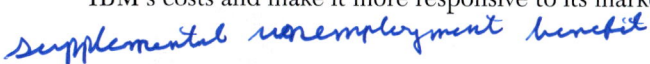

supplemental unemployment benefit

IBM

> Shortly after John F. Akers assumed the chairmanship of IBM, the computer industry went into a severe slump. Worse, from IBM's perspective, domestic competitors had gained strong footholds, and Japanese competitors loomed just over the horizon.[38] Sales and profits stalled. Compounding IBM's situation further, the company honored a "no-layoff" policy that prevented layoffs to reduce costs. Within these constraints, a variety of human resource actions were taken.
>
> Domestic employment was frozen at 242,000. Overtime was cut from five percent of total hours to one percent, the equivalent of cutting 1,000 jobs. Summer student help was reduced, and 4,000 temporary workers were not reemployed when their contracts ended. Some of the 10 billion dollars' worth of work normally done by IBM's 35,000 subcontractors was done in-house. At a cost of $550 million, employees were trained or retrained, with 10,000 employees trained for new jobs. Although some employees joke that IBM (International Business Machines) stands for "I've Been Moved," 7,300 employees changed locations at a cost of $60,000 each to rebalance staffing needs.[39] Even the hiring of college students was cut from 6,100 to only 1,000. Further rebalancing occurred by merging five marketing staffs into one, which freed another 2,500 people to join 4,000 surplus people released by laboratories and plants to boost IBM's sales force to 28,000.[40]

9. ORIENTATION AND PLACEMENT

A typical trimmed-down division, says IBM's director of organization and planning, Keith Austin, has shrunk from eight layers of management to six. "Historically," Austin explains almost casually, "managers would provide technical support. . . ." Now, the worker, with his personal computer, can generally find what he is looking for on his own.

And the pruning isn't finished. "We will continue to move in the direction of fewer layers," Austin says.[41]

Warn Act

The *Worker Adjustment and Retraining Notification Act* of 1988 requires employers to give affected workers (or their union representatives) written notice of layoffs 60 days in advance. This applies to employers with 100 or more workers when a closed or discontinued facility affects 50 employees. A layoff of more than 50 people if that constitutes a third of the work force at one site, or a layoff of 500 or more requires notification, even if a facility is not to be closed or discontinued. This law further underscores the importance of human resource planning to affected human resource departments.[42]

International issues

In international operations, layoffs are often more complicated. In Japan, especially among the very large, well-known firms, employment for men is considered to be for life—or at least until the company's retirement age. Severe morale and public relations pressures virtually eliminate layoffs as an option in these firms. In Western Europe, legislation severely restricts the use of layoffs as a method of reducing the work force. These approaches force employers to carefully plan work force growth and utilization, leading many firms to become export-oriented to offset domestic economic cycles. Nevertheless, layoffs may be required when attrition is insufficient. Though harsh for the affected employees, the alternative may be bankruptcy, affecting an even larger number of employees.[43] Most developed nations cushion the blow of layoffs and terminations with unemployment insurance, which may be supplemented by vacation pay, continued health insurance, or other supplemental unemployment benefits.

Down-sizing, reducing the levels of an organization, has been a feature of the 1980s and early 1990s. IBM and many others have been forced to down-size to reduce costs. Although down-sizing can leave emotional scars on those who remain,[44] a side benefit is often greater responsibility and greater organizational responsiveness since changes must go through fewer levels of approval. Of course, fewer people and the continuing pressures of competition usually mean more work, too.

The impact of down-sizing on human resource departments at companies like IBM has been that many more placement decisions, separations, orientations, and revised succession and human resource plans (discussed in Chapter 6, "Human Resource Planning") have been required. "Flatter" organizations also have meant fewer career opportunities. Although some people get new responsibilities and challenges, many human resource departments use lateral transfers, overseas assignments, and other placement approaches to motivate, stimulate, and retain employees, who in the past would have received promotions.

Mergers and acquisitions require different, but equally extensive, orientation and placement activities.[45] In fact, many merger and acquisitions specialists are coming to realize that blending different organizational cultures may be their most important challenge. Sophisticated orientation efforts, like Metropolitan Life's and Exxon's, and intelligent placement decisions, like IBM's, can reduce the emotional impact and help unify the company culture during down-sizing or mergers and acquisitions.[46]

Termination

Of course, employees may be separated by termination of the employment relationship. *Termination* is a broad term that encompasses the permanent separation from the organization for any reason. Usually this term implies that the person was fired as a form of discipline. When people are discharged for business or economic reasons, it is commonly, although not always, called a layoff. Sometimes, however, the employer needs to separate some employees for business reasons and has no plans to rehire them. Rather than being laid off, those people are simply terminated.

Employment-at-will doctrine

The employer's historical right to terminate an employee at any time without cause is known as the *employment-at-will doctrine*. This doctrine argues that owners (or their agents, management) have property rights that supersede an employee's right to his or her job. Simply stated, an employee can be fired for any reason, including "no reason." In recent years, however, courts have looked to employee handbooks, management promises, and other sources to find implied employment contracts which might serve to protect employees against at-will terminations. Additionally, discipline is restricted by:

➤ Conditions controlled by equal opportunity laws—such as race, religion, national origin, sex, pregnancy, and age (older than 40)[47]

➤ Union activities, as determined by law[48]

➤ The Occupational Safety and Health Act

➤ The right of an employee to refuse to perform an unusual work assignment that the employee believes is hazardous or even life-threatening

➤ The right of an employee to refuse to perform an act that is clearly in violation of law, such as cooperating in a price-fixing scheme.[49]

Other termination restrictions also may apply, depending on the circumstances and local laws. In general, a dismissal may be challenged if it is arbitrary or unjust. It also cannot be contrary to clear public policy. For example, one employee was fired for serving on a jury after the employer asked the worker to try to avoid jury service. The court decided in favor of the employee because jury duty is a high public obligation.[50]

When termination is not the fault of the employee, he or she may receive severance pay and outplacement assistance.

Severance pay is money—often equal to one or more week's salary—that is given to employees who are being permanently separated. Many organizations give severance pay only for involuntary separations and only to employees who have been performing satisfactorily. For example, if a factory is going to close or operations are to move to another state, employees who are terminated may be given an extra week's salary for each year they have worked for the company.[51] One study of 325 firms found that 84.6 percent have severance pay policies.[52] It is unlikely that someone who is being fired for poor performance or for other disciplinary reasons will receive severance pay or outplacement assistance.

Herman Miller's "silver parachutes"

Herman Miller, Inc., the world's second largest manufacturer of office furniture, developed a novel approach to severance pay, called a "silver parachute." Unlike the "golden parachutes" offered only to senior executives at firms likely to be targets of a takeover, the "silver parachutes" extend to all 35,000 of the company's employees. "The parachute would be activated in the event of a hostile takeover, and the ripcord would be pulled if a worker's job were eliminated, salary reduced, or working conditions or benefits altered."[53]

This unusual form of severance pay would be paid within ten days of termination. Those employees with between one and five years of service would receive twice their previous twelve-month compensation. Longer-service employees would receive 2.5 times their salary for the previous twelve months. Besides assuring employees of severance pay should they lose their jobs in a hostile takeover, this benefit makes the company a less attractive takeover target. And, if the silver parachute is not activated, it has no cost to the company.[54]

Outplacement

Outplacement assistance includes those efforts made by the employer directly or indirectly through a private firm to help the recently separated worker find a job. Not only do such efforts help the former employee, but they also assure the remaining employees of management's commitment to their welfare if a further reduction in force is necessary. Although outplacement is a relatively new benefit, it gained widespread support in the 1970s and early 1980s and is offered by 73.6 percent of the employers surveyed in one study.[55]

ISSUES IN PLACEMENT

Three placement decisions that are of overriding concern to a human resource department are effectiveness, legal compliance, and prevention of separations.

III. DEVELOPMENT AND EVALUATION

1. Effectiveness

The effectiveness of a placement decision depends on minimizing disruption to the employee and the organization. To reduce disruption, promotions and transfer decisions should be made in accordance with the selection steps outlined in Chapter 8. Likewise, demotions should be well-documented and follow the rules of effective discipline discussed in Chapter 17. Once the placement has been made, the new employee should get an orientation to reduce personal anxieties and speed up the socialization process.

2. Legal Compliance

For many years, employment relationships that were not based on formal, written contracts were considered to be *employment-at-will* relationships. Employment was at the will (or discretion) of either party and continued by mutual agreement. All either party had to do to end the relationship was notify the other. Over the years, however, government and the courts have limited the employment-at-will doctrine.[56]

Besides well-known laws that prevent discrimination on the basis of race, religion, national origin, age, sex, pregnancy, veteran status, or handicaps that can be accommodated, other laws and court interpretations have further limited the employment-at-will doctrine. As a matter of public policy, adverse placement decisions (primarily transfers, demotions, or separations) are restricted when applied to employees who are exercising their rights under other laws, such as the *Fair Labor Standards Act*, which specifies minimum wage and overtime pay, or the *National Labor Relations Act*, which gives some employees the right to form unions and collectively bargain with management. Beyond employment-related laws, courts and government agencies often protect *whistle-blowers*, employees who report employer violations of occupational safety and health laws, insider trader violations of Securities Exchange Commission regulations, or similar violations of public policy. Simply put, the courts are likely to reverse and penalize employers who make placement decisions that thwart employees' efforts to force employer compliance with laws or public policy.[57]

This employment-at-will doctrine has been further limited in instances where the courts have found that employment contracts have been created by past actions. For example, promises made during recruitment and commitments made in new-employee orientation programs and handbooks have been considered the base for implied employment contracts. Courts have even forced employers to reverse their placement decisions because company procedures were not followed carefully.[58]

When a placement decision is mutually supported or favorable to the employee (a promotion, for example), legal entanglements are unlikely—assuming the decision did not have negative consequence for others. However, unfavorable transfers, demotions, or involuntary separations should be arranged in accordance with laws, company procedure, and only for justifiable business reasons. Even then, the *Comprehensive Omnibus Budget Reconciliation Act* of

1986 requires employers to extend health-care coverage to former employees who are separated from the employer, regardless of the reasons. Failure to comply with employment-related laws may lead to costly suits, as one Japanese subsidiary discovered.

Quasar

> *In what is believed to be the first such verdict, a federal judge . . . found Quasar, a unit of Matsushita Electric, guilty of racial discrimination against American employees. Quasar was ordered to pay nearly $2.5 million in damages to three former Quasar executives, all in their 50s, who brought charges of age and racial discrimination against the consumer-electronics company after they and 63 other American managers—but no Japanese executives—were fired. . . .* [59]

3. Prevention of Separations

One of the more creative areas of personnel management is the prevention of separations. Obviously, anything that the personnel department can do to lessen unwanted separations benefits the organization. Restated, when personnel departments can prevent their organizations from losing valuable human resources, the moneys invested in recruitment, selection, orientation, and training are not lost. Although a minimum amount of attrition ensures a flow of new people into the organization and promotional opportunities for those already there, each departing employee is a lost investment.

To reduce the loss of valuable human resources, personnel departments can undertake a variety of actions. Through proactive programs, employee losses through voluntary resignations, retirement, death, layoffs, and terminations can be reduced.

Voluntary resignations. Voluntary resignations are reduced by a satisfying work environment, a challenging job, high-quality supervision, and personal opportunities for growth. Personnel departments are involved with these issues through supervisor training, career planning, and other activities. As described in Chapter 5, "Job Analysis and Design," for example, the personnel department can play an especially powerful role as an adviser to line managers who seek better ways to redesign the jobs they supervise. Realistic job previews and orientation programs are two other ways the department can reduce voluntary turnover. In a survey of human resource directors and top executives about why good employees quit, one study found that:

> Forty-seven percent of valued employees who quit their jobs do so because advancement opportunities are not available. Additional reasons why good employees resign include:

294 III. DEVELOPMENT AND EVALUATION

- Lack of recognition, 26%
- Dissatisfaction with management, 15%
- Inadequate salaries or benefits, 6%
- Boredom with job responsibilities, 6%[60]

Retirement. Retirement is another type of separation. Some companies offer part-time work to retiring employees as a means of helping them move from work to retirement while at the same time retaining access to the employee's valued skills and knowledge.[61]

Equitable Life Assurance Society's part-time program for retirees is called "Retiree Talent Bank." Salaried employees who have retired are used to staff temporary openings instead of hiring workers from temporary help providers or consultants. Retirees may work up to 780 hours per year while drawing full-time retirement benefits.

Equitable Life

Death. Even death as a source of separation can be targeted by progressive human resource departments through safety, preventative health care, and wellness programs designed to keep employees healthy.

Sentry Insurance Company, for example, installed a multimillion-dollar recreational complex in its western regional office in Scottsdale, Arizona. Part of the plan for this combination of weight rooms, jogging tracks, tennis courts, and other athletic facilities is to encourage employees to maintain better physical health in order to continue working longer.

Layoffs. Layoffs are minimized in some companies by careful human resource planning. By projecting employment needs several years into the future, employers like State Farm Insurance Company have avoided layoffs even during the worst recessions. Then, as the needed skill mix of their businesses changes, training and transfers help these organizations adjust to economic challenges, while providing secure employment for their employees.

Companies such as Control Data, Motorola, and IBM take another step to protect their full-time workers. As Figure 9-5 illustrates, Control Data Corporation uses a "rings of defense" approach. In the center ring are the prized full-time Control Data employees. In the next level are permanent part-time employees who would be put on layoff before the full-timers. Before permanent part-timers are laid off, temporary employees would be given their notices to

9. ORIENTATION AND PLACEMENT 295

Figure 9-5

"Rings of Defense" at Control Data Corporation

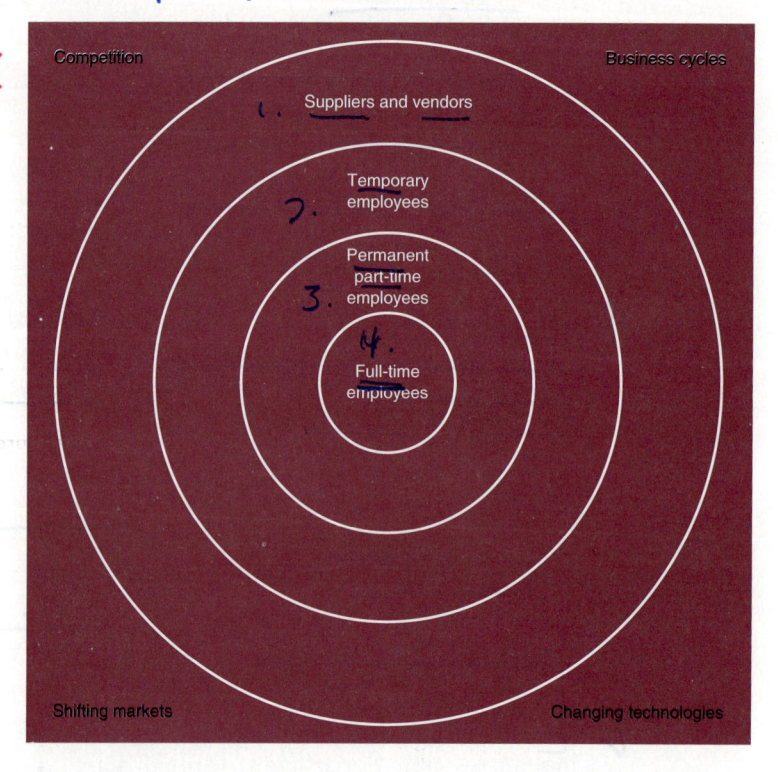

Competition — Business cycles — Shifting markets — Changing technologies

1. Suppliers and vendors
2. Temporary employees
3. Permanent part-time employees
4. Full-time employees

leave. Suppliers and vendors become the first line of defense because Control Data (along with Motorola, IBM, and other companies) contracts out some jobs that its own people could do. Before Control Data employees would be separated, janitorial, maintenance, and other jobs that are now done by contractors would be done by Control Data employees.

Layoffs also can be reduced through other approaches.[62] One method that has gained popularity is the use of reduced workweeks or *part-time layoffs*, which allow employers to lay off workers for part of each week. In such cases, the employees can collect a pro rata share of their weekly unemployment benefits. A person must usually be out of work for an entire week to collect unemployment compensation; however, new laws allow employees to collect unemployment insurance if they are put on a short-time or reduced workweek. For example, employees whose workweeks are reduced from five to four days can collect unemployment compensation for the one day they are "unemployed." This approach spreads the available work among employees while allowing the employer to retain the work force without traditional layoffs.

Part-time layoffs

Job sharing allows two or more workers to do the same job by each working part-time. Although most workers who want full-time work may find a part-time

III. DEVELOPMENT AND EVALUATION

job unacceptable, job sharing may be preferable to a layoff, especially if the job sharing is of short duration or if both employees want part-time work.

Terminations. In a nationwide study of why people were fired,

Research summary: why people are fired

The reasons include: incompetence (39%); inability to get along with coworkers (17%); dishonesty or lying (12%); negative attitude (10%); lack of motivation (7%); and failure or refusal to follow instructions (7%).

"An employer's perception of incompetence may arise from a mismatch of a candidate's professional skills and personality with the actual requirements of the job," notes Max Messmer, the chairman of Robert Hall International. He suggests that thorough reviews of corporate interviewing, reference checking, and job specification procedures would significantly reduce the high percentage of hiring mistakes and the unfortunate consequences for employees and employer alike.[63]

Besides assuring that the human resource information system is accurate and using the proper selection procedures described in the previous chapter, the department can reduce terminations among new hires through orientation. Progressive discipline that is designed to correct (not punish) poor performance is another important approach to avoiding terminations.

Another approach to reducing terminations for poor performance is training. Through effective training, new and long-service employees can be taught how to do their jobs successfully. The training and development of human resources are so important to the success of most firms that the next chapter will discuss these functions in detail. Chapter 10 clarifies the distinction between training and development and examines different training approaches.

SUMMARY

Once the selection process is completed, new employees must be oriented in order to become productive contributors. Orientation not only improves the rate at which employees are able to perform their jobs but also helps employees satisfy their personal desires to be a part of the organization's social fabric. The human resource department generally orients newcomers to broad organizational issues and fringe benefits. Supervisors complete the orientation by introducing new employees to coworkers and others involved in the job. The supervisory orientation also explains the job's duties, safety requirements, and relationship to other jobs. The purpose of orientation is to expedite the socialization process through which the employee absorbs the values, beliefs, and traditions of the organization. Proactive human resource departments follow up after the orientation to ensure that the employees do not have any remaining questions and to check on the quality of the orientation.

When job openings are filled internally, the placement process also should include an orientation. This orientation, however, tends to be informal and focuses on job-related issues, since the employee is already familiar with the organization and its benefits. When the placement decision involves moving people across international borders, however, they should receive an extensive orientation that also considers cultural and other international differences.

The process of placing present employees in different jobs or separating them from the organization is often a decision made by line managers in consultation with the human resource department. Placement decisions include promotions, transfers, and demotions. Although promotions come about in a variety of ways, they usually result from merit, seniority, self-nomination, or some combination of these approaches. Transfers and demotions also call for the advice of the human resource department. Demotions, although rare, are a particularly sensitive issue and require careful planning and employee counseling. Separations from the organization may result from disciplinary, economic, or business reasons. The department's job is to minimize the harm done to the organization and to the individual. Separations may be caused by attrition, layoffs, and terminations.

Terms for Review

- Cognitive dissonance
- Socialization
- Orientation program
- Employee handbook
- Buddy system
- Placement
- Promotions
- Merit-based promotions
- Peter Principle
- Seniority-based promotions
- Transfers
- Demotions
- Job-posting programs
- Attrition
- Employment freeze
- Early retirement
- Layoffs
- Severance pay
- Job sharing
- Comprehensive Omnibus Budget Reconciliation Act (COBRA)
- Employment-at-will
- Whistle-blowers
- Part-time layoffs

Review and Discussion Questions

1. If employees are properly selected, there should be no need for an orientation program. Do you agree or disagree with this statement? Why?

2. What are the benefits to the employee of a comprehensive orientation program? To the organization?

3. If you were going to design an orientation program for a retail store, describe the issues that would be covered by the human resource department and the issues that would be covered by the first-level supervisor.

4. When employees are being moved across international borders to fill internal openings, what unique orientation considerations arise?

5. Why would a human resource department use seniority-based promotions, and what problems might result?

6. Why have a job-posting program? How does it work?

7. In Japan, the United States, and Western Europe, layoffs are permitted, but each faces different limitations. Describe how layoffs differ in these three places.

8. How can organizations improve the stability of the employment they offer and minimize the use of layoffs?

INCIDENT 9-1
Orientation at International Warehousing, Inc.

International Warehousing owns and leases a variety of warehouse facilities at major seaports and airports around the world. Most of their facilities are concentrated in North America, Japan, Korea, Hong Kong, and throughout the European Common Market. Most employees are hired locally to work as stockers, loaders, and equipment operators. Likewise, many staff professionals—such as accountants, systems analysts, and human resource professionals—are local hires, too.

However, the warehouse and sales managers in each location are considered to be executives within the company. Although many have worked their way up from the loading docks, most have received extensive education through the company's training department and outside universities and institutes. As new facilities are planned in different regions of the world, teams of executives from adjoining areas serve as project leaders and advisers in designing, building, and leasing warehouse space. Most executives claim to enjoy occasional trips to nearby countries or cities to work on these projects, but, when a new facility is about to open, the human resource department often faces great difficulty in convincing an experienced executive to move to the new operation to help ensure a smooth startup. Those who do move typically request a transfer to their home country after the startup period is over.

1. If you were advising the human resources department, what explanations could you give for the reluctance of these executives to move to new locations?

2. What procedures would you recommend that the human resource department implement to help ensure a better supply of internal talent for international openings?

EXERCISE 9-1
Reductions in Force at Chrysler Corporation

The economic difficulties faced by the Chrysler Corporation in the late 1970s and early 1980s had a variety of causes, both domestic and foreign. The reality faced by top management was that the size of the organization—in both physical and human assets—was too big. For the level of sales that could be expected, the company had too many facilities and too many people. Systematically, top management began to shrink the size of the corporation until the early 1980s, by which time the company was about one-half its original size. This radical transformation and the short-run survival of the corporation could not depend on attrition because attrition was too slow, especially since other automobile makers and parts suppliers were, in general, not hiring. As a result, Chrysler put thousands of workers on layoff status. Most may never again work for Chrysler, or for any other car maker, because the industry is rapidly automating and foreign producers have won a larger share of the market.

For the purposes of this exercise, assume that you were asked to draw up a plan to reduce the work force from 15,000 to 10,000 employees at one very large factory.

1. What programs discussed in this chapter would you consider suggesting to the vice president of human relations before the actual layoffs begin?

2. Once people have to be given their "notice of layoff," what other actions could the company take to assist those who would be separated?

References

1. Karen N. Gaertner, "Managers' Careers and Organizational Change," *The Academy of Management Executive* (Nov. 1988), p. 317.

2. John P. Wanous, *Organization Entry: Recruitment, Selection and Socialization of Newcomers* (Reading, Mass.: Addison-Wesley Publishing Co., Inc., 1979), p. 171.

3. Susan Berger and Karen Huchendorf, "Ongoing Orientation at Metropolitan Life," *Personnel Journal* (Dec. 1989), pp. 28–35.

4. Dan R. Dalton and William D. Todor, "Turnover: A Lucrative Hard Dollar Phenomenon," *Academy of Management Review* (April 1982), pp. 212–218.

5. L. Festinger, *A Theory of Cognitive Dissonance* (Evanston, Ill.: Row, Peterson, 1957).

6. Bruna Nota, "The Socialization Process at High-commitment Organizations," *Personnel* (August 1988), pp. 20–23. See also Kenneth Oldfield, "Survival of the Newest," *Personnel Journal* (March 1989), pp. 53–59.

7. Craig Mello, "A Delayered Big Blue," *Business Month* (Jan. 1990), p. 13. See also Carol J. Loomis, "IBM's Big Blues: A Legend Tries to Remake Itself,"*Fortune* (Jan. 19, 1987), p. 52; and Charles L. Hughes and Vincent S. Flowers, "Why Employees Stay Is More Critical Than Why They Leave," *Personnel Journal* (Oct. 1987), pp. 19, 22, 24, 28.

8. William H. Mobley, "Some Unanswered Questions in Turnover and Withdrawal Research," *Academy of Management Review* (Jan. 1982), pp. 111–116.

9. Earl G. Gomersall and M. Scott Myers, "Breakthrough in On-the-Job Training," *Harvard Business Review* (July–August 1966), pp. 66–72.

10. George F. Dreher, "The Role of Performance in the Turnover Process," *Academy of Management Journal* (March 1982), pp. 137–147. See also Gareth R. Jones, "Socialization Tactics, Self-Efficacy, and Newcomers' Adjustments to Organizations," *Academy of Management Journal* (June 1986), pp. 262–279.

11. Nota, op. cit.; Oldfield, op. cit.; and Wanous, op. cit.

12. Milan Moravec and Kevin Wheeler, "Speed New Hires into Success," *Personnel Journal* (March 1989), pp. 74–75. See also Nigel Nicholson, "A Theory of Work Role Transitions," *Administrative Science Quarterly* (June 1984), pp. 172–191.

13. Claudia Reinhardt, "Training Supervisors in First-day Orientation Techniques," *Personnel* (June 1988), pp. 24, 26, 28.

14. Ronald E. Smith, "Employee Orientation: 10 Steps to Success," *Personnel Journal* (Dec. 1984), pp. 46–48.

15. Steven L. McShane and Trudy Baal, *Employee Socialization Practices of Canada's West Coast: A Management Report* (Vancouver, B.C.: Simon Fraser University, 1984).

16. Kenneth Oldfield and Nancy Ayers, "Avoid the New Job Blues," *Personnel Journal* (August 1986), pp. 49–56.

17. "ASPA-BNA Survey No. 32," op. cit., p. 5. See also Richard Pascale, "Fitting New Employees into the Company Culture," *Fortune* (May 1984), pp. 28, 30, 34, 38–40.

18. Gomersall and Myers, op. cit.

19. Ibid.

20. Thomas K. Meier and Susan Hough, "Beyond Orientation: Assimilating New Employees," *Human Resource Management* (Spring 1982), pp. 27–29.

21. Richard S. Savich and Raymond Rodgers, "Assignment Overseas: Easing the Transition Before and After," *Personnel* (August 1988), pp. 44–48.

22. Carole Gould, "A Checklist for Accepting a Job Abroad," *The New York Times* (July 17, 1988), sec. 4, p. 2.

23. Cecil G. Howard, "How Relocation Abroad Affects Expatriates' Family Life," *Personnel Administrator* (Nov. 1980), pp. 71–78.

24. Rosalie L. Tung, "Career Issues in International Assignments," *The Academy of Management Executive* (August 1988), pp. 241–244.

25. Michael C. Harvey, "The Other Side of Foreign Assignments: Dealing with the Repatriation Dilemma," *Columbia Journal of World Business* (Spring 1982), pp. 53–59. See also Savich and Rodgers, op. cit.

26. Alfred W. Swinyard and Floyd A. Bond, "Who Gets Promoted?" *Harvard Business Review* (Sept.–Oct. 1980), pp. 6–8, 12, 14, 18.

27. Ronald W. Clement, George E. Stevens, and Daniel Brenenstuhl, "Promotion Practices in American Business Colleges: A Comprehensive Investigation," *Manhattan College Journal of Business* (Spring 1986), pp. 9–15.

28. Laurence J. Peter and Raymond Hull, *The Peter Principle* (New York: William Morrow & Co., Inc., 1969).

29. Amy Saltzman, "Sidestepping Your Way to the Top," *U.S. News and World Report* (Sept. 17, 1990), pp. 60–61. See also Larry Reibstein, "The Not-So-Fast Track: Firms Try Promoting Hotshots More Slowly," *The Wall Street Journal*, Western ed. (March 24, 1986), p. 21.

30. David B. Stephens and John P. Kohl, "Demotion As a Human Resource Management Practice: An Analysis of the Oil and Gas Industry," *Journal of Managerial Issues* (Fall 1989), pp. 35–43. The demotion of a 52-year-old employee was ruled to be the equivalent of a discharge because of the physical demands of the new job. A suit brought under the Age Discrimination in Employment Act was successful against the employer, Caterpillar Tractor Company. See "Employment Update: Demotion of Employee Constitutes Constructive Discharge," *Resources* (Nov. 1985), p. 3.

31. Gary G. Wallrapp, "Job Posting for Nonexempt Employees: A Sample Program," *Personnel Journal* (Oct. 1981), pp. 796–798. See also J. Robert Garcia, "Job Posting for Professional Staff," *Personnel Journal* (March 1981), pp. 189–192.

32. "Job Posting Gains Favor in Private Firms as an Affirmative Action Tool," *The Wall Street Journal*, Western ed. (Nov. 22, 1977), p. 1.

33. Michael J. Withey and William H. Cooper, "Predicting Exit, Voice, Loyalty, and Neglect," *Administrative Science Quarterly* (Dec. 1989), pp. 521–539.

34. John Merwin, "The Logical Leader," *Forbes* (Nov. 2, 1983), p. 157.

35. James B. Shaw and Lisa L. Grubbs, "The Process of Retiring: Organizational Entry in Reverse," *Academy of Management Review* (Jan. 1981), pp. 41–47.

36. Reed E. Nelson, "Common Sense Staff Reduction," *Personnel Journal* (August 1988), pp. 50–57.

37. Carol Hymowitz, "Merged Firms Often Fire Workers the Easy Way—Not the Best Way," *The Wall Street Journal*, Western ed. (Feb. 24, 1986), p. 35.

38. Loomis, op. cit.

39. Marilyn A. Harris, "A Lifetime at IBM Gets a Little Shorter for Some," *Business Week* (Sept. 29, 1986), p. 40.

40. Ibid. See also Loomis, op. cit.

41. Mello, op. cit. See also Eric Rolfe Greenberg, "The Latest AMA Survey on Downsizing," *Personnel* (Oct. 1989), pp. 38–44.

42. Paul D. Staudohar, "New Plant Closing Law Aids Workers in Transition," *Personnel Journal* (Jan. 1989), pp. 87–90. See also Betty Southard Murphy, Wayne E. Barlow, and D. Diane Hatch, "Employers Must Notify Employees of Plant Closure," *Personnel Journal* (Oct. 1988), p. 22.

43. Carrie R. Leana, "Layoffs: How Employees and Companies Cope," *Personnel Journal* (Sept. 1988), pp. 31–24. See also Loretta D. Foxman and Walter L. Polsky, "Layoffs: Selecting Who Stays and Who Goes," *Personnel Journal* (Sept. 1988), pp. 26–27.

44. "Downsizing Falls Out of Favor," *Personnel Journal* (June 1989), p. 14.

45. Hymowitz, op. cit.

46. Phillip L. Hunsaker and Michael W. Coombs, "Mergers and Acquisitions: Managing the Emotional Issues," *Personnel* (March 1988), pp. 56–63.

47. Janis Klotchman and Linda L. Neider, "EEO Alert: Watch Out for Discrimination in Discharge," *Personnel* (Jan.–Feb. 1983), pp. 60–66.

48. Edward L. Harrison, "Legal Restrictions on the Employer's Authority to Discipline," *Personnel Journal* (Feb. 1982), pp. 136–141.

49. David W. Ewing, "Your Right to Fire," *Harvard Business Review* (March–April 1983), pp. 33–42.

50. Jeffrey C. Pingpank and Thomas B. Mooney, "Wrongful Discharge: A New Danger for Employers," *Personnel Administrator* (March 1982), pp. 31–35.

51. Stephanie Lawrence, "Trends in Severance," *Personnel Journal* (May 1988), p. 8. See also Stephenie Overman, "Westinghouse Loses Case on Severance Pay," *Resource* (May 1989), p. 11; and Angelo J. Kinicki, "Personal Consequences of Plant Closings: A Model and Preliminary Test," *Human Relations*, vol. 38, no. 3 (1985), pp. 197–212.

52. "Most Firms Have Severance Pay Programs," *Resource* (October 1986), p. 2.

53. " 'Silver Parachute' Protects Work Force," *Resource* (Jan. 1987), p. 3.

54. Ibid.

55. Elaine M. Duffy, Richard M. O'Brien, William P. Brittain, and Stephen Cuthrell, "Behavioral Outplacement: A Shorter, Sweeter Approach," *Personnel* (March 1988), pp. 28–33. See also Loretta D. Foxman and Walter Polsky, "Outplacement Results in Success," *Personnel Journal* (Feb. 1990), pp. 30, 32, 36–37.

56. Raymond L. Hilgert, "How At-Will Statements Hurt Employers,"*Personnel Journal* (Feb. 1988), pp. 75–76. See also Daniel J. Koys, Steven Briggs, and Jay Grenig, "State Court Disparity on Employment at-Will," *Personnel Psychology*, vol. 40 (1987), pp. 565–577; and David A. Bradshaw and Barbara C. Strikker, "Wrongful Termination: Keeping the Right to Fire-at-Will," *Personnel Journal* (Sept. 1986), pp. 45–47. See also David W. Ewing, "Your Right to Fire," *Harvard Business Review* (March–April 1983), pp. 32–42.

57. George E. Stevens, "The Fading of Firing-at-Will," *MW* (March 1985), pp. 8–12. See also "Employers Defend Laws on Firing," *The Miami Herald* (Nov. 11, 1985), pp. 1, 12–13.

58. Nancy Croft Baker, "The Need for Caution in Handbook Changes," *Resource* (Dec. 1988), p. 6. See also "At-Will Doctrine and Discipline," *Impact* (July 30, 1986), p. 6.

59. "Ex-Quasar Execs Win a Bias Suit," *Business Week* (Dec. 24, 1990), p. 59.

60. "Lack of Opportunity Causes Key Workers to Quit," *Small Business Reports* (Dec. 1988), p. 12.

61. "Bring 'Em Back to Work," *The Arizona Republic* (Jan. 17, 1983), p. a14. See also "When Retirees Go Back on the Payroll," *Business Week* (Nov. 22, 1982), pp. 112–116; and William B. Werther, Jr., "Part-timers: Overlooked and Undervalued," *Business Horizons* (Feb. 1975), pp. 13–29.

62. Alan H. Locher, "Short-time Compensation: A Viable Alternative to Layoffs," *Personnel Journal* (March 1981), pp. 213–216. See also Kim Watford, "Shorter Workweeks: An Alternative to Layoffs," *Business Week* (April 14, 1986), pp. 77–78.

63. "Why Are Workers Fired?" *Personnel Journal* (June 1989), p. 14.

The broad mix of social, technical, economic, and organizational changes has dramatically expanded the scope and shifted the structure of training.
LOUIS A. FERMAN, MICHELE HOYMAN, JOEL CUTCHER-GERSHENFELD, AND ENREST J. SAVOIE[1]

10

TRAINING AND DEVELOPMENT

CHAPTER OBJECTIVES

After studying this chapter, you should be able to:
1. **DISTINGUISH** between the training and the development of human resources.
2. **IDENTIFY** the employee and organizational benefits of training.
3. **EXPLAIN** the different approaches to needs analysis in designing training and development programs.
4. **DISCUSS** how work force diversity and the trend toward global businesses impact training and development.
5. **DESCRIBE** the major learning principles associated with each training technique.
6. **DEVELOP** an evaluation process to assess the results of a training and development program.

AFTER A comprehensive orientation and proper job placement, new employees may not be able to perform satisfactorily. Often they must be trained in the duties they are expected to do. Even experienced employees in new jobs need training to improve their performance. Capabilities and job demands must be balanced by orientation and training, as shown in Figure 10-1. Orientation or training alone is insufficient; both are needed.

Training versus development

Although *training* helps employees do their present jobs, the benefits of training may extend throughout a person's entire career and may help *develop* that person for future responsibilities.[2] *Development*, on the other hand, helps the individual handle future responsibilities, with less emphasis on present job duties. Since the distinction between training (now) and development (in the future) is often blurred and primarily one of intent, both are discussed together throughout the chapter, with significant differences noted where important. To illustrate the developmental impact of training, consider one human resource director's observations.

> When I was first promoted to head all the job analysts many years ago, I did not know the first thing about supervising. So I was sent to a supervisory training program for new supervisors. In that seminar I learned a lot of things, but the section on delegation really impressed me the most. I have relied on that knowledge ever since. Probably the reason I head the personnel department today is because that training helped to develop me into a manager.

When looked at from the overall corporate perspective, the distinction between training for a present job and development for future ones blurs even further. Consider the training program at one company.

Corning Glass

> "At the Corning Glass Works plant in Harrodsburg, Kentucky, we adopted a systematic approach in the development of a plant-wide training program. Our concept of training focuses on the individual. We at the Harrodsburg plant believe all employees, regardless of salary grade, position, or department assignment, can benefit from quality training."[3]
>
> The training program at Corning has four phases. The first phase is called *individual training*. Included here is an extensive orientation program for new employees and on-the-job training for those who have transferred to a new job. The second phase is *departmental training*. Hourly and management employees receive specialized courses that are intended to increase departmental productivity. These courses focus primarily on standard operation procedures used to run specific operations in the department. The third phase, *plant or facilities training*, contains information of general interest to those at the plant. Safety training and courses for personal or professional development are included in this category. The final phase is corporate and outside training and development. It includes training and development efforts done

Figure 10-1

The Balance between New Employee Capabilities and Job Demands

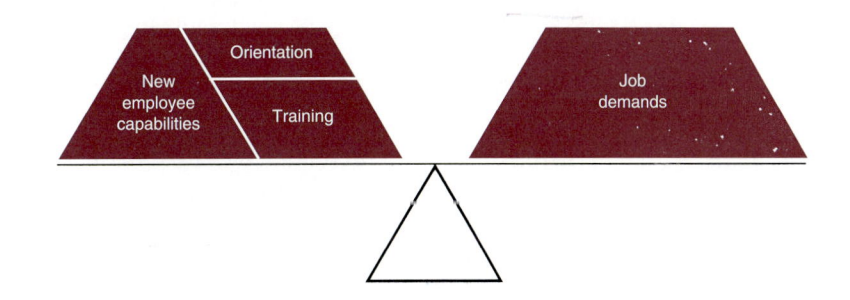

[Diagram: A balance scale. Left side shows a trapezoid divided into "New employee capabilities," "Orientation," and "Training." Right side shows a trapezoid labeled "Job demands."]

by the corporate offices, private consultants, and universities. These courses tend to be more general and more developmental in nature.

To support these various levels of training the plant training coordinator develops a master training schedule that is published monthly on a department-by-department basis. It shows the name, type, and appropriate audience for each training session to be held that month. This calendar is supplemented by a catalog that shows whether the training subject is an operational, safety, departmental, or plantwide session.[4]

This range of learning opportunities includes some very specific training modules that teach people the company's procedures for doing specific jobs. At the other end of the course spectrum are seminars that grapple with broad developmental issues that upwardly mobile managers at Corning can expect to face during their careers. Many of the other seminars are training employees for their present jobs while helping others develop their skills for future jobs at Corning. Neither the training coordinator nor the students are much concerned whether a class is intended to be "training" or "development."

The more appropriate concern is whether the seminars help the employees and the organization. Corning believes that its approach to training and development benefits both employees and the company. And judging from some of the results that Corning has been able to report, the training and development have had some identifiable payoffs in productivity and in quality of work life.

As the personnel assistant and plant training coordinator at Corning asked: "So, where have over two hundred various courses for our employees taken us? First, we have increased productivity."[5] In one department, record production runs were achieved following the formalized on-the-job training of some departmental employees. Workplace practices also have become more standardized, and employees have an in-plant means of self-improvement.[6]

10. TRAINING AND DEVELOPMENT 307

Training also played an important role when Corning opened a new facility in Blacksburg, Virginia, to make automobile filters.

Corning's Virginia operations

> After sorting through 8,000 job applicants to identify potential workers with the best problem-solving skills and a willingness to work in teams, Corning hired 150 employees. Even though most had at least one year of college, they were put through extensive training in both technical and interpersonal subjects. In the first year of operation, 25 percent of all hours worked were devoted to training, at a cost of $750,000.[7]

The training provided by Corning was directed at employees at all levels in both the Kentucky and Virginia operations. However, in many companies, these activities are concentrated among managers and professionals,[8] unlike companies in Japan and Europe, where greater attention is given to the skills training of workers. The result, according to one researcher, is that only 35 percent of Americans receive upgrading on the job.[9] At the same time, many organizations provide remedial education—teaching reading, writing, and arithmetic skills to workers. These workers may be part of the nearly 14 percent of 18- to 21-year-olds who lack high school degrees,[10] compared to six percent in Japan.[11] Restated, one in seven American adults (totaling about 25 million) is functionally illiterate.[12]

As businesses becomes more global, competition demands a more competent work force. When a nation's educational system does not provide sufficiently educated workers, the burden falls to businesses. As a result, it has been estimated that U.S. businesses spend more than $30 billion annually on training and development.[13] A survey by the American Society for Training and Development found that firms should invest at least two percent of payroll in training and development.[14] Some leading companies spend even more; for example, Hewlett-Packard spends five percent of revenues on training.[15] IBM, Motorola, Xerox, McDonalds, Ford, and others have actually built education centers to meet their commitment to the training and development of their work force. These and other companies have been called "learning organizations" because they treat training and development as investments in their future, not just as an expense. As Paul Banas, Ford's manager of human resource strategies and planning explains,

Estimated training costs

Ford

> If education and training are seen as a cost, then in tough times when costs are cut, education and training budgets disappear. However, if a corporation has developed a set of values and principles that view employees as an important asset, then the education and training remain even during corporate downswings.[16]

A company's training and development pays dividends to the employee and the organization, as suggested in Figure 10-2. Though no single training program yields all the benefits presented in the figure, the organization which devotes

III. DEVELOPMENT AND EVALUATION

Figure 10-2

The Benefits of Employee Training

How Training Benefits the Organization

- Leads to improved profitability and/or more positive attitudes toward profit orientation.
- Improves the job knowledge and skills at all levels of the organization.
- Improves the morale of the work force.
- Helps people identify with organizational goals.
- Helps create a better corporate image.
- Fosters authenticity, openness and trust.
- Improves the relationship between boss and subordinate.
- Aids in organizational development.
- Learns from the trainee.
- Helps prepare guidelines for work.
- Aids in understanding and carrying out organizational policies.
- Provides information for future needs in all areas of the organization.
- Organization gets more effective decision making and problem solving.
- Aids in development for promotion from within.
- Aids in developing leadership skill, motivation, loyalty, better attitudes, and other aspects that successful workers and managers usually display.
- Aids in increasing productivity and/or quality of work.
- Helps keep costs down in many areas, e.g., production, personnel, administration, etc.
- Develops a sense of responsibility to the organization for being competent and knowledgeable.
- Improves labor-management relations.
- Reduces outside consulting costs by utilizing competent internal consulting.
- Stimulates preventive management as opposed to putting out fires.
- Eliminates suboptimal behavior (such as hiding tools).
- Creates an appropriate climate for growth, communication.
- Aids in improving organizational communication.
- Helps employees adjust to change.
- Aids in handling conflict, thereby helping to prevent stress and tension.

Benefits to the Individual Which in Turn Ultimately Should Benefit the Organization

- Helps the individual in making better decisions and effective problem solving.
- Through training and development, motivational variables of recognition, achievement, growth, responsibility and advancement are internalized and operationalized.
- Aids in encouraging and achieving self-development and self-confidence.
- Helps a person handle stress, tension, frustration and conflict.
- Provides information for improving leadership knowledge, communication skills and attitudes.
- Increases job satisfaction and recognition.
- Moves a person toward personal goals while improving interaction skills.
- Satisfies personal needs of the trainer (and trainee!).
- Provides trainee an avenue for growth and a say in his/her own future.
- Develops a sense of growth in learning.
- Helps a person develop speaking and listening skills; also writing skills when exercises are required.
- Helps eliminate fear in attempting new tasks.

Benefits in Personnel and Human Relations, Intra and Intergroup Relations and Policy Implementation

- Improves communication between groups and individuals.
- Aids in orientation for new employees and those taking new jobs through transfer or promotion.
- Provides information on equal opportunity and affirmative action.
- Provides information on other governmental laws and administrative policies.
- Improves interpersonal skills.
- Makes organization policies, rules and regulations viable.
- Improves morale.
- Builds cohesiveness in groups.
- Provides a good climate for learning, growth, and coordination.
- Makes the organization a better place to work and live.

Source: From M.J. Tessin, "Once Again, Why Training?" *Training* Feb. 1978, p.7, Reprinted by permission.

---

itself to training and development enhances its human capabilities and strengthens its competitive edge. At the same time, the employee's personal and career goals are furthered, generally adding to his or her abilities and value to the employer. Ultimately, the objectives of the human resource department are also furthered. However, training and development are not universal solutions to every company need. Effective job designs, selection, placement, and other activities are necessary, too. Nevertheless, training can make a substantial contribution when done properly.

STEPS TO TRAINING AND DEVELOPMENT

To accrue the benefits listed in Figure 10-2, human resource specialists and managers must assess the needs, objectives, content, and learning principles associated with training. Figure 10-3 diagrams the sequence that should be followed before training and development begin. As implied by the figure, the person who is responsible for the training or development (usually a trainer) must assess the needs of the employee and the organization in order to learn what objectives should be sought. Once objectives are set, specific content and learning principles are considered. Whether guided by trainers in the human resource department or by first-level supervisors, these preliminary steps should be undertaken to create an effective program.

Needs Assessment

What's needed

Many companies allocate large sums of money to training and development. IBM, for example, spends more than one-half billion dollars per year educating and training workers.[17] Some money goes to train 10,000 workers for new jobs. Other expenditures update the knowledge and skills of technical and scientific workers.[18] Still other outlays prepare workers and managers for future challenges. If IBM is to get maximum benefit for this staggering expenditure, its efforts must concentrate on the people and situations that will benefit the most. To decide what training and development is needed, IBM's trainers assess organizational and individual needs, as do 27 percent of the companies in one survey.[19]

Needs assessment diagnoses present problems and future challenges to be met through training and development. Changes in the external environment, for example, may present an organization with new challenges. To respond effectively to these changes, employees may need training. The comments of one training director illustrate the impact of the external environment:

ADA

After the *Americans with Disabilities Act of 1990* changed the Civil Rights Act of 1964, we had to train every interviewer in the personnel department. This training was needed to ensure that our interviewers would not ask questions that might violate federal laws. When managers in other departments heard of the training, they, too, wanted to sign up. We decided that since they interviewed recruits, they should also be trained. What was to be a one-time seminar became a monthly session for nearly three years.

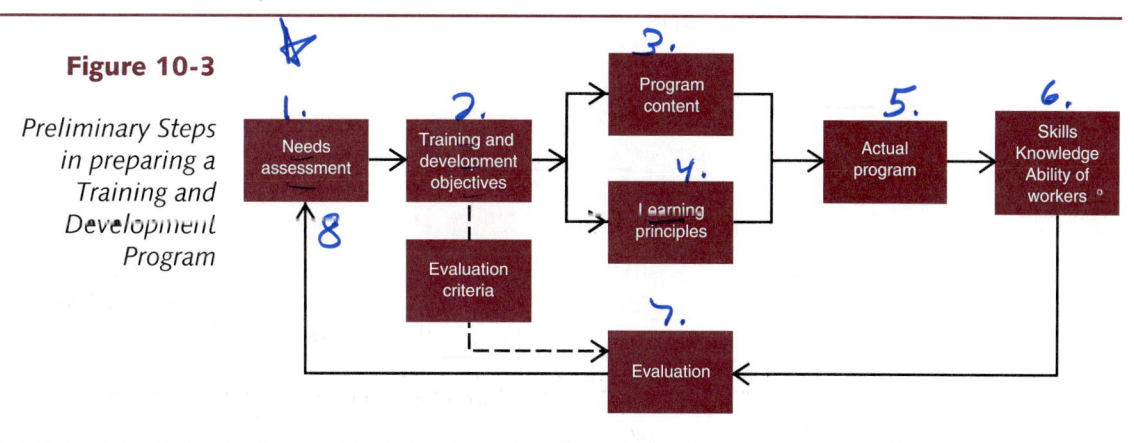

Figure 10-3

Preliminary Steps in preparing a Training and Development Program

Sometimes a change in the organization's strategy can create a need for training. For example, new products or services usually require employees to learn new procedures. Xerox encountered this challenge when it decided to produce computers. Sales personnel, programmers, and production workers had to be trained to produce, sell, and service this new product line. Training also can be used when high scrap or accident rates, low morale and motivation, or other problems are diagnosed. Although training is not an organizational cure-all, undesirable trends may be evidence of a poorly prepared work force.

Regardless of these challenges, needs assessment must consider each person.[20] His or her needs may be determined by the human resource department, by supervisors, or by self-nomination. The department may find weaknesses among those who are hired or promoted. Supervisors see employees on a daily basis; therefore, they are another source of recommendation for training. However, supervisors may use training sessions as a means to banish troublemakers or to "hide" surplus employees who are temporarily not needed. Since these are not valid reasons, the personnel department often reviews supervisory recommendations to verify the need for training. Likewise, the department also reviews self-nominations to learn if the training actually is needed. In one research study, more training attendees were chosen through supervisor recommendation than through self-nomination.[21] Self-nomination appears to be less common for training situations but more common for developmental activities, such as getting an M.B.A. degree under the employer's tuition reimbursement program.

Even when employees are allowed to nominate themselves for available training programs, training directors have little assurance that their courses fit the needs of the workers. To better narrow the range of courses and to define their content, more refined approaches to needs assessment are used. One approach is task identification. Trainers begin by evaluating the job description to identify the salient tasks that the job requires. Then, with an understanding of these tasks, specific plans are developed to provide the necessary training so that job incum-

10. TRAINING AND DEVELOPMENT 311

bents can perform the tasks.[22] The individual and departmental training phases of the Corning Glass Works training program are an example of a task identification approach.

Another approach is to survey potential trainees to identify specific topical areas about which they want to learn more.[23] The advantage of this method is that trainees are more likely to see the resulting programs as relevant and are thus more likely to be receptive to training. Of course, this approach presumes that those surveyed know what training they need. For new employees at Corning, for example, this method is not likely to be successful. However, for the more general needs that are found at Corning's facilities, group recommendations may be the best way to identify training needs. The groups' expertise may be tapped through a group discussion, questionnaire, Delphi procedure, or nominal group meeting (which were discussed in Chapter 6, "Human Resource Planning").

Trainers are alert for other sources of information that may indicate a need for training. Production records, quality control reports, grievances, safety reports, absenteeism and turnover statistics, and exit interviews among departing employees may evidence problems that should be addressed through training and development efforts. Training needs may also become apparent from performance appraisal reviews or career planning discussions, which are covered in Chapters 11 and 12.

Needs assessment as a diagnostic tool

Needs assessment reveals shortcomings that can be traced to other human resource activities. Inappropriate placement, orientation, selection, or recruiting may lead to workers with deficiencies, and errors in these activities may stem from faulty human resource planning, job designs, or the department's human resource information system. Although training and development may be needed to bolster worker performance, proactive departments treat assessment information as feedback on other human resource activities. By uncovering repeated shortcomings, the department can modify other activities to ensure a better fit between people and performance.

Needs assessment also must consider international issues. Training may be wasted if poor performance stems from cultural or language barriers. For example, employees in developing nations may have different views about time, which range from problems with punctuality and attendance to attitudes that value interpersonal relationships more highly than timely performance. A common reaction is to provide more training in how to do the job; however, when cultural imperatives dictate that performance is secondary to customs, skills training may be inappropriate.[24]

The success of the remaining steps in Figure 10-3 depends on the accuracy of the needs assessment process. The results of that process are translated into objectives.

Training and Development Objectives

Goals of training

Needs result in training and development objectives. These objectives should state the desired behavior and the conditions under which it is to occur. Objectives also serve as the standard against which individual performance and a training program can be measured. For example, the objectives for an airline reservationist might be stated as follows:

1. Provide flight information to call-in customers within thirty seconds

2. Complete a one-city, round-trip reservation in two minutes after all information is obtained from the customer.

Objectives like these for a reservationist give the trainer and the trainee specific goals that can be used to evaluate their success. If the objectives are not met, failure gives the personnel department feedback on the training program and on the participants.

Program Content

The content of the program is shaped by the needs assessment and by the learning objectives. This content may seek to teach specific skills, provide needed knowledge, or simply try to influence attitudes. Whatever its content, the program must meet the needs of the organization and the participants. If company goals are not furthered, resources are wasted. And participants must view the content as relevant to their needs, or else their motivation to learn may be low.

When successful completion of a training program is a prerequisite to selection, retention, or placement, training content must be valid. The Equal Employment Opportunity Commission's Uniform Guidelines on Employee Selection Procedures requires that selection criteria be job-related.[25] This requirement does not apply to all training and development activities. It applies in those cases where the training program is a selection criterion for initial hiring, retention, or internal placement. When a training program is one such criterion, trainers should validate the job-relatedness of the content.[26]

Learning Principles

Learning guidelines

Learning curve

Although the learning process is widely studied, little is known about it. Part of the problem is that learning cannot be observed; only its results can be measured. From studies of learning, however, researchers have sketched a broad picture of the learning process and have developed some tentative principles of learning. Perhaps the best way to understand learning is through the use of a *learning curve*, shown in Figure 10-4. As the curve illustrates, learning takes place in bursts (from points A to B) and in plateaus (from points B to C). Trainers should establish two goals related to the shape of each employee's learning curve. First, trainers want the learning curve to reach a satisfactory level of performance. This level is shown as the dashed line in the figure. Second, they want the learning

10. TRAINING AND DEVELOPMENT

Figure 10-4

A Typical Learning Curve

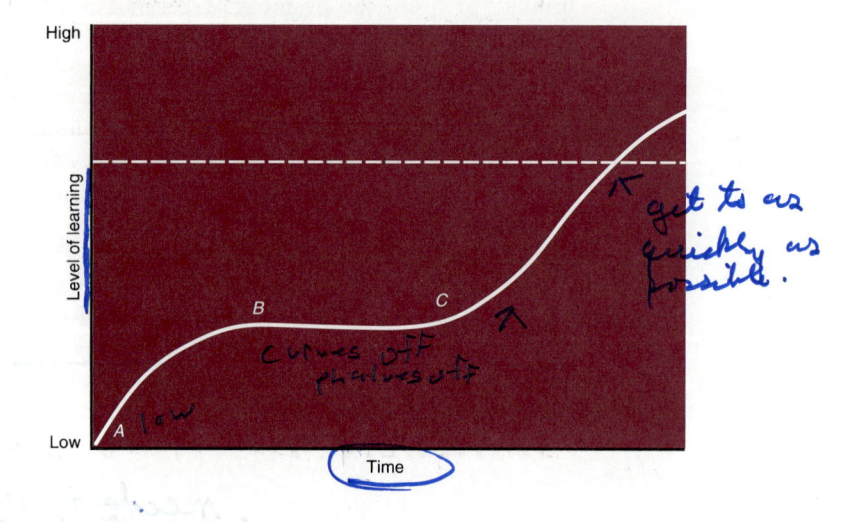

curve to get to the satisfactory level as quickly as possible. Although the rate at which an individual learns depends upon the person, the use of various learning principles helps speed up the learning process.

Learning principles are the guidelines to the ways in which people learn most effectively. The more these principles are reflected in training, the more effective training is likely to be. These principles are participation, repetition, relevance, transference, and feedback. Research suggests that they apply equally to domestic and international training situations.

1. **Participation.** Learning usually is quicker and more long-lasting when the learner can participate actively. Participation improves motivation and apparently engages more senses that help reinforce the learning process. As a result of participation, we learn more quickly and retain that learning longer. For example, most people never forget how to ride a bicycle because they actively participated in the learning process.

2. **Repetition.** Although seldom fun, *repetition* apparently etches a pattern into our memory. Studying for an examination, for example, involves repetition of key ideas so that they can be recalled during the test. Likewise, most people learned the alphabet and the multiplication tables by repetition.

3. **Relevance.** Learning is helped when the material to be learned is meaningful. For example, trainers usually explain the overall purpose of a job to trainees before explaining specific tasks. This explanation allows the worker to see the relevance of each task and the relevance of following the correct procedures.

III. DEVELOPMENT AND EVALUATION

4. **Transference.** The closer the demands of the training program match the demands of the job, the faster a person learns to master the job.[27] For example, pilots usually are trained in flight simulators because the simulators very closely resemble the actual cockpit and flight characteristics of the plane. The close match between the simulator and the plane allows the trainee to *transfer* quickly the learning in the simulator to actual flight conditions.

5. **Feedback.** Learners are given information on their progress. With feedback, motivated learners can adjust their behavior to achieve the quickest possible learning curve. Without feedback, the learners cannot gauge their progress and may become discouraged. Test grades are, for example, feedback on the study habits of test takers.

TRAINING AND DEVELOPMENT APPROACHES

Training considerations

Before reviewing the various training and development approaches, it is important to remember that any method may be applied to both training and development. For example, a class on management techniques may be attended by supervisors and by workers who are likely to be promoted to these positions. For supervisors, the class is training in how to do their present jobs better. For workers who have no management responsibilities, the classes are intended to develop these employees into supervisors. The classroom instruction is identical for both groups, but it has two different intents: training for supervisors and development for workers.

In selecting a particular technique to use in training or development, there are several tradeoffs. That is, no one technique is always best; the best method depends upon:

- ▶ Cost-effectiveness
- ▶ Desired program content
- ▶ Appropriateness of the facilities
- ▶ Trainee preferences and capabilities
- ▶ Trainer preferences and capabilities
- ▶ Learning principles.

The importance of these six tradeoffs depends upon the situation. For example, cost-effectiveness may be a minor factor when training an airline pilot in emergency maneuvers. But whatever method is selected, it has certain learn-

Figure 10-5

Learning Principles in Different Training and Development Techniques

	PARTICIPATION	REPETITION	RELEVANCE	TRANSFERENCE	FEEDBACK
ON-THE-JOB TECHNIQUES					
Job instruction training	Yes	Yes	Yes	Yes	Sometimes
Job rotation	Yes	Sometimes	Yes	Sometimes	No
Apprenticeships	Yes	Sometimes	Yes	Sometimes	Sometimes
Coaching	Yes	Sometimes	Yes	Sometimes	Yes
OFF-THE-JOB TECHNIQUES					
Lecture	No	No	No	Sometimes	No
Video presentation	No	No	No	Yes	No
Vestibule training	Yes	Yes	Sometimes	Yes	Sometimes
Role playing	Yes	Sometimes	Sometimes	No	Sometimes
Case study	Yes	Sometimes	Sometimes	Sometimes	Sometimes
Simulation	Yes	Sometimes	Sometimes	Sometimes	Sometimes
Self-study	Yes	Yes	Sometimes	Sometimes	No
Programmed learning	Yes	Yes	No	Yes	Yes
Laboratory training	Yes	Yes	Sometimes	No	Yes

Source: From *Training in Industry: The Management of Learning*, by B.M. Bass and J.A. Vaughn. Copyright © 1966 by Wadsworth Publishing Company, Inc. Reprinted by permission of the publisher, Brooks/Cole Publishing Company, Monterey, Calif.

ing principles associated with it. Figure 10-5 lists the most common training and development techniques and the learning principles each involves. As the figure reveals, some techniques make more effective use of learning principles than others. Even those approaches that use few learning principles, such as the lecture, are valuable tools because they may satisfy one of the other six tradeoffs listed above. For example, a lecture may be the best way to communicate some academic content in the most cost-effective manner, especially if the classroom is large and does not lend itself to other approaches. Although these tradeoffs affect the methods used, personnel specialists must be familiar with all the techniques and learning principles found in Figure 10-5.[28]

Job Instruction Training

"OJT"

Job instruction training is received directly on the job, so it is often simply called "on-the-job" training. It is used primarily to teach workers how to do their present jobs. A trainer, supervisor, or coworker serves as the instructor. When it is properly planned and executed, this method includes each of the learning principles shown in Figure 10 5. In most cases, however, the trainer's focus is on making a product, not on good training technique.

On-the-job training (or OJT) has several steps. First, the trainee receives an overview of the job, its purpose, and its desired outcomes, with emphasis on the relevance of the training. Then the trainer demonstrates the job to provide the employee with a model to copy. Since the employee is shown the actual actions that the job requires, the training is transferable to the job. Next the employee is allowed to mimic the trainer's example. Demonstrations by the trainer and practice by the trainee are repeated until the job is mastered by the trainee. Repeated demonstrations and practice provide the advantage of repetition and feedback. Finally, the employee performs the job without supervision, although the trainer may visit the employee to see if there are any lingering questions.[29]

Job Rotation

To cross-train employees in a variety of jobs, some trainers will move the trainee from job to job. Each move normally is preceded by job instruction training. Besides giving workers variety in their jobs, cross-training helps the organization when vacations, absences, and resignations occur. Learner participation and high job transferability are the learning advantages to job rotation. Although rotation is most often associated with hourly employees, it can be used for jobs on many levels within the organization.

McDonnell Douglas

McDonnell Douglas Corporation is a major defense contractor, employing more than 100,000 people. As a company, it is committed to being a learning organization that devotes an average of 40 hours of training per year for each employee. To ensure development of key employees, the company created a "High Potential" program as part of its management succession planning. The program seeks to identify and develop employees who are assessed as having high potential. The centerpiece of the program is job rotation.

McDonnell's rotation program has three parts. The "Corporate Rotation" program intends to develop top executives with a wide breadth of experience. The "Functional Rotation" program seeks to give people with a background in accounting, human resources, or other functions broad exposure within the function. The "Intracompany Rotation" program targets those below middle management for two-year rotational assignments within the organization.[30]

Each of these programs seeks to give employees exposure to a variety of assignments. Among hourly employees, job rotation is an effective way to train workers and give management greater flexibility in making job assignments. Among managerial, technical, and professional employees, job rotation can afford a broader perspective, often developing employees for potential career advancement.

Apprenticeships and Coaching

Apprenticeships involve learning from a more experienced employee or employees. This approach to training may be supplemented with off-the-job classroom training. Most craft workers, such as plumbers and carpenters, are trained through formal apprenticeship programs. Assistantships and internships are similar to apprenticeships. These approaches use high levels of participation by the trainee and have high transferability to the job.

Coaching is similar to apprenticeships because the coach attempts to provide a model for the trainee to copy. Most companies use some coaching. It tends to be less formal than an apprenticeship program because there are few formal classroom sessions, and the coaching is provided when needed rather than as part of a carefully planned program. Coaching is almost always handled by the supervisor or manager and not by the personnel department. Participation, feedback, and job transference are likely to be high in this form of learning.[21]

An employee who is coached by someone else to learn that person's specific job is called an understudy. The star of a theater production often will have an understudy, for example. Likewise, a senior executive may designate his or her replacement well before retirement so that person can serve as an understudy.

Assignments to task forces or committees may help develop people in much the same way that apprenticeships and coaching do. Through periodic staff meetings or working with task forces and committees, a manager develops interpersonal skills, learns to evaluate information, and gains experience in observing other potential models.

Lecture and Video Presentations

Lecture and other off-the-job techniques tend to rely more heavily on communications than on the modeling approach used in on-the-job programs. Lecture is a popular approach because it offers relative economy and a meaningful organization of materials. However, participation, feedback, transference, and repetition are often low. Feedback and participation can be improved when discussion is permitted along with the lecture process.

Television, films, slides, and filmstrip presentations are similar to lectures. A meaningful organization of materials is a potential strength, along with initial audience interest. Growth of video presentations is encouraged by the use of satellite communications to bring courses into the work site, particularly in engineering and other technical fields.[31] Lecture and video approaches are applied in both training and development.

III. DEVELOPMENT AND EVALUATION

Vestibule Training

So that instruction does not disrupt normal operations, some organizations use *vestibule training*. Separate areas or vestibules are set up with equipment similar to that used on the job. This arrangement allows transference, repetition, and participation. The meaningful organization of materials and feedback is also possible with this approach.

Best Western motels

At the corporate training facilities of Best Western motels and hotels, vestibules have been set up that duplicate a typical motel room, a typical front counter, and a typical restaurant kitchen. This allows trainees to practice housekeeping, front counter, and kitchen skills without disrupting the operations of any one property.

Role Playing and Behavior Modeling

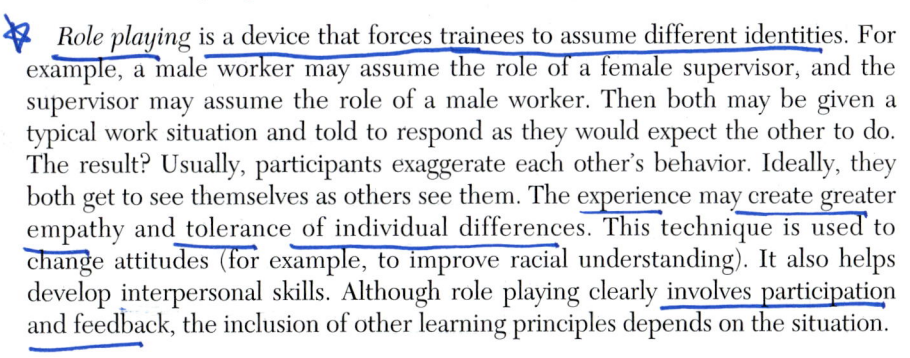

Role playing is a device that forces trainees to assume different identities. For example, a male worker may assume the role of a female supervisor, and the supervisor may assume the role of a male worker. Then both may be given a typical work situation and told to respond as they would expect the other to do. The result? Usually, participants exaggerate each other's behavior. Ideally, they both get to see themselves as others see them. The experience may create greater empathy and tolerance of individual differences. This technique is used to change attitudes (for example, to improve racial understanding). It also helps develop interpersonal skills. Although role playing clearly involves participation and feedback, the inclusion of other learning principles depends on the situation.

U.S. Navy

The U.S. Navy has used role playing to reduce racial tensions. Friction among sailors of different races—within the limited confines of ships on extended patrol duty—not only harmed morale and crew efficiency but also caused low rates of reenlistment among highly trained personnel. High turnover impaired the Navy's ability to function.

The role-playing exercises required small groups of black and white sailors to assume the role of the opposite race. The role-playing leader gave the members of each group an assignment and then directed them to carry it out as they thought members of the other race would. As the other group watched, each group in turn acted out the behavior of the others. Through these exercises and the subsequent discussions, members of both races were able to learn how their behavior and attitudes affected one another.

Closely related to role playing and apprenticeships is *behavior modeling*. *Behavior modeling* was described by two writers as follows:

Behavior modeling

Modeling is one of the fundamental psychological processes by which new patterns of behavior can be acquired, and existing patterns can be altered. The fundamental characteristic of modeling is that learning takes place, *not through actual experience, but through observation or imagination of another individual's experience*. Modeling is a "vicarious process," which implies sharing in the experience of another person through imagination or sympathetic participation.[32]

Whether behavior modeling is referred to as "matching" or "copying," "observational learning" or "imitation," all of these terms imply that a behavior is learned or modified through the observation of some other individual. . . ."[33] Employees may learn a new behavior by observing a new or novel behavior and then imitating it. The re-creation of the behavior may be videotaped so that the trainer and the trainee can review and critique it. When reviewing behavior, the trainee often can also see the negative consequences that result from not using the behavior as recommended. By observing positive and negative consequences, the employee receives vicarious reinforcement that encourages the correct behavior. One area where this approach has been used successfully is in teaching supervisors how to discipline employees.[34]

In the supervisory training program of a large unionized steel company, supervisors were put through a half-day disciplinary training session that used videotape-based behavior modeling. After a short lecture on the principles of discipline, trainees were shown a brief tape of a supervisor conducting a disciplinary interview incorrectly and another tape in which the discipline was handled properly. Then the supervisors were paired into groups of two. Each supervisor was told to "discipline" his or her partner using the correct method they had just observed. These mock discipline sessions were filmed and played back—often to the horror of the participants. Each saw how others saw him or her during a disciplinary interview.

After a brief and largely positive critique from the trainer, each supervisor conducted a second and a third discipline session that was followed by a critique. By the end of the morning, each supervisor was capable of conducting a disciplinary interview in the correct manner. Whether this training was actually transferred to their day-to-day behavior on the job was not evaluated by the training department nor by the shop manager.

Case Study

By studying case situations, trainees learn about real or hypothetical circumstances and the actions others take under those circumstances. Besides learning from the content of the case, trainees can develop decision-making skills from this approach. When cases are meaningful and similar to work-related situations, case studies provide some transference. They also offer the advantage of partici-

Cases in advertising

pation through discussion. At Ogilvy & Mather International, a major advertising agency, new recruits are assigned to a specific account, which becomes a "live" case and which is discussed at three lunch-time seminars each week.[35] Although feedback and repetition are usually lacking in this approach, research indicates that this technique is most effective for developing problem-solving skills.[36]

Simulation

Simulation exercises are in two forms. One form involves a mechanical simulator that replicates the major features of the work situation. Driving simulators used in driver's education programs are an example. This training method is similar to vestibule training, except that the simulator more often provides instantaneous feedback on performance.

Computer simulations are another technique. For training and development purposes, this method often takes the form of games. Players make a decision, and the computer determines the outcome, given the conditions under which it was programmed. This technique is used most commonly to train managers, who otherwise might have to use trial and error to learn decision making.[37]

Self-study and Programmed Learning

Carefully planned instructional materials can be used to train and develop employees. These are particularly useful when employees are dispersed geographically or when learning requires little interaction. Self-study techniques range from manuals to prerecorded cassettes or videotapes. Several learning principles are included in this type of training.

Pepsi Cola

The Pepsi Cola Management Institute is responsible for training bottlers all over the world. To contend with this dispersion, it created a network of videotape recorders and supplied bottlers with videotaped materials. The institute also uses other techniques.

Programmed learning materials are another form of self-study. Usually these are printed booklets that contain a series of questions and answers. After reading and answering a question, the reader can immediately turn to the correct response. If it matches the reader's answer, the reader proceeds. If not, the reader is directed to review accompanying materials.

Of course, computer programs with visual displays may be used instead of printed booklets. The Control Data Corporation, for example, has spent hundreds of millions of dollars on an interactive computer-based system called "PLATO." It allows a large number of users to interact with the system to learn at their own pace. Similarly, with the growth in personal computers, programmed learning materials on floppy disks are growing in popularity. Programmed materials do provide learner participation, repetition, relevance, and feedback. Transference, however, tends to be low. Illiteracy, whether in industrial or developing nations, limits the feasibility of this approach, especially among entry-level employees.[38]

Laboratory Training

Laboratory training is a form of group training primarily used to enhance interpersonal skills. It, too, can be used to develop desired behaviors for future job responsibilities. Participants seek to improve their human relationship skills by better understanding themselves and others. Laboratory training involves sharing experiences and examining the feelings, behaviors, perceptions, and reactions that result. A trained professional usually serves as a facilitator. The process relies on participation, feedback, and repetition. One popular form of laboratory training is sensitivity training, which seeks to improve a person's sensitivity to the feelings of others.

EVALUATION OF TRAINING AND DEVELOPMENT

The implementation of training and development serves as a transformation process. Untrained employees are transformed into capable workers, and present workers are developed to assume new responsibilities. To verify a program's success, personnel managers increasingly demand that training and development activities be evaluated systematically.

The lack of evaluation may be the most serious flaw in most training and development efforts. Simply stated, personnel professionals too seldom ask, "Did the program achieve the objectives established for it?" They often assume it had value because the content seemed important. Or trainers may rely on the evaluations of the trainees, who reported how enjoyable the experience was for them, rather than evaluate the content themselves.

The criteria used to evaluate training effectiveness focus on outcomes. Trainers are concerned about training effects that relate to:

Training outcomes

1. The *reactions* by trainees to the training content and process

2. The *knowledge* or learning acquired through the training experience

3. Changes in *behavior* that result from the training

4. Measurable *results or improvements* in the individuals or organization, such as lower turnover, accidents, or absenteeism.[39]

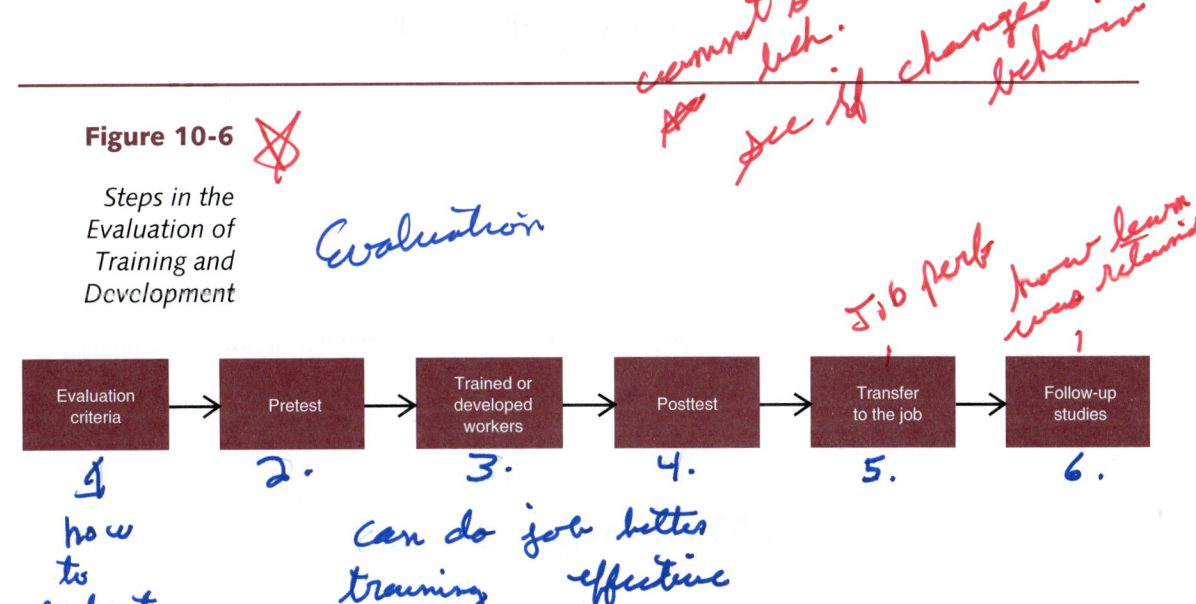

Figure 10-6

Steps in the Evaluation of Training and Development

| Evaluation criteria | → | Pretest | → | Trained or developed workers | → | Posttest | → | Transfer to the job | → | Follow-up studies |

Evaluation of training and development should follow the steps in Figure 10-6. First, evaluation criteria should be established before training begins, and often are similar to the training and development objectives in Figure 10-3. Then participants should be given a pretest. That is, they should be tested to establish their level of knowledge before the program begins. Sometimes selection tests can serve this purpose. If those tests are not practical, as when looking for a behavioral change, pretraining performance may be determined by supervisory evaluations. After the training or development is completed, a posttest or posttraining evaluation should reveal improvement that resulted from the program. If the improvement is significant, that is, if it did not result from chance, it can be assumed that the program actually made a difference. The program is a success if the improvement met the evaluation criteria and is transferred to the job. Transference is best measured by improved job performance. Follow-up studies may be conducted months later to see how well learning was retained.[40]

Transference to the job

Plagued by a disturbing number of accidents, a local home builder contracted with a management consulting firm to set up a safety training program. The training included a variety of techniques, but the builder wanted "proof" that it was effective without waiting to see if accidents declined. A safety quiz was given to the builder's field employees. The average score was 39. After training, a posttest revealed that the average score was 67, a result that was not likely due to chance.

The consultant claimed that the posttest proved that the training was successful. The builder's human resource manager correctly argued: "The training is a qualified success. The posttest reveals that the training did increase knowledge of safety. But the only measure of success is whether that new knowledge results in behavioral changes—namely, the lowering of the

10. TRAINING AND DEVELOPMENT

frequency and severity of accidents. We won't know if the training was successful until we get the quarterly accident reports. In fact, I would like to run a follow-up study in a year to see if the knowledge was retained."

As this example illustrates, posttests do not prove the success of the training. Success is best illustrated by behavioral changes. Therefore, the evaluation criteria should be stated in behavioral terms whenever possible. For the home builder's example, the learning objectives and the evaluation criteria might have read as follows:

A reduction of the frequency and severity of work-related accidents per 10,000 work hours during the subsequent calendar quarter.

The posttest is still useful to determine if the information was communicated. It may also be useful to evaluate which applicants failed to understand the materials. However, the success of a program eventually is measured against specific behavioral changes that occur on the job.[41]

DEVELOPMENT OF HUMAN RESOURCES

The long-term development of human resources—as distinct from training for a specific job—is of growing concern to human resource departments. Through the development of present employees, the department reduces the company's dependence on hiring new workers. If employees are developed properly, the job openings found through human resource planning are more likely to be filled internally. Promotions and transfers also show employees that they have a career, not just a job. The employer benefits from increased continuity in operations and from employees who feel a greater commitment to the firm.

Human resource development is also an effective way to meet several challenges, including employee obsolescence, international and domestic work force diversity, technical changes, affirmative action, and employee turnover. By meeting these challenges, the department can help maintain an effective work force.

Employee Obsolescence

Obsolescence

Obsolescence results when an employee no longer possesses the knowledge or abilities to perform successfully. In rapidly changing and highly technical fields, such as engineering and medicine, obsolescence can occur quickly. Among managers, the change may take place more slowly and be more difficult to discern. Other people in the organization may not notice obsolescence until it is advanced. Too often, favorable opinions about a manager, which are formed over years of association, prevent others from seeing telltale signs of obsolescence, such as inappropriate attitudes or poor performance. Obsolescence may result from failure to adapt to new technology, new procedures, or other changes. The more rapidly the environment changes, the more likely it is that employees will become obsolete.[42]

Some employers are reluctant to take strong action and fire obsolete employees, particularly if they have been with the company for a long time. Instead, such workers may be given jobs in which their obsolescence does not matter as much or in which their skills are not as obsolete. For example, when top executives fail to perform satisfactorily, they sometimes are "promoted" to vice chairperson of the board, where they may play an advisory role or attend ceremonial functions such as banquets for retiring employees. For lower-level workers, the solution is often additional development programs.

To avoid obsolescence before it occurs is a major challenge for the human resource department. By assessing the needs of employees and giving them programs to develop new skills, the department can use development programs proactively. If programs are designed reactively, after obsolescence occurs, they are likely to be less effective and more costly. For example, consider the situation faced by a regional airline.

> Sam Oliver had been a ground crew chief in the Air Force for many of his 20 years in the service. After retirement, he joined a regional airline as a mechanic. Since he had extensive supervisory experience, he was promoted to ground crew chief. Sam had been successful in the Air Force by giving direct orders with little explanation, and he followed the same leadership style in his civilian job.
>
> The human resource department realized something was wrong when an unusually large number of grievances were filed with the union by Sam's ground crew. To correct the problems, Sam was enrolled in an intensive sixteen-week supervisory training program at the local community college. Although he changed his approach after the program, Sam now showed resentment.

Had the department been proactive before Sam was promoted, rather than reacting to his obsolescence, his resentment might have been avoided.

Career plateau

When an employee reaches a career plateau, obsolescence may even be more likely. A *career plateau* occurs when an employee does well enough not to be demoted or fired, but not so well as to be promoted.[43] When the employee realizes that he or she is at this plateau, the motivation to stay current may be reduced.[44]

Many companies use continuing education for middle- and upper-level management to combat obsolescence. Western Electric conducts "Corporate Symposiums on Emerging Issues" at its corporate education center in Hopewell, New Jersey. General Electric operates the GE Management Institute outside New York City. IBM runs the IBM Country Club and Management Institute on Long Island, and the federal government operates the Federal Executive

Institute in Virginia.[45] These opportunities are supplemented by educational leaves at companies like IBM and Xerox and by university-based programs that typically last from four to 14 weeks. Phillips Petroleum Company provides an example of one company's approach.[46]

> On the basis of performance and future promotability, Phillips Petroleum selects 30 middle managers with high potential to go to its internal management training program. About one-fourth of the time is devoted to issues in the external environment—macroeconomics, international economics, public policy formulation, congressional dynamics, and ethics. The remainder of the four weeks deals with business management subjects such as planning, financial management, marketing, individual and organizational behavior, and the like.
>
> The purpose of the four-week program is not to replace university-based education, which is still used. Instead, the intent of the training is to give these high-potential managers a broader perspective on Phillips and the business environment. One of the purposes of this training is to help these managers identify areas where they need further training and development. The $3,000 cost per participant is not cheap; however, the broadened perspective and the intellectual stimulation of these key middle managers can help Phillips deal with the issue of obsolescence. And if the attendees are motivated by the experience to further their education, obsolescence may be avoided entirely.[47]

International and Domestic Work Force Diversity

Adjusting to diversity

The trends toward global businesses and the diversity of the work force also challenge the human resource department. For example, cultural attitudes about women in the work force have caused many companies to redesign their development programs to put women in jobs largely held previously by men. The diversity of educational attainment among workers has led companies to provide increasing amounts of remedial education in reading, writing, arithmetic, and English as a second language. And, with the large number of non-English speaking workers in some firms, training materials are sometimes adapted to a second or third language.

When providing training for foreign nationals, the content and delivery must consider local customs and expectations, even down to seating arrangements, duration and ending times, meals, and accommodations. Longer-range management development is even more complicated. When an international move is involved, some companies facilitate the process with in-house mentoring programs. At Colgate-Palmolive, for instance, the mentor is usually at or above the level of vice president. Dow assigns a high-level person in the individual's specialty.[48] The assignment of mentors can be crucial because the development of international managers generally involves job rotation across borders. As one commentator observes,

III. DEVELOPMENT AND EVALUATION

To complicate matters, many executives steer clear of overseas assignments because they feel that their absence from their company's headquarters will hurt their chances for career advancement and that good jobs will not be waiting for them at home when they do repatriate.[49]

Mentors serve to reduce these fears and facilitate the move by providing both guidance and contacts.

Technological Change

Rapid changes in technology require technically-based firms to engage in nearly continuous development. Technological changes have made AT&T and IBM major competitors.[50] The improvements in information handling and transmission technology have opened up new markets for these two ultralarge organizations. At the same time, society decreed a greater deregulation of businesses. This deregulation caused AT&T to spin off most of its assets that were tied up in basic phone service in order to become deregulated and compete with IBM in the emerging information industry. These technological changes are having a profound impact on training and development, increasing the need to assess the developmental requirements of current and future managers, professionals, and technical people. Not only are the social and technological forces changing quickly, but in the case of AT&T, this once largely regulated monopoly is now trying to adjust its corporate culture to that of a market-oriented, technology-driven competitor. These marketing changes are further compounding the complexities faced by AT&T training and development specialists.

Development and Affirmative Action

Companies like AT&T and IBM also face the challenge of equal opportunity. AT&T redesigned an existing program for outside craft workers to enable more women to qualify for outside jobs, such as installer and line worker, that previously had been dominated by men. The changes brought about by equal employment opportunity and the company's affirmative action program even led to a redesign of the equipment used by outside craft people in order to better accommodate more female workers.

The Civil Rights Act prohibits discrimination with respect to terms, conditions, or privileges of employment. As a result, training and development activities must be conducted in a way that does not discriminate against protected classes.[51] When passing a training program or course is a condition of employment or promotion, for example, the human resource department must be able to show that the training requirements are related to job success. If the training or development activities are not validated, the employer may be charged with violations of the act. Even admission into a training or development program can be discriminatory if the admission criteria have an adverse impact on members of protected classes. Likewise, the training or development program itself may have

10. TRAINING AND DEVELOPMENT **327**

a discriminatory impact if barriers to successful completion of training are not related to subsequent job success. (For example, women had significant difficulty passing the training for outside craft positions at AT&T subsidiaries. Part of the problem was that some of the training equipment had been designed for the larger feet of men, thus causing a disproportionate number of women and smaller men to fail the course.) Still another problem may occur when the scores obtained from various parts of the training program are used for future placement decisions. Under these circumstances, the burden falls on the human resource department to show that these scores are in fact valid criteria for placement.[52]

Key case

In *United Steel Workers and Kaiser Aluminum and Chemical Corporation v. Weber*, the U.S. Supreme Court recognized that affirmative action may require a disproportionately high number of minorities to be admitted to training programs. If this form of "reverse discrimination" occurs to achieve the goals of an affirmative action plan, the courts consider it legal.

Employee Turnover

Turnover—the willingness of employees to leave one organization for another—creates a special challenge for human resource development. Because these departures are largely unpredictable, development activities must prepare employees to succeed those who leave. Although research shows that executives of very large industrial companies spend nearly all of their careers with one firm, the same research found that mobility is widespread among managers of other firms.[53] Therefore, development programs must prepare other employees to replace these mobile managers. Employers with excellent development programs sometimes find that these programs actually *contribute* to employee turnover.

T & D-caused turnover

> Ironically, the widely recognized development programs of such companies as General Electric, Procter & Gamble, General Motors, and IBM partially cause some employee mobility. Their programs produce such high-quality results that recruiters from other companies are attracted to these employees. These companies realize, however, that it is better to have some trained employees who leave than to have an untrained work force that stays.

And yet as Roger B. Smith, former chairman and CEO of General Motors, observes:

GM's view

> Money and technology alone won't solve our problems—we know that. We also need the key ingredient—people. The computerization of an industry is only another sophisticated tool. Without the right people given the right training to correctly use the system and make the right decisions, technology only gives us the opportunity to make scrap faster. We still have to manage technology. And we need top, trained people at all levels to help us to do it.[54]

However, for training and development to be effective, they must be integrated into the other human resource activities discussed throughout this book. As two professionals connected with New York Telephone's training efforts observe:

> Instead of management training standing alone, it should be part of a total development operation that's linked to the whole training process. Although that's not a new thought, experience shows that in most situations, management training isn't connected to other developmental processes, such as career pathing, special assignments, selection procedures, appraisals, and reward systems.[55]

SUMMARY

AFTER WORKERS are selected and oriented, they still may lack the necessary skills, knowledge, and abilities to perform successfully. Most workers require some training to do their jobs properly. If the organization wishes to use these employees in more responsible positions in the future, then developmental activities also will have to take place. For most workers and trainers, individual learning sessions are a blend of training and development.

Most large organizations make available a broad array of educational opportunities. However, trainers should conduct a needs assessment to determine if the training is truly needed and, if it is needed, what the training should cover. Training and development, or learning, objectives result from the needs assessment. Trainers can plan the content of the course from these objectives and incorporate as many learning principles as is feasible.

To merely conduct training—even when a careful needs assessment has been undertaken—is insufficient. Experienced trainers seek to evaluate the impact of training and development activities. Often this involves pretesting, posttesting, and follow-up studies to see if the learning was transferred to the job.

Human resource development prepares individuals for future job responsibilities. At the same time, it attempts to contend with employee obsolescence, international and domestic work force diversity, technological changes, affirmative action, and employee turnover.

Terms for Review

- ✓ Needs assessment
- ✓ Learning curve
- ✓ Learning principles
- ✓ Repetition
- ✓ Job rotation
- ✓ Transference
- ✓ Feedback
- ✓ Job instruction training
- ✓ Vestibule training
- ✓ Role playing
- ✓ Behavior modeling
- ✓ Laboratory training
- ✓ Obsolescence
- ✓ Career plateau

Review and Discussion Questions

1. Why is needs assessment an important first step in any training program? Explain three ways that a trainer might learn about the training needs of employees.

2. What purpose do learning objectives serve?

3. If you had an employee who had been working for six or seven years in the same job, what signs would you look for to tell if this person was becoming obsolete?

4. Which training techniques do you recommend for each of the following occupations? Why?

    a. A cashier in a grocery store

    b. A welder

    c. An assembly-line worker

    d. An inexperienced supervisor

5. If you were directed to design a managerial development program that made use of all five learning principles, which two training techniques would you combine? Why?

6. Suppose you were a supervisor in an accounting department and the training manager wanted to implement a new training program to teach bookkeepers how to complete some new accounting forms. What steps would you recommend to evaluate the effectiveness of the training program?

7. Assume you were hired to manage a research and development department. After a few weeks you noticed that some researchers were more effective than others and that the less effective ones received little recognition from their more productive counterparts. What forms of development would you consider for both groups?

INCIDENT 10-1
Developing a Training Program at Johnson Wax Company

"How can we develop a training program which will have a significant impact on new first-line supervisors, experienced supervisors (first- and second-level), and on staff personnel, both new and experienced?"

This was the question we faced at the Johnson Wax Company, Racine, Wisconsin . . . at an initial task force meeting of seven middle managers (section managers). The challenge had been issued to the task force by the two vice presidents of major divisions (manufacturing and distribution) to build a practical, participative, results-oriented training program for newly appointed unit managers, our title for first-line supervisors.[56]

1. Describe the steps you would go through before actually designing the content of the training.

2. How would you evaluate the final training modules to determine how effective each was?

3. Do you think these line managers were the right people to design the training program? Who else would you add, if anyone, to this group?

INCIDENT 10-2
Development of Human Resources at CT-General Hospital

Clayton Dahl was appointed director of human resource development at CT-General. The hospital director, Andrea Hess, suggested that Clayton could best familiarize himself with the hospital's development needs by compiling a report about past development efforts.

In gathering the information for the report, Clayton made several interesting observations:

➤ Development activities had been limited to preparing nonprofessionals to assume supervisory positions.

➤ Most department managers and staff directors took the attitude that it was easier to hire talent as it was needed rather than develop present employees.

➤ Those managers who supervised professional hospital employees took the attitude that development is the responsibility of each professional.

Development of Human Resources at CT-General Hospital

Clayton Dahl was appointed director of human resource development at CT-General. The hospital director, Andrea Hess, suggested that Clayton could best familiarize himself with the hospital's development needs by compiling a report about past development efforts.

In gathering the information for the report, Clayton made several interesting observations:

➤ Development activities had been limited to preparing nonprofessionals to assume supervisory positions.

➤ Most department managers and staff directors took the attitude that it was easier to hire talent as it was needed rather than develop present employees.

➤ Those managers who supervised professional hospital employees took the attitude that development is the responsibility of each professional.

➤ Most other managers viewed voluntary attendance at management development programs as an admission of inability.

➤ During each of the last three years, the development budget had been cut by about 10 percent.

1. What would you recommend if you were in Clayton's position?

2. What type of support should Clayton seek from the hospital administrator?

3. If a new development program is offered, what type of attendance policy should Clayton set? Why? What types of problems will your answer cause?

References

1. Louis A. Ferman, Michele Hoyman, Joel Cutcher-Gershenfeld, and Ernest J. Savoie, "Editors' Introduction," in *New Developments in Worker Training: A Legacy for the 1990s*, (Madison, Wi.: Industrial Relations Research Association, 1990), p. 6.

2. Donald B. Miller, "Training Managers to Stimulate Employee Development," *Training and Development Journal* (Feb. 1981), pp. 47–53; and Anthony P. Carnevale and Harold Goldstein, *Employee Training: Its Changing Role and an Analysis of New Data* (Washington, D.C.: ASTD Press, 1983).

3. John D. Dickey, "Training with a Focus on the Individual," *Personnel Administrator* (June 1982), p. 35.

4. Ibid., pp. 35, 37.

5. Ibid., p. 38.

6. Ibid., p. 37.

7. John Hoerr, "Sharpening Minds for a Competitive Advantage," *Business Week* (Dec. 17, 1990), p. 72.

8. John Hoerr, "With Job Training, A Little Dab Won't Do Ya," *Business Week* (Sept. 24, 1990), p. 95.

9. Diane E. Kirrane, "Training: HR's Number One Priority," *Personnel Administrator* (Dec. 1988), pp. 70–74.

10. Sar A. Levitan and Frank Gallo, "Uncle Sam's Helping Hand: Educating, Training, and Employing the Disadvantaged," in Ferman et al., op. cit., p. 226.

11. Gary S. Becker, "Why Don't We Value Schooling As Much As the Asians Do?", *Business Week* (Dec. 12, 1988), p. 22.

12. "Fight Workplace Illiteracy," *Personnel Journal* (August 1988), p. 18.

13. Dominic J. DiMattia and Raymond J. Yeager, "Emotional Barriers to Learning," *Personnel Journal* (Nov. 1989), pp. 86–89.

14. "Training As an Investment," *Small Business Reports* (Dec. 1988), p. 11.

15. "Worker Training Gets High Priority at Companies," *The Wall Street Journal*, Eastern ed. (Nov. 22, 1988), p. 1.

16. Gerald L. McManis and Michael S. Leibman, "Management Development: A Lifetime Commitment," *Personnel Administrator* (Sept. 1988), pp. 53–58.

17. Aaron Bernstein, Scott Ticer, and Jonathan B. Levine, "IBM's Fancy Footwork to Sidestep Layoffs," *Business Week* (July 7, 1986), pp. 54–55.

18. "Burdick: Inside Look at IBM," *Resource* (July 1986), p. 11.

19. Lise M. Saari, Terry R. Johnson, Steven D. McLaughlin, Denise M. Zimmerle, "A Survey of Management Training and Education Practices in U.S. Companies," *Personnel Psychology*, vol. 41 (1988), pp. 731–743. See also Richard Beckhard, "The Changing Shape of Management Development," *Journal of Management Development*, vol. 1, no. 1 (1982), pp. 51–62.

20. John W. Lawrie, "A Guide to Customized Leadership Training and Development," *Personnel Journal* (Sept. 1979), pp. 593–596.

21. J. Kevin Ford and Raymond Noe, "Self-assessed Training Needs: The Effects of Attitudes toward Training, Managerial Level, and Function," *Personnel Psychology*, vol. 40 (1987), pp. 39–53. See also "Employee Training," *Personnel Management: Policies and Practices* (Englewood Cliffs, N.J.: Prentice-Hall Inc., 1979), p. 9.

22. Kenneth N. Wexley and Gary P. Latham, *Developing and Training Human Resources in Organizations* (Glenview, Ill.: Scott, Foresman & Co., 1981), p. 35.

23. Mariless S. Niehoff and M. Jay Romans, "Needs Assessment As Step One toward Enhancing Productivity," *Personnel Administrator* (May 1982), pp. 35–39. See also John W. Newstrom, "HRD and the Rule of Four," *Training* (Sept. 1987), pp. 61–65.

24. Irene Chew Keng Howe, Anthony Tsai-pen Tseng, and Adrian Teo Kim Hong, "The Role of Culture in Training in a Multinational Context," *The Journal of Management Development* (Special Issue: Management Development in Asia), vol. 9, no. 5. (1990), pp. 51–57. See also Faneuil Adams, Jr., "Developing an International Workforce," *Columbia Journal of World Business* (Jan. 1989), pp. 23–25.

25. Equal Employment Opportunity Commission, Department of Labor, "Uniform Guidelines on Employee Selection Procedures," *Federal Register,* vol. 43, no. 166 (1978), pp. 38290–38315.

26. J. Kevin Ford and Steven P. Wroten, "Introducing New Methods for Conducting Training Evaluation and for Linking Training Evaluation to Program Redesign," *Personnel Psychology,* vol. 37 (1984), pp. 651–665. See also I.L. Goldstein, "Training in Work Organizations," *Annual Review of Psychology,* vol. 31 (1980), pp. 229–272.

27. Kenneth N. Wexley and Timothy T. Baldwin, "Posttraining Strategies for Facilitating Positive Transfer: An Empirical Exploration," *Academy of Management Journal,* vol. 29, no. 3 (1986), pp. 503–520. See also Lennie Copeland, "Skills Transfer and Training Overseas," *Personnel Administrator* (June 1986), pp. 107–117; and Elaine I. Berke, "Keeping Newly Trained Supervisors from Going Back to Their Old Ways," *Management Review* (Feb. 1984), pp. 14–16; and John W. Newstrom, "Leveraging Management Development through the Management of Transfer," *Journal of Management Development*, vol. 5, no. 5 (1986), pp. 33–45.

28. Margaret Magnus, "Training Futures," *Personnel Journal* (May 1986), pp. 60–71.

29. "On-the-Job Training," *Resource* (Dec. 1986), p. 8.

30. Mary Settle, "Up Through the Ranks at McDonnell Douglas," *Personnel* (Dec. 1989), pp. 17–22.

31. David Green, "Business Television: A Dynamic New Training Channel," *Personnel* (Oct. 1988), pp. 62–66. See also "On-the-Job Training," op. cit. See also Robert Neff, "Videos and Starring in More and More Training Programs," *Business Week* (Sept. 7, 1987), pp. 108–110.

32. Henry P. Sims, Jr., and Charles C. Manz, "Modeling Influence on Employee Behavior," *Personnel Journal* (Jan. 1982), p. 58.

33. Ibid.

34. William M. Fox, "Getting the Most from Behavior Modeling Training," *National Productivity Review* (Summer 1988), pp. 238–245; and James S. Russel, Kenneth N. Wexley, and John E. Hunter, "Questioning the Effectiveness of Behavior Modeling Training in an Industrial Setting," *Personnel Psychology*, vol. 37 (1984), pp. 465–481. See also Herbert H. Meyer and Michael S. Raich, "An Objective Evaluation of a Behavior Modeling Training Program," *Personnel Psychology*, vol. 36 (1983), pp. 755–761.

35. Marian L. Salzman, "The 10 Best Company Training Programs," *Business Week's Guide to Careers* (Spring/Summer 1985), p. 26.

36. John W. Newstrom, "Evaluating the Effectiveness of Training Methods," *Personnel Administrator* (Jan. 1980), pp. 55–60.

37. Stephen B. Wehrenberg, "Simulations: Capturing the Experience of the Real Thing," *Personnel Journal* (April 1986), pp. 101–105. See also Bernard Keys, "Improving Management Development through Simulation Gaming," in John R. Schermerhorn, Jr., ed., *Management Development for Productivity, Journal of Management Development* (special issue), vol. 5, no. 2 (1986), pp. 41–50.

38. Ralph E. Ganger, "Computer-based Training Improves Job Performance," *Personnel Journal* (June 1989), pp. 116–123. See also Arnold Packer, "America's New Learning Technology," *Personnel Administrator* (Sept. 1988), pp. 62–67.

39. George M. Alliger and Elizabeth A. Janak, "Kirkpatrick's Levels of Training Criteria: Thirty Years Later," *Personnel Psychology*, vol. 42 (1989), pp. 331–343. See also D.L. Kirkpatrick, "Evaluation of Training," in R.L. Craig and L.R. Bittel, eds., *Training and Development Handbook* (New York: McGraw-Hill Book Company, 1967), pp. 87–112.

40. Wexley and Latham, op. cit., pp. 78–100. See also Frank Hoy, W. Wray Buchanan, and Bobby C. Vaught, "Are Your Management Development Programs Working?" *Personnel Journal* (Dec. 1981), pp. 953–957. See also Charles Margerison, "How To Avoid Failure and Gain Success in Management Development," *Journal of Management Development*, vol. 1, no. 1 (1982), pp. 3–17.

41. Jonathan S. Monat, "A Perspective on the Evaluation of Training and Development Programs," *Personnel Administrator* (July 1981), pp. 47–54. See also John W. Newstrom, "Confronting Anomalies in Evaluation," *Training and Development Journal* (July 1987), pp. 56–60.

42. Jeffrey S. Bracker and John N. Pearson, "Worker Obsolescence: The Human Resource Dilemma of the '80s," *Personnel Administrator* (Dec. 1986), pp. 109–117.

43. Christopher M. Dawson, "Will Career Plateauing Become a Bigger Problem?" *Personnel Journal* (Jan. 1983), pp. 78–81. See also Richard A. Payne, "Mid-Career Block," *Personnel Journal* (April 1984), pp. 38–40, 42, 44, 46–48.

44. Morley D. Glicken, "A Counseling Approach to Employee Burnout," *Personnel Journal* (March 1983), pp. 222–228. See also Jack Brewer and Carol Dubnicki, "Relighting the Fire with an Employee Revitalization Program," *Personnel Journal* (Oct. 1983), pp. 812–818; and Jay W. Lorsch and Haruo Takagi, "Keeping Managers Off the Shelf," *Harvard Business Review* (July–August 1986), pp. 60–65.

45. Matt M. Starcevich and J. Arnold Sykes, "Internal Advancement Programs for Executive Development," *Personnel Administrator* (June 1982), pp. 27–33.

46. Beverly McQuigg-Martinetz and Edward E. Sutton, "New York Telephone Connects to Training and Development," *Personnel Journal* (Jan. 1990), pp. 64–71.

47. Starcevich and Sykes, op. cit. See also Stanley Truski, "Guidelines for Conducting In-house Management Development," *Personnel Administrator* (July 1981), pp. 25–27.

48. Paul L. Blocklyn, "Developing the International Executive," *Personnel* (March 1989), pp. 44–47.

49. Ibid.

50. "In the News," *Fortune* (Feb. 27, 1979), pp. 15–16.

51. Donald W. Myers, "The Impact of a Selected Provision in the Federal Guidelines on Job Analysis and Training," *Personnel Administrator* (July 1981), pp. 41–46.

52. Wexley and Latham, op. cit., pp. 17–22.

53. William B. Werther, Jr., "Management Turnover Implications of Career Mobility," *Personnel Administrator* (Feb. 1977), pp. 63–66.

54. Roger B. Smith, "The 21st Century Corporation," an address before the Economic Club of Detroit (Sept. 9, 1985).

55. McQuigg-Martinetz and Sutton, op. cit.

Performance appraisal continues to be a perennial irritant to a substantial number of organizational members.
WILLIAM M. FOX[1]

Performance appraisal is an increasingly important personnel practice in both the public and private sectors.
RONALD W. CLEMENT AND GEORGE E. STEVENS[2]

PERFORMANCE APPRAISAL

CHAPTER OBJECTIVES

After studying this chapter, you should be able to:
1. IDENTIFY the issues that influence selection of a performance appraisal system.
2. EXPLAIN the uses of performance appraisals.
3. DISCUSS rater biases in performance appraisals.
4. DESCRIBE commonly used appraisal methods.
5. DISCUSS the role of evaluation interviews in the appraisal process.
6. EXPLAIN how the results of performance appraisal affect other human resource management activities.

Appraisals and feedback

PERFORMANCE APPRAISAL is the process by which organizations evaluate job performance. When done correctly, employees, their supervisors, the human resource department, and, ultimately, the organization all benefit.

Employees seek feedback on their performance as a guide to future behavior. This need for guidance is most obvious among newcomers who are trying to understand their jobs and the work setting. Longer-service workers want positive feedback on the good things they do, although they may resent corrective feedback that feels like criticism.[3]

Supervisors and managers need to evaluate performance in order to know what actions to take. Detailed and specific feedback enables them to better guide employee performance and needed training. Specific feedback also better enables members of management to make comparative judgments about pay increases, promotions, and other placement decisions. Performance feedback is compared with standards, prompting the leader to reinforce desired outcomes and take corrective action for poor performance.

Patterns of performance

Human resource departments also use the information gathered through performance appraisals. Patterns of good or bad evaluations give feedback about the success of recruitment, selection, orientation, placement, training, and other activities. Although informal and ongoing appraisals on a day-to-day basis are necessary to a smooth operation, these methods are insufficient for the human resource department's needs. Formal appraisals are sought by the department to help managers with placement, pay, and other human resource decisions.

One study of 324 organizations in Southern California found that 94 percent of the organizations had a formal appraisal system. This survey research revealed that the major uses of appraisals were for compensation (74.9 percent), performance improvement (48.4 percent), feedback (40.4 percent), placement-related decisions (40.1 percent), and documentation (30.2 percent).[4] Figure 11-1 describes these and other uses.

Ultimately the organization benefits because feedback enables corrective action to be taken when the focus of the appraisal is past performance. When the appraisal process addresses future performance—as is sometimes the case with managerial and professional employees—the process can facilitate goal-setting and other actions that guide future behavior. Yet even in otherwise well-managed organizations, the appraisal system may encounter problems. Supervisors and managers often view formal appraisals as unneeded. And why not? They believe that they already know how their employees are performing. So why spend precious time going through some form developed by the human resource department? In addition, the design of the system may encourage unintended actions by employees and supervisors, as happened in one part of Xerox.

Xerox

Xerox's main copier organization, the Reprographic Business Group, was getting few benefits from its formal, systematic performance appraisal approach, which had been in place for more than twenty years. The old system provided annual performance reviews based upon employees'

III. DEVELOPMENT AND EVALUATION

Figure 11-1

Uses of Performance Appraisals

➤ *Performance improvement.* Performance feedback allows the employee, m personnel specialists to intervene with appropriate actions to improve performance.

➤ *Compensation adjustments.* Performance evaluations help decision makers determine who should receive pay raises. Many firms grant part or all of their pay increases and bonuses based upon merit, which is determined mostly through performance appraisals.

➤ *Placement decisions.* Promotions, transfers, and demotions are usually based on past or anticipated performance. Often promotions are a reward for past *performance.*

➤ *Training and development needs.* Poor performance may indicate the need for retraining. Likewise, good performance may indicate untapped potential that should be developed.

➤ *Career planning and development.* Performance feedback guides career decisions about specific career paths one should investigate.

➤ *Staffing process deficiencies.* Good or bad performance implies strengths or weaknesses in the personnel department's staffing procedures.

➤ *Informational inaccuracies.* Poor performance may indicate errors in job analysis information, human resource plans, or other parts of the personnel management information system. Reliance on inaccurate information may have led to inappropriate hiring, training, or counseling decisions.

➤ *Job design errors.* Poor performance may be a symptom of ill-conceived job designs. Appraisals help diagnose these errors.

➤ *Equal employment opportunity.* Accurate performance appraisals that actually measure job-related performance ensure that internal placement decisions are not discriminatory.

➤ *External challenges.* Sometimes performance is influenced by factors outside the work environment, such as family, financial, health, or other personal matters. If uncovered through appraisals, the human resource department may be able to provide assistance.

➤ *Feedback to human resources.* Good or bad performance throughout the organization indicates how well the human resource function is performing.

---

documentations of their accomplishments during the previous year. Managers developed written appraisals and a numerical rating, ranging from 1 (unsatisfactory performance) to 5 (exceptional performance). The higher the rating, the higher an employee's raise.

Under the old system, more than 95 percent of all ratings were a 3 ("meets and sometimes exceeds expected performance") or 4 ("consistently exceeds expected performance"), with the majority being a 4. In fact, so many people received a rating of 4 that a rating of 3 was seen as substandard. Also contributing to the ratings problem was the lack of objectives among managers and subordinates at the beginning of the evaluation year. And since ratings were tied to compensation, the inflated numerical rating meant a higher raise was more likely.

In order to overcome these problems, a new process called "Performance Feedback and Development" was created by a task force of senior personnel and middle managers. The new system requires employee objectives to be set at the outset of the year and approved by a second-level manager. An interim review is conducted after six months to discuss good and bad performance, update objectives, and review progress.

> *Discussion of pay increases is no longer coupled to the performance review; raises are discussed one or two months later. The numerical rating was dropped altogether, although a written summary is included with the evaluation.*
>
> *When setting out the next year's targets, financial and people-related goals are discussed. But so too are developmental objectives that relate both to one's professional specialty and to general skills such as time management, human relations, and communications.*[5]

As this example emphasizes, an organization cannot have just *any* appraisal system. It must be effective and accepted. If effective and accepted, it can identify developmental (Chapter 10) and career planning (Chapter 12) needs. It also can help with replacement summaries (discussed in Chapter 6, "Human Resource Planning") along with the other uses illustrated in Figure 11-1.

ELEMENTS OF THE PERFORMANCE APPRAISAL SYSTEM

Figure 11-2 shows the elements of an effective appraisal system. The approach must identify performance-related standards, measure those criteria, and then give feedback to employees and to the human resource department. The end result, of course, is to improve performance. If performance standards or measures are not job-related, the evaluation can lead to inaccurate or biased results.[6] Without feedback, improvement in human behavior is not likely and the department lacks accurate records in its human resource information system upon which to base other personnel decisions, ranging from job design to compensation.

The department usually designs and administers the performance appraisal system for employees in all departments. Centralization is done to ensure uniformity, which means results are more likely to be comparable among employees. Although the department may develop different approaches for managers, professionals, workers, and other groups, uniformity within each group is needed to ensure useful results. Although the department usually designs the appraisal system, it seldom evaluates actual performance. Instead, according to one study, the employee's immediate supervisor performs the evaluation 92 percent of the time.[7] Although others may rate performance, the immediate supervisor is often in the best position to make the appraisal. However, multiple raters—including peers and even subordinates—offer additional perspectives.

Typical performance

The appraisal should create an accurate picture of an individual's *typical* job performance. Appraisals are not just to uncover poor performance; acceptable and good performances also need to be identified. To achieve this goal, appraisal systems should be job-related and practical, have standards, and use dependable measures.[8] *Job-related* means that the system evaluates critical behaviors that constitute job success. These behaviors normally are identified as part of the job analysis process, described in Chapter 5. If the evaluation is not job-related, it is

Figure 11-2

Key Elements of Performance Appraisal Systems

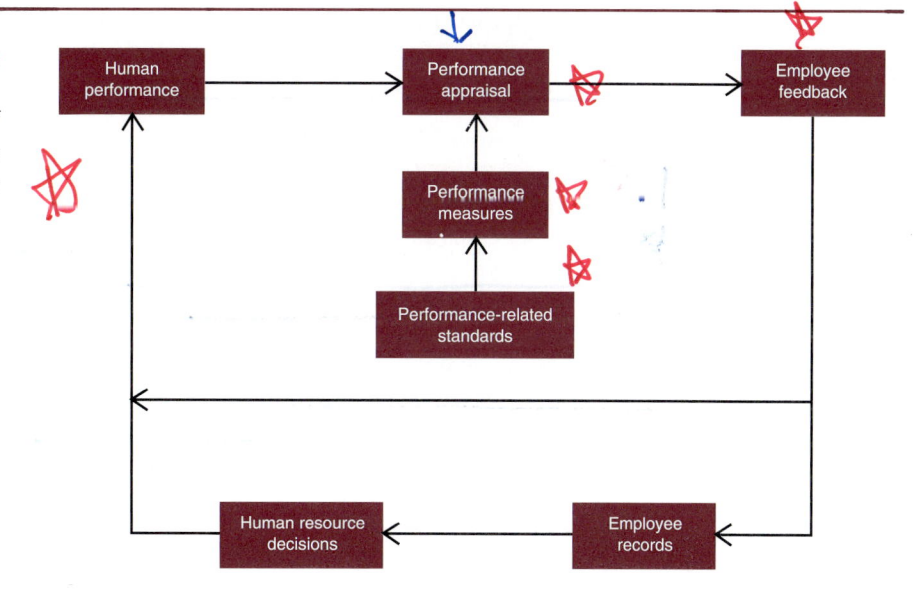

[Diagram showing flow: Human performance → Performance appraisal → Employee feedback → Employee records → Human resource decisions → (back to Human performance); with Performance-related standards → Performance measures → Performance appraisal]

invalid. Without validity and reliability, the system may discriminate in violation of equal opportunity laws. Even when discrimination does not occur, appraisals may be inaccurate and useless if they are not job-related.

Practicality

A *practical* system is understood by evaluators and employees. A complicated, impractical approach may cause resentment, confusion, and nonuse.

Standardization

A *standardized* system is helpful because it allows uniform practices to be established. Standardization among firms across different industries does not exist. However, two authorities believe that an emerging standard may be found in the *Civil Service Reform Act* of 1978, which is enforced in the federal sector by the Office of Personnel Management. These authors believe that the act is noteworthy because its approach to performance appraisal is straightforward and eventually may be applied by the courts to private-sector organizations to replace invalid systems.[9] Section 430 of the act encourages employee participation in developing performance standards based upon the critical elements of the jobs to be appraised. The method of identifying these elements would most likely be through job analysis procedures. But whatever method is used, there must be a written record of the standards. The employee also must be advised of these standards before the evaluation occurs, not afterward. The appraisal of each employee's performance must be based upon actual performance of the critical elements.[10] The new Xerox system described earlier in this chapter meets these standards.

Measures

Ideally, dependable *measures* would allow others using the same measures applied against the same standards to reach the same conclusions about performance. The application of these measures to the standards takes place through a

11. PERFORMANCE APPRAISAL

variety of approaches. Before specific approaches can be examined, standards and measures merit further discussion because the heart of the appraisal process is measuring performance against the standards.

1. Performance Standards

Standards

Performance evaluation requires *performance standards*, which are the benchmarks against which performance is measured. To be effective, they should relate to the desired results of each job. They cannot be set arbitrarily. Knowledge of these standards is collected through job analysis.[11] As discussed in Chapter 5, job analysis uncovers specific performance criteria by analyzing the performance of existing employees.

Perhaps no better example of detailed work standards exists than at United Parcel Service. At UPS, more than 1,000 industrial engineers study and time every aspect of worker performance. In establishing standards for drivers, consider this quote from the *Wall Street Journal*:

UPS

> Joseph Polise . . . bounds from his brown delivery truck and towards an office building. . . . A few paces behind him, Marjorie Cusack, a UPS industrial engineer, clutches a digital timer.
> . . . She counts his steps and times his contact with customers, traffic, detours, doorbells, walkways, stairways, and coffee breaks.
> "We don't use the standards as hammers, but they do give accountability," says Larry P. Breakiron, the company's senior vice president for engineering. "Our ability to manage labor and hold it accountable is the key to our success."[12]

As two researchers observe:

> It is important that management carefully examine the characteristics of effective performance. Job analysis coupled with a detailed performance analysis of existing employees should begin to identify what characteristics are required by a job and which of those are exhibited by "successful" employees. It is possible that such an investigation may reveal that what management has used in the past to define successful performance is inadequate or misleading. This should not deter management from the task of defining the criteria, but should reinforce management for the "housecleaning" which is being undertaken. This must be a careful scrutiny with an eye to what the performance criteria should be in the future, rather than what criteria have been used in the past.[13]

From the duties and standards listed in the job description, the analyst can decide which behaviors are critical and should be evaluated. When this information is lacking or unclear, standards are developed from observation of the job or discussions with the immediate supervisor.[14]

2. Performance Measures

Performance evaluation also requires dependable *performance measures*, the ratings used to evaluate performance. To be useful, they must be easy to use, reliable, and report on the critical behaviors that determine performance. For example, a telephone company supervisor must observe each operator's:

Telephone operator example

➤ Use of company procedures—staying calm, applying tariff rates for phone calls, and following company rules and regulations

➤ Pleasant phone manners—speaking clearly and courteously

➤ Call-placement accuracy—placing operator-assisted calls accurately.

These observations can be made either directly or indirectly. *Direct observation* occurs when the rater actually sees the performance. *Indirect observation* occurs when the rater can evaluate only substitutes for actual performance. For example, a supervisor's monitoring of an operator's calls is direct observation; a written test for telephone operators about company procedures for handling emergency calls is indirect observation. Indirect observations are usually less accurate because they evaluate substitutes, or *constructs*. Since constructs are not exactly the same as actual performance, they may lead to errors.

Constructs

To test how well operators might respond to emergency calls, an independent telephone company developed a paper-and-pencil test. The test was intended to determine if each operator knew exactly how to proceed with emergency calls. After several hundred operators were tested, it was noticed that fast readers scored better. The human resource department decided to scrap the test and use false emergency calls to evaluate the operators.

Objective measures

Another dimension of performance measures is whether they are objective or subjective. *Objective performance measures* are those indications of job performance that are verifiable by others. For example, if two supervisors monitor an operator's calls, they can count the number of misdialings. The results are objective and verifiable since each supervisor gets the same call-placement accuracy percentage. Objective measures are usually quantitative. They typically include items such as units produced, net units approved by quality control, scrap rates, number of complaints, or some other mathematically precise measure of performance.[15]

With more than 13 million workers using video-display terminals, new ways of objectively measuring employee performance are emerging. About one-third of these workers are in jobs that can be scrutinized automatically by

Computer measures

computer. With program modifications, most master computers can "not only process information from each employee's terminal but also measure, record, and tabulate dozens of details about how efficiently the worker is putting information into the machine."[16]

"Airline-reservation computers, for example, closely measure how long individual clerks take to handle each customer and the amount of time . . . between calls."[17]

Of course, having "Big Brother" constantly monitoring performance can be psychologically oppressive. Human resource specialists will need to consider the impact on morale. Otherwise, legislation or union efforts may force changes in these direct and objective measurement approaches that emerge from the computerization of the work force.[18]

Subjective measures

Subjective performance measures are those ratings that are based on the personal standards or opinions of those doing the evaluation. Generally, such ratings are not verifiable by others. Figure 11-3 compares the accuracy of objective and subjective measures. It shows that subjective measures are low in accuracy. When subjective measures are also indirect, accuracy becomes even lower. For example, measurement of an operator's phone manners is done subjectively; supervisors must use their personal opinions of good or bad manners. Since the evaluation is subjective, accuracy is usually low even if the supervisor directly observes the operator. Accuracy is likely to be even lower when the rater uses an indirect measure, such as an essay test of phone manners. Whenever possible, specialists prefer objective and direct measures of performance. When objective and direct measures are not available, inaccuracies and additional challenges can arise.

PERFORMANCE APPRAISAL CHALLENGES

The design of the performance appraisal system often contributes directly or indirectly to the challenges facing human resource professionals. Important challenges include legal constraints, rater biases, and appraisal acceptance.

Legal constraints

Performance appraisals must be free from discrimination. Whatever form of evaluation the department uses, it should be both valid and reliable, as explained in Chapter 4, "Equal Employment Opportunity." Otherwise, placement decisions may be challenged because they violate equal employment or other laws. Nowhere are such suits more likely than in case of "wrongful discharge," which occurs when someone is improperly fired. They also arise when decisions involve a layoff, demotion, or failure to promote.[19]

344   III. DEVELOPMENT AND EVALUATION

Figure 11-3

Types and Accuracy of Performance Measures

TYPES OF PERFORMANCE MEASURES	RELATIVE DEGREE OF ACCURACY	
	DIRECT	INDIRECT
OBJECTIVE	Very high	High
SUBJECTIVE	Low	Very low

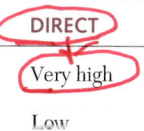

Key case

"General Motors, for example, was found guilty of discrimination in Rowe v. General Motors because a supervisor used an appraisal method that relied almost entirely on subjective evaluations of initiative and attitude. The courts ruled that a company could not rely solely on the recommendations of supervisors in selecting employees for promotion where standards used by the foremen were vague and subjective."[20]

Rater Biases

The problem with subjective measures is the opportunity for bias. *Bias* is the inaccurate distortion of a measurement. Although training in the conduct of performance appraisals can help reduce bias,[21] it is usually caused by raters who fail to remain emotionally detached while they evaluate employee performance. The most common rater biases include:

Biases

➤ The halo effect

➤ The error of central tendency

➤ The leniency and strictness biases

➤ Cross-cultural biases

➤ Personal prejudice

➤ The recency effect.[22]

The halo effect. The *halo effect* occurs when the rater's personal opinion of the employee sways the rater's measurement of performance. For example, if a supervi-

11. PERFORMANCE APPRAISAL

sor likes or dislikes an employee, that opinion may distort estimates of the employee's performance. This problem is most severe when raters must evaluate personality traits[23] (instead of behaviors), their friends, or those they strongly dislike.[24]

2. **The error of central tendency.** Some raters do not like to rate employees as effective or ineffective, and so ratings are distorted to make each employee appear average. On rating forms, this distortion causes evaluators to avoid checking extremes—very poor or excellent. Instead they place their marks near the center of the rating sheet. Thus the term *error of central tendency* has been applied to this bias. Human resource departments sometimes unintentionally encourage this behavior by requiring raters to justify extremely high or low ratings.

3. **The leniency and strictness bias.** The *leniency bias* results when raters tend to be easy in evaluating the performance of employees. Such raters see all employee performance as good and rate it favorably. The *strictness bias* is just the opposite. It results from raters being too harsh in their evaluations. Sometimes the strictness bias results because the rater wants others to think that he or she is a "tough judge" of people's performance. Both leniency and strictness errors more commonly occur when performance standards are vague.[25]

4. **Cross-cultural biases.** Every rater holds expectations about human behavior based upon his or her culture. When people are expected to evaluate others from different cultures, they may apply their cultural expectations to someone who has a different set of beliefs. In many Eastern cultures, the elderly are treated with greater respect and are held in higher esteem than in many Western cultures. If a young worker is asked to rate an older subordinate, this cultural value of "respect and esteem" may bias the rating. Likewise, in some Arabic cultures, women are expected to play a very subservient role, especially in public. Assertive women may receive biased ratings because of these cross-cultural differences. With the greater cultural diversity and the movement of employees across international borders, this potential source of bias becomes more likely.

5. **Personal prejudice.** A rater's dislike for a group or class of people may distort the ratings those people receive. For example, some human resource departments have noticed that male supervisors give undeservedly low ratings to women who hold "traditionally male jobs." Sometimes raters are unaware of their prejudice, which makes such biases even more difficult to overcome. Nevertheless, specialists should pay close attention to patterns in appraisals that suggest prejudice. Such prejudice prevents effective evaluations and may violate antidiscrimination laws. Where the halo bias affects one's judgment of an individual, prejudice affects entire groups. When prejudice affects the ratings of protected class members, this form of discrimination can lead to equal employment violations.[26]

6. **The recency effect.** When using subjective performance measures, ratings are affected strongly by the employee's most recent actions. Recent actions—either good or bad—are more likely to be remembered by the rater.

7. **Reducing rater biases**. When subjective performance measures must be used, biases can be reduced through training, feedback, and the proper selection of performance appraisal techniques. Training for raters should involve three steps. First, biases and their causes should be explained. Second, the role of performance appraisals in employee decisions should stress the need for impartiality and objectivity. Third, if subjective measures are to be used, raters should be required to apply them as part of their training. For example, classroom exercises may require that the trainer evaluate performance in videotapes showing workers and various working situations. Mistakes uncovered during simulated evaluations then can be corrected through additional training or counseling.

Merck & Company

Merck & Company, a worldwide pharmaceutical company developed a new performance appraisal system and pilot tested it in three divisions. Before it was made the company-wide program, a formal training program was developed for all salaried employees. The training explained the new forms, rating criteria, and how the approach would relate to the company's compensation program. Higher-level employees were trained in how to review the ratings of others and administer the program.[27]

Once subjective performance measures move out of the classroom and into practice, raters should get feedback about their previous ratings.[28] When ratings prove relatively accurate or inaccurate, feedback helps raters adjust their behavior accordingly. Human resource departments also can reduce distortion through the careful selection of performance appraisal techniques.[29] For ease of discussion, these techniques are presented in two groups—those that focuses on past and those that focus on future performance.

PAST-ORIENTED APPRAISAL METHODS

The importance of performance evaluations has led academicians and practitioners to create many methods to appraise past performance. Most of these techniques are a direct attempt to minimize particular problems found in other approaches. No one technique is perfect; each has advantages and disadvantages.[30]

Past-oriented approaches have the advantage of dealing with performance that has already occurred and can, to some degree, be measured. The obvious disadvantage is that past performance cannot be changed. But by evaluating past performance, employees can get feedback that may lead to renewed efforts at improved performance. The most widely used appraisal techniques that have a past orientation include:

Past-oriented approaches

- Rating scales
- Checklists
- Forced choice method
- Critical incident method
- Behaviorally anchored rating scales
- Field review method
- Performance tests and observations
- Comparative evaluation approaches

Rating Scales

Perhaps the oldest and most widely used form of performance appraisal is the *rating scale*, which requires the rater to provide a subjective evaluation of an individual's performance along a scale from low to high. An example appears in Figure 11-4. As the figure indicates, the evaluation is based solely on the opinions of the rater. And in many cases, the criteria are not directly related to job performance. Although subordinates or peers may use it, the form is usually completed by the supervisor, who checks the most appropriate response for each performance dimension. Responses may be given numerical values to enable an average score to be computed and compared for each employee. The number of points attained may be linked to salary increases, whereby so many points equal a raise of some percentage. Other advantages of this method are that it is inexpensive to develop and administer, raters need little training or time to complete the form, and it can be applied to a large number of employees.[31]

Biases are likely

Disadvantages are numerous. A rater's biases are likely to be reflected in a subjective instrument of this type. Specific criteria may be omitted to make the form applicable to a variety of jobs. For example, "maintenance of equipment" may be left off the form because it applies only to a few workers, yet for some employees equipment maintenance may be the most important part of the job. This and other omissions tend to limit specific feedback. These evaluations also are subject to individual interpretations. Furthermore, when specific performance criteria are hard to identify, the form may rely on irrelevant personality traits that dilute the meaning of the evaluation. Finally, like the subjective evaluations in the General Motors case discussed earlier, rating scales may prove to be discriminatory.

Checklists

The *checklist* method requires the rater to select a word or statement that best describes the employee's performance and characteristics. Again, the rater is usually the immediate superior. Without the rater's knowledge, however, the human resource department may assign weights to different items on the checklist, according to each item's importance. The result is called a *weighted checklist*.

Weighted checklist

The weights allow the rating to be quantified so that total scores can be determined. Figure 11-5 shows a portion of a checklist. The weights for each item are in parentheses but usually are omitted from the form the rater uses. If the list contains enough items, it may provide an accurate picture of employee perfor-

III. DEVELOPMENT AND EVALUATION

Figure 11-4

A Sample Rating Scale for Performance Evaluation

Instructions: For the following performance factors, please indicate on the rating scale your evaluation of the named employee.

Employee's Name _____ Department _____

Rater's Name _____ Date _____

	Excellent 5	Good 4	Acceptable 3	Fair 2	Poor 1
1. Dependability	___	___	___	___	___
2. Initiative	___	___	___	___	___
3. Overall Output	___	___	___	___	___
4. Attendance	___	___	___	___	___
5. Attitude	___	___	___	___	___
6. Cooperation	___	___	___	___	___
. .	•	•	•	•	•
. .	•	•	•	•	•
. .	•	•	•	•	•
20. Quality of Work					
Results	___	___	___	___	___
Totals	___ +	___ +	___ +	___ +	___ = ___

Total Score

mance. Although this method is practical and standardized, the use of general statements reduces its job-relatedness.[32]

The advantages of a checklist are economy, ease of administration, limited training of raters, and standardization. The disadvantages include susceptibility to rater biases (especially the halo effect), use of personality criteria instead of performance criteria, misinterpretations of checklist items, and the use of improper weights by the human resource department. Another disadvantage of this approach is that it does not allow the rater to give relative ratings. For example, on item 1 in the figure, employees who gladly work overtime get the same score as those who do so unwillingly.

3. Forced Choice Method

The *forced choice method* requires the rater to choose the most descriptive statement in each pair of statements about the employee being rated. Often both statements in the pair are positive or negative. For example:

1. Learns quickly................Works hard
2. Work is reliable................Performance is a good example for others
3. Absent too often..............Usually tardy

Figure 11-5

An Example of a Weighted-Performance Checklist

Instructions: Check each of the following items that apply to the named employee's performance.

Employee's Name _____   Department _____

Rater's Name _____   Date _____

Weights		Check Here
(6.5)	1. Employee works overtime when asked.	_____
(4.0)	2. Employee keeps work station or desk well organized.	_____
(3.9)	3. Employee cooperatively assists others who need help.	_____
(4.3)	4. Employee plans actions before beginning job.	_____
•	• •	•
•	• •	•
•	• •	•
(0.2)	30. Employee listens to others' advice but seldom follows it.	_____
100.0	Total of all weights.	

Sometimes the rater must select the best statement (or even pair of statements) from four choices. However the form is constructed, human resource specialists usually code the items on the form into predetermined categories—such as learning ability, performance, interpersonal relations, and the like. Then effectiveness can be computed for each category by adding up the number of times each category is selected by the rater. The results then show which areas need further improvement. Again, the supervisor is usually the rater, although peers or subordinates may make the evaluation.

The forced choice method has the advantages of reducing rater bias because employees must be ranked relative to each other, preventing all employees from being rated superior. This approach also is easy to administer, and fits a wide variety of jobs. Although practical and easily standardized, the general statements may not be specifically job-related. Thus it may have limited usefulness in helping employees improve their performance. Even worse, an employee may feel slighted when one statement is checked in preference to another. For example, if the rater checks "learns quickly" in number 1 above, the worker may feel that his or her hard work is overlooked. This method is seldom liked by either the rater or ratee because it provides little useful feedback.[33]

Critical Incident Technique

The critical incident technique requires the rater to record statements that describe extremely good or bad employee behavior related to performance. The statements are called *critical incidents*. These incidents are usually recorded by

Figure 11-6

A Critical Incidents Record for a Lab Assistant

[Handwritten annotations: "identifies problem. Need to record throughout evaluation period positives + negatives. Benefits - specifics, feedback, reduces recency bias, time consuming & don't work."]

Instructions: In each category below, record specific incidents of employee behavior that were either extremely good or extremely poor.

Employee's Name: Kay Watts   Department: Chemistry Lab
Rater's Name: Nat Cordoba   Rating Period of 10/1 to 12/31

Control of Safety Hazards

Date	Positive Employee Behavior
10/12	Report broken rung on utility ladder and flagged ladder as unsafe.
10/15	Put out small trash fire promptly.

Date	Negative Employee Behavior
11/3	Left hose across storeroom aisle.
11/27	Smoked in chemical storeroom.

Control of Material Scrap

Date	Positive Employee Behavior
10/3	Sorted through damaged shipment of glassware to salvage usable beakers.

Date	Negative Employee Behavior
11/7	Used glass containers for strong bases ruining glass.
11/19	Repeatedly used glass for storage of lye and other bases.
	Poured acid into plastic container ruining counter top.

[Handwritten annotation: "Too much negatives aspects"]

Specific feedback

the supervisor during the evaluation period for each subordinate. Recorded incidents include a brief explanation of what happened. Several typical entries for a laboratory assistant appear in Figure 11-6. As shown in the figure, both positive and negative incidents are recorded and classified (either as they occur or later by the human resource department) into categories such as control of safety hazards, control of material scrap, and employee development.[34]

The critical incident technique is extremely useful for giving employees job-related feedback. It also reduces the recency bias, if raters record incidents throughout the rating period. Of course, the main drawback is that supervisors often do not record incidents as they occur. Many start out recording incidents faithfully, gradually lose interest and then, just before the evaluation period ends, add new entries. When this happens, the recency bias is exaggerated, and employees may feel that the supervisors are building a case to support their subjective opinions. Even when the form is filled out over the entire rating period, employees may feel that the supervisor is unwilling to forget negative incidents that occurred months earlier.[35]

Behaviorally Anchored Rating Scales

Behaviorally anchored rating scales are a family of evaluation approaches that identify and evaluate relevant job-related behaviors. Specific, named behaviors are used to give the rater reference points in making the evaluation. Since job-related behaviors are used, validity is more likely than with bipolar rating scales or forced choice methods.[36] The most popular approaches are called behavioral expectation scales and behavioral observation scales.[37]

Behavioral expectation scales (BES) use specific, named behaviors as benchmarks to help the rater. This method attempts to reduce some of the subjectivity and biases found in other approaches to performance measurement. From descriptions of good and bad performance provided by incumbents, peers, and supervisors, job analysts or knowledgeable employees classify behaviors into major categories of job performance. For example, a listing of job-related behaviors for a bartender in the category of customer relations appears in Figure 11-7. Other rating sheets would be assembled for other aspects of the bartender's job, such as the ability to maintain equipment, to keep the bar area clean, and to mix drinks. Specific behaviors are ranked along a scale, from 1 to 7 in Figure 11-7, by the analyst or by a group of knowledgeable workers.

Behavioral expectation scales are expressed in terms with which the rater and the employee are familiar. The rater, usually the supervisor, can review the identified behavioral anchors and indicate those items that the bartender needs to improve. Since these scales are anchored by specific behaviors within each category, the supervisor is better able to provide specific feedback to each bartender. If the rater also collects specific incidents during the rating period, the evaluation is apt to be more accurate and more legally defensible, and is likely to be a more effective counseling tool.[38] One serious limitation is that raters only look at a limited number of performance categories, such as, in the case of a bartender, customer relations or drink mixing. And each of these categories has only a limited number of specific behaviors. Like the critical incident technique, most supervisors are reluctant to maintain records of specific incidents, which reduces the effectiveness of this approach when it comes time to counsel the employee.

Behavioral observation scales (BOS) use specific, named behaviors as benchmarks and require the rater to report the frequency of these behaviors. The behavioral expectation scales discussed above are primarily concerned with defining poor to superior performance; *behavioral observation scales* ask the rater to indicate the *frequency* of the identified behavioral anchors, usually along a five-point scale from "almost never" to "almost always." These differences between the behavioral expectation scales and the behavioral observation scales can best be seen by contrasting Figures 11-7 and 11-8. In Figure 11-8, the quality levels used in Figure 11-7 have been converted into frequency ranges.[39]

Figure 11-7

A Behavioral Expectation Scale for a Bartender's Customer Relations

Behavioral Expectation Rating Scale for Hotel Bartender

Performance Category: Customer Relations

Rating	Score	Description
Extremely Outstanding Performance	7	You can expect this bartender to help customers in need
Good Performance	6	You can expect this bartender to calm down arguments before they erupt into fights
Fairly Good Performance	5	You can expect this bartender to use discretion about whether to continue serving intoxicated customers who are with other patrons
Acceptable Performance	4	You can expect this bartender to stop serving drinks to those who are intoxicated and alone
Fairly Poor Performance	3	You can expect this bartender to make idle conversation with customers who are alone
Poor Performance	2	You can expect this bartender to check identification of young customers on their first time in the bar
Extremely Poor Performance	1	You can expect this bartender to pick up customers' drinks, finished or not, with little or no warning at closing time

One pair of researchers found that a year after BOS were implemented in a company, senior management reported satisfaction with this method. They believed it minimized personality disputes, enabled raters to explain low ratings, led to comprehensive reviews, and improved feedback between raters and workers.[40]

Behaviorally anchored rating scales are complex to develop and administer. Because they address specific, job-related behaviors, their validity is more defensible than ratings based on subjective personality traits. However, this close job-relatedness makes them costly and time-consuming to develop; they must be developed for each job.

Field Review Method

Whenever subjective performance measures are used, differences in rater perceptions cause bias. To provide greater standardization in reviews, some employers use the *field review method*. In this method, a skilled representative of the human resource department goes into the "field" and assists supervisors with their ratings. The personnel specialist solicits from the immediate supervisor

11. PERFORMANCE APPRAISAL

Figure 11-8
Behavioral Observation Scales for a Bartender's Customer Relations

1. You can expect this bartender to help customers in need:

ALMOST NEVER				ALMOST ALWAYS
1	2	3	4	5

2. You can expect this bartender to calm down arguments before they erupt into fights:

ALMOST NEVER				ALMOST ALWAYS
1	2	3	4	5

•
•
•

7. You can expect this bartender to pick up customers' drinks, finished or not, with little or no warning at closing time:

ALMOST NEVER				ALMOST ALWAYS
1	2	3	4	5

Costly approach

specific information about the employee's performance. Then the specialist prepares an evaluation based on this information. The evaluation is sent to the supervisor for review, changes, approval, and discussion with the employee who was rated. The expert then records the rating on whatever specific type of rating form the employer uses. Since a skilled professional is completing the form, evaluations are likely to be more reliable and comparable. However, the use of skilled professionals makes this approach costly and impractical for many firms, and, since the supervisor is the primary source of information, bias may still exist.

Performance Tests and Observations

With a limited number of jobs, performance appraisals may be based upon a test of knowledge or skills. The test may be of the paper-and-pencil variety or an actual demonstration of skills. The test must be reliable and validated to be useful. Even then, performance tests are apt to measure potential more than actual performance. In order for the test to be job-related, observations should be made under circumstances likely to be encountered. Practicality may suffer if costs of test development or administration are high.

Pilots of all major airlines are subject to evaluation by airline raters and by the Federal Aviation Administration. Evaluations of flying ability are usually

III. DEVELOPMENT AND EVALUATION

Flight simulators

made in a flight simulator and in actual flight. The evaluation is based on how well the pilot follows prescribed flight procedures and safety rules. Although testing is expensive, public safety makes this approach practical, job-related, and standardized.

Comparative Evaluation Approaches

Comparative evaluation approaches are a collection of different methods that compare one worker's performance with that of coworkers. Comparative appraisals are usually conducted by the supervisor. Because these appraisals can result in a ranking of employees from best to worst, they are useful for deciding merit pay increases, promotions, and organizational rewards. The most common forms of comparative evaluations are the ranking method, forced distributions, the point allocation method, and paired comparisons, all of which are described in the following pages. Although these methods are practical and easily standardized, they, too, are subject to bias and offer little job-related feedback. They are usually based on the rater's overall, subjective evaluation of the employee's performance.

FP & L

Companies can lessen these disadvantages. Florida Power and Light, which uses an elaborate group evaluation method, is a case in point. Biases are reduced at this utility by using multiple raters, and some feedback results from managers and professionals learning how they compared with others on each critical factor.[41] However, many of the comparative examples described in this section offer employees little, if any, feedback. Comparative results often are not shared with employees in the interest of creating an atmosphere of cooperation among employees. Sharing comparative rankings may lead instead to internal competition. However, two arguments in favor of comparative approaches merit mention before discussing specific methods.

Arguments for a comparative approach are simple and powerful. The simple argument is that organizations do it anyway, all the time. Whenever personnel decisions are made, the performance of those being considered is ranked. People generally are promoted not because they achieve their objectives, but rather because they achieve their objectives *better* than others.

The second reason for using comparative as opposed to noncomparative methods is that they are far more reliable because reliability is controlled by the rating process itself, not by rules, policies, and other external constraints.[42]

1. **Ranking method.** The *ranking method* has the rater place all employees in order from best to worst. All the human resource department learns from this method is that certain employees are better than others. It does not know by how much. The employee ranked second may be almost as good as the one who was ranked first, or perhaps considerably worse. This method is subject to the halo and recency effects, although rankings by two or more raters can be averaged to help reduce biases. Its advantages include ease of administration and explanation.

11. PERFORMANCE APPRAISAL   **355**

Figure 11-9

The Forced Distribution Method of Appraisal of Ten Subordinates

CLASSIFICATION: OVERALL PERFORMANCE

Best 10% of Subordinates	Next 20% of Subordinates	Middle 40% of Subordinates	Next 20% of Subordinates	Lowest 10% of Subordinates
A. Wilson	G. Carrs M. Lopez	B. Johnson E. Wilson C. Grant T. Valley	K. McDougal L. Ray	W. Smythe

2. Forced distributions. *Forced distributions* require raters to sort employees into different classifications. A certain proportion of employees usually must be put in each category. Figure 11-9 shows how a rater might classify ten subordinates. Although the criterion shown in the figure is for overall performance, this method can be used for other performance criteria, such as reliability and control of costs. As with the ranking method, specific differences among employees are not given, but this method does overcome the biases of the error of central tendency, leniency, and strictness. Some workers and supervisors at American Express's Western Regional Operations Center strongly dislike this method because some employees received lower ratings than they or their supervisor-rater thought were correct; however, the department's forced distribution method required that some employees be rated low.

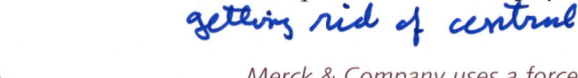

Merck & Company

Merck & Company uses a forced distribution system that is based on a bell-shaped curve, where employee evaluations are distributed as follows:

Exceptional within Merck	5%
Merck standard with distinction	15%
High Merck standard	70%
Merck standard with room for improvement	8%
Not adequate for Merck	2%

Adjustments are made through "roll-up" meetings, which allows supervisors to meet with their common manager to argue why their evaluations should be allowed to deviate from the expected distribution. These "roll-up" meetings allow supervisors with an exceptionally high-performing team to receive evaluations skewed toward the upper end. The manager can then permit adjustments among the groups so that the resulting distribution follows the company norms.[43]

Figure 11-10

The Point Allocation Method of Appraisal

Instructions: Allocate all 100 points to all employees according to their relative worth. The employee with the maximum points is the best employee.

Points	Employee
17	A. Wilson
14	G. Carrs
13	M. Lopez
11	B. Johnson
10	E. Wilson
10	C. Grant
9	T. Valley
6	K. McDougal
5	L. Ray
5	W. Smythe
100	

3. **Point allocation method.** The *point allocation method* requires the rater to allocate a fixed number of points among employees in the group, as shown in Figure 11-10. Good performers are given more points than poor performers. The advantage of the point allocation method is that the rater can recognize the relative differences between employees, although the halo effect and the recency bias remain.

4. **Paired comparisons.** *Paired comparisons* force raters to compare each employee with all other employees who are being rated in the same group. An example of paired comparisons appears in Figure 11-11. The basis for comparison is usually overall performance. The number of times each employee is rated superior to another can be totaled to develop an index. The employee who is preferred the most is the best employee on the criterion selected. In the figure, A. Wilson is selected nine times and is the top-ranking worker. Although subject to halo and recency effects, this method overcomes the leniency, strictness, and central tendency errors because some employees must be rated better than others.

FUTURE-ORIENTED APPRAISALS

The use of past-oriented approaches is like driving a car by looking through the rearview mirror; you only know where you have been, not where you are going. Future-oriented appraisals focus on future performance by evaluating employee potential or setting future performance goals. In practice, many past-oriented approaches include a section for the supervisor and employee to record future plans.[44] Four common approaches to future performance are:

Figure 11-11

The Paired Comparison Method of Evaluating Employees

Instructions: Compare each employee on overall performance with every other employee. For each comparison, write the number of the employee who is best in the intersecting box. Each time an employee is found superior to another employee, the better employee receives one point. Employees then can be ranked according to the number of times each is selected as best by the rater.

Employee	2	3	4	5	6	7	8	9	10
1. G. Carrs	1	1	4	1	1	1	1	9	1
2. C. Grant		3	4	2	2	2	2	9	2
3. B. Johnson			4	3	3	3	3	9	3
4. M. Lopez				4	4	4	4	9	4
5. K. McDougal					6	5	8	9	10
6. L. Ray						6	8	9	10
7. W. Smythe							8	9	10
8. T. Valley								9	10
9. A. Wilson									9
10. E. Wilson									

➤ Self-appraisals
➤ Management by objectives
➤ Psychological appraisals
➤ Assessment centers

Self-appraisals

Getting employees to conduct self-appraisals can be a useful evaluation technique if the goal of evaluation is to further self-development. When employees evaluate themselves, defensive behavior is less likely to occur; self-improvement is thus more likely. When self-appraisals are used to determine areas of needed improvement, this method can help users set personal goals for the future. With any employee, there is the risk that he or she will be too lenient or too critical of his or her performance. If self-appraisals are used among a diverse or international work force, home-office human resource specialists must be aware of cultural differences that may lead to evaluations that over- or understate performance and future plans. Obviously, self-appraisals can be used with any evaluative approach, past- or future-oriented. The important dimension of self-appraisal is the employee's involvement and commitment to the improvement process.[45]

Bechtel Company

At the Bechtel Company, the largest privately held construction and engineering firm in the world, the performance planning system involves the employees in a process of self-appraisal. The process starts with the supervisors telling the employees what is expected. Then the employees get a work sheet on which they write down their understanding of the job. About ten to fifteen days before a performance evaluation is to be done, the employees complete the work sheet by filling in the portions that relate to job accomplishments, performance difficulties, and suggestions for improvement. Not only does the work sheet get the employees involved in forming a self-appraisal of improvement areas, but it also indicates to the supervisors what they need to do in the future to "eliminate roadblocks to meeting or exceeding job standards."[46]

2. Management by Objectives

The heart of the *management by objectives* (MBO) approach is that both employee and superior jointly establish mutual performance goals for the future.[47] Ideally, these goals are mutually agreed upon and objectively measurable. If both of these conditions are met, the employees are apt to be more motivated to achieve their goals since they participated in setting them. Moreover, since they can measure their progress, employees can adjust their behavior to ensure attainment of the objectives. However, in order to adjust their efforts, employees must receive performance feedback on a timely basis.

When future objectives are set, employees gain the motivational benefit of a specific target toward which to organize and direct their efforts. Objectives also help the employee and supervisor discuss the specific development needs of the employee, which can make future training and development efforts appear more relevant to the employee. When done correctly, performance discussions focus on the job's objectives and not on personality variables. Biases are reduced to the extent that goal attainment can be measured objectively.

In practice, MBO programs have encountered difficulties. Objectives are sometimes either too ambitious or too narrow. The result is frustrated employees or overlooked areas of performance. For example, employees may set objectives that are quantitatively measurable to the exclusion of subjectively measurable objectives that may be equally important. The classic illustration is quantity versus quality of work. Objectives may focus on quantity to the exclusion of quality because quality is often more difficult to measure. When employees and managers do focus on subjectively measured objectives, special care is needed to ensure that biases do not distort the manager's evaluation.

Xerox

At Xerox's Reprographic Business Group, objectives are set between the manager and employee annually. A second-level manager reviews and approves those objectives. They are then subjected to an interim review after six months by the manager and employee. Adjustments, if any, are made. At

11. PERFORMANCE APPRAISAL **359**

the end of the year, a written appraisal evaluates performance against the objectives. The appraisal then serves as a basis for setting the next year's performance and developmental objectives.[48]

3. Psychological Appraisals

Some (mostly very large) organizations employ full-time industrial psychologists. When psychologists are used for evaluations, they assess an individual's future potential, not past performance. The appraisal normally consists of in-depth interviews, psychological tests, discussions with supervisors, and a review of other evaluations. The psychologist then writes an evaluation of the employee's intellectual, emotional, motivational, and other work-related characteristics that suggest individual potential and may predict future performance. The evaluation by the psychologist may be for a specific job opening for which the person is being considered, or it may be a global assessment of his or her future potential. From these evaluations, placement and development decisions may be made to shape the person's career. Because this approach is slow and costly, it is usually reserved for bright young managers who others think may have considerable potential within the organization. Since the quality of these appraisals depends largely on the skills of the psychologists, some employees object to this type of evaluation, especially if cross-cultural differences exist.[49]

4. Assessment Centers

Assessment centers are another method of evaluating future potential, but they do not rely on the conclusions of one psychologist. *Assessment centers* are a standardized employee appraisal technique that relies on multiple types of evaluation and multiple raters.[50] The assessment center method is usually applied to managers who appear to have potential to perform more responsible jobs. The members of the assessment group often meet first at a hotel or training facility. During their stay they are individually evaluated.

The process puts selected employees through in-depth interviews, psychological tests, personal background histories, peer ratings by other attendees, leaderless group discussions, ratings by psychologists and managers, and simulated work exercises to evaluate future potential. The simulated work experiences usually include in-basket exercises, decision-making exercises, computer-based business games, and other job-like opportunities that test the employee in realistic ways. These activities usually are concentrated during a few days at a location physically removed from the job site. During this time, the psychologists and managers who do the rating attempt to estimate the strengths, weaknesses, and potential of each attendee at the center. They then pool their estimates to arrive at some conclusion about each member of the group.[51]

Assessment centers are both time-consuming and costly. Not only are the candidates away from their jobs while the company pays for travel and lodging, but the evaluators are often company managers who are assigned to the assessment center for short durations. These managers are often supplemented by psychologists and personnel professionals who run the center and also make evaluations.[52] Some critics question whether the procedures used are objective and job-related, especially since rater biases may help form the subjective opinions of attendees.[53] Nevertheless, assessment centers have gained widespread use, and researchers are finding ways to validate the process.

The results of these sessions inform management development and placement decisions. From composite ratings, a report is prepared on each attendee. This information goes into the human resource information system to assist human resource planning (particularly the development of replacement charts) and other human resource decisions. Interestingly, research indicates that the results of assessment centers are a good prediction of actual on-the-job performance.[54] Consider how the process works at Johnson Wax:

Johnson Wax

For years, the Consumer Products Division of S.C. Johnson & Son, Inc. ran a traditional assessment center. Twice a year, selected managers from each division in the company attended the assessment center for five days and were evaluated on a variety of skills. On the fourth day, the candidates attended a debriefing and career development session while the raters wrote their final evaluations. On the fifth day, attendees received a report of their performance and counseling. The assessment process was successful in helping select those for promotion. However, the results of the center tended to be overemphasized; people were seen to have "passed" or "failed" the process. Those who "failed" became dissatisfied because they believed their career potential had been severely limited. Many people who attended the center "failed" because field management had few guidelines about who should be sent and at what stage of their career development. Likewise, few programs existed to prepare people for the assessment center process.

To overcome these shortcomings, a project group was formed that included people in human resource, field sales management, and a consultant. It changed the thrust of Johnson Wax's assessment center by recommending that results be given less emphasis and be used to identify strengths and weaknesses in individual skills. The group also recommended that field management become more involved with career and development activities. The project group also made sure that management knew what the purpose of the center was and gave them guidelines for recommending people to attend the center. A voluntary program for skill development was also undertaken. Even the name of the center reflects this focus: the Management Skill Identification Center.[55]

"Today, the MSI Center results are but one element in the 'management promotion equation.' This equation consists of four weighted elements which are used by management to make a promotion determination: (1) the individual's record of performance on the job; (2) the individual's sales experience

11. PERFORMANCE APPRAISAL

level; (3) the individual's previous job-related experience (i.e., previous employment experience, education experience, etc.); and (4) the individual's MSI Center results."[56]

As this example illustrates, assessment center results must be kept in perspective. If they are the sole determinant of future career progress in the organization, people will see the assessment process as threatening. However, if the results are used to appraise an individual's strengths and weaknesses, while offering that individual a way of improving areas of deficiency, the center can be a positive force for developing future talent.[57] Training and career development benefits are a justification of the high costs associated with assessment centers. As a result of the process, the future training needs for candidates are often clearly identified.

To reduce the expense but still capture some of the benefits associated with assessment centers, some companies use "mail-in" assessments. A package of tests, exercises, and required reports is mailed to the individual, who mails it to the raters for subsequent evaluation. Not only does this method cost less, but raters and employers do not spend time away at a centralized location.

IMPLICATIONS OF THE APPRAISAL PROCESS

A successful performance appraisal system requires more than a good technique. It depends on a consistent approach for comparability of results, clear standards and measures, and bias-free ratings. Using multiple raters, even peers,[58] suggests multiple viewpoints, which may reduce biases and offer a better evaluation. If nothing else, employees may feel the process is fair, although being graded may still be uncomfortable.[59] Monsanto, Massachusetts Mutual Life Insurance, and other companies are even experimenting with employees evaluating their bosses. As the chief operating office of the Waldorf Corporation observed, "Who better to tell you what kind of manager you are than your subordinates?"[60]

Mail-in assessments

Regardless of the method used, it must be implemented, usually among operating and staff managers who have other priorities. Since these managers already believe they know who their good and poor performers are, formal appraisals may seem neither important nor urgent. Nevertheless, successful appraisal almost always depends on management involvement and support. Building involvement, through a task force at Xerox, for example, or multiple raters in an assessment center at Johnson Wax, reaches only a few people in a large organization. For widespread understanding and support, training may be needed.

✦ Training Raters and Evaluators

Whether a simple comparative method or a sophisticated assessment center is used, the evaluators need knowledge of the system and its purpose. Just knowing whether the appraisal is to be used for compensation or for placement may change the rater's evaluation because different criteria may be weighted for different uses.

Two major problems are evaluator understanding and consistency of evaluations. Human resource departments provide raters with written instructions in 82 percent of the organizations and 60 percent provide training in one study.[61] Guidelines for conducting the evaluation or for providing ratees with feedback often are included, as well as definitions for key terms—such as "shows initiative" or "provides leadership."

Companies like Bechtel and Glendale Federal Savings and Loan Association are part of the 60 percent of the firms that solve this knowledge gap through training. The training workshops are usually intended to explain to raters the purpose of the procedure, the mechanics of "how to do it," likely pitfalls or biases they may encounter, and answers to their questions. The training may include trial runs evaluating other classmates just to gain some supervised experience. Bechtel and Glendale even use videotapes and role-playing evaluation sessions to give raters both experience and insight into the evaluation process. During the training, the timing and scheduling of evaluations are discussed. Typically, most companies do formal evaluations annually, near the date of the individual's employment anniversary. For new employees or for those with performance problems, evaluations may be done more frequently as part of the department's formal program or as the supervisor sees fit. Consider how the vice president and manager of human resources at Glendale Federal Savings and Loan viewed the implementation of his firm's program:

With the new appraisal process and related forms in place, the next major step was educating managers and supervisors in the use of the program. Mandatory one-day training workshops were given, providing each manager an opportunity to review, discuss, and understand the objectives of the program. The appraisal forms were reviewed in detail with an explanation of how to use the various sections of each form. A videotaped appraisal discussion was presented to demonstrate how performance appraisal worked. And finally, during the workshops, managers were given role-play situations using the new appraisal forms.[62] Then, on the biweekly payroll sheets that listed everyone in the department or branch, the manager received a notification of who was due to be evaluated during the next month. If the review date had passed, a reminder would appear on the payroll sheets, showing that the review date for the indicated employee was past due. As a result, managers knew how to complete the forms, and few delinquencies occured. The human resource department at Glendale Federal also has valuable data that allow it to anticipate and respond to training needs and employee concerns.[63]

Figure 11-12

Guidelines for Effective Performance Evaluation Interviews

1. *Emphasize* positive aspects of employee performance.
2. *Tell* each employee that the evaluation session is to improve performance, not to discipline.
3. *Conduct* the performance review session in private with minimum interruptions.
4. *Review* performance formally at least annually and more frequently for new employees or those who are performing poorly.
5. *Make* criticisms specific, not general and vague.
6. *Focus* criticisms on performance, not personality characteristics.
7. *Stay* calm and do not argue with the person being evaluated.
8. *Identify* specific actions the employee can take to improve performance.
9. *Emphasize* the evaluator's willingness to assist the employee's efforts and to improve performance.
10. *End* the evaluation sessions by stressing the positive aspects of the employee's performance.

Once evaluators are trained, the appraisal process can begin. But the results of the appraisal do little to improve employee performance unless employees receive feedback. This feedback process is called the evaluation interview.

Evaluation Interviews

Giving feedback

Evaluation interviews are performance review sessions that give employees feedback about their past performance or future potential. This feedback is essential for improvement to occur. Its importance demands preparation.[64] This preparation normally includes a review of previous appraisals, identification of specific behaviors to be reinforced during the evaluation interview, and a plan or approach to be used in providing the feedback.

The evaluator may provide this feedback through several approaches: tell-and-sell, tell-and-listen, and problem-solving.[65] The *tell-and-sell approach* reviews the employee's performance and tries to convince the employee to perform better. It is best used with new employees. The *tell-and-listen method* allows the employee to explain reasons, excuses, and defensive feelings about performance. It attempts to overcome these reactions by counseling the employee on how to perform better. The *problem-solving approach* identifies problems that are interfering with employee performance. Then, through training, coaching, or counseling, goals for future performance are set to remove these deficiencies.

Regardless of which approach is used to give employees feedback, the guidelines listed in Figure 11-12 can help make the performance review session more effective.[66] The intent of these suggestions is to make the interview a positive, performance-improving dialogue. By stressing desirable aspects of employee performance, the evaluator can give the employee renewed confidence in her or his ability to perform satisfactorily. This positive approach also enables the employee to keep desirable and undesirable performance in perspective because it prevents the individual from feeling that performance review sessions are

III. DEVELOPMENT AND EVALUATION

Figure 11-13

The Personnel Management Process

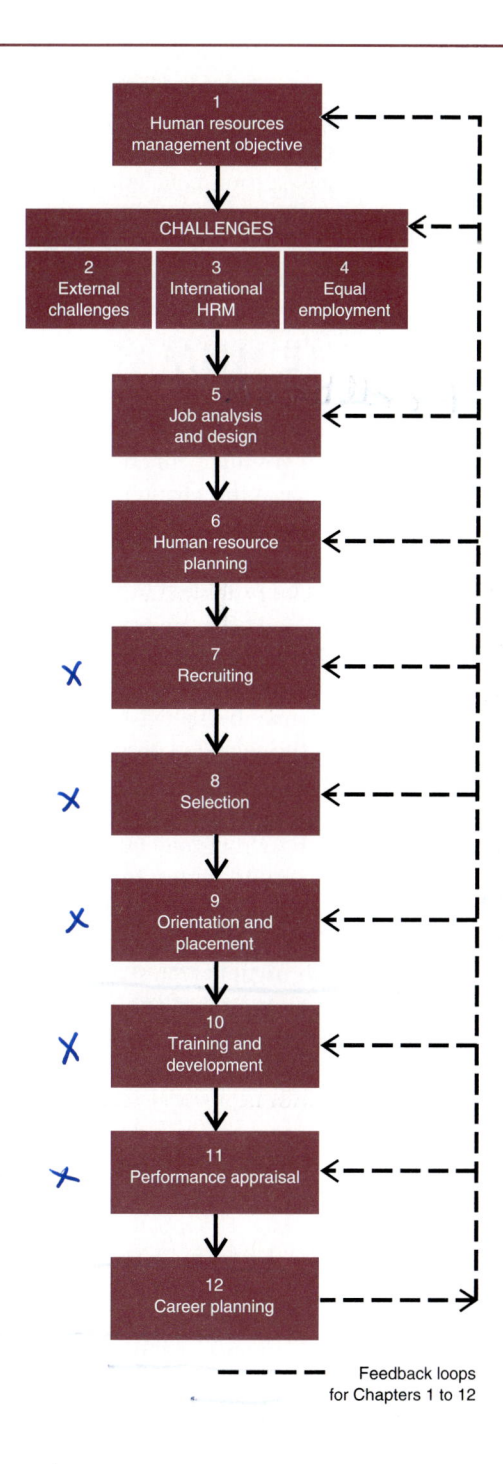

```
                    ┌──────────────────────┐
                    │          1           │
                    │   Human resources    │◄─────────┐
                    │ management objective │          │
                    └──────────┬───────────┘          │
                               ▼                      │
         ┌─────────────────CHALLENGES─────────────┐   │
         │    2           3             4         │◄──┤
         │ External   International   Equal       │   │
         │challenges      HRM       employment    │   │
         └─────────────────┬──────────────────────┘   │
                           ▼                          │
                    ┌──────────────┐                  │
                    │      5       │                  │
                    │ Job analysis │◄─────────────────┤
                    │  and design  │                  │
                    └──────┬───────┘                  │
                           ▼                          │
                    ┌──────────────┐                  │
                    │      6       │                  │
                    │Human resource│◄─────────────────┤
                    │   planning   │                  │
                    └──────┬───────┘                  │
                           ▼                          │
                    ┌──────────────┐                  │
                    │      7       │                  │
                    │  Recruiting  │◄─────────────────┤
                    └──────┬───────┘                  │
                           ▼                          │
                    ┌──────────────┐                  │
                    │      8       │                  │
                    │   Selection  │◄─────────────────┤
                    └──────┬───────┘                  │
                           ▼                          │
                    ┌──────────────┐                  │
                    │      9       │                  │
                    │ Orientation  │◄─────────────────┤
                    │and placement │                  │
                    └──────┬───────┘                  │
                           ▼                          │
                    ┌──────────────┐                  │
                    │     10       │                  │
                    │ Training and │◄─────────────────┤
                    │ development  │                  │
                    └──────┬───────┘                  │
                           ▼                          │
                    ┌──────────────┐                  │
                    │     11       │                  │
                    │ Performance  │◄─────────────────┤
                    │  appraisal   │                  │
                    └──────┬───────┘                  │
                           ▼                          │
                    ┌──────────────┐                  │
                    │     12       │                  │
                    │   Career     │──────────────────┘
                    │   planning   │
                    └──────────────┘

                    ─ ─ ─ ─  Feedback loops
                             for Chapters 1 to 12
```

entirely negative. When negative comments are made, they focus on work performance and not on the individual's personality. Specific, not general and vague, examples of the employee's shortcomings are used so that the individual knows exactly which behaviors need to be changed.[67]

The review session concludes by focusing on actions that the employee may take to improve areas of poor performance. In that concluding discussion, the evaluator usually offers to provide whatever assistance the employee needs to overcome the deficiencies discussed.

FEEDBACK FOR THE HUMAN RESOURCE FUNCTION

The performance appraisal process also provides insight into the effectiveness of the human resource function. Figure 11-13 summarizes the major concepts discussed so far in this chapter. As can be seen, performance appraisal serves as a "quality control check." If the appraisal process indicates that poor performance is widespread, many employees are excluded from internal placement decisions. They will not be promoted or transferred. In fact, they may be excluded through termination.

Feedback on the HR function

Unacceptably high numbers of poor performers may indicate errors elsewhere among human resource management functions. For example, human resource development may be failing to fulfill career plans because the people who are hired during the selection process are poorly screened. The human resource plan may be in error insofar as the job analysis information is wrong or the affirmative action plan seeks the wrong objectives. Sometimes the human resource function is pursuing the wrong objectives. Or the appraisal system itself may be faulty because of management resistance, incorrect performance standards or measures, or a lack of constructive feedback.

Wherever the problem lies, personnel specialists need to monitor carefully the results of the organization's performance appraisal process. These results can serve as a barometer of the entire human resource function. Furthermore, performance appraisals serve as a foundation for career planning and development, compensation, and other activities discussed in subsequent chapters.

SUMMARY

PERFORMANCE APPRAISAL is a critical activity of human resource management. Its goal is to provide an accurate picture of past and/or future employee performance. To do this, performance standards are established. Standards are based on job-related criteria that best determine successful job performance. Where possible, actual performance then is measured directly and objectively. From a wide variety of appraisal techniques, specialists select those methods that most effectively measure employee performance against the previously established standards. Techniques can be selected both to review past performance and to anticipate performance in the future.

The appraisal process is usually designed by the human resource department, often with little input from other parts of the organization. When it is time to implement a new appraisal approach, those who do the rating may have little idea about the appraisal process or its objectives. To overcome this shortcoming, the department can design and conduct appraisal workshops to train managers.

One necessary requirement of the appraisal process is employee feedback in the form of an evaluation interview. The interviewer tries to balance areas of positive performance with areas in which performance is deficient, so that the employee receives a realistic view. Perhaps the most significant challenge raised by performance appraisals is the feedback they provide about the department's performance. Human resource specialists need to be keenly aware that poor performance, especially when it is widespread, may reflect problems with previous human resource management activities.

Terms for Review

- Performance standards
- Performance measures
- Constructs
- Halo effect
- Error of central tendency
- Recency effect
- Rating scale
- Paired comparisons
- Forced choice method
- Critical incident method
- Behaviorally anchored ratings scales
- Field review method
- Comparative evaluation approaches
- Management by objectives
- Assessment centers
- Evaluation interviews

Review and Discussion Questions

1. What are the uses of performance appraisals?

2. Suppose the company you work for uses a rating scale. The items on the scale are general personality characteristics. What criticisms do you have of this method?

3. If you were asked to recommend a replacement for the rating scale, what actions would you take before selecting another appraisal technique?

4. If the dean of your college asked you to serve on a committee to develop a performance appraisal system for evaluating the faculty, what performance criteria would you identify? Of these criteria, which ones do you think are most likely to determine a faculty member's success at your school? What standards would you recommend to the dean, regardless of the specific evaluation instrument selected?

5. If you were designing a performance appraisal system for use in multiple, overseas locations, what factors would you consider in preparing to implement the new system?

6. If your organization were to use subjective measures to evaluate employee performance, what instructions would you give evaluators about the biases they might encounter?

7. Describe how you would conduct a typical performance evaluation interview.

8. How do the results of performance appraisals affect other human resource management activities?

INCIDENT 11-1
Global Banking's Decentralized Human Resource Function

Global Banking operates in three states and several countries, including all major money centers: New York, London, Hong Kong, Tokyo, and three locations in Switzerland. Because of different cultures and different laws, each office has its own human resource department. Although these offices report directly to the manager of each bank, the home-office human resource department in New York exercises functional authority to ensure uniformity in procedures, requiring each office to coordinate its policies with the home office human resource department.

With the growing internationalization of business, the bank has a strategy that requires senior managers to maintain relationships with key clients. When a senior executive or a client is reassigned, the bank sometimes tries to reassign its senior manager to maintain the personal and banking relationship. Although this is an unusual tactic, the bank has been able to retain and acquire major accounts through this process.

To ensure that reassignments involve capable people who can ascend to higher levels, all senior banking executives are to go through Global's assessment center, which is in the early planning stages. Of particular concern are cultural issues among different countries and the diversity among Global's domestic and international workers. Another concern is the cost of running an international assessment center.

Assume you are assigned to the corporate planning committee that is to design the assessment center.

1. Describe your recommendations about who should be selected to serve on this planning committee.

2. Describe what considerations should be weighed, given the international composition of those who are to be evaluated.

References

1. William M. Fox, "Improving Performance Appraisal Systems," *National Productivity Review* (Winter 1987–88), p. 20.

2. Ronald W. Clement and George E. Stevens, "The Performance Appraisal Interview: What, When, and How?" *Review of Public Personnel Administration* (Spring 1984), p. 43.

3. Kenneth Blanchard and Spencer Johnson, *The One-Minute Manager* (New York: William Morrow & Co., Inc., 1982), p. 100.

4. Alan H. Locher and Kenneth S. Teel, "Appraisal Trends," *Personnel Journal* (Sept. 1988), pp. 139–145.

5. Norman R. Deets and D. Timothy Tyler, "How Xerox Improved Its Performance Appraisal," *Personnel Journal* (April 1986), pp. 50–52.

6. John B. Miner, "Management Appraisal: A Review of Procedures and Practices," in W. Clay Hamner and Frank L. Schmidt, eds., *Contemporary Problems in Personnel* (Chicago: St. Clair, 1977), p. 228. See also Michael H. Schuster and Christopher S. Miller, "Performance Appraisal and the Age Discrimination in Employment Act," *Personnel Administrator* (March 1984), pp. 48–50, 52, 54–56; and Robert Dipboye, "Some Neglected Variables in Research Discrimination in Appraisals," *Academy of Management Review*, vol. 10, no. 1 (1985), pp. 116–127.

7. Locher and Teel, op. cit.

8. Christina G. Banks and Kevin R. Murphy, "Toward Narrowing the Research-practice Gap in Performance Appraisal," *Personnel Psychology* (1985), pp. 335–345.

9. Gary P. Latham and Kenneth N. Wexley, *Increasing Productivity through Performance Appraisal* (Menlo Park, Calif.: Addison-Wesley Publishing Co. Inc., 1981), pp. 28–29.

10. Ibid. See also Robert G. Pajer, "Performance Appraisal: A New Era for Federal Government Managers," *Personnel Administrator* (March 1984), pp. 81–82, 84–86, 88–89; and H. John Bernardin, "Subordinate Appraisal: A Valuable Source of Information about Managers," *Human Resource Management* (Fall 1986), pp. 421–439.

11. James A. Buford, Jr., Bettye B. Burkhalter, and Grover T. Jacobs, "Link Job Descriptions to Performance Appraisals," *Personnel Journal* (June 1988), pp. 132–140.

12. Daniel Machalaba, "Up to Speed: United Parcel Service Gets Deliveries Done by Driving Its Workers," *The Wall Street Journal,* Eastern ed. (April 22, 1986), pp. 1, 26.

13. James M. McFillen and Patrick G. Decker, "Building Meaning into Appraisal," *Personnel Administrator* (June 1978), pp. 78–79.

14. Frank Krzystofiak, Robert Cardy, and Jerry Newman, "Implicit Personality and Performance Appraisal: The Influence of Trait Inferences on Evaluations of Behavior," *Journal of Applied Psychology*, vol. 73 (1988), pp. 515–521. See also Thomas C. Alewine, "Performance Appraisals and Performance Standards," *Personnel Journal* (March 1982), pp. 210–213; and Robert Giles and Christine Landauer, "Setting Specific Standards for Appraising Creative Staffs," *Personnel Administrator* (March 1984), pp. 35–36, 38–41, 47.

15. Martin G. Friedman, "Ten Steps to Objective Appraisals," *Personnel Journal* (June 1986), pp. 66–72.

16. Stephen Koepp, "The Boss That Never Blinks," *Time* (July 28, 1986), p. 38.

17. Ibid., pp. 38–39.

18. Ibid. See also Cathy Trost, "Computer Monitoring of Workers Increases, but Critics Cry Foul," *The Wall Street Journal*, Eastern ed. (May 20, 1986), p. 1.

19. Patricia S. Eyres, "Legally Defensible Performance Appraisal Systems," *Personnel Journal* (July 1989), pp. 58–62. See also Robert W. Goddard, "Is Your Appraisal System Headed for Court?" *Personnel Journal* (Jan. 1989), pp. 114–118; and Gerald V. Barrett and Mary C. Kernan, "Performance Appraisal and Terminations: A Review of Court Decisions since Brito v. Zia with Implications for Personnel Practices," *Personnel Psychology*, vol. 40 (1987), pp. 489–503.

20. Mary Green Miner and John B. Miner, Employee Selection within the Law (Washington, D.C.: Bureau of National Affairs, 1978), p. 27. See also Ronald G. Wells, "Guidelines for Effective and Defensible Performance Systems," *Personnel Journal* (Oct. 1982), pp. 776–782.

21. Jerry W. Hedge and Michael J. Kavanagh, "Improving the Accuracy of Performance Evaluations: Comparison of Three Methods of Performance Appraiser Training," *Journal of Applied Psychology*, vol. 73 (1988), pp. 68–73. See also Stephen B. Wehrenberg, "Train Supervisors to Measure and Evaluate Performance," *Personnel Journal* (Feb. 1988), pp. 77–79.

22. Robert J. Wherry, Sr., and C. J. Bartlett, "The Control of Bias in Ratings: A Theory of Rating," *Personnel Psychology* (1982), pp. 521–551. See also Dipboye, op. cit.

23. Krzystofiak, Cardy, and Newman, op. cit.

24. Sebastiano A. Fisicaro, "A Reexamination of the Relation Between Halo Error and Accuracy," *Journal of Applied Psychology*, vol. 73 (1988), pp. 239–244. See also Rick Jacobs and Steve W. J. Kozlowski, "A Closer Look at Halo Error in Performance Ratings," *Academy of Management Journal*, vol. 28, no. 1 (1985), pp. 201–212.

25. Dipboye, op. cit. See also Jiing-Lih Farh and Gregory H. Dobbins, "Effects of Self-esteem on Leniency Bias in Self-Reports of Performance: A Structural Equation Model Analysis," *Personnel Psychology*, vol. 42 (1989), pp. 835–848.

26. Ibid.

27. "Merck's New Performance Appraisal/Merit Pay System Is Based on a Bell-Shaped Distribution, E. Jeffrey Stoll, Director, Corporate Personnel Relations Says," *Ideas & Trends in Personnel Management*, issue 195 (May 17, 1989), pp. 88–92.

28. McFillen and Decker, op. cit. See also Kevin R. Murphy and William K. Balzer, "Rater Errors and Rating Accuracy," *Journal of Applied Psychology*, vol. 74 (1989), pp. 619–624.

29. Cynthia Lee, "Increasing Performance Appraisal Effectiveness: Matching Task Types, Appraisal Process, and Rater Training," *Academy of Management Review*, vol. 10, no. 2 (1985), pp. 322–331.

30. Martin Levy, "Almost-Perfect Performance Appraisals," *Personnel Journal* (April 1989), pp. 76–83.

31. Lee, op. cit.

32. Wherry and Bartlett, op. cit.

33. Ibid.

34. John C. Flanagan, "The Critical Incident Technique," *Psychological Bulletin*, vol. 51 (1954), pp. 327–358.

35. Fox, op. cit.

36. Toni S. Locklear, Barbara B. Granger, and John G. Veres III, "Evaluation of a Behaviorally-based Appraisal System," *Journal of Managerial Issues* (Fall 1989), pp. 66–75. See also Kevin R. Murphy and Joseph I. Constans, "Behavioral Anchors As a Source of Bias in Rating," *Journal of Applied Psychology*, vol. 72 (1987), pp. 573–577; and Kevin R. Murphy and Virginia A. Pardaffy, "Bias in Behaviorally Anchored Rating Scales: Global or Scale-specific," *Journal of Applied Psychology*, vol. 74 (1989), pp. 343–346.

37. George Rosinger et al., "Development of a Behaviorally-based Performance Appraisal System," *Personnel Psychology* (1982), pp. 75–88.

38. Angelo J. Kinicki, Brendan D. Bannister, Peter Hom, and Angelo S. Denisi, "Behaviorally Anchored Rating Scales v. Summated Rating Scales: Psychometric Properties and Susceptibility to Rating Bias," *Educational and Psychological Measurement* (1985), pp. 535–549.

39. Uco Wiersma and Gary Latham, "The Practicality of Behavioral Observation Scales, Behavioral Expectation Scales, and Trait Scales," *Personnel Psychology* (1986), pp. 619–628.

40. Ibid., p. 627.

41. "Tapping Managerial and Professional Talent at FPL," *The Career Development Bulletin*, vol. 3, no. 3 (1982), pp. 4–6.

42. J. Peter Graves, "Let's Put Appraisal Back in Performance Appraisal: II," *Personnel Journal* (Dec. 1982), p. 918.

43. "Merck's New Performance Appraisal/Merit Pay System . . .," *Ideas & Trends in Personnel Management*, op. cit.

44. Richard R. Goodell, "Room for Improvement," *Personnel Administrator* (June 1988), pp. 132–142.

45. Donald J. Campbell and Cynthia Lee, "Self-appraisal in Performance Evaluation: Development versus Evaluation," *Academy of Management Review*, vol. 13 (1988), pp. 302–314. See also H. John Bernardin, "Subordinate Appraisal: A Valuable Source of Information About Managers," *Human Resource Management* (Fall 1986), pp. 421–439; and Jing-Lih Farh, James D. Werbel, Arthur G. Bedeian, "An Empirical Investigation of Self-appraisal-based Performance Evaluation," *Personnel Psychology*, vol. 41 (1988), pp. 141–156.

46. Milan Moravec, "How Performance Appraisal Can Tie Communication to Productivity," *Personnel Administrator* (Jan. 1981), pp. 51–52.

47. William B. Werther, Jr., and Heinz Weihrich, "Refining MBO through Negotiations," *MSU Business Topics* (Summer 1975), pp. 53–58. See also Deets and Tyler, op. cit.

48. Deets and Tyler, op. cit.

49. Ann Marie Ryan and Paul R. Sackett, "A Survey of Individual Assessment Practices by I/O Psychologists," *Personnel Psychology*, vol. 40 (1987), pp. 455–489.

50. Michael M. Harris and John Schaubroeck, "A Meta-analysis of Self-Supervisor, Self-Peer, and Peer-Supervisor Ratings," *Personnel Psychology*, vol. 41 (1988), pp. 43–62.

51. Douglas W. Bray, "Fifty Years of Assessment Centers: A Retrospective and Prospective View," *Journal of Management Development*, vol. 4, no. 4 (1985), pp. 4–11.

52. Paul R. Sackett and Ann Marie Ryan, "A Review of Recent Assessment Center Research," *Journal of Management Development*, vol. 4, no. 4 (1985), pp. 13–25.

53. Paul R. Sackett, "Assessment Centers and Content Validity: Some Neglected Issues," *Personnel Psychology*, vol. 40 (1987), pp. 13–25. See also Peter Rea, Julie Rea and Charles Moomaw, "Use Assessment Centers in Skill Development," *Personnel Journal* (April 1990), pp. 126–131; and Hubert S. Field and William H. Holley, "The Relationship of Performance Appraisal System Characteristics to Verdicts in Selected Employment Discrimination Cases," *Academy of Management Journal* (June 1982), pp. 392–406. See also George F. Dreher and Paul S. Sackett, "Some Problems with Applying Content Validity Evidence to Assessment Center Procedures," *Academy of Management Review* (Oct. 1981), pp. 551–560; Steven D. Norton, "The Assessment Center Process and Content Validity: A Reply to Dreher and Sackett," *Academy of*

Management Review (Oct. 1982), pp. 561–566; Paul R. Sackett and George F. Dreher, "Some Misconceptions about Content-oriented Validation: A Rejoinder to Norton," *Academy of Management Review* (Oct. 1981), pp. 567–568.

54. Glenn M. McEvoy and Richard W. Beatty, "Assessment Centers and Subordinate Appraisals of Managers: A Seven-year Examination of Predictive Validity," *Personnel Psychology*, vol. 42 (1989), pp. 37–52. See also Sackett and Ryan, op. cit.

55. Leland C. Nichols and Joseph Hudson, "Dual-role Assessment Center: Selection and Development," *Personnel Journal* (May 1981), pp. 380–386.

56. Ibid., p. 382.

57. Jeffery S. Schippmann, Garry L. Hughes, and Erich P. Prien, "Raise Assessment Standards," *Personnel Journal* (July 1988), pp. 69–79.

58. Glenn M. McEvoy, Paul F. Buller, and Steven R. Roghaar, "A Jury of One's Peers," *Personnel Administrator* (May 1988), pp. 94–101. See also Ryan and Sackett, op. cit.

59. Jim Laumeyer and Tim Beebe, "Employees and Their Appraisal," *Personnel Administrator* (Dec. 1988), pp. 76–80

60. Walter Kiechell III, "When Subordinates Evaluate the Boss," *Fortune* (June 19, 1989), pp. 102. See also Glenn M. McEvoy, "Evaluating the Boss," *Personnel Administrator* (Sept. 1988), pp. 115–120.

61. Locher and Teel, op. cit., p. 145.

62. William J. Birch, "Performance Appraisal: One Company's Experience," *Personnel Journal* (June 1981), pp. 456–460. For another view see Virginia Bianco, "In Praise of Performance," *Personnel Journal* (June 1984), pp. 40–45, 47–48, 50.

63. Birch, op. cit. See also Timothy R. Athey and Robert M. McIntyre, "Effect of Rater Training on Rater Accuracy: Levels-of-Processing Theory and Social Facilitation Theory Perspectives," *Journal of Applied Psychology*, vol. 72 (1987), pp. 567–572; and Brian L. Davis and Michael K. Mount, "Effectiveness of Performance Appraisal Training Using Computer Assisted Instruction and Behavior Modeling," *Personnel Psychology*, vol. 37 (1984), pp. 439–452.

64. John Lawrie, "Prepare for a Performance Appraisal," *Personnel Journal* (April 1990), pp. 132–136.

65. Norman R.F. Maier, *The Appraisal Interview: Three Basic Approaches* (La Jolla, Calif.: University Associates, 1976).

66. Ibid. See also Robert L. Taylor and Robert A. Zawacki, "Trends in Performance Appraisal: Guidelines for Managers," *Personnel Administrator* (March 1984), pp. 71–72, 74, 76, 78–80; Brian L. Davis and Michael K. Mount, "Design and Use of a Performance Appraisal Feedback System," *Personnel Administrator* (March 1984), pp. 91–97; and Stanley B. Silverman and Kenneth N. Wexley, "Reaction of Employees to

Performance Appraisal Interviews as a Function of Their Participation in Rating Scale Development," *Personnel Psychology*, vol. 37 (1984), pp. 703–710.

67. Clement and Stevens, op. cit., pp. 43–58.

The large organization generally creates career patterns through which people move, become committed to the organization, and become capable of managing larger parts of the business.
KAREN N. GAERTNER[1]

12

CAREER PLANNING

CHAPTER OBJECTIVES

After studying this chapter, you should be able to:
1. ADVISE someone about the major points in career planning.
2. DESCRIBE how human resource departments encourage and assist career planning.
3. DISCUSS career planning issues related to work force diversity and international employees.
4. IDENTIFY the major advantages of career planning.
5. EXPLAIN the relationship between career planning and career development.
6. LIST the major actions that aid career development.

As a consultant to several companies, one of the authors of this book is frequently asked the following questions:

Common concerns

➤ "How do I get ahead in this company?"

➤ "Why hasn't my boss given me career counseling?"

➤ "Don't you think that most promotions are based on luck and knowing the right people?"

➤ "Do I need a degree for that job?"

➤ "Do company training programs help my chances for a promotion?"

Nearly everyone asks these questions at some point during their working life. Performance appraisals provide some of the answers. And the answers to these questions help identify the actions needed to further an employee's career. Actions may involve placements into new jobs within the organization, professional certifications, a new degree, or other training and development activities discussed in Chapter 10. If the department has accurate human resource plans, knowledge of the firm's future staffing needs can make it an important source of career planning information and assistance.

Career defined

A *career* is all the jobs that are held during one's working life. For some people, these jobs are part of a careful plan. For others, their career is simply a matter of luck. Merely planning a career does not guarantee career success. Superior performance, experience, education, and some occasional luck play important roles. When people rely largely on luck, however, they seldom are prepared for career opportunities that arise. Successful people identify their career goals, plan, and then take action.

People who fail to plan their careers may do so because they think that their company or their boss will assume that responsibility, or because they are unaware of the basic career planning concepts described in Figure 12-1. Without an understanding of career goals[2] and career paths,[3] planning is unlikely. Some people argue, "Who can look ten, twenty, or thirty years into the future and predict where my career will lead? I never thought it would lead to where I am now!" True, an accurate prediction that far into the future is impossible. However, by asking, "What are my career goals?" and "What is my first step?" a career plan can be started.[4]

Key questions

Employees must take responsibility for asking these questions. Although the department can facilitate the process and help answer questions about appropriate career paths, the employee remains ultimately responsible for his or her career progress.[5] In fact, some departments offer no formal career planning assistance because they lack the sophistication to do so (as is the case in many small

Figure 12-1

Selected Career Planning Terms

- *Career.* A career is all the jobs that are held during one's working life.
- *Career path.* A career path is the sequential pattern of jobs that forms one's career.
- *Career goals.* Career goals are the future positions one strives to reach as part of a career. These goals serve as benchmarks along one's career path.
- *Career planning.* Career planning is the process by which one selects career goals and the path to those goals
- *Career development.* Career development is those personal improvements one undertakes to achieve a personal career plan.

organizations). Even in some large businesses, senior managers view career planning as the responsibility of the employee, not the company.[6] Nevertheless, more and more sophisticated organizations see career planning assistance as a means to help ensure an adequate supply of internal talent. As one writer observes:

> During the past 30 years, career development programs have become an important and vital activity in business and industry. Career development is now an accepted human resource strategy among training and development administrators, personnel officers, and organizational consultants. The principal aim of such programs has been to help employees analyze their abilities and interests to better match personnel needs for growth and development with the needs of the organization. In addition, career development is a critical tool through which management can increase productivity, improve employee attitudes toward work, and develop greater worker satisfaction.[7]

And, effective career planning programs may reduce turnover, especially among those who have the greatest career mobility—the best employees.[8]

Dow Jones

Dow Jones & Company, Inc., is the publisher of the Wall Street Journal, Barron's, and other business information sources. During the 1980s, the vice president for staff development created a task force that designed the "Druthers Program" for the company. Endorsed by top management and the union that represents most of the company's clerical and professional employees, this program puts responsibility for career development where it belongs: on employees.

An employee initiates the "Druthers Program" by writing a letter to his or her manager. The letter identifies a specific career objective and, if known, the next job being sought. Then the letter describes relevant education and experience and may discuss willingness to travel or relocate. The style and content of the letter give an indication of the writer's logic and writing skills.

These letters are kept on file for 12 months by the manager. If a job is sought outside the department, a copy of the letter goes to the national coordinator of the program, the director of employment and career planning.

When a job opening occurs, the letters are reviewed. If suitable candidates are not on file, referrals are sought from the program coordinator. Although managers may recruit outside the firm, they are encouraged to review internal candidates first.

The "Druthers Program" is supported by the department in several ways. Seminars give employees insight into career planning and self-assessment. Briefings about career options and appropriate job requirements are done by people from key departments. Seminars even show employees how to present their qualifications in writing and in person.

Employees receive The Dow Jones Job Information Handbook that describes the various departments and jobs within the company, including summaries of job responsibilities, locations, and qualifications. Dow Jones employees also can get a booklet entitled Writing Your Own Success Story—A Guide to Using the Druthers System. It answers questions about the Dow Jones career development and placement service and gives sample Druthers letters along with the biographies of those who wrote them.[9]

The Dow Jones program gives employees a way to express their preferences, or "druthers," about the work they want to do. The department's role includes creating, publicizing, and maintaining the program through training and information. But the responsibility for career planning and development stays with the employee because he or she is the person most keenly interested. And since each person's career is unique, only the employee can decide if the company's career path is appropriate for him or her.

Although each person's career is unique, consider the insights contained in one executive's career path. This executive's name and the name of his employers have been changed to protect his privacy, so we will call him "Joe."[10] Joe was in banking for 41 years. His career progress is summarized in Figure 12-2 and explained below:

After graduation from college and three years in the Marine Corps, Joe joined the First National Bank as a teller trainee. At that point in his career, his goal was to become a banking executive. He had no idea of the career path he would follow. But Joe realized that his first step was to become a supervisor. This career planning prompted him to enroll in the bank's supervisory management training program. After being promoted to teller, he enrolled in other training programs and also took some noncredit courses from the American Banking Institute. These programs were the first of many career development actions he undertook. Two promotions later he became head teller.

Figure 12-2

The Career Path for a Retired Executive Vice President in the Banking Industry

JOB NUMBER	JOB LEVEL	JOB TITLE	TYPE OF JOB CHANGE	YEARS IN JOB	ENDING AGE
1	Worker	Teller Trainee	—	1/2	24
2	Worker	Teller	Promotion	3 1/2	28
3	Worker	Asst. Head Teller	Promotion	2	30
4	Supervisory	Head Teller	Promotion	4	34
5	Supervisory	New Account Supervisor	Transfer	3	37
6	Management	Asst. Branch Manager for Loans	Promotion	3	40
7			Educational leave (finish M.B.A.)	1	41
8	Management	Asst. Branch Manager	Transfer	1	42
9	Management	Branch Manager	Promotion	3	45
10	Management	Branch Manager	Transfer	4	49
11	Management	Loan Officer	Transfer	5	54
12	Management	Chief Loan Officer	Promotion	3	57
13	Executive	Vice President Operations Center	Resignation/Promotion (joins another bank)	3	60
14	Executive	Senior Vice President for Operations	Promotion	1	61
15	Executive	Executive Vice President	Promotion	4	65
16			Retired		

After four years, Joe felt his career plan was stalled, so he accepted a transfer into the bank's new account department. Although the transfer was not a promotion and did not even include a raise, Joe needed some diversification in his background to increase his chances of becoming an assistant branch manager. Three years later he became assistant branch manager for loans.

After three years as an assistant branch manager for loans, Joe again felt that his career progress was too slow, so he took an educational leave and finished his master of business administration degree (M.B.A.). With the M.B.A., he returned to the bank as an assistant manager in a new branch. A year later he was promoted to branch manager. To gain a wider breadth of skills, Joe transferred to another branch as manager and then to the home office as a loan officer. In five years he became chief loan officer, and three years later he achieved his goal by accepting a job as vice president in a competing bank. His success as an executive led to two more promotions before he retired as an executive vice president at age 65.

Figure 12-3

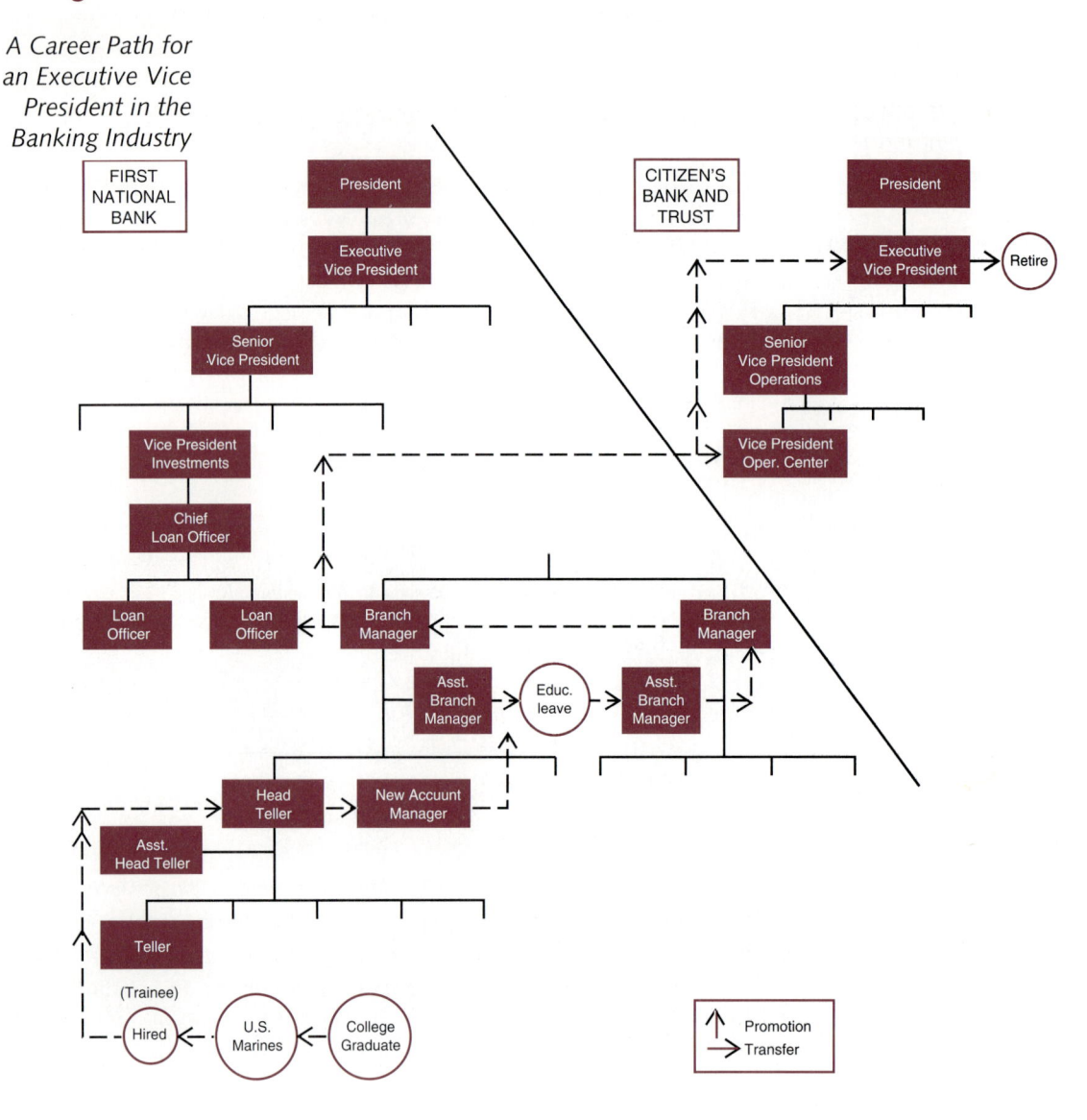

A Career Path for an Executive Vice President in the Banking Industry

As a review of Figure 12-2 indicates, Joe's career plan involved well-timed transfers and an educational leave. Figure 12-3 superimposes Joe's career changes on the organizational charts of the two banks for which he worked. As the organizational charts show, career progress is seldom straight up in an organization. Lateral transfers, leaves, and even resignations are used. When Joe started as a teller trainee at age 24, he could not have predicted the career path he would follow. But through career planning, he reassessed his career progress and then undertook developmental activities to achieve intermediate career goals, such as becoming a supervisor. As a result of ongoing career planning and development, Joe's career path led him to his goal of becoming an executive in the banking industry.

CAREER PLANNING AND EMPLOYEE NEEDS

During the 40 years of Joe's career, human resource departments in banks and other organizations gave little support to career planning. When promotable talent was scarce, employers usually reacted with crash training programs or additional recruitment. Human resource planning and career planning seldom occurred. Instead of seeking proactive solutions, organizations and employees simply reacted to new developments.[11] This limited role for the department is understandable historically because career plans were seen as an individual matter.[12] Even when human resource managers wanted their departments to provide assistance, they often lacked the resources to become involved. As a result, only a few (mostly large) organizations encouraged career planning by employees.[13]

Internal staffing help

Today, an increasing number of human resource experts see career planning as a way to meet their internal staffing needs.[14] Although career planning assistance is generally reserved for managerial, professional, and technical employees because of available funds, ideally, all workers would have access to this advice, as they do at the Dow Jones Company. When employers encourage career planning, employees are more likely to set career goals and work toward them. In turn, these goals may motivate employees to pursue further education, training, and other developmental activities, which gives the department a larger internal pool of qualified applicants.

But what do employees want? A study of one group of employees revealed five factors of concern.[15] These include:

Research summary: what employees want

➤ *Career equity.* Employees want equity in the promotion system with respect to career advancement opportunities.

➤ Supervisory concern. Employees want their supervisors to play an active role in career development and to provide timely performance feedback.

➤ Awareness of opportunities. Employees want knowledge of the career advancement opportunities.

➤ Employee interest. Employees need different amounts of information and have different degrees of interest in career advancement depending on a variety of factors.

➤ Career satisfaction. Employees, depending on their age and occupation, have different levels of career satisfaction.

12. CAREER PLANNING

381

Effective career programs must consider these different perceptions and desires among employees.[16] What workers expect from the career programs developed by the department will vary according to age, sex, occupation, education, and other variables. In short, whatever approach the department undertakes, it must be flexible and proactive. One personnel manager, associated with the Hanes Group in Winston-Salem, North Carolina, comes to this conclusion:

> Flexibility in career development programs is paramount if the goals of improved productivity, increased personal satisfaction, growth, and ultimately increased organizational effectiveness are to be achieved. In many cases, this will require the modification of basic existing programs to address the specific needs of a particular group of employees.[17]

HUMAN RESOURCE DEPARTMENTS AND CAREER PLANNING

For corporations to implement their business strategies requires an appropriate mix of human talents. The department's human resource plans serve to translate corporate strategy into employment needs.[18] To fulfill the organization's future employment requirements with internal candidates, the department uses placement decisions, training and development, performance appraisals, and career planning assistance. As organizations seek to project a global presence, the department can use career planning assistance to encourage employees to prepare for international openings.

Human resource departments become involved in career planning for other reasons. Departmental experts are more likely to be aware of training and other developmental opportunities. Of course, individual managers also should assist employees with career planning. However, if specialists leave career planning to managers, it may not get done. Not all managers take a strong interest in their employees' careers, although 68 percent of the firms in one study do have formal succession plans.[19]

The primary risk for the department and the company is the creation of career expectations that cannot be met by the company. Offering career guidance to employees suggests that if they follow the advice, career opportunities will follow. However, company growth, down-sizing, or changes in business strategies may prevent opportunities from materializing. Disappointment may lower morale and performance and may lead to resignations.

Down-sizing and careers

As organizations seek to down-size, the career opportunities of those remaining shrink. The department can use career planning to help employees identify other career opportunities, ranging from lateral transfers to special task forces that challenge employees to continue their development. If successful, these efforts can convince remaining employees that they have a future with the company. Since those remaining are usually viewed as the "best" employees, it is essential that these employees remain with the company and remain motivated.

The involvement of the Human Resource department in career planning has grown during recent years because of its benefits. Here is a partial list of those benefits:

Career planning benefits

➤ *Aligns strategy and internal staffing requirements.* By assisting employees with career planning, the department can better prepare them for anticipated job openings identified in the human resource plan. The result can be a better mix of talents needed to implement company strategies.

➤ *Develops promotable employees.* Career planning helps to develop internal supplies of promotable talent to meet openings due to retirement, resignation, or growth.

➤ *Facilitates international placement.* Global organizations use career planning to help identify appropriate assignments and prepare employees for placement across international borders.

➤ *Assists with work force diversity.* By providing career planning assistance, workers with diverse backgrounds can learn about the organization's expectations for self-growth and development and become better integrated into the mainstream of the company.

➤ *Lowers turnover.* The increased attention and concern for individual careers generate more organizational loyalty and, therefore, lower employee turnover.

➤ *Taps employee potential.* Career planning encourages employees to tap more of their potential abilities because they have specific career goals. Not only does this prepare employees for future openings, it can lead to better performance among incumbents in their present jobs.

➤ *Furthers personal growth.* Career plans and goals motivate employees to grow and develop.

➤ *Reduces hoarding.* Without career planning, it is easier for managers to hoard key subordinates. Career planning causes employees, managers, and the human resource department to become aware of employee qualifications.

➤ *Satisfies employee needs.* With less hoarding and improved growth opportunities for employees, an individual's esteem needs, such as recognition and accomplishment, are more readily satisfied.

➤ *Assists affirmative action plans.* Career planning can help members of protected groups prepare for more important jobs. This preparation can contribute to meeting affirmative action timetables.

To realize these benefits, companies are supporting career planning, through career education, information, and counseling.

Career Education

Surprisingly, many employees know very little about career planning. They are often unaware of the need for and advantages of career planning. And once made aware, they often lack the necessary information to plan their careers successfully. Human resource departments are suited to solve both of these shortcomings, and they can increase employee awareness through a variety of educational techniques. For example, speeches, memoranda, and position papers from top executives stimulate employee interest at low cost to the employer. If executives communicate their belief in career planning, other managers are likely to do the same.

Workshops and seminars increase employee interest by pointing out the key concepts associated with career planning.[20] Workshops also help the employee set career goals, identify career paths, and uncover specific career development activities. These educational efforts may be supplemented by printed or taped information. The John Deere Company offers one example of the varied approaches to career education.

John Deere

The John Deere Harvester Works has been in East Moline, Illinois, since the company moved into the "new" technology of combine harvesting around the turn of this century. Although many employees have decades of service, the company has hired many newcomers. Not all of these employees have the loyalty of their long-service coworkers and are more prone to ask, "What is the company doing for my career?"

At this operation, members of the human resource department have taken the view that career planning and development are the responsibility of the employee. With that philosophy, a four-hour career planning workshop was developed. Attendance is voluntary. Employees go to the workshop on their own time and do not receive any pay for attending. This "on-your-own-time" approach is intended to reinforce the point that career development rests with the individual. Instructors from the department are not paid either; the fact that they volunteer to do the sessions helps to convey the idea that the department is interested in the participants as people, not only as employees.

Figure 12-4 lists the goals of these career information seminars. As the seminars begin, participants are assigned to teams. Introductions and a discussion about the confidentiality of the sessions follow. Then the groups discuss career planning and list enjoyable and not-so-enjoyable activities as a step to creating a personal inventory and identifying alternatives. Discussions also center on making internal staffing decisions—an exercise in which the teams are asked to fill hypothetical openings immediately. As two members of the department observed: *"The arguments which are created in this exercise are*

Figure 12-4

Goals of the Career Information Seminar at John Deere

JOHN DEERE HARVESTER WORKS

Career Information Seminar

Goals

1. To help employees better understand how their jobs and careers at John Deere can contribute to their goals
2. To provide employees with an approach to individualized career planning.
3. To define the roles of employees, their supervisors, and the personnel department in career planning and personal development.
4. To provide realistic job and career information upon which to build career plans.

Source: Reprinted, with permission, from Karl A. Hickerson and Richard C. Anderson, "Career Development: Whose Responsibility?" *Personnel Administrator,* June 1982, p. 45. Copyright © 1982, the American Society for Personnel Administration, 30 Park Drive, Berea, Ohio 44017.

---

highly beneficial for promoting acceptance of the management perspective on internal selection and promotion, a perspective which many have not previously considered. Many participants realize for the first time that being passed over only means someone else was slightly better qualified—not that they're in disfavor with the company."[21]

When the department lacks the necessary staff to design and conduct educational programs, public programs conducted by local colleges or consultants may help.

TPF & C consultants

One worldwide consulting firm—Towers, Perrin, Forster & Crosby—provides its clients with a four-step package. The packaged program develops (1) a strategy for the organization to solve its unique needs, (2) support systems, based upon the present personnel management information system, to give employees the data they need to plan their careers, (3) workbooks that allow employees to perform career planning, and (4) a career resource center that offers employees assistance with their career planning.

Competition and down-sizing have put cost pressures on many human resource departments. To keep career planning information flowing, some departments have enlisted the support of line managers instead of staff in the department:

> "At Anheuser-Busch, certain employees receive five days of training, which equips them to run two-day career management workshops for fellow employees.
> B.F. Goodrich's Career Growth System includes a 12-hour training program . . . to enhance managers' ability to handle career-related discussions with employees."[22]

Many companies still rely on staff-run centers and staff-provided information on career planning:

> 3M has a company-funded Career Information Center that provides continuing education and training, job vacancy information, individual assessments, and counseling, along with . . . career growth workshops that are attended on company time.[23]

Information about Career Planning

Regardless of the educational strategy the department selects, it should provide employees with other information they need to plan their careers. Much of the needed career information is already a part of the department's human resource information system.[24] For instance, job descriptions and specifications can be quite valuable to someone who is trying to estimate reasonable career goals at a firm like Dow Jones and Company. Human resource specialists can also share their knowledge of potential career paths. For example, they are often keenly aware of the similarities between seemingly unrelated jobs.

> Consider the possible career paths faced by a clerk-typist at the *Wall Street Journal*, for example. In this type of work, the jobs of typist, word processor, and Teletype or Linotype operator share a common characteristic: finger dexterity. But a clerk-typist in the advertising department may not realize that similar skills applied to a Linotype machine may earn three times as much as the other jobs.

When different jobs require similar skills, they form *job families*. Career paths within a job family demand little additional training, since the skills of each job are closely related. If information about job families is made available, employees can find feasible career paths. They then can assess the career paths by talking to those who already hold these jobs. One problem with job families is that employees may want to skip less pleasant or lower-paying jobs. To prevent employees from rejecting some jobs in a job family the department may establish a sequential progression of jobs. A *job progression ladder* is a partial career path where some jobs have prerequisites, as shown in Figure 12-5. The job progression

Figure 12-5

Four Jobs with Similiar Requirements Grouped into a Job Family

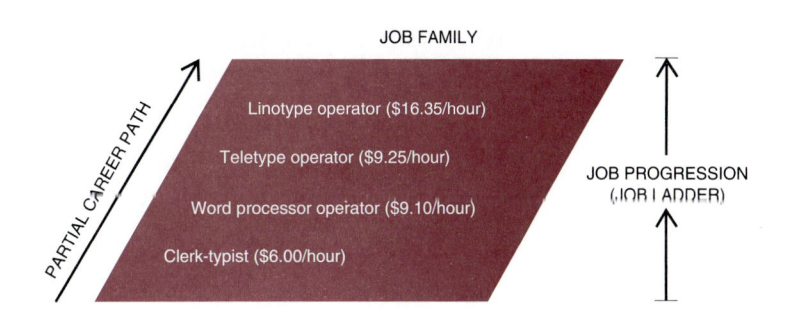

JOB FAMILY

PARTIAL CAREER PATH

Linotype operator ($16.35/hour)
Teletype operator ($9.25/hour)
Word processor operator ($9.10/hour)
Clerk-typist ($6.00/hour)

JOB PROGRESSION (JOB LADDER)

ladder shown in the figure requires a clerk-typist to become a word processor and then a Teletype operator before moving to the better-paying job of Linotype operator. This requirement assures the department of an ample internal supply of Teletype operators because this job is a prerequisite to a better-paying ones.

The department also can encourage career planning by providing information about alternative career paths. Figure 12-5 shows that clerk-typists face multiple career paths. If a particular clerk-typist does not want to become a Linotype operator, human resource specialists can provide information about alternatives. At a newspaper, for example, a clerk-typist might prefer a career in editorial, secretarial, or advertising occupations because these careers offer more long-term potential.

At the John Deere Harvester Works, the department provides an extensive brochure that describes every factory job below the level of management. However, the brochure is only available through the career information seminar.[25]

Career Counseling

To help employees establish career goals and find appropriate career paths, some departments offer *career counseling*. The career counselor may simply be someone who listens to the employee's interests and provides the specific job-related information.[26] Or the counselor may help employees uncover their interests by administering and interpreting aptitude and skills tests. Two tests in particular—the *Kuder Preference Record* and the *Strong Vocational Interest Blank*—are useful for guiding people into occupations that are likely to be of interest. Other tests also are available to measure individual abilities and interests in specific types of work. But to be truly successful, career counselors must get employees to assess themselves and their environment.

Vocational interest blanks

Employee self-assessment. Career counselors realize that a career is only a part of one's life. It may be a large part or even a central part. But it is only a part of one's life plan. A *life plan* is that often ill-defined series of hopes, dreams, and personal goals that each person carries through life. For example, broad objectives to be happy, healthy, and successful combine with specific goals to be a good spouse, parent, student, citizen, neighbor, and manager. Together these roles form one's life plan. Ideally, a career plan is an integral part of one's life plan. Otherwise, career goals become ends (sometimes dead ends!) rather than means toward fulfilling a life plan.[27] An example can be drawn from an overworked movie plot:

> The husband struggles for decades to achieve a degree of career success. When that success is within reach, he realizes his personal life—friendships, marriage, and paternal relationships—is in shambles. It is in shambles because career plans were pursued to the exclusion of an integrated life plan.

Besides a life plan, self-assessment includes a self-inventory. Components of a self-inventory are listed in Figure 12-6. If a career counselor can get employees to complete detailed and honest self-evaluations, they help to focus their thinking about themselves. Then employees can match their interests and abilities with the career information available to them from the human resource department.[28] Likewise, they can match their aptitudes and career goals with their life plans.

Environmental assessment. A career plan that matches employee interests with likely career paths actually may do a disservice to the employee if environmental factors are overlooked. A return to the choices faced by clerk-typists at the newspaper provides an example.

> The job family of clerk-typist, word processor, Teletype, and Linotype operator may appear to comprise a reasonable career path since clerk-typists possess the basic typing skills needed for all four jobs. But technological changes in the newspaper industry have reduced the need for Linotype operators. Photographic and computer developments are quickly replacing the use of Linotype machines in newspaper printing. If career counselors in the human resource department do not point out this development, clerk-typists may find their careers stalled in the job of Teletype operator.

Regardless of the match between one's skills and the organization's career paths, counselors need to inform employees of likely changes that will affect their occupational choices. Occupational information is readily available from the U.S. Department of Labor's Bureau of Labor Statistics.

Figure 12-6

A Self-Inventory for Career Planning

WORK INTERESTS AND APTITUDES

	Low 1	2	3	4	High 5
Physical work (fixing, building, using hands)	___	___	___	___	___
Written work (writing, reading, using words)	___	___	___	___	___
Oral work (talking, giving speeches, using words)	___	___	___	___	___
Quantitative work (calculating, doing accounting, using numbers)	___	___	___	___	___
Visual work (watching, inspecting, using eyes)	___	___	___	___	___
Interpersonal work (counseling, interviewing)	___	___	___	___	___
Creative work (inventing, designing, ideas)	___	___	___	___	___
Analytical work (doing research, solving problems)	___	___	___	___	___
Managerial work (initiating, directing, coordinating)	___	___	___	___	___
Clerical (keeping records)	___	___	___	___	___
Outdoor work (farming, traveling, doing athletics)	___	___	___	___	___
Mechanical (repairing, fixing, tinkering)	___	___	___	___	___

WORK SKILLS AND ABILITIES

List below specialized skills, unique personal assets, enjoyable experiences, and major accomplishments. Then evaluate.

PHYSICAL | WRITTEN | ORAL | QUANTITATIVE | VISUAL | INTERPERSONAL | CREATIVE | ANALYTICAL | MANAGERIAL | CLERICAL | OUTDOOR | MECHANICAL

Career counseling process. One of the problems often encountered by career counselors is employee reaction to the counseling process. Counseling about careers is a very sensitive, potentially explosive issue. Employees may see only parts of some jobs that pay much better and think that they are qualified. When the counselor tries to explain the need for additional skills that are not apparent, employees may feel that they are not being treated fairly. "If old Mary can do that job, certainly I can do it," is a typical reaction. Even if that reaction is true, others who are even more qualified may be better choices. Or when the counselor points out necessary steps to become qualified for a job, the employee may resist additional training or schooling. Finally, the mere presence of career counselors may be a trap. Employees might think that someone else is taking responsibility for their career planning and development. Returning to the observations of two human resource specialists at John Deere Harvester Works:

John Deere

We find, for example, there is a great unspoken lesson about the nature of competition for "career" advancement at the moment people gather on their own time at the workplace on a Saturday morning. All they have to do is look around.

"Looking around" emphasizes that there are other people who are interested in advancing, too. Although a counselor can point this out, seeing thirty or forty people at the plant on a Saturday morning probably makes a deeper impression. The group training sessions also can illustrate some issues that counseling may not be able to do as well. When the personnel specialists state during the seminar that people who are flexible, energetic, and willing to improve their skills have an advantage, there is less defensive behavior than when those comments are made in a private counseling session.[29]

Stalled Careers

A particularly difficult issue in career planning assistance is addressing stalled careers. As two researchers observe:

Research summary

... retaining employees with critical skills, creating career paths to help senior employees break out of career plateaus, and retraining senior employees whose skills have become outdated will pose special challenges to human resource managers.[30]

Slow growth and restructuring through down-sizing have eliminated many career opportunities for otherwise good, hard-working employees.[31] Simply put, many people have found their careers stalled through no fault of their own. Since many companies have scaled back their levels of middle management and staff, finding career advancement opportunities outside the firm involves considerable competition. At the same time, the human resource department needs to keep remaining employees motivated and developing.[32] With fewer levels of jobs between entry-level positions and senior management in many firms, human resource departments have focused on planning that includes lateral job transfers, or job rotation, among staff members and middle managers. Assigning greater responsibility also has helped develop those who remain on the payroll. The trend toward connecting pay to performance has also helped serve as a motivator.

When stalled careers result from limited skills, knowledge, abilities, or personal attributes of employees, the department faces a different set of challenges. When the problem is a simple deficiency of knowledge, skills, or abilities, retraining is required.[33] Often, however, these shortcomings may be combined with issues of motivation or personal attributes that preclude advancement even with training. Furthermore, as organizations attempt to accommodate work force diversity, affirmative action plans may stall otherwise promotable employees.

Some people reach a career plateau beyond which they are not capable of advancing, even with training and development. Yet these same employees may be good performers in their present jobs and important to the continued smooth operation of the organization.[34]

Others may experience burnout. *Burnout* is a condition of mental, emotional, and sometimes physical exhaustion that results from substantial and prolonged stress.[35] Stress-reduction training may help to eliminate or reduce the problem before or after it occurs. However, people experiencing burnout are not likely candidates for advancement to jobs with greater responsibility and, perhaps, greater stress. Even after the feelings of burnout pass, personal motivation or the reputation of having gone through a period of burnout may eliminate the person from consideration for advancement.

CAREER DEVELOPMENT

The implementation of career plans requires career development. Career development is comprised of those personal improvements one undertakes to achieve a career plan. These actions may be sponsored by the human resource department, or they may be activities that employees undertake independent of the department. This section reviews the tactics employees may use to achieve their career plans and then discusses the department's role in career development.

Individual Career Development

Personal responsibility

Each person must accept his or her responsibility for career development, or career progress is likely to suffer. Once this personal commitment is made, several career development actions may prove useful. These actions involve:

- ➤ Job performance
- ➤ Exposure
- ➤ Resignations
- ➤ Organizational loyalty
- ➤ Mentors and sponsors
- ➤ Key subordinates
- ➤ Growth opportunities
- ➤ International experience.

Job performance. The most important action an individual can undertake to further his or her career is good, ethical job performance. The assumption of good performance underlies all career development activities. When performance is substandard, regardless of other career development efforts, even modest career goals are usually unattainable. Those who perform poorly are disregarded quickly by decision makers. *Career progress rests largely upon performance.*

Exposure. Career progress also is furthered by exposure.[36] *Exposure* means becoming known (and, it is hoped, held in high regard) by those who decide on promotions, transfers, and other career opportunities. Without exposure, good performers may not get a chance at the opportunities needed to achieve their career goals. Managers gain exposure primarily through their performance, written reports, oral presentations, committee work, and even the hours they work. Exposure also comes from furthering the organization's social responsibility through involvement in professional associations and non-profit community groups, such as the United Way, Chambers of Commerce, and other civic-minded groups. Simply put, exposure makes an individual stand out from the crowd—a necessary ingredient to career success, especially in large organizations.[37] For example, consider how one management trainee gained some vital exposure early in her career:

> *Paula Dorsey noticed that two executives worked on Saturday mornings. As one of 12 new management trainees, she decided that coming to work on Saturday mornings would give her additional exposure to these key decision makers. Soon these two executives began greeting her by name whenever they passed in the halls. While still in the training program, she was assigned to the product introduction committee, which planned strategy for new products. At the end of the training program, Paula was made an assistant product manager for a new line of phones. The other 11 trainees received less important jobs.*

In small organizations, exposure to decision makers is more frequent and less dependent upon reports, presentations, and the like. In some situations, especially in other nations, social status, school ties, and seniority can be more important than exposure.

Resignations. When an individual sees greater career opportunities elsewhere, a resignation may be the only way to meet one's career goals. Some employees—professionals and managers in particular—change employers as part of a conscious career strategy. If done effectively, these resignations usually result in a promotion, a pay increase, and a new learning experience. Resigning in order to further one's career with another employer has been called *leveraging*.[38] Astute managers and professionals use this technique sparingly because too many moves can lead to the label of "job hopper." Those who leave seldom benefit their previous organization because they almost never return with their new experiences.

> *In a study of 268 mobile executives conducted by one of the authors of this book, only 3 percent (7 of the executives) ever returned to an organization that they had left during their careers.[39] This finding means that organizations seldom benefit from the return of managers who quit and go elsewhere. Thus*

personnel departments must work to develop the loyalty of their employees to reduce turnover and retain valuable human resources.

Organizational loyalty. In many organizations, people put loyalty to their career above loyalty to their organization. Low levels of organizational loyalty are common among recent college graduates (whose high expectations often lead to disappointment with their first few employers) and professionals (whose first loyalty is often to their profession).[40] Career-long dedication to the same organization complements the human resource department's objective of reducing employee turnover. Sometimes employers try to "buy" this loyalty with high pay or benefits. Other organizations may limit mobility by requiring employees to sign noncompete contracts that prohibit them for working for competitors, usually for one or more years. Still other organizations try to build employee loyalty through effective human resource practices, including career planning and development. By offering careers, not just jobs, many organizations nurture a pool of talent that allows them to staff senior management positions internally. And many employees use their dedication and loyalty to the company as a career tactic. For example, one study showed that of the 100 largest industrial companies in the United States, 51 percent of their chief executive officers spent their entire careers with the same organization.[41] In Japan, employees tend to be very loyal to their employer because many firms will hire only entry-level workers. And in many large firms, men are given lifetime employment. Thus, changing jobs to another Japanese firm to further one's career is seldom done.

Dedication

Mentors and sponsors. Many employees quickly learn that a *mentor* can aid their career development. A mentor is someone who offers informal career advice. Neither the mentor nor the employee always recognize the relationship exists. Instead, a junior worker simply knows someone who gives good advice.[42]

If the mentor can nominate the employee for career development activities—such as training programs, transfers, or promotions—then the mentor becomes a sponsor. A *sponsor* is someone in the organization who can create career development opportunities. Often an employee's sponsor is the immediate supervisor, although others may serve as nominators.[43]

Japanese approach

Many Japanese firms rely on senior managers to use their storehouse of insights and wisdom to help junior managers with career development. In a relationship based on school ties or on some other non-work-related factor, the senior manager serves as a career counselor, mentor, and sponsor for the junior employee, who often works in a different department. In return, the senior manager's actions are reinforced by the respect received from other managers.

Key subordinates. Successful managers rely on subordinates who aid the managers' performance. The subordinates may possess highly specialized knowledge or skills that the manager may learn from them. Or the employee may perform a crucial role in helping a manager achieve good performance. In either case, employees of this type are *key subordinates.* They exhibit loyalty to their bosses and a high ethical standard. They gather and interpret information, offer skills that supplement those of their managers, and work unselfishly to further their managers' careers. They benefit by also moving up the career ladder when the manager is promoted and by receiving important delegations that serve to develop their careers. These people complement human resource department objectives through their teamwork, motivation, and dedication. But when a manager resigns and takes a string of key subordinates along, the results can be devastating.[44]

Crucial subordinates

> *A small West Coast research firm had a 10-month lead in developing a new type of memory component for computers. A major electronics company hired away the project manager, the chief engineer, and their key subordinates. With this loss, the small firm was forced to recruit replacements at a higher salary and at a cost of several months' delay.*

As a career strategy, perceptive subordinates are careful not to become attached to an immobile manager. One researcher calls such immobiles "shelf-sitters."[45] Not only do shelf-sitters block promotion channels, but their key subordinates can become unfairly labeled as shelf-sitters, too. Although working for a shelf-sitter may develop an employee's skill, such a label can arrest one's career progress.

Growth opportunities. When employees expand their abilities, they complement the organization's objectives. Enrolling in a training program, taking noncredit courses, pursuing an additional degree, or seeking a new work assignment can contribute to employee growth. These growth opportunities aid both the department's objective of developing internal replacements and the individual's personal career plan.

> *Rachael Holmes was the chief recruiter in the employment department of Brem Paper Products. Her department manager was 60 years old and had indicated that he planned to retire at age 65. At 37, with three years experience as a recruiter, Rachael felt she was in a dead-end job. She obtained a transfer to the wage and salary department. Two years later the company planned a new facility and made Rachael the personnel manager for it. She was selected because of her broad experience in recruiting and compensation—two major concerns in starting the new operation.*

Rachael initiated the transfer through self-nomination because she wanted to further her career development. But the real opportunity she obtained from the transfer was a chance to grow—a chance to develop new skills and knowledge.

Besides self-nomination, other groups outside the organization may help one's career. For years, men have used private clubs and professional associations to form "old-boy networks," which afforded growth opportunities and often a fair amount of exposure among organizational decision makers. Many of these organizations now admit women, but some do so grudgingly. Whether excluded or admitted grudgingly, women who are excluded from the informal networks in an organization can miss the exposure and visibility needed to gain career advancement. The result may be a "glass ceiling" where women can see the higher rungs on the corporate ladder but are blocked from reaching them.[46] However, a short piece in the *Wall Street Journal* notes:

Women's groups

Women's groups spring up in a variety of occupations to aid members. These groups tend to push career advancement rather than general women's issues. Women in Information Processing, Washington, D.C., helps its 4,000 members achieve industry visibility in part by lining up speaking engagements. The National Association of Professional Saleswomen, Sacramento, stresses education for members. Its chapters in 35 cities hold monthly meetings to discuss sales training. Formed in 1980 with 900 members, it now has 5,000 saleswomen. The National Association of Black Women Entrepreneurs, Detroit . . . helps its 3,000 members get information about business opportunities for minorities.[47]

Community service activities provide opportunities for both growth and recognition. United Way campaigns, chamber of commerce committees, arts organizations, and other community groups offer even junior managers growth opportunities to use their leadership skills. Learning to work with other volunteers uncovers different management skills and exposes one to different styles of leadership. Accounting, law, consulting, and other professional service firms often expect their members to be active as a means of developing new business. In large organizations, community involvement may be an effective way of gaining visibility within the company. And the network of contacts outside the company may be useful in looking for another job or beginning an entrepreneurial venture.

International experience. For those who aspire to senior operating or staff positions, international experience is becoming an increasingly important growth opportunity. Among major domestic corporations, a growing percentage of sales are often derived from international operations, particularly in such industries as pharmaceuticals, computers, electronics, and aerospace. As the proportion of international sales and operations grows, the importance of international experi-

Figure 12-7

Accepting an Overseas Job

Career development increasingly means gaining international experience, especially for those working in large, global corporations. Unlike Europeans, for example, who are exposed to different cultures and languages, North Americans—and particularly United States citizens—often have little exposure to foreign nationals, foreign culture, and different languages. Europeans are typically educated in more than just their native tongue. It is not uncommon, for example, for educated Europeans to know two or three languages and to have been exposed to other cultures within Europe. Although the language of business and science is dominated by the use of English throughout the world, language abilities are important for managers who seek to truly understand the non-English speaking countries and cultures in which they may work. Language is also an important key to understanding other cultures, too. In seeking international job experience, language skills are an important career development consideration, causing the human resource department to arrange intensive language and cultural education courses.

Although the acceptance of an international job often comes with additional compensation to adjust for living costs, many human resource departments also assist transferees with moving, housing, language training, child education, job location assistance for spouses, and other needs peculiar to overseas assignments. Considering an international move also requires consideration to the impact such move can have on family members. These considerations range from finding suitable housing, which is of particular concern in developing countries, to finding traditional foods of expected quality. Even the availability of household appliances may be different, requiring more frequent shopping or different approaches to household chores.

Legal conditions change, too. Tax laws can be considerably different, for example. In many developed countries, taxes are much higher. These often include higher income taxes and much higher sales taxes that are sometimes called value added taxes, which can substantially increase the cost of major consumer purchases such as automobiles. Living in another country does not always eliminate home-country taxes, leading some transferees to face considerable tax increases. For example, selling a home in the United States before moving overseas can lead to capital gains taxes on any profits. Some relocation plans by human resource departments do include "tax equalization" adjustments so that the extra taxes associated with foreign work do not add an extra burden to the employee. Even relatively simple matters of reviewing wills and a leaving power-of-attorney should be considered.

The human resource department also needs to adjust benefits to comply with various national laws and appropriate coverages, especially with respect to health care. Travel benefits, such as return trips to the home country for vacations, business, and emergencies should be reviewed.

When accepting a job for a foreign employer, whether in the home country or overseas, many of these same considerations apply. Although work with a foreign company can be a developmental experience, some unique issues can arise. For example, working for a foreign company in the home country side steps many of the legal and tax concerns. However, learning the employer's home country language often becomes crucial for those who aspire to senior positions. Otherwise, informal acceptance—and, therefore, career progress—is almost certain to be limited. In many foreign companies, the senior-most positions are reserved for home country nationals, creating a "glass ceiling" on career progress. Likewise informal rules and formal assistance from the human resource department may be considerably different. For example, salaries in foreign companies are often considered highly confidential; to even discuss one's salary among peers can be seen as highly inappropriate even though such conversations may be common in North American-based firms.

For both the human resource department and the transferee, an international assignment or work with a foreign employer may be a powerful career development experience. However, such opportunities involve complex considerations.

ence increases, becoming a virtual prerequisite in many global corporations, such as Coca-Cola, Eli Lily, Procter and Gamble, Ford, and General Dynamics. Being overseas, however, does not mean losing touch with the home office or home-country managers.

Whether international experience is gained by working internationally for a company based in one's home country or working for a foreign company, there are a variety of considerations that affect the human resource department and the individual.[48] Figure 12-7 suggests some of these issues.

Human Resource-Supported Career Development

Career development should not rely solely on individual efforts. Career development often involves the human resource department for assistance. Perhaps even more important than assistance is guidance. Without coaching from operating managers or the human resource department, employees may take actions that are not in the best interest of the company or the employee or both. For example, employees may move on to another employer, as in the West Coast research example. Or employees may simply be unaware of opportunities to further their careers.

John Deere

The John Deere career information seminar offers a good example. It helps employees with education and information. The brochure handed out to attendees describes the range of jobs that are available at the job site. Personnel representatives also are available. But since the meetings are voluntary and on the employee's own time, the department is able to emphasize that career development is the employee's responsibility.

There can be little doubt that employees want such company-based programs if the results from John Deere are representative. In the first two weeks after the program was announced, 50 percent of the eligible salaried employees enrolled in the program. For employees who attended the seminar, there was a 50 percent improvement in their understanding of career planning, compared with a control group that did not participate. And comments from participants have been favorable.[49]

Human resource departments do more to help employee careers than just conduct career information seminars. For example, the training and development programs discussed in Chapter 10 are big stepping-stones in most people's careers.[50]

HR goals

Human resource departments seek many goals through their career planning activities in addition to helping employees. A key goal is to develop an internal pool of talent. Career planning can help trainers identify training needs among employees. It also can be used to help guide members of protected classes into jobs where the employer has an underutilization of women and minorities.

Improvements in performance, loyalty to the company, and motivation also may be outcomes of career planning. Simply put, career planning can make good business sense; it can enhance profits, productivity, and the quality of the employees' work life, as the following example underscores:

> *One bank's career counseling program saved $1.95 million in a year. This estimate, based on tabulations by an industrial engineer, reflected a 65 percent reduction in turnover, 25 percent increase in productivity, and 75 percent increase in promotability.*[51]

However, for the benefits of career planning and development to accrue to the organization and its people, the department must enlist the support of management, particularly top management.

Management support. Efforts by the department to encourage career development have little impact unless supported by managers. Commitment by top management is crucial. Without it, middle-level managers may show much less support of their subordinates' careers. This commitment must go beyond mere permission; top management must lead through example by taking an active interest in the career plans of middle-level managers. When executives show an active concern, other managers will emulate that behavior. Without broad-based support among all levels of management, others in the organization are likely to ignore career development and devote their attention elsewhere. Many North American and European managers do not have a tradition of giving meaningful peer recognition to those who voluntarily support employee development, but such recognition is common among managers in Japan.

One way more North American firms are showing support for career development activities is by monitoring the progress of *fast trackers*, those who seem destined to make rapid career progress. The act of identifying, tracking, and evaluating those likely to be on the way up the organizational hierarchy sends a message to those involved that they have more than just a job, that they have career potential.

7-Eleven

> *Southland Corp., parent company to the 7-Eleven convenience store chain, has managers file reports twice a year about the promotability of their subordinates. Reports are consolidated on a computer to identify future shortages of talent. These deficits are then addressed through career development activities.*
>
> *Gulf & Western Industries tracks 125 high-potential executives, and John Deere & Company uses a computer program to track more than 1,000 managers.*[52]

Support for the career development of employees varies widely from company to company. Some organizations take the view that career planning is the employee's responsibility and that company involvement would be an intrusion of the employee's privacy. Others fear that career development may raise employee expectations about rapid promotions and lead to disappointment if those promotions do not materialize. However, among the leading companies, the development of successful employees is considered a hallmark of the organization. These successes could not exist without long-term support from generation after generation of top management. Some other examples include McGraw-Hill, the publisher of this book:

> *At McGraw Hill* "The corporate point of view . . . is that management's involvement in career planning helps to ensure that the individual career plans of the employees mesh with the . . . goals of the corporation. In essence, the organization tries to ensure that 'the grass is greener at home than across the street.' "[53]
>
> "In a 10-year period, General Electric produced a highly admirable earnings growth record while 61 of its 360 vice presidents became presidents of other companies. This means GE is producing talent for other companies.
>
> "Donald Burnham was not the first chief engineer at GM to become the head of another company. He left . . . to lead Westinghouse.
>
> "And finally . . . IBM. They give their employees such good training and experience that after five years these individuals can go to almost any company and name their price."[54]

Feedback. Without feedback about their career development efforts, it is difficult for employees to sustain the years of preparation sometimes needed to reach career goals. Human resource departments can provide this information in several ways. One way is to give employees feedback about job placement decisions. An employee who pursues career development activities and is passed over for promotion may conclude that career development is not worth the effort. Unsuccessful candidates for internal job openings should be told why they did not get the career opportunity they sought. This feedback has three objectives:

1. *To assure* bypassed employees that they are still valued and will be considered for future promotions if they are qualified.

2. *To explain* why they were not selected.

3. *To indicate* what specific career development actions they should undertake.

Figure 12-8

A Career Planning and Development Framework

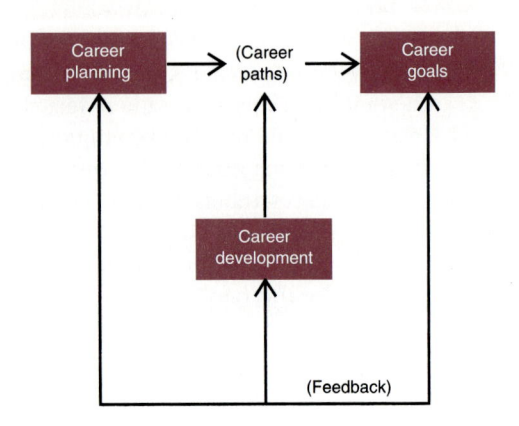

```
Career          (Career          Career
planning  →     paths)    →      goals
   ↑              ↑                ↑
   |              |                |
   |           Career              |
   |         development           |
   |              ↑                |
   |              |                |
   |          (Feedback)           |
```

Care should be exercised not to imply that these actions automatically will mean a promotion. Instead, the individual's *candidacy* for selection will be influenced by appropriate career development actions.

Feedback about job performance is perhaps the most important feedback an employee gets. As stated earlier in the chapter and worth emphasizing, career success rests largely upon performance. In the long run, there can be no substitute for doing the job well. None. Although objective measures of performance are sometimes absent and some promotions are based on "whom you know," most managers are rational. They want to promote people who can do the job. If their subordinates are successful, they look good, too. To give employees feedback about their job performance, many human resource departments develop formal performance evaluation procedures. The resulting feedback allows the employee to adjust his or her performance and career plans. Job placement decisions and developmental opportunities that meet the organization's future needs and employees' desires can then be sought. Among those desires are the compensation that accompanies career advancement. Compensation is discussed in the following chapters.

SUMMARY

CAREER PLANNING and development are relatively new concepts to human resource departments. In recent years, these departments have begun to recognize the need for more proactive efforts in this area. As a result, some departments provide career education, information, and counseling. But the primary responsibility for career planning and development rests with the individual employee.

Figure 12-8 illustrates an overview of career planning and development. The planning process enables employees to identify career goals and the paths to those goals. Then, through developmental activities, workers seek ways to improve themselves and to further their career goals. Even today, most developmental activities are individual and voluntary. Individual efforts include good job performance, favorable exposure, leveraging, and the building of alliances. Human resource departments become involved by providing information and obtaining management support. The department helps make career planning a success for both the employees and the organization.

Career planning does not guarantee success. But without it, employees are seldom ready for career opportunities that arise. As a result, their career progress may be slowed, and the human resource department may be unable to fill openings internally.

Terms for Review

Career
Career path
Career planning
Career development
Job families
Job progression ladder

Career counseling
Life plan
Exposure
Mentor
Sponsor
Key subordinates

Review and Discussion Questions

1. Why should a human resource department be concerned about career planning, especially since employee plans may conflict with the organization's objectives? What advantages can the department expect to receive from assisting career planning?

2. In what ways can the department assist career planning?

3. If you were interested in making a career out of your ability to play a musical instrument, what types of career goals would you set for yourself? How would you find out about the career prospects for musicians before you took your first job?

4. Suppose you are in a management training position after completing college. Your career goal is not very clear, but you would like to become a top manager in your firm. What types of information would you seek from the human resource department to help you develop your career plan?

5. Why is international job experience growing in importance to employees and the human resource department?

6. Suppose you are assigned to develop a career planning and development program in a large organization with a diverse work force. What unique concerns might you have because of this diversity.

7. What challenges do the slow growth and down-sizing that has occurred in many companies present for the human resource department? How and why should the department help?

8. Suppose a hard-working and loyal employee is passed over for promotion. What would you tell this person?

INCIDENT 12-1
Career Planning at Diverse, Inc.

Diverse, Inc. is well named. It is a major, multi-billion dollar food broker that operates primarily in the United States but maintains sales offices throughout the world, including China, the C.I.S., and many other countries in Asia, Europe, Africa, and South America. Its primary business is buying and selling food grains, such as wheat, corn, and rice. These sales are in bulk quantities with extremely narrow profit margins in the face of intense competition. Futures buyers lock in favorable prices and the string of worldwide sales offices sell these bulk goods to food processors and foreign governments.

The employees of the company hold many diverse jobs, ranging from ship loaders to highly specialized commodity buyers and sellers. Top management was concerned that many employees, particularly those in key buying and selling positions, were quitting to go to work for competitors. Not only were replacements costly to find, but employees also took with them vital information about company procedures and prices. Additionally, top management wanted to move key employees across borders to balance its work force to meet changing patterns of international trade. To build loyalty to the company and enhance morale, the human resource department was directed to begin a career planning program for employees throughout the company.

1. Given the diversity of the company's work force, what unique problems would you expect the human resource department to encounter?

2. What other career development actions could the human resource department undertake in the short-run to address the loss of key people?

INCIDENT 12-2
Going Global at Casefile, Inc.

Casefile, Inc. is a medium-size maker of business furniture, having begun in 1947 by making fire-resistant file cabinets. As the business and its markets matured, the company expanded into a full line of office furniture, ranging from expensive executive desks and chairs to mass-produced computer furniture. In the early 1990s, the company realized that its main markets—the United States and Canada—were becoming very mature and offered few prospects for rapid growth. Sales gains increasingly resulted from "doing battle" with larger companies. Growth was slow and profit margins were narrow as the North American economy continued in recession during early 1992.

The president of the company convened the senior management for a three-day retreat to map out a strategy to enter the European market before the increased unification of the European Economic Community took place on December 31, 1992. At the end of the meeting, he made a variety of assignments to his key vice presidents. Each was expected to write a short report on the implications for their department in "going global." These reports were to be forwarded to the vice president of human resources so she could evaluate the human resource planning and career development needs of the company. Before those reports arrived, the president asked the vice president of human resources to put together a broad outline of the "type of things that would have to change in career development and other areas of human resource management for the company to become a successful, international operation."

Assuming you have been asked to provide the vice president of human resources an outline of the key issues:

1. What additional training and development activities do you think would be needed in support of career development?

2. What career objectives could be suggested to offset employee reluctance to be transferred overseas?

References

1. Karen N. Gaertner, "Manager's Careers and Organizational Change," *Academy of Management Executive* (Nov. 1988), p. 311.

2. Lewis Newman, "Career Management: Start with Goals," *Personnel Journal* (April 1989), pp. 91–92.

3. William J. Kuchta, "Options in Career Paths," *Personnel Journal* (Dec. 1989), pp. 28, 31–32.

4. Lorraine M. Carulli, Cheryl L. Noroian, and Cindy Levine, "Employee-driven Career Development," *Personnel Administrator* (March 1989), pp. 67–68, 70.

5. Ibid.

6. Jack Keller and Chris Piotrowski, "Career Development Programs in Fortune 500 Firms," *Psychological Reports*, vol. 61 (1987), pp. 920–922.

7. Jerry W. Gilley, "Career Development As a Partnership," *Personnel Administrator* (April 1988), pp. 62–68.

8. Phil Farish, "Why People Leave," *Personnel Administrator* (August 1988), p. 18.

9. Richard K. Broszeit, "If I Had My Druthers . . .," *Personnel Journal* (Oct. 1986), pp. 84–90.

10. Two interesting articles offer added richness to the example of "Joe." The first is a conversation with Bob Beck, the senior human resource executive at Bank of America; the second article offers a 30-year perspective on "making it to the top." Martha I. Finney, "A Matter of Balance," *Personnel Administrator* (Oct. 1988), pp. 66–70; and Joel E. Ross and Darab Unwalla, "Making It to the Top: A Thirty-Year Perspective," *Personnel* (April 1988), pp. 71–78.

11. John J. Leach, "The Career Planning Process," *Personnel Journal* (April 1981), pp. 283–287. See also Manuel London, "Toward a Theory of Career Motivation," *The Academy of Management Review* (Oct. 1983), pp. 631–639; Caela Farren and Beverly Kaye, "The Principles of Program Design: A Successful Career Development Model," *Personnel Administrator* (June 1984), pp. 109–118; Joseph A. Raelin, "An Examination of Deviant/Adaptive Behaviors in the Organizational Careers of Professionals," *Academy of Management Review*, vol. 9, no. 3 (1984), pp. 413–427; and William L. Mihal, Patricia A. Sorce, and Thomas E. Conte, "A Process Model of Individual Career Decision Making," *Academy of Management Review*, vol. 9, no. 1 (1984), pp. 95–103.

12. This individual/organization dichotomy is useful for distinguishing between the role of the individual and the role of the personnel department. For a more detailed discussion of this distinction, see Dorothy Heider and Elliot N. Kushell, "I Can Develop My Management Skills By: _____," *Personnel Journal* (June 1984), pp. 52–54; and Warren R. Wilhelm, "Helping Workers to Self-manage Their Careers," *Personnel Administrator* (August 1983), pp. 83–88.

13. Friedman, op. cit., pp. 191–213.

14. Ellryn Mirides and Andre Cote, "Women in Management: Strategies for Removing the Barriers," *Personnel Administrator* (April 1980), pp. 25–28, 48; Friedman, op. cit., pp. 191–213.

15. William F. Rothenbach, "Career Development: Ask Your Employees for Their Opinions," *Personnel Administrator* (Nov. 1982), pp. 43–46, 51.

16. Loretta D. Foxman and Walter L. Polsky, "Aid in Employee Career Development," *Personnel Journal* (Jan. 1990), pp. 22, 24.

17. Ibid., p. 51.

18. Bernadette Steele, Jerold R. Bratkovich, and Thomas Rollins, "Implementing Strategic Redirection through the Career Management System," *Human Resource Planning*, vol. 13, no. 4 (1991), pp. 241–263.

19. Friedman, op. cit., p. 200.

20. Douglas T. Hall, *Careers in Organizations* (Pacific Palisades, Calif.: Goodyear Publishing Co., 1976); Frank W. Archer, "Charting a Career Course," *Personnel Journal* (April 1984), pp. 60–64; Broszeit, op. cit.

21. Karl A. Hickerson and Richard C. Anderson, "Career Development: Whose Responsibility?" *Personnel Administrator* (June 1982), p. 46.

22. "HRM Update," *Personnel Administrator* (March 1987), p. 26.

23. Ibid., p. 28.

24. Amiel T. Sharon, "Skills Bank Tracks Talent, Not Training," *Personnel Journal* (June 1988), pp. 44–49.

25. Hickerson and Anderson, op. cit.

26. Edward G. Verlander, "Incorporating Career Counseling into Management Development," *Journal of Management Development*, vol. 5, no. 3 (1986), pp. 36–45; Peter C. Cairo, "Counseling in Industry: A Selected Review of the Literature," *Personnel Psychology*, vol. 36 (1983), pp. 1–18.

27. Douglas T. Hall and Judith Richter, "Balancing Work Life and Home Life: What Can Organizations Do To Help?" *Academy of Management Executives* (August 1988), pp. 213–223.

28. Cairo, op cit.

29. Hickerson and Anderson, op. cit.

30. Benson Rosen and Thomas H. Jerdee, "Middle and Late Career Problems: Causes, Consequences, and Research Needs," *Human Resource Planning*, vol. 13 (1991), pp. 59–70.

31. Joseph Weber, Lisa Dricall, and Richard Brandt, "Farewell Fast Track," *Business Week* (Dec. 10, 1990), pp. 192–200.

32. Ronald E. Gerevas, "Keeping Good Managers Happy on a Slower Track," *Business Month* (May 1989), p. 79.

33. Paul L. Blocklyn, "Employee Retraining Programs," *Personnel* (Nov. 1988), pp. 64–66.

34. Amy Saltzman, "Sidestepping Your Way to the Top," *U.S. News & World Report* (Sept. 17, 1990), p. 61.

35. Roy Bailey, "'Burn-Out,' Counseling, and the Health Professions," *Health Care Management*, vol. 3, no. 1 (1988), pp. 5–8.

36. Eugene E. Jennings, *The Mobile Manager* (New York: McGraw-Hill Book Company, 1976).

37. Eugene E. Jennings, "How to Develop Your Management Talent Internally," *Personnel Administrator* (July 1981), pp. 20–23; Teresa Carson and John A. Byrne, "Fast-track Kids," *Business Week* (Nov. 10, 1986), pp. 90–92.

38. Jennings, The Mobile Manager, op. cit.; Walter L. Polsky and Loretta D. Foxman, "Career Counselors," *Personnel Journal* (Dec. 1986), pp. 35–38.

39. William B. Werther, Jr., "Management Turnover Implications of Career Mobility," *Personnel Administrator* (Feb. 1977), pp. 63–66. See also Ellen F. Jacofsky and Lawrence H. Peters, "The Hypothesized Effects of Ability in the Turnover Process," *Academy of Management Review* (Jan. 1983), pp. 46–49.

40. Joseph A. Raelin, "Two-track Plans for One-track Careers," *Personnel Journal* (Jan. 1987), pp. 96–101.

41. Werther, op. cit.

42. Raymond A. Noe "An Investigation of the Determinants of Successful Assigned Mentoring Relationships," *Personnel Psychology*, vol. 41 (1988), pp. 457–479. Several chief executive officers express their views about mentors and careers in Roy Rowan, "America's Most Wanted Managers," *Fortune* (Feb. 3, 1986), pp. 18–25. See also Kathy E. Kram and Lynn A. Isabella, "Mentoring Alternatives: The Role of Peer Relationships in Career Development," *Academy of Management Journal*, vol. 28, no. 1 (1985), pp. 110–132.

43. Jennings, "How to Develop Your Management Talent Internally," op. cit.

44. Jennings, The Mobile Manager, op. cit. See also John F. Veiga, "Plateaued versus Nonplateaued Managers: Career Patterns, Attitudes, and Path Potential," *Academy of Management Journal* (Sept. 1981), pp. 566–578.

45. Jennings, *The Mobile Managers*, op. cit.

46. Jaclyn Fierman,"Why Women Still Don't Hit the Top," *Fortune* (July 30, 1990), pp. 40–62.

47. Robert S. Greenberger, "Women's Groups Spring Up in a Variety of Occupations to Aid Members," *The Wall Street Journal*, Western ed. (Jan. 11, 1983), p. 1.

48. Claudia H. Deutsch, "Getting the Brightest To Go Abroad," *The New York Times*, National ed. (June 17, 1990), sec. 3, part 2, p. 25.

49. Hickerson and Anderson, op. cit.

50. Beverly Kaye, "Career Development Puts Training in Its Place," *Personnel Journal* (Feb. 1983), pp. 132–137.

51. Milan Moravec, "A Cost-Effective Career Planning Program Requires a Strategy," *Personnel Administrator* (1982), p. 28.

52. William M. Bulkeley, "The Fast Track: Computers Help Firms Decide Whom to Promote," *The Wall Street Journal*, Eastern ed. (Sept. 18, 1985), p. 25.

53. "Is Career Development the Answer?" *Training and Development Journal* (March 1981), pp. 81–82.

54. Jennings, "How to Develop Your Management Talent Internally," op. cit., p. 20. See also Manual London, "The Boss's Role in Management Development," *Journal of Management Development*, vol. 5, no. 3 (1986), pp. 25–35.

IV

COMPENSATION AND PROTECTION

13 Compensation Management
14 Incentives and Gainsharing
15 Employee Benefits and Services
16 Security, Safety, and Health

EMPLOYEES MUST be compensated for their efforts. But compensation goes beyond just wages and salaries. It may include incentives that help relate labor costs to productivity. A wide range of benefits and services is almost always part of the total compensation package each worker receives. Financial and physical security also are provided to employees because of a variety of federal and state laws that impose social responsibilities on employers in a variety of areas.

These concerns play an important role in any human resource department's efforts to obtain, maintain, and retain an effective work force. Understanding the role of the human resource department in compensation and protection is important for your own well-being as an employee and also for the well-being of your present or future employees.

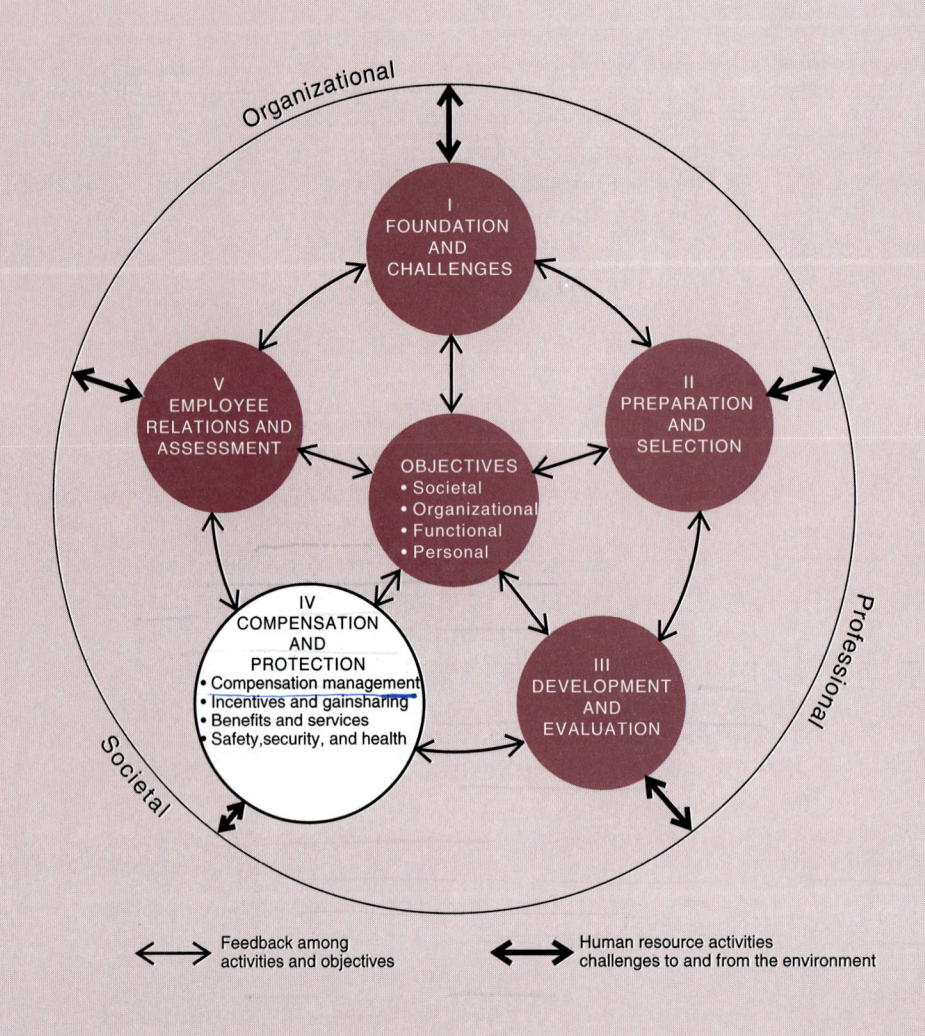

A Model of Human Resource Management

```
                    Organizational
                    ↕
                    ┌─────────────┐
                    │      I      │
                    │ FOUNDATION  │
                    │    AND      │
                    │ CHALLENGES  │
                    └─────────────┘
          ┌──────────┐         ┌──────────┐
          │    V     │         │    II    │
      ↔   │ EMPLOYEE │         │PREPARATION│ ↔
          │RELATIONS │         │   AND    │
          │   AND    │ OBJECTIVES SELECTION│
          │ASSESSMENT│ • Societal└──────────┘
          └──────────┘ • Organizational
                       • Functional
                       • Personal
          ┌──────────┐         ┌──────────┐
          │   IV     │         │   III    │
          │COMPENSATION│       │DEVELOPMENT│
          │   AND    │         │    AND   │
          │PROTECTION│         │EVALUATION│
          │•Compensation management
          │•Incentives and gainsharing
          │•Benefits and services
          │•Safety, security, and health
          └──────────┘         └──────────┘
      Societal                      Professional
```

↔ Feedback among activities and objectives

↔ Human resource activities challenges to and from the environment

For a large percentage of the work force..., earnings are determined by and in organizations, which has led to growing interest in the wage-determination process within organizations.
ALISON M. KONRAD AND JEFFREY PFEFFER[1]

Comparable worth pressure is just the tip of a quiet revolution occurring in pay practice.
ROSABETH MOSS KANTER[2]

13

COMPENSATION MANAGEMENT

CHAPTER OBJECTIVES

After studying this chapter, you should be able to:
1. DISCUSS the consequences of mismanaged compensation programs.
2. EXPLAIN the objectives of effective compensation management.
3. EXPLAIN the major laws and other challenges that impact pay plans.
4. DESCRIBE how wages and salaries are determined.
5. EVALUATE the advantages and disadvantages of comparable worth.
6. IDENTIFY key concerns in international compensation.

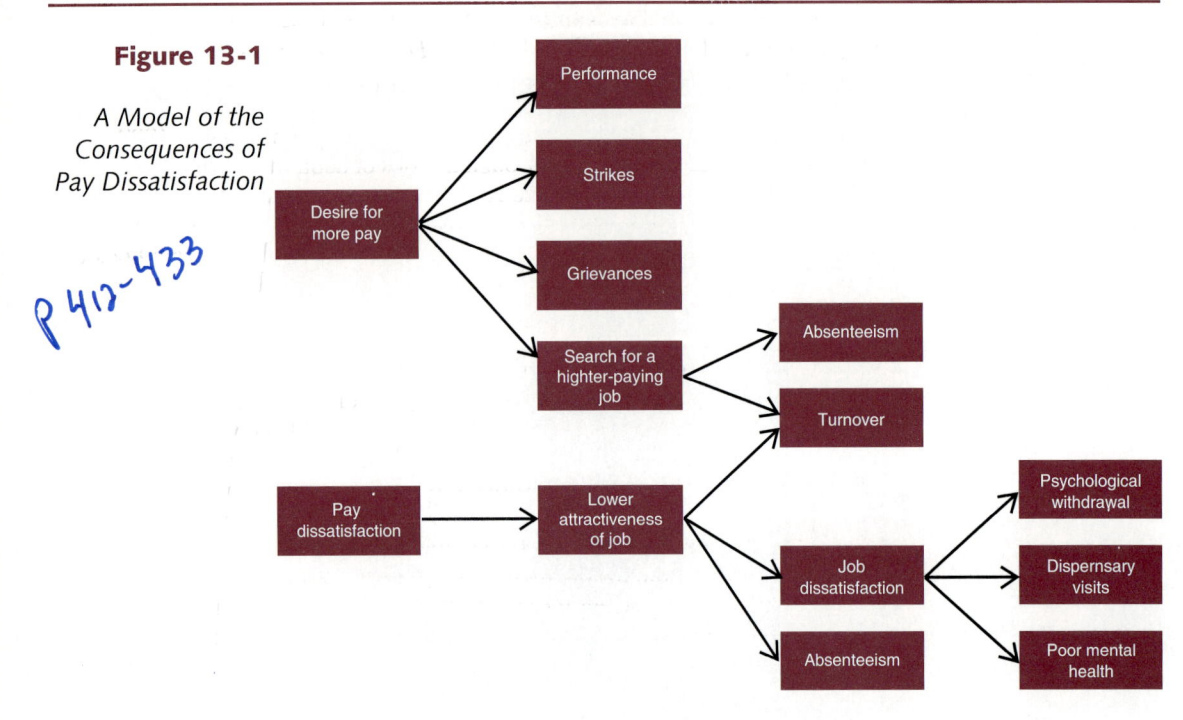

Figure 13-1

A Model of the Consequences of Pay Dissatisfaction

Source: Edward E. Lawler III, *Pay and Organizational Effectiveness: A Psychological View,* New York: McGraw-Hill Book Company, 1971, p. 233. Used with permission of the McGraw-Hill Book Company.

C OMPENSATION IS what employees receive in exchange for their contribution to the organization. Compensation management helps the organization obtain, maintain, and retain a productive work force. Without adequate compensation, current employees are likely to leave, and replacements will be difficult to recruit. Other implications of pay dissatisfaction are diagrammed in Figure 13-1.

The outcomes of pay dissatisfaction shown in Figure 13-1 may detract from the organization's productivity and suggest a decline in the quality of work life. In severe cases, pay issues may lower performance, increase grievances, or cause workers to quit. Poorly compensated jobs can lead to absenteeism and other forms of employee withdrawal, too. Even overpayment can harm the organization and its people, causing anxiety, guilt, and discomfort.[3] High compensation costs also reduce the firm's competitiveness and its ability to provide jobs. This balance between satisfaction and competitiveness underlies most of the department's compensation efforts.

Human resource departments can contribute to the organization's strategic objectives through this balance of satisfaction and competitiveness in the firm's compensation program. An example comes from one of the largest banks in the United States, the Marine Midland Bank. As *Fortune* describes it:

Marine Midland

> The Marine Midland Bank has always been an oddity. Founded in 1929, Marine grew over the decades through a series of acquisitions in which 75 local and regional banks in upstate New York were loosely joined with a money-center bank in New York City. With headquarters in Buffalo, Marine has had trouble attracting the kind of talented young employees who flock to such slick, big-city banks as Morgan Guaranty and Citibank. Marine also has enjoyed little success in attracting the more lucrative kinds of customers—large corporations and wealthy individuals. . . . Now all this is changing. . . .[4]

Given the turbulent banking environment in recent years, the bank is transforming itself through its policies, strategies, and organization design to develop a more assertive organizational culture that will allow the bank to become a dominant force in its markets. To change employee attitudes and become more assertive, Marine Midland is revamping its approach to compensation management. Salaries and benefits are increasing rapidly. But these improvements are being tied to employee performance, which makes top performers eligible for big increases in their compensation. By rewarding employees and management for actions that match the bank's new direction, Marine Midland plans to grow faster and make a bigger impact on the financial community.[5]

By rewarding desired results, such as providing incentives to bank officers who further Marine's social responsibility through their community involvement, compensation policies reinforce those behaviors that support the bank's strategies. Compensation is not the only way to align performance with strategy. Human resource planning, recruiting, selection, placement, development, performance appraisals, and career planning also help align individual efforts and strategy. But unlike staffing and development activities, compensation programs can be quickly modified and linked with new strategies.[6]

Direct versus indirect compensation

The flexibility and responsiveness of "compensation management"[7] comes from its broad scope. Compensation management embraces *direct* compensation, which includes wages and salaries and, increasingly, incentives and gainsharing; and *indirect* compensation, which includes fringe benefits. These areas can be adjusted to support the strategic efforts of the company or more traditional day-to-day activities.

This chapter examines direct compensation, wages and salaries. Chapter 14 discusses other forms of direct compensation, incentives and gainsharing. Chapters 15 and 16 describe indirect compensation, primarily the employer-provided benefits and services discussed in Chapter 15 and legally mandated benefits and services explained in Chapter 16. Underlying direct and indirect compensation are a variety of objectives.

13. COMPENSATION MANAGEMENT 413

Figure 13-2

Objectives Sought through Effective Compensation Management

▶ *Acquire qualified personnel.* Compensation needs to be high enough to attract applicants. Pay levels must respond to supply and demand of workers in the labor market since employers compete for workers. Premium wages are sometimes needed to attract applicants who are already working for others.

▶ *Retain present employees.* Employees may quit when compensation levels are not competitive, resulting in higher turnover.

▶ *Ensure equity.* Compensation management strives for internal and external equity. *Internal equity* requires that pay be related to the relative worth of jobs, so that similar jobs get similar pay. *External equity* means paying workers what comparable workers at other firms in the labor market pay.

▶ *Reward desired behavior.* Pay should reinforce desired behaviors and act as an incentive for those behaviors to occur in the future. Effective compensation plans reward performance, loyalty, experience, responsibilities, and other behaviors.

▶ *Control costs.* A rational compensation system helps the organization obtain and retain workers at a reasonable cost. Without effective compensation management, workers could be over- or underpayed.

▶ *Comply with legal regulations.* A sound wage and salary system considers the legal challenges imposed by government and ensures the employer's compliance.

▶ *Facilitate understanding.* The compensation management system should be easily understood by human resource specialists, operating managers, and employees.

▶ *Further administrative efficiency.* Wage and salary programs should be designed to be managed efficiently, making optimal use of the human resource information system, although this objective should be a secondary consideration compared with other objectives.

OBJECTIVES OF COMPENSATION MANAGEMENT

Compensation management must meet several objectives.[8] Sometimes these objectives, listed in Figure 13-2, conflict with one another, and tradeoffs must be made.[9] For example, to retain employees and to ensure equity, wage and salary analysts pay similar amounts for similar jobs. But a recruiter may want to offer an unusually high salary to attract a qualified recruit. At this point, the human resource manager must make a tradeoff between the recruiting objective and the objective of consistency. Other objectives of compensation include rewarding desired behavior and controlling costs. These objectives too, can conflict.[10] For example, Marine Midland's top management wants to reward outstanding performance with raises, but every raise adds to costs.

Legal compliance

Regardless of the tradeoffs, an overriding objective is to maintain legal compliance. *The Fair Labor Standards Act of 1938*, for example, requires employers to pay minimum wages and time and a half for overtime. Congress periodically raises the minimum wage, and employers must comply regardless of their other objectives. Likewise, the *Equal Pay Act* requires employers to provide equal pay for equal work without regard to the employee's sex.[11] Discrimination in pay among workers 40 years of age and older is outlawed by the *Age Discrimination in Employment Act*. And Title VII of the 1964 *Civil Rights Act* prohibits discrimination in pay because of race, sex, religion, or national origin. (Each of these

IV. COMPENSATION AND PROTECTION

Figure 13-3

Major Phases of Compensation Management

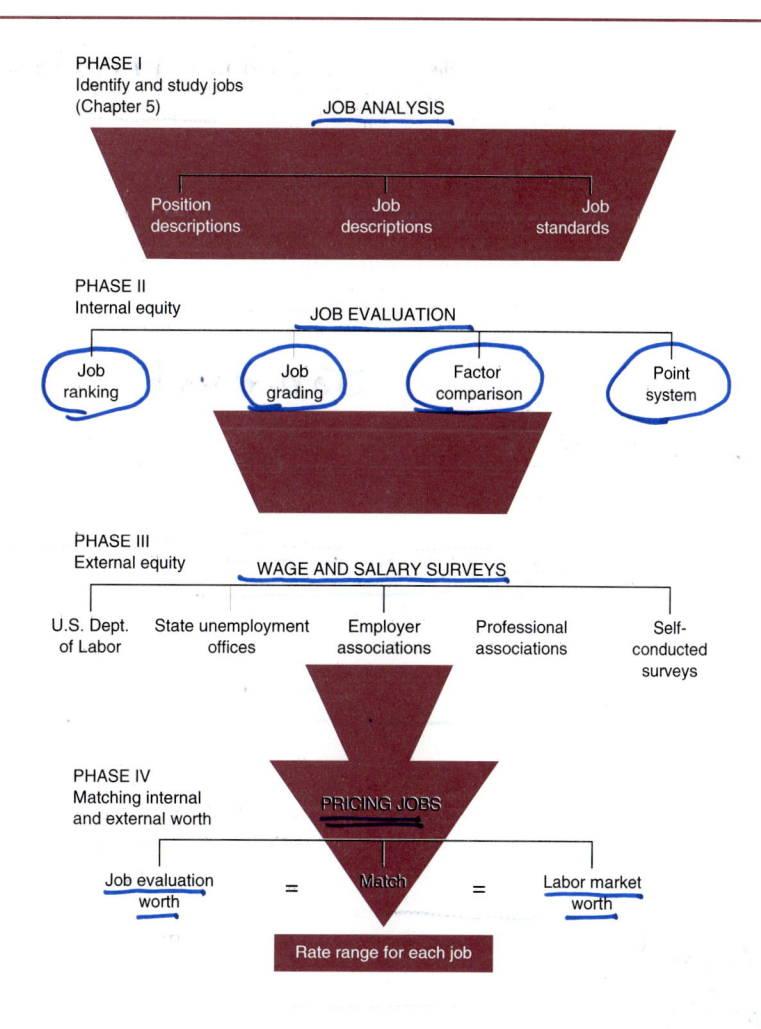

PHASE I
Identify and study jobs
(Chapter 5)

JOB ANALYSIS
- Position descriptions
- Job descriptions
- Job standards

PHASE II
Internal equity

JOB EVALUATION
- Job ranking
- Job grading
- Factor comparison
- Point system

PHASE III
External equity

WAGE AND SALARY SURVEYS
- U.S. Dept. of Labor
- State unemployment offices
- Employer associations
- Professional associations
- Self-conducted surveys

PHASE IV
Matching internal and external worth

PRICING JOBS

Job evaluation worth = Match = Labor market worth

Rate range for each job

---

nondiscrimination laws is discussed in Chapter 4, "Equal Employment Opportunity.") Regardless of its strategy, each company must comply with the laws that affect compensation.

Compensation objectives are not rules. They are guidelines. But the better the objectives in Figure 13-2 are followed, the more effective wage and salary administration will be. To meet these objectives, compensation specialists evaluate every job, conduct wage and salary surveys, and price each job.[12] Through these steps, the pay level for each job is determined. Figure 13-3 depicts these three major phases of compensation management, which are discussed in the following sections.

JOB ANALYSIS

As discussed in Chapter 5, job analysis collects information about jobs (through surveys, observation, and discussions among workers and supervisors) to produce job and position descriptions. This information also helps provide the basis for job standards. With the job analysis information provided as part of the department's human resource information system, compensation specialists have the minimum information they need to begin the next phase of compensation management, job evaluations.

Back to the HRIS

JOB EVALUATIONS

Job evaluations are systematic procedures used to determine the relative worth of jobs. Although there are several different approaches to job evaluation, each one considers the responsibilities, skills, efforts, and the working conditions of the job. The purpose of job evaluation is to decide which jobs are worth more to the organization than other jobs.[13] Without job evaluations, employers would be unable to arrive at a rational approach to paying the diversity of jobs found in many companies.

Since evaluation is subjective, it is conducted by specially trained personnel, called job analysts or compensation specialists. When a group of managers or specialists is used, the group is called a *job evaluation committee*.[14] The committee reviews job analysis information to learn about the duties, responsibilities, and working conditions of each job. With this knowledge, jobs are put in a hierarchy according to their relative worth, through the use of a job evaluation method. The most common methods are job ranking, job grading, factor comparison, and the point system.[15]

Job Ranking

The simplest and least precise method of job evaluation is *job ranking*. Specialists review the job analysis information and then appraise each job subjectively according to its general importance in comparison with other jobs. These are overall rankings, although raters may consider individually the responsibility, skill, effort, and working conditions of each job. It is quite possible that important elements of some jobs may be overlooked while unimportant items are weighted too heavily. More damagingly, these rankings do not differentiate specific degrees of *relative* importance between jobs. For example, the job of janitor may be ranked as a 1, the secretary's job may get a 2, and the office manager be ranked a 3. But the secretarial position may be three times as important as the janitorial job and half as important as the job of office manager. Pay scales based on these broad rankings ensure that more important jobs are paid more, but this may not accurately capture the relative differences between jobs. As a result, pay levels may be inaccurate.[16]

Crude approach

416   IV. COMPENSATION AND PROTECTION

Figure 13-4

A Job Classification Schedule for Use with the Job Grading Method

Directions: To determine appropriate job grade, match standard description with job description.

JOB GRADE	STANDARD DESCRIPTION
I	Work is simple and highly repetitive, done under close supervision, requiring minimal training and little responsibility or initiative.
	Examples: Janitor, file clerk
II	Work is simple and repetitive, done under close supervision, requiring some training or skill. Employee is expected to assume responsibility or exhibit initiative only rarely.
	Examples: Clerk-typist I, machine cleaner
III	Work is simple, with little variation, done under general supervision. Training or skill required. Employee has minimum responsibilities and must take some initiative to perform satisfactorily.
	Examples: Parts expediter, machine oiler, clerk-typist II
IV	Work is moderately complex, with some variation, done under general supervision. High level of skill required. Employee is responsible for equipment or safety; regularly exhibits initiative.
	Examples: Machine operator I, tool and die apprentice
V	Work is complex, varied, done under general supervision. Advanced skill level required. Employee is responsible for equipment and safety; shows high degree of initiative.
	Examples: Machine operator II, tool and die specialist

Job Grading

Job grading, or *job classification*, is a slightly more sophisticated method than job ranking, though still not very precise. It works by assigning each job a grade, as illustrated in Figure 13-4. In the figure, the standard description that most nearly matches the job description determines the job's grading. Once again, more important jobs are paid more, but the lack of precision can lead to inaccurate pay levels. The largest user of this approach has been the U.S. Civil Service Commission, which gradually is replacing this method with more sophisticated approaches.[17]

Factor Comparison Method

Little-used approach

The *factor comparison method* requires the job evaluation committee to compare critical or compensable job components. The compensable components are those factors common to all the jobs being evaluated—such as responsibility, skill, mental effort, physical effort, and working conditions.[18] Each factor is compared, one at a time, with the same factor for other key jobs. This evaluation

Figure 13-5

The Apportionment of Wages for Key Jobs

KEY JOBS

COMPENSABLE OR CRITICAL FACTORS	MACHINIST	FORKLIFT DRIVER	SECRETARY	JANITOR	FILE CLERK
Responsibility	$3.20	$1.80	$2.40	$.80	$1.40
Skill	4.00	1.80	2.00	.80	1.30
Mental effort	3.00	1.20	1.80	.50	1.40
Physical effort	2.00	1.80	.70	2.70	.90
Working conditions	.70	.60	.60	1.90	.60
Total	$12.90	$7.20	$7.50	$6.70	$5.60
Wage rate	$12.90	$7.20	$7.50	$6.70	$5.60

allows the committee to determine the relative importance of each job. The factor comparison method involves the following five steps:

Step 1: Determine the compensable factors. Analysts must first decide which factors are common and important in a broad range of jobs. The critical factors shown in Figure 13-5 are the ones most commonly used. Some organizations use different factors for managerial, professional, sales, and other types of jobs.

Step 2: Determine key jobs. Key jobs are those that are commonly found throughout the organization and are common in the employer's labor market.[19] Common jobs are selected because it is easier to discover the market rate for them. Ideally, these benchmark jobs should be accepted by employees as key jobs and should encompass a wide variety of critical factors to be evaluated.

Step 3: Apportion present wages for key jobs. The job evaluation committee then allocates a part of each key job's current wage rate to each critical factor, as shown in Figure 13-5. The proportion wage assigned to each of the different compensable factors depends on the importance of the factor.

For example, assume that a janitor receives $6.70 an hour. This amount is apportioned in Figure 13-5 as follows: $0.80 for responsibility, $.80 for skill, $0.50 for mental effort, $2.70 for physical effort, and $1.90 for working conditions. In apportioning these wage rates, the evaluation committee must make two comparisons. First, the amount assigned to each factor should reflect its importance when compared with other factors of the job. For

IV. COMPENSATION AND PROTECTION

example, in apportioning wage rates for a machinist, if $4 is assigned to skill and $2 is assigned to physical effort, this implies that the skill factor is two times as important as the physical effort. Second, the amount allocated to a single factor should reflect the relative importance of that factor among different jobs. For example, if the responsibility of a secretary is three times that of a janitor, then the money allocated to a secretary for responsibility ($2.40) should be three times that allocated to a janitor (80 cents).

Step 4: Place key jobs on a factor comparison chart. Once the wage rates are assigned to the compensable factors of each key job, this information is transferred to a factor comparison chart, such as the one shown in Figure 13-6. Key job titles are placed in the factor columns according to the rate of wages assigned to the job for each critical factor. In the responsibility column, for example, the secretary title is placed on the $2.40 rate line to reflect how much the secretary's responsibility is worth to the organization. This job title also appears under the other critical factors according to the relative worth of these factors in the job of secretary. The same assignment process takes place for every other key job.

Step 5: Evaluate other jobs. The titles of key jobs in each column of Figure 13-6 serve as benchmarks. Other, nonkey jobs are then evaluated by fitting them on the rate scale under each factor column.

For the nonkey job of maintenance mechanic, the evaluation committee compares the responsibility of the mechanic with the responsibility of other key jobs already on the chart. It is decided subjectively that the mechanic's responsibility is between that of the forklift driver and the secretary. And since the mechanic's job requires about three-fourths of the machinist's skills, the mechanic job is placed one-quarter below that of the machinist in the skill column. This procedure is repeated for each compensable factor. When the task is completed, the committee can determine the worth of the mechanic's job, which is:

Responsibility	$2.10
Skill	3.00
Mental effort	2.70
Physical effort	1.90
Working conditions	1.30
TOTAL WAGE	$11.00

13. COMPENSATION MANAGEMENT

Figure 13-6

Factor comparison chart (handwritten)

A Factor Comparison Chart

RATE	RESPONSI-BILITY	SKILL	MENTAL EFFORT	PHYSICAL EFFORT	WORKING CONDITIONS
4.00		Machinist			
	Machinist				
3.00		MECHANIC	Machinist		
			MECHANIC	Janitor	
2.50	Secretary				
	MECHANIC			Machinist	
2.00		Secretary		MECHANIC	Janitor
	Forklift driver	Forklift driver	Secretary	Forklift driver	
1.50	File clerk				
		File clerk	File clerk		MECHANIC
			Forklift driver		
1.00			File clerk	File clerk	
	Janitor	Janitor			
				Secretary	Machinist
.50			Janitor		Forklift driver
					Secretary
					File clerk
.00					

determine salary rate (handwritten)

By using this same procedure, the committee can rank every other job according to its relative worth as indicated by its wage rate. These rankings should be reviewed by department managers to verify their appropriateness.

Figure 13-7

A Point System Matrix

COMPENSABLE OR CRITICAL FACTORS	MINIMUM I	LOW II	MODERATE III	HIGH IV
1. Responsibility				
a. Safety of others	25	50	75	100
b. Equipment and materials	20	40	60	80
c. Assisting trainees	5	20	35	50
d. Product/service quality	20	40	60	80
2. Skill				
a. Experience	45	90	135	180
b. Education/training	25	50	75	100
3. Effort				
a. Physical	25	50	75	100
b. Mental	35	70	105	150
4. Working conditions				
a. Unpleasant conditions	20	40	60	80
b. Hazards	20	40	60	80
Total points				1000

LEVELS

Point System

Common approach

Research shows that the point system is used more than any other method.[20] This system evaluates the compensable factors of each job. But instead of using wage rates, as the factor comparison method does, it uses points. Although more difficult to develop initially, the point system is more precise than the factor comparison method because it can handle critical, compensable factors in more detail.[21] This system requires six steps and is usually implemented by a job evaluation committee or by an individual analyst.

Step 1: Determine critical factors. The point system can use the same factors as the factor comparison method, but it usually adds more detail by breaking down these factors into subfactors. For example, Figure 13-7 shows how the factor of responsibility can be broken down into (a) safety of others, (b) equipment and materials, (c) assisting trainees, and (d) product and/or service quality.

Step 2: Determine the levels of factors. Since the amount of responsibility, or other factors, may vary from job to job, the point system creates several levels associated with each factor. Figure 13-7 shows four levels, although more or

13. COMPENSATION MANAGEMENT 421

Figure 13-8

A Point Manual Description of "Responsibility: Equipment and Materials"

1. RESPONSIBILITY
   b. *Equipment and materials.* Each employee is responsible for conserving the company's equipment and materials. This includes reporting malfunctioning equipment or defective materials, keeping equipment and materials cleaned or in proper order, and maintaining, repairing, or modifying equipment and materials according to individual job duties. The company recognizes that the degree of responsibility for equipment and material varies widely throughout the organization.

   Level I.   Employee reports malfunctioning equipment or defective materials to immediate superior.

   Level II. Employee maintains the appearance of equipment or order of materials and has responsibility for the security of such equipment or materials.

   Level III. Employee performs preventive maintenance and minor repairs on equipment or corrects minor defects in materials.

   Level IV. Employee performs major maintenance or overhauls of equipment or is responsible for deciding type, quantity, and quality of materials to be used.

---

fewer may be used. These levels help analysts reward different degrees of responsibility, skill, and other critical factors.

Step 3: Allocate points to subfactors. With the factors listed down one side of Figure 13-7 and the levels placed across the top, the result is a point system matrix. Starting with level IV, the job evaluation committee subjectively assigns the maximum possible points to each subfactor. This allocation allows the committee to give very precise weights to each element of the job. For example, if safety (100) is twice as important as assisting trainees (50), then it gets twice as many points.

Step 4: Allocate points to levels. Once the total points for each job element are assigned under level IV, analysts allocate points across each row to reflect the importance of the different levels. For simplicity, equal point differences usually are assigned between levels, as was done for "safety of others" (100, 75, 50, and 25) in Figure 13-7. Or point differences between levels can be variable, as shown for "assisting trainees" (50, 35, 20, and 5). Both approaches are used depending on the importance of each level of each subfactor.

Step 5: Develop the point manual. Analysts then develop a point manual. It contains a written explanation of each job element, as shown in Figure 13-8 for responsibility for equipment and materials. It also defines what is expected for the four levels of each subfactor. This information is needed to assign jobs to their appropriate levels.

Step 6: Apply the point system. When the point matrix and manual are ready, the relative value of each job can be determined. This process is subjective. It requires specialists to compare job descriptions with the point manual for each subfactor. The match between the job description and the point manual statement reveals the level and points for each subfactor of every job. The points for each subfactor are added to find the total number of points for the job. Here, for example, is the matching process for a machine operator I:

The role of job descriptions

The job description of a machine operator I states that the "operator is responsible for performing preventive maintenance (such as cleaning, oiling, and adjusting belts) and minor repairs." The sample point manual excerpt in Figure 13-8 states, "Level III: . . . performs preventive maintenance and minor repairs. . . ." Since the job description and the point manual match at level III, the points for the equipment responsibility subfactor are 60. Repeating this matching process for every subfactor yields the total points for the job of machine operator I.

After the total points for each job are known, the jobs are ranked. As with the job ranking, job grading, and factor comparison systems, this relative ranking should be reviewed by department managers to ensure that it is appropriate.

Beyond the four job evaluation methods discussed in this section, many other variations exist. Large organizations often modify standard approaches to create unique in-house variations. The Salt River Project, a large quasi-government utility, for example, has been working to make its job evaluation methods even more objective than a traditional point system.[22] The "Hay Plan" is another variation widely used by U.S. and Canadian firms. This proprietary method is marketed by a large consulting firm, Hay and Associates, and relies on a committee evaluation of critical job factors to determine each job's relative worth.[23] Although other job evaluation approaches exist, all effective job evaluation schemes attempt to determine a job's relative worth to ensure internal equity.[24]

WAGE AND SALARY SURVEYS

Equity

All job evaluation techniques result in a ranking of jobs based upon their relative worth. This ensures *internal equity*. That is, jobs that are worth more will be paid more. But how much should be paid? What constitutes *external equity*?[25]

To determine a fair rate of compensation, most firms rely on *wage and salary surveys*. These surveys discover what other employers in the *same* labor market are paying for specific key jobs. The *labor market* is the area from which the employer recruits. Generally, it is the area within commuting distance from the employer. However, some firms may have to compete for some workers in a labor market that extends beyond their communities. Consider how the president of one large university views the labor market:

13. COMPENSATION MANAGEMENT

Our labor market depends on the type of position we are trying to fill. For the hourly paid jobs such as janitor, clerk, typist, and secretary, the labor market is the surrounding metropolitan community. When we hire professors, our labor market is the entire country. We have to compete with universities in other parts of the country to get the type of faculty member we seek. When we have the funds to hire a distinguished professor, our market is the world.

Sources of Compensation Data

Wage and salary survey data are benchmarks against which analysts compare compensation levels. This survey information can be obtained in several ways. One source is the U.S. Department of Labor. It periodically conducts surveys in major metropolitan labor markets. Sometimes these surveys are out of date in a fast-changing labor market, and other sources may be needed. Many state unemployment offices also compile this information for employers. If compiled frequently, this information may be current enough for use by compensation analysts. A third source of compensation data may be an employer association, which surveys member firms. Employer associations, or a fourth source—professional associations—may be the only source of compensation data for highly specialized jobs.

The major problem with all of these published surveys is comparability. Analysts cannot always be sure that their jobs match the jobs reported in the survey. Matching job titles may be misleading. Federal, state, or association job descriptions may be considerably different, even though the jobs have the same title. Since most published surveys rely on the *Dictionary of Occupational Titles* (DOT), the company's descriptions should be compared with those in the DOT.

The central paradox of surveys is that each firm watches what the others in its labor market pay. An increase by one is likely to be detected by the others and may influence their pay plans. These changes, in turn, may trigger another round of changes.

Survey Procedures

To overcome the limitations of published surveys, some human resource departments conduct their own wage and salary surveys.[26] Since surveys are expensive, usually only key jobs are used. A sample of firms from the labor market is selected, and they are contacted by phone or mail to learn what they are paying for the key jobs. Most companies are willing to cooperate since they, too, need this information. Professional associations, such as the Society for Human Resource Management or the American Compensation Association, can further aid this process. Again, comparisons should use similar jobs, not just similar titles.

For international jobs, especially at higher levels, a survey may not be effective because of the uniqueness of the jobs or the limited nature of the comparisons. Most firms pay a salary similar to that received in the home country and then add a supplement for the extra costs of an international assignment.

Figure 13-9

The Development of a Wage-Trend Line

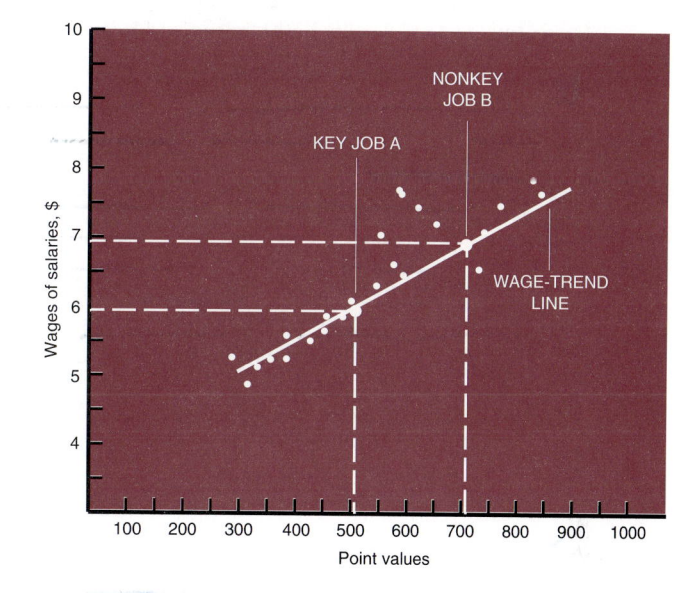

[Scattergram showing Wages of salaries ($) on vertical axis (4 to 10) vs Point values on horizontal axis (100 to 1000), with KEY JOB A at ~500 points/$6, NONKEY JOB B at ~700 points/$7, and a WAGE-TREND LINE fitted through the data points.]

As a result of the job evaluation process, all jobs are ranked according to their relative worth. Through surveys, the rate for key jobs in the labor market also is known. This leaves the last phase of wage and salary administration: pricing jobs.

PRICING JOBS

In pricing jobs, the job evaluation worth is matched with labor market worth. Two activities are involved: establishing the appropriate pay level for each job, and grouping different pay levels into a structure that can be managed effectively.

Pay Levels

The appropriate pay level for any job reflects its worth. A job's relative worth is determined by its ranking through the job evaluation process and by what the labor market pays for similar jobs.

To set the right pay level, the internal rankings and the survey wage rates are combined through the use of a graph called a *scattergram*. As Figure 13-9 shows, the vertical axis is pay rates. If the point system is used, the horizontal axis is for points. The scattergram is created by plotting the total points and wage levels for all *key jobs*. Each dot represents the intersection of the point value and the

13. COMPENSATION MANAGEMENT 425

market-determined wage rate for a particular key job. For example, key job A in Figure 13-9 is worth 500 points and is paid $6 an hour.

Through the dots that represent key jobs, a *wage-trend line* is drawn as close to as many points as possible, using a statistical technique called the *least squares method*.[27] It relates point values (internal worth) to wage rates in the labor market (external worth).

The wage-trend line then helps determine the wage rates for nonkey jobs. There are two steps involved. First, the point value for the nonkey job is located on the horizontal axis. Second, a line is traced vertically to the wage-trend line, then horizontally to the dollar scale. The amount on the vertical scale is the appropriate wage rate for the nonkey job.

> For example, in Figure 13-9, nonkey job B is worth 700 points. By tracing a vertical line up to the wage-trend line and then across to the vertical (dollar) scale, it can be seen that the appropriate wage rate for job B is $7 per hour.

The Compensation Structure

Setting a framework

An employer with 2,000 workers and 325 individual jobs would present the wage and salary analyst with complex problems. The existence of 325 separate wage rates would be meaningless because the differences between each job might be only few cents.

Compensation analysts find it more convenient to lump jobs together into *job classes*. In the job grade approach, jobs are already grouped into predetermined categories. With other methods, the grouping is done by creating job grades based on the previous ranking, pay, or points. In the point system, for example, classifications are based on point ranges: 0 to 100, 101 to 150, 151 to 200, and so forth. This grouping causes the wage-trend line to be replaced by a series of ascending dashes, as shown in Figure 13-10. Thus all jobs in the same class receive the same wage rate. A job valued at 105 points, for example, receives the same pay as a job with 145 points. Too many grades defeat the purpose of grouping; and too few grades result in jobs of widely varying importance receiving the same pay. As has recently been reported, down-sizing can reshape the optimal number of groupings.

General Electric

Since General Electric . . . compressed 10 layers of management into 4, the company has replaced its long-standing 29-tier pay scale with a 5-level scheme. Pay grades 8 through 11, for example, have been compressed into a single band ranging from $33,000 to $74,000. The broader bands make lateral movement easier. A finance manager at the old level 9 who wanted to try marketing would have been stymied if the post he coveted was a level 8. With the wider bands, the manager can try a new area but avoid taking a step down.[28]

Figure 13-10

The Impact of Job Classes on the Wage-Trend Line

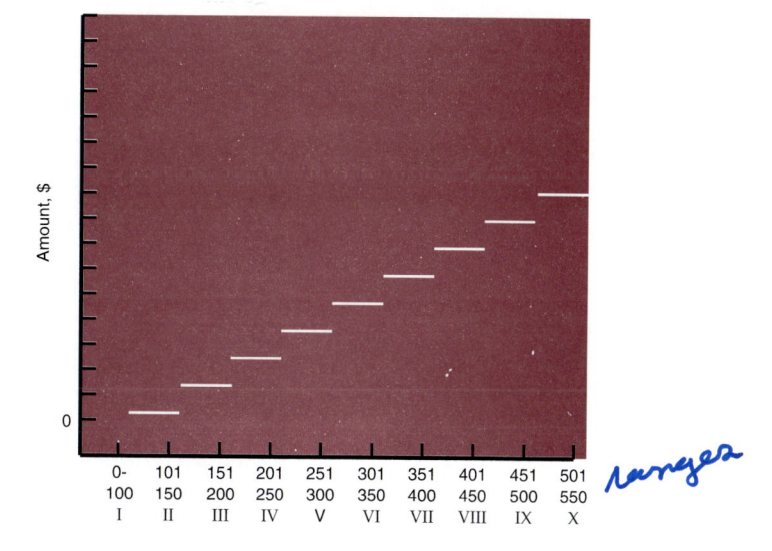

[Chart showing Amount ($) on y-axis and job class ranges on x-axis: 0-100 (I), 101-150 (II), 151-200 (III), 201-250 (IV), 251-300 (V), 301-350 (VI), 351-400 (VII), 401-450 (VIII), 451-500 (IX), 501-550 (X), with stepped horizontal lines ascending across classes.]

The problem with flat rates for each job class means that to give a worker a *merit increase*—which is a raise in pay for performance—requires moving the employee into a higher job class.[29] This upsets the entire balance of internal equity that has been developed. To solve these problems, most firms use rate ranges for each class.

Rate ranges are simply pay ranges for each job class. For example, suppose the wage-trend line indicates that $8 is the average hourly rate for a particular job class. Every employee in that class gets $8 if a flat rate is paid. With a rate range of $1 for each class, a new or marginal performer can be paid $7.50 at the bottom range, as indicated in Figure 13-11. Then an average performer is placed at the midpoint in the rate range, or $8. When performance appraisals indicate above-average results, the employee may be given a merit raise of, say, 25 cents per hour. If this performance continues, another merit raise of 25 cents can be granted. Once the employee reaches the top of the rate range, no more wage increases will be forthcoming. Either a promotion or a general across-the-board pay raise must occur to exceed $8.50. An across-the-board increase moves the entire wage-trend line upward.

As new jobs are created, analysts perform new job evaluations and assign the jobs to appropriate job classes. If rate ranges are used, the new incumbent will start at the bottom of the range.

Figure 13-11

Varying Wage Rates for Job Classes

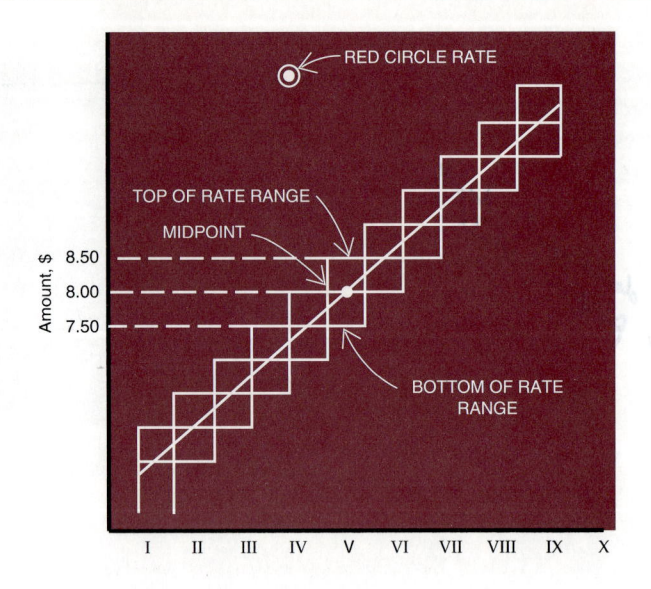

CHALLENGES AFFECTING COMPENSATION

Even the most rational methods of determining pay must be tempered by several challenges. The implications of these demands may cause analysts to make further adjustments to compensation.

Prevailing Wage Rates

Market forces may cause some jobs to be paid more than their relative worth.[30] In the 1980s and early 1990s, a shortage of nurses occurred. Fitting these jobs onto a wage-trend line often resulted in a wage rate below the *prevailing (or market) wage rate*. Since demand outstripped supply, market forces caused wage rates for nurses to rise above their relative worth when compared with other jobs. Organizations that needed these talents were forced to pay a premium. Diagrammatically, these rates appear on a wage chart as a *red-circle rate* (Figure 13-11). The term "red-circle rate" arises from the practice of marking out-of-line rates with a red circle on the chart.[31] Pay raises for red-circle rate jobs are often frozen when the supply of talent catches up with demand.

Union Power

Unions

When unions represent a portion of the work force, they may be able to use their power to obtain wage rates that are out of proportion to the relative worth of the jobs. For example, wage and salary studies may determine that $15.00 an hour is appropriate for a nurse. But if the nurses union insists on $17.00, the human resource department may believe that paying the higher rate is less expensive than a strike. Higher wages may lead to more automation, fewer benefits, or a loss of the firm's competitive position. Sometimes the union controls most or all of a particular skill, such as carpentry or plumbing. This enables the union to raise the prevailing rate for those jobs. If the industry is subject to competition from foreign producers or nonunion startups, unionized firms may be forced to reduce labor costs by laying off workers or by producing their products in other countries.

Government Constraints

The *Fair Labor Standards Act* (FLSA) of 1938 is the most comprehensive law affecting compensation management. It sets minimum-wage, overtime pay, equal pay, child labor, and record-keeping requirements. The minimum-wage and overtime provisions require employers to pay at least a minimum hourly rate of pay regardless of the worth of the job. (When the minimum is increased by law, it may mean that the wages of those who already earn above the minimum are adjusted accordingly.[32] If those just above minimum wage do not also get raises, wage differentials are squeezed together. This is called *wage compression*.)

Wage compression

Overtime pay also is regulated. For every covered job, the organization must pay one and a half times the employee's regular pay rate for all hours worked over 40 per week.[33] Executive, administrative, professional, outside sales personnel, and others are exempt from the overtime provisions, although the burden falls on the employer to justify the exemption based on the employee's actual duties, not just the job title.[34] Interestingly, 38 percent of the firms in one study reported paying some form of overtime to exempt employees.[35] These provisions are enforced by the Wage-Hour Division of the Department of Labor, which can initiate an investigation without receiving complaints. Failure to comply can lead to serious back-pay claims. For example, the U.S. Postal Service agreed to pay $400 million to 800,000 present and past employees after it underpaid them for a five-year period.

Equal Pay Act

In 1963, the FLSA was amended by the *Equal Pay Act*, as discussed in Chapter 4. This amendment was passed to eliminate sex-based discrimination in pay. It requires employers to pay men and women equal wages when their jobs are equal in skill, effort, and responsibility and are performed under similar conditions.[36] The equal pay concept requires an employer to pay men and women the same wage or salary when they do the same work. Exceptions are allowed when a valid seniority or merit system exists. Employers can pay more to senior workers or to workers who perform better and merit higher pay. Exceptions also are allowed when pay is determined by the employee's productivity, such as in-the case of sales commissions.³⁷ As explained more fully in Chapter 4, the federal government enforces these provisions by requiring wrongdoers to equalize pay and make up past discrepancies. In one incident, for example, American Telephone and Telegraph was required to pay $6,300,000 to 6,100 female employees whose pay suffered because of their gender.³⁸

Comparable Worth and Equal Pay

An important issue in compensation management and in equal opportunity is *comparable worth*. According to this idea, jobs of comparable value to the organization should be paid equally. Comparable worth goes beyond equal pay for equal work. It requires employers to pay equal wages for jobs of *comparable* value. Under the Equal Pay Act, for example, a male and female nurse would have to be paid the same if seniority and merit matched. But a female nurse and a male electrician would probably be paid different rates since their jobs are not the same. And even if male-dominated electricians make more and the female-dominated nurses make less, the *Equal Pay Act* is not violated. Under comparable worth, however, if a nurse and an electrician both receive approximately the same number of points under a job evaluation point system, they have to be paid the same, subject, presumably, to merit and seniority differences as the *Equal Pay Act* now permits.³⁹

Comparable worth is sought as a means of eliminating the historical gap between the incomes of men and those of women. (In the United States women earn about 60 percent as much as men do.) This gap exists, in part, because women have traditionally found work in lower-paying occupations—such as teaching, retailing, and nursing. Part of the difference in earnings also results from women leaving the work force to have and care for children, thus having to re-start careers at a later date. And part of the difference may result from discrimination. Although comparable worth approaches may reduce the gap, this compensation theory ignores the marketplace. If, in the previous example, nurses were paid $30,000 a year and electricians were paid $40,000, comparable worth would require paying the nurses $40,000, even though salary surveys showed the market rate to be $30,000. (To pay the electricians $30,000 would be appropriate under the comparable worth doctrine but impractical if their market rate was $40,000 a year.) If legislative bodies or the courts mandate comparable worth, analysts will face a major challenge in restructuring their compensation plans to comply while trying to obtain, maintain, and retain a cost-effective work force.⁴⁰ In recent years, however, less interest in this subject has been shown by researchers and legislatures.

State and local governments

What experience has been had with comparable worth doctrines has come almost exclusively from the public sector. More than 100 state and local government initiatives in support of comparable worth have been launched. Minnesota, for example, has a statute that mandates implementation of comparable worth in each political subdivision in the state.⁴¹ Not subject to the direct marketplace pressures faced by for-profit organizations, political subdivisions may have greater latitude to experiment.

Research into comparable worth shows that different job evaluation approaches can widen or narrow the gap in pay for comparable jobs.[42] For example, consider the critical factors, of responsibility, skill, effort, and the like, used in job evaluation studies. If analysts select as benchmarks male-dominated jobs (such as electrician), factors common to female-dominated jobs (such as nurse) may be given less weight. So, the tendency of a factor comparison or point system may be to devalue skills found in female-dominated occupations. For example, interpersonal or communication skills are important in such female-dominated occupations as bank teller, public school teacher, or nurse. But a review of a traditional factor comparison chart (Figure 13-6) or point system matrix (Figure 13-7) does not directly acknowledge these skills, presumably lumping them under "responsibility" and "mental effort." As one pair of researchers concludes:

Research conclusion

> In short, analyses of equity in pay structures are highly sensitive to differences in job evaluation methods.
> ... comparable worth initiatives tend to ignore the fact that there is no definitive test of the fairness of a pay structure. Equity in a pay structure is like beauty—in the eye of the beholder.[43]

Wage and Salary Policies and Adjustments

Most organizations have policies that cause wages and salaries to be adjusted. One common policy is to give nonunion workers the same raises that are given to the unionized employees. Premiums or bonuses for international assignments are another adjustment. Some companies, particularly large ones, have a policy of paying a premium above the prevailing wages.[44] Also, some employers, such as State Farm Insurance Companies, have automatic cost-of-living clauses that give employees automatic raises when the U.S. Department of Labor's cost-of-living index increases.[45] Raises or policies that increase employee compensation move the wage-trend line upward.

International Compensation Challenges

The growing globalization of business means greater movement of employees among countries. As employees are relocated, compensation specialists are challenged to make adjustments that are fair to the employee and the company. Most commonly, these challenges affect executive compensation, although professional, managerial, and technical workers are increasingly affected.

When international assignments are temporary, that is, under a year, the employee is generally paid his or her regular salary plus adjustments. These additional amounts typically cover transportation, temporary living quarters, and cost-of-living differentials. Educational supplements may be added if children

Greater complexity

join the employee. Bonuses may also be used to compensate for hardships, particularly if the employee is sent to a less than desirable location. For extended stays, relocation expenses may also include the purchase of the employee's residence at the appraised value, company-paid trips back to the home country, legal expenses for adjusting wills, supplements to offset higher taxes in the new country, and other adjustments to income.[46]

Additional compensation costs may include benefits not common in the home country but commonly provided to employees overseas. For example, the high taxes in many developed nations have led to a long list of nonpay (and, therefore, nontaxed) benefits, especially for senior managers—such as company cars (with drivers), servants, and club memberships—being provided in lieu of the high salaries drawn by U.S. executives.[47]

Productivity and Costs

Regardless of company or social policies, employers must make a profit to survive. Without profits, they cannot attract sufficient investors to remain competitive. Therefore, a company cannot pay its workers more than the workers give back to the firm through their productivity. However, if a company does find itself paying more than productivity affords (because of scarcity of workers or union power), the company must either redesign those jobs, train new workers to increase their supply, automate, go out of business, or innovate.[48]

Two-tiered wages

Two-tiered wages and bonuses are innovations that became widespread during the 1980s. As the name implies, employers created two wage structures, usually one for current employees and one for future recruits. Current employees often retain their current wages and rate ranges, or even receive a modest increase. Future employees, however, are paid a lower rate to start. The lower starting rate—often combined with a lower midpoint and maximum in the rate range—assures the employer lower labor costs as current employees leave and are replaced by lower-cost recruits.[49] These two tiers are most commonly found in unionized companies, especially those that have faced extreme cost-cutting within their industry. Meat packing, automobile, trucking, and airline are a few of the more widely publicized industries with two-tiered wage structures.[50] This approach allows union leaders to maintain the wages of their current (and voting) members while enabling employers to reduce their labor costs. Since some two-tiered systems allow recruits to catch up to the first-tier rates over two, five, or ten years, these savings may be temporary.[51] In recent years, the use of two-tiered wage approaches has declined in popularity because workers and researchers have raised questions about the equity of different rates for the same work.[52]

Other innovations help employer productivity and costs. Instead of wage increases that permanently raised workers' pay levels, some employers give lump-sum bonuses.[53] These bonuses are not part of the employees' base pay. If sales, productivity, or profits falter the following year, bonuses are not given, thus providing a cushion of lower labor costs in years of poor performance.[54] And since lump-sum bonuses do not raise the base wage, future merit or across-the-board raises start from a lower base pay. Likewise, overtime, pensions, disability insurance, and other benefits are usually linked to base pay. By using lump-sum bonuses instead of increasing the hourly rate, General Motors alone might save as much as $86 million in one year.[55]

Of course, productivity and cost innovations are not limited to wages only. Outdated work rules have been changed by union-management negotiators in return for pay increases (or in return for no pay cuts). Narrow job classifications, for example, may be expanded, giving operating managers more flexibility in job assignments and giving compensation specialists broader job groupings, with the savings allowing the employer to maintain, and even improve, compensation.[56]

Two other productivity and cost-related areas merit mention. First, fringe benefits—especially medical costs—have been a major target of cost-reducing efforts. These areas of cost improvement are addressed more fully in Chapter 15, "Benefits and Services." Second, more and more employers are trying to increase productivity and relate pay increases to gains in productivity through incentives and gainsharing, the topics of Chapter 14, which follows.

SUMMARY

employee compensation, if properly administered, is an effective tool to obtain, maintain, and retain a productive work force. And since compensation can signal what behaviors are most valued, it has the potential of influencing both strongly individual productivity and the strategic direction of the company. If it is mismanaged, the compensation program may result in high turnover, increased absenteeism, more grievances, job dissatisfaction, poor productivity, and unfulfilled strategic plans.

For the pay component of compensation programs to be appropriate, wages and salaries must be internally and externally equitable. Through job evaluation techniques, the relative worth of jobs is determined. This ensures internal equity. Wage and salary surveys then determine external equity.

With internal and external equity determined, jobs are priced at specific pay levels, which may be grouped into rate ranges for easier administration. The actual amounts paid may be further influenced by such challenges as union power, compensation policies, government constraints, and worker productivity. The Fair Labor Standards Act is the major federal law affecting compensation management. It regulates minimum wages, overtime, and child labor laws. The Equal Pay Act seeks to eliminate sex-based pay differentials.

Terms for Review

- ✓ Job evaluations
- ✓ Job ranking
- ✓ Job grading
- ✓ Factor comparison method
- ✓ Key jobs
- → Internal equity
- → External equity
- → Scattergram
- ✓ Point system
- ✓ Wage and salary surveys
- ✓ Rate ranges
- ✓ Merit raise
- ✓ Prevailing wage rates
- ✓ Red-circle rate
- ✓ Fair Labor Standards Act
- ✓ Wage compression
- ✓ Equal Pay Act
- ✓ Comparable worth
- ✓ Two-tiered wages

Review and Discussion Questions

1. Suppose you manage a small business with 30 employees. You discover that some employees are motivated by money, while others are motivated by security. For those who want more money, you provide merit raises in which their income is determined by their productivity. The other employees have a fair salary. What problems might arise?

2. What role does job analysis information (discussed in Chapter 5) play in the job evaluation process?

3. Assume your company has a properly conducted compensation program. If several employees ask you why they receive different hourly pay rates even though they perform the same job, how would you respond?

4. Why are the factor comparison and the point system methods of job evaluation more widely used than job ranking or job grading approaches?

5. Assume you wanted to learn what different jobs in your community paid. What sources of information would you turn to?

6. Even after jobs are priced using a wage-trend line, what other challenges might cause you to adjust some rates upward? Downward?

7. Explain why equal pay does not mean comparable worth.

8. Provide examples of what changes in compensation might have to be made for someone assigned to an international job.

INCIDENT 13-1
Compensation Issues at Southmore Hospital

Southmore Hospital is a major, regional medical center. It operates a 24-hour-a-day emergency room and provides a wide range of health services on an in- and out-patient basis. The human resource department has had a difficult time attracting sufficient applicants to fill its needs for nurses and technologists. The hospital has even joined a consortium of other health care providers in its community to recruit overseas.

Part of the problem is turnover. Each year nearly one-third of the nurses and technologists quit. When they are interviewed before leaving, nearly all report leaning toward "higher pay." A review of governmental wage and salary surveys shows Southmore to be competitive in pay.

1. What recommendations would you make to the head of the compensation committee at the hospital?

2. Given that the hospital handles many charity cases that do not pay, costs are a major concern. An across-the-board raise would increase labor costs, the hospital's major expense. What alternative approaches to increasing compensation might meet the employee's needs for more income without saddling the hospital with permanently higher labor costs?

References

1. Alison M. Konrad and Jeffrey Pfeffer, "Do You Get What You Deserve? Factors Affecting the Relationship between Productivity and Pay," *Administrative Science Quarterly*, vol. 35 (1990), pp. 258–285.

2. Rosabeth Moss Kanter, "From Status to Contribution: Some Organizational Implications of the Changing Basis for Pay," *Personnel* (Jan. 1987), p. 12.

3. Edward E. Lawler III, *Pay and Organizational Effectiveness: A Psychological View* (New York: McGraw-Hill Book Company, 1971), p. 71.

4. Arthur M. Louis, "In Search of Style at the 'New Marine,' " *Fortune* (July 25, 1982), p. 40.

5. Ibid., p. 44.

6. Mary Ann Von Glinow, "Reward Strategies for Attracting, Evaluating, and Retaining Professionals," *Human Resource Management* (Summer 1985), pp. 191–206.

7. Daniel J.B. Mitchell, "Wage Flexibility: Then and Now," *Industrial Relations* (Spring 1985), pp. 266–279.

8. Eddie C. Smith, "Support Objectives Using Base Compensation," *Personnel Journal* (Feb. 1990), pp. 86–90.

9. *Elements of Sound Pay Administration* (Berea, Oh.: The American Society for Personnel Administration and the American Compensation Association, 1981), pp. 1–2.

10. Mary A. Konovsky and Daniel S. Fogel, "Innovation in Employee Evaluation and Compensation," *Personnel Administrator* (Dec. 1988), pp. 92–95.

11. George W. Bohlander, "A Statistical Approach to Assessing Minority/White Pay Equity," *Compensation Review* (Fourth Quarter 1980), pp. 15–24.

12. Thomas M. Robertson, "Fundamental Strategies for Wage and Salary Administration," *Personnel Journal* (Nov. 1986), pp. 120–132.

13. John D. McMillan and Cynthia G. Biondi, "Job Evaluation: Generate the Numbers," *Personnel Journal* (Nov. 1986), pp. 56–63.

14. Robert M. Madigan and David H. Hoover, "Effects of Alternative Job Evaluation Methods on Decisions Involving Pay Equity," *Academy of Management Journal* (March 1986), pp. 84–100.

15. Marvin G. Dertien, "The Accuracy of Job Evaluation Plans," *Personnel Journal* (July 1981), pp. 566–570.

16. McMillan and Biondi, op cit., pp. 59–60.

17. Ibid., pp. 58–60.

18. Ibid., p. 58. See also Charles M. Cumming, "New Directions in Salary Administration," *Personnel* (Jan. 1987), pp. 68–69.

19. Madigan and Hoover, op. cit.

20. Edward E. Lawler, "What's Wrong with Point-factor Job Evaluation," *Personnel* (Jan. 1987), p. 41. See also McMillan and Biondi, op. cit.

21. Robert J. Sahl, "How to Install a Point-factor Job-evaluation System," *Personnel* (March 1989), pp. 38–42.

22. Dertien, op. cit.

23. Edward E. Lawler III, "Compensation: Forces of Change," *1985 Conference Highlights* (Scottsdale, Ariz.: American Compensation Association, 1986), pp. 8–14.

24. Gerald V. Barrett and Dennis Doverspike, "Another Defense of Point-factor Job Evaluation," *Personnel* (March 1989), pp. 33–36.

25. Wayne L. Wright, "Overcoming Barriers to Productivity," *Personnel Journal* (Feb. 1987), pp. 28, 31. See also Robertson, op. cit.; and Herbert Z. Halbrecht, "Compensation Surveys: Misleading Guideposts," *Personnel Journal* (March 1987), pp. 122–124.

26. Michael A. Conway, "Salary Surveys: Avoid the Pitfalls," *Personnel* Journal (June 1984), pp. 62–65.

27. The least squares method is explained in most introductory statistics books.

28. Joseph Weber, Lisa Driscoll, and Richard Brandt, "Farewell Fast Track," *Business Week* (Dec. 31, 1990), p. 200.

29. Frederick S. Hills, Robert M. Madigan, K. Dow Scott, and Steven E. Markham, "Tracking the Merit of Merit Pay," *Personnel Administrator* (March 1987), pp. 50–57. See also Lawrence B. Chonko and Ricky W. Griffin, "Tradeoff Analysis Finds the Best Reward Combination," *Personnel Administrator* (May 1983), pp. 45, 47, 99.

30. Paul R. Reed and Mark J. Kroll, "Red-circle Employees: A Wage Scale Dilemma," *Personnel Journal* (Feb. 1987), pp. 92–95; Robert J. Greene, "Characteristics of an Ideal Direct Pay Program," *1985 Conference Highlights* (Scottsdale, Ariz.: American Compensation Association, 1986), pp. 1–7. See also Lawler, "Compensation: Forces of Change," op. cit.; Cumming, op. cit.; and Frederic W. Cook, "Rethinking Compensation Practices in Light of Economic Conditions," *Personnel* (Jan. 1987), pp. 46–60.

31. Paul R. Reed and Mark J. Kroll, "Red-circle Employees: A Wage Scale Dilemma," *Personnel Journal* (Feb. 1987), pp. 92–93, 95.

32. E. James Brennan, "Increasing Minimum Wages Without Maximum Cost," *Personnel Journal* (August 1988), pp. 91–92.

33. In the public sector, workers can be compensated by receiving 1.5 hours off for each hour of overtime, under the 1985 amendments to the Fair Labor Standards Act. These amendments were passed to reduce the impact of the U.S. Supreme Court decision in *Garcia v. San Antonio Transit Authority*, 1985, which forced state and local governments to comply with the FLSA. See "Garcia Bill Seen As Relief for Government HRM," *Resource* (Jan. 1986), p. 3.

34. John A. Dantico, "Wage-Hour Law Clarifies Exempt/Non-Exempt," *HR News* (Jan. 1990), pp. 3, 12. See also "How To Determine Exemptions from FLSA," *Resource* (April 1988), p. 3.

35. David Gold and Beth Madigan, "More than One-Third Pay Overtime to Exempt," *Resource* (July 1989), p. 5.

36. *Elements of Sound Pay Administration*, op. cit., p. 23.

37. Ibid.

38. Ibid., p. 10.

39. Carl C. Hoffman and Kathleen P. Hoffman, "Does Comparable Worth Obscure the Real Issues?" *Personnel Journal* (Jan. 1987), pp. 83–95. See also Kanter, op. cit.

40. Judy B. Flughum, "The Employer's Liabilities under Comparable Worth," *Personnel Journal* (May 1983), pp. 400–404, 406, 408, 410, 412. See also Thomas A. Mahoney, "Approaches to the Definition of Comparable Worth," *The Academy of Management Review* (Jan. 1983), pp. 14–22; John R. Schnebly, "Comparable Worth: A Legal Overview," *Personnel Administrator* (April 1982), pp. 43–48, 90; George L. Whaley, "Controversy Swirls over Comparable Worth Issue," *Personnel Administrator* (April 1982), pp. 51–61, 92; and Gary R. Siniscalo and Cynthia L. Remmers, "A Special Update: Comparable Worth," *Employee Relations Law Journal* (Winter 1983–1984), pp. 496–499.

41. Madigan and Hoover, op. cit., p. 84.

42. Ibid., p. 91. See also McMillan and Biondi, op. cit., pp. 56–63.

43. Ibid., pp. 96–97.

44. "Large Employers Pay Higher Wages, on Average, than Smaller Employers Pay—but We Don't Know Why," *ISR Newsletter* (Fall 1990), p. 10.

45. During the rapid deflation in early 1983, COLA caused some wages to drop. "The Wage Spiral Has Lost Its Bounce," *Business Week* (April 11, 1983), p. 28.

46. Lin P. Crandall and Mark I. Phelps, "Pay for a Global Work Force," *Personnel Journal* (Feb. 1991), pp. 28, 30–32.

47. Graef S. Crystal, "The Wacky, Wacky World of CEO Pay," *Fortune* (June 6, 1988), p. 78.

48. Lester Thurow, "Productivity Pay," *Newsweek* (May 3, 1982), p. 69.

49. James E. Martin and Melanie M. Peterson, "Two-tier Wage Structures: Implications for Equity Theory," *Academy of Management Journal* (June 1987), pp. 297–315. See also Mollie H. Bowers and Roger D. Roderick, "Two-tier Pay Systems: The Good, the Bad and the Debatable," *Personnel Administrator* (June 1987), pp. 101, 102, 104, 106, 108, 110, 112.

50. Daniel J. B. Mitchell, "Why Are Wage Concessions So Prevalent?" *Personnel Journal* (August 1986), p. 131.

51. Ibid., pp. 131–133.

52. James E. Martin and Melanie M. Peterson, "Two-tier Wage Structures: Implications for Equity Theory," *Academy of Management Journal* (June 1987), pp. 297–315.

53. Suzanne L. Minken, "Does Lump-Sum Pay Merit Attention?" *Personnel Journal* (June 1988), pp. 77–83.

54. Mitchell, op. cit., pp. 131–133.

55. Susan Gelfond, "A Pile of Cash That Doesn't Stack Up to a Raise," *Business Week* (Dec. 23, 1985), p. 33. The issue of paying overtime or bonuses may require rethinking overtime pay. See, for example, Gina Ameci, "Bonuses and Commissions: Is Your Overtime Pay Legal?" *Personnel Journal* (Jan. 1987), pp. 107–110.

56. Clemens P. Work, Jack A. Seamonds, and Robert F. Black, "Making It Clear Who's Boss," *U.S. News & World Report* (Sept. 8, 1986), p. 45. See also Richard W. Walton, "From Control to Commitment in the Workplace," *Harvard Business Review* (March–April 1985), p. 82.

The issue of how to reward high performers is one of the perennial problems in the field of compensation.
STEVEN E. MARKHAM[1]

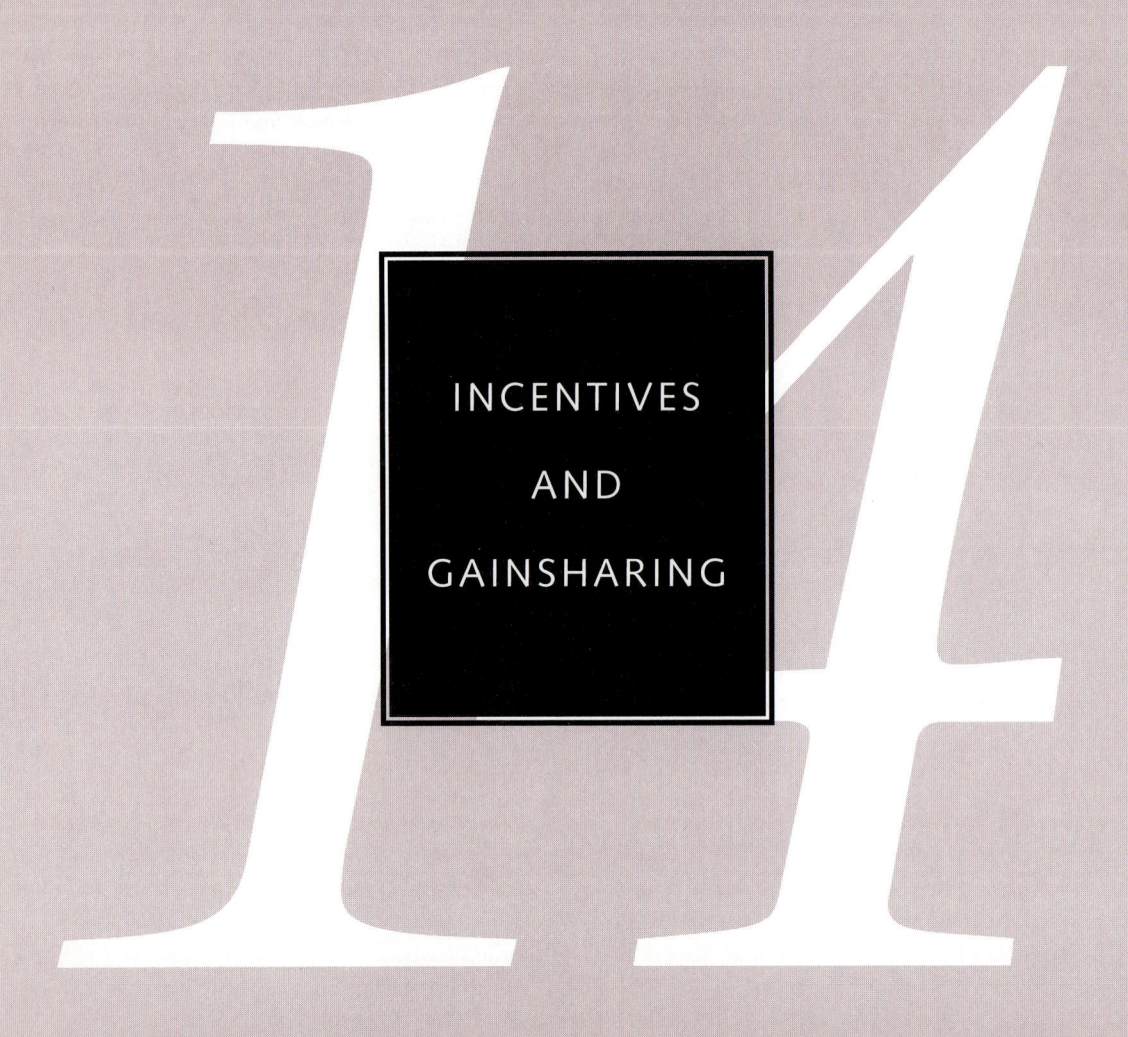

14

INCENTIVES AND GAINSHARING

CHAPTER OBJECTIVES

After studying this chapter, you should be able to:
1. DISTINGUISH between incentives and gainsharing.
2. EXPLAIN why incentives and gainsharing are growing in popularity.
3. DISCUSS the major challenges in developing incentives and gainsharing for international operations.
4. IDENTIFY nonmonetary incentives.
5. EXPLAIN what the key factors are in executive incentives.
6. DISTINGUISH between gainsharing approaches that employees can control versus those controlled by the external environment.

Definitions

INCENTIVES AND gainsharing are compensation approaches that reward specified outcomes. *Incentive systems* link compensation and performance by rewarding employees for performance, not for seniority or hours worked. Although incentives may be given to a group, they often reward individual behavior. Many farm workers are paid for each pound or bag of fruit they pick, for example. *Gainsharing* matches an improvement (*gain*) in the company's performance to some distribution (*sharing*) of the benefits with employees. Usually, gainsharing applies to a group of employees, rather than an individual. Both incentives and gainsharing supplement the more traditional wage and salary approaches discussed in Chapter 13.[2]

Although performance-based compensation has a long history, it often is considered a nontraditional compensation approach, since most people receive wages and salaries. The interest in performance-based compensation stems from the growing challenges of increased competition.[3] Consider, for example, the benefits of nontraditional compensation cited by two researchers:

> In recent years, hundreds of organizations, from manufacturing concerns and services to government agencies, have developed and adopted new, nontraditional reward systems to:
>
> ➤ Tie pay to performance, productivity, and quality
>
> ➤ Reduce compensation costs
>
> ➤ Improve employee commitment and involvement
>
> ➤ Increase teamwork and a sense of common fate.[4]

Creating a sense of common fate or destiny gives people a feeling that they need to cooperate to prosper. Incentives and gainsharing can give employees a feeling of shared destiny. The result can be a greater commitment to improving performance, productivity, and quality through teamwork.[5] And even though individual compensation may increase, overall labor costs may actually *drop* as the same number of workers (inputs) produce more goods and services (outputs). Consider a classic example, the Lincoln Electric Company.

Lincoln Electric

> The Lincoln Electric Company is a manufacturer of arc-welding and electric motor products. Its equipment is considered to be among the best in the world because productivity and quality are so good. Lincoln's employees are two and a half to three times as productive as their counterparts in similar settings.[6] And much of this advantage is attributed to the company's use of incentives and gainsharing.
>
> Each year the gainsharing process begins with a commitment to employees, "guaranteeing" each worker a minimum of 30 hours of work per week during

the next year. (The company actually aims at 42 to 43 hours per week, adjusting that number up or down to match sales). The company honors its employment pledge by using extensive overtime rather than hiring new workers who might have to be put on layoff during a recession. Applicants are screened so that they fit Lincoln's strong "promote-from-within" policy. Even then, they are considered probationary for two years before they receive "guaranteed" employment.

Lincoln's compensation program has four parts: traditional wages and salaries, incentives, gainsharing, and fringe benefits. Wages are comparable to those in the Cleveland area. Managers' salaries, however, are fixed at about 80 percent of what similar jobs pay. About 90 percent of the workers are on an incentive system. Salespeople, interestingly, are salaried and not on commission. All employees—whether receiving salaries, wages, or piece rates—are part of the merit and bonus system. This system has resulted in bonuses that have averaged 97.6 percent of regular earnings since 1934. On average, Lincoln employees receive annual bonus checks about equal to their year-long income. Fringe benefits are also provided.

The bonus amount equals total profits less taxes, reinvestment reserves, and stockholders' dividends. Individual bonuses, however, are determined by merit. In twice-a-year reviews, workers are evaluated on the quality and quantity of their output, their dependability, and their ideas and cooperation. With input from other departments, the supervisor allocates a predetermined pool of points among workers to determine each person's bonus.[7]

Although this is a unique example, research shows that nontraditional pay plans are gaining popularity. One study of 1,600 companies found that 75 percent of them implemented reward and incentive systems during the preceding five years.[8] Another study found that:

Research summary

> Directors of top firms favor a stronger pay/performance link, according to a national survey of directors, CEOs, and human resource executives. More than 70 percent of all directors and 74 percent of HR managers rated "more effectively relating pay to performance" as the most important issue facing large companies....
> One out of five respondents to the survey conducted by Gibson & Co. said "pay without performance" is the most worrisome abuse of a company's payroll....[9]

Chapter 13, "Compensation Management," discusses how analysts ensure internal pay equity among employees and external pay equity between the employees and the labor market. This chapter addresses how incentives and gainsharing link pay and performance. Chapters 15 and 16 cover fringe benefits.

Figure 14-1

Key Considerations in Designing Incentives and Gainsharing Approaches

ISSUES	KEY CONSIDERATIONS
Purpose of nontraditional compensation	➤ Why is nontraditional compensation under consideration?
	➤ What are the key goals of this nontraditional compensation program?
Eligibility	➤ Who will be covered under the nontraditional compensation program?
Coverage	➤ Where will nontraditional compensation be applied? All facilities?
Payout standard	➤ What will trigger an incentive or gainsharing bonus?
	➤ When will it be paid?
Administration	➤ How will the program be administered? By personnel? By line management? Both?

INCENTIVE AND GAINSHARING ISSUES

Lincoln Electric

Faced with a slump in demand . . . companies often . . . can't cut wages; instead, they lay off workers.
Lincoln Electric . . . hasn't laid off a worker in more than three decades, according to Richard Sabo, assistant to the chief executive officer. Even during the severe recession of 1982, when the company's sales plummeted 40%, employment stayed steady. Workers reduced their hours, and bonus payments fell from a total of $59 million in 1981 to $26.5 million in 1983. The combined result: the average production worker's pay fell from $44,000 in 1981 to $22,500 in 1983.[10]

Besides providing greater flexibility in matching labor costs to organizational success, incentives and gainsharing raise issues that should be considered *before* selecting a particular approach. Human resource specialists should understand the purpose, the eligibility and coverage, the payout standards, and the administration of pay-for-performance plans.[11] These issues are summarized in Figure 14-1 and discussed below.

The Purpose of Nontraditional Compensation

Employees who work under a financial incentive system find that their performance determines, in whole or in part, their income. As a result, incentives reinforce performance on a regular basis. Unlike raises and promotions, the reinforcement is generally quick and frequent—usually with each paycheck.

Since the worker sees the results of the desired behavior quickly, that behavior is more likely to continue. Employers benefit because payouts are in proportion to productivity. And, if the system motivates employees to expand their output, recruiting expenses for additional employees and capital outlays for new workstations are minimized.

Incentives and cooperation

With fixed wages individual workers also have little incentive to cooperate with management or to take the initiative in suggesting new ideas for raising productivity. At the level of the individual worker, higher productivity has no immediate payoff—wages are fixed for the length of the contract. The immediate effect of higher productivity is, in fact, negative. Less labor is needed, and the probability of layoffs rises.

The higher productivity growth rates of the Japanese may also be due to their bonus system that encourages labor to take a direct interest in raising productivity.[12]

Many experts believe that bonuses contribute to Japan's success. More than one-fourth of an industrial worker's pay may arrive as an annual bonus, tied to company profits. Some economists think that this form of payment helps explain why Japan's savings rate is triple that of the United States. And since companies can adjust labor costs by adjusting their bonuses, layoffs may not be necessary; this may help explain why unemployment levels in Japan seldom rise above 3 percent.[13]

Eligibility and Coverage

Who gets incentives?

Who is eligible to participate in incentives, gainsharing, or other forms of nontraditional compensation? The extent of coverage is crucial because it affects motivation, teamwork, and perceptions of equity. Eligibility may differ for different programs, even in the same firm. As is the case at Lincoln Electric, hourly paid workers get individual incentives (piece rates), while managers and other workers share in the profits. Individual incentives, such as sales commissions, work best when cooperation and teamwork are less important to success. When success requires cooperation and coordination among those doing the work, group incentives and gainsharing work best. Coverage must be defined broadly enough to facilitate equity and teamwork and yet narrowly enough to include just those who affect results. Answering *who* is eligible largely determines *where* coverage will be found in the company. But, as two compensation consultants caution:

> Our experience has been that most organizations can identify several groups whose needs can only be met through separate plans. Across-the-board profit-sharing plans may be appreciated, but a program tailored to the results of a small team or group tends to be the most effective in modifying behavior

and getting results. The tendency to include various groups for "equity" should be avoided.[14]

Payout Standards

Standards for paying

Besides answering why, who, and where, nontraditional compensation plans must also answer *what* and *when*. What triggers the payout? When? With individual and even group incentives, the trigger is usually one or two clearly stated standards. For example, under piece rates, workers are paid for each unit produced. For gainsharing, the standard is usually some percentage of the cost savings or increased profits.

When should the payout occur? In agriculture, pickers are often paid daily. In production or sales, the payout is added to the weekly or biweekly paycheck. Gainsharing may delay the payout to quarterly or even annual payments. The delay in gainsharing helps smooth out seasonal and even monthly variations caused by sales and production. Although longer delays separate the reward from the performance, the resulting bonuses may be larger and more significant.

Administration

The administration of an incentive system can be complex. As with any control system, standards have to be established and results measured. For many jobs, the standards and measures are too imprecise or too costly to develop. This means that the incentive system may result in inequities. For example, sometimes workers make more money than their supervisors, who are on salary. Or employees may not achieve the standard because of uncontrollable forces, such as work delays or machine breakdowns.

Union reactions

Unions often resist incentive systems because they fear management will change the standard, and employees will have to work harder for the same pay. This fear of a speedup often leads to peer pressure against anyone who exceeds the group's output norms. The advantages of the incentive system are essentially lost when peer pressure restricts output.

Who should compute the payout? Should the payout be included with the regular paycheck, or should it be a separate payment? Should payments be made frequently to quickly relate performance to pay, or should payouts be larger and less frequent?[15] These and other questions must be answered in designing nontraditional plans. The answers depend upon the purpose, eligibility, coverage, and payout standards for each form of nonstandard compensation. When employees can estimate their additional income from their work effort or results—as when a real estate agent can estimate sales commissions, for example—greater confidence exists that the payout is correct. Including the extra income in the regular paycheck may dilute its impact because it is not separated from regular earnings of wages or salaries and is diminished by payroll deductions, such as taxes. The timing of payouts should follow the performance as quickly as is administratively feasible. Here the goal is quick reinforcement. However, daily or weekly payouts may be so small that they provide limited incentive for extra effort.

The development of performance standards and measures, tracking performance measures against those standards, and the associated administrative and clerical support often adds to the costs and complexity of compensation management. If competitive, technological, or other changes lead to a redesign of the firm's nontraditional compensation, additional expenses are incurred. And, if employees see these changes as cutting their payouts, trust, morale, and even productivity could suffer. The remainder of this chapter will examine different approaches to incentives and gainsharing, beginning with incentives.

INCENTIVE SYSTEMS

Incentive systems exist for almost every type of job from manual labor to professional, managerial and executive work. The more common incentives are discussed in the following pages.

Piecework

Per unit payments

Piecework is an incentive system that compensates the worker for each unit of output. Daily or weekly pay is determined by multiplying the output in units times the rate per unit. For example, in agricultural labor, workers are often paid a specific amount per bushel of produce picked. Piecework compensation does not always yield higher productivity, however. Group norms may have a more significant impact if peer pressure works against higher productivity. And it may be difficult to measure the employee's contribution (for example, the receptionist's), or the employee may not be able to control the output (as with an assembly-line worker, for example).

Production Bonuses

Pay and bonuses

Production bonuses are incentives paid to workers for exceeding output goals. They are used to supplement base pay. Under one approach, the employee receives a base pay. Then through extra effort that results in output above the standard, they get a supplemental bonus, usually figured at a given rate for each unit of production over the standard. Another variation rewards the employee for saving time. For example, if the standard time for replacing an automobile transmission is four hours and the mechanic does it in three, the mechanic may be paid for four hours. A third method combines production bonuses with piecework by compensating workers on an hourly basis, plus an incentive payment for each unit produced. For example, the employee may be paid $9.00 an hour plus $0.25 per unit. A stepped or tiered bonus might pay $0.35 for each unit over 30 per day.

Figure 14-2

Maturity Curves for Professionals with Varying Degrees of Performance

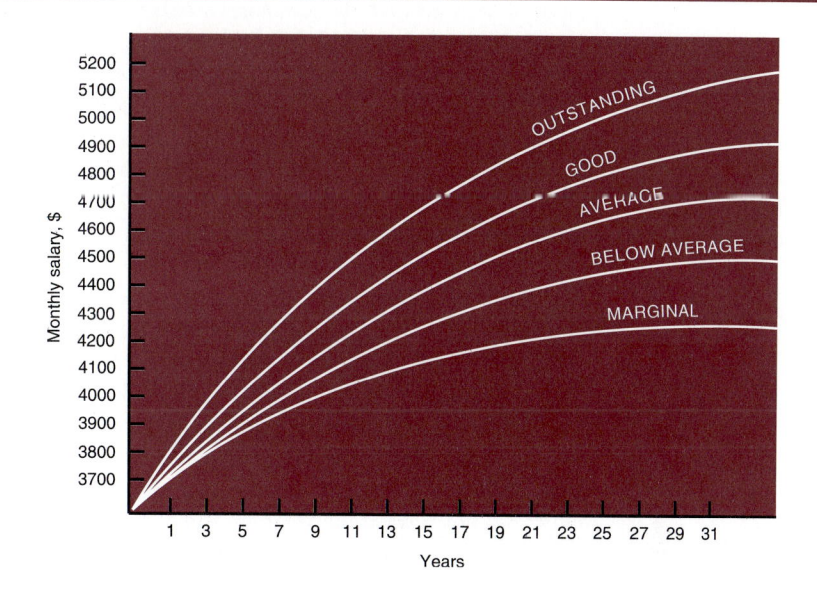

[Graph: Monthly salary ($) vs Years (1–31), with curves labeled OUTSTANDING, GOOD, AVERAGE, BELOW AVERAGE, MARGINAL. Y-axis from 3700 to 5200.]

Commissions

In sales jobs, the seller may be paid a percentage of the selling price or a flat amount for each unit sold. When no base compensation is paid, total earnings come from commissions. Real estate agents and automobile sellers are often on this form of "straight commission," as are a growing number of retail clerks.[16]

Maturity Curves

What happens when technical or scientific employees reach the top of their rate range? To provide an incentive for technical people, some companies have developed *maturity curves*, which are adjustments to the top of the rate range for selected jobs. Employees are rated on productivity and on experience. Outstanding contributors are assigned to the top curve, as shown in Figure 14-2. Good, but less outstanding, performers are placed on the next-to-top curve. Through this technique, high-performing professionals continue to be rewarded for their efforts without being required to seek a management position to increase their earnings.

Merit Raises

As discussed in Chapter 13, *merit raises* are pay increases given according to an evaluation of performance. These raises are usually decided by the employee's immediate supervisor, often in conjunction with superiors. Although merit raises reward above-average performance, they are seldom tied to any specific payout standard. This lack of clear standards has prompted some companies to rely on a management by objectives approach. This approach is used to create standards against which merit raises can be given, particularly among administrative and managerial employees whose productivity is less subject to objective measurement.

Because the productivity of some employees is difficult to measure objectively, merit raises are subject to many of the biases discussed in Chapter 11, "Performance Appraisal."[17] These biases create problems in administration. When raises are distorted by biases, meritorious performance goes unrewarded. Furthermore, employees are sent incorrect messages about what is expected of them. For example, if a company values quality but merit raises are given to those managers who exceed their production goals regardless of quality, the other managers soon realize that quality is not valued as highly as quantity. When merit raises are severely limited, some managers give an equal raise to everyone, which really does not reward merit. If, on the other hand, the manager gives meaningful raises to only a few of the best performers, dissatisfaction among those who received no raises may become a serious morale problem.[18]

Pay-for-knowledge Compensation

Pay-for-knowledge compensation systems provide employees higher pay as an incentive for each new skill or job they learn.

An emerging innovation

"Most organizations have traditionally designed their compensation systems around specific jobs. The wage and salary structure of these systems has typically been based on job analyses and evaluations; this process determines a job's worth and salary range. In recent years, however, a new alternative to this job-based approach has been developed; this new system pays employees for the skills and knowledge they possess, rather than for the job they do or a particular job category."[19]

Whether called knowledge-based pay, skill-based pay, or pay-for-knowledge, pay levels are based not on what an employee *does*, but rather on the range of jobs the employee *can* do.[20] Employees are rewarded for each new job or skill. Pay-for-knowledge evaluates the employee's worth to the employer. Increased skills and job mastery give management greater staffing flexibility. The increased employee knowledge also may reduce the total number of workers needed and may lead to higher-quality results. The higher pay and greater diversity of work may mean higher levels of satisfaction and, therefore, lower absenteeism and turnover. In short, employees are paid more because they are worth more.[21]

To the extent that operations like those of Westinghouse in College Station, Texas, benefit from this nontraditional approach, the idea is likely to spread.

Westinghouse

Westinghouse's College Station facility makes electronic assemblies for military radar. Each worker averages 12 assemblies a day, compared with a more traditional operation in Baltimore where employees average 1 1/2 assemblies per day. Although part of the difference stems from the College Station plant's investment in automated equipment and its use of teamwork, some of the difference can be attributed to the plant's pay-for-knowledge compensation system. Under this site's pay-for-knowledge approach, employees can increase their annual salaries by 60 percent in three years, depending on how many jobs they master. As each new job is mastered, the employee receives a pay increase.[22]

Nonmonetary Incentives

Noncash rewards

Incentives usually mean money. However, performance incentives may come in other forms.[23] For example, many companies have recognition programs where employees receive plaques, novelty items (from key chains to baseball caps), certificates, time off, vacations, and other noncash incentives for job performance, suggestions, and even community service.[24] These *nonmonetary incentives* are particularly common among salespeople, who may already be eligible for commissions or other financial incentives. Nonmonetary incentives serve to encourage extra or more narrowly focused efforts.

Beyond specific rewards for specific behaviors, changes in the job or the work setting may serve as an incentive to improved performance. As discussed more fully in subsequent chapters, people may be motivated to apply for employment or work diligently to retain their present jobs because of fringe benefits. For example, health insurance for those with sickly family members or tuition waivers for university employees with college-age children may be a powerful incentive.[25]

Efforts at job redesign (see Chapter 5) such as job rotation, enlargement, and enrichment, also may be viewed as incentives to induce improved performance. Instead of money, other incentives include increased responsibility, autonomy, or some other effort to empower workers and enhance the quality of their work life.

Executive Incentives

Incentives—especially executive incentives—need to achieve a balance between short-term results and long-term performance. Although incentives that relate to long-term improvements were found in 45 percent of the 112 firms researched in one study,[26] most companies still tie executive bonuses to annual profits, which are considered to be short-term improvements.[27] In some companies, this short-term orientation may lead to reductions in product quality and cuts in outlays for research and development, advertising, new capital equipment, employee development, and other long-term investments. As a report from the management consulting firm of Towers, Perrin, Forster & Crosby concludes:

The point is simple: If you're intent on maximizing current earnings, there are myriad ways to do it. And some of them, to use the Surgeon General's words, are dangerous to your health.

Faced with the results of this short-term thinking, most companies began to take action:

Short- versus long-term comp

➤ They either cut down on the size of their short-term incentives or they cut down on the degree to which incentive payments would respond to changes in short-term profits.

➤ They beefed up their long-term incentive programs; in some cases, designing entirely new programs.[28]

At the same time, incentives must be matched to the needs of executives. Young and middle-aged executives are likely to desire *cash bonuses* to meet the needs of a growing or maturing family. Older executives often seek to defer incentive compensation to build retirement savings. In Europe, where tax rates on income are often higher than in the United States, executives frequently receive nontaxable benefits as rewards for good performance. A chauffeured limousine paid for by the company is a common incentive for superior performance. In Japan, expensive club memberships and liberal expense accounts are common perks of the executive life.

Sometimes, executives are granted *stock options*—the right to purchase the company's stock at a predetermined price. This price may be set at, below, or above the market value. Thus the executive has an incentive to improve the company's performance. (In recent years, stock options and other incentives have been pushed further down the organization. At PepsiCo, for example, stock options equal to 10 percent of compensation are now available to all 100,000 employees.[29])

Stock options

Other forms of incentives exist, including those that allow executives to design their own compensation packages. The common element in most executive plans, however, is their relation to the performance of the organization. When these systems do not relate the incentive to performance, no matter what they are called, they are not incentive plans. And many plans have been criticized when executive incentives have been paid while company performance or stock prices have declined.[30]

To overcome these criticisms, companies are trying to tie the executive incentive to gains for shareholders. As two writers observe:

> The new reward systems are being built around performance measures that will constantly propel managers to obtain long-term benefits for the companies.
> According to compensation experts, a top manager's salary should be based on:

➤Company size

➤Profitability

➤Return to shareholders of the company

➤The complexity and importance of the job.[31]

Weighted incentive systems

Given the volatility of the stock market, incentives might be more effective if tied to improvements in key, organizationwide measures that executives do control. For example, *weighted incentive systems* reward executives on the basis of improvements in multiple areas of business performance. Depending on the weights used, part of the incentive bonus can be tied to improvements in market share, profit margin, return on assets, cash flow, or other indexes.[32] Some companies even weight their bonuses according to executive contributions to social responsibility, such as accident or pollution prevention.

Deferred stock incentive systems award stock to executives gradually over several years. This method not only creates an incentive for the executive to stay until the stock is owned, but stock value depends on what the executive team does to improve the company's performance during this time. Corning Glass Works, for example, uses stock incentives that take four years for complete ownership by executives.[33]

International Incentives

To attract, retain, and motivate international executives and key employees, many global companies are setting up incentives for international employees. Some companies find it advantageous to pay foreign housing, transportation, and taxes directly rather than pay allowances and incentives to work overseas.[34] Other companies prefer to use pay-for-performance plans. In one study, 32 of 40 U.S. multinational corporations have created long-term plans that reward improvements in performance.[35] One expert recommends that international incentives be based on financial and strategic goals within the control of the host country manager. Payouts and eligibility should be flexible to accommodate individual and national differences. Some companies even give equity ownership in foreign subsidiaries. As one consultant observes:

> Designing and implementing long-term incentive and direct ownership programs is a complex task. The companies that are putting them in place, however, are realizing significant benefits. They've found that the program development process has itself been valuable as an "audit" of their international executive compensation programs. They've also taken advantage of the opportunity to improve the linkages between the human resources function and the management of the international business. Finally, they're confident

that programs tailored to local needs will help ensure that long-term incentives are an integral part of the management process worldwide.[36]

GAINSHARING APPROACHES

Sharing the gains

Gainsharing matches an improvement in company performance to some distribution of benefits to employees. This approach has experienced explosive growth, with nearly three out of every four plans installed during the 1980s.[37] This rapid growth appears to be a response to competitive pressures and the resulting need for higher productivity. Employers with gainsharing were likely to share financial and nonfinancial information with employees much more frequently (65 percent) than were companies without gainsharing (37 percent).[38] And 84 percent of the firms in another study report that employees view gainsharing favorably,[39] while still another study found 25 to 35 percent productivity gains.[40]

Although gainsharing should be customized for individual plants or specific groups, most gainsharing falls into four broad categories: employee ownership, production-sharing, profit-sharing, and cost reduction plans.

Employee Ownership

Perhaps the ultimate gainsharing approach is for employees to own the company. Many companies have stock purchase plans that allow workers to buy shares in the company, thus "owning" a fractional part of the company and sharing in the firm's success.

ESOPs

A revolutionary approach by which employees may own their company is called an ESOP—*employee stock ownership plan*. Although it may be created in a variety of ways, an ESOP is a means for employees to buy stock in the company. Stock is "sold" to employees, who often "pay" for the stock by accepting stock shares instead of pay or pay raises. Or employees may simply pledge to buy stock as a way of helping a company pay off a debt. ESOPs can be used in other ways that can be called "creative financing." The ESOP, as a separate, legal entity, may:

➤Buy the stock with borrowed money secured by the stock and employee pledges

➤Buy the stock with the funds from a tax-deductible contribution made by the company (An owner wanting to sell may authorize a tax-deductible contribution to the ESOP so the ESOP can buy the stock, paying the owner with cash.)

➤Create a new employee benefit when the company contributes new stock issues to the plan

➤ Make public companies private, spin off or divest subsidiaries, or even save failing companies.[41]

Perhaps the most widely publicized ESOP involves National Steel Corporation's creation of Weirton Steel Corporation.

> *The National Steel Corporation created an ESOP to divest its steelworks in Weirton, West Virginia. National assumed $5 million dollars in unfunded pension liabilities and loaned money to Weirton. Weirton employees took a 20 percent cut in wages and benefits and agreed to a six-year freeze in their wage levels. As employees bought stock, National was repaid. The following year Weirton posted a profit, which was the largest profit per ton of steel among the six major steel companies.*
>
> *When the final distribution of shares is made, employees will have control of 80 percent of the Weirton stock. The Weirton Steel Corporation will be substantially owned and controlled by employees.*[42]

With employee ownership, workers may accept lower wages since they are entitled to share in company profits. After the spin-off from National, for example, Weirton employee participation teams were created to enhance communications and tap employee ideas. Such employee-oriented actions may cause them to continue their present productivity at the reduced wages.

Not all ESOPs result in such a positive outcome. Often stock sales to ESOPs are only partial ones, leaving control of the operation in the hands of others. The ESOP may be used to shelter the company from corporate raiders, since employees might be reluctant to support a corporate raider and an uncertain fate. Or, as was the case at National, the ESOP may be a way to divest an unprofitable operation with dim prospects. And, yet, even under the worst conditions, turnarounds were achieved as a result of ESOPs at Weirton, at Bridgeport Brass, at a division of the Great Atlantic & Pacific Tea Company, and others.[43] Still further, according to the National Center of Employee Ownership, ESOP employers have faster sales growth than non-ESOP companies, averaging 6.3 percent contrasted with 2.7 percent growth.[44]

Production-sharing Plans

Production-sharing plans allow groups of workers to receive bonuses for exceeding predetermined levels of output. The plans tend to be short-ranged and related to very specific production goals. For example, a team may get a bonus for meeting a specific goal. One well-publicized example comes from Nucor Corporation.

Nucor

Nucor's management transformed the company into a steel producer in the late 1960s, when the North American steel industry was beginning to face strong competition from European and Japanese producers. Nucor's strategy was to "build plants economically and run them very efficiently with high productivity."[45]

Nucor's nonunion production workers earn a base wage below that of employees in the United Steelworkers Union. But if they reach progressively higher production targets, they can supplement their weekly pay with bonuses of from 100 to 200 percent of their base wage. If production does not reach the target, no bonuses are paid.

The results? Workers are motivated as a team to find ways to improve productivity. Employees who do not do their share receive considerable peer pressure. Workers earn about 20 percent more than their unionized counterparts and about 250 percent more than the average production worker in South Carolina, the home of Nucor's flagship steel mill. The company has been able to add mills in Texas, Nebraska, and Utah while producing steel at prices equal to or below those charged by foreign producers.[46]

Profit-sharing Plans

Profit-sharing plans share profits with the workers. The effectiveness of these plans may suffer because profitability is not always related to the employee's performance. A recession or new competitors may have a significant impact. Or employees may not perceive their efforts as making much difference. Some plans divert the payouts into retirement plans, reducing the immediate reinforcement value. However, when these plans work well, they can create trust and a feeling of common fate among workers and management.

Cost Reduction Plans

Some critics of group incentive plans argue that profit-sharing schemes, such as those found at Lincoln Electric, do not always reward the employees' efforts. For example, the pay received by workers at Lincoln Electric fell from $44,000 one year to $22,500 two years later because of a slowdown in the economy. The reasons for the drop were largely beyond the employees' control.

Incentives to cut costs by sharing savings

Another approach is to reward workers for something they can control: labor costs. As part of this approach, employee committees are formed to facilitate the communication of new ideas and employee involvement in the firm's day-to-day operations, usually through periodic meetings. Perhaps the best known of these approaches is the *Scanlon Plan*, which bases bonuses on improvements in labor costs as compared with historical norms.[47] See the first column of Figure 14-3.

Under the Scanlon Plan employees aim to reduce costs and share in the savings that result. If, for example, productivity increases at a company that uses Scanlon, such as the American Valve and Hydrant Manufacturing Company,

Figure 14-3

A Comparison of Scanlon, Rucker, and Improshare Gainsharing Approaches

	SCANLON	RUCKER	IMPROSHARE
PURPOSE	Improve labor costs and/or quality	Improve labor and/or material costs	Reduce labor hours
CREATION	By vote of employees	By management or optional vote	By management
TYPE OF EMPLOYERS	Usually goods producers	Usually goods producers	Usually goods producers
COVERAGE	Production areas	Company or facility-wide or smaller groups	Usually entire firm or facility
ELIGIBILITY	Production workers	Usually all employees excluding senior management	Usually all employees excluding senior management
PAYOUT STANDARD	Reductions in historical labor costs as a percentage of sales revenue, adjusted for inventory	Reductions in labor costs as a percentage of sales, adjusted for inventory, materials, and supplies	Reduction in labor hours for unit of output
FREQUENCY OF PAYOUT	Monthly bonus as a percentage of wages with a reserve for year-end bonus and seasonality	Monthly bonus as a percentage of wages with reserves for seasonality	Usually weekly (or payroll period) or a four-week moving average
EMPLOYEE INVOLVEMENT IN PROCESS	Extensive through formal suggestion system; also weekly department production committee and a monthly screening committee composed of production committee representatives, both of which review suggestions	Extensive through formal suggestion system and Rucker committees composed of employees and managers to improve communications about suggestions and problems	Limited primarily to employees figuring out how to reduce the number of hours needed to produce a standard of output

labor costs drop as a percentage of net sales revenue. These savings are then shared with employees in the form of bonuses.

Rucker and *Improshare plans* are similar to the Scanlon approach, but they differ in how bonuses are calculated and in other administrative matters. All three differ from profit-sharing in that they focus on something that the employee can influence (costs) and not on something that the employee may control only indirectly (profits). A summary of the differences among these three plans appears in Figure 14-3 and is discussed in the following paragraphs.

Scanlon, Rucker, and Improshare plans primarily aim to reduce costs and create improved commitment from workers through various approaches. Improshare, for example, focuses on reducing labor hours as a means of reducing costs. Rucker plans reward reductions in labor and material costs by including these savings in the calculations of gainsharing bonuses. The Scanlon Plan focuses primarily on labor costs and quality. Employees usually get to vote for a one-year trial of the Scanlon Plan. A subsequent vote at the end of the trial period determines whether it is made a permanent form of compensation. Rucker is sometimes instituted as a result of an employee vote, but it and Improshare are commonly initiated by management. Although these plans can work in service industries, they are more common in goods-producing ones.[48] Scanlon Plans normally cover production areas, making production employees eligible. Rucker and Improshare typically extend to an entire facility or firm, excluding senior management.

Scanlon and Rucker are, perhaps, more accurately seen as management philosophies that stress employee suggestions and review of those suggestions by employee committees. The involvement helps build employee interest and commitment. Although Improshare uses less employee involvement, it rewards gains in performance by sharing the benefits, as do Scanlon and Rucker. The success of these plans often hinges on managers allowing employees to influence the job and job setting. As two economists observe:

Redistribution of power

> The real problem with establishing meaningful worker participation programs that contribute to greater productivity is that they require a redistribution of power within the workplace. The traditional management perspective is that the retention of control and final decision-making authority is essential to profit maximization. Although some employers may seek the advice of their employees in order to solve production problems, management in general is more likely to want workers to "feel" involved rather than actually to help make policy.[49]

Ways for the human resource department to help build employee involvement and commitment are examined in Part V, "Employee Relations and Assessment." Before discussing those approaches, however, the next two chapters examine indirect and legally mandated benefits and services, the compensation that extends beyond wages, salaries, and bonuses. Remuneration includes an ever-growing list of fringe benefits and services. Although these benefits are referred to as noncash compensation, they are a significant part of most employers' total labor costs. Chapter 15 describes the range of fringe benefits and services offered by employers.

SUMMARY

INCENTIVES AND gainsharing are compensation approaches that reward specified outcomes. Incentives usually link individual performance and rewards, while gainsharing usually embraces groups of employees. These nontraditional compensation approaches have gained popularity in recent years as a means of stimulating increased productivity. They also help employers relate pay to performance while improving employee commitment.

Nontraditional compensation approaches must consider the purpose, eligibility, coverage, payout standard, and administrative issues.

Many different incentive systems exist. They include merit raises, piecework, production bonuses, commissions, maturity curves, pay-for-knowledge compensation, and nonmonetary and executive incentives.

Gainsharing approaches share the benefits of an improvement in company performance with employees. These approaches include production- and profit-sharing plans. Also popular are cost-reduction methods such as Scanlon, Rucker, and Improshare.

Terms for Review

Incentive systems
Gainsharing
Employee stock ownership plans (ESOPs)
Payout standards
Piecework
Production bonuses
Pay-for-knowledge compensation systems
Maturity curves

Merit raises
Nonmonetary incentives
Weighted incentive systems
Deferred stock incentive systems
Production-sharing plans
Profit-sharing plans
Scanlon plan
Rucker plan
Improshare plan

Review and Discussion Questions

1. Why are incentive and gainsharing approaches rapidly gaining in popularity?

2. If you were hired as a consultant by Lincoln Electric, what suggestions could you offer that might further improve upon the company's successful approach?

3. What factors make international compensation unique?

4. What are maturity curves? When are they used? Why are they considered an incentive?

5. In what fundamental ways do pay-for-knowledge compensation systems differ from traditional compensation approaches?

6. If you became a manager of an assembly-line operation and wanted to improve performance, what type of incentives or gainsharing would you select? Why? What would you do if your boss said you could not give monetary incentives or gainsharing bonuses?

7. Executive incentives should consider many factors and tradeoffs. What are the major ones you would keep in mind?

INCIDENT 14-1
Incentives at Karma Records

Joe Karma had owned and operated Karma Records since its founding in 1982. Joe was often heard to say, "I believe in paying people for what they do, not for how many hours they work." This management philosophy was expressed through a variety of incentive plans that Joe designed himself. Although he was firmly committed to the use of incentives, he hired a management consulting team to make recommendations about his compensation program.

To help the consultants, Joe wrote down the major features of each incentive program. His notes were as follows:

a. Executives do not own any stock. But they each get $1,000 for every dollar the stock price increases from the previous year.

b. Every time sales go up 10 percent, all the hourly employees get a day off with pay, or they can work one day at double-time rates.

c. Production workers get paid 18 cents for each record they press and 3 cents for each record they package.

d. Sales personnel get a $50 savings bond each time a new record store or department store starts stocking Karma records.

1. What problems do you see with the incentives for (a) executives, (b) hourly workers, (c) production workers, (d) salespeople?

2. If you were a member of the consulting team, what incentives would you recommend for each group?

References

1. Steven E. Markham, "Pay-for-performance Dilemma Revisited: Empirical Example of the Importance of Group Effects," *Journal of Applied Psychology*, vol. 73, no. 2 (1988), pp. 172–180.

2. Timothy L. Ross and Warren C. Hauck, "Gainsharing in the United States," *Industrial Management* (March–April 1984), pp. 9–14.

3. Carla O'Dell and Jerry McAdams, *Major Findings from People, Performance and Pay* (Houston: American Productivity Center, 1986), pp. 10–12. See also Victoria A. Hoevemeyer, "Performance-based Compensation: Miracle or Waste?" *Personnel Journal* (July 1989), pp. 64–68.

4. Carla O'Dell and Jerry McAdams, "The Revolution in Employee Rewards," *Management Review* (March 1987), p. 30.

5. Joyce E. Santora, "DuPont Builds Stakeholders," *Personnel Journal* (Dec. 1989), pp. 72–76. See also Jerry McAdams, "Performance-based Reward Systems: Toward a Common-fate Environment," *Personnel Journal* (June 1988), pp. 103–107, 111–113.

6. "The Lincoln Electric Company," Case Study 48 (Houston: American Productivity Center, 1985), p. 5. See also Alan Murray, "Democrats Latch Onto Bonus Pay System in Search of New Ideas," *The Wall Street Journal*, Eastern ed. (April 28, 1987), p. 1.

7. "The Lincoln Electric Company," op. cit., pp. 1–8; Murray, op. cit.

8. "Nontraditional Pay Plans Gaining Popularity, Study Shows," *Resource* (Dec. 1986), pp. 1, 6.

9. "Directors of Top Firms Favor a Stronger Pay/Performance Link," *Resource* (Nov. 1986), p. 10.

10. Murray, op. cit.

11. Hoyt Doyel and Thomas Riles, "Considerations in Developing Incentive Plans," *Management Review* (March 1987), pp. 34–37.

12. Lester Thurow, "Productivity Pay," *Newsweek* (May 3, 1982), p. 69.

13. Murray, op. cit.

14. Doyel and Riles, op. cit.

15. Ross and Hauck, op. cit.

16. Amy Dunkin and Kathleen Kerwin, "Now Salespeople Really Must Sell for Their Supper," *Business Week* (July 31, 1989), pp. 50, 52.

17. Ross and Hauck, op. cit.; Jon L. Pearce, William B. Stevenson, and James L. Perry, "Managerial Compensation Based on Organizational Performance: A Time Series Analysis of the Effects of Merit Pay," *Academy of Management Journal* (June 1985), pp. 261–278; Dow Scott, Fred Hills, and Gayel Pitchford, "An Evaluation of a Merit Pay Program: A Case Study," unpublished paper presented at the American Management Association's 58th Annual Human Resources Conference, New York (March 30, 1987).

18. Frederick S. Hills, Robert M. Madigan, K. Dow Scott, and Steven E. Markham, "Tracking the Merit of Merit Pay," *Personnel Administrator* (March 1987), pp. 50–57. See also Lawrence B. Chonko and Ricky W. Griffin, "Tradeoff Analysis Finds the Best Reward Combination," *Personnel Administrator* (May 1983), pp. 45, 47, 99.

19. Fred Luthans and Marilyn L. Fox, "Update on Skill-based Pay," *Personnel* (March 1989), pp. 26–31.

20. Nina Gupta, G. Douglas Jenkins, Jr., and William P. Curington, "Paying for Knowledge: Myths and Realities," *National Productivity Review* (Spring 1986), p. 107.

21. Earl Ingram II, "The Advantages of Knowledge-based Pay," *Personnel Journal* (April 1990), pp. 138–140. See also Jerry Franklin, "For Technical Professionals: Pay for Skills and Pay for Performance," *Personnel* (May 1988), pp. 20–28.

22. "Yesterday's Despair Can Be Tomorrow's Triumph," *Behavioral Science Newsletter* (Sept. 8, 1986), p. 1.

23. Richard L. Bunning, "Rewarding a Job Well Done," *Personnel Administrator* (Jan. 1989), pp. 60–64.

24. Lynne F. McGee, "Keeping Up the Good Work," *Personnel Administrator* (June 1988), pp. 68–72.

25. Peter W. Stonebraker, "Flexible and Incentive Benefits: A Guide to Program Development," *Compensation Review* (Second Quarter 1985), pp. 40–53.

26. Sumer C. Aggarwal and Sudhir Aggarwal, "A Management Rewards System for the Long- and Short-terms," *Personnel Journal* (Dec. 1986), pp. 115–126.

27. Ibid. See also Graef S. Crystal, "Rendering Long-term Incentives Less Risky for Executives," *Personnel* (Sept. 1988), pp. 80–84.

28. *Paying for Divisional Executive Performance* (New York: Towers, Perrin, Forster & Crosby, 1985), p. 1.

29. "How You'll Be Paid in the 1990's," *Fortune* (April 9, 1990), p. 11.

30. Pearl Merey, "Executive Compensation Must Promote Long-term Commitment," *Personnel Administrator* (May 1983), pp. 37–38, 40, 42. See also Carl J. Loomis, "The Madness of Executive Compensation," *Fortune* (July 12, 1982), pp. 42–46; Daniel Seligman, "Believe It or Not, Top-Executive Pay May Make Sense," *Fortune* (June 11, 1984), pp. 57–62; and Graef S. Crystal, "Too Many Make-Any-Excuse C.E.O.s," *Fortune* (July 21, 1986), pp. 116–117.

31. Aggarwal and Aggarwal, op. cit., p. 115.

32. Ibid., p. 118.

33. Ibid.

34. Lin P. Crandall and Mark I. Phelps, "Pay for a Global Work Force," *Personnel Journal* (Feb. 1991), pp. 28, 30–33.

35. Brian J. Brooks, "Long-term Incentives: International Executives," *Personnel* (August 1988), pp. 40–42.

36. Ibid.

37. O'Dell and McAdams, *Major Findings from People, Performance and Pay*, op. cit., p. 8.

38. O'Dell and McAdams, "The Revolution in Employee Rewards", op. cit., p.32.

39. "Does Your Pay Plan Demotivate?" *Personnel Journal* (June 1988), p. 10.

40. Thomas Owens, "Gainsharing," *Small Business Reports* (Dec. 1988), pp. 19–28.

41. *NCEO Membership Services and Publications* (Arlington, Va.: The National Center for Employee Ownership, 1986), p. 1.

42. "Making Money—and History—at Weirton," *Business Week* (Nov. 12, 1984), pp. 136, 138, 140.

43. Robert Kuttner, "Worker Ownership: A Commitment That's More Often a Con," *Business Week* (July 6, 1987), p. 16.

44. Clemens P. Work and Jack A. Seamonds, "Making It Clear Who's Boss," *U.S. News & World Report* (Sept. 8, 1986), p. 45. See also *NCEO Membership Services and Publications* and other publications of the National Center for Employee Ownership.

45. Richard I. Kirkland, Jr., "Pilgrims' Profits at Nucor," *Fortune* (April 6, 1981), p. 44.

46. Ibid., pp. 43–44, 46. See also John Savage, "Incentive Programs at Nucor Corporation Boost Productivity," *Personnel Administrator* (April 1981), pp. 33–36, 49.

47. Robert J. Schulhop, "Five Years with the Scanlon Plan," *Personnel Administrator* (June 1979), pp. 55–60, 62, 92. See also John Hoerr, "Why Labor and Management Are Both Buying Profit Sharing," *Business Week* (Jan. 10, 1983), p. 84; and Richard I. Henderson, "Designing a Reward System for Today's Employee," *Business* (July–August 1982), pp. 2–12.

48. O'Dell and McAdams, *Major Findings from People, Performance and Pay*, op. cit.

49. Sar A. Levitan and Diane Wernke, "Worker Participation and Productivity Change," *Monthly Labor Review* (Sept. 1984), p. 32.

As organizations move toward the new millennium, they . . . are seriously looking for ways to retain and develop their people.
FRED LUTHANS AND ROBERT WALDERSEE[1]

Compensation—and, more particularly, benefits—practices are more dynamic, visible, and competitive than ever before.
PETER W. STONEBRAKER[2]

BENEFITS AND SERVICES

CHAPTER OBJECTIVES

After studying this chapter, you should be able to:
1. DESCRIBE the objectives of indirect compensation.
2. IDENTIFY policies that minimize the costs of fringe benefits.
3. EXPLAIN the key issues in designing pension plans.
4. IDENTIFY problems in administering employee benefits and services, especially when international workers are involved.
5. EXPLAIN how flexible benefits and services work.
6. CITE benefits and services that are likely to become more common in the future.

Figure 15-1

The Elements of Total Compensation

THE ELEMENTS OF TOTAL COMPENSATION

INDIRECT COMPENSATION	SECURITY, SAFETY AND HEALTH (Legally Mandated Benefits)	Chapter 16
	BENEFITS AND SERVICES ("Fringe" Benefits)	Chapter 15
DIRECT COMPENSATION	INCENTIVES AND GAINSHARING (Pay-for-Performance)	Chapter 14
	COMPENSATION MANAGEMENT (Base Wages and Salaries)	Chapter 13

tOTAL COMPENSATION consists of direct and indirect compensation, as Figure 15-1 suggests. The previous two chapters addressed direct compensation in the forms of base wages and salaries (Chapter 13) and incentives and gainsharing (Chapter 14). This chapter and the next describe indirect compensation in the forms of "fringe" benefits and services (Chapter 15) and legally mandated security, safety, and health requirements (Chapter 16).

Fringes misnamed

"Fringe" benefits and services are misnamed, since the cost of these voluntarily provided types of compensation often represent about 40 percent of total labor costs. Consider just *some* of the fringe benefits one electronics firm provides its employees.

Intel

> The Intel Corporation is a billion-dollar company that produces sophisticated microelectronics and electronic components for the computer, communications, automotive, and other industries. This fast-growing, profitable company is responsible for some of the significant breakthroughs in the computer-on-a-chip technology. Along the way, however, Intel has encouraged innovation by giving employees rewards and security through its benefit program.
> Some of its fringe benefits include group life insurance, supplemental life insurance, business travel accident insurance, dependent life insurance, accidental death and dismemberment insurance, a voluntary short-term disability plan, a long-term disability plan, medical insurance, dental insurance, a stock purchase plan, tuition reimbursement, vacation and personal absence time, holidays, a profit-sharing retirement plan, sabbaticals, subsidized cafeterias, free parking, rest breaks, and legally required services (social security, unemployment insurance, workers' compensation, and safe work

IV. COMPENSATION AND PROTECTION

environments). Moreover, most of these benefits and services are fully paid for by the company. And, with the exception of sabbaticals, most large employers would be able to produce a similar list.

The point of this Intel illustration is that "fringes" embrace a broad range of benefits and services that employees receive as part of their total compensation package. As with most employers, pay—or *direct compensation*—at Intel is based on critical job factors and performance. Benefits and services, however, are *indirect compensation* because they are usually extended as a condition of employment and are not directly related to performance.

This chapter describes the role of indirect compensation in an organization's overall compensation program. Then the discussion turns to common benefits and services—including insurance, security, time off, and scheduling benefits, in addition to educational, financial, and social services. The chapter ends with an explanation of benefit administration. Legally required benefits and services are covered in Chapter 16.

THE ROLE OF INDIRECT COMPENSATION

Employee benefits and services address societal, organizational, and employee objectives.

1. Societal Objectives

Nonbusiness objectives

Europe, Japan, and North America have changed from rural nations of independent farmers and ranchers to urban nations of interdependent wage earners. This interdependence was illustrated forcefully by mass unemployment during the Great Depression in the 1930s and during the recession of the early 1980s. As a result, these societies sought solutions to societal problems.

To provide security for interdependent wage earners, governments rely on the support of employers.[3] Through favorable tax treatment, employees can receive most benefits tax-free, while employers can deduct the cost of benefits as a regular business expense. The result has been a rapid growth in indirect compensation.[4] Although tax breaks reduce government receipts, health-care, disability, life insurance, and retirement benefits lower the burden on society when ill-health, retirement, or death occur. Even if these tax breaks were eliminated, benefits are so widely used that they would be almost certain to continue.

2. Organizational Objectives   *Benefits package*

What do employers gain from these large outlays for fringe benefits? Besides the desires of many companies to be socially responsible, employers such as Intel must offer some fringe benefits if they are to recruit successfully in the labor

reduces turnover

15. BENEFITS AND SERVICES 465

market. If Intel did not offer health insurance and paid vacations, for example, recruits and present employees might favor Motorola, Texas Instruments, National Semiconductor, or other competitors who do offer these "fringes." Similarly, many employees will stay with a company because they do not want to give up a benefit, and so employee turnover is lowered. For example, an employee who has been at Intel for 6 ½ years might stay through the seventh year to earn his or her eight-week sabbatical. Likewise, employees at other companies may stay to save pension credits or their rights to the extended vacations that typically come with greater seniority.

Vacations, along with holidays and rest breaks, help employees reduce fatigue and may enhance productivity during the hours employees do work. Similarly, retirement, health-care, and disability benefits may allow workers to be more productive by freeing them of concern about medical and retirement costs. If these benefits were not available, employees might elect to form a union and collectively bargain with the employer. (Although collective action is legal, many nonunion employers such as Intel prefer to remain nonunion.) So, it is accurate to state that indirect compensation may:

▶ Reduce fatigue

▶ Discourage labor unrest

▶ Satisfy employee objectives

▶ Aid recruitment

▶ Reduce turnover

▶ Minimize overtime costs.

3. Employee Objectives

Employees usually seek employer-provided benefits and services because of lower costs and availability. For example, insurance benefits are usually less expensive because the employer may pay some or all of the costs, as Intel does. Group plans save the cost of administering and selling many individual policies. The insurer also can reduce the risk of *adverse selection*, which occurs when individuals sign up for insurance because they are heavy users. Actuaries—the specialists who compute insurance rates—can pass along these savings in the form of lower premiums, even if workers pay the entire premium.

Another employee objective is to cut taxes. For example, an employee in a 28 percent tax bracket has to earn $1,000 to buy a $720 policy. But for $1,000, the company can buy the same $720 policy and give the worker a $280 raise. The employee has a policy and a $280 raise, while the employer is no worse off. And

Inflation protection

in many cases the company can negotiate a lower cost for the insurance policy. So the policy might cost only $600 instead of $720. Whether the tax advantages of company-provided benefits will continue is uncertain because government deficits may lead to the taxation of these fringes in the future.

When the employer pays for a benefit, the employee also gets "inflation protection." For example, a two-week paid vacation is not reduced in value by inflation. The employee still gets two weeks off with pay. Or if a completely employer-paid insurance premium rises from $720 to $900, the worker is protected (although pay raises may be smaller). For some people, the primary objective of employment may be to obtain benefits, such as health insurance, which might otherwise be unaffordable or unavailable—especially if they have a preexisting medical condition that limits their eligibility for insurance. In Canada, Sweden, and other developed nations, health insurance may be of less importance because of government-provided health insurance or care.

The objectives of society, organizations, and employees have encouraged rapid growth of benefits and services. This growth has affected all areas of fringe benefits and services including insurance, security, time-off, and work scheduling benefits.

INSURANCE BENEFITS

Insurance benefits disperse the financial risks encountered by employees and their families. These risks are shared by pooling funds in the form of insurance premiums. Then when insured events occur, the covered employees or their families are compensated.

Health-related Insurance

Health care

Health-related coverage is a common form of insurance provided by employers. In one survey of 1,000, mostly large companies, 99 percent reported making payments for health insurance.[5] Contrast this finding in the United States with Europe, where, since health care is provided by the government, many firms face no direct medical insurance costs. However, an estimated 35 million Americans lack health coverage because they are unemployed or work for (mostly small) employers that do not provide affordable coverage. Concern for the uninsured and underinsured has created a national debate about whether there should be a government-led change in how health care costs are paid. Though chronic budget deficits probably preclude national health insurance in the immediate future, federal legislation is likely to change how health care and health insurance are provided in the United States during the 1990s.

Medical insurance. Medical insurance pays for sickness, accident, and hospitalization expenses, up to the dollar limits of the policy. In addition, most policies contain a schedule of benefits. This schedule sets forth which sickness, accident, or hospitalization costs are covered and how much of these expenses will be paid. Otherwise, the insurer agrees to pay "reasonable and customary" expenses.

If the company pays part or all of the premiums, human resource managers should require a deductible or coinsurance clause in addition to a ceiling on the policy's benefits. A *deductible clause* requires the covered employee to pay a specified amount (usually $100, $200, or more) before the insurer is obligated to pay. Xerox, for example, pays 100 percent of medical costs after a deductible equal to 4 percent of annual wages or salary. The deductible clause has two significant cost advantages. First, if each minor illness resulted in a claim, premium costs would soar because of the added administrative burden. Second, a deductible discourages employees from abusing the benefit through overuse. A *coinsurance clause* requires the employee to pay a percentage of the medical expenses—typically, a copayment equal to 20 percent of the expenses. These clauses often specify a maximum liability for the employee but require cost-sharing to discourage malingering and give employees a reason to hold down these costs.

Even when deductibles, coinsurance, and policy ceilings have been used, premiums have continued to increase rapidly. As a health-care adviser to the White House observed, "The cost of health care has risen so high for employers, it's undermining industrial efficiency and international competitiveness. . . ."[6] For example, the National Association of Manufacturers reports that health-care costs amount to 37.2 percent of net profits.[7] As a result, human resource managers find that holding down medical insurance costs is a major concern. And the growing AIDS epidemic means even more attention to health-care costs.

Benefit administrators constantly seek to meet the basic health-care needs of employees in ways that minimize the costs to the employer. Some of the more innovative efforts include requirements for second opinions on nonemergency surgery, more extensive outpatient surgery, preadmission testing to reduce time spent as a costly hospital inpatient, and a greater analysis of medical claims costs. Through analysis of claims costs, employers try to identify the most cost-effective doctors and hospitals in their areas.

Some employers pay employees not to get sick. Companies such as Mobil, Chemical Bank, and Quaker Oats are using a method whereby the company sets aside a cash amount that employees can keep if they do not use those moneys for health care.[8]

Cost savers

Quaker Oats

The Quaker Oats plan is a combination of a flexible spending account and a group plan. Each of the 6,000 Quaker Oats employees gets $300 beyond medical insurance that can be applied to medical-related expenses. If an employee does not need the $300 for medical-related expenses, he or she keeps what is left. If employees reduce their medical expenses and Quaker Oats does not spend the planned $1,535 per employee, the unspent balance is

IV. COMPENSATION AND PROTECTION

shared among employees. The director of employee benefits at Quaker estimates that each employee could receive as much as $200 while reducing the company's total outlays for medical care and insurance premiums.[9]

Besides Quaker's incentive-based approach to health cost reductions, many successful efforts have been tried by others. Southern California Edison operates 10 clinics with its own doctors and buys pharmaceuticals in bulk, saving 40 percent on its drug purchases alone. Caterpillar negotiates lower hospital and doctor costs for its employees.[10] Preventative or "wellness" care seeks to keep employees healthy through "quit-smoking," weight-reduction, exercise, and other programs.

General Electric

General Electric, for example, reports saving one million dollars annually at its aircraft engine headquarters in Cincinnati since installing voluntary fitness programs. "In a study, GE tracked the health-care costs of 800 fitness center members of similar age, gender and work classification. . . . In the six months before the members-to-be joined the health club, their medical costs averaged 35% higher than those of nonmembers.

But in the year after they joined, . . . their annual health costs plunged 38% to $757. For nonmembers, costs jumped 21% to $841."[11]

The Health Research Institute reports that for every dollar spent on wellness, savings average $3.44.[12]

WHAT ARE HMO'S

HMOs

Health maintenance organizations. The *Health Maintenance Act* of 1973 required firms of 25 or more employees to offer their employees *health maintenance organization (HMO)* coverage, if it is available in their area and if the employer offers other forms of health benefits. HMOs are organizations that provide their own staff of doctors and facilities. A company's covered employees and their dependents can usually use the HMO's services for any health-related problem. Most large employers in metropolitan areas (where most HMOs are located) offer this alternative to encourage preventive rather than remedial health care. The hope for HMOs is that through better management, preventive care, and fewer unneeded tests, exams, and other medical procedures, costs will be slowed. The attraction of HMOs for employees is that they offer "well care," such as free or "low-cost" physical examinations and usually have a small ($5.00 to $15.00) charge or no charge at all for office visits. Most large employers offer both HMOs and indemnity plans. Indemnity plans reimburse the employee for medical expenses according to the company's medical insurance plan, often giving the employee greater freedom in selecting health care providers but making the employee pay a larger share of each health care bill. Employers are split, however, on whether HMOs really do provide lower costs. One study found that 31 percent of employers thought HMO costs were *higher*, while 38 percent thought they were *lower*.[13]

PPOs

Closely related to HMOs are preferred-provider organizations (PPOs). HMOs generally operate clinic-like facilities where members receive service from those employed by the HMO. PPOs allow subscribers to select doctors and hospitals from an approved list, helping to assure cost containment because those on the list usually agree to discount their services. If the member uses another health-care provider, the cost may not be fully reimbursable. HMOs and PPOs encourage affiliated health-care providers to minimize tests, hospital admissions, and other sources of rising medical-care costs. Simply put, these alternative delivery systems provide *managed care*, intended to reduce medical-care costs. Alternative delivery systems (ADS) give employees the options of choosing among indemnity, HMO, or PPO health-care providers. One survey found that:

> ... employees tend to have the highest satisfaction levels (86%) with the quality of care they receive through traditional indemnity plans; the lowest satisfaction levels (75%) with PPOs; and a nominal satisfaction level (80%) with HMOs. ADS were not rated.[14]

Other types of health-related benefits have gained in popularity during recent years, including vision, dental, and mental health insurance.

Vision insurance. Vision care—often including examinations and eyeglasses—is a developing benefit, although it represents well below 1 percent of benefit outlays.[15] As with other insurance, deductibles, copayments, and policy limits usually apply. Some plans limit benefits to 12- to 24-month intervals for services such as new glasses. The availability and cost of this benefit are likely to grow, since the need for eye correction grows with age and the average age in the work force is increasing. And because more than two-thirds of the work force needs vision correction, vision insurance is likely to be an increasingly popular benefit.[16]

Dental insurance. Dental insurance benefit plans pay for most preventive care and for a portion of needed dental work—sometimes including false teeth and braces. Policies tend to be narrow in scope. Besides deductibles and coinsurance clauses, most plans have benefit ceilings of $1,000 per year or less. On the average, dental insurance costs employers less than one-half of 1 percent of payroll.[17]

Intel

Intel's dental plan, for example, pays for 90 percent of all routine care for employees who have been with the company for three years or more. It pays 70 percent in the first year and 80 percent in the second year. The plan has a one-time deductible of $25 and an annual maximum benefit of $1,000 per *year per person. Orthodontia is not covered, and other major costs are covered 50 percent by the company and 50 percent by the employee.*

Mental health insurance. Mental health coverage pays for psychiatric care and counseling. Although most policies have special limits, there does appear to be a trend toward comprehensive, employer-provided mental health insurance. At Intel, for example, the coverage for outpatient psychiatric care is 50 percent of usual, customary, and reasonable charges up to a $25 benefit for each of fifty visits per year.[18]

Life Insurance

Life insurance was the first form of insurance offered to workers by employers. Although some firms provide a flat amount for all workers, the majority of firms pay a multiple of the employee's salary. For example, the multiple at Intel is 2, so a $30,000-a-year worker has $60,000 of coverage. Unlike health insurance, employer-provided life insurance is not typically extended to the worker's family members. Most human resource managers and benefits experts reason that life insurance is to protect the family from the loss of the worker's income. Since group life insurance is considerably cheaper than most private policies, supplemental life policies also may be available. These policies allow employees to increase their coverage or to include dependents. However, the employees must pay the premiums.

Disability Insurance

What happens when an employee is disabled and unable to work? Short-term disabilities usually are handled through the company's time-off benefits and *accident and sickness* policies, which usually provide a partial replacement of wages or salaries for up to six months or a year. But if the worker is unable to work for a prolonged time, most companies provide some form of *long-term disability insurance* (LTD). LTD policies generally have a long waiting period (usually six months). They pay the employee only a fraction (usually 50 to 60 percent) of their wages or salaries and usually end within a few years unless the insured is unable to perform any type of work. All these features protect the worker and hold down employer costs, without encouraging malingerers. In one study of 366 firms, 90 percent offer LTD coverage and three-quarters offer short-term disability plans.[19] In Canada, Britain, and Scandinavian countries, long-term disability is largely provided by local or national governments.[20] At Intel, there is a 180-day wait, after which the employee receives 65 percent of his or her base monthly earnings up to a maximum of $4,000 a month. The payment is reduced by any social security or workers' compensation payments.

Cost-saving measures may not discriminate against protected classes under equal employment laws. For example, disability payments must be extended to

Foreign approaches

15. BENEFITS AND SERVICES

pregnant women if such payments are made to other workers for non-job-related disabilities. Human resource departments that discriminate against pregnant women in their disability policies (or in medical benefits) may be in violation of equal employment laws.[21]

Other Related Benefits

The economies of group plans have led a few companies to provide a variety of other insurance programs. Some employers offer group home owners' and group automobile insurance. Since individual rates vary widely, and not all employees have houses or cars, employers seldom contribute to the cost of these premiums. However, Procter & Gamble, Honeywell, Control Data, and others do provide financial assistance to employees who adopt children.[22]

Legal insurance

Another benefit that is likely to become more widespread is group *legal insurance*. Under these plans employees gain access to low-cost legal aid. It is like group medical programs, which pool prepaid amounts, allowing members to obtain legal assistance at rates that might not be readily available to individuals. Human resource departments usually control costs by maximum dollar limits on total services received per year or by a dollar limit on each type of legal service, such as selling a house, handling a divorce, or drawing up a will. At present, unions are encouraging these plans through their negotiations with employers.[23]

EMPLOYEE SECURITY BENEFITS

In addition to insurance, there are noninsurance benefits that enhance employee security. These benefits seek to ensure an income before and after retirement.

Employment Income Security

Severance pay

Discharges or layoffs hold potentially severe economic consequences for an employee. They can be cushioned by employer-provided benefits. *Severance pay benefits entitle the worker to a lump-sum payment at the time of separation from the company.* The payment is either a flat amount equal to a few weeks' pay or a graduated amount based on salary and length of service with the employer. For top executives, the figure can exceed six months' or a year's pay. Personnel policies may limit severance pay to situations where the employee leaves involuntarily and has done nothing wrong, such as in the case of a layoff, plant closing, or job elimination caused by a merger.

When International Harvester restructured itself to become Navistar, several managers were asked to sell or liquidate parts of the firm that included

472   IV. COMPENSATION AND PROTECTION

International Harvester

their jobs. They were compensated with employment contracts guaranteeing them up to two years' salary and benefits.[24]

Fearful that a hostile takeover attempt might cause valued executives to leave rather than fight the takeover, many companies have created "golden parachutes." *Golden parachutes* are agreements by the company to compensate executives with bonuses and benefits if they should be displaced by a merger or acquisition. The agreements allow executives to focus on their duties with little concern about financial security or the need to search for new jobs as soon as merger talks begin. Often these "parachutes" bestow significant cash bonuses on the senior managers, but seldom make provisions for others in the organization. An exception to this trend (and an attempt to make the company less attractive to raiders) comes from the second largest producer of office furniture manufacturers, Herman Miller, Inc.

Golden parachutes

Herman Miller, Inc.

On the basis of the employees' years of continuous, full-time employment with the company, each worker (regardless of title or position) would be compensated if harmed within two years of a takeover. If a worker's job is eliminated, or the compensation package (salary and benefits) is reduced, or working conditions are changed, the worker will be eligible for a "silver parachute."

Compensation must be paid within 10 days of termination and in amounts equal to 2.5 times the total compensation during the previous 12 months for employees who have been employed for more than five years. Employees with shorter service receive a smaller compensation package.[25]

Of the 325 firms surveyed in one study, 84.6 percent have severance pay policies for some or all of their employees. Almost half of these firms (47.9 percent) provide employees outplacement assistance—that is, help in finding other jobs. The frequency of severance pay and outplacement help was found to be more common among larger firms.[26]

Layoffs overseas

In Europe, layoffs are less common because of severance requirements and legislation. By contrast, Japan's largest firms typically offer lifetime employment (usually for adult males only) and historically steady growth to avoid layoffs.

Layoffs also may be eased by accrued vacation pay. A few companies go so far as to provide a *guaranteed annual wage* (GAW). These plans ensure that the worker receives a minimum amount of work or pay. For example, employees may be promised a minimum of 1,500 hours of work or pay a year (compared with the "normal" 52 40-hour weeks for a total of 2,080 hours). Some employers guarantee 30 hours per week. Even on layoff, the employees draw some income. Lincoln Electric has such a plan, for example.

SUB

The auto industry is a leader in another benefit: *supplemental unemployment benefits* (SUB). When employees are out of work, state unemployment benefits

15. BENEFITS AND SERVICES

are supplemented by the employer from moneys previously paid to the SUB fund. This ensures covered employees of an income almost equal to their previous earnings for as long as the SUB fund remains solvent. Take the case of Alfredo Sedona:

> Alfredo Sedona was put on indefinite layoff. Under the SUB plan, he is entitled to 95 percent of his previous take-home pay, less $12.50 that would otherwise go for commuting, lunches, and other work-related expenses. He typically took home $380 a week; therefore he will get $348.50; [($380 x .95) - $12.50]. Since the state unemployment benefits will pay Alfredo $98.50 a week, the SUB plan will pay him $250 a week ($348.50 - 98.50 = $250). Alfredo will get $348.50 until the SUB fund is depleted, he finds another job, or he is called back to work.

Although SUB plans are expensive, a very high percentage of workers are available for work when recalled. This high return rate occurs because few employees find jobs that pay as much as they receive while on layoff. One societal drawback is that these unemployed workers have little incentive to find other work, and so they may continue to draw public unemployment funds for a longer period of time than do unemployed workers who have no access to a SUB plan.

Retirement Security

Retirement plans originally were designed to reward long-service employees. Through employer generosity and union pressures, retirement plans have grown in scope and in coverage.

Key questions in retirement

Developing a retirement plan. When a human resource department develops a retirement plan, several critical questions must be answered. One concern is: Who shall pay for it? In a *noncontributory plan*, the employer pays the entire amount. *Contributory plans* require both the employee and the employer to contribute. Another question is: When will the pension rights vest? *Vesting* gives a worker the right to pension benefits even if he or she leaves the company. Pension rights usually vest after several years of service. If an employee leaves before pension benefits are vested, the worker has no rights except to regain his or her contributions to the plan. Some pensions have *portability clauses*, which allow accumulated pension rights to be transferred to another employer.

A third question is: How will the firm meet its financial obligations? Some companies pay pensions out of current income when employees retire. This is called an *unfunded plan. Funded plans* require the employer to accumulate moneys in advance so that the employer's contribution plus interest will cover the pension obligation.

474   IV. COMPENSATION AND PROTECTION

How much monies should be put aside by the employer depend on whether the pension is a defined contribution or a defined benefit plan. With a *defined contribution* plan, the employer agrees to contribute a specific amount into an account. Often this amount is a percentage of the employee's pay. A *defined benefit* plan is more complicated. This plan obligates the employer to pay the retiree a specific amount at retirement. For example, the employer may agree to calculate an employee's average salary for the last five years. Then the employee is paid two percent of that salary for each year he or she worked for the firm. Thus, the annual retirement income for an employee who had been employed for 20 years would be 40 percent (20 years times 2%) of his or her average annual pay during the last five years of work. Since retirement may be many years away for some employees, the retirement income obligations of the firm are difficult to calculate accurately. As a result, overfunding or underfunding of the company's pension obligations is more likely to occur under a defined benefit program.

Another important question is: Will the plan be trusted or insured? The *trusted plan* calls for all monies to be deposited into a trust fund, usually in a bank. The bank manages and protects the funds; it does not guarantee that the employer's pension liabilities will be met. With an *insured plan*, the pension monies are used to buy employee annuities from an insurer. Each annuity represents an insurance company's pledge to pay the worker a given amount per month upon retirement.

Two significant problems have developed in the administration of pension plans. First, some employers go out of business, leaving the pension plan unfunded or only partially funded. Second, some companies minimize their pension costs by having very long vesting periods. Thus an employee who quits or is fired often has no pension rights. Since both of these problems may impose hardships on employees and on the nation's welfare burden, Congress passed the *Employee Retirement Income Security Act* of 1974 (ERISA).[27]

ERISA

ERISA. ERISA, and the *Tax Reform Act* of 1986, impose restrictions on the operation of pension plans. As can be seen by Figure 15-2, this pension reform law sets forth participation, vesting, and funding requirements. To protect workers in the event of employer insolvency, employers are required to participate in a federal insurance program.

The insurance aspect of ERISA provides employees with a guarantee of a pension even if the employer should go out of business before the pension plan is fully funded. But ERISA is more than just an insurance plan. It requires employers to have their plans funded and vested. Moreover, it requires trustees to apply the "prudent man" rule when investing pension funds and to report annually on the plan's operations.[28] For example, the fiduciary standards set by ERISA prohibit the pension plan from investing in stock or real estate above a fixed level. When the Grumman Corporation put more than 10 percent of its pension fund assets into its own stock to avoid a takeover by the LTV Corporation, the U.S. Department of Labor successfully sued Grumman for violating ERISA.

Portability

Portability is also encouraged by the act. *Portability* allows the pension credits earned in one employer's retirement plan to be transferred into another retire-

15. BENEFITS AND SERVICES 475

3 primary things to know ↓

Figure 15-2

Highlights of the Pension Reform Act, as Amended

	MAJOR PROVISIONS
PARTICIPATION	Prohibits plans from requiring service eligibility over 1 year; 2 years of eligibility is permitted if plan vests 100 percent immediately.
VESTING	Plan vesting provision must be: 1. 100 percent vested after 5 years of service 2. 20 percent vested after 3 years of service, increasing yearly by 20 percent until fully vested in a total of 7 years.
FUNDING	The plan must fund current year's benefit accruals and must amortize any unfunded costs over 30 years (40 years for existing plans and multi-employer plans).
FIDUCIARY STANDARDS	Establishes the "prudent man" rule as the basic standard of conduct, outlaws various transactions between parties-in-interest, and prohibits investment of more than 10 percent of fund assets in employer securities or real estate.
REPORTING AND DISCLOSURE	Requires the plan to provide participants with a comprehensive booklet describing pension plan provisions and to report annually to the Secretary of Labor on numerous operating and financial details of the plan.
PLAN TERMINATION INSURANCE	Creates a federal insurance organization to protect beneficiaries against loss of vested pension on plan termination where assets are inadequate.
PORTABILITY	Encourages some voluntary portability by allowing a worker, if the employer agrees to it, to transfer his or her pension rights tax free from one employer pension fund to another by establishing a tax free individual retirement account.
JOINT AND SURVIVORSHIP OPTION	Unless a married worker specifically requests the plan's normal retirement benefit, the worker is required to receive a pension payable for his or her lifetime and continuing in 50 percent of that amount to the spouse if the spouse survives the employee. The worker's normal retirement benefit may be actuarially reduced to pay for the cost of this provision.

Source: Adapted from *The American Federationist,* October 1975, p. 19 (used by permission); Employee Retirement Income Security Act of 1974; and the 1986 Tax Reform Act.

---

ment plan when the worker changes companies. About 10 million, mostly unionized, employees have portability in their pension plans.

Lockheed

In the defense contracting industry, for example, engineers change employers when the government contracts they are working on come to an end. As a result, many of them never stay with an employer long enough to earn a vested pension. Lockheed Engineering & Management Services Company recognized this problem and modified its pension plan to make it a more attractive recruiting tool. Their retirement program now offers immediate vesting once an employee joins the plan, and it allows portability when the employee leaves.[29]

Early Retirement. As retirement plans mature, companies tend to liberalize them. Increasingly, this has meant early retirement provisions, which allow workers to retire before the traditional retirement age of 65.[30] Benefits are normally reduced for early retirement because the employee draws benefits longer, and the employer has less time to fund its contribution. Some pensions—those used by the military, for example—pay the retiree an amount based on years of service, regardless of age. When economic conditions require a layoff, the company may encourage senior employees to retire early by reducing or eliminating the penalty for early retirement. This lowers the employer's staffing costs in a voluntary manner and explains why the average retirement age has declined to 62. Since this benefit is often based on the employee's age, age discrimination suits may result if these early retirement programs are not properly designed and implemented.[31]

Du Pont

Du Pont, in an attempt to reduce its employment levels, used an early retirement option as part of its first companywide employee-reduction program. The result was that 11,200 employees, or about 8 percent of its work force, departed.[32]

As the number of new entrants into the work force decreases and the number of retirees increases after the turn of the century, early retirement policies may fade away. As two researchers observe:

> Currently, human resource policies in many organizations encourage early retirement. Senior employees have been offered early retirement as an alternative to layoffs . . . as an alternative to possible termination . . . and . . . as a way to unclog career channels and create affirmative action promotion opportunities.
>
> Looking toward the future, however, the policy emphasis on early retirement may prove quite shortsighted. With changing workforce demographics, organizations are likely to encounter critical shortages among technical, professional, and managerial personnel.[33]

Retirement counseling. As part of the retirement program, some employers offer preretirement and postretirement counseling. The primary purpose of *preretirement counseling* is to encourage an employee to plan for retirement. The sooner counseling occurs, the more able the worker is to prepare emotionally and financially. These sessions also are used to explain the nature of the employee's retirement program and to indicate the probable adjustments a retiree may face.[34] Ultimately, preretirement counseling encourages employees to grapple with such questions as, "How much money do I need to retire?" and "How will I arrange to have a sufficient retirement income?"

An important part of preretirement planning is to consider the spouse. ERISA allows survivorship options, enabling the surviving spouse to receive 50 percent

15. BENEFITS AND SERVICES

REA

of the worker's pension. The prevalence of divorce left some spouses without any pension rights until Congress passed the *Retirement Equity Act* (REA) of 1984. This act allows divorce settlements to include court orders called *qualified domestic relations orders* (QDRO). These court orders require the pension plan administrator to reduce an employee's retirement benefits by a specified amount. This amount then goes to the divorced spouse when the worker retires. The result is to help assure that long-married spouses can receive some share of pension benefits as part of their divorce settlements.[35]

Postretirement counseling is designed to ease the transition from worker to retiree. The retiree is made aware of community and company programs for retired people. Retired employees of Mountain Bell Telephone Company, for example, can join an organization of other retired telephone workers. This type of association provides social contacts, community projects, and recreational opportunities.[36]

TIME-OFF BENEFITS

Time-off benefits include breaks, sick days, holidays and vacations, and leaves of absence.

1. On-the-Job Breaks

Some of the most common forms of time-off benefits are those which occur during working hours. Examples include rest breaks, meal breaks, and wash-up time. A rest from the physical and mental effort of a job may renew employee energy and increase productivity. The major problem for personnel and line managers is the tendency of employees to stretch these time-off periods.

> When one manager was confronted by a supervisor with the problem of stretched breaks, she suggested a simple solution. Each employee was assigned a specific break time—from 9:15 to 9:30 a.m. or 9:30 to 9:45 a.m., for example—but could not leave for break until the preceding employee returned. Since each clerk was anxious to go on break, the peer group policed the length of breaks and the stretched breaks ended.

2. Sick Days and Well Pay   *most abused.*

Some absences from work are unavoidable. Today, most companies pay workers when they are absent for medical reasons by granting a limited number of sick days per year. Unfortunately, this fringe benefit is often abused when workers take the attitude that these are simply extra days off. If the personnel policy prohibits employees from crediting unused sick leave to next year's account, absences increase near the end of the year.[37] To minimize abuses, some

478   IV. COMPENSATION AND PROTECTION

Well pay

companies require medical verifications of illness or pay employees for unused sick leave. Payment for unused sick leave is sometimes called *well pay*, which may serve as an incentive for attendance. In Sweden, however, employees receive sick pay reimbursements of 90 percent of their salaries directly from the government, giving companies less incentive to reduce absenteeism than if the employer paid for sick days. This policy may explain why the average Swedish worker takes 27 sick days per year.[00]

Personal leave days

A few firms avoid the abuse question by granting *personal leave days*, as Intel does, for example. This approach allows an employee to skip work for any reason and get paid, up to a specified number of days per year. *Sick leave banks* allow employees to "borrow" extra days above the specified number when they use up their individual allocations. Then, when they earn additional days off, the borrowed days are repaid to the sick leave bank.

3. Holidays and Vacations

The median company grants 10 paid holidays per year.[39] Like sick days, however, this benefit is subject to abuse. Employees sometimes try to stretch the holiday by missing the workday before or after it. Personnel policies that require attendance the day before and after the holiday as a condition of holiday pay lessen this problem. Other firms ignore this issue of "stretched holidays" by using the personal leave days concept instead of holidays or sick days. Paterson Food in the United Kingdom grants "working holidays" that pay employees to visit vendors as a bonus for long service. Other companies provide *contingent time off* in the form of paid "holidays" to workers who meet productivity or other goals.[40]

Stretched holidays

Vacations usually are based on the employee's length of service—for example, one week for one year of service, two weeks for two years of service, three weeks for five or ten years of employment, and so on. Policies for vacations vary widely. Some companies allow employees to use vacation days a few at a time. Other companies insist that the workers take the vacation all at once. A few employers actually close down during designated periods and require vacations to be taken during that time. (This "plant shutdown" approach is sometimes required to perform major maintenance on equipment.) Still other companies completely negate the reason for vacations by allowing employees to work and receive vacation pay as a bonus.

Intel created a sabbatical leave policy that is one of the more unusual industrial time-off benefits. It gives permanent U.S. and Canadian employees eight weeks off with full pay after seven years of service. And with executive staff management approval, employees can get up to six months leave with pay for public service, teaching, or exceptional educational opportunities.

Leaves of Absence

Leaves of absence are often granted for pregnancy, extended illness, accidents, summer military camps, military reservists called to active duty, jury duty, funeral services, and other reasons specified in a company's personnel policies. Extended leaves are normally without pay. Shorter absences—especially for jury duty or for funerals of close relatives—are often with pay. Under the *Pregnancy Discrimination Act* of 1978, employers may not discriminate against pregnant women by treating pregnancy leave differently from other types of leaves of absence. AT&T, for example, grants one-year unpaid leaves to employees for the care of infants or ill dependents.[41] A growing number of companies are creating "Mommy" and "Daddy" career tracks that grant leaves or reductions in the workweek to accommodate new mothers and fathers who want to actively participate in childrearing. In Sweden and other countries, maternity and paternity leaves are mandated by law.

Pregnancy discrimination

WORK SCHEDULING BENEFITS

The length of the typical workweek has declined significantly since the early days of the industrial revolution, as illustrated by Figure 15-3. The norm of a five-day forty-hour workweek remained relatively unchanged from the 1930s to the early 1970s. During the 1970s, however, several new approaches to work scheduling gained popularity: the shorter workweek, flextime, and job sharing.[42]

Shorter Workweeks

A *shorter workweek* compresses 40 hours of work into less than five full days. Some plans even shorten the workweek to less than 40 hours, with a growing number of companies moving to 37.5 or even 35 hours per five-day week. One version has been 40 hours of work compressed into four days. This version can present child-care problems for working parents and fatigue in physically demanding jobs.

Flextime

The introduction from Europe of *flextime* may have contributed to the slower growth of four-day weeks.[43] Flextime abolishes rigid starting and ending times for the workday. Instead, employees are allowed to report to work and end work at any time during a range of hours each day, as long as they work 40 hours (or whatever is defined as a full-time workweek). For example, starting time may be from 7 A.M. to 9 A.M. with all employees expected to work the *core hours* of 9 A.M. to 3 P.M. and work, say, 40 hours each week.

The outcome of a flextime program, however, depends upon the nature of the firm's operations. For example, the major disadvantage of flextime is the difficulty in meeting minimum staffing needs early and late in the day. Assembly-line

Core hours

480   IV. COMPENSATION AND PROTECTION

Figure 15-3

A Typical Work Schedule before the Civil War

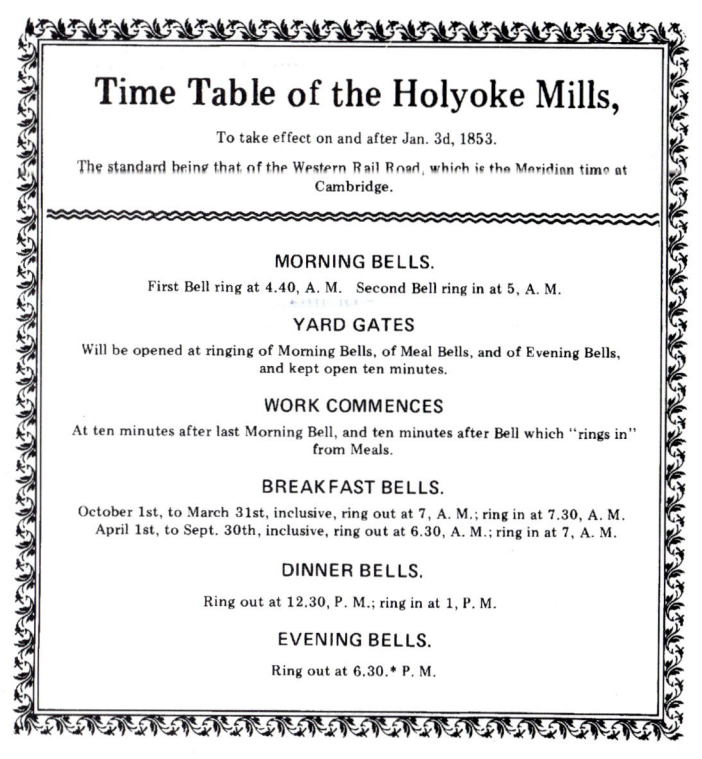

Time Table of the Holyoke Mills,

To take effect on and after Jan. 3d, 1853.

The standard being that of the Western Rail Road, which is the Meridian time at Cambridge.

MORNING BELLS.
First Bell ring at 4.40, A. M.   Second Bell ring in at 5, A. M.

YARD GATES
Will be opened at ringing of Morning Bells, of Meal Bells, and of Evening Bells, and kept open ten minutes.

WORK COMMENCES
At ten minutes after last Morning Bell, and ten minutes after Bell which "rings in" from Meals.

BREAKFAST BELLS.
October 1st, to March 31st, inclusive, ring out at 7, A. M.; ring in at 7.30, A. M.
April 1st, to Sept. 30th, inclusive, ring out at 6.30, A. M.; ring in at 7, A. M.

DINNER BELLS.
Ring out at 12.30, P. M.; ring in at 1, P. M.

EVENING BELLS.
Ring out at 6.30.* P. M.

Source: *Labor's Long, Hard Road,* Air Line Employees Association, International, p.4. Used by permission.

and customer service operations find this problem especially significant. But in most clerical operations, some users have reported noteworthy successes. For example, Public Law 97-221 allows 325,000 federal employees to work longer hours on certain days in order to have other days, or partial days, off.[44]

Job Sharing

A third approach to employee scheduling that has gained popularity is job sharing. *Job sharing* involves one or more employees doing the same job but working different hours, days, or even weeks. Most commonly, two people handle the duties of one full-time job.

Karen and Bob Rosen both taught English at Lincoln High School. After Karen had her first child one summer, Karen, Bob, and their principal agreed

15. BENEFITS AND SERVICES

to a job-sharing arrangement. Bob taught three classes of English literature and composition in the morning. He then drove home and gave Karen the car, and she returned to school and taught three English classes in the afternoon. The school benefited because teachers normally had five classes and a planning period. With job sharing, the school received six classes of English instruction. Bob and Karen also were able to share in raising their child with neither of them completely giving up his or her career.

The major advantage claimed for job sharing is increased productivity. Problems arise, however, from the increased administrative burden associated with two employees doing the job of one. Another problem is benefits. Personnel specialists are forced to decide whether job sharers should be given benefits equal to those of other employees or whether the benefits should be scaled down in proportion to the employee's hours. Most state unemployment offices will not scale down unemployment benefits when job sharers are put on layoff status; instead, job sharers simply are considered ineligible for unemployment compensation. In Europe, unions are lobbying for full benefits for part-timers as part of the current effort to standardize employment practices in the European Common Market.[45]

EMPLOYEE SERVICES

Some companies go beyond pay and traditional benefits and provide services for their employees. The most common ones are educational, financial, and social programs.

Educational Assistance

Tuition refund programs are among the more common employer services, with 97 percent of the 617 companies in one survey reporting this assistance.[46] These programs partially or completely reimburse employees for furthering their education but may be limited to courses that are related to the employee's job. Some companies make the amount of reimbursement contingent upon grades. Beckman Instruments, Inc., for example, refunds 100 percent of the college tuition for an A or a B, 50 percent for a C, and nothing for grades of D or F. In the future, more companies may follow the lead of Kimberly-Clark Corporation:

Kimberly-Clark

Kimberly-Clark created an educational savings account for employees and their dependents. The company gives employees credits for each year of service. Then, when an employee or dependent wants to go to college, he or she can be reimbursed partially from the educational savings account established by the company.

IV. COMPENSATION AND PROTECTION

Financial Services

Probably the oldest service is the employee discount plan. These programs—common among retail stores and consumer goods manufacturers—allow workers to buy products from the company at a discount. For example, employees of Broadway Department Stores may buy clothes from the store at a 10 percent discount.

Credit unions are another well-established employee service. The interest collected on loans and investments is distributed to members in the form of dividends. The dividends (interest payments) are allocated in proportion to the amount employees have in their share (savings) account. The lower interest rate on loans, the higher interest on deposits, and the payroll deductions are the major employee advantages.

Stock purchase programs enable employees to buy company stock—usually through payroll deductions. In some programs, employee outlays may be matched by company contributions, or the stock may be purchased by employees at a discount from its market value. At Intel, for example, employees in the purchase plan can buy company stock at 85 percent of its market price.

ESOPs

An *employee stock option plan* (ESOP) enables the employer to raise money and also encourages employee ownership of stock. The employer sells a block of stock to an employee group, which uses it as collateral for a loan. The proceeds from the loan then repay the company for the stock. The dividends and purchases of stock by employees from the ESOP retire the loan. Employees end up with stock in the company and share in its prosperity. Of course, if the company faces hard times, the employees may find that their jobs *and* their investments are at risk.[47]

Social Services

EAPs

A wide range of social services is provided by employers. At one extreme are simple interest groups such as bowling leagues and baseball teams. At the other extreme are comprehensive *employee assistance programs* (EAPs) designed to help employees with personal problems.[48] The introduction of Xerox's booklet about its employee assistance program states:

Xerox

The Xerox Employee Assistance Program (XEAP) is a benefit for employees, retirees and their families. Its purpose is to help people suffering from alcohol or drug misuse, as well as other emotional or family problems.

In the home, these problems surface as marital discord, parent/child conflict and financial troubles. If left unchecked, they can devastate a family.

On the job, these problems can also be serious and costly. They impair work relationships, erode individual job performance and result in the loss of valuable work time.[49]

15. BENEFITS AND SERVICES

The XEAP program is available to employees, retirees, and their families. It entitles users to two free diagnostic visits for problems related to substance abuse, family, or emotional issues. The company pays 80 percent of the first eight outpatient therapy sessions related to drug or alcohol problems. Other medical or therapy needs are covered through Xerox's medical plan.

The XEAP is not limited to drug and alcohol problems. Individual emotional problems and problems related to marriage, children, and finances also are covered.

Access to the program is provided through referral by the personnel department or by calling a toll-free number given to all employees. To assure confidentiality, the use of the XEAP and the nature of the employee's problem do not become part of the employee's records. In fact, Xerox contracts with another organization, Family Service America, to provide counseling and referral.[50]

Even though EAPs are not a universal benefit, 79 percent of a 409-company survey report providing them.[51] They exist because human resource managers and executives realize that workers' problems affect their performance. Xerox's program is typical of those found in major corporations, although many early EAPs began as alcohol (and then drug) rehabilitation programs.

General Motors

General Motors Corporation evaluated the job performance of 71 alcoholic employees who had been treated in an alcoholic rehabilitation program. The results of a several-month-long experiment showed more than an 85 percent decline in time lost by employees and a 72 percent reduction in accident and sickness benefits claims.[52] Whether these savings repaid the company's outlays was not reported. However, this limited study indicates that positive benefits accrue to employers who sponsor such programs either separately or as part of a comprehensive employee assistance plan.

Du Pont and child care

Child care. Child care is fast becoming an important benefit. During the 1990s, 18 million working mothers will be in the work force. More than 50 percent of women who have children during their careers are returning to work within one year. The need is obvious. Some employers, like the American Bankers Insurance Company, provide on-site child care. Other companies subsidize off-site providers, hoping to avoid the liability and ill feelings should an accident on company property harm an employee's child (as well as avoiding the cost of providing facilities that meet state and local standards). Du Pont, for example, spent half a million dollars renovating a building and gave it to the local YMCA to become a child-care center for their employees and the public.[53] Since child-care expenses average 10 percent of a family's gross income, employer-provided child care appears to offer strong recruiting and retention value.

Intermedics, Inc., a Texas manufacturer of heart pacemakers, reported a 23 percent drop in turnover and approximately a 2 percent decline in absenteeism since offering its heavily subsidized child care benefit.[54]

Elder care.

Elder care. Elderly parents present a special problem because of the limited day-care options faced by their working children. As *Fortune* magazine concludes, ". . . elder care could soon replace child care as the hottest employee benefit."[55] Researchers at the University of Bridgeport's Center for the Study of Aging have found that almost a fourth of employees age 40 and over provide some form of elder care, and half of them are the chief providers.[56] Although EAPs may provide referrals to locate sources of day care, a growing number of employees are part of a "sandwich" generation, having responsibility for both children and aging parents.

Relocation programs. Relocation programs are the support in dollars or services that a company provides to its transferred or new employees. At a minimum, this benefit includes payment for moving expenses. Some employees receive fully paid house-hunting trips with their spouses to the new location before the move, temporary living expenses, subsidized home mortgages, placement assistance for working spouses, and even family counseling to reduce the stress of the move. A transferred employee also may be able to sell his or her home to the employer for the appraised value. As a result, the half-million employees relocated annually cost employers an average of $37,000 per home-owning family.[57] Of particular difficulty to human resource professionals are dual-career families, which contribute to the three out of eight employees who reject transfer offers.[58] Not only are married employees with career-oriented spouses less likely to move, but when they do, the human resource department is often called upon to help the spouse find a job. And, when international transfers are undertaken, relocation expenses increase—fueled by language training, bonuses, cost-of-living and tax-equalization adjustments, educational allowances, and other outlays associated with international relocations.[59]

Social service leave programs. Social service leave programs are not widespread, but such leading organizations as IBM, Xerox, and others allow fully paid leaves to employees who wish to work full-time in a community program.

At Xerox, employees are loaned out at full salary and benefits to nonprofit organizations. Employees initiate proposals to the community and the Employee Programs manager. The proposal outlines the employee's project,

Xerox

relevant skills, a description of the organization, and a letter of support from the sponsoring organization. Leaves may last from one to 12 months. In one year, the review committee received about 60 applications to which it allocated a total of 264 months of leave. This program costs Xerox $300,000 to $350,000 each year.[60]

ADMINISTRATION OF BENEFITS AND SERVICES

A serious shortcoming of human resource management has been poor administration of indirect compensation. Even in otherwise well-managed departments, benefits and services have grown in a haphazard manner. These costly supplements have been added in response to social trends, union demands, employee pressures, and management wishes, and so human resource departments have seldom established objectives, systematic plans, and standards to determine the appropriateness of the programs. This patchwork of benefits and services has caused several problems.

Problems in Administration

The central problem in indirect compensation is a lack of employee participation. Once a fringe benefit program is designed by the company (and labor union, if there is one), employees have little discretion. For example, the same pension and maternity benefits usually are granted to all workers. Younger employees see pensions as distant and largely irrelevant; older workers feel that maternity benefits are unneeded. The uniformity of benefits fails to recognize work force diversity. Admittedly, uniformity leads to administrative and actuarial economies; but when employees receive benefits they neither want nor need, these economies are questionable.

Since employees have little choice in their benefit packages, most workers are unaware of all the benefits to which they are entitled. As three researchers at the University of Arizona conclude after studying employee valuation of medical insurance:

Research summary

One hundred eighty-two University of Arizona employees each participated in one of two field studies of the valuation of fringe benefits. Findings include: (*a*) a lack of employee knowledge regarding employer cost and market value of the studied benefit, and (*b*) significant undervaluation of the benefit by employees. These findings are consistent with the hypothesis that employee benefit valuations anchor on employee contributions [not employer costs].[60]

This lack of knowledge often causes employees to request more benefits to meet their needs. For example, older workers may want improved retirement plans, while younger workers seek improved insurance coverage for dependents. The result is often a proliferation of benefits and increased employer costs. And perhaps even worse, employee confusion can lead to complaints and dissatisfaction about their fringe benefit packages, particularly, as the University of Arizona researchers observe, when employees do not have to contribute financially.

Traditional Remedies

The traditional remedy to benefit problems has been to increase employee awareness, usually through publicizing employee benefits.[61] This publicity starts with orientation sessions and employee handbooks. Company newspapers, special mailings, employee meetings, and bulletin-board announcements are used to further publicize the benefit package.

Mass Mutual

The Massachusetts Mutual Life Insurance Company has developed an interesting variation of these traditional approaches. With the consent of the employer, this insurer evaluates the benefits each employee receives and provides a booklet that summarizes this information. A representative of the insurer explains the booklet and indicates gaps in the employee's coverage (with the object of selling the worker any needed insurance).

Publicizing benefits and services only attacks the symptoms of the problem: employee disinterest and growing costs. Moreover, this reactive approach adds to the costs of administration through increased "advertising" expenses. As a result, some employers have reduced their contributions or benefits, especially in the area of health care. Though cost reductions follow, employee participation and understanding remain limited, and cuts can lead to reduced employee morale. In fact, during recent years, many strikes by unions have been attempts to reduce these cuts. A more proactive approach has been the growing use of flexible benefits.

Cafeteria Benefits: A Proactive Solution

Flex benefits

Cafeteria benefits, or flexible benefit programs, allow employees to select benefits and services that match their individual needs. Workers are provided a benefit and services account with a specified number of dollars in it. With the money from this account, employees choose and "purchase" specific benefits from among those offered by the employer. (To ensure minimum coverage, some flex-plans require all employees to take a set of "core benefits," such as life and health insurance.) The types and prices of benefits are provided to each worker in the form of a computer printout. This cost sheet also describes each benefit. From this cost sheet, employees elect their package of benefits and services for the coming year, as illustrated in Figure 15-4.

Figure 15-4 indicates how two different workers might spend the $8,600 the company grants each employee. Workers A and B elect two different sets of

Figure 15-4

Hypothetical Benefit Selection by Two Different Workers

	WORKER A Age 27, female, married with one child. Husband in graduate school.		WORKER B Age 56, male, married with two grown and married children. Wife does not work.
		Health insurance:	
	$ 345	Maternity	0
	2435	$100 deductible	0
	0	$1000 deductible	$2025
		Life insurance:	
	100	$20,000 for worker	100
	150	$10,000 for spouse	0
	1600	Vacations	1900
	700	Holidays	900
	1200	Pension plan	2270
	0	Jury duty pay	0
	200	Disability insurance	200
	<u>1870</u>	Sick pay	<u>1205</u>
	$8600	Total	$8600

benefits because their personal situations differ dramatically. Worker A is a young parent who is supporting a family and her husband. If she were to have another child or if her family had some other health-related expense, it might seriously affect their plans, and so she has elected to be well insured for pregnancy and health costs. Worker B can more easily afford unexpected medical expenses, and so he bought health insurance with a larger deductible and allocated fewer dollars for sick pay. Instead, he put a large portion of his benefit monies into the company pension plan.

Although this approach creates additional administrative costs and an obligation for the human resource department to advise employees, advantages exists. The main advantage is employee participation. Through participation, workers understand exactly what benefits the employer is offering and can better match their benefits with their needs.[62]

Beyond the wide range of benefits and services described in this chapter, employers are required to provide social security, workers' compensation, and a workplace free from recognizable safety and health hazards. These legally imposed benefits and services are described in Chapter 16, which concludes this part of the book.

SUMMARY

EMPLOYEE BENEFITS and services are the fastest-growing component of compensation. Employers have sought to expand them to discourage labor unrest, respond to employee pressures, and remain competitive in the labor market. Employees have desired to obtain benefits and services through their employer because of the low costs, tax advantages, and inflation protection they provide.

Benefits are classified into four major types: insurance, security, time-off, and scheduling benefits. Services include educational, financial, and social programs. This diversity contributes to several serious administrative problems. The most significant problem is the orientation of managers and personnel specialists toward cost savings. In pursuit of administrative and actuarial economies, most companies and unions do not allow individualized benefit packages in indirect compensation programs, although flexible benefits are gaining popularity.

Terms for Review

- Adverse selection
- Coinsurance clause
- Self-funding
- Health maintenance organizations (HMOs)
- Long-term disability insurance (LTD)
- Legal insurance
- Severance pay
- Golden parachutes
- Guaranteed annual wage (GAW)
- Supplemental unemployment benefits (SUB)
- Contributory plans
- Vesting
- Indirect compensation
- Portability clauses
- Employee Assistance Programs (EAPs)
- Employee Retirement Income Security Act (ERISA)
- Well pay
- Personal leave days
- Shorter workweek
- Flextime
- Cafeteria benefit programs

Review and Discussion Questions

1. What factors have contributed to the rapid growth of fringe benefits as a percentage of most employers' total payroll costs?

2. Given that health and disability insurance costs are some of the fastest-growing expenses for most employers, what ideas do you have to slow the growth in these costs?

3. Suppose you were requested to explain why employees are better off receiving pay and benefits rather than just getting larger paychecks that include the monetary value of benefits. What arguments would you use?

4. Briefly describe the benefits that an organization might give employees to provide them with greater financial security.

5. Why was the Employee Retirement Income Security Act needed? What are its major provisions?

6. For each of the following groups of employees, what types of problems are likely to occur if a company goes from a five-day 40-hour week to a four-day 40-hour week: (*a*) working mothers, (*b*) laborers, (*c*) assembly-line workers?

7. A growing number of employees are reluctant to accept geographic transfers. What factors contribute to this reluctance? What types of services would a human resource department be likely to provide for a transfer? What additional concerns affect international transfers?

8. If you were asked to increase employee awareness of fringe benefits, what actions would you take without changing the way the company provides benefits? If you could change the entire benefits program, what other methods might you use to increase employee awareness?

INCIDENT 15-1
Flexibility at Steelcase, Inc.

Steelcase, Inc. is a Grand Rapids-based manufacturer of office furniture. While paying modest wages, the company offers extensive bonus opportunities, ranging from piecework to profit-sharing. During the 1980s, Steelcase rethought its approach to employee benefits.

Perhaps the most radical changes were in its approaches to being flexible with employees. About 20 percent of the office employees are on flexible schedules and 40 employees share 20 jobs. Fringe benefits are "cafeteria style," with eight medical and three dental options. Long- and short-term disability plans and life insurance are also offered. Monies left over can be put into tax-free accounts to cover out-of-pocket health care or off-site day care.

Company officials like to stress those advantages to workers. "People are becoming good at choosing what they need, as opposed to us playing God," says James Soule, vice president for human resources. But the cafeteria plan will also save Steelcase a good deal of money. It stipulates that as health-care costs go up, benefit dollars will increase only 80 percent as quickly, leaving employees to fill the 20 percent gap.[63]

1. Since employees can change their benefit election each year, what type of abuses might occur?

2. Even though the flexibility provided to employees appears desirable, what problems might result from having 20 percent of the office workers on flexible work schedules?

3. If Steelcase were to open operations in a foreign country, what parts of the benefit program would need rethinking?

References

1. Fred Luthans and Robert Waldersee, "What Do We Really Know about EAPs?" *Human Resource Management* (Fall 1989), p. 385.

2. Peter W. Stonebraker, "Flexible and Incentive Benefits: A Guide to Program Development," *Compensation Review* (Second Quarter 1985), p. 41.

3. Daniel J.B. Mitchell, "Employee Benefits and the New Economy: A Proposal for Reform," *California Management Review* (Fall 1990), pp. 113–130.

4. J.H. Foegen, "The Creative Flowering of Employee Benefits," *Business Horizons* (May–June 1982), pp. 9–13.

5. *Employee Benefits 1985* (Washington, D.C.: Chamber of Commerce of the United States, 1986), p. 5.

6. Susan J. Duncan, "What's Next on Health Cost Control," *Nation's Business* (Nov. 1982), p. 24. See also "Shifting Health Costs to Employees 'More Expensive,' " *Resource* (June 1984), p. 12.

7. "Perspectives," *Personnel Journal* (July 1989), p. 8.

8. Ronald Bujan, "A Primer on Self-funding Health Care Benefits," *Personnel Administrator* (April 1983), pp. 61–64. There is even a National Wellness Association, which publishes a quarterly newsletter called *Wellness Management*, at the National Wellness Institute of the University of Wisconsin—Stevens Point.

9. "Paying Employees Not To Go To the Doctor," *Business Week* (March 21, 1983), p. 150. See also Thomas N. Fannin and Teresa Ann Fannin, "Coordination of Benefits: Uncovering a Buried Treasure," *Personnel Journal* (May 1983), pp. 386–391.

10. Glenn Kramon, "Four Health Care Vigilantes," *The New York Times*, National Ed. (Sept. 24, 1989), pp. 1, 6.

11. Hilary Stout, "Fitness Center Gets Couch Potatoes Moving," *The Wall Street Journal*, Eastern Ed. (April 12, 1991), p. b1.

12. Leonard Abramson, "Boost to the Bottom Line," *Personnel Administrator* (July 1988), pp. 36–39.

13. "Employer Perceptions of HMOs: Survey Shows Mixed Feelings on Effectiveness As Cost Saving Vehicles," *Medical Benefits* (April 30, 1987), p. 1.

14. Douglas C. Harper, "Control Health Care Costs," *Personnel Journal* (Oct. 1988), pp. 65–70. See also Frederic R. Curtiss, "How Managed Care Works," *Personnel Journal* (July 1989), pp. 38–53; Stuart Gannes, "Strong Medicine for Health Bills," *Fortune* (April 13, 1987), pp. 70–72, 74; "Case Management: Can It Help Cut the Cost of Care?" *Resource* (Nov. 1986), pp. 5–6.

15. Employee Benefits 1985, op. cit., p. 22. See also Jesse Rosenthal, Barry J. Baresi, and Mordachai Soroka, "The New Focus on Vision Care Plans," *Personnel Journal* (August 1986), pp. 136–138.

16. Rosenthal, Baresi, and Soroka, op. cit.

17. Employee Benefits 1985, op. cit., p. 11. See also Carroll Roarty, "Biting Dental Insurance Costs," *Personnel Administrator* (Nov. 1988), pp. 68–71.

18. Sharon George-Perry, "Easing the Costs of Mental Health Benefits," *Personnel Administrator* (Nov. 1988), pp. 62–76. See also John S. Montgomery, "Shrinking Mental Health Care Costs," *Personnel Journal* (May 1988), pp. 86–91.

19. "Most Employers Offer Disability Leaves," *Resource* (Dec. 1988), p. 4.

20. Martin Tolchin, "Other Countries Do Much More for Disabled," *The New York Times*, National Ed. (March 29, 1990), p. 9.

21. Aaron Bernstein, "Business and Pregnancy: Good Will Is No Longer Good Enough," *Business Week* (Feb. 2, 1987), p. 37. See also Nancy Norman and James T. Tedeschi, "Paternity Leave: The Unpopular Benefit Option," *Personnel Administrator* (Feb. 1984), pp. 39–40, 42–43.

22. "More Companies Aid Employees on Adoptions," *The New York Times* (August 18, 1982), pp. c1, c13.

23. Kevin J. O'Donnell and Kathy A. Lawler, "Group Legal Services Plans," *Personnel Administrator* (March 1987), pp. 92–97.

24. Nancy Russell, "Compensation Key in Navistar Restructuring," *Resources* (Dec. 1986), p. 7.

25. "'Silver Parachute' Protects Work Force," *Resource* (Jan. 1987), p. 3.

26. "Most Firms Have Severance Pay Programs," *Resource* (Oct. 1986), p. 2.

27. Alfred Klein, "Why You Can't Afford To Ignore ERISA," *Personnel Journal* (June 1986), pp. 73–83.

28. Stephenie Overman, "Regulating Retirement Fund Plans," *Personnel Administrator* (Nov. 1989), pp. 43–44, 96.

29. "Pension Plans Get More Flexible," *Business Week* (Nov. 8, 1982), pp. 82, 87. See also Larry Lang, "The Impact of Job-hopping on Retirement Benefits," *Personnel Administrator* (Feb. 1984), pp. 55–56, 58–60.

30. The elimination of the age 70 cap in the Age Discrimination in Employment Act (which was effective January 1, 1987) is estimated to have kept 200,000 additional workers on the job who would have otherwise retired. See "Retirement Age Law to Keep 200,000 on Job," *Resource* (Nov. 1986), p. 3. Benefit calculations and pension accruals were also affected. See "Changes in Mandatory Retirement and Benefit Accounts Take Effect," *Personnel Journal* (Jan. 1987), pp. 24–25. See also "Securing Corporate America," *Personnel Administrator* (Oct. 1988), pp. 56–61.

31. "Median Age of Retirement Drops to 62," *Resource* (Jan. 1987), p. 15. See also David R. Godofsky, "Early Retirement Pensions: Penalty or Perk?" *Personnel Journal* (August 1988), pp. 69–73.

32. Alex M. Freedman, "Du Pont Trims Costs, Bureaucracy to Bolster Competitive Position," *The Wall Street Journal*, Eastern ed. (Sept. 25, 1985), p. 1.

33. Benson Rosen and Thomas H. Jerdee, "Retirement Policies for the 21st Century," *Human Resource Management* (Fall 1986), p. 405.

34. Philip H. Turnquist, Walter B. Newsom, and Daniel S. Cochran, "More Than a Gold Watch," *Personnel Administrator* (April 1988), pp. 54–56.

35. Robert J. Schnitzer, "Divorced Spouses Have Won New Rights to Pension Benefits," *Personnel Administrator* (Jan. 1987), pp. 90, 92, 94–95.

36. Eugene H. Seibert and Joanne Seibert, "Retirement: Crises or Opportunity?" *Personnel Administrator* (August 1986), pp. 43–49.

37. Barron H. Harvey, "Two Alternatives to Traditional Sick Leave Programs," *Personnel Journal* (May 1983), pp. 374, 376–378. See also Richard E. Kopelman, George O. Schneller IV, and John J. Silver, Jr., "Parkinson's Law and Absenteeism: A Program to Rein in Sick Leave Costs," *Personnel Administrator* (May 1981), pp. 57–58, 60, 62, 64.

38. Larry Eichel, "Model Welfare State Succumbs to Chill of Economics," *The Miami Herald* (Nov. 2, 1990), p. 19a.

39. "How Many Annual Paid Holidays Do Companies Normally Grant to Employees?" *Resource* (April 1988), p. 3.

40. Larry F. Cluff and D. Neil Ashworth, "Contingent Time Off," *Personnel Administrator* (Dec. 1988), pp. 44–47, 100.

41. "AT&T: All in the Family," *Newsweek* (June 12, 1989), p. 45.

42. Shirley J. Smith, "The Growing Diversity of Work Schedules," *Monthly Labor Review* (Nov. 1986), pp. 7–13.

43. Earl F. Mellor, "Shift Work and Flextime: How Prevalent Are They?" *Monthly Labor Review* (Nov. 1986), pp. 14–21.

44. "New Laws You May Have Missed," *U.S. News & World Report* (Oct. 4, 1982), p. 74.

45. Jonathan Kapstein, Blanca Riemer, and Richard A. Melcher, "Workers Want Their Piece of Europe Inc." *Business Week* (Oct. 29, 1990), pp. 46–47.

46. "Most Companies Offer Tuition Aid," *Resource* (August 1988), p. 3.

47. D. Keith Denton, "An Employee Ownership Program That Rebuilt Success," *Personnel Journal* (March 1987), pp. 114–120. See also Joan Szabo, "E.S.O.P.'s Fables & Other Pension Choices," *Personnel Administrator* (Nov. 1989), pp. 38–42.

48. Paul V. Lyons, "EAPs: The Only Real Cure for Substance Abuse," *Management Review* (March 1987), pp. 38–40.

49. "You, Your Family, and XEAP: The Xerox Employee Assistance Program" (an internal company brochure), *n.d.*, p. 1.

50. Ibid.

51. "79% of Companies Have EAPs; Most Use Community Sources," *Resource* (April 1989), p. 2. See also Diane Kirrane, "EAPs: Dawning of a New Age," *HRMagazine* (Jan. 1990), pp. 30–34.

52. "More Help for Emotionally Troubled Employees," *Business Week* (March 12, 1979), p. 102. See also Robert Witte and Marsha Cannon, "Employee Assistance Programs: Getting Top Management's Support," *Personnel Administrator* (June 1979), pp. 23–28.

53. "Day Care, Inc." *American Demographics* (May 1989), p. 19.

54. "Child Care Grows as a Benefit," *Business Week* (Dec. 21, 1981), pp. 60, 63. See also Sandra E. LaMarre and Kate Thompson, "Industry-sponsored Day Care," *Personnel Administrator* (Feb. 1984), pp. 53–55, 58, 60, 62, 64–65.

55. "Your Next Employee Benefits," *Fortune* (March 30, 1987), pp. 8–9.

56. Cathy Trost, "Aiding Aging Relatives Is a Task Companies Seek To Ease for Employees," *The Wall Street Journal* (August 12, 1986), p. 1. See also William B. Werther, Jr., "Childcare and Eldercare Benefits," *Personnel* (Sept. 1989), pp. 42–46.

57. Carol Hymowitz, "Lures for Relocation Come in New Shapes," *The Wall Street Journal*, Eastern ed. (March 1, 1990), p. b1.

58. Ibid.

59. Linda K. Strob, Anne H. Reilly, and Jeanne M. Brett, "New Trends in Relocation," *HRMagazine* (Feb. 1990), pp. 42–44.

60. Marie Wilson, Gregory B. Northcraft, and Margaret A. Neale, "The Perceived Value of Fringe Benefits," *Personnel Psychology*, vol. 38 (1985), p. 309.

61. Catherine Murino, "What Benefit Is Communication?" *Personnel Journal* (February 1990), pp. 64–69.

62. Albert Cole, Jr., "Flexible Benefits Are a Key to Better Employee Relations," *Personnel Journal* (Jan. 1983), pp. 49–53. See also William B. Werther, Jr., "A New Direction in Rethinking Employee Benefits," *MSU Business Topics* (Winter 1974), pp. 36–37.

63. Bob Cohn, "A Glimpse of the 'Flex' Future," *Newsweek* (August 1, 1988), pp. 38–39.

The criminal prosecution of corporate executives in connection with deaths or serious injuries in the workplace . . . is back on the front burner.
MICHAEL A. VERESPEJ[1]

16

SECURITY, SAFETY, AND HEALTH

CHAPTER OBJECTIVES

After studying this chapter, you should be able to:
1. DISCUSS the role of government in furthering work place security.
2. EXPLAIN the need for a proactive approach to employee security, safety, and health by the human resource department.
3. DESCRIBE the different approaches to mandated employee security.
4. LIST the objectives of safety and health programs.
5. DESCRIBE how OSHA helps employers reduce the burden of its regulations.
6. SUMMARIZE the safety and health responsibilities of employers and employees.

CHAPTER 15 described the benefits and services that employers voluntarily give to their employees. This chapter examines legally required benefits and services that are imposed upon an organization by government. They include social security, unemployment compensation, extended medical insurance, workers' compensation, and occupational safety and health.

Since governments further societal objectives through laws, employers must comply or face legal sanctions. These laws help employees alter work-related hardships and protect them from future workplace hazards. Industrial nations decided long ago that the consequences of unregulated employment relationships imposed burdens on society. For example, before workers' compensation laws required payment for job-related injuries, the burden for job injuries fell on society through government or charitable organizations. Today employers must compensate workers for their on-the-job injuries. These mandated coverages are expensive and common in developed nations.

International wage costs

Supplemental non-wage costs—for social security, workers' compensation, and unemployment insurance—add a staggering 85% to direct compensation, making Germany's cost of industrial labor ($19 an hour all told) the world's highest. The comparable figure in the U.S. is $14.40 and in Japan, $15.78.[2]

The challenge for human resource specialists becomes how to comply proactively with the least costs to the employer and the greatest benefit to the employees. In the area of employee safety and health, for example, Du Pont has been a proactive leader.

Du Pont

Du Pont's nylon fiber plant in Seaford, Delaware provides an example of the company's safety efforts. The last accident at the plant that was serious enough to cause an employee to miss a day happened when an employee tripped in the parking lot and fractured her wrist. "Like any other accident serious enough to keep one of Du Pont's 140,000 employees off the job for a day or more, this one was reported to Du Pont's chairman within 24 hours."[3] Since that accident, the plant has operated for more than two years without a lost-time case.

This commitment to safety by top management is reflected by other managers within Du Pont. The plant manager at the Seaford plant, for example, has his staff conduct regular one-hour safety tours that look for deviations from sound safety practices. On one tour, the three safety defects that were found included a worker without his hearing protectors, a ladder leaning against a wall without anyone attending to it, and an open desk drawer that could trip someone. Although these items are seemingly minor in a large nylon plant, attention to such minor "safety defects" prevents them from growing into accidents.

16. SECURITY, SAFETY, AND HEALTH

This level of attention to safety does not just happen because top management is notified of accidents. Employee safety and health must be part of an ongoing concern by top management that is built into the firm's culture. Du Pont has been fortunate to have had that concern from its beginning: Pierre Samuel Du Pont founded the American branch of the family and set an early example of top-management involvement. In 1817 he left his sickbed at age 77 to help put out a fire at a gunpowder mill. Today, that aspect of Du Pont's organizational character is reflected in the regular Friday meetings of Du Pont's top management in Wilmington, Delaware; safety is the first agenda item at each meeting. This pattern occurs at lower-level management meetings, too. People inside the company realize that to do a job right, it must be done safely. Supervisors and managers also realize that promotions are hindered by poor safety records.

Has all this attention to safety paid off? "Du Pont, which probably has the lowest accident rate of any major manufacturer, counts savings in the tens of millions a year from its safety programs."[4] For example, in one year, Du Pont had 129 lost-time accidents at all of its operations, for an annual rate of 0.12 accidents per 100 workers. This accident rate was 1/23 of the National Safety Council's average for all manufacturers. If Du Pont's rate had been average, its workers' compensation and related costs would have been $26 million higher. That $26 million is equivalent to 3.6 percent of Du Pont's profits. Said another way, Du Pont would have had to sell another $500 million worth of products to make as much money as its safety program saved the company.[5]

The apparent key to Du Pont's successful safety record is top management's active commitment. That commitment cascades down the organization to all levels of management. But not all organizations exhibit the commitment that Du Pont does. The result has been government-imposed measures that provide a base level of financial security along with safe and healthy working conditions. The primary sources of financial and physical protection for workers are outlined in Figure 16-1.

None of the sources of protection shown in the figure fully meet the needs of workers. Instead, employees are provided a floor of protection that is supplemented by individual efforts and voluntarily provided company benefits and services. The objective of providing financial security is to ease the monetary burdens of retirement, death, long-term disability, and injury. The loss of income from these causes is cushioned by social security. The financial problems of involuntary unemployment are lessened by unemployment compensation. And job-related injuries and death are compensated under workers' compensation laws. The objective of providing physical security is to protect employees from unhealthy and injury-causing situations. These goals are partially achieved through health and safety legislation.

Legally required benefits and services are important to the human resource department for four reasons. First, top management holds the department

Figure 16-1

Sources of Financial and Physical Protection for Workers

PROTECTION FOR WORKERS	SOURCES OF PROTECTION
FINANCIAL SECURITY	
Retirement	Social Security Act, 1935
Survivors and dependents	1939 amendments to Social Security
Total disability	1956 amendments to Social Security
Involuntary unemployment	Title IX of the 1935 Social Security Act
Industrial accidents	State workers' compensation acts
Post-employment medical coverage	Consolidated Omnibus Budget Reconciliation Act, 1986
PHYSICAL SECURITY	
Unsafe situations and unhealthful work environments	OSHA — Occupational Safety and Health Act, 1970, and its enforcement agency, the Occupational Safety and Health Administration

[Handwritten notes: H.R
1. Top management holds the dep. resp. for meeting legal oblig.
2. If oblig. not handled, hardship for employees, fines, taxes, higher insur.
3. help dept. cont. to org. object.
4. Good impression of company.]

Legally mandated benefits

responsible for meeting these legal obligations. If the department is to meet this responsibility, it must keep the firm in compliance. Second, if the obligations are improperly handled, the result can be severe hardship for employees, along with fines, more taxes, or higher insurance premiums for the company. Third, effective management of these legal requirements can help the department contribute to the organization's objectives, as the safety program at Du Pont illustrates. And fourth, for international companies like Du Pont, good treatment of employees creates a favorable impression of the company, even though foreign-controlled firms are not always welcomed by local residents.

FINANCIAL SECURITY

Developed nations consist of workers financially dependent on a paycheck. Anything that keeps people from earning a paycheck threatens their financial security. If enough people are affected, the well-being of society is harmed, and government action becomes likely. Because retirement, disability, layoffs, and injuries limit the earning power of many citizens, government has intervened with social security, unemployment compensation, and workers' compensation acts. Each of these interventions into the employment relationship will be discussed.

Social Security *[WHAT is SS for?]*

In the United States, *social security* is one of the most comprehensive and least understood social programs ever enacted. Although it is a cornerstone of financial security, to some, it is a high-priced pension. Others see it as a wide-

16. SECURITY, SAFETY, AND HEALTH 499

Figure 16-2

Nonretirement Provisions of the Social Security Act, as Amended

▶ *Disability benefits.* After a six-month waiting period, disabled workers can collect social security checks. To qualify, the disability must prevent the individual from working and be expected to last twelve months or result in death.

▶ *Death benefits.* The surviving spouse or other family member may receive a lump-sum payment upon the death of a worker. This nominal amount is designed to assist with the burial expenses.

▶ *Survivors benefits.* Dependents of a retired, disabled, or deceased worker may also receive monthly social security checks. Such payments generally are limited to dependent children, parents, or spouse.

▶ *Health insurance benefits.* Medicare is the portion of social security that helps those over 65 (or under 65 if disabled) meet the costs of health care. Medicare coverage includes hospital insurance (to pay hospital costs), medical insurance (to pay physicians and other nonhospital costs), and payment for kidney transplants or dialysis.

---

ranging program of social insurance. Since social security results in payroll deductions, questions and complaints often end up in the human resource department.[6] The department must then contend with widely differing views, such as the following:

Chuck DeLeon: With five children and a wife to support, I can't afford social security, even if it is a good deal. More money is taken out of my paycheck every week for social security than for income taxes. My grandfather gets a check every month that amounts to around $540. If he didn't live with my parents, how would he survive? I pay in nearly $200 a month. If I put $200 in a bank every month until I'm 65, I would get a lot more than $540 a month when I retire. I'm against social security.

Martha Kearny: Social security is a great bargain. My parents, who retired last year, receive $890 every month and that goes up with inflation! Even their medical bills are paid by the Medicare provisions of social security. I even know one 29-year-old man who gets social security checks because he is disabled.

Social security's scope

Social security is more than a compulsory retirement plan, although it does provide an income for life at retirement. Figure 16-2 shows other aspects of social security. These provisions give covered workers and their families disability, death, survivor, and health insurance benefits.

Coverage and administration. The *Social Security Act* of 1935 covers virtually all workers in the United States. Benefits are determined by the amount and duration of the worker's earnings. The more an employee earns (up to a limit that changes annually), the more the payroll department is required to deduct from

IV. COMPENSATION AND PROTECTION

Fully insured

each paycheck. This figure is matched by the employer and paid to the federal government.

Employees with contributions for 40 quarters (10 years) are *fully insured workers*. They are eligible for a pension at retirement and for all the benefits explained in Figure 16-2. Those who are fully insured and have paid in at the highest rate receive the largest benefits. The total benefits received may be more or less than the amount credited to the individual's social security account. There also are certain eligibility requirements. For example, if a retired employee takes a part-time job, that employee may lose social security income or have it reduced. This federal program is administered by the Social Security Board in the Department of Health and Human Services. Generally, northern European countries, such as Scandinavia and Germany, provide more liberal benefits than those found in the United States, while Japan's benefits are lower.

Implications for the human resource department. The implications of social security for the departments are several. First, departmental specialists need to explain social security to workers. Some employees do not realize that the employer must make these deductions by law. Other employees—especially those with large families and low incomes, like Chuck DeLeon in the previous example—do not understand why social security is a bigger deduction than income tax. Like many people, he also appears to be unaware of the nonretirement benefits explained in Figure 16-2. Specialists can reduce employee confusion and morale-lowering resentment by explaining how social security works. This explanation is an especially important part of preretirement counseling programs,[6] which are discussed in Chapter 15. The local social security administration office often is able to provide informative booklets that can be used in orientation and preretirement counseling sessions.

A second implication is the need to consider social security when designing other benefits and services.[7] For example, one hospital discovered an unintended outcome of its pension plan:

Exit interviewer:	Why are you taking early retirement at age 62?
Housekeeper:	I cannot afford to stay here. I can make more money if I retire.
Exit interviewer:	How can that be? According to our retirement plan, you are eligible for only 80 percent of your average salary based on the last three years. That's still 20 percent less than you earn now.
Housekeeper:	Not if you consider social security. Even with the lower social security rates of early retirement at age 62, I figure I will make seven dollars more a week by not working. If I stay and work, the government will reduce my social security benefits.

This hospital's retirement plan probably was not intended to encourage retirement in this way. A less expensive program might have freed resources for other employee benefits and services. Likewise, thought should be given to social security when designing health insurance.[8] Kidney dialysis and transplants should be excluded from the company's major medical policy since both types of treatment are covered under social security.

The wave of post-World War II "baby boomers" will start to retire shortly after the turn of the century. The proportion of workers to retirees will drop dramatically and the system will be severely strained. If surpluses are not created before the baby boomers retire or if existing funds are used to expand other social security benefits, such as Medicare, the high taxes that concern Chuck DeLeon in the example will rise sharply in the future.[9]

Unemployment Compensation

Unemployment compensation represents payments to those who lose their jobs. It began as a voluntary fringe benefit in such companies as General Electric and Eastman Kodak.[10] But with the massive unemployment of the 1930s, Congress decided that unemployment compensation should become widely available.

Legally required unemployment compensation began in 1935 under the Social Security Act and was modelled after similar legislation in Great Britain. The federal government imposed a tax of three percent on payrolls. The tax applied to the first $3,000 of each covered employee's annual earnings. To encourage state participation, employers could reduce this federal tax from 3.0 percent to 0.3 percent if they paid the difference (2.7 percent) into a qualified state unemployment plan. This tax-offset feature prompted *every* state to create an unemployment compensation program. The monies collected by each state created the funds from which unemployment compensation claims are paid. The federal share finances the U.S. Employment Service and supports emergency funds against which states can borrow during severe economic downturns. This state-federal partnership still works the same way. However, the tax rate and the tax base have changed. The U.S. Employment Service determines the federal tax rate and tax base and allows each state to set its own tax rates and tax base.[11]

Unemployment criteria

Coverage and administration. Employers with four or more employees must participate in their state unemployment program.[12] Their employees are eligible for compensation if they meet two tests. First, the employee must be *involuntarily separated*. That is, the employee's actions must not have caused the unemployment. For example, if a drop in sales causes an employee to be laid off, the employee is considered involuntarily separated. Applicants for unemployment compensation who quit or who are fired for just cause may be denied payments.

The second test requires that the applicant must make a *good-faith attempt* to secure *suitable employment*. A good-faith attempt means that the individual is

502   IV. COMPENSATION AND PROTECTION

willing and able to accept employment. Willingness is usually evidenced by actively looking for another job. This means at least pursuing job interviews arranged by a counselor at the state unemployment office. Being able means being available, which explains why full-time college students are often denied unemployment compensation.

The phrase "willing and able" does not require acceptance of just any job. Only suitable employment must be accepted. An unemployed engineer cannot be told to accept the job of a janitor, for example, because the job of janitor is not suited to the engineer's training and experience. If an unemployed individual rejects a suitable job, that person is considered unavailable for employment and, therefore, ineligible for unemployment compensation. However, some states have amended their laws to permit unemployment compensation for striking workers.[13]

When a claim is received by a state unemployment office, the employer is allowed to challenge the claim. Certainly, the employer should challenge the claim if the termination was the employee's fault. If the employer can show that the unemployment was caused by the employee's actions, the claim may be denied or, if paid, not charged to the employer. If the claim appears proper, the worker receives weekly compensation until another job is found or for the maximum duration of benefits. Weekly payments typically range between half and two-thirds of a worker's previous pay, except for highly paid workers who receive up to their state's maximum benefit, which is likely to be far below one-half of their previous income. Benefits do not continue indefinitely. An unemployed worker only receives benefits for a specified period or until a new job is found. During periods of severe unemployment, Congress often extends the duration of benefits for states with high levels of unemployment. As a result, benefits vary from state to state.

Experience rating

Lowering unemployment taxes

Implications for human resource management. The unemployment tax is controllable. Employers pay the maximum tax rate in their state *minus* credits for favorable experience. The use of *experience rating* encourages employers to stabilize employment to pay a lower payroll tax. By stabilizing employment, the department can lower the unemployment tax. Simply put, fewer layoffs mean lower taxes because the employer has a more favorable experience.

There are six major ways a human resource department can lower the unemployment tax rate.[14] First, as explained in Chapter 6, human resource planning minimizes overhiring and subsequent layoffs; shortages and surpluses of employees are anticipated. Then retraining or attrition can lead to proper staffing levels without layoffs. Second, the department can educate decision makers—particularly production planners and schedulers—who may not realize that "hire-then-layoff" policies increase payroll taxes. Third, the department can review all discharges to make sure that they are justified. Unjustified dismissal decisions by supervisors can be reversed or changed into intracompany transfers in order to prevent higher payroll taxes.

16. SECURITY, SAFETY, AND HEALTH

4. A fourth approach is to challenge all unjustified claims for unemployment compensation made against the employer. Claims that are successfully challenged may reduce the employer's costs in the future.

> Kevin Hirtsman was fired for stealing from the company. (The employee manual stated that stealing was grounds for immediate dismissal.) When his claim for unemployment insurance was sent to the company for its comments, the human resource manager replied that Kevin was terminated for cause. Kevin's claim for unemployment compensation was denied. Had there been no objection to Kevin's claim, the company's unemployment tax rate might have increased.

5. A fifth way to reduce the tax is to use workweek reductions instead of layoffs. When a company must lower its labor costs, a reduction in everyone's hours rather than a partial layoff does not create claims for unemployment compensation under the plans in most states. The smaller paycheck for a short workweek usually exceeds unemployment compensation. In some states, such as California, rules permit employees to collect unemployment compensation for a reduced workweek. For example, if an employer needs to reduce labor expenses by 20 percent, workers may be put on layoff one day a week, collecting four-fifths of their regular earnings. Employees in states that allow unemployment compensation for reduced workweeks then can collect unemployment compensation for the day they are on layoff.

6. A final means of reducing the unemployment tax is to adopt the "rings of defense" strategy used by Control Data and other companies. As described at the end of Chapter 9, the company contracts some tasks to outside firms. When the amount of work for permanent full-time workers is insufficient, they are assigned jobs previously handled by outside contractors.

3. Extended Medical Insurance under COBRA

COBRA

Changes in employment, marital, or dependency status affect insurance coverage. To prevent these changes from causing an involuntary lapse of protection, Title 10 of the Consolidated Omnibus Budget Reconciliation Act (COBRA) of 1986 offers employees and their families an opportunity for a temporary extension of health coverage at group rates in situations that would otherwise cause insurance to end. COBRA requires an employer to continue offering health insurance to employees and their dependents after a covered worker's employment status changes.[15]

Coverage and administration. COBRA applies to employers who provide health insurance and have 20 or more employees. Employees and their depen-

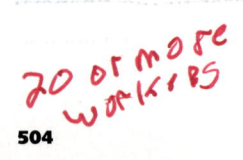

504   IV. COMPENSATION AND PROTECTION

dents (spouses and children) are eligible for COBRA coverage if they notify the employer within 60 days of a qualifying event. A qualifying event includes:

➤ Employee's employment is terminated (for reasons other than gross misconduct).

➤ Employee's hours are reduced.

➤ Employee dies (making dependents eligible).

➤ Employee is divorced or legally separated (making dependents eligible).

➤ Employee becomes eligible for Medicare.

➤ Employee's dependent child loses dependency status (making the son or daughter eligible).

After being notified of a qualifying event, the plan administrator has 14 days in which to inform qualified beneficiaries that they are eligible for coverage. Once notified, the person has 60 days in which to elect coverage and another 45 days from that decision to pay the premium. A continuation of prior coverage must be extended to qualified beneficiaries for 18 months when employees are terminated or their hours are reduced. All other qualifying events (death, marital status change, Medicare eligibility, or loss of dependency status) require coverage to be extended for 36 months.

Not covered under this act are small employers (those with fewer than 20 employees), church employers (such as church-sponsored hospitals, universities, and other operations), and certain government employers (such as the federal government, U.S. territories, and Washington, D.C.).

Implications for human resource management. More than 12 percent of eligible employees elect COBRA coverage. The most common problems for the human resource department are recordkeeping and collecting the premiums, since the department must set up a collection system to take in payments from those who elect coverage.[16] Whether done by the department or an outside vendor, recordkeeping for notices, payments, reimbursements, and policy changes confronts human resource managers with a new burden.[17]

Workers' Compensation

Work-related accidents and illnesses are another threat to the financial security of employees. In the nineteenth century a worker could get compensation for an industrial accident or illness only by suing the employer. With the cost of medical treatment, the loss of income, or the loss of a wage earner, many workers or their families found it financially impossible to bring these suits. The result was a severe burden on society in general and on the affected workers and their families in particular.

Purpose

Once again the problem became widespread and government acted, by requiring *workers' compensation*. Starting in 1908, states began passing *workers' compensation laws*. Today, every state has these laws, which are designed to compensate employees at least partially, under a wide range of situations. Covered under these laws are the following:

➤ Medical expenses

➤ Lost income due to total disabilities that prevent working (Such disabilities may be temporary—such as, sprains, burns, or broken limbs, or permanent—such as loss of limbs or blindness.)

➤ Death benefits, including funeral allowances and survivor benefits.

For example, every state requires at least partial payment of the medical bill that results from a work-related accident or illness; and most states require that the entire bill be paid. Every state pays disabled employees between 55 and 75 percent of their average weekly earnings up to a limit. And all states pay benefits to survivors in the event of death. The actual operation of the law is straightforward. A covered employee with a compensable injury or illness files the proper documentation with the state agency, insurer, or employer. After a waiting period of three to seven days, the employee is compensated at the rate determined by the state.

Coverage and administration. Most employees in the United States are covered under workers' compensation laws. The major exceptions are farm workers, domestics, casual labor, athletes, and small businesses with less than five full-time workers. Since these laws vary from state to state, there are some significant differences in how the law is administered. Most states have compulsory laws, although a few have elective laws. Regardless of which approach is followed, the employer ultimately pays.

Compulsory laws require employers to comply fully with the decision of the state agency that administers the law. Some states administer their own insurance fund and compel the employer to contribute to it. Other states permit employers to buy policies from insurance companies or allow the employer to be self-insuring by paying compensation claims out of reserves or company income. Regardless of how the fund is financed, the employer must compensate affected employees according to the decision of the state agency.

Elective laws allow the employer to refuse coverage under the state's workers' compensation laws. In these states, the decision of the state agency that adminis-

506   IV. COMPENSATION AND PROTECTION

ters these laws is *not* binding on the employer. If the employer rejects the state agency's decision on the amount of compensation for an affected worker, the worker can sue.[18]

Implications for human resource management. Workers' compensation claims are expensive. If the employer is self-insured or uses some other insurance pool, the funds devoted to workers' compensation increase with each injured or disabled employee. Efforts to restrain these costs are an ongoing concern to those in human resource management in small and large organizations alike because these outlays are some of the fastest growing costs employers face. Figure 16-3 outlines specific recommendations for minimizing workers' compensation costs. Additionally, specialists must stay alert to suspicious situations that suggest malingering. Some examples suggested by one expert include:

Suspicious situations

▶ A high frequency of work-related back strains at 10 A.M. on Monday morning during weekend softball season

▶ The rash of tendonitis on one assembly line on one shift of one plant in a company with three shifts in three plants doing identical work under the same conditions

▶ A sudden surge in medical disabilities just before a major layoff

▶ The employee who never wanted to work, gets into a minor auto accident and then files a permanent total disability claim for chronic pain arising from a soft tissue injury unsubstantiated by observable medical evidence

All of these cases smack of malingering. . . .[19]

Malingering

Malingering is more likely after worker compensation reimbursement increases; one study found that a 10 percent increase in benefits meant a three to four percent increase in recovery time.[20] Even company sports teams can be a source of workers' compensation claims:

Edward Carr, a lawyer at insurance broker Alexander & Alexander, Inc., says companies that organize or benefit from athletic programs may be liable under worker compensation laws for any injuries. And the risk can be significant, he says. At a large division of a major corporation that he declines to identify, more than half the worker compensation costs stemmed from company athletic team injuries, he contends.

16. SECURITY, SAFETY, AND HEALTH

Figure 16-3

Ten Ways to Protect Employers under Workers' Compensation Laws

1. *Know your state law:*
   - ➤ Posting requirements
   - ➤ Time limits
   - ➤ Application
   - ➤ Coverage
   - ➤ Insurance requirements
   - ➤ Related laws

2. *Have clear rules on the scope of employees' duties:*
   - ➤ On/off the clock
   - ➤ Use of company vehicle
   - ➤ More than one employee
   - ➤ Personal business in the workplace
   - ➤ No horseplay
   - ➤ "Outside" staff
   - ➤ Injuries during breaks

3. *Develop a communication program.* It is important to maintain a consistent and effective communication program with employees on workers' compensation problems.

4. *Investigate accidents early.* Investigate accidents promptly and thoroughly. Always get affidavits from witnesses. Promptly contest a claim if the employee is at fault.

5. *Pay valid claims without delay.* Employers have a legal and moral obligation to do so. This practice ensures good employee relations.

6. *Keep accurate records.* Maintain a file on all claims. Keep on file all witness affidavits obtained.

7. *Coordinate claims with your labor attorney.* Consider all other labor cases that are pending with the same employee, such as wage and hour, unemployment insurance, wrongful discharge and discrimination claims, and so on. One case can affect another.

8. *Do not reemploy the worker without a doctor's letter.* Any injury serious enough for workers' compensation payments is serious enough for a doctor's letter vouching for the employee's ability to return to work.

9. *Do not change the employee's position on staff without a doctor's letter.* Take nothing for granted. Protect yourself from future claims before reassigning an employee.

10. *Fight frivolous claims.* The best way to discourage frivolous claims is to fight each one. Employees must know that you investigate all claims, promptly pay valid claims, and dispute frivolous and questionable cases.

Source: From "The Preventive Program," copyrighted by the law firm of Stokes, Lazarus & Carmichael, Atlanta, Ga. Used by permission.

> Many corporations, pooh-poohing the risk, say there's more to be gained through improved employee health and morale than is lost. . . . "There are very, very few injuries," says Burlington Industries.[21]

Beyond these specific examples, many courts view stress-related disabilities with growing sympathy. Disabilities caused by stress appear to be the fastest-growing source of workers' compensation claims, and a growing number of these claims are coming from workers who use video display terminals.[22] Given the relative youth of some claimants, the costs to the employer may be significant. For example,

Raytheon

Helen J. Kelly, a Raytheon Co. employee with 22 years' seniority, suffered a nervous breakdown when told she would be transferred to another department. The Massachusetts Supreme Judicial Court ruled four to three that she was entitled to workers' compensation benefits. Her breakdown was a "personal injury arising out of and in the course of . . . employment," the court explained.

Harry A. McGarrah, an Oregon deputy sheriff, blamed his depression on the belief that his supervisor was persecuting him. The Oregon Supreme Court upheld his claim for workers' compensation benefits.

Kelly collected $40,000 and McGarrah $20,000.[23]

Besides providing a safe and healthy work environment, personnel professionals can help restrain workers' compensation costs by getting injured employees back on the job as quickly as possible. Not only does returning to work stop the costly benefit payments, but the sooner the employee returns to the workplace, the less likely that the injury will become a permanent disability. In other words, the sooner the injured employee returns—even if it is not to his or her "old job"—the less likely that the employee will become used to receiving compensation without working.

The IAM and Boeing

The International Association of Machinists Union and Boeing used some federal funds to retrain 200 disabled ex-Boeing workers. The union provided job counseling information about rehabilitation programs and then worked with Boeing to find jobs for these people. The injury may mean that the employee cannot do his or her previous job. But if other jobs that require different physical attributes are available and if those who are disabled are reached soon enough with retraining, the company may be able to reduce the number of short-term disabilities that become long-term ones. As one union counselor said, "We try to get them within six months of their accident, before they learn to live on compensation payments and lose their work habits."[24]

Another concern for human resource specialists is that employees often are only vaguely aware of these compensation laws and even less aware of their rights. Consider the comments of one employee:

The "shock" of coverage

It really came as a shock to learn that the state would only pay me 60 percent of my wages while I was unable to work. On top of that, the state paid nothing for the first seven days I was out. I guess I am lucky that the disability wasn't permanent or else my weekly benefit would have been even lower.

16. SECURITY, SAFETY, AND HEALTH

As this incident illustrates, employees are sometimes shocked by workers' compensation rules that pay only a fraction of the regular paycheck. For example, every state pays disabled claimants only part of their regular pay to discourage self-inflicted accidents or malingering. Also to encourage a speedy return to work, payments are less than wages. Another universal state rule includes a waiting period to lessen claims for trivial accidents. Payments eventually are reduced or even discontinued to encourage the permanently disabled to seek rehabilitation.

The inadequacy of workers' compensation coverage holds two related implications for human resource departments. First, workers need to be informed by the department of the limited financial security provided by these laws. Second, gaps in the employee's financial security need to be closed with supplemental disability and life insurance. These voluntary actions by human resource departments help to illustrate a genuine concern for employee welfare. The department also needs to be concerned about reducing accidents to lower the cost of workers' compensation.

Safety incentives

Oceaneering International, the largest underwater service contractor, offered bonuses to employees for safely conducted dives. The average $2,000 bonuses reduced lost-time accidents from 31 to 18, saving between $340,000 to $500,000 compared to the $170,000 paid-out in bonuses.[25]

Beyond cost considerations, many managers feel an obligation to provide a safe working environment, as is the case at Oceaneering, above, and Du Pont, discussed earlier in this chapter.[26] Unfortunately, few employers have achieved such dramatic success as Du Pont, so government involvement has resulted in safety laws that encourage safer practices and conditions in some workplaces.

PHYSICAL SECURITY

OSHA

Workers' compensation programs have a serious defect: they are after-the-fact efforts. These laws attempt to compensate employees for accidents and illnesses that have already occurred. Once again, the government intervened and passed a comprehensive law: the *Occupational Safety and Health Act (OSHA)* of 1970. The statistical support justifying this safety legislation was overwhelming. In 1970, Congress considered annual figures such as these:

▶ Job-related accidents accounted for more than 14,000 worker deaths.

▶ Nearly 2 1/2 million workers were disabled, either temporarily or permanently.

Figure 16-4

Total Number of Lost-Workday and Nonlost-Workday Injuries for 1972 and 1989

INCIDENCE RATES PER 100 FULL-TIME WORKERS

YEAR	TOTAL INJURIES		NONFATAL INJURIES WITHOUT LOST WORKDAYS		LOST WORKDAY INJURIES
1972	10.5	=	7.3	+	3.2
1989	8.6	=	4.6	+	4.0

Source: "BLS Reports on Survey of Occupational Injuries and Illnesses in 1989," *News*, U.S. Department of Labor, Nov. 14, 1990, p. 5.

▶ Ten times more workdays were lost from job-related disabilities than from strikes.

▶ Estimated new cases of occupational diseases totaled 300,000.[27]

Injury trends

Figure 16-4 tells the story of workplace injuries since OSHA began collecting injury statistics in 1972. The trend from 1972 to 1989 shows that total injuries per 100 full-time workers have declined from 10.5 to 8.6. The incidence of injuries without lost workdays has declined also, from 7.3 to 4.0. However, the injuries that have led to lost workdays have actually increased from 3.2 to 4.6 incidents per 100 full-time workers. Part of the increase in lost workday figures may be due to more accurate recording and reporting of *lost-time accidents.*[28]

Implications of OSHA for the Workplace

Congressional purpose

In passing OSHA, Congress declared its purpose was "to assure so far as possible every working man and woman in the nation safe and healthful working conditions and to preserve our human resources." Congress imposed upon covered employers a general duty to provide a safe and healthy workplace. Figure 16-5 summarizes the major objectives of this legislation. As the figure indicates, Congress sought improved attention to safety and health by employees and employers. It also sought to enforce tough safety standards and to uncover causes of accidents. OSHA has been one of the most far-reaching efforts by government to control the work environment. Since OSHA directly affects employees, the human resource department typically is responsible for compliance.

Coverage and administration. OSHA covers all workers except those who are self-employed, those who are protected under other federal agencies or statutes, and those who work on family-owned and -operated farms. It is administered and

Figure 16-5

Objectives of OSHA

1. To encourage employers and employees to reduce safety and health hazards
2. To encourage employers and employees to perfect safety and health programs
3. To authorize the Secretary of Labor to establish mandatory occupational health and safety standards
4. To create an Occupational Safety and Health Review Commission to hear appeals under the act
5. To provide health and safety research through the National Institute for Occupational Safety and Health
6. To discover the causal connections between diseases and work, and to establish appropriate standards to eliminate industrial disease
7. To establish medical criteria to assure no employee will suffer diminished health, ability, or life expectancy
8. To implement training programs to improve the quantity and quality of people engaged in the safety and health field
9. To provide an effective program of enforcement of safety and health standards
10. To encourage the states to assume responsibility for administration and enforcement of safety and health regulations
11. To provide appropriate reporting procedures with regard to safety and health
12. To encourage joint labor-management efforts to reduce injuries and disease.

Source: The Occupational Safety and Health Act of 1970.

---

enforced by the secretary of labor through the *Occupational Safety and Health Administration* (also called OSHA). This organization conducts safety and health inspections according to its targeting system. Besides cases of serious accident, fatality, or complaint, the agency's inspectors focus their efforts on high-hazard industries. Within these industries, OSHA inspectors concentrate on those firms with injury rates above the national average. These inspections help the agency directly meet some of the objectives in Figure 16-5.

Employers want to reduce safety and health hazards through effective programs. However, many line managers and personnel professionals have found some aspects of OSHA burdensome, such as the government reporting requirements, the on-site OSHA inspections, and the fines for violations. To meet these objections, OSHA has eliminated some of the more trivial safety requirements, exempted some low-hazard industries from routine inspection, allowed some industries to drastically reduce their reporting requirements, and even exempted some employers from routine safety inspections and allowed them to begin their own self-policing of work site safety and health. Mobil Chemical Company provides an example of a voluntary worker protection program called *Star.*

With about one-half of Mobil Chemical's plants covered under OSHA's Star program, it is easy to see why the company seeks 100 percent Star coverage.

512   IV. COMPENSATION AND PROTECTION

Mobil Chemical

The *Star* program allows self-policing of qualified companies, permitting OSHA to better focus on other employers. The program requires Mobil to adhere to safety and health standards as rigorous as OSHA's. OSHA inspects company records as part of a triennial inspection, unless an employee complaint or serious problem causes an inspection to be needed sooner.

Mobil's safety system is so good that OSHA's compliance officers audit Mobil's training program as part of their training.

Employees get recognition for their safety efforts, weaknesses in the company's efforts are uncovered, and the number and severity of injuries have declined along with the number of lost workdays. In one year, workers' compensation costs dropped in half, from $2.4 million to $1.2 million.[29]

Besides the Star program, OSHA also has *Try* and *Praise* programs. The Try program allows employers like Mobil to implement experimental safety efforts that may differ from traditional approaches. The Praise program attempts to recognize the lowest-hazard firms in low-hazard industries. It is a performance recognition program by OSHA for firms that have exceptional safety and health programs but do not normally receive inspections because they are in low-hazard industries.[30]

Inspection situations

Inspections. A variety of situations can lead to an OSHA inspection, although only two percent of the six million workplaces in the U.S. are inspected in a given year.[31] When an inspection occurs, the employer *and* an employee representative normally accompany the OSHA compliance officer.[32] Situations of interest to OSHA that lead to inspections are summarized below.

1. *Imminent danger*. Conditions likely to cause death or serious injury if allowed to continue merit OSHA's highest priority for inspection. Included are situations that could cause severe bodily damage, disability, or life-shortening illness. Improperly shored ditches, machines with open gears, and toxic fumes and dust are examples. Compliance officers must seek an immediate voluntary solution or obtain a court order to correct any imminent dangers.

2. *Catastrophes and fatal accidents*. Catastrophes, deaths, or accidents resulting in hospitalization of five or more employees merit a high priority from compliance officers. The compliance officer determines if any OSHA standards have been violated and how similar events can be avoided in the future.

3. *Employee complaints*. Employees can complain to OSHA about safety violations or about unsafe or unhealthy conditions; these allegations receive OSHA's attention and an inspection. Employees have the right under OSHA to request an inspection when they believe improper safety and health conditions exist. When complaints of imminent danger are made, the employee's name is withheld from the employer if the employee wishes.

4. *Programmed high-hazard inspections.* Occupations, industries, or substances that lead to high levels of accidents or illnesses receive special attention and extra inspections under OSHA. Meat cutting, sheet metal working, logging, and their associated industries are examples of target occupations and industries. Asbestos and lead are examples of hazardous health substances. To encourage all employers to comply with the act, inspections are conducted randomly among firms in hazardous industries, with emphasis on those employers whose safety records are worse than industry norms.

5. *Follow-up inspections.* Employers who have been cited for violations of OSHA are reinspected to ensure that hazards have been corrected and that compliance is maintained.[33]

Standards and appeals. The standards to which employers must adhere are extremely detailed. Although the safe cowboy caricatured in Figure 16-6 is an obvious exaggeration, OSHA does have jurisdiction over every chemical substance, piece of equipment, and work environment that poses even a potential threat to worker health or safety. To conduct research and develop additional safety and health standards, the act also created the *National Institute of Occupational Safety and Health* (NIOSH).[34] Although NIOSH's standards are sometimes viewed by industry as arbitrary, those standards can be the basis for serious fines or jail sentences.

Safety and health standards

Jail time

Three executives of Film Recovery Systems, Inc., were sentenced to 25 years in jail for causing the death of an employee who was exposed to cyanide on the job. Testimony revealed that employees worked without adequate protection and that management took no actions even after repeated complaints.[35]

Hazard communications

Because of incidents like the one just described at Film Recovery Systems, OSHA requires employers to give employees *hazard communications*. More popularly known as "right-to-know" laws, these OSHA regulations require the employer to inform employees of known risks associated with the hazardous materials encountered on the job. Employers must develop written orientation and training programs to communicate these hazards to employees. In addition, hazardous materials must be so labeled. OSHA's hazard communication ruling also requires the employer to maintain material safety data sheets for each hazard item handled by employees. These sheets specify the maker, characteristics, health risks, and precautions associated with the product. Employees must have access to this information. Had these procedures been in effect and followed at Film Recovery Systems, Inc., the employee fatality might have been avoided.[36]

Figure 16-7 summarizes the type and extent of fines that are imposed on a noncomplying employer. Note that fines are imposed for *each* violation, no matter how many violations are discovered per inspection. If an employer wants

514   IV. COMPENSATION AND PROTECTION

Figure 16-6

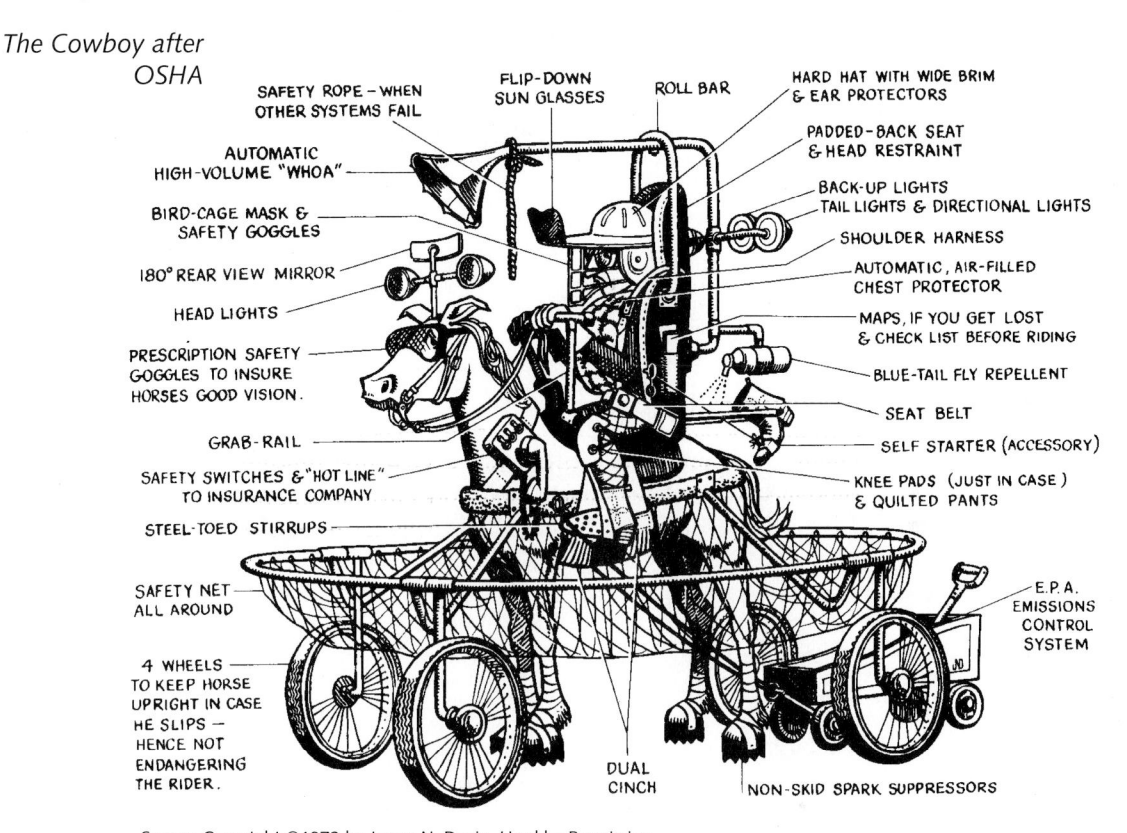

The Cowboy after OSHA

Source: Copyright ©1972 by James N. Devin, Used by Permission

to challenge a citation, a "notice of contest" can be filed with the nearest area director of OSHA. This appeal is reviewed by a judge from the *Occupational Safety and Health Review Commission*. The judge's decision can be appealed to the review commission and even to the federal courts.

Participation by other governments. As with unemployment compensation, state involvement was encouraged under the Occupational Safety and Health Act. Any state that wanted to assume the duties of enforcing safety and health standards could submit a qualified plan to the U.S. Department of Labor. If the state plan was considered "at least as effective as" the federal program, the department allowed the state to have jurisdiction. Fifty percent of the operating costs of a qualified state plan is paid for by the federal government.

Federal and state involvement

16. SECURITY, SAFETY, AND HEALTH

Figure 16-7

Violations and Penalties under OSHA

TYPE	DESCRIPTION	PENALTY
DE MINIMIS	Violation with no direct or immediate relationship to job safety or health.	None
NONSERIOUS VIOLATION	Violation of safety or health standards that would not likely cause serious physical harm or death.	Up to $1000 per day beyond the abatement period allowed by OSHA. Penalty is discretionary and may be reduced because of the employer's size, past actions, and good-faith cooperation.
SERIOUS VIOLATION	Violation likely to cause death or serious injury due to hazard of which the employer was, or should have been aware.	A $1000 mandatory penalty that can be reduced by 50 percent because of the employer's size, past actions, and good-faith cooperation.
IMMINENT DANGER	Violation that is expected to cause death or serious physical harm immediately or before usual enforcement procedures can eliminate the danger.	Immediate voluntary abatement or court order closing the operations. Financial penalties same as serious violation, unless a willful or repeated violation.
WILLFUL OR REPEATED	Intentional or continuous violations of safety and health standards.	Up to $70,000 per violation. A willful violation that leads to death of an employee can be fined up to $70,000 and/or six months imprisonment. These maximums are doubled for second convictions.
FALSIFYING RECORDS	Any improper and willful falsification of records.	Fine of up to $70,000 and six months in jail.
POSTING VIOLATIONS	Failure to post OSHA notices after violations are cited by OSHA.	Civil penalty of up to $1000.
INTERFERING WITH COMPLIANCE	Assaulting a compliance officer or otherwise resisting or obstructing a safety inspection.	Fine of up to $5000 and up to three years imprisonment.

In the name of employee safety and health, many local governments have become involved, primarily by passing specific, workplace-related ordinances. For example, San Francisco has passed a law to address the hazards of extended work at video display terminals.[37] Although generally considered safe, the concern with VDT workers is *repetitive strain injury*, which emerges in a wide variety of jobs that require repeated actions over an extended time (such a typing, meatpacking, and textile work). In fact, the Bureau of Labor Statistics reported that nearly half of all workplace illnesses involve a repetitive strain injury.[38] Likewise, some state and municipal ordinances restrict smoking in the workplace because of potential hazards associated with secondary cigarette smoke.[39]

Implications of OSHA for Human Resource Management

The act requires that an employer:

1. shall furnish to each of his employees . . . a place of employment . . . free from recognized hazards that are . . . likely to cause death or serious physical harm to his employees;

2. shall comply with occupational safety and health standards promulgated under this Act.[40]

Likewise, the Act imposes certain duties on employees:

Each employee shall comply with occupational safety and health standards and all rules, regulations, and orders issued pursuant to this Act.[41]

These two quotes from the Act hold several implications for human resource managers: they must obtain organizationwide compliance, maintain records, seek consistent enforcement, and permit workers to exercise their rights without punishment.

Compliance. Organizationwide compliance requires a detailed safety program. To be effective, the program should have several characteristics.[42] Top-management support is crucial because without it, other managers often fail to make the necessary commitment of time and resources. The Du Pont example presented earlier in this chapter illustrates how strong top-management commitment can lead to organizationwide compliance.

With this support, the human resource or safety department needs to conduct a self-inspection so that health and accident hazards can be eliminated and unsafe practices corrected. Then training should include safety awareness programs for both employees and supervisors, whose support is essential. Firm enforcement of safety rules by the supervisor quickly establishes a safety-conscious work environment. Supervisory commitment also requires that rewards (such as pay increases and promotions) depend on a good safety record, as they do at Du Pont. Finally, the department must communicate directly with employees about safety. Not only do communications elevate safety awareness, but they reinforce supervisory actions as well. Some companies even develop safety slogan contests or offer rewards to employees to increase safety awareness.

In Gainesville, Florida, a city-owned utility conducted a successful safety program managed by a city employee who had been seriously injured on his job as a utility lineman. Once a week, he changed a large sign in the office

16. SECURITY, SAFETY, AND HEALTH

Figure 16-8

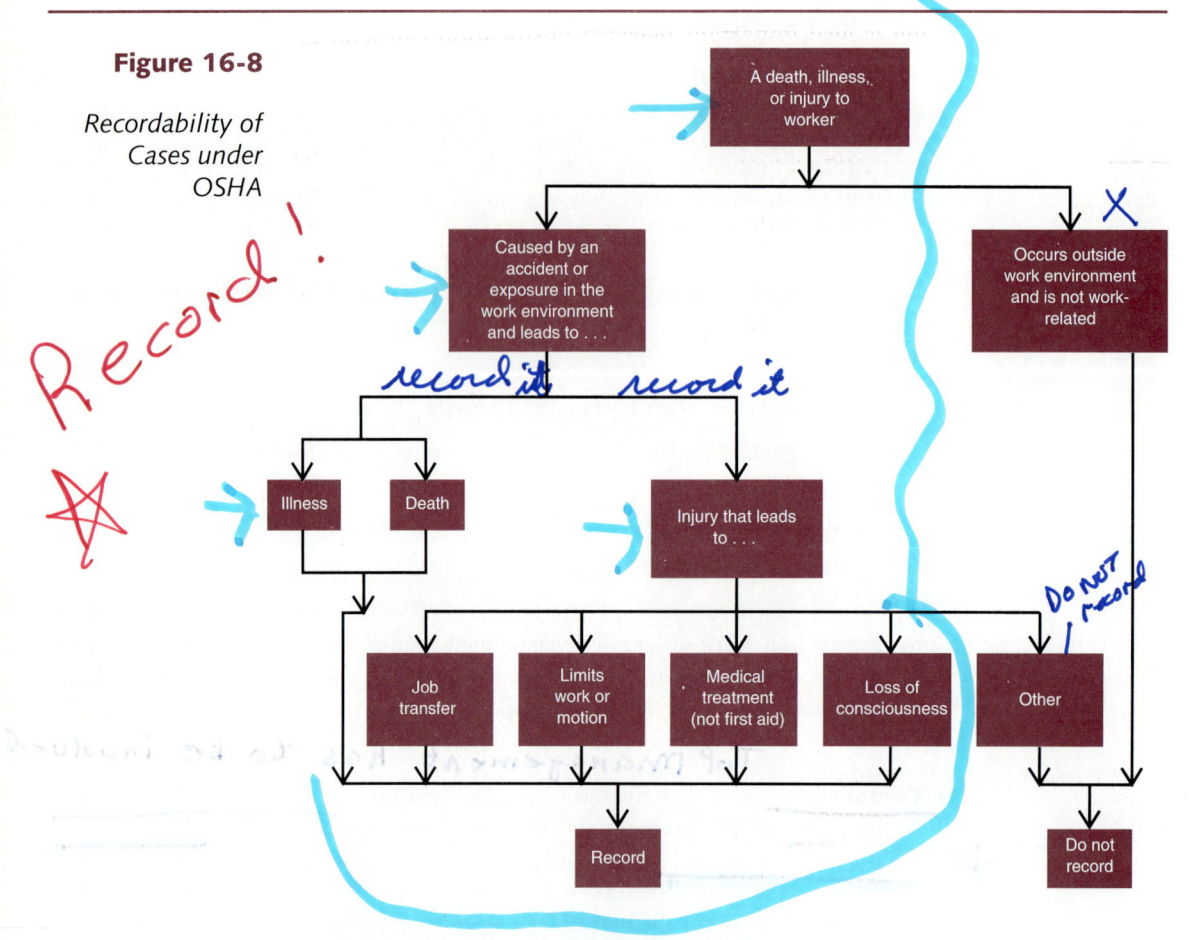

Recordability of Cases under OSHA

```
                    ┌─────────────────┐
                    │ A death, illness,│
                    │   or injury to  │
                    │     worker      │
                    └────────┬────────┘
              ┌──────────────┴──────────────┐
              ▼                             ▼
   ┌─────────────────┐              ┌─────────────────┐
   │   Caused by an  │              │ Occurs outside  │
   │    accident or  │              │ work environment│
   │  exposure in the│              │ and is not work-│
   │ work environment│              │     related     │
   │  and leads to...│              └────────┬────────┘
   └────────┬────────┘                       │
       ┌────┼──────────────┐                 │
       ▼    ▼              ▼                 │
   ┌──────┐┌──────┐  ┌───────────────┐       │
   │Illness││Death│  │Injury that leads      │
   │      ││      │  │     to...     │       │
   └──┬───┘└──┬──┘  └───┬───┬───┬───┬┘       │
      │       │         │   │   │   │        │
      │  ┌────┼─────┬───┼───┼───┼───┼──┐     │
      ▼  ▼    ▼     ▼   ▼   ▼   ▼   ▼  ▼     ▼
   ┌─────┐┌──────┐┌────────┐┌──────┐┌─────┐┌──────┐
   │ Job ││Limits││Medical ││Loss of││Other│
   │trans││work or││treatment││consc.│
   │ fer ││motion││(not first││      │
   │     ││      ││  aid)   ││      │
   └──┬──┘└───┬──┘└────┬───┘└───┬──┘└──┬──┘
      └───────┴────────┼────────┘      │
                       ▼               ▼
                   ┌────────┐     ┌────────┐
                   │ Record │     │ Do not │
                   └────────┘     │ record │
                                  └────────┘
```

Source: *What Every Employer Needs to Know about OSHA Recordkeeping*, U.S. Department of Labor, 1975, p. 2.

showing how many total hours had been worked since the last departmental accident. When the figure reached 10,000 hours (about every three months), every employee and spouse was entitled to a free dinner at any restaurant in the city. This program succeeded because safety was reinforced weekly by the sign and quarterly by the free dinners.

Records. The department must maintain proper records, as shown in Figure 16-8. Not only are records required by OSHA, but they can be used to identify the causes of accidents. From these records, safety experts can detect patterns of accidents or illnesses and then undertake corrective action. Accurate recordkeep-

post them up after recording them.
keep for five years.

ing is also important because falsification can lead to severe fines and jail sentences.

Chrysler Corporation

> The U.S. Department of Labor . . . cited Chrysler Corporation for 182 alleged willful violations of the Occupational Safety and Health Administration's recordkeeping requirements and proposed fines totalling $910,000.
>
> The citations, issued . . . at Chrysler's assembly plant at Belvidere, Ill., follow a thorough review of the plant's injury records. . . . The review began when an OSHA inspector noticed numerous discrepancies in the company's injury records during the course of a fatality investigation. . . .
>
> In announcing the citations, Assistant Secretary of Labor for Occupational Safety and Health John A. Pendergrass said the action "was a necessary response to an apparent pattern of disregard for OSHA's recordkeeping requirements."
>
> "We cannot allow complacency by some employers in maintaining accurate and dependable injury reports," Pendergrass said. "Recordkeeping must be the cornerstone of any successful safety and health program."
>
> Although the Belvidere plant employs an estimated 3,900 people, a review of its records indicated an unusually low number of injuries were reported. The agency found 182 instances of work-related injuries that had not been recorded on the log, as required by federal regulations, including 133 workers' compensation cases.
>
> OSHA proposed penalties of $5,000 for each of the 182 alleged recordkeeping violations.
>
> As a result of the recordkeeping investigation, OSHA ... started a comprehensive safety inspection of the entire Chrysler facility at the Belvidere plant.[43]

Records for evaluation + correction of Safety + health problems

Recordkeeping violations are treated with severe fines because accurate records are necessary for evaluation and correction of safety and health problems. At the same time, managers may see such reports as taking up too much of their schedules and diverting them from other responsibilities. Pressure from senior management and the human resource department may turn out to be an incentive not to record every incident, especially those that are seen as "minor" by line managers.

Have to enforce.

Enforcement. Another implication of OSHA is consistent enforcement of safety and health rules. Is management too harsh when it fires a worker who refused to wear safety shoes? Probably not. If safety policies allow one worker to violate the rules, others may do the same. If an accident results, it is the employer that is fined by OSHA. By being firm—even if this means discharge—management quickly convinces employees that safety is important. Sometimes just the threat

16. SECURITY, SAFETY, AND HEALTH

Figure 16-9

Worker Rights under OSHA

IT'S AGAINST THE LAW FOR YOUR EMPLOYER TO PUNISH YOU FOR EXERCISING YOUR OSHA RIGHTS

Section ELEVEN-C of the OSHA law was written to protect you from discrimination or punishment by your employer if you do such things as:

► Complain to your employer about job safety or health conditions.
► Discuss health or safety matters with other workers.
► Participate in union activities concerning health and safety matters.
► Participate in workplace health and safety committee activities.
► File health or safety grievances.
► File a complaint about workplace health or safety hazards with OSHA, state agencies, your local health department or fire department, or any other government agency.
► Participate in OSHA inspections.
► Testify before any panel, agency, or court about job hazards.
► File ELEVEN-C complaints.
► Give evidence in connection with ELEVEN-C complaints.
► Refuse a dangerous task, but only under certain conditions.

Section ELEVEN-C of the OSHA law makes it illegal for your employer to do any of the following as punishment for exercising your OSHA rights:

► Fire you.
► Demote you.
► Assign you to an undesirable job or shift.
► Take away your seniority.
► Deny you a promotion.
► Deny you benefits you've earned, such as sick leave or vacation time.
► Spy on you.
► Harass you.
► Blacklist you with other employers.
► Take away your company housing.
► Try to cut off your credit at banks or credit unions.

OSHA can protect you from these and other punishments only if they result from your exercising OSHA rights. If you want to protest discrimination or punishment which is not related to your OSHA rights, you should contact your union or the appropriate government agency. OSHA cannot protect you if you are disciplined solely for refusing to comply with OSHA regulations or valid health or safety rules established by your employer.

Source: "OSHA: Your Workplace Rights in Action," U.S. Department of Labor, 1980, pp. 2–3.

of discipline is sufficient to get employees to comply with safety regulations. And a strong record of enforcing safety rules also may convince OSHA to reduce penalties when citations are received.

Employee rights. Figure 16-9 explains the last major implication of OSHA: employee rights to safe working conditions. To ensure the effectiveness of OSHA, the law permits employees to refuse to work when working conditions are unsafe. This is not an unqualified right. Employees first are expected to ask the employer to correct the situation if it is reasonable to do so. They may also request an OSHA inspection and have an employee representative accompany the inspector. When employees exercise their rights under the act, they are protected from discrimination by the employer. Management may not retaliate against workers who have sought changes in unsafe or unhealthful working conditions.[44]

SUMMARY

LEGALLY REQUIRED benefits and services are imposed by government to further societal objectives. The government—primarily the federal government—seeks to provide workers with financial and physical security.

Financial security is achieved partially through such benefits as social security, unemployment compensation, extended medical coverage, and workers' compensation. Social security provides income at retirement or upon disability. It also provides the family members of a deceased worker with a death benefit and a survivor's annuity, under certain conditions.

Unemployment compensation pays the worker a modest income to reduce the hardship of losing a job. These payments go to employees who are involuntarily separated from their work. Payments last until the worker finds suitable employment or until the worker receives the maximum number of payments permitted by the state.

Extended benefits coverage under COBRA ensures that workers or their dependents will continue to receive medical-related insurance coverage after their employment, marital, or dependent status changes.

Workers' compensation pays employees who are injured in the course of their employment. The payments are made to prevent the employee from having to sue to be compensated for injuries. If an employee dies, benefits are paid to the survivors.

The government has tried to provide physical security through the Occupational Safety and Health Act of 1970. This act imposes a duty on employers to provide a safe and healthy place of employment. Violations of this law, which can lead to serious injuries or to industrial diseases, are subject to severe penalties. The success of a department's program depends heavily on top management's support and commitment to employee safety and health.

16. SECURITY, SAFETY, AND HEALTH

Terms for Review

- ✓ Social security
- ✓ Fully insured workers
- ✓ Unemployment compensation
- ✓ Suitable employment
- ✓ Experience rating
- ✓ Workers' compensation
- ✓ Occupational Safety and Health Act (OSHA)
- ✓ Occupational Safety and Health Administration
- ✓ Imminent danger
- ✓ Lost-time accidents
- ✓ National Institute of Occupational Safety and Health (NIOSH)
- ✓ Occupational Safety and Health Review Commission (OSHRC)
- ✓ Hazard communication
- ✓ Repetitive strain injury

Review and Discussion Questions

1. Why has government been interested in providing financial security to workers through laws? What areas do you think are likely to receive federal attention to ensure employee financial security in the future?

2. Some people feel that social security is greatly overpriced for the benefits it delivers. But many people who are retired or permanently disabled think it is an excellent social program. What is your opinion of social security? Why?

3. Explain why someone from the human resource department should follow up on employees who are injured on the job and who are beginning to receive workers' compensation checks at home.

4. Suppose a friend of yours contracted lead poisoning on the job. What sources of income could this person rely on while recovering during the next two months? What if it took two years for your friend to recover? Are other sources of income available? If you worked at the same lead processing plant as your ill friend, what actions would you take?

5. Assume your company began using a new chemical for its photocopier and FAX machines. What information would you want from the supplier? As a human resources manager, what other actions should you take to inform employees?

6. Indicate whether each of the following people would be eligible for unemployment compensation and why: (*a*) a worker who took voluntary retirement at age 62, (*b*) a disabled employee who was confined to a hospital bed, (*c*) a soldier who is on active duty.

7. When must an accident or illness be recorded by an employer?

8. Although most OSHA penalties are in the form of fines, when can criminal penalties apply?

INCIDENT 16-1
Cutting the K & D Company's Tax Bill

Karen Carrea, a personnel specialist, recently was hired by the K & D consulting firm. The president of the firm was concerned about the taxes the company paid for such employee benefits as social security, workers' compensation, and unemployment compensation. The president assigned Karen to uncover ways by which the firm could legally reduce its labor costs by reducing tax liability.

Karen's report contained several novel solutions. To reduce workers' compensation costs, she suggested that the personnel department request OSHA to inspect the company's printing shop, which produced the firm's reports and most of its accidents. To reduce unemployment compensation costs, Karen suggested that personnel change its policy of hiring additional consultants on a project basis. She had found that every time a project ended, the temporary consultants were laid off and filed for unemployment compensation. She suggested that the company subcontract its overload to free-lance consultants at the nearby university. Since the consultants would be independent contractors, their loss of consulting business would not reflect on the firm's unemployment insurance taxes, and as independent consultants they would pay their own social security taxes. Karen was unable to suggest any other way that social security taxes could be lowered, since they were a percentage of payroll.

1. What is your evaluation of Karen's suggestions?

2. What other methods might Karen suggest to hold down the cost of these required benefits?

INCIDENT 16-2
Safety and Health and the Bank Operations Center

A large Midwestern bank ran its own operations center, which processed more than 10,000 checks a day. The keyboard operators verified each check, encoding the checks with the amount and date. Items were then batched for shipment to local banks or the Federal Reserve for clearance. Accuracy and speed were stressed by management, and bonuses were based on these factors.

Jobs were organized in a job ladder, progressing from mail room clerk, to sorter, to bundler, to encoder. A strong policy of promotion-from-within was followed to encourage people to stay and work their way up to the encoder's position, which was the best hourly paying job. Skilled encoding operators were expected to undertake minor maintenance, such as changing the ink and ink rollers in the machines.

Although there were hardly ever any injuries, the major employee complaints concerned the great pressure they felt to increase their encoding efficiency.

Complaints about headaches, backaches, and sore wrists would emerge occasionally, usually leading to one or two days off under the companies liberal sick leave (with pay) policies.

1. Assuming you were responsible for safety and health in the bank's operations center, what concerns would you raise?

2. Given the nature of the jobs in the center, what recommendations would you have to lessen the possibility of repetitive strain syndrome?

References

1. Michael A. Verespej, "Execs Could Be Tried for Murder," *Industry Week* (March 6, 1989), p. 61.

2. Louis S. Richman, "Managing for a Second Miracle," *Fortune* (April 22, 1991), pp. 221–226.

3. Jeremy Main, "When Accidents Don't Happen," *Fortune* (Sept. 6, 1982), p. 62.

4. Ibid.

5. Ibid., pp. 62, 64, 68.

6. Richard Schultz, Peter J. Ferrara, and Richard C. Keating, "Social Security: Three Points of View," *Personnel Administrator* (May 1981), pp. 45–49.

7. Patrick J. Montana, "Preretirement Planning: How Corporations Help," *Personnel Administrator* (June 1986), pp. 121–128.

8. Michael J. Boskin, ed., *The Crisis in Social Security: Problems and Prospects*, 2d ed. (San Francisco: Institute for Contemporary Studies, 1979).

9. Howard Gleckman, Susan B. Garland, and Paula Dwyer, "Social Security's 'Dirty Little Secret,'" *Business Week* (Jan. 29, 1990), pp. 66–67.

10. Russell L. Greenman and Eric J. Schmertz, *Personnel Administration and the Law* (Washington, D.C.: Bureau of National Affairs, 1972), p. 129.

11. "The Hidden Crisis in Jobless Pay," *Business Week* (Jan. 24, 1977), p. 21.

12. Allan N. Nash and Stephen J. Carroll, Jr., *The Management of Compensation* (Monterey: Brooks/Cole Publishing Co., 1975), p. 230.

13. Craig S. Weaver, "Should Workers Be Paid To Strike?" *Personnel Administrator* (June 1988), pp. 108–111.

14. Philip Kaplan, "Unemployment Taxes Are Variable, Controllable Expenses Which Employers Must Recognize as Growing Profit Drain," *Personnel Journal* (April 1976), pp. 170–172, 184–185.

15. Betty Southard Murphy, Wayne E. Barlow, and D. Diane Hatch, "COBRA Takes Effect," *Personnel Journal* (Jan. 1987), pp. 12, 14.

16. "Companies Report Administrative Problems with COBRA," *Small Business Reports* (Dec. 1988), p. 7. See also Gary B. Kushner and Gina Williams, "COBRA: Answers to the Most-asked Questions," *Legal Report* (Fall 1990), pp. 1–8.

17. Sidney H. Simon, "Benefits Administration That Complies with COBRA," *Personnel Journal* (March 1987), pp. 44, 46.

18. Greenman and Schmertz, op. cit., pp. 152–153.

19. Paul R. Lees-Haley, "How to Detect Malingerers in the Workplace," *Personnel Journal* (July 1986), pp. 106, 108, 110.

20. Gene Koretz, "Does Better Workers' Comp Mean Longer Absences?" *Business Week* (Jan. 28, 1991), p. 22.

21. Selwyn Feinstein, "Labor Letter: Company Sports Teams Often Are Winners, but a Fumble Can Be Expensive," *The Wall Street Journal*, Midwest ed. (Sept. 30, 1986), p. 1.

22. "More Workers' Compensation Claims for Stress, Costs Rising," *Resource* (Dec. 1989), p. 19. See also Resa W. King and Irene Pave, "Stress Claims Are Making Business Jumpy," *Business Week* (Oct. 14, 1985), pp. 151, 154.

23. Ibid., p. 151. See also Philip R. Voluck and Herbert Abramson, "How to Avoid Stress-related Disability Claims," *Personnel Journal* (May 1987), pp. 95–96, 98.

24. "Disabled Workers Get Training to Begin New Careers in a Union Program," *The Wall Street Journal*, Western ed. (July 7, 1981), p. 1. See also Resa W. King, "The Worsening Ills of Worker's Comp.," *Business Week* (Oct. 12, 1987), p. 46.

25. Laurel B. Calkins, "No Pain, Some Gain," *Business Month* (Oct. 1989), p. 21.

26. Bruce S. Vanner, "Cut beneath the Abuse of Workers' Compensation," *Personnel Journal* (April 1988), pp. 30, 35–36.

27. *All about OSHA* (U.S. Department of Labor, 1985), p. 1.

28. "Occupational Injuries and Illnesses in 1981," *News* (U.S. Department of Labor, Nov. 17, 1982), p. 4. See also "BLS Reports on Survey of Occupational Injuries and Illnesses in 1989," *News* (U.S. Department of Labor, Nov. 14, 1990), pp. 1–7.

29. "HRM Update: Safety Stars," *Personnel Administrator* (June 1986), p. 22.

30. Barbara Gray Gricar and H. Donald Hopkins, "How Does Your Company Respond to OSHA?" *Personnel Administrator* (April 1983), pp. 53–57.

31. Susan B. Garland, "A New Chief Has OSHA Growling Again," *Business Week* (August 20, 1990), p. 57.

32. Mary Hayes, "What Can You Do When OSHA Calls?" *Personnel Administrator* (Nov. 1982), pp. 65–66.

33. *All about OSHA*, op. cit., pp. 19–23.

34. Richard E. Gallagher, "Setting Priorities for NIOSH Research," *Monthly Labor Review* (March 1975), pp. 41–43. See also James P. Carty, "The Politics of Regulation: Understanding the Regulatory Complex," *Personnel Administrator* (June 1980), pp. 25–30.

35. Peter A. Susser, "Criminal Prosecution for Workplace Safety Problems," *Personnel Administrator* (July 1986), pp. 34, 36, 38.

36. Bruce D. May, "Hazardous Substances: OSHA Mandates the Right to Know," *Personnel Journal* (August 1986), pp. 128–130.

37. "San Francisco Has Nation's Sole VDT Law," *The Miami Herald* (Dec. 28, 1990), p. 10a. See also "Landmark VDT Law Adopted in New York," *AFL-CIO News* (June 18, 1988), pp. 1–2.

38. Barbara Kantrowitz and Rebecca Crandall, "Casualties of the Keyboard," *Newsweek* (August 20, 1990), p. 57.

39. John D. Adams, "A Healthy Cut in Costs," *Personnel Administrator* (August 1988), pp. 42–47.

40. Occupational Safety and Health Act of 1970.

41. Ibid.

42. Randall S. Schuler, "Occupational Health in Organizations: Strategies for Personnel Effectiveness," *Personnel Administrator* (Jan. 1982), pp. 47–55.

43. "OSHA Cites Chrysler Corporation for 182 Alleged Willful Violations, Proposes $910,000 in Penalties," *News* (U.S. Department of Labor, Nov. 5, 1986), pp. 1–2.

44. John J. Hoover, "Workers Have New Rights to Health and Safety," *Personnel Administrator* (April 1983), pp. 47–51. See also "New OSHA Poster Alerts Workers to Job Safety and Health Rights," *News* (U.S. Department of Labor, Nov. 14, 1989), pp. 1–2.

V

EMPLOYEE RELATIONS AND ASSESSMENT

17 Employee Relations Challenges
18 Dispute Resolutions and Unions
19 Assessing Performance and Prospects

*P*ROACTIVE HUMAN resource departments contribute to the organization's bottom line by creating a productive and satisfying work environment through effective employee relations. Quality work life results from employee relations practices that meet organizational objectives and employee needs. When unions are present, employee relations efforts face new challenges from laws, labor agreements, and past practices. The department must search for new ways to help the firm and its people. Through an audit of its activities, and by helping the firm and its people anticipate future challenges in an ethical manner, the department helps the firm meet its employee and social responsibilities.

The last three chapters of the book describe the department's role in employee relations, whether a union is present or not. Although human resource departments conduct organizationwide activities to facilitate good employee relations, your success as a manager depends on effective employee relations among your peers. As a manager or human resource professional, audits give you feedback on how you perform, and so they may change the way you manage in the future.

Organizational

I FOUNDATION AND CHALLENGES

II PREPARATION AND SELECTION

III DEVELOPMENT AND EVALUATION

IV COMPENSATION AND PROTECTION

V EMPLOYEE RELATIONS AND ASSESSMENT
- Employee relations challenges
- Union-management relations
- Assessing performance and prospects

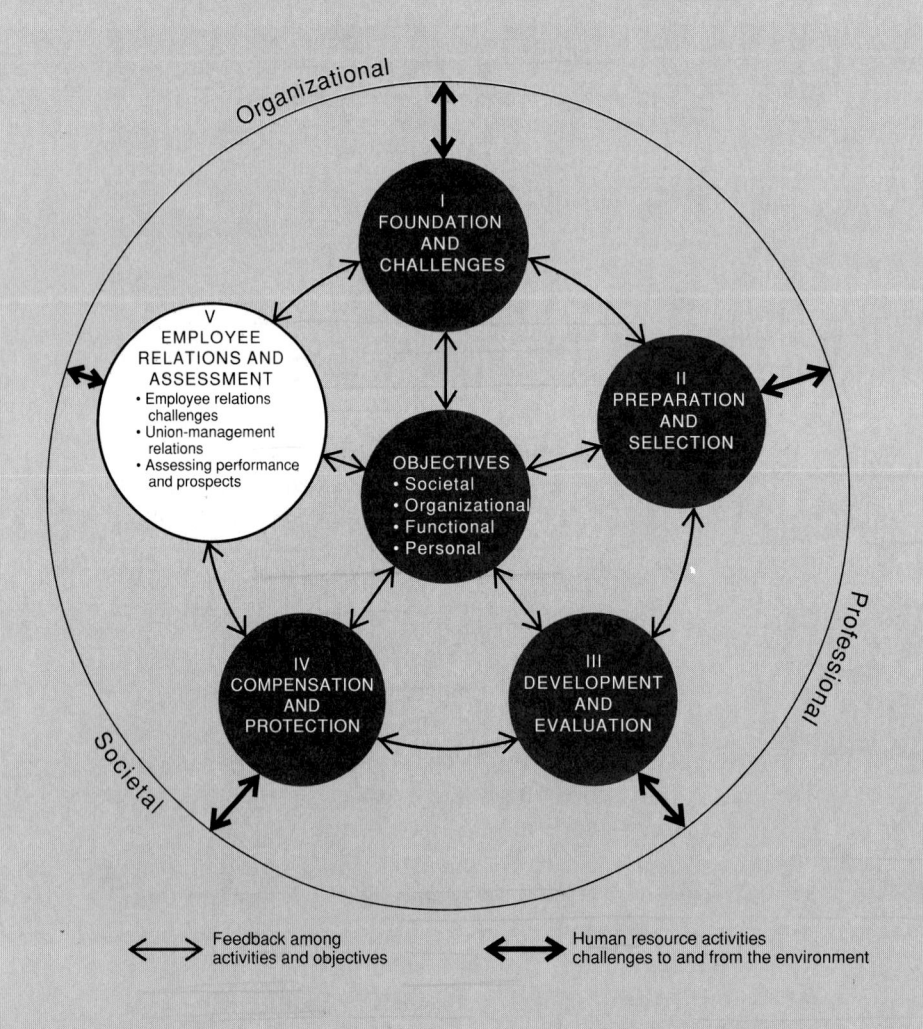

OBJECTIVES
- Societal
- Organizational
- Functional
- Personal

Professional

Societal

⟷ Feedback among activities and objectives

⟷ Human resource activities challenges to and from the environment

> Although managers are not expected to be able to solve all employee problems, they should concern themselves with correcting poor job performance by helping employees work through their own problems.
> VICKI PAWLIK AND BRIAN H. KLEINER[1]

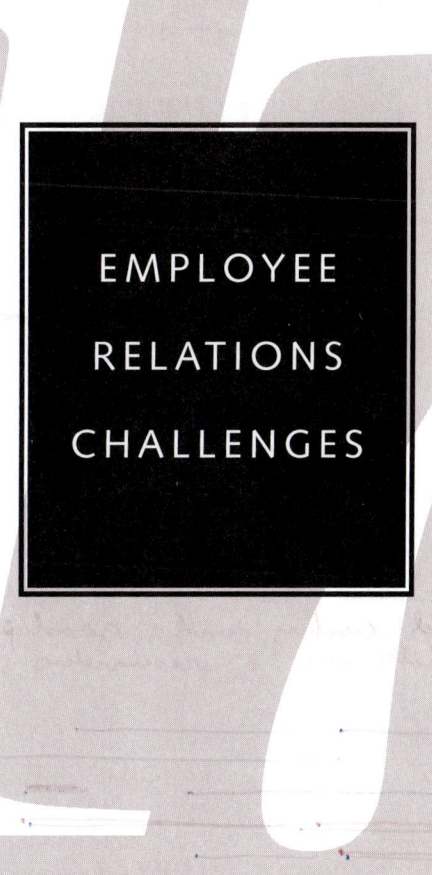

17

EMPLOYEE RELATIONS CHALLENGES

CHAPTER OBJECTIVES

After studying this chapter, you should be able to:
1. EXPLAIN why there is a growing interest in the use of employee relations to improve quality of work life (QWL).
2. DESCRIBE the human resource department's role in QWL.
3. DISCUSS the common forms of upward and downward communication used by human resource departments.
4. IDENTIFY the balance between production and QWL concerns needed for high productivity.
5. EXPLAIN how progressive discipline works.
6. DISCUSS differences between preventive and corrective discipline.

VIGOROUS DOMESTIC and international competition drive organizations to be more productive. Proactive managers and human resource departments respond to this challenge by finding new ways to improve productivity. Some strategies rely heavily upon new capital investment and technology. Others seek changes in employee relations practices. Contrast General Motor's approach with the one used by the Ford Motor Company.

GM versus Ford

F. Alan Smith, chief financial officer at General Motors, estimated that in response to competitive pressures (especially from Japan), GM spent more than $40 billion on new plants and equipment. In an attempt to use capital investment and technology to leapfrog the quality and cost advantages of Japanese carmakers, GM spent more money than it would have cost to buy Toyota and Nissan. And the general depreciation charges on all this invested capital at GM exceeds Chrysler's entire fixed asset base. Even more telling, GM's market share fell from 48 percent in the late 1970s to 35 percent by the early 1990s.[2]

Ford, on the other hand, made smaller capital investments and created its "Quality is 'Job 1' " program, where small groups of employees were formed into teams, often led by a coworker. These teams were empowered to find areas of quality or productivity improvement and make changes.[3] The result? GM needed 41 worker-hours to assemble a mid-size car, while Ford built Taurus and Sable models in 25 worker-hours.[4] The lesson is ". . . that 'brains and wits will beat capital spending ten times out of ten.' "[5]

QWL

Human resource departments are involved with efforts to improve productivity through changes in employee relations. The success reported by Ford comes from tapping the ideas and enthusiasm of employees by providing employees with a good *quality of work life* (QWL). QWL means having good supervision, good working conditions, good pay and benefits, and an interesting, challenging, and rewarding job. High QWL is sought through an employee relations philosophy that encourages the use of *QWL efforts*, which are systematic attempts by an organization to give workers greater opportunities to affect their jobs and their contributions to the organization's overall effectiveness.[6] That is, a proactive human resources department finds ways to empower employees so that they draw on their "brains and wits," usually by getting the employees more involved in the decision-making process.

Empower employees

THE HUMAN RESOURCE DEPARTMENT'S ROLE

The role of the human resource department in QWL efforts varies widely. In some organizations, such as TRW, Bank of America, Control Data, and NASA, top management appoints an executive to ensure that QWL and productivity

Figure 17-1

Influence of the Human Resource Function on Motivation and Satisfaction

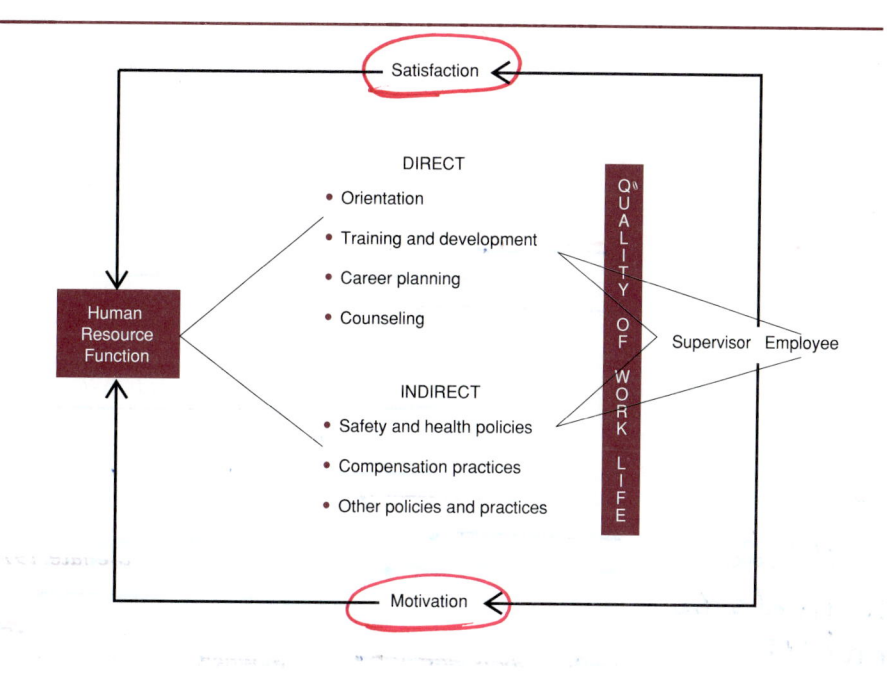

```
                              Satisfaction
                                   ↓
                        DIRECT
                        • Orientation        Q
                                             U
                        • Training and       A
                          development        L
          Human                              I
          Resource      • Career planning    T
          Function                           Y
                        • Counseling
                                             O   Supervisor  Employee
                                             F
                        INDIRECT
                                             W
                        • Safety and         O
                          health policies    R
                                             K
                        • Compensation
                          practices          L
                                             I
                        • Other policies     F
                          and practices      E

                              Motivation
```

efforts occur throughout the organization.[7] In most cases, these executives have a small staff and must rely on the human resource department for help with employee training, communications, attitude survey feedback, and similar assistance.[8] In other organizations, the department is responsible for initiating and directing the firm's QWL and productivity efforts.

Perhaps the most crucial role for the department is winning the support of key managers. Management support—particularly top-management support—appears to be an almost universal prerequisite for successful QWL programs.[9] By substantiating employee satisfaction and bottom-line benefits, which range from lower absenteeism and turnover to higher productivity and fewer accidents, the department can help convince doubting managers.[10] Sometimes documentation of QWL can result from studies of performance before and after a QWL effort. Ohio Bell, for example, achieved better sales from its phone installers, a reduction in lost inventory, fewer strikes, better employee attitudes, and improved productivity as a result of its QWL effort. Without documentation of these results, top management might not have continued its strong support.

Ohio Bell

The department also has both a direct and an indirect influence on employee motivation and satisfaction. As Figure 17-1 illustrates, the department makes direct contact with employees and supervisors through orientation, training and development, career planning, and counseling activities. At the same time, these activities may help a supervisor do a better job of motivating employees.[11]

The policies and practices of the department also influence motivation and satisfaction indirectly. Rigorously enforced safety and health programs, for

17. EMPLOYEE RELATIONS CHALLENGES   533

example, can give employees and supervisors a greater sense of safety from accidents and industrial health hazards. Likewise, compensation policies may motivate and satisfy employees through incentive plans, or they may harm motivation and satisfaction through insufficient raises or outright salary freezes. The motivation and satisfaction of employees act as feedback on the organization's QWL and on the department's day-to-day activities.

Motivation

Motivation is a complex subject. It involves the unique feelings, thoughts, and past experiences of each of us as we share a variety of relationships within and outside organizations. To expect a single motivational approach to work in every situation is probably unrealistic. In fact, even the theorists and researchers take different points of view about motivation. Nevertheless, *motivation* can be defined as a person's drive to take an action because that person wants to do so. People act because they feel that they have to. However, if they are motivated, they make the positive choice to act for a purpose—because, for example, it may satisfy some of their needs.

Job satisfaction

Job satisfaction is the favorableness or unfavorableness with which employees view their work. As with motivation, it is affected by the environment. As discussed in Chapter 5, job satisfaction is impacted by job design. Jobs that are rich in positive behavioral elements—such as autonomy, variety, task identity, task significance, and feedback—contribute to an employee's satisfaction. Likewise, orientation, emphasized in Chapter 9, is important because the employee's acceptance by the work group contributes to satisfaction. In short, each element of the environmental system can add to, or detract from, job satisfaction.

Rewards satisfaction and performance

A basic issue is whether satisfaction leads to better performance, or whether better performance leads to satisfaction. Which comes first? The reason for the apparent uncertainty about the relationship between performance and satisfaction is that rewards intervene, as shown at the top of Figure 17-2. Whether satisfaction is going to be improved depends on whether the rewards match the expectations, needs, and desires of the employee, as shown at the bottom of the figure. If better performance leads to higher rewards and if these rewards are seen as fair and equitable, then improved satisfaction results.[12] On the other hand, inadequate rewards can lead to dissatisfaction. In either case, satisfaction becomes feedback that affects one's self-image and motivation to perform. The total performance-satisfaction relationship is a continuous system, making it difficult to assess the impact of satisfaction on motivation or on performance, and vice versa.

This chapter describes how managers and human resource departments meet the challenge of higher productivity and QWL through a variety of QWL efforts that empower employees. Then the discussion focuses on three important practices: communications, counseling, and discipline.

QWL THROUGH EMPLOYEE INVOLVEMENT

One of the most common methods used to create QWL is employee involvement. *Employee involvement* (EI) consists of a variety of systematic methods that

534   V. EMPLOYEE RELATIONS AND ASSESSMENT

Figure 17-2

A Reward Performance Model of Motivation

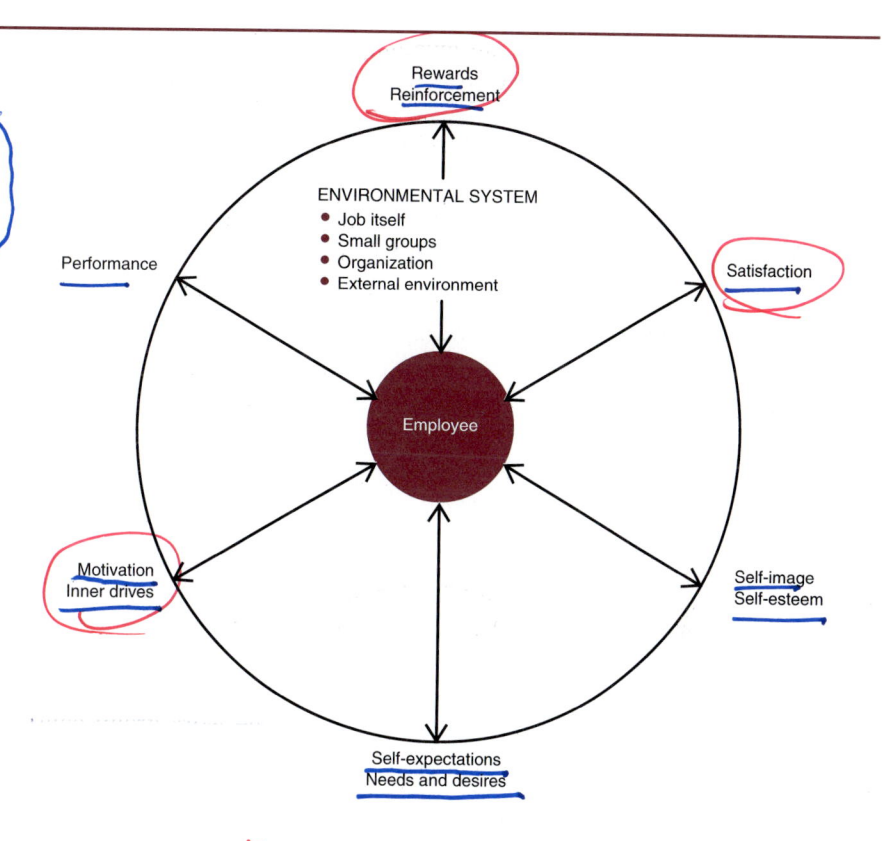

- Rewards / Reinforcement
- ENVIRONMENTAL SYSTEM
  - Job itself
  - Small groups
  - Organization
  - External environment
- Performance
- Satisfaction
- Employee
- Motivation / Inner drives
- Self-image / Self-esteem
- Self-expectations / Needs and desires

"Ownership"

empower employees to participate in the decisions that affect them and their relationship with the organization. Through EI, employees feel a sense of responsibility, even "ownership" of decisions in which they participate. To be successful, however, EI must be more than just a systematic approach; it must become part of the organization's culture by being part of management's philosophy.[13] Some companies have had this philosophy ingrained in their corporate structure for decades; Hewlett-Packard, IBM, and Tektronix are examples. Other companies, like USX, General Motors, and Ford are trying to create a high QWL corporate culture through employee empowerment approaches. Consider, for example, Ford's Sharonville operation.

Ford

The Sharonville plant was built in 1957. Over the years it had developed a "confrontational" form of labor-management relations. Plant management was autocratic, and employment had dropped from 5,000 in 1979 to 2,500 within a few years. A new plant manager who was not satisfied with the old autocratic style observed, "Times have changed and we have to take a new approach."[14]

17. EMPLOYEE RELATIONS CHALLENGES 535

Shortly after his arrival, he proposed a joint union-management coordinating committee to be cochaired by the head of the union's bargaining group and a top-ranking management employee. This committee helped create several groups of six or seven hourly employees each. To each group was added a representative from quality control and one from process engineering. They were formed to find solutions to workplace problems. One of the hourly members was elected leader, and meetings were held for one hour each week.

Soon members of the original committee could no longer keep up with the demand for creating and training more groups. Additional "minicoordinators" were used, and within two years the small problem-solving groups existed throughout the entire plant. "In effect, a parallel organization overlay the regular hierarchical structure. EI had become a permanent process interlocking at all points with the formal organization."[15]

Efforts like these at Ford—or similar ones at IBM, AT&T, Westinghouse, Motorola, Texas Instruments, Citibank, TRW, NASA, Reynolds Metals, and many others shown in Figure 17-3—indicate that interest in improving the quality of work life is no accident. It parallels and, some might say, reflects growing international competitive forces and growing workforce diversity.[16] In Europe this trend is often labeled *industrial democracy*.[17]

Industrial democracy

The implications for managers and human resource specialists are to create an organizational culture that truly treats people as though they are experts at their jobs and empowers them to use that expertise. When management does this, a *Pygmalion effect* may result, which occurs when people live up to the high expectations that others have of them.[18] If management further assumes that people want to contribute and seeks ways to tap that contribution, better decisions, improved productivity, and a higher QWL are likely.

Pygmalion effect

The economic dominance of the United States during the post–World War II period created little need for evolutionary changes in the way people were managed. However, in Europe and in Japan, national economic survival during the late 1940s and early 1950s meant that new, innovative methods of human resource management were needed. Some of these innovations began in the legislative halls, while other developments started on the shop floor. Most of these approaches were based upon sound behavioral and sociological research, much of which had been initially conducted in the United States and Canada but which was first applied in Japan and in northern Europe. During subsequent decades these EI approaches to QWL were modified and in many cases "imported" back into North America. Some of the more commonly used approaches to attain QWL through EI are discussed in the following pages.

QWL AND EI INTERVENTIONS

A wide variety of companies have undertaken interventions to create employee involvement or improved QWL.[19] Examples include Ford's Sharonville

Figure 17-3

A Partial List of North American Organizations Concerned with Quality of Work Life and Employee Involvement

Allen Bradley Company	General Telephone and Electric Co.
American Express, Inc.	General Tire Company
American Telephone and Telegraph	Honeywell, Inc.
AmHoist, Inc.	Ideal Basic Industries
Arizona Public Service	Inland Steel Company
Atwood Vacuum Machine Company	International Business Machine Co.
Arcata Redwood Company	Lincoln Electric Company
Babcock & Wilcox	Motorola, Inc.
Bank of America	N.A.S.A.
Beech Aircraft Corporation	Owens-Illinois, Inc.
Bendix Company	Penn Central, Inc.
Boeing, Inc.	Pennzoil, Inc.
Boise Cascade Company	Philadelphia Electric Company
Citibank Corporation	Phillips Petroleum Company
City of Phoenix	Reynolds Metals Company
Champion International	Tektronix, Incorporated
Chrysler Corporation	Texas Instruments, Inc.
Consolidated Foods, Inc.	TRW, Inc.
Control Data Corporation	Union Carbide
Flemming Foods, Inc.	Valley National Bank
Ford Motors Company	Waters Associates Inc.
General Dynamics, Inc.	Western Electric
General Electric Company	Westinghouse, Inc.
General Motors Company	W.R. Grace and Company

Boeing's "tiger teams"

plant and Motorola's participative management program discussed in Chapter 2. Boeing uses a single-focus task force approach called "tiger teams." Generally these teams are assembled to solve some production-delaying problem that the supervisor and employees cannot overcome. Various approaches to team building share a common underlying philosophy: Groups of people usually are better at solving problems than an individual. And even though the "purpose" of these approaches may be to find a solution, a by-product is improved quality of work life.[20]

Quality Circles

Quality circles

Quality circles are small groups of employees who meet regularly with their common leader to identify and solve work-related problems.[21] They are a highly specific form of team building, which are common in Japan and gained popularity in North America in the late 1970s and early 1980s. By the 1980s most medium- and large-sized Japanese firms had quality control circles for hourly employees. This effort began as a quality improvement program but has since become a routine procedure for many Japanese managers and a cornerstone of QWL efforts in many Japanese firms.

Unique features

Several characteristics make this approach unique. First, membership in the circle is voluntary for both the leader (usually the supervisor) and the members (usually hourly workers).[22] Second, the creation of quality circles is usually preceded by in-house training. For supervisors these sessions typically last for two or three days. Most of the time is devoted to discussions of small-group dynamics, leadership skills, and indoctrination in the QWL and quality circle philosophies. About a day is spent on the different approaches to problem-solving. Employees are usually given one day of intensive training in problem-solving techniques. The workers also receive an explanation of the supervisor's role as the group's discussion leader and information on the quality circle concept. Third, as is pointed out in the training, the group is permitted to select the problems it wants to tackle. Management may suggest problems of concern, but the group is empowered to decide which ones to select. Ideally, the selection process is not by democratic vote but is arrived at by consensus, whereby everyone agrees on the problem to be tackled. (If management has pressing problems that need to be solved, these problems can be handled in the same way that they were resolved before the introduction of quality circles.)

Solar Turbines

At Solar Turbines International (a Caterpillar Tractor Company subsidiary), employees were frustrated by the lack of power hand tools. They studied the lost production time caused by waiting for tools and showed management how to save more than $30,000 a year by making a $2,200 investment in additional hand tools.

The employees did not select this problem to save management money; they did it because of the inconvenience that insufficient tools caused them. The fact that the solution saved more than a dozen times what it cost was the type of by-product that many companies report from successful quality circle efforts.

When employees are allowed to select the problems they want to work on, they are likely to be more motivated to find solutions. And they are also more likely to be motivated to stay on as members of the circle and solve additional problems in the future.

Sociotechnical Systems

Another intervention to improve QWL is the use of sociotechnical systems. *Sociotechnical systems* are interventions in the work situation that restructure the work, the work groups, and the relationship between workers and the technologies they use to do their jobs. More than just enlarging or enriching a job, these approaches may result in more radical changes in the work environment.

Germany's Siemens

At a Siemens plant in Karlsruhe, Germany, workers assembling electronics products used to perform simple tasks over and over, spending less than one minute on each unit as it moved along a conveyor belt. Today many employees work in teams of three to seven at well-designed "work islands," where they can avoid boredom by rotating jobs, socializing, and working in job cycles of up to 20 minutes rather than a few seconds.[23]

This rearrangement of the social and technical relationships on the job offers workers an opportunity for greater QWL. Efforts to humanize the workplace seem to be most advanced in Germany, where the government funds 50 percent of selected work restructuring and retraining efforts of private industry. Shell Canada Ltd. and Procter & Gamble provide North American examples.[24]

Ergonomics

Germany also has done considerable work in the area of ergonomics. *Ergonomics* is the study of the biotechnical relationships between the physical attributes of workers and the physical demands of the job. The objective is to reduce physical and mental strain in order to increase productivity and QWL. The Germans have made considerable strides in reducing the strain of lifting, bending, and reaching through their ergonomic approach to structuring jobs, arranging equipment, and lighting.[25]

Raising or lowering work surfaces slightly, shifting handles to more convenient locations, or just tilting a parts bin can all reduce worker strain. Those are the initial findings of a four-year, $2.5 million project of Ford Motor Co. and the University of Michigan's Center for Ergonomics, which studies the physical relationship between workers and machines. Ford claims quality and productivity are up at plants where ergonomic changes were made. Workers also report feeling better on the job. The program is "... an everybody-wins situation."[26]

Codetermination

Union-management involvement

One of the early attempts at industrial democracy on a broad scale occurred in Germany under the name *codetermination*. Through formal sessions with company management, codetermination allows workers' representatives to discuss and vote on key decisions that affect the workers. This form of industrial democracy has since spread throughout most of the European Economic Community. As a result, decisions to close plants or to lay off large numbers of employees meet with far more formal resistance in Europe than they do in North America. However, European firms are forced to plan their human resource needs more carefully and to seek export markets to offset national economic cycles. Since major North American corporations operate in Europe under codetermination, human resource management in multinational corporations is affected. For international human resource experts, codetermination is a consideration in the design of overseas jobs. In North America, the first steps toward codetermination may have begun in the 1980s when Chrysler Corporation appointed the president of the United Automobile Workers to its board of directors.

Autonomous Work Groups

Leaderless work teams

A more common, albeit still rare, approach to employee involvement is the use of autonomous work groups. As discussed in Chapter 5, *autonomous work groups are teams of workers, without a formal company-appointed leader, who decide among themselves most decisions traditionally handled by supervisors.*[27] The key feature of autonomous work groups is a high degree of self-determination by employees in the management of their day-to-day work. Typically this includes collective control over the pace of work, distribution of tasks, organization of breaks, and collective participation in the recruitment and training of new members. Direct supervision is often unnecessary.[28]

Classic applications

Two early classic experiments with autonomous work groups were at the Gaines Pet Food plant in Topeka, Kansas, and at the Volvo plant in Kalmar, Sweden. (These experiments are summarized in Figure 17-4.)[29] Similar innovations intended to increase employee commitment have been undertaken by Cummins Engine in Jamestown, New York; Procter & Gamble in Lima, Ohio; and General Motors plants in Mississippi, Michigan, and New York. More attention will have to be paid by human resource experts to changing the sociotechnical relationship in order to meet changing expectations about jobs. Improving the quality of work life may mean completely redesigning factories and workplaces—as Volvo and Gaines have done to satisfy the efficiency, environmental, and behavioral requirements of jobs.

QWL is more likely to improve as workers demand jobs with more behavioral elements. These demands will probably emerge from an increasingly diverse and educated work force that expects more challenges and more autonomy in its jobs—such as worker participation in decisions traditionally reserved for management. Through codetermination, this trend has lasted more than 30 years in Europe and is still growing in popularity. And experiments by Gaines, Volvo, TRW, and other employers indicate that such new arrangements are economically feasible.[30]

EMPLOYEE RELATIONS PRACTICES

HR and employee relations

Beyond structural interventions in the way people work together, virtually everything the human resource department does impacts employee relations directly or indirectly. Many activities are largely unnoticed by employees, including, for example, recruitment, selection, benefits administration, and other important functions. Other activities only affect employees periodically, such as performance and salary review sessions. However, the department directly

540 V. EMPLOYEE RELATIONS AND ASSESSMENT

Figure 17-4

A Summary of Gaines and Volvo Experiences with Autonomous Work Groups

GAINES PET FOOD

At the Gaines Pet Food plant in Topeka, Kansas, jobs were radically changed. No longer are workers assigned specific tasks in traditional jobs. Instead, teams of workers are held responsible for a group of tasks that previously constituted several separate jobs. For example, the work group is held responsible for packing and storing the completed products, instead of each worker having a narrow job that includes only a few tasks in the packaging and storing operations. Employees are assigned to a work group, not a job. They are free to participate in the group decision-making processes. Members develop work schedules, interview new employees, perform quality control checks, maintain machinery, and perform other diverse activities. The work-group enrichment led to reduced overhead, higher productivity, better product quality, and lower turnover and absenteeism. And labor costs are 7 percent lower than those at a sister plant in Kankakee, Illinois.

VOLVO'S KALMAR PLANT

Volvo, the Swedish automobile producer, sought to design a more humane car production environment. It built the Kalmar plant around the concept of work teams, rather than the traditional assembly line. Again, workers are assigned to teams, not jobs. Teams build subsystems of the car: doors, cooling systems, engines, and other key components. Buffer stocks of partially completed cars reduce the dependence of one group on another. The physical work environment is as quiet as the latest technology permits.

Volvo claims higher satisfaction levels among employees because of the design changes, and production costs are 25 percent lower than those at Volvo's conventional plants. On the basis of the Kalmar experience, the company is building a new plant at Uddevalla.

---

impacts individual QWL and employee involvement through its communications, counseling, and disciplinary practices.

Employee relations activities are shared with supervisors because of the growing complexity of organizations, laws, and union-management relations. Earlier in this century, for example, supervisors were solely responsible for employee relations practices and hiring, which led to unethical practices, such as favoritism and kickbacks to supervisors. Today, with the need for uniform, legal, and corporationwide approaches, human resource specialists are given considerable responsibility for employee relations. The result is a dual responsibility between the department and supervisors. Of course, supervisors remain responsible for communicating task-related requirements. They are also responsible for counseling and disciplining their employees, within the guidelines established by the department. But, when serious problems are uncovered in counseling or a major disciplinary action is planned, human resource specialists are commonly involved to ensure fairness and uniformity of treatment.

Employee Communication

Information is the engine that drives organizations.[31] Information about the organization, its environment, its products and services, and its people is essential to management and workers. Without information, managers cannot make effec-

Information flows

tive decisions about markets or resources, particularly human resources. Likewise, insufficient information may cause stress and dissatisfaction among workers. This universal need for information is met through an organization's communication system.[32] *Communication systems* provide formal and informal methods to move information through an organization so that appropriate decisions can be made. Consider an example from IBM.

IBM

IBM excels in the management of its human resources. Long ago top management at IBM realized that the company's future success rested with the people who developed its technology and sold its products. One example of IBM's commitment to its workers is a 1940s policy, still in effect, against putting full-time permanent employees on layoff.[33]

The management at IBM recognizes that the treatment of human resources must be approached from a systems viewpoint. To tie its various employee relations activities together and to facilitate motivation and satisfaction, IBM relies heavily on communication. Some of its approaches include extensive career planning information and assistance, attitude surveys, suggestion systems, open-door policies, daily newspapers at some sites, and near-daily bulletins on educational opportunities and promotions.

"Trolling for open doors"

Beyond these formal methods, informal communications also occur. For example "management by walking around" is known at IBM as "trolling for open doors." IBM has an open-door policy whereby employees are free to walk into any manager's office with their problems. However, IBM management realizes that most workers are reluctant to take a problem to their boss's boss.[34] Therefore, human resource specialists and line managers leave their offices and go out among the employees to learn what problems exist. As one IBM executive explains, "The only open-door policy that works is one where the manager gets up from the desk and goes through the door to talk to employees."

All organizations have human resource communication systems. Most organizations use a blend of formal, systematically designed communication efforts and informal, ad hoc arrangements. For convenience, most of these approaches can be divided into downward communication systems, which exist to get information *to* employees, and upward communication systems, which exist to get information *from* employees.

Downward communication systems. Human resource departments operate extensive communication systems to keep people informed. They try to facilitate an open, two-way flow of information, although most messages are of the top-down variety. *Downward communication* is information that begins at some point in the organization and cascades down the organizational hierarchy to inform or influence others. Top-down methods are necessary to execute decisions and give

542   V. EMPLOYEE RELATIONS AND ASSESSMENT

employees knowledge about the organization and feedback on how their efforts are perceived.

Organizations use a variety of downward communications because the diversity of multiple channels is more likely to overcome barriers and reach the intended receivers. Some common examples of downward communication include house organs (such as company newspapers), information booklets, employee bulletin boards, prerecorded messages, and jobholder reports and meetings, which inform employees about company developments.

IBM

IBM's Boulder, Colorado facility publishes a daily paper called Boulder Today, plus almost daily flyers about promotions and educational opportunities. In addition, the Information Systems Division at the Boulder site prints its own newspaper every two months. These local house organs are supplemented by other divisional and corporate publications that try to keep IBM employees in Boulder informed. Similar house organs are published at other IBM facilities around the world.

Chevron

At Chevron Corporation, more than 60 newsletters called "bluetops" were produced during the year following its merger with Gulf Corporation, which at the time was the largest corporate merger in history. In addition, 20-minute videos, recorded phone updates, seminars, and "town hall" meetings with Chevron's leader, George Keller, were used.[35]

When operating internationally, communications need to be modified to fit local benefits and programs. In addition, to send publications that are written in the home-country language indicates an insensitivity to the employees who speak only their native language.

Upward communication systems. Perhaps no area of communication is more in need of improvement than upward communication.[36] *Upward communication* consists of information initiated by people who seek to inform or influence those higher up in the organization's hierarchy. The cornerstone of all such messages is the employee and the supervisor.[37] When a free flow of information travels between an employee and the supervisor, informal day-to-day communications are often sufficient for most situations. Consider one tragic example of blocked, upward communications:

Challenger disaster

"If the decision-makers had known all of the facts, it is highly unlikely they would have decided to launch."

With that sentence, the blue-ribbon commission investigating the explosion of the space shuttle Challenger summed up perhaps the most haunting element in the tragedy: not the fatal flaws in NASA's ultrasophisticated rockets but the human failure to follow one of the oldest rules in the book.

17. EMPLOYEE RELATIONS CHALLENGES

Despite the weaknesses in Challenger's technology, its seven crew members would probably still be alive today if shuttle officials had only spoken more candidly to their superiors and if their superiors had only been willing to listen.[38]

An employee may have a good, open relationship with the supervisor about job-related matters such as supplies, work performance, quality of outputs, and the like. However, that same employee may not be able to discuss interpersonal issues such as peer relations or career expectations. If the human resource department is to help build effective communication, then it must provide additional channels through which messages can flow, such as IBM's active open-door policy. Although no universal formula exists, a common element of effective upward communications is a genuine concern for employee well-being combined with meaningful opportunities for ideas to flow up the organization's hierarchy. Some of the more common upward communication channels include the grapevine, in-house complaint procedures, rap sessions, suggestion systems, and attitude survey feedback.

Grapevine communication is an informal system that arises spontaneously from the social interaction of people in the organization. It is the people-to-people system that arises naturally from the human desire to make friends and share ideas. When two employees chat at the water fountain about their trouble with a supervisor, that is a grapevine communication. The human resource department has an interest in the grapevine because it provides useful, off-the-record feedback from employees, if human resource specialists are prepared to listen, understand, and interpret the information. And, according to a study reported in the *Wall Street Journal*, "The office grapevine is 75% to 95% accurate and provides managers and staff with better information than formal communications. . . ."[39] Some of the types of grapevine feedback that come to the department are shown in Figure 17-5.

In-house complaint procedures are formal methods through which an employee can register a complaint. These procedures are normally operated by the human resource department and require the employee to submit the complaint in writing. Then an employee relations specialist investigates the complaint and advises its author of the results.

IBM's "Speak Up!"

IBM's program is called "Speak Up!" It uses a confidential form designed as a prepaid envelope. On the inside the employee completes a home address section and then writes the complaint, opinion, or question. When the Speak Up! administrator receives the envelope, the name and address sections are removed, and the issue is investigated. Answers are mailed to the employee's home address. If the employee is not satisfied, an interview with an executive from corporate headquarters will be arranged, regardless of where the employee works.

V. EMPLOYEE RELATIONS AND ASSESSMENT

Grapevine

Figure 17-5

Types of Grapevine Feedback to the Human Resource Department

- Information about the problems and anxieties that employees have
- Incorrect feedback that is evidence of breakdowns in communication
- Insights into goals and motivation of employees
- Identification of job problems that have high emotional content, because intense feelings encourage grapevine communication
- Information about the quality of labor relations, including grievance settlements
- Information about the quality of supervision. Complaints about supervision often are brought informally to the attention of personnel specialists with the hope that they will do something
- Information about areas of job dissatisfaction
- Feedback about acceptance of new policies and procedures

Managers at IBM "troll for open doors" to avoid Speak Ups! that cause executives to visit disgruntled employees. If that employee is dissatisfied with some improper management action and talks to an executive about it, the manager's career with IBM may be adversely affected. What makes IBM's complaint procedure and open communications so effective is that IBM executives support the program with their actions; they are willing to get on an airplane and fly to a meeting with a dissatisfied employee.

Rap sessions

Rap sessions are meetings between managers and groups of employees to discuss complaints, suggestions, opinions, or questions. These meetings may begin with some information sharing by management to tell the group about developments in the company. However, the primary purpose is to encourage upward communication, often with several levels of employees and lower-level management in attendance at the same time. When these meetings are face-to-face informal discussions between a higher-level manager and rank-and-file workers, the process may be called *deep-sensing* if it attempts to probe in some depth the issues that are on the minds of employees.[40] These sessions also are called *vertical staffing meetings* because they put higher-level managers directly in touch with employees. Constructive suggestions sometimes emerge from these meetings, as the president of Hyatt Hotels discovered.

Hyatt Hotels

In one eight-month period, Patrick Foley, president of Hyatt Hotels Corporation, held a dozen meetings with hotel employees. "Sometimes he hears of serious problems that require immediate attention. More often, he hears seemingly trivial complaints—but they concern matters that can make day-to-day life miserable. 'Every time I do one of these meetings, I realize it's the little things that most often affect morale,' Mr. Foley says. 'This is a way to make the employee feel like we care.' "[41]

17. EMPLOYEE RELATIONS CHALLENGES 545

Figure 17-6

Steps in a Suggestion System

Employee idea → Discussion with supervisor → Completion of form → Supervisory review and signoff → Submission to suggestion office → Receipt and acknowledgment →

Evaluation → Decision → Discussion with supervisor → Implementation → Discussion with supervisor / Savings to employer

Suggestion systems are a formal method for generating, evaluating, and implementing employee ideas. Figure 17-6 shows the key steps in a successful suggestion system. It begins with the employee's idea and a discussion with the supervisor. Once the suggestion form is completed, the supervisor reviews and signs the form, indicating awareness but not necessarily approval of the suggestion. The suggestion system office or committee then receives the idea and sends an acknowledgment to the employee through company mail. The idea is then evaluated and the decision is communicated to the employee. If it is a good idea, implementation follows, and the employee receives recognition and usually an award, typically equal to 10 percent of the first year's savings.

This method is likely to succeed if management provides prompt and fair evaluations, if supervisors are trained to encourage employee suggestions, and if top management actively supports the program. Unfortunately, evaluations often take months to process or supervisors see suggestions as too much work for them with few personal benefits. As a result, many company suggestion plans exist on paper but are not very effective.[42]

Attitude surveys and feedback

Attitude surveys are systematic methods of determining what employees think about their organization. These surveys may be conducted through face-to-face interviews, but they are usually done through anonymous questionnaires. An attitude survey typically seeks to learn what employees think about working conditions, supervision, and personnel policies. Questions about new programs or special concerns to management may also be asked. The resulting information

546   V. EMPLOYEE RELATIONS AND ASSESSMENT

can be used to evaluate specific concerns, such as how individual managers are perceived by their employees.

Attitude surveys can be a frustrating experience for employees if they do not see any results.[43] Therefore, a summary of upward communication should be provided to employees for their reactions. When this feedback loop is closed, the overall process is called *attitude survey feedback*. However, feedback is not enough. Action is needed. Employees need to see that the survey resulted in the resolution of problems.[44] Feedback of the results and action on the problem areas make attitude survey feedback a powerful communication tool. However, providing feedback in a constructive manner may require considerable assistance from the human resource department, especially for first-level supervisors who may have little experience in running meetings and listening to employee criticisms.

Bendix

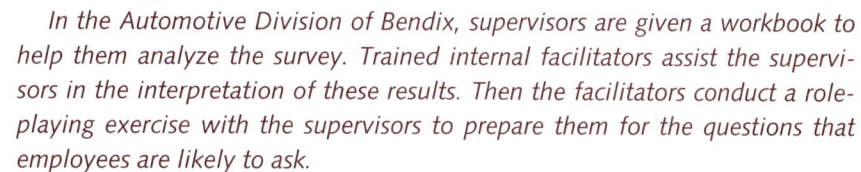

In the Automotive Division of Bendix, supervisors are given a workbook to help them analyze the survey. Trained internal facilitators assist the supervisors in the interpretation of these results. Then the facilitators conduct a role-playing exercise with the supervisors to prepare them for the questions that employees are likely to ask.

After the role playing, the supervisor meets with the employees and presents the results. Together, problems are identified and solutions are sought. From this meeting a prioritized list is drawn up with completion dates indicated for each action item. Bendix's approach to attitude survey feedback not only gives employees an explanation of what the results showed but develops an action plan to resolve the problems that emerged from the process.

Employee Counseling

Counseling is the discussion of a problem with an employee, with the general objective of helping the worker either resolve or cope with it. Stress and personal problems are likely to affect both performance and an employee's general life adjustment; therefore, it is in the best interests of all those concerned (employer, employee, and community) to help the employee return to full effectiveness. Counseling is a useful tool to help accomplish this goal. The success rate from counseling programs often is substantial, as described in the Kimberly-Clark example that follows:

Kimberly-Clark

Kimberly-Clark, a paper and forest products firm, compared the records of participants for one year before and one year after their involvement in its counseling program. These workers had a 43 percent reduction in absences and a 70 percent reduction in accidents.[45]

EAPs

Counseling programs usually are administered by the human resource department, which uses various combinations of in-house and external counseling services.⁴⁶ Often referred to as *Employee Assistance Programs*, EAPs usually rely on a blend of in-house administration and external counselors to advise employees about work or personal problems. Community services are especially useful to smaller firms that would be unable to employ a full-time counselor. An example of a comprehensive employee counseling service is Control Data Corporation's Employee Advisory Resource (EAR) program.⁴⁷

Control Data

> One of the program's slogans is: "Employees are bright and well-trained enough to handle just about any problem—except their own." The program is available to employees and their families, and it covers both personal and work-related problems. It maintains a 24-hour hot line and uses both company counselors and community agencies. The service is strictly confidential.
>
> An average of 750 employees use the service each month. Many successes have been reported, although the program is unable to solve every employee problem. Control Data's more specific study of alcoholic employees reported a remarkable 85 percent reduction in lost work hours, a 47 percent reduction in sick leave, and a 72 percent reduction in sickness and accident benefit payments. In one survey, 93 percent of the employees reported that they believe EAR is a worthwhile service.

Counseling is strictly a confidential relationship, and records of it should be restricted to persons directly involved in solving the counseling problem. These practices are necessary to protect employee privacy and to protect the employer from possible lawsuits for such liabilities as invasion of privacy or alleged slander. The policy of some firms is to refer all marital and family counseling to community agencies. These companies believe that, for reasons of employee privacy, they should not be involved in these problems. Employers also must be certain that their counseling programs comply with EEO regulations by providing equal counseling services to all protected employee groups.

Discipline

Counseling does not always work. Sometimes the employee's behavior is inappropriately disruptive or performance is unacceptable. Under these circumstances, discipline is needed. *Discipline* is management action to encourage compliance with organizational standards. There are two types of discipline: preventive and corrective.

Discipline approaches

Preventive discipline is action taken to encourage employees to follow standards and rules so that infractions are prevented. The basic objective is to encourage self-discipline, and the human resource department plays an important role. For example, it develops programs to control absences and grievances.

548   V. EMPLOYEE RELATIONS AND ASSESSMENT

Figure 17-7

A Progressive Discipline System

1. Verbal reprimand by supervisor
2. Written reprimand, with a record in personnel file
3. One- to three-day suspension from work
4. Suspension for one week or longer
5. Discharge for cause

It communicates standards to employees and encourages workers to follow them. And it encourages employee participation in setting standards, since workers will give better support to rules that they have helped create. Employees also will give more support to standards stated positively instead of negatively, such as "Safety first!" rather than "Don't be careless!" Effective discipline is a system relationship, and the department needs to be concerned with all parts of the system.[48]

Corrective discipline is an action that follows a rule infraction. It seeks to discourage further infractions and to ensure future compliance with standards. Typically the corrective or *disciplinary action* is a penalty, such as a warning or suspension without pay. These actions are usually initiated by an employee's immediate supervisor but may require approval by a higher-level manager or the human resource department. Approvals exist to guard against subsequent labor union or legal actions and to assure uniform application of rules throughout the organization. Any appeals then go to higher levels in the company and in the union hierarchy. At Motorola, for example, a senior vice president must approve the discharge of anyone who has worked for the company for 10 years or more.

Most employers apply a policy of *progressive discipline*, which means that there are stronger penalties for repeated offenses. The purpose is to give an employee an opportunity to take corrective action before more serious penalties are applied. A typical progressive discipline system is shown in Figure 17-7, and more detailed examples may be found in most labor union contracts. The first infraction leads to a verbal reprimand by the supervisor. The next infraction leads to a written reprimand, with a record placed in the files. Further infractions build up to stronger discipline, leading finally to discharge. The department is usually involved in step 3 or sooner in order to ensure that company policy is followed consistently in all departments.

Government is increasing its regulation of discipline, making it more difficult to justify. Due process for discipline is required by courts of law, arbitrators, and labor unions, especially where employee handbooks, labor agreements, or even verbal promises apply. *Due process* means that established rules and procedures for disciplinary action are followed and that employees have an opportunity to respond to charges made against them.[49] Compliance with due process rules and procedures usually falls to the human resource department.

Due process

If challenged, the department must have sufficient documentation to support its decisions for all disciplinary actions.[50] Even in employment-at-will states

17. EMPLOYEE RELATIONS CHALLENGES 549

discussed in Chapter 9, documentation of disciplinary action should be specific—beginning with the date, time, and location of an incident. Specific rules and regulations that relate to the incident should also be identified. It should state what the manager said to the employee and how the employee responded, including specific words and acts. All documentation must be recorded promptly while the supervisor's memory is still fresh. It should be objective, complete, precise, accurate, and based on observations, not on impressions. If there were witnesses, they should be identified, too.

EMERGING EMPLOYEE RELATIONS CHALLENGES

The growing diversity of the work force and the increased globalization of many companies present unique employee relations challenges to human resource departments. Departmental policies and practices—even those based on experience and sound research—may have to be modified or even discarded when dealing with different groups. Domestic goals of equal opportunity may conflict with laws or cultures in other countries. For example, separation of women from men or members of different ethnic or tribal groups may be a practical, even legal necessity in many developing nations. Domestically and internationally, employee relations may be strained by perceptions of discrimination and "reverse discrimination," which may occur when job assignments, promotions, or rewards favor one group over another. And this problem is not limited to North America. Arab employees may resent being replaced by immigrants in Israel, as may British and French workers who see jobs going to immigrants from previous colonies. As loosening borders in the European Economic Community present fewer barriers to immigration, resentments are likely to grow throughout Europe, especially in the more industrially advanced nations.

Employee relations specialists will also face growing challenges from employee concerns about AIDS-infected coworkers,[51] exposure to hazardous materials,[52] eye strain and radiation exposure from work with video display terminals, smoking policies and air quality at work,[53] and issues of privacy as computers are increasingly used to measure employee productivity.[54] All of these challenges can be expected to grow in importance during the remainder of the 1990s. Perhaps even more disturbingly, simple answers to these complex workplace issues involve tradeoffs that are likely to be unsatisfactory to at least some employees. Communications, counseling, and even discipline may be needed to ensure a work environment that balances employee relations concerns with the pressing competitive pressures for productivity and quality performance.

SUMMARY

QUALITY OF work life efforts are systematic attempts by organizations to give workers a greater opportunity to affect the way they do their jobs and the contributions they make to their organization's overall effectiveness. These efforts are not a substitute for good, sound human resource practices and policies. However, effective QWL programs can supplement other departmental actions and provide improved employee motivation, satisfaction, and productivity. QWL is most commonly improved through employee involvement. Whether that involvement is in solving workplace problems or in merely participating in the design of one's job, it gives people a feeling that their contributions matter. People want to know that they make a difference.

Many EI and QWL interventions exist. Team building and other quality of work life approaches must have top management support and be adjusted to the organization's needs and culture. One of the most popular is an import from Japan: quality circles, which rely on small groups of employees from the same work area who meet regularly with their supervisors to identify and solve workplace problems. Other forms of team building are similar to quality circles, although different groupings or objectives might be sought. Sociotechnical systems seek to change the human and technical relationship that exists in the workplace. Codetermination gives workers a formal voice in management decisions. Although common in Europe, it is almost nonexistent in North America. Autonomous work groups also are uncommon in North America, though they are more widely used in the United States than codetermination. These work groups consist of employees who collectively assume the supervisor's role in determining work schedules, job assignments, and so forth.

In many ways, this entire book has been about employee relations. How well the personnel department handles human resource planning, staffing, placement, development, evaluation, compensation, and quality of work life largely determines the state of employee relations. A mistake in any one of these areas can harm the employee-employer relationship. However, even when these activities are performed properly, solid employee relations demand careful attention to organizational communication, employee counseling, and discipline.

Terms for Review

- Quality of work life (QWL)
- Employee involvement (EI)
- Quality circles
- Industrial democracy
- Sociotechnical systems
- Ergonomics
- Codetermination
- Autonomous work groups
- Open-door policy
- Grapevine communication
- In-house complaint procedures
- Suggestion programs / Systems
- Preventive discipline
- Corrective discipline
- Attitude survey feedback
- Progressive discipline

Review and Discussion Questions

1. Describe the forces that are causing organizations and human resources departments to pursue EI and QWL strategies.

2. Since many QWL efforts are initiated by top management or by other line managers, what is the human resource department's role in a QWL effort?

3. Identify QWL and EI efforts that had their origins overseas and briefly explain each, addressing their origins and intents.

4. Suppose you are a plant or division manager and you want to create a high QWL environment. Why could you not simply order it done and expect a high QWL environment almost immediately?

5. If TRW and Gaines Pet Food have had successes with autonomous work groups, why, in your opinion, have so few other employers used this innovative method?

6. List and discuss different programs that the personnel department manages in order to improve communications. How could personnel professionals use company policies to improve communication among employees as one way to further the company's strategy?

7. Discuss differences between preventive and corrective discipline. What examples of either one were applied to you on the last job you had?

8. Discuss different government restrictions on an employer's right to discipline or dismiss an employee "at will." Why do you think each of these restrictions probably exists?

INCIDENT 17-1
Cooperation, QWL, and Space

Psychologists Joseph Brady and Henry Emurian at Johns Hopkins Hospital have been doing research to learn how to increase productivity and reduce friction on future space missions. Under research grants from NASA, they are "studying the psychological and physiological effects of prolonged confinement on two- and three-person 'microsocieties.' Their goal is to develop behavioral guidelines for the most productive individual and group performance, with the least social friction, on future space and underwater missions."[55]

Their studies have revealed the not too surprising conclusion that rewards and incentives are better motivators than sanctions and controls. Cooperation leads to greater individual performance and greater satisfaction in the group.

Assume that these findings are applicable to larger societies called organizations.

1. What implications do you see in these studies for improving the QWL in organizations?

2. If you were a supervisor with six employees working for you, how could these findings make teamwork more effective? On the basis of this brief summary of Brady and Emurian's findings, suggest specific actions you would implement to improve the effectiveness of your team.

INCIDENT 17-2
The Machinist's Abusive Comments

William Lee, a machine operator, worked as a machinist for supervisor Horace Gray. Horace told William to pick up some trash that had fallen from William's work area, and William replied, "I won't do the janitor's work."

Horace replied, "When you drop it, you pick it up." William became angry and abusive, calling Horace a number of names in a loud voice and refusing to pick up the trash. All employees in the department heard William's comments.

Horace had been trying for two weeks to get his employees to pick up trash in order to have a cleaner workplace and prevent accidents. He talked with all employees in a weekly department meeting and to each employee individually at least once. He stated that he was following the instructions of the superintendent. Only William objected.

William had been in the department for six months and with the company for three years. Horace had spoken to him twice about excessive horseplay, but otherwise his record was good. He was known to have a quick temper.

After William's abusive outburst, Horace told him to come to the office and suspended him for one day for insubordination and abusive language to a supervisor. The discipline was within company policy, and similar behavior had been disciplined in other departments.

When William walked out of Horace's office, Horace called the personnel director, reported what he had done, and said that he was sending a copy of his action for William's file.

1. If you were the director of human resources, what comments would you make?

2. What follow-up actions should the director take or recommend that Horace take? For example, do you recommend counseling for William? Would you reconsider disciplinary procedures and policies?

References

1. Vicki Pawlik and Brian H. Kleiner, "On-the-job Employee Counseling: Focus on Performance," *Personnel Journal* (Nov. 1986), p. 31.

2. Anne B. Fisher, "GM Is Tougher than You Think," *Fortune* (Nov. 10, 1986), p. 58.

3. William B. Werther, Jr., " 'Job 1' at Ford: Employee Cooperation," *Employee Relations*, vol. 7, no. 1 (1985), pp. 10–16.

4. Fisher, op. cit.

5. Ibid.

6. Lisa Copenhaver and Robert H. Guest, "Quality of Work Life: The Anatomy of Two Successes," *National Productivity Review* (Winter 1982–1983), p. 5.

7. William B. Werther, Jr., and William A. Ruch, "Chief Productivity Officer," *National Productivity Review* (Autumn 1985), pp. 397–410.

8. William A. Ruch and William B. Werther, Jr., "Productivity Strategies at TRW," *National Productivity Review* (Spring 1983), p. 116.

9. William B. Werther, Jr., "Out of the Productivity Box," *Business Horizons* (Sept.–Oct. 1982), p. 56.

10. Werther, "Out of the Productivity Box," op. cit., pp. 51–52.

11. Edward E. Lawler III and Gerald E. Ledford, Jr., "Productivity and the Quality of Work Life," *National Productivity Review* (Winter 1982–1983), pp. 23–36. See also Erwin S. Stanton, "A Critical Reevaluation of Motivation, Management and Productivity," *Personnel Journal* (March 1983), pp. 208–214.

12. See Edward E. Lawler III and Lyman W. Porter, "The Effect of Performance on Job Satisfaction," *Industrial Relations* (Oct. 1967), pp. 20–28. See also Lyman W. Porter and Edward E. Lawler, *Managerial Attitudes and Performance* (Homewood, Ill.: Richard D. Irwin, Inc., 1968).

13. William B. Werther, Jr., "Productivity Improvement through People," *Arizona Business* (Feb. 1981), pp. 14–19. See also Marion E. Haynes, "Partnerships in Management: Employee Involvement Gets Results," *Personnel Journal* (July 1986), pp. 47–55.

14. Copenhaver and Guest, op. cit., p. 11.

15. Ibid.

16. Ted Mills, "Human Resources—Why the New Concern?" *Harvard Business Review* (March–April 1975), pp. 120–134. See also Cary L. Cooper, "Humanizing the

Work Place in Europe: An Overview of Six Countries," *Personnel Journal* (June 1980), pp. 488–491.

17. Mills, op. cit.

18. J. Sterling Livingston, "Pygmalion in Management," *Harvard Business Review* (July–August 1969), pp. 81–89.

19. Rosabeth Moss Kanter, "The New Workforce Meets the Changing Workplace: Strains, Dilemmas, and Contradictions in Attempts to Implement Participative and Entrepreneurial Management," *Human Resource Management*, vol. 25, no. 4 (1986), pp. 515–537.

20. Dutch Landen, "Beyond Quality Circles," *Productivity Brief 12* (American Productivity Center, April 1982), pp. 1–7.

21. William B. Werther, Jr., "Quality Circles: Key Executive Issues," *Journal of Contemporary Business*, vol. 11, no. 2, n.d., pp. 17–26. See also Frank Shipper, "Quality Circles Using Small Group Formation," *Training and Development Journal* (May 1983), p. 82.

22. Shipper, op. cit.

23. "Moving beyond Assembly Lines," *Business Week* (July 27, 1981), pp. 87, 90.

24. Ibid. See also John Hoerr, Michael A. Pollock, and David E. Whiteside, "Management Discovers the Human Side of Automation," *Business Week* (Sept. 29, 1986), pp. 70–75.

25. "Ergonomics" (adapted from *Ergonomics Handbook* of the IBM Corporation), *Personnel Journal* (June 1986), pp. 95–101.

26. Sana Siwolop, "Making the Assembly Line Easier on the Joints," *Business Week* (May 12, 1986), p. 67.

27. Briane Dumaine, "Who Needs a Boss?" *Fortune* (May 7, 1990), pp. 52–60.

28. Toby D. Wall, Nigel J. Kemp, Pauly R. Jackson, and Chris W. Clegg, "Outcomes of Autonomous Workgroups: A Long-term Field Experiment," *Academy of Management Journal*, vol. 29, no. 2 (1986), pp. 280–281.

29. Jonathan Kapstein and John Hoerr, "Volvo's Radical New Plant: 'The Death of the Assembly Line'?" *Business Week* (August 28, 1989), pp. 92–93. See also Hoerr, Pollock, and Whiteside, op. cit.

30. Daniel Zwerdling, *Democracy at Work* (Washington, D.C.: Association for Self-management, 1978). See also Steve Lohr, "Making Cars the Volvo Way," *The New York Times* (June 23, 1987), p. d1.

31. Everett M. Rogers and Rekha Agarwala-Rogers, *Communication in Organizations* (New York: The Free Press, 1976), p. 26.

32. William Arnold and Lynne McClure, *Communication Training & Development* (New York: Harper & Row Publishers, Inc., 1989).

33. "Techniques of Appraising Performance," *IBM Fundamentals of Management Course,* sec. 4, p. 1.

34. Walter D. St. John, "Successful Communications between Supervisors and Employees," *Personnel Journal* (Jan. 1983), p. 73.

35. Cathy Trost, "Labor Letter: Major Changes Put Demands on Corporate Communicators," *The Wall Street Journal,* Western ed. (May 20, 1986), p. 1.

36. Valorie A. McClelland, "Upward Communication: Is Anyone Listening?" *Personnel Journal* (June 1988), pp. 124–130.

37. Robert W. Hollmann and Mary Ellen Campbell, "Communications Strategies for Improving HRM Effectiveness," *Personnel Administrator* (July 1984), pp. 93, 95–98.

38. Gaylord Shaw, "NASA Managers Broke Oldest Rule in the Book," *Los Angeles Times* (June 10, 1986), p. 1.

39. Carol Hymowitz, "Spread the Word: Gossip is Good," *The Wall Street Journal,* Eastern ed. (Oct. 4, 1988), p. b1. See also Alan Zaremba, "Working with the Organizational Grapevine," *Personnel Journal* (July 1988), pp. 38–42.

40. Richard E. Walton, "From Control to Commitment in the Workplace," *Harvard Business Review* (March–April 1985), pp. 77–84. See also "Deep Sensing: A Pipeline to Employee Morale," *Business Week* (Jan. 29, 1979), pp. 124–128.

41. Lawrence Rout, "Hyatt Hotels' Gripe Sessions Help Chief Maintain Communications with Workers," *The Wall Street Journal,* Western ed. (July 16, 1981), p. 25.

42. Bill Saporito, "The Revolt against 'Working Smarter,' " *Fortune* (July 21, 1986), pp. 58–65.

43. Paul Sheibar, "The Seven Deadly Sins of Employee Attitude Surveys," *Personnel* (June 1989), pp. 66–71.

44. Brian S. Morgan and William A. Schiemann, "Employee Attitude: Then and Now," *Personnel Journal* (Oct. 1986), pp. 100–106.

45. David Hill, "Employee Assistance Programs: The Helping Hand That's Good for All," *Corporate Fitness and Recreation* (Oct.–Nov. 1982), pp. 43–49.

46. Robert C. Ford and Frank S. McLaughlin, "Employee Assistance Programs: A Descriptive Survey of ASPA Members," *Personnel Administrator* (Sept. 1981), pp. 29–35. See also Beverly L. Wolkind, "North American Congress on EAPs Comes Through," *EAP Digest* (Sept./Oct. 1986), pp. 44–48.

47. David J. Reed, "One Approach to Employee Assistance," *Personnel Journal* (August 1983), pp. 648–652; and information supplied to the authors by Control Data Corporation.

48. "Employee Discipline: Firm but Fair," *Business Update* (Sept. 1985), pp. 1–15.

49. David W. Ewing, "Due Process: Will Business Default?" *Harvard Business Review* (Nov.–Dec. 1982), pp. 114–122.

50. Ira G. Asherman and Sandra Lee Vance, "Documentation: A Tool for Effective Management," *Personnel Journal* (August 1981), pp. 641–643.

51. George E. Stevens, "Understanding AIDS," *Personnel Administrator* (August 1988), pp. 84–88.

52. "Workplace Issues," *Inc.* (March 1990), p. 91.

53. Dexter Hutchins, "The Drive to Kick Smoking at Work," *Fortune* (Sept. 15, 1986), pp. 42–44.

54. Jeffrey Rothfeder, Michele Galen, and Lesa Driscoll, "Is Your Boss Spying on You?" *Business Week* (Jan. 15, 1990), pp. 74–75.

55. For a more detailed explanation of this study, see Berkeley Rice, "Space-Lab Encounters," *Psychology Today* (June 1983), pp. 50–58.

... quality workplaces are those built on foundations of trust and mutual respect between labor and management.
ELIZABETH DOLE[1]

Collective bargaining is inherently an adversary relationship.
DANIEL J. B. MITCHELL[2]

13

UNION – MANAGEMENT RELATIONS

CHAPTER OBJECTIVES

After studying this chapter, you should be able to:
1. EXPLAIN the relationship between unions, employers, and government.
2. IDENTIFY illegal management and union activities.
3. DISCUSS the impact of unions on managers and human resource professionals.
4. DESCRIBE common techniques to resolve grievances.
5. IDENTIFY the human resource department's role in dispute resolution.
6. LIST the steps that facilitate cooperation.

WHETHER EMPLOYEES are represented by a union, human resource professionals and line managers remain responsible for employee relations. Unions do not mean the end of an organization's success nor the end of sound human resource practices. Many successful companies have one or more unions and continue to perform the human resource activities discussed in this book.

Line managers and human resource specialists find that their roles change when a union is present. Both unions and managers must comply with new rules that emerge from the union-management framework. Some changes are mandated by law; other changes come from agreements between the union and management officials. Because of the many constraints that a unionized work force places on an organization, some companies try to avoid unions.

Emerson Electric's "southern strategy"

For many years, the Emerson Electric Company was a high-cost producer of fans, motors, tools, and defense equipment. However, during the 20-year reign of W.R. "Buck" Persons, Emerson became a low-cost manufacturer and consistently outperformed other firms in the electrical and electronics industry.

Part of this transformation was achieved by Persons's "southern strategy," which involved opening small new factories throughout the rural South. (Most of Emerson's 116 plants are located in the mid-South.) As another part of its strategy, the company bases 10 percent of the division managers' bonuses on keeping their plants union-free.[3]

Emerson resists unionization because it must operate in an industry that is only partially unionized. By staying nonunion, it hopes to retain lower labor costs through lower wages and greater management flexibility in the day-to-day operations of its plants. However, in industries that are largely unionized, management often takes a more conciliatory view of the union-management relationship. Consider the approach taken by General Motors and its major union, the United Automobile Workers, to provide greater security for union members.

GM and the UAW

"Throughout the 1980s, the United Auto Workers watched with mounting frustration as General Motors Corp. lost market share—and union jobs to foreign rivals. Union leaders tried to limit the damage by demanding more job security in every labor agreement. But nothing worked. GM's product troubles and stiff competition from Japanese plants in the U.S. slashed its sales from 41% of the domestic market to 36%...."[4]

By the early 1990s, it became apparent that "if GM can't sell cars, the union won't have jobs."[5] *Guarantees against plant closings in the 1980s had failed, so the union and management agreed to provide wage and income guarantees to union members when down-sizing and plant closings cause jobs to be lost. Workers with 10 years of seniority will be assured of receiving 95 percent of their pay for three years, while less senior union members will have the same benefits for up to 18 months. In addition, the company agreed to use early retirement incentives to induce 20,000 other workers to leave voluntarily.*[6]

The differences between Emerson Electric and GM are common in industry. Some employers view unions as outsiders; others see them as another component of the business environment that must be addressed. However, changes in the environment affect the strategies of unions and management, which often challenge employee and union relations. This chapter discusses the three major challenges that shape union-management relations: international competition, the labor-management system, and dispute resolution.

INTERNATIONAL COMPETITION

As Elizabeth Dole, former secretary of labor under President Bush, observed:

> ... the United States is facing its stiffest economic competition in history. The Pacific Rim nations continue their remarkable economic expansion. Western Europe will soon be united in one common market with a GNP larger than that of the United States. And the newly emerging free-market economies of Eastern Europe are hoping to take their place at the table.
>
> America's ability to compete in this complex global market may well be determined by our success in providing quality workplaces. ...[7]

Increased international competition demands higher productivity and quality from North American organizations. Companies like Emerson Electric seek a competitive advantage by locating in small southern towns, avoiding the constraints that unions can impose and gaining the benefits of higher productivity and lower wage costs. GM has been forced to drastically reduce its workforce to lower costs and bring production in line with sales, having announced plans to shrink by 74,000 workers and close 21 plants or other facilities during the first half of the 1990s. Still other firms have relocated operations to lower-wage countries, such as Mexico, or simply have imported needed parts or products.

The impact of international competition has meant a reduction in growth possibilities and even contractions among North American unions. The United Auto Workers, for example, lost 500,000 members, or about one-third of its membership, during the 1980s. From the mid-1950s to the early 1990s, union membership dropped from about 36 percent to 12 percent of private-sector workers. When government employees are included, unions only represent about 16 percent of the United States' workforce.[8] Parallel to the drop in membership has been a drop in the political strength of unions to influence employee relations laws.

Human resource professionals, however, would be badly mistaken if they assume that unions in other countries have suffered the same fate. Among major

Research summary

560   V. EMPLOYEE RELATIONS AND ASSESSMENT

Figure 18-1

The Interdependence of Unions, Management, and Government

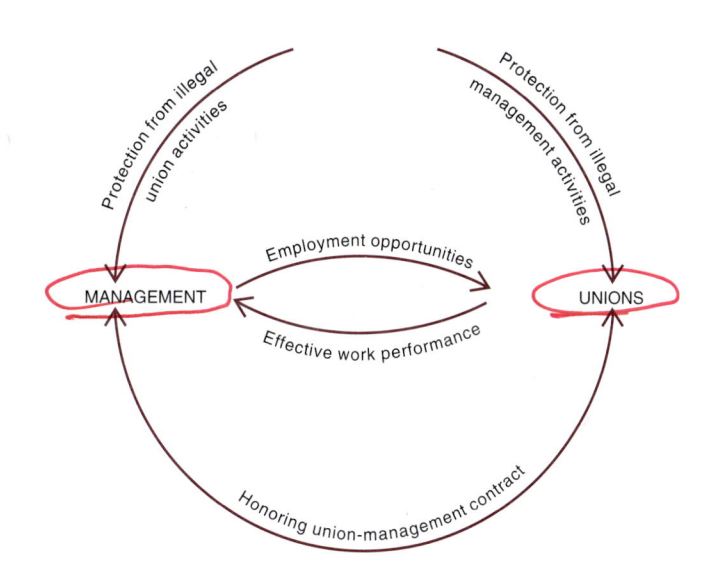

[Figure: Circular diagram showing MANAGEMENT and UNIONS with arrows indicating: Protection from illegal union activities; Protection from illegal management activities; Employment opportunities; Effective work performance; Honoring union-management contract]

Union and nonunion wage gaps

industrial countries, union membership grew during the 1970s and 1980s, today averaging 53 percent of all workers.⁹ Experts attribute the international difference to the smaller wage gap between union and nonunion workers abroad. In most industrialized countries, the difference between union and nonunion worker wages is about 10 percent or less; in the United States the difference is often 20 to 25 percent. As a result, United States firms—such as Emerson Electric—have been more active in resisting union attempts to organize workers.¹⁰

THE LABOR-MANAGEMENT SYSTEM

Although the size and power of unions have changed in recent years, unions remain a powerful political and economic force, particularly in highly industrialized regions and within industries that have a high percentage of unionized workers. The electric utility, manufacturing, trucking, telephone, and aerospace industries, and the government are, for example, highly unionized.

Union-management framework

Within the context of international competition and the changing prospects for unions, union-management relations continue to take place within a well-defined system of laws and past practices. The union-management framework is an interdependent system that consists of three principal sets of actors: workers and their representatives (unions); managerial employees (management); and government representatives in the legislative, judicial, and executive branches (government).¹¹ Each of these parties depends upon the other, as shown in Figure 18-1. For

18. UNION-MANAGEMENT RELATIONS

Figure 18-2

Union Philosophy and Objectives

The groundwork principle of America's labor movement has been to recognize that first things must come first. The primary essential in our mission has been the protection of the wage-worker, now; to increase his wages; to cut hours off the long workday, which was killing him; to improve the safety and the sanitary condition of the work-shop; to free him from the tyrannies, petty and otherwise, which serve to make his existence a slavery. These, in the nature of things, I repeat, were and are the primary objects of . . . unionism.

Our great Federation has uniformly refused to surrender this conviction and to rush to the support of any one of the numerous society-saving or society-destroying schemes which decade by decade have been sprung upon this country. A score of such schemes . . . have gone down behind the horizon and are now but ancient history. But while our Federation has thus been conservative, it has . . . had its face turned toward whatever reforms in politics or economics could be of direct and obvious benefit to the working class. It has pursued its avowed policy with the conviction that if the lesser and immediate demands of labor could not be obtained now from society as it is, it would be mere dreaming to preach and pursue that will-o'-the-wisp, a new society constructed from rainbow materials—a system of society on which even the dreamers themselves have never agreed. These demands of organized labor are comprehended in this larger and ultimate ideal—to enrich, enlarge, and magnify humanity. . . .

Source: Samuel Gompers, *Labor and the Common Welfare,* Freeport, N.Y.: Books for Libraries Press, 1919, p. 20.

---

example, the union relies on management to run the business and provide jobs—although in some countries, such as Germany, union officials commonly sit on boards of directors. Management and unions depend on the government for protection of legal rights. Managers rely on unions to honor their obligations and, increasingly, to assist management in cooperative ventures to increase productivity and quality. In turn, government relies on both the other parties to meet society's needs through productive organizations.

Unions and Human Resource Management

Labor unions do alter the work environment. Managers face new constraints on how they manage. While remaining responsible for employee relations, profits, sales, production, and other traditional functions, managers and human resource departments gain an additional responsibility: dealing with the union. The increased formality of employee relations often leads to greater centralization of decision making about employee relations. The human resource department becomes more deeply involved with decisions that affect compensation, hours, and other terms and conditions of employment to ensure uniformity of treatment among unionized workers. In short, management must still manage; and the union does not assume the responsibilities of the personnel department.

Unions as open social systems Like other organizations, unions are open social systems that pursue objectives and are influenced by their external environment. The financial strength of the employer, gains of rival unions, inflation and unemployment rates, government, and, as already discussed, international competition influence union objectives.

Figure 18-3

Tradeoffs Faced by Unions under Business and Social Unionism

PHILOSOPHICAL APPROACHES	TRADEOFFS BETWEEN UNION OBJECTIVES		
BUSINESS UNIONISM	Maximize number of employed members	OR	Maximize pay and benefits of members.
SOCIAL UNIONISM	Maximize welfare of members	OR	Maximize welfare of working people

Objectives of unions

Nevertheless, a core of widely agreed upon objectives exists. These objectives were stated by Samuel Gompers, the first president of the American Federation of Labor quoted in Figure 18-2. Although published in 1919, Gompers's philosophy remains valid today.[12] He sought to protect workers, increase their pay, and improve their working conditions.

Business and social unionism

Gompers's approach became known as *business unionism* because he recognized that a union can survive only if it delivers what members want in a businesslike manner. Gompers also realized that unions must address larger social issues of politics and economics when in the best interest of members. This approach is called *social unionism*. Figure 18-3 contrasts the sometimes conflicting tradeoffs faced by unions under business and social unionism. Business unionism focuses on membership or pay, while social unionism addresses the welfare of members or of working people. Early unions often focused too heavily on social unionism issues and, thus, lost the support of members who saw too few direct benefits. While business unionism directs its attention to the bargain between the employer and the union, human resource departments have been affected by social unionism when unions have lobbied for employment relations laws, such as the Occupational Safety and Health and Civil Rights Acts. Even when employees are not in a union, human resource departments are affected by gains in union wages, benefits, and other changes that must be met by nonunionized employers to remain competitive in the labor market.

Union Structure and Functions

Some writers believe that as organizations grew, employees lost direct contact with owners, and so unions emerged to help workers influence workplace decisions.[13] Through unions, workers were able to exert control over "their jobs" and "their work environment."[14] Then when attempts were made by employers to cut wages, the employees relied on their unions to resist these actions.[15] (Today, pressures for wage cuts may have an opposite impact, causing different factions to emerge within the union.[16])

Early attempts to control the work environment were local efforts because most companies were small operations. As employers—particularly the railroads—began to span city and then state boundaries, labor organizations

18. UNION-MANAGEMENT RELATIONS

formed national unions composed of locals from all over the country. When social problems affected several national unions at once, these unions joined together and formed multiunion associations. The most successful of these has been the *American Federation of Labor* and the *Congress of Industrial Organizations* (AFL-CIO). A brief review of the three levels—local, national, and multiunion associations, as represented by the AFL-CIO—illustrates the functions and structure of unions as seen by the human resource department.[17]

1. **Local Unions.** For human resource directors, the *local unions* are the most important part of the union structure.[18] They provide the members, the revenue, and the power of the entire union movement. There are three types of local unions: craft, industrial, and mixed locals. *Craft unions* are composed of workers who possess the same skills or trades. These include, for example, all the carpenters who work in the same geographical area. *Industrial unions* include the unskilled and semiskilled workers employed at the same location. When an employer has several unionized locations, employees at each location are usually represented by a different local union. Such is the case with the United Automobile Workers, for example. A local may even combine both unskilled and skilled employees. This arrangement is common in the electric utility industry, in which the International Brotherhood of Electrical Workers includes skilled, semiskilled, and unskilled workers, which results in a *mixed local*.

Figure 18-4 shows the structure of a typical local. The *steward* is the first level in the union hierarchy and usually is elected by the workers. Stewards help employees present their problems to management. If the steward of an industrial or mixed local cannot help a worker, then the problem is given to a *grievance committee*, which takes the issue to higher levels of management or to the human resource department.[19] In craft unions, the steward—who is also call the representative—usually takes the issue directly to the *business agent*, who is a full-time employee of the union. This process of resolving employee problems, called the *grievance procedure*, limits the authority of human resource specialists and line managers because it challenges their decisions. If the challenge is successful, the results may serve as a precedent that limits future decisions.

Human resource specialists also find that employee perceptions of the local union's administration can influence worker attitudes, satisfaction, and even complaints to the department about the union. After surveying 3,000 members of nine different locals, one researcher concluded:

Margin notes: Craft unions; Industrial unions; Mixed locals; Steward; Grievance committee; Research summary

> Union members were largely satisfied with contract terms, with the communications and informational materials received from officials, and with the opportunity to participate in local union affairs. Members were moderately satisfied with the effectiveness of union leadership, the overall worth of union meetings, and the administration of grievances. The main dissatisfactions uncovered were in the areas of adequacy of union training, the willingness of union leaders to act on the personal views of constituents, and the usefulness of union meetings to serve job-related needs.[20]

Figure 18-4

Organization Structure of a Typical Local Union

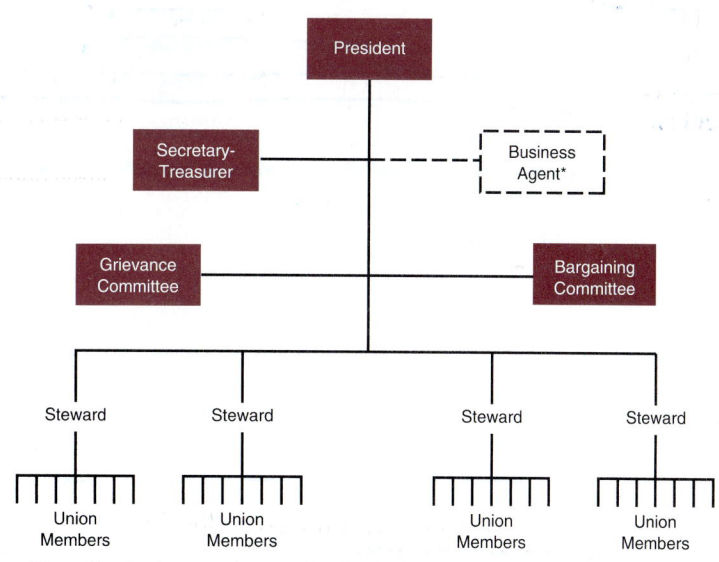

[Organization chart: President at top; Secretary-Treasurer and Business Agent* below; Grievance Committee and Bargaining Committee; four Stewards, each with Union Members.]

*The position of business agent is common in craft union locals.

An even more important limitation on supervisors and human resource specialists is the labor contract. It normally specifies wages, hours, working conditions, and related issues, such as grievance procedures, safety standards, probationary periods, and benefits. It usually is negotiated between the local union's *bargaining committee* and the human resource or industrial relations department.

Bargaining committee

National unions. Most local unions are chartered by a larger association called the *national union*, which organizes and helps the locals. National unions also pursue social objectives of interest to their members and maintain a staff that helps the local unions with legal assistance, negotiations, training of local officials, grievance handling, and expert advice. In return, locals share their dues with the national union, and they must obey its constitution and bylaws. Among craft unions, the national tends to leave many decisions to the locals. Industrial nationals, though, are more likely to be involved with their locals. For example, a national union may require that locally bargained contracts receive the national's approval to ensure consistent treatment among locals and to create a floor under wages. Sometimes the national union actually may bargain a companywide contract, as is the case with the United Automobile Workers, which leaves the locals to negotiate issues related to the particular work site.[21]

3. **Multiunion associations.** The AFL-CIO is the principal multiunion association. It is composed of affiliated national unions, and most major unions are members. The AFL-CIO is not a union; it is an association of unions. Its primary purpose is to further the social unionism goals of organized labor. Through lobbying, education, and research efforts, it supports new laws and social changes that benefit workers and affect human resource management. The AFL-CIO's influence over national unions is limited. It charges them small per capita dues to finance its programs. Any national union that fails to pay the dues or fails to support the AFL-CIO's policies may be removed as a member. At one time the United Automobile Workers union was expelled for nonpayment of dues. It has subsequently reaffiliated with the AFL-CIO.

Government and Labor Relations Law

Government shapes the union-management framework through laws and their interpretation. Government's role comes from the obligation to protect the welfare of society and from the authority found in Section VIII of the U.S. Constitution, which states that Congress shall have the power "to regulate commerce . . . among the . . . states. . . ." Congress has used that authority several times to regulate union-management relations.

U.S. Constitution

National Labor Relations Act. The *National Labor Relations Act* (NLRA), also knows as the Wagner Act, became law in 1935. It was passed during the Great Depression in an attempt to minimize the disruption of interstate commerce caused by strikes.[22] The act gives employees the right to collective action free of employer interference, except in small businesses that have little or no impact on interstate commerce. It allows employees to form labor organizations and to bargain with management about wages, hours, and working conditions. To prevent employers from interfering with these new employee rights, the law prohibits five *unfair labor practices* by management. These legal prohibitions are summarized in Figure 18-5. The act requires that management neither interfere with nor discriminate against employees who undertake collective action. Unfair labor practices also include the firing or "blacklisting" of employees for exercising their rights and "yellow dog" contracts.

ULPs

"Yellow dog" contracts

A common personnel policy before 1935 was to require new employees to sign a "yellow dog" contract. This employment contract meant that if a worker assisted a union in any way, that person could be fired. Those who agreed to these contracts were often called "yellow dogs." The NLRA made yellow dog contracts illegal, as well as outlawing the management practice of "blacklisting" employees by giving negative references because of union activities.

566   V. EMPLOYEE RELATIONS AND ASSESSMENT

Figure 18-5

Unfair Labor Practices by Management

The National Labor Relations Act makes it an unfair labor practice for members of management to:

1. *Interfere*, restrain, or coerce employees who desire to act collectively or refrain from such activities
2. *Dominate* or interfere with the formation or administration of any labor organization by contributing money or other support to it
3. *Discriminate* against anyone in hiring, stability of employment, or any other condition of employment because of their union activity or lack of involvement
4. *Discharge*, discipline, or otherwise discriminate against employees who have exercised their rights under the act
5. *Refuse* to bargain in good faith with employee representatives

---

The law also prohibits employers from discriminating against anyone who brings charges against a company for violating the law. To make the result of unionization meaningful, employers must bargain with the union in good faith over wages, hours, and working conditions. Refusal to do so is a violation of the act, as the National Football League owners discovered.

NFL

> The NFL owners were charged with a violation of their duty to bargain in good faith, according to a formal complaint issued against them. The complaint stemmed from a strike by the National Football League Players Association. It charged that the players' strike "was caused and has been prolonged by the unfair labor practices of respondents—the NFL management council." The owners had failed to give the union required "information essential to bargaining, changing working conditions . . . coercing players and interfering with their rights, as well as attempting to bypass the union in dealing with individual players."[23]

NLRB

To make the NLRA work, Congress also created the *National Labor Relations Board* (NLRB) to enforce it. This federal agency prosecutes violators and conducts secret-ballot elections among employees. It was the NLRB that filed the complaint against the NFL owners, for example.

The enforcement procedures of the NLRB are summarized in Figure 18-6. This agency does not search for violations until someone files a complaint with one of the local NLRB offices, which are located in major cities.[24] Then the complaint is investigated. If a violation appears to have occurred, a judge from the NLRB hears the case and renders a decision. A guilty employer must refrain from these illegal actions in the future. If an employee was fired as a result of the violation, that person is entitled to back pay, plus interest, and reinstatement with no loss of seniority.

Figure 18-6

NLRB Procedures to Redress Unfair Labor Practices

1. The aggrieved individual or organization contacts the nearest NLRB regional office and explains the alleged violation.

2. If the case appears to have merit, the regional director assigns the case to an NLRB employee for investigation.

3. The investigator determines if the facts are accurate.

4. The NLRB employee reports the findings to the regional director. If a violation appears to have occurred, the wrongdoer is charged with a violation of the act.

5. The local NLRB office prosecutes the alleged violator (who is defended by counsel) before an administrative law judge who renders an opinion after receiving final written arguments from both sides.

6. If innocent, the procedure ends. If guilty, the party may appeal the case to a five-member board in Washington, D.C.

7. If the board's ruling upholds the original finding, the guilty party may appeal to the federal courts.

When charges are filed against the employer, the human resource department usually assists the company's attorney in preparing the case. The department compiles performance appraisals, attendance records, and other documents that help the company prove its case. Sometimes the department's investigation reveals that the company is guilty. At this point, time and legal costs are saved by admitting guilt and accepting the NLRB's proposed settlement.

Human resource departments also become involved when the NLRB holds an employee election. This NLRB function takes place when a substantial number of employees (at least 30 percent of the eligible employees in an organization) request a government-supervised election to determine if the workers want a union. Through its local offices, the NLRB conducts a secret-ballot election at the employer's place of business. To win, the union must get a majority of the votes. If the union loses, another election among the same employees cannot be held for one year. If the union wins, the human resource department must be prepared to bargain with the union to reach a labor agreement.

Elections

LMRA

Labor Management Relations Act. After World War II, the public objected to the inflationary conditions, strikes, and the lack of legal constraints on unions. As a result, Congress passed the *Labor Management Relations Act* (LMRA) in 1947.

> One illustration of this lack of constraint concerns a powerful union that arranged for a large number of its unemployed members to picket a small trucking firm. The pickets so severely interfered with deliveries that the owner was forced to recognize the union against the wishes of his employees.
>
> When negotiations over the first contract began, the union leader refused to meet with the company's attorney. The owner was told to pick someone

Figure 18-7

Unfair Labor Practices by Unions

The Labor Management Relations Act made it an unfair labor practice for unions to:

1. *Restrain* or coerce employees or employers in the exercise of their legal rights.
2. *Force* an employer to discriminate against an employee because of that employee's membership or nonmembership in the union.
3. *Refuse* to bargain with an employer in good faith.
4. *Engage* in strikes or threats to force members of management to join a union (usually to collect large initiation fees) or to force an employer to cease doing business with another employer.
5. *Require* an employer to bargain with a union other than the one employees have selected.
6. *Demand* excessive or discriminatory initiation fees.
7. *Picket* an employer in order to force it to recognize the union as the employees' representative without requesting a government election within a reasonable time period.

else to represent the firm. Having no legal remedies and fearing more disruption, the owner hired a new attorney. The union then presented the lawyer with a completed contract and said, "Sign or we strike." There were no negotiations, and the company signed.[25]

Although most unions did not abuse their power, isolated cases such as this example contributed to the legal restrictions found in the LMRA.

Taft-Hartley

The Taft-Hartley Act, as the LMRA also is called, amended the earlier NLRA by prohibiting unfair labor practices by unions. These prohibitions appear in Figure 18-7. The act makes it illegal for unions to force employees to join them or to interfere with an employer's selection of its collective bargaining representatives. It also requires unions to bargain with management in good faith, and it outlaws union picketing and strikes under certain circumstances. This law also leaves to the individual states the right to pass "right-to-work" laws, which ensure that new employees are not required to join an already established union as a condition of retaining their jobs. Violations of the Taft-Hartley Act are prosecuted by the NLRB.

Taft-Hartley allows employers and human resource departments to deal with unions on a more equal basis. No longer can unions legally force one employer to stop doing business with another as a way for the union to win its demands. Unions can no longer threaten employees with high initiation fees if they do not actively support the union's organizing efforts. Although some union leaders called Taft-Hartley the "slave labor act," the law means that unions have to organize employees on the merits of unionization, not through unfair economic pressures on workers or their employers. To further minimize the disruptions caused by strikes, the Labor Management Relations Act made two other changes in union-management practices. It created the Federal Mediation and Conciliation Service, and it authorized Taft-Hartley injunctions.

"Slave labor" act

18. UNION-MANAGEMENT RELATIONS

FMCS

As its name implies, the *Federal Mediation and Conciliation Service* (FMCS) helps union and management bargainers to remain friendly (FMCS conciliates) during the process of bargaining a contract.[26] When bargaining leads to deadlocks, the agency suggests compromises (mediates). Although it has no power to force a settlement of disputes, the agency helps both sides reach an agreement without the need for a strike. When serious strikes threaten national security or create a national emergency, the Taft-Hartley Act allows the president of the United States to seek a court-ordered injunction to delay the strike for 80 days. During this "cooling-off" period, the government investigates the facts surrounding the dispute. The results of the fact-finding activities are turned over to union and management representatives, and the office of the president urges a negotiated settlement. If no settlement is reached at the end of 80 days, the strike can resume. Public pressure and the potential for congressional action usually cause both sides to find a solution even if the strike does start up again at the end of the 80-day cooling-off period.

Taft-Hartley injunction

Cooling-off period

Labor-Management Reporting and Disclosure Act. During the 12 years following the passage of the Taft-Hartley Act, it became evident that a few union leaders were not properly representing their members' interests. To correct this problem, the *Labor-Management Reporting and Disclosure Act* was passed in 1959.[26]

Figure 18-8 summarizes the major provisions of the act. In general, the law sought two broad objectives. First, it made union officials responsible for properly using union funds by establishing detailed reporting requirements. It backed up these requirements with the possibility of prison sentences for those found guilty of serious violations. Second, the act sought to make unions more democratic by providing members with certain rights. In fact, Title I of the law is often referred to as the union members' "bill of rights." If an employee has a complaint about the union's treatment, the human resource department need not get involved. Instead, it can direct workers to the nearest office of the Department of Labor. Specialists within the department then investigate the complaint to ensure that employee rights are not being ignored or abused by their union leaders.[27]

LMRDA

Union members' "bill of rights"

COOPERATION AND DISPUTE RESOLUTION

Given the increased competition faced by North American organizations and the growing complexity of labor relations laws, competitive success—even economic survival—depends upon cooperation and the successful resolution of disputes. Labor-management relations do not occur in isolation. The day-to-day treatment that employees receive from their supervisors, the employer's compensation program, and the personnel department's employee relations efforts all shape the workers' feelings about the organization, whether a union exists or not. With a union, however, employees can take collective action.

The actions that employees take depend upon the treatment they have received. When that treatment is perceived to be unacceptable to nonunionized

V. EMPLOYEE RELATIONS AND ASSESSMENT

Figure 18-8

Major Provisions of the Labor-Management Reporting and Disclosure Act

▶ *Title I* created a bill of rights for union members in dealing with their union. It assured members equal rights, freedom of speech and assembly, the right to sue the union, and other safeguards.
▶ *Title II* imposed detailed reporting requirements upon those who handle union funds.
▶ *Title III* established safeguards to ensure that the rights of members to elect leaders will not be lost when a national union takes over a local union and creates a trusteeship.
▶ *Title IV* requires that fair elections for union officers be held periodically.
▶ *Title V* sets forth the fiduciary responsibility of union officers and prohibitions against certain people from holding union office (primarily convicted felons).
▶ *Title VI* grants the Secretary of Labor the right to conduct investigations into possible abuses under this act.
▶ *Title VII* includes a series of miscellaneous provisions that limit strikes, picketing, and boycotts.

---

employees, a union is one likely outcome. If a union already exists, members seek to negotiate an agreement that changes the worse features of their relationship. When negotiations fail to resolve the major causes of friction, a strike is likely. Consider the situation surrounding a strike by 11,000 federal employees.

Air Traffic Controllers' strike

After members of the Professional Air Traffic Controllers' Organization (PATCO) went on strike, they were fired and barred from further federal employment because strikes by U.S. government workers are illegal. The traditional economic motives of most strikes were not the primary cause for the action taken by these Federal Aviation Administration (FAA) employees. According to research done by the University of Michigan's Institute for Social Research, the strike "was bred in and precipitated by the deteriorating conditions created by the Federal Aviation Administration's own organizational and management practices."[28]

A survey of more than 33,000 FAA employees revealed that morale among air traffic controllers was low. Strikers and nonstrikers alike produced similarly negative assessments of their jobs. "FAA employees holding managerial positions gave relatively high approval to an autocratic, no-questions-asked style of management, while the generally younger technicians and controllers—strikers and nonstrikers alike—strongly rejected such a style."[29]

Discontent was caused by the controllers' belief that little concern was shown for their well-being, rewards, work loads, or satisfaction. Many felt that ability had little to do with promotions. The principal researcher concluded: "A less directive bureaucratic style would have buffered the problem of the strike . . . and a participative style would have solved it. The implementation of participatory management . . . can go far toward prevent-

18. UNION-MANAGEMENT RELATIONS

ing future labor relations disasters like the massive federal strike and employee dismissals suffered by the FAA."[30]

The economic warfare of strikes extends to innocent victims, too. The PATCO strike meant restrictions on air traffic during the peak summer flying season. Passengers were inconvenienced, airlines lost money, and many employees were laid off for lack of work. And since the strike was illegal, the Federal Labor Relations Authority (which administers federal-sector labor regulations) decertified PATCO. This meant that the union could no longer represent air traffic controllers. For most PATCO leaders and employees, the strike-caused decertification meant a loss of their jobs, too.

Since these actions, the air traffic controllers have formed another union because many of their complaints and concerns remained unaddressed.

The PATCO strike is an example of a dispute that erupted over negotiations of an agreement between labor and management. Although most contract negotiations do not result in strikes, when they do, they can have serious effects on both parties along with those who depend upon them, such as the traveling public and the airline industry in the case of the PATCO strike. Disputes also arise during the administration of the labor agreement after it is negotiated. Although these contract interpretation disputes almost never lead to a strike, employee relations and organizational performance can be disrupted while dispute resolution procedures are applied. Even though one side or the other may "win" the dispute, cooperation is needed to minimize the need for dispute resolution. And, in truly progressive union-management relations, cooperation can be the basis for improved organizational performance that can benefit the management and union, along with customers, suppliers, and the general public.[31]

Since most disputes arise from the negotiation or administration of the labor agreement, the remainder of this chapter will provide an overview of the collective bargaining process and conclude with discussions of dispute resolution, cooperation, and the attendant challenges to human resource management.

Collective Bargaining

Figure 18-9 summarizes the collective bargaining process. Preparation for contract negotiations is often an ongoing activity in sophisticated companies such as General Motors. In other organizations, serious preparations begin three to six months before the expiration of the old contract or as soon as it looks like a union will successfully organize the previously nonunionized employer. The human resource department starts by studying recent trends in the economy and other labor negotiations. A plan is developed that outlines the company's position on wages, hours, and other terms and conditions of employment. The company's bargaining team may be supplemented by outsiders, most often a labor attorney. Once top management has approved the plan and strike preparations are under-

Figure 18-9

Stages of Collective Bargaining

1. PREPARATION   2. BARGAINING   3. ADMINISTRATION

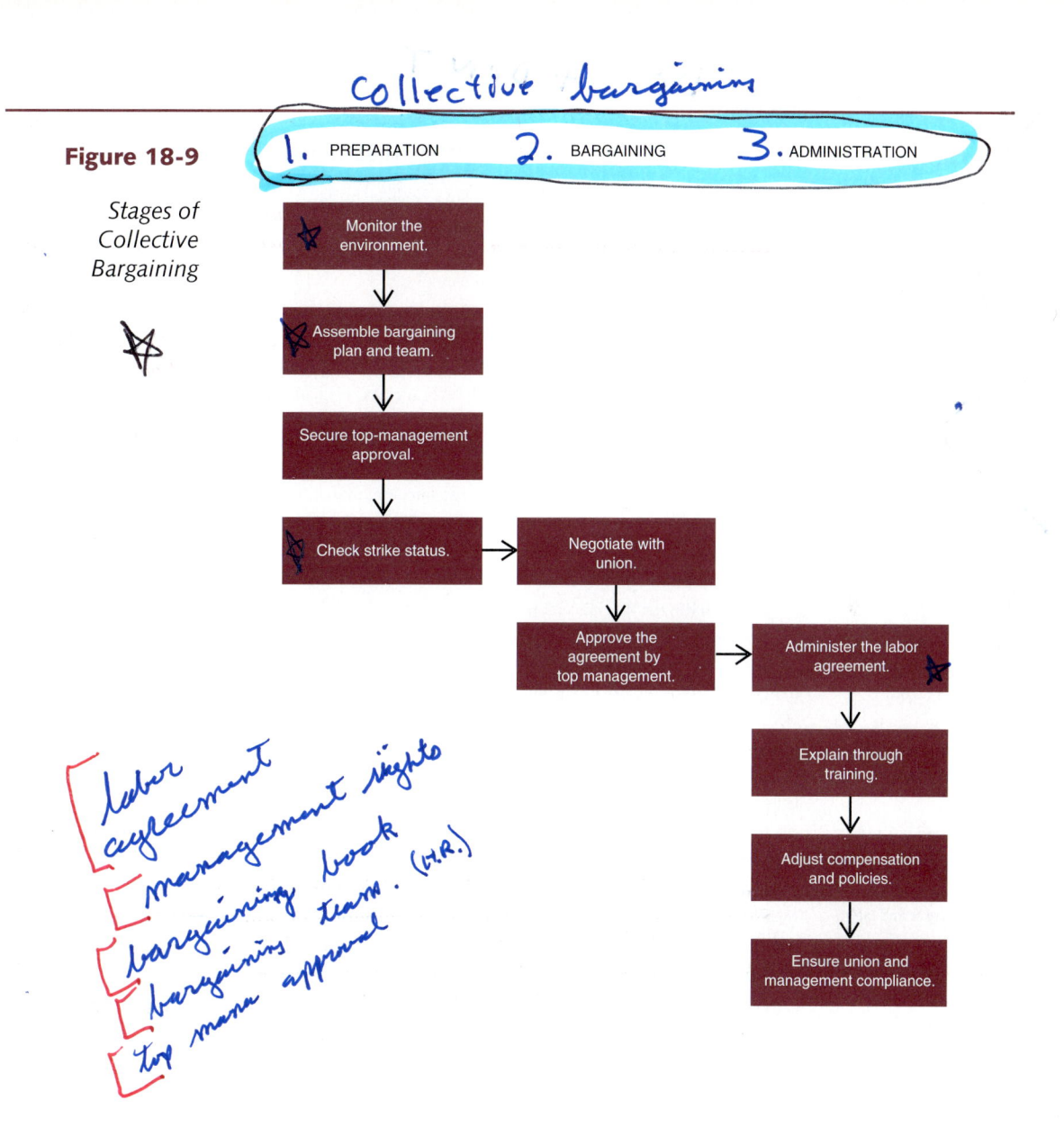

- Monitor the environment.
- Assemble bargaining plan and team.
- Secure top-management approval.
- Check strike status.
- Negotiate with union.
- Approve the agreement by top management.
- Administer the labor agreement.
- Explain through training.
- Adjust compensation and policies.
- Ensure union and management compliance.

way, negotiations begin several weeks or months before the expiration date of the labor agreement.

Negotiations with the union bargaining committee continue until a mutually satisfactory agreement is reached. Figure 18-10 identifies some of the traditional guidelines for successfully negotiating a labor contract. If the old contract expires, the union may elect to strike the company in an attempt to increase the pressure for its position. Once the contract is approved by top management and by a vote of the union members, the contract administration phase begins.

The final contract determines the terms and conditions of employment. Figure 18-11 captures the main topics found in a labor agreement. Although these documents can range from a few, photocopied pages to multivolume,

18. UNION-MANAGEMENT RELATIONS

Figure 18-10

Guidelines for Negotiations

THE "DOS" OF NEGOTIATIONS

1. Do seek more (or offer less) than you plan to receive (or give).
2. Do negotiate in private, not through the media.
3. Do let both sides win; otherwise the other side may retaliate.
4. Do start with easy issues.
5. Do remember that negotiations are seldom over when the agreement is concluded; eventually the contract will be renegotiated.
6. Do resolve deadlocks by stressing past progress, another point, or counterproposals.
7. Do enlist the support of the Federal Mediation and Conciliation Service if a strike seems likely.

THE "DON'TS" OF NEGOTIATIONS

1. Do not make your best offer first; that is so uncommon that the other side will expect more.
2. Do not seek unwanted changes; you may get them.
3. Do not say "no" absolutely, unless your organization will back you up absolutely.
4. Do not violate a confidence.
5. Do not settle too quickly; union members may think a quick settlement is not a good one.
6. Do not let the other side bypass your team and go directly to top management.
7. Do not let top management actually participate in face-to-face negotiations; they are often inexperienced and poorly informed.

Dayton Power and Light

printed books, most agreements address the topics in Figure 18-11. As the union-management relationship matures, each of these points is typically defined in greater and greater detail. At Dayton Power and Light, the union agreement had grown to 141 pages and was dominated by a "rule-book" mentality that sought to specify rights and responsibilities in increasing detail over the years. However, growing economic pressures led the company and the union to seek a more cooperative relationship, which has led to a 14-page document that stresses mutual goals and has led to greater trust. As a result, lost-time accidents have dropped by more than half and grievances have fallen by nearly 85 percent. Even in cooperative relationships based on trust, the need for dispute resolution remains.[32]

Dispute Resolution

Grievance resolution

Contract administration requires the company and the union to abide by the terms and conditions they have negotiated. Even in cooperative relationships, disputes arise over interpretation of the contract. Alleged violations of the agreement require a resolution of the resulting complaint, or grievance.

Either management or the union may file a grievance when the contract is violated. But since most decisions are made by management, there are few

Figure 18-11

Common Provisions in Union-Management Agreements

▶ *Union recognition.* Normally near the beginning of a contract, this clause states management's acceptance of the union as the sole representative of designated employees.

▶ *Union security.* To ensure that the union maintains members as new employees are hired and present employees quit, a union security clause commonly is demanded by the union. Forms of union security include:

    a. *Union shop.* All new workers must join the union shortly after being hired, usually within 60 or 90 days.

    b. *Agency shop.* All new workers must pay to the union an amount equal to dues.

    c. *Checkoff.* Upon authorization, management agrees to deduct the union dues from each union member's paycheck and transfer the monies to the union.

▶ *Wage rates.* The amount of wages to be paid to workers (or classes of workers) is specified in the wage clause.

▶ *Cost of living.* Increasingly, unions are demanding and receiving automatic wage increases for workers when price levels go up. For example, a common approach is for wages to go up by one cent an hour for each 0.3 or 0.4 percent increase in the consumer price index.

▶ *Insurance benefits.* This section specifies which insurance benefits the employer provides and how much the employer contributes toward these benefits. Frequently included benefits are life, hospitalization, and surgical insurance.

▶ *Pension benefits.* The amount of retirement income, years of service required, penalties for early retirement, employer and employee contributions, and vesting provisions are described in this section if a pension plan exists.

▶ *Income maintenance.* To provide workers with economic security, some contracts give guarantees of minimum income or minimum work. Other income maintenance provisions include severance pay and supplements to state unemployment insurance.

▶ *Time-off benefits.* Vacations, holidays, rest breaks, wash-up periods, and leave-of-absence provisions typically are specified in this clause.

▶ *Strikes/Lockouts.* It is common to find clauses in which the union promises not to strike for the duration of the contract in return for management's promise not to lock employees out of work during a labor dispute.

▶ *Seniority clause.* Unions seek contract terms that cause personnel decisions to be made on the basis of seniority. Often senior workers are given preferential treatment in job assignments, promotions, layoffs, vacation scheduling, overtime, and shift preferences.

▶ *Management rights.* Management must retain certain rights to do an effective job. These may include the ability to require overtime work, decide on promotions into management, design jobs, and select employees. This clause reserves to management the right to make decisions that management thinks are necessary for the organization's success.

▶ *Discipline.* Prohibited employee actions, penalties, and disciplinary procedures are either stated in the contract or included in the agreement by reference to those documents that contain the information.

▶ *Dispute resolution.* Disagreements between the union and management are resolved through procedures specified in the contract.

---

opportunities for the union to break the agreement. More commonly, unions file grievances because of alleged violations by management. The *grievance procedure* consists of an ordered series of steps to resolve disputes. Figure 18-12 describes the steps through which an employee's grievance typically passes. The actual number of steps in the grievance procedure depends upon the size of the organization. A three-step grievance procedure is most common. In very large

18. UNION-MANAGEMENT RELATIONS

Figure 18-12

Typical Steps in a Union-Management Grievance Procedure

▶ *Preliminary discussion.* The aggrieved employees discuss the complaint with the immediate supervisor with or without a union representative.

▶ *Step 1.* The complaint is put in writing and formally presented to the first-level supervisor. Normally, the supervisor must respond in writing within a contractually specified period, usually two to five days.

▶ *Step 2.* The union representative or the union grievance committee takes the written complaint to the supervisor's boss or the personnel department. A written response is required, usually within a week.

▶ *Step 3.* The local union president or other high-ranking union official takes the complaint to a member of top management or the personnel director. Again, a written response typically is required.

▶ *Step 4.* The company and the union present its viewpoints to an outside neutral arbitrator who hears the case and renders a decision much as a judge would do.

---

firms (often in manufacturing), four and even five steps are possible. The extra steps reduce the number of cases reaching top union and company officials.

Types and causes of grievances. Although personnel may not handle grievances in their early stages, the department plays an important role. Each supervisor sees only a small number of complaints, but personnel has an organizationwide view from which it can identify the types and causes of grievances. With this information, the department can create programs to improve grievance handling.[33] Grievances can be legitimate, imagined, or political. *Legitimate grievances* occur when there is a reasonable cause to think that there has been a contract violation. Even in a cooperative environment, contract clauses have different meanings to different people.

Imagined grievances occur when employees believe that the agreement has been violated even though management is exercising its contract rights in a reasonable manner. Again, misunderstanding is the primary cause of these grievances. A cooperative union can help settle such complaints quickly by explaining management's rights. Otherwise, when a manager says that the complaint is without merit, the worker may think that management is trying to save face for a bad decision.

Political grievances are the most difficult to solve. They are most common just before contract negotiations and union elections. They also occur when a complaint is pursued to further someone's political aspirations. For example, a union representative may be reluctant to tell union members that their grievances are without merit. To do so may mean a loss of political support in the next union election. Instead, the union leader may process a worthless grievance. Likewise, management also files political grievances.[34]

Handling grievances. Once a grievance is submitted, management should seek to resolve it fairly and quickly. Failure to do so can be seen as a disregard for

V. EMPLOYEE RELATIONS AND ASSESSMENT

Cautions

employee needs. In time, morale, motivation, performance, and company loyalty may be damaged.

In resolving grievances, several precautions should be followed.[35] Most importantly, grievances should be settled on their own merits. Political considerations by either party weaken the grievance system. Complaints need to be carefully investigated and decided on the basis of facts, not on emotional whim. Otherwise, damaging precedents may result. Second, the cause of each grievance should be recorded. Many grievances coming from one or two departments may indicate personality conflicts or a poor understanding of the contract. Third, employees should be encouraged to use the grievance procedure. Problems cannot be solved unless management and union officials know what they are. But before employees can use the grievance process, it must be explained through meetings, employee handbooks, or bulletin-board notices. And finally, whatever the solution may be, it needs to be explained to those affected. Even though union leaders do this, management should not fail to explain *its* reasoning to workers.[36]

Arbitration

Arbitration is the submission of a dispute to a neutral third party. Both sides of the issues are heard by an arbitrator, who acts as judge and jury. After weighing the facts, the arbitrator renders a decision.

Types of arbitration

In *advisory arbitration,* the arbitrator's opinion is intended to guide the parties toward a fair resolution without compelling them to accept the arbitrator's recommendations. *Last-offer arbitration* is usually binding and requires the arbitrator to select either labor's or management's position, whichever seems most reasonable. Both advisory and last-offer arbitration are most commonly used in resolving disputes that arise during contract negotiations. *Binding arbitration* requires both parties to accept the arbitrator's decision. When a grievance procedure does not result in a mutually acceptable solution, binding arbitration is called for in 96 percent of all labor agreements.[37]

Arbitration clauses are common because they allow a complaint to be resolved once and for all. Although a court action would have the same result, arbitration has several advantages. Unlike court decisions, an arbitrator's ruling usually is not subject to several levels of appeal. The lack of extensive appeals means a quicker decision. Since arbitration also is private, it is not an open proceeding as court cases are. Best of all, arbitration is less expensive than a court case.[38]

Arbitration holds two potential problems for personnel administrators: costs and unacceptable solutions. Although the employer and the union usually share the expenses, each case may cost several hundred to several thousand dollars. Admittedly, court costs and legal fees usually are more. Nevertheless, personnel needs to consider the costs involved. Another potential problem occurs when an arbitrator renders a decision against management's best interests. Since the ruling is binding, it may drastically alter management's rights. Suppose, for example, that management lays off several hundred workers, and the union convinces an arbitrator that management did not follow the contract's layoff procedure. The arbitrator may rule that all workers get their jobs back with back pay. Or if an arbitrator accepts the union's argument of extenuating circumstances in a disciplinary case, those extenuating circumstances may be cited in future cases. For instance, consider what happened in a chain of convenience markets.

> The Quick Foods Market had a policy that stealing from the company was grounds for immediate discharge. Sam Anglin, a new employee, took a sandwich and a beer from the cooler and consumed them without paying for them. He was fired when caught by the store manager. The union argued that Sam should get a second chance since he was a new employee. The arbitrator upheld management but added that discharge for such a minor theft might have been too harsh a penalty had Sam not been a probationary employee. If a senior employee is ever caught stealing, the union may use this opinion to claim that discharge is the wrong penalty. And another arbitrator might agree.

In cases like Sam's, a prompt arbitration decision is essential. The employee may be reluctant to look for a new job, and personnel may be reluctant to train a replacement until a final decision is made. To speed up the arbitration process, the company and the union may agree to use *expedited arbitration*. Under this approach the arbitrator usually gives an oral opinion at the end of the hearing or a written decision within a few days. Otherwise, arbitrators usually are allowed 30 days in which to render their decisions, and some arbitrators take considerably longer.[39]

It is important for personnel specialists to seek a solution with the union before arbitration. By so doing they may avoid additional costs, delays, and the possibility of an unsatisfactory decision. When arbitration is unavoidable, personnel specialists should follow the guidelines in Figure 18-13. These guidelines suggest the best chance of winning a favorable decision. If these guidelines reveal serious flaws in the employer's case, a compromise solution with the union before arbitration is usually advised.

UNION-MANAGEMENT COOPERATION

Although dispute resolution techniques stop most complaints from erupting into strikes, they are after-the-fact measures. Even the "winner" of a favorable arbitration decision loses the time and money it took to argue the case. Through cooperation, both parties can replace reactive measures with proactive approaches. Proactive efforts benefit the union and the company by saving time and expenses. These savings can mean higher profits for the employer and better contracts for the union.[40]

Figure 18-13

Preparation Guidelines for Arbitration Hearings

1. Study the original grievance and review its history through every step of the grievance machinery.
2. Determine the arbitrator's role. It might be found, for instance, that while the original grievance contains many elements, the arbitrator is restricted by the contract to resolving only certain aspects.
3. Review the collective bargaining agreement from beginning to end. Often, other clauses may be related to the grievance.
4. Assemble all documents and papers you will need at the hearing. Where feasible, make copies for the arbitrator and the other party. If some of the documents you need are in the possession of the other party, ask in advance that they be brought to the arbitration.
5. Make plans in advance if you think it will be necessary for the arbitrator to visit the plant or job site for on-the-spot investigation. The arbitrator should be accompanied by representatives of *both* parties.
6. Interview all witnesses. Make certain that they understand the whole case and the importance of their own testimony within it.
7. Make a written summary of what each witness will say. This serves as a useful check-list at the hearing to make certain nothing is overlooked.
8. Study the case from the other side's point of view. Be prepared to answer the opposing evidence and arguments.
9. Discuss your outline of the case with others in your organization. A fresh viewpoint often will disclose weak spots or previously overlooked details.
10. Read as many articles and published awards as you can on the general subject matter in dispute. While awards by other arbitrators for other parties have no binding precedent value, they may help clarify the thinking of parties and arbitrators alike.

Source: *Labor Arbitration Procedures and Techniques,* New York: American Arbitration Association, 1972, pp. 15–16. Used with permission.

Oregon Logging

As personnel manager for the Oregon Logging Company, Joe Von Kampen spent about 40 percent of his time on some phase of dispute resolution. Although the Teamsters represented only 125 of Oregon Logging's employees, there were usually 275 to 300 grievances a year. About 10 percent of these cases went to arbitration. The cost of arbitration seriously affected the company's profitability, which forced the union to accept the lowest wage rates in the area. To improve the situation, the town's mayor offered to help.

The mayor devised a training program that consisted of the union leader and the personnel manager taking turns reading the contract to an audience of supervisors and union representatives. After each paragraph, the personnel manager and union leader both summarized what the paragraph meant. The mayor did not let them go on to the next paragraph until both agreed on the meaning of the previous one. After several sessions, the entire contract was reviewed. Lower-ranking union and management officials learned what the contract meant and that they were expected to cooperate with each other. The following year, 14 grievances were filed and only one went to arbitration. The company's profitability improved dramatically, and the local union obtained its largest wage increase in the next negotiations.

Union-Management Attitudes

Severe conflicts between the company and the union often can be traced to the attitudes each holds about the other.⁴¹ In the Oregon Logging example, supervisors felt that the union was intruding on their rights. When the supervisors, in turn, denied workers their rights, the union fought back with grievances. Union members sometimes get so frustrated that they conduct *wildcat strikes*. These strikes are spontaneous acts that take place in violation of the contract, regardless of the objections raised by union leaders. Even after the strike is over, the underlying problems still have to be settled.⁴²

If the attitudes between the parties remain hostile, the organization suffers from poor performance. Serious disruptions can even affect the survival of the organization and the union. Sometimes extreme disruptions may require both parties to cooperate in order to prevent bankruptcy and massive layoffs.⁴³

Building Cooperation

Proactive human resource departments cannot wait for disaster to occur before attempting to build cooperation with the union. Such departments realize that cooperation is not automatic and must be initiated by human resource specialists. However, there are several obstacles to cooperation.

Obstacles to cooperation. Human resource specialists often seek union cooperation to improve the organization's effectiveness. But effectiveness usually is far less important to union leaders. Quite naturally, these officials are more concerned about the welfare of their members and winning reelection to union office. So, when cooperation fails to be attractive politically, union leaders have little incentive to cooperate. In fact, if leaders do cooperate, they may be accused by workers of forgetting the union's interests. These accusations can mean defeat by political opponents within the union. Thus cooperation may not be in the leader's best interest.

For many years, negotiations in the steel industry were marked by strikes and threats of strikes. The result was lower profitability and even a loss of markets to foreign producers. In turn, many members of the United Steelworkers Union were laid off. Both the union and the steel companies were suffering.

Both parties reached a cooperative arrangement called the Experimental Negotiations Agreement. This agreement called for concessions from the steel producers and no nationwide strikes by the union. The cooperative move was

Figure 18-14

Methods of Building Union-Management Cooperation

Managers and personnel specialists can build cooperation between the employer and the union through:

- *Prior consultation* with union leaders to defuse problems before they become formal grievances
- *Sincere concern* for employee problems and welfare even when management is not obligated to do so by the labor agreement
- *Training programs* that objectively communicate the intent of union and management bargainers and reduce biases and misunderstandings.
- *Joint study committees* that allow management and union officials to find solutions to common problems
- *Third parties* who can provide guidance and programs that bring union leaders and managers closer together to pursue common objectives.

---

intended to benefit both the union and employees. But some members saw it as a loss of rights, particularly the right to strike. In the union's national elections, a splinter group was able to mount a serious, but subsequently unsuccessful challenge to the established leadership by attacking this cooperative agreement.

Besides political obstacles, union leaders may mistrust the human resources department. For example, bitter remarks made by the department during organizing drives may convince union officials that personnel specialists are antiunion. Within this climate, cooperative gestures by the department may be seen as tricks. If mistrust increases, cooperation usually fails.

Cooperative methods. Once human resource specialists realize the political concerns and suspicions of union leaders, several cooperative methods can be tried. These techniques are summarized in Figure 18-14 and are explained in the following paragraphs.

One of the most basic actions human resources departments can take is *prior consultation* with the union. Not every management decision must be approved by the union, but actions that affect the union or its leaders may cause a grievance unless explained before the action is taken. Suppose, for instance, that a senior employee was passed over for promotion because the use of profanity by this employee could mean a loss of customers. Suppose further that the personnel department explained to union leaders that the use of profanity by the most senior worker could mean a loss of valuable business and jobs for union members. The union leaders might accept the promotion of the junior worker. The union president would be less likely—at least politically, to challenge the promotion decision. Some managers even ask union leaders to talk to problem employees before management has to take action that might lead to grievances.

Management and personnel also can build cooperation through a *sincere concern* for employees. This concern may be shown through the prompt settlement of grievances, regardless of who wins. Or management can bargain sincerely with the union to reduce the need for a strike. Even when a strike occurs, management can express its concern for workers. For example, during one strike at General Motors, GM continued to pay the strikers' insurance premiums to prevent a lapse in coverage. Sometimes this concern is initially expressed by management's acceptance of the union. The disciplining of a member of management for a flagrant violation of the union's rights is one example of such an expression. Ford Motor Company provides another:

Ford

> *The president of Ford Motor Company issued a policy letter to all Ford divisions, subsidiaries, and affiliated companies. In that policy letter, entitled "Employee Involvement," he stated: "It is the policy of the Company to encourage and enable all employees to become involved in and contribute to the success of the Company. A work climate should be created and maintained in which employees, at all levels, can achieve individual goals and work satisfaction by directing their talents and energies toward clearly defined Company goals.*
>
> ▶*Methods of managing should encourage employee participation in identifying and solving work-related problems.*
>
> ▶*Communications programs and procedures should be implemented that encourage frequent, timely and constructive two-way communications with employees concerning work-related problems."*[44]

Training programs are another way to build cooperation. After a new contract is signed, the personnel department usually trains managers so that they understand the contract terms. The union does the same for its leaders. As a result, both sides continue their biases and misunderstandings. If the human resource department sponsors training for both the union and management, then a common understanding of the contract is more likely. The training can be as simple as taking turns paraphrasing the contract, or neutral trainers outside the company can be hired to conduct the training. Either way, supervisors and union officials end the training with a common understanding of the contract and a new basis for cooperation.

Joint study committees

When a complex problem confronts the union and the employer, *joint study committees* are sometimes formed.[45] For example, the three largest automobile companies agreed to create separate committees with the United Auto Workers union to study health-care costs, and find ways to slow its rapid rise.[46] Productivity committees are another common form of union-management cooperation.

According to the Department of Labor, 97 of 1,550 contracts surveyed had provisions for union-management committees to study production.[47]

A final method of building cooperation is through *third parties,* such as consultants or government agencies, who may act as catalysts. For example, the Federal Mediation and Conciliation Service (FMCS), discussed earlier in this chapter, has a program entitled *relations by objectives* (RBO).

RBO at the FMCS

In a series of meetings, which at first are held separately with labor and management, FMCS staff members determine company and union viewpoints on what the "other party" should do to improve relations, and then on what each party should do itself. Following these sessions, meetings are held, attended by all management officials—including top executives and line supervisors—and by all union officials, including shop stewards. Respective viewpoints are discussed, clarified, and incorporated into mutually acceptable lists of objectives for improvement of labor-management relations.

The list then is discussed by the two parties separately and jointly. The joint sessions develop an agreement on action steps for attaining each objective, assigning responsibility for starting and completing steps, and implementing a timetable for achievement of each objective.[48]

> *Dayton Power and Light Company faced a dramatic slowdown in its growth prospects because of a serious decline in new customers. Hundreds of employees were laid off. The union reacted by filing 450 grievances and unfair labor practice charges with the National Labor Relations Board. Morale and productivity suffered.*
>
> *The FMCS had previously begun a relationship by objectives program that had begun to open communication channels between labor and management. Monthly meetings were set up in 40 departments, and 90 percent of the work force was trained in analytical decision-making approaches. Although hostile relations between the union and management remained, over the following years cooperation and trust emerged and grew. Through the participation of union officials and rank-and-file members with various levels of management, joint committees attacked mutual problems.*
>
> *The results have been a dramatic drop in accidents, grievances, and negative attitudes. Productivity and morale have improved. And, the detailed, 141-page contract that sought to control the relationship in minute detail gave way to a 14-page compact that outlines the new relationship in more positive terms.[49]*

Labor-management cooperation grew dramatically during the 1980s and early 1990s in response to international and domestic pressures for greater productivity.[50] Success with participative and other cooperative approaches means that this trend is likely to continue and spread, as these innovations are institutionalized and diffused in the economy.[51] These trends toward greater cooperation are already appearing in the public sector, too.[52] As a member of the Public

18. UNION-MANAGEMENT RELATIONS

Employee Department of the AFL-CIO observes, "Generally, wherever there is a fairly sophisticated labor-management relationship, the chances are that the parties have developed some type of cooperative program."[53]

THE CHALLENGES TO HUMAN RESOURCE MANAGEMENT

HR challenges

Unions are at a crossroads. During recent years they have experienced a steady decline in membership, political power, and prestige. Nevertheless, unions represent a significant challenge to personnel professionals and operating managers. Within companies with unions, compliance with labor laws, contract provisions, and past practices limit managers' flexibility. Even when no unions are present, proactive employee relations are needed to assure a productive work force. And if a company wants to remain nonunion, additional pressures fall on employee relations specialists and operating managers, especially supervisors.

Whether unions will rebound and reclaim their role as a powerful actor in the economic and political systems of developed nations is uncertain. What does seem certain, however, is that unions will seek innovative approaches to reverse these trends. Some examples include efforts to organize nontraditional groups, such as white-collar, service, government, and professional workers. Other examples include offering new services—from charge cards to health-care advice—to supplement more traditional collective bargaining efforts and fringe benefits.[54]

At the same time, many human resource managers and union leaders perceive government intervention as a potential threat to the traditional freedoms that they have all enjoyed. Their common concern rises out of the fear that more laws will control their affairs. And since existing laws are enforced by agencies with the power to "make laws" by their interpretation of existing ones, regulations are bound to grow.

Effective HR policies

To meet the challenges of increased union innovation and government intrusion into the workplace, personnel professionals need to be proactive. Effective human resource policies and practices provide the best stance for meeting the challenges of unions and government involvement with a productive work force. More specifically, personnel specialists (within the constraints of organizational effectiveness and efficiency, law, technology, and other challenges) must carefully do the following:

➤ *Design* jobs that are personally satisfying to workers

➤ *Develop* plans that maximize individual opportunities and minimize the possibility of layoffs

➤ *Select* workers who are qualified

➤ *Establish* fair, meaningful, objective standards of individual performance

▶ *Train* workers and managers to enable them to achieve expected levels of performance

▶ *Evaluate* and reward behavior on the basis of actual performance.

In other words, human resource managers need to apply proactively the ideas discussed in earlier chapters of this book! Failure to implement sound human resource policies and practices provides the justification *and* motivation for workers to be less productive, to form unions, or to seek the help of government regulatory agencies.

Organizationally, when unions are present, the department is expanded by the addition of a labor relations section. This section allows labor specialists to deal with such critical areas as negotiations and contract administration, while other human resource professionals attend to their more traditional roles. In fact, personnel and labor relations may form two equal divisions within a broader department, typically called *industrial relations*.

Operationally, the personnel section seeks sound employee relations through effective practices. Open-door policies and in-house complaint procedures are two examples. The labor relations section has a complementary role. It seeks to minimize restrictions on management by diligent negotiations and fair administration of the union contract. Or, to use a sports analogy, personnel serves as the offensive team and labor relations is the defensive team.

SUMMARY

UNIONS ARE open systems—affected by their environment—and political organizations which are influenced by the needs and wishes of members. Increased global competition has put pressure on many firms to reduce costs, whether the result be lower wages for employees or lower labor costs through better productivity. Some organizations seek to avoid unions, such as Emerson Electric. Other employers seeks ways to prosper with a union through contract negotiations, dispute resolution procedures, and various cooperative approaches.

The labor-management system means additional constraints for operating managers and human resource professionals. However, management remains responsible for the economic success of the firm and its employee relations. Government plays a crucial role by setting the legal rules under which the collective bargaining relationship occurs. It outlaws unfair labor practices and provides mechanisms through the National Labor Relations Board to conduct representation elections and resolve allegations of unfair labor practices.

Dispute resolution relies on contractual terms and cooperation of labor and management. Grievance procedures, culminating in binding arbitration, exist to resolve contract interpretation disputes. Although strikes are rare, they allow both parties to exercise their economic strength to pressure the other side when negotiating a labor agreement. Although cooperation is determined by the nature of the union-management relationship, international and domestic competitive pressures have forced many unions and employers to find ways to cooperate in order to prosper during these turbulent economic times.

Terms for Review

- Business unionism
- Social unionism
- National Labor Relations Act (NLRA)
- National Labor Relations Board (NLRB)
- Federal Mediation and Conciliation Service
- American Federation of Labor and Congress of Industrial Organizations (AFL-CIO)
- Labor-Management Reporting and Disclosure Act
- Local unions
- Labor Management Relations Act (LMRA)
- Craft unions
- Industrial unions
- National unions
- Unfair labor practices
- Labor agreement
- Management rights
- Grievance procedure
- Arbitration
- Mixed unions
- Wildcat strike
- Grievance committee

Review and Discussion Questions

1. In your own words, summarize the primary objectives of unions.

2. What distinguishes craft, industrial, and mixed unions from one another?

3. Suppose you are a personnel specialist and you are having the following problems. For each problem, which government agency would you turn to for assistance?

   a. The union is trying to get the personnel department to fire a union critic.

   b. An employee complains to you that the union will not allow members to speak up at the local union meeting.

   c. The company and the union are deadlocked over the terms of a new labor agreement.

4. In your own words, explain why unions usually file the most grievances.

5. How are local and national unions impacted by international competition?

6. When an employee has a complaint about a management action in a unionized operation, how does she or he go about resolving it?

7. What are the advantages and disadvantages of using arbitration?

8. Since labor-management cooperation is important to the economic success of the business and, eventually, the union's ability to negotiate wage gains and other benefits for members, what are some of the ways you could recommend to improve labor-management cooperation?

INCIDENT 18-1
In-Flight Food Services Company

The In-Flight Food Services Company provides prepared meals for several airlines at a major airport in the Southeast. Food handlers cook and package meals to be reheated in airplane galleys for service to passengers while in flight. Most of the 535 food handlers belong to the Independent Food Handlers Union, which has represented these employees for over five years.

Each year, the industrial relations department noticed that the number of grievances filed by members of the union had increased about 15 percent. The time spent by union representatives, employees, and supervisors as a result of these grievances was affecting productivity in the company's cafeteria. The general manager was concerned that the company's costs and low productivity could lead to a loss of several key contracts with major airlines.

The industrial relations department studied all the grievances during the past year and provided the following analysis.

A. Total grievances filed	803
Number settled at:	
First-level supervision	104
Second-level supervision	483
General manager level	205
Arbitration	11

Although some grievances involved more than one issue, most of them were single-issue matters. When the industrial relations department classified the grievances, the following results were reported:

B. Tardiness or absence control	349
Overtime disputes	265
Other discipline or discharge	77
Incorrect job schedules	75
Multiple-issue disputes	37

1. How would you approach the local union for help?

2. Assuming the industrial relations director asked you to design a training program to reduce the high number of grievances, who do you think should attend the training sessions?

3. What topics would you cover in the training?

References

1. Elizabeth Dole, "Facing Tomorrow Together," *Labor Relations Today* (May–June 1990), p. 1.

2. Daniel J.B. Mitchell, "Compensation: Why Are Wage Concessions So Prevalent?" *Personnel Journal* (August 1986), p. 135.

3. "Emerson Electric: High Profits from Low Tech," *Business Week* (April 4, 1983), p. 60.

4. David Woodruff, "The UAW Veers Closer to Reality," *Business Week* (Oct. 1, 1990), p. 33.

5. Ibid.

6. Ibid.

7. Dole, op. cit.

8. Gene Koretz, "Why Unions Thrive Abroad," *Business Week* (Sept. 10, 1990), p. 26.

9. Ibid.

10. Ibid.

11. John T. Dunlop, *Industrial Relations Systems* (New York: Henry Holt, 1958), pp. 7–8; J.W. Miller, Jr., "Power, Politics, and the Prospects for Collective Bargaining: An Employer Viewpoint," in Stanley M. Jacks, ed., *Issues in Labor Policy* (Cambridge: MIT Press, 1971), pp. 144–157.

12. Samuel Gompers, *Labor and the Common Welfare* (Freeport, N.Y.: Books for Libraries Press, 1919).

13. Frank Tannenbaum, *The Labor Movement: Its Conservative Functions and Consequences* (New York: Alfred A. Knopf, Inc., 1921).

14. Selig Perlman, *A Theory of the Labor Movement* (New York: Macmillan Publishing Co., 1928).

15. John R. Commons et al., *History of Labor in the United States* (New York: Macmillan Publishing Co., 1918). See also A. H. Raskin, "From Sitdowns to Solidarity," *Across the Board* (Dec. 1981), pp. 22–25.

16. Jonathan Tasini, "Unions Divided: The Revolt of the Rank and File," *Business Week* (August 11, 1986), pp. 72–73.

17. Reed C. Richardson, *American Labor Unions, An Outline of Growth and Structure*, 2nd ed. (Ithaca: New York State School of Industrial and Labor Relations, Cornell University, 1970), p. 19.

18. Leonard Sayles and George Strauss, *The Local Union* (New York: Harcourt, Brace & World, 1967).

19. Harry Graham and Brian Heshizer, "The Effect of Contract Language on Low Level Settlement of Grievances," *Labor Law Journal* (July 1979), pp. 427–432.

20. George W. Bohlander, "How the Rank and File Views Local Union Administration—A Survey," *Employee Relations Law Journal* (Autumn 1982), p. 232.

21. "Labor's Marriage of Convenience," *Business Week* (Nov. 1, 1982), pp. 28–29.

22. Irving Berstein, *A History of the American Worker, 1933–1941: Turbulent Years* (Boston: Houghton Mifflin Co., 1971), p. 332.

23. "NLRB Complaint Blames Football Owners," *AFL-CIO News* (Oct. 30, 1982), p. 8.

24. John S. Irvin, Jr., "Why Do We Need a Labor Board?" *Labor Law Journal* (July 1979), pp. 387–395.

25. Perry A. Zirkel and J. Gary Lutz, "Characteristics and Functions of Mediators: A Pilot Study, *The Arbitration Journal* (June 1981), pp. 15–20.

26. George W. Bohlander and William B. Werther, Jr., "The Labor-Management Reporting and Disclosure Act Revisited," *Labor Law Journal* (Sept. 1979), pp. 528–589.

27. Ibid.

28. "Management vs. Labor," *ISR Newsletter* (Autumn 1982), p. 3.

29. Ibid.

30. Ibid.

31. Joel Cutcher-Gershenfeld, Robert B. McKersie, and Kristen R. Weaver, *The Changing Role of Union Leaders* (Washington, D.C.: U.S. Department of Labor, 1988).

32. Phil Farish, "HRM Update: New-Style Pact," *Personnel Administrator* (Oct. 1988), p. 12.

33. William B. Werther, Jr., "Reducing Grievances through Effective Contract Administration," *Labor Law Journal* (April 1974), pp. 211–216. See also Deborah M. Kolb and Priscilla A. Glidden, "Getting to Know Your Conflict Options," *Personnel Administrator* (June 1986), pp. 77–78, 80–86, 88, 90.

34. Ross Stagner and Hjalmar Rosen, *Psychology of Union-Management Relations* (Belmont, Calif.: Wadsworth Publishing Co., 1965), pp. 110–111.

35. Thomas F. Gideon and Richard B. Peterson, "A Comparison of Alternate Grievance Procedures," *Employee Relations Law Journal* (Autumn 1979), pp. 222–233. See also "The Antiunion Grievance Play," *Business Week* (Feb. 12, 1979), pp. 117, 120; and George W. Mauer and Jeanne Flores, "From Adversary to Advocate," *Personnel Administrator* (June 1986), pp. 53–58.

36. George W. Bohlander, "Fair Representation: Not Just a Union Problem," *Personnel Administrator* (March 1980), pp. 36–40, 82.

37. *Basic Patterns in Union Contracts* (Washington, D.C.: Bureau of National Affairs, 1975), p. 37.

38. William B. Werther, Jr., and Harold C. White, "Cost Effective Arbitration," *MSU Business Topics* (Summer 1978), pp. 59–64. See also Mollie H. Bowers, "Grievance-Mediation: Another Route to Resolution," *Personnel Journal* (Feb. 1980), pp. 132–136, 139.

39. Werther and White, op. cit.

40. *Labor-Management Cooperation: 1989 State-of-the-Art Symposium* (Washington, D.C.: U.S. Department of Labor, 1989). See also Steve Donahue, "New Ways to Divide the Pay Pie," *Labor Relations Today* (Oct./Nov./Dec. 1988), pp. 1–2.

41. Joseph Tomkiewicz and Otto Brenner, "Union Attitudes and the 'Manager of the Future,'" *Personnel Administrator* (Oct. 1979), pp. 67–70, 72. See also William B. Werther, Jr., "Government Control vs. Corporate Ingenuity," *Labor Law Journal* (June 1975), pp. 360–367.

42. "In Wildcat Strikes, Court Rules: Union Leaders Safe from Discipline," *Resource* (May 1983), pp. 1, 10. See also Dana P. Swinehart and Mitchell A. Sherr, "A Systems Model of Labor-Management Cooperation," *Personnel Administrator* (April 1986), p. 87.

43. Richard E. Walton and Robert B. McKersie, *A Behavioral Theory of Labor Negotiations* (New York: McGraw-Hill Book Company, 1965), pp. 13–46. See also Thomas F. O'Boyle and Terence Roth, "War and Peace: Labor Relations Vary at Two Steelmakers," *The Wall Street Journal*, Western ed. (Sept. 17, 1985), pp. 1–24.

44. Phillip Caldwell, "Policy Letter 13–14, Subject: Employee Involvement," Ford Motor Company (internal document) (Nov. 5, 1979), p. 1. See also Denise Tanguay and Gregory E. Huszczo, *Forging a Partnership through Employee Involvement: The Case of the GM Hydramatic Willow Run Plant and UAW Local 735 Joint Activities* (Washington, D.C.: U.S. Department of Labor, 1988).

45. Edgar Weinberg, "Labor-Management Cooperation: A Report on Recent Initiatives," *Monthly Labor Review* (April 1976), p. 13.

46. "A Joint Look at Cutting Health Care Costs," *Business Week* (Nov. 17, 1975), p. 49.

47. Weinberg, op. cit. See also David C. Mowery and Bruce E. Henderson, *The Challenge of New Technology to Labor-Management Relations* (Washington, D.C.: U.S. Department of Labor, 1989).

48. National Center on Productivity and Quality of Working Life, *Recent Initiatives in Labor-Management Cooperation* (Washington, D.C.: U.S. Government Printing Office, 1976).

49. Phyllis Lehmann McIntosh, "Labor Compact Key to New Employee-Management Partnership at Dayton Power and Light," *Labor-Management Cooperation Brief*, (Jan. 1988), pp. 1–7. See also Farish, op. cit.

50. Richard Shore, "Regaining the Productive Edge," *Labor Relations Today* (Sept./Oct. 1989), pp. 1–2.

51. Thomas A. Kochan and Joel Cutcher-Gershenfeld, *Institutionalizing and Diffusing Innovations in Industrial Relations* (Washington, D.C.: U.S. Department of Labor, 1988).

52. Donna St. John, "A Unique Labor-Management Partnership Has Made Dade County Public Schools a Model in Education Reform," *Labor-Management Cooperation Brief* (June 1989), pp. 1–7.

53. John R. Stepp, "Making Public Service Work Better," *Labor Relations Today* (May/April 1989), p. 1. See also Jan Abott, "New Approaches to Collective Bargaining and Workplace Relations: Do They Work?" *Readings on Labor-Management Relations* (Washington, D.C.: U.S. Department of Labor, 1990).

54. Jonathan Tasini and Jim Hurlock, "Big Labor Tries the Soft Sell," *Business Week* (Oct. 13, 1986), p. 126. See also Cathy Trost, "Rejuvenating Organized Labor Is the Aim of a Three-State Pilot Project," *The Wall Street Journal*, Western ed. (July 16, 1986), p. 1; "Unions Must Adapt, Labor Leader Says," *Resource* (Oct. 1986), p. 7; Cathy Trost, "What They Preach to Cut Health-Care Costs," *The Wall Street Journal*, Eastern ed. (August 12, 1986), p. 1.

Employers who use human resources auditing stand a greater chance of avoiding . . . suits and, should they arise, are better positioned to defend against them.
PAUL J. CHAMPAGNE AND R. BRUCE MCAFEE[1]

. . . managers are focusing on improved human resources management as a means of restoring the competitive position of their companies in an increasingly challenging global marketplace.
RAYMOND E. MILES AND CHARLES C. SNOW[2]

ASSESSING PERFORMANCE AND PROSPECTS

CHAPTER OBJECTIVES

After studying this chapter, you should be able to:
1. IDENTIFY the benefits of a human resource audit.
2. DESCRIBE the most common approaches to audits.
3. LIST the research tools used in a human resource audit.
4. EXPLAIN the major challenges facing human resource practitioners in the future.
5. DESCRIBE how third parties cause changes in human resource management.
6. LIST major workplace innovations that are likely to occur by the year 2000.

Figure 19-1

A Human Resource Management Model

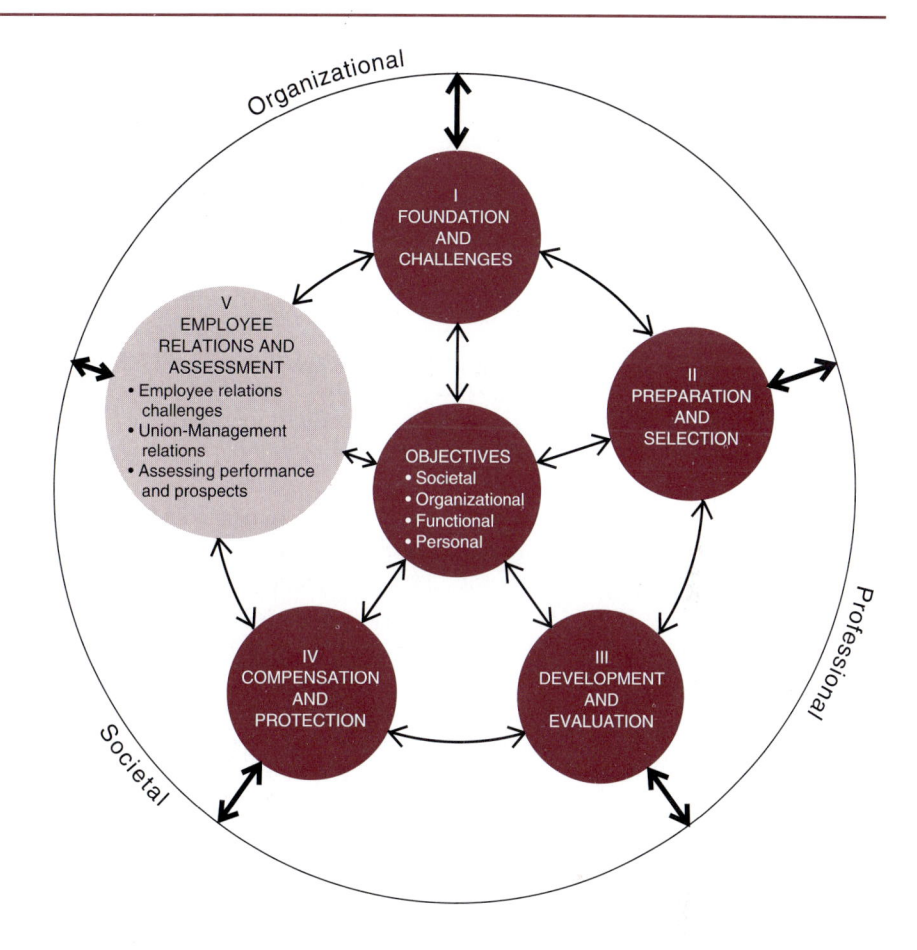

A circular diagram titled with axes "Organizational," "Professional," and "Societal" surrounding five interconnected nodes:

- **I FOUNDATION AND CHALLENGES**
- **II PREPARATION AND SELECTION**
- **III DEVELOPMENT AND EVALUATION**
- **IV COMPENSATION AND PROTECTION**
- **V EMPLOYEE RELATIONS AND ASSESSMENT**
  - Employee relations challenges
  - Union-Management relations
  - Assessing performance and prospects

Center: **OBJECTIVES**
- Societal
- Organizational
- Functional
- Personal

xecutive expectations, international and domestic competition, and the growing diversity of the work force are challenging the role of human resource management. More than ever, the department is expected to contribute to the firm's competitive advantage. As a result, the importance of the human resource function and its impact have grown dramatically. However, the department's contribution is also challenged by the multiple objectives first identified in Chapter 1 and shown in Figure 19-1.

Consider the findings from a research project that interviewed 71 executives:

> Top executives say that people are an increasingly important factor in distinguishing one company from another. As a result, many now consider the human resource function . . . critical to business success.

CEOs and HR

> CEOs . . . are looking to their human resource departments for help on such "people" issues as productivity improvement, succession planning and culture change. . . .
>
> Some CEOs are attempting to reshape the mandate of the human resource function according to their companies' future business needs.[3]

Besides furthering the organizational objective of competitive advantage, the department also must address societal, functional, and personal objectives. Societal objectives—often in the form of laws—must be met to ensure fair treatment and legal compliance. Functional objectives add professional and ethical challenges to the department's constraints. And the personal objectives of employees gain in importance and complexity as the growth in the work force slows and the work force becomes more diverse.

Strategic contribution

For modern human resource departments to make a strategic contribution[4] and better meet other objectives, their efforts must respect the importance and dignity of human beings, the human resource approach discussed in Chapter 1. At the same time, specialists must not lose sight of the systems approach, which *subordinates* the departmental subsystem to the larger system of the organization. The organization's success, not the department's, is the first priority. Achieving the organization's objectives also depends on providing service to managers and employees through a proactive approach. The department does not usurp each manager's human resource responsibilities. Instead, a professional management approach assumes a dual responsibility between the worker's immediate supervisor and the human resource department, with the department playing a major and proactive role in those areas outlined in Figure 19-1.

Self-audits

At the same time, the department cannot assume that everything it does is correct. Errors happen. Policies and practices become outdated. By auditing itself, the department finds problems before they become serious.[5] Done correctly, the evaluation process can build rapport between the department and operating managers, and it can reveal outdated assumptions that can be changed to meet the department's objectives and future challenges. Of course, the problems with any self-audit center on the ability of department members to be objective when they evaluate their performance, even though most of the audit involves evaluating line management's compliance.[6]

The scope of the department's responsibilities is broad, as suggested by this book and Figure 19-1. Of course, not every human resource department deals with each item discussed in this book. Through a comprehensive audit, human resource departments assess the subsystems of the overall model in Figure 19-1. But an effective audit does more than just assess the subsystems; it ensures that the subsystems mesh to form a rational approach to the creation and delivery of services.

This chapter examines the scope, approaches, and tools used in human resource audits and research. It concludes with a review of future challenges that are likely to confront the human resource professionals.

Figure 19-2

Benefits of a Human Resource Management Audit

➤ *Identifies* the contributions of the personnel department to the organization.
➤ *Improves* the professional image of the personnel department.
➤ *Encourages* greater responsibility and professionalism among members of the personnel department.
➤ *Clarifies* the personnel department's duties and responsibilities.
➤ *Stimulates* uniformity of personnel policies and practices.
➤ *Finds* critical personnel problems.
➤ *Ensures* timely compliance with legal requirements.
➤ *Reduces* human resource costs through more effective personnel procedures.
➤ *Creates* increased acceptance of needed changes in the personnel department.
➤ *Requires* a thorough review of the department's information system.

THE SCOPE OF HUMAN RESOURCE AUDITS

HR audits

A *human resource audit* evaluates the personnel activities used in an organization. The audit may include one division or an entire company. It gives feedback about the function to operating managers and human resource specialists. It also provides feedback about how well managers are meeting their human resource duties. In short, the audit is an overall quality control check on human resource activities in a division or company and on how those activities support the organization's strategy.[7]

Several benefits result from a human resource audit. Figure 19-2 lists the major ones. An audit reminds members of the department and others of its contribution. It also creates a more professional image of the department among managers and specialists. The audit helps clarify the department's role and leads to greater uniformity, especially in the geographically scattered and decentralized human resource functions of large firms. Perhaps most important, it finds problems and ensures compliance with a variety of laws and the strategic plans of the organization.

The scope of an audit extends beyond the department's actions. The department's success depends on how well it performs *and* on how well its programs are carried out by others in the organization. For example, consider how supervisors at the American Guard Agency reduced the effectiveness of the performance appraisal process.

American Guard Agency

To become a sergeant at the American Guard Agency, employees need two years of good or superior performance evaluations. The agency uses a critical incident appraisal form, which requires that supervisors record both positive and negative incidents as they occur. In practice, supervisors stressed employee mistakes when they recorded incidents. As a result, few guards *received good enough ratings to qualify for sergeant. Many of them blamed the department's appraisal process for their lack of promotions.*

An audit uncovered the misuse of the program and recommended additional training for supervisors in the use of the critical incident method. If the audit had not uncovered this problem, employee dissatisfaction may have grown worse.

As this example illustrates, people problems seldom are confined to the human resource department. Thus audits should be broad in scope to be effective. They should evaluate the personnel function, the use of its procedures by managers, and the impact of these activities on employees.

In recent years, however, this "inward-looking perspective" has become insufficient. Human resource professionals find that the scope of the audit must transcend even the concerns of the department and operating managers. Although not all human resource audits review corporate strategy and its fit with the external environment, these broader concerns merit mention.[8]

Audit of Corporate Strategy

Human resource professionals do not set corporate strategy, but they strongly determine its success.[9] Corporate strategy concerns how the organization is going to gain a competitive advantage. By assessing the firm's internal strengths and weaknesses and its external opportunities and threats, for example, senior management devises ways of gaining an advantage. Whether the company stresses superior marketing channels (State Farm), service (IBM), innovation (3M), low-cost production (Emerson Electric), or some other approach, human resource management is affected.[10] Understanding the strategy has strong implications for human resource planning, staffing, compensation, employee relations, and other human resource activities.

Strategy-environment fit

The strategy-environmental fit cannot be ignored. Members of the department can learn about the firm's strategy through interviews with key executives, reviews of long-range business plans, and systematic environmental scans designed to uncover changing trends.[11] They must audit their function, managerial compliance, and employee acceptance of human resource policies and practices against the firm's strategic plans. For example, high turnover in entry-level jobs may keep wages near the bottom of the rate range, lowering labor costs. Thus, employee turnover in a "Big Six" accounting firm may be a low-cost way to keep overall labor costs competitive. An audit, however, might reveal considerable dissatisfaction among recent accounting graduates about the number of billable hours required of them each week. Knowledge of the firm's strategy (to hire excess entry-level accountants) affects the value of audit information (about employee satisfaction, for example).

Figure 19-3

Major Areas Covered by a Human Resource Functions Audit

HUMAN RESOURCE INFORMATION SYSTEM

AFFIRMATIVE ACTION PLANS
- Underutilization and concentration
- Affirmative action goals
- Progress toward goals

HUMAN RESOURCE PLANS
- Supply and demand estimates
- Skills inventories
- Replacement charts and summaries

JOB ANALYSIS INFORMATION
- Job standards
- Job descriptions
- Job specifications

COMPENSATION ADMINISTRATION
- Wage, salary, and incentive levels
- Fringe benefit package
- Employer-provided services

STAFFING AND DEVELOPMENT

RECRUITING
- Sources of recruits
- Availability of recruits
- Employment applications

SELECTION
- Selection ratios
- Selection procedures
- Equal opportunity compliance

TRAINING AND ORIENTATION
- Orientation program
- Training objectives and procedures
- Learning rates

CAREER DEVELOPMENT
- Internal placement success
- Career planning program
- Human resource development effort

ORGANIZATION CONTROL AND EVALUATION

PERFORMANCE APPRAISALS
- Standards and measures of performance
- Performance appraisal techniques
- Evaluation interviews

LABOR-MANAGEMENT RELATIONS
- Legal compliance
- Management rights
- Dispute resolution problems

HUMAN RESOURCE CONTROLS
- Employee communications
- Discipline procedures
- Change and development procedures

HUMAN RESOURCE AUDITS
- Human resource function
- Operating managers
- Employee feedback on personnel

Audit of the Human Resource Function

Audits logically review the department's work.[12] Figure 19-3 lists the major areas covered. An audit touches on virtually every subject discussed in this book. To review only a few aspects of the human resource management system may ignore topics that affect the department's performance.

For each item in the figure, the audit team should:

Audit teams

> ➤ *Identify* who is responsible for each activity

> ➤ *Determine* the objectives sought by each activity

> ➤ *Review* the policies and procedures used to achieve these objectives

> ➤ *Sample* the records in the human resource information system to learn if policies and procedures are being followed correctly

> ➤ *Prepare* a report commending proper objectives, policies, and procedures

> ➤ *Develop* an action plan to correct errors in objectives, policies, and procedures

> ➤ *Follow up* on the action plan to see if it solved the problems found through the audit.[13]

Admittedly, an audit of every activity is time-consuming. As a result, small firms use ad hoc arrangements that often evaluate only selected areas.[14] Very large organizations have *audit teams* similar to those used to conduct financial audits. These teams are especially useful when the department is decentralized into regional or field offices, as is the case with the State Farm Insurance Companies. Through the use of audits, the organization maintains consistency in its practices even though there are several offices in different locations. And the mere existence of a corporate audit team encourages compliance and self-audits by the regional offices between visits.[15]

> Cliff Swain, a regional personnel manager, realized that his chances for promotion to the corporate headquarters depended on how well his region's offices performed. The corporate audit team reviewed his region's performance every June. In preparation for the audit, he had each human resource office in the southwest region conduct a self-audit in April. Then in early May, the administrators from the four branches met in Phoenix to review the results. Errors uncovered through the audit were corrected if possible. When the corporate audit team completed its review in June, it always gave Cliff's region high marks for compliance with company policies and employment laws.

Audit of Managerial Compliance

Auditing management compliance with HR

An audit also reviews how well managers comply with human resource policies and procedures. If managers ignore policies or violate employee relations laws, the audit should uncover these errors so that corrective action can be started.[16] Compliance with laws is especially important. When equal opportunity, safety, compensation, or labor laws are violated, the government holds the company responsible.[17]

Besides ensuring compliance, the audit can improve the department's image and contribution to the company. Operating managers may gain a higher respect for the department when an audit team seeks their views. If the comments of managers are acted upon, the department will be seen as more responsive to their needs. And since it is a service department, these actions may improve its contribution to organizational objectives. For example, consider what one audit team learned when it talked to managers of local claims offices.

> *After several interviews with claims office managers, the audit team discovered a pattern to their comments. Most managers believed that the human resource department filled job vacancies quickly. The major criticism was that the department did not train recruits before assigning them to a claims office. The day-to-day pressures in the claims offices caused training to be superficial and led to many errors by new adjusters. Most managers felt that the training should be done by the human resource department at the regional office.*
>
> *After reading the team's report, the regional human resource manager felt confident that the selection process was satisfactory. To solve the complaints about field training, she created a two-week program for claims adjusters with her next budget increase.*

Audit of Employee Satisfaction

Auditing employee perceptions

Effective departments meet both company objectives and employee needs. When employee needs are unmet, turnover, absenteeism, and union activity are more likely. To learn how well employee needs are met, the audit team gathers data from workers. The team collects information about wages, benefits, supervisory practices, career planning assistance, and the feedback employees receive about their performance.[18]

> *The audit team of an automobile parts distributor received one common complaint from employees: they felt isolated because they worked in retail stores or in warehouses located all over the Midwest. They had little sense of belonging to the large company of which they were a part. To bolster sagging morale and to help employees feel that they were members of a fast-growing and dynamic organization, the department started a biweekly "Payroll Action Newsletter." The two-page letter was stuffed into every pay envelope each payday. It gave tips on new developments at headquarters and at different field locations. In this way, the department used the audit to make the firm more responsive to its employees' needs.*

Figure 19-4

Research Approaches to a Human Resource Audit

▶ *Comparative approach.* The audit team compares its firm (or division) with another firm (or division) to uncover areas of poor performance. This approach commonly is used to compare the results of specific activities or programs. It helps to detect areas of needed improvement.

▶ *Outside authority approach.* The audit team relies on the expertise of a consultant or published research findings as a standard against which activities or programs are evaluated. The consultant or research findings may help diagnose the cause of problems.

▶ *Statistical approach.* From existing records, the audit team generates statistical standards against which activities and programs are evaluated. With these mathematical standards, the team may uncover errors while they are still minor.

▶ *Compliance approach.* By sampling elements of the human resource information system, the audit team looks for deviations from laws and company policies or procedures. Through their fact-finding efforts, the team can determine whether there is compliance with company policies and legal regulations.

▶ *MBO approach.* When an MBO approach is applied to the human resource area, the audit team can compare actual results with stated objectives. Areas of poor performance can be detected and reported.

RESEARCH APPROACHES TO AUDITS

HR research

Human resource activities are evaluated through research. At times, the research may be advanced, relying on sophisticated designs and statistics.[19] Whether informal or rigorous, research seeks to improve the department's performance. Applications-oriented efforts are called *applied research*. The most common forms of applied human resource research are described in Figure 19-4 and explained in the following paragraphs.

Perhaps the simplest form of research is the *comparative approach*. It uses another division or company as a model. The audit team then compares their results or procedures with those of the other organization. This approach often is used with absence, turnover, staffing levels, and salary data. It also makes sense when a new procedure is being tried for the first time. For example, if a company installs an alcoholic rehabilitation program, it may copy a similar program at another firm or division. Then the results of both programs are compared. IBM conducts a "Common Staffing Study" to compare employment levels among its various plants and facilities.

Or the department may rely on an *outside authority approach*. Standards set by a consultant or by published research findings serve as a benchmark for the audit team. For example, the consultant or industrywide research may indicate that the human resource budget is usually about three-fourths of 1 percent of gross sales. This figure then serves as a rough guidepost when evaluating the department's overall budget.

A third approach is to develop statistical measures of performance based on the company's existing information system. For example, records reveal absenteeism and turnover rates. These data indicate how well human resource activities and operating managers control these problem areas. A *statistical approach* usually is supplemented with comparisons against external information, which may be gathered from other firms or industry sources, such as surveys conducted by industry associations. This information often is expressed as ratios that are easy to compute and use. For example, if eight employees out of a work force of 200 miss work on a particular day, the absenteeism rate is 4 percent. Likewise, a company that averages 200 employees during the month and has 12 quit finds that its turnover rate is 6 percent per month, or 72 percent a year.

Roy Rogers Restaurants

Roy Rogers Restaurants, a major division of Marriott Corporation, operates 657 restaurants, primarily in the northeastern part of the United States. Entry-level managers are drawn largely from workers age 20 to 24. However, that age group will experience a decline well into the mid-1990s. Making matters worse, company audits reveal an annualized turnover rate of 80 to 90 percent, the costs of which are conservatively estimated at three million dollars a year.

A survey of field managers in the restaurant industry revealed that 58 percent of the turnover is seen as beyond their control. They attributed 31 percent of the reasons for turnover to the human resource department. Armed with this knowledge, the department was able to address the managers' perceptions and begin addressing the turnover problem before the targeted labor pool of 20- to 24 year-olds shrunk further.[20]

The *compliance approach* is another audit strategy. This method reviews past practices to determine if those actions followed legal requirements and company policies and procedures. Often the audit team examines a sample of employment, compensation, discipline, and employee appraisal forms. The purpose of the review is to ensure that field offices and operating managers comply with internal rules and legal regulations.

A final approach is for specialists and operating managers to set objectives in their areas of responsibility. This *MBO (management by objectives) approach* creates specific goals against which performance can be measured. Then the audit team researches actual performance and compares it with the objectives. For example, field managers at Roy Rogers may set a goal of reducing turnover to below 50 percent in one year. Then the audit evaluates the trends in this area.

Mixed approaches

No one of these audit approaches can be applied to all parts of human resource management.[21] More commonly, audit teams use several of these strategies, depending on the specific activities under evaluation. Then, as Figure 19-5 suggests, the audit team gives feedback on activities to the department, to operating managers, and to employees. Unfavorable feedback leads to corrective action that improves the contribution of human resource activities.

Figure 19-5

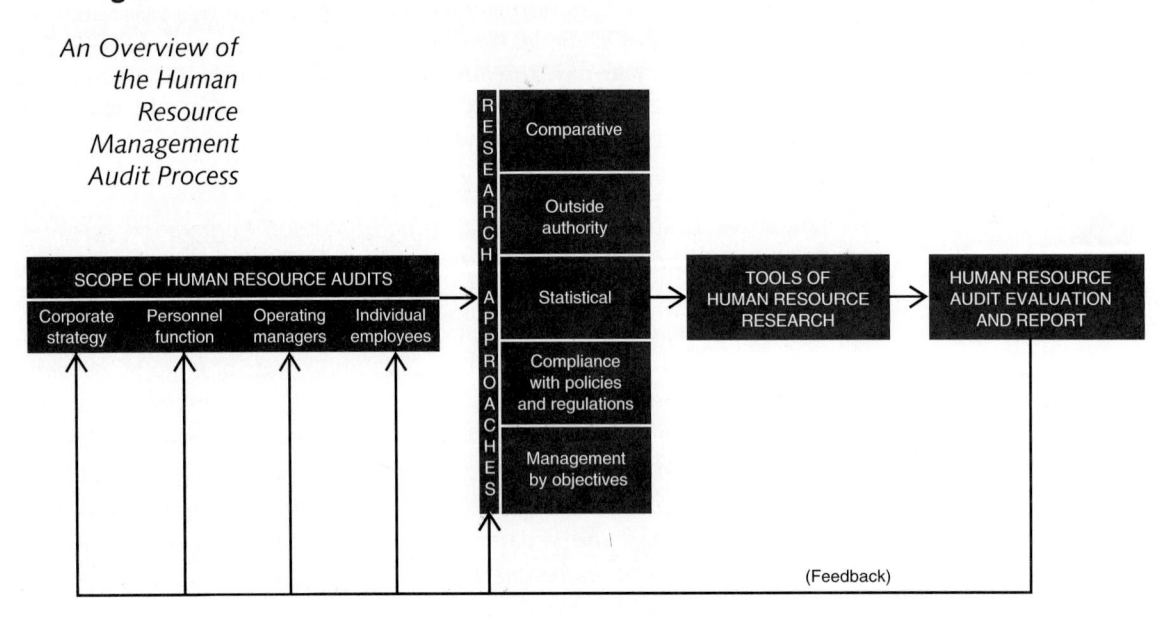

An Overview of the Human Resource Management Audit Process

```
SCOPE OF HUMAN RESOURCE AUDITS
  Corporate    Personnel   Operating    Individual
  strategy     function    managers     employees
```

RESEARCH APPROACHES:
- Comparative
- Outside authority
- Statistical
- Compliance with policies and regulations
- Management by objectives

→ TOOLS OF HUMAN RESOURCE RESEARCH → HUMAN RESOURCE AUDIT EVALUATION AND REPORT

(Feedback)

TOOLS OF HUMAN RESOURCE RESEARCH

Data-gathering tools

Several techniques serve as information-gathering tools to collect data about the firm's human resource activities. Each tool provides partial insight into the firm's activities. If these tools are used skillfully, the team can weave these insights into a clear picture of the organization's human resource activities. The tools include:

➤ Interviews

➤ Surveys

➤ Historical analysis

➤ External information

➤ Human resource research

➤ International audits.

Figure 19-6

An Exit Interview Form

Employee's Name _____   Date Hired _____
Interviewed by _____   Interviewed on _____
Supervisor's Name _____   Department _____

1. Were your job duties and responsibilities what you expected? _____
   If not, why: _____

2. What is your frank and honest opinion of: _____
   a. Your job? _____
   b. Your working conditions? _____
   c. Your orientation to your job? _____
   d. Your training provided by the company? _____
   e. Your pay? _____
   f. Your company-provided benefits and services? _____
   g. Your treatment by your manager? _____

3. What is your major reason for leaving the company? _____
   _____

4. What could we have done to keep you from leaving? _____
   _____

5. What could be done to make this a better place to work? _____
   _____

Interviews

Interviews with employees and managers are one source of information about human resource activities. Employees' and managers' comments help the audit team find areas that need improvement. For example, when the turnover problem at Roy Rogers was identified, the director of resources and a consultant conducted interviews with field managers to learn about the turnover issue. Criticisms and comments from interviews can help pinpoint perceptions and causes that serve as a basis for departmental actions. Likewise, suggestions by managers may reveal ways to provide them with better service. When the criticisms are valid, changes should be made. But when the criticism is unwarranted, the department may have to educate others in the firm by explaining the procedures that are being questioned.[22]

Exit interviews

Another useful source of information is the exit interview.[23] *Exit interviews* are conducted with departing employees to learn their views of the organization.

Figure 19-7

Critical Concerns to Be Answered by Attitude Surveys

EMPLOYEE ATTITUDES ABOUT SUPERVISORS

➤ Are some supervisors' employees exceptionally satisfied or dissatisfied?
➤ Do specific supervisors need training in supervisory and human relations skills?
➤ Have attitudes improved since the last survey?

EMPLOYEE ATTITUDES ABOUT THEIR JOBS

➤ What are common elements of jobs that cause negative attitudes? Positive attitudes?
➤ Can jobs that cause poor attitudes be redesigned to improve satisfaction?
➤ Can jobs that cause poor attitudes be given alternative work schedules (such as shorter workweeks or flextime)?

PERCEIVED EFFECTIVENESS OF THE HUMAN RESOURCE DEPARTMENT

➤ Do employees think they work for a good or bad employer?
➤ Do employees think they merely have a job or a career?
➤ Do employees think they have some place to turn in order to solve problems besides their immediate superior?
➤ Do employees feel informed about company developments?
➤ Do employees know what is expected of them in their jobs?
➤ Are employees satisfied by the amount and type of feedback they get about their performance?
➤ Are employees satisfied by their pay? Benefits?

Figure 19-6 lists the typical questions that are asked. The workers' comments are recorded and later reviewed during the audit to find the causes of employee turnover, dissatisfaction, and other issues. Since many employees are reluctant to criticize, the exit interviewer must take time to probe and listen carefully. Then the results must be studied to uncover trends among departments, divisions, or managers.[24]

Surveys

Many human resource departments use questionnaires because interviews are time-consuming, costly, and often limited to only a few people. Through questionnaire surveys, a more comprehensive picture of employee treatment can be developed. Questionnaires may also lead to more candid answers than face-to-face interviews.[25] As discussed in Chapter 17, attitude survey feedback can generate answers to the concerns found in Figure 19-7.

Responses to the issues suggested by the Figure give insight into the perceptions of the department. Of particular importance are trends revealed through repeated, periodic administration of questionnaires. The discovery of research-

Figure 19-8

Records Commonly Reviewed as Part of a Human Resource Audit

SAFETY AND HEALTH RECORDS

➤ Determine differences before and after programs aimed at lowering accident rates.
➤ Are there patterns or discernable causes? By jobs? By shift?
➤ Is the firm in compliance with OSHA recordkeeping requirements?

GRIEVANCE RECORDS

➤ Are there patterns to grievances arising from specific contract clauses or supervisors?
➤ Are there sections of the agreement that are unclear to union or management officials?

COMPENSATION STUDIES

➤ Are wages externally and internally equitable?
➤ Are fringe benefits understood by employees?
➤ Does the fringe benefit package compare favorably with local firms and national competitors?

AFFIRMATIVE ACTION PLANS

➤ Is the firm in compliance with all equal employment laws?
➤ Does the affirmative action plan address those areas where the firm is not in compliance?
➤ Has the firm made acceptable progress toward meeting its affirmative action goals?

PROGRAM AND POLICY STUDIES

➤ Does each human resource program meet its stated goals?
➤ Are policies and procedures being followed by the human resource department and line managers?

SCRAP RATES

➤ Determine if training, bonuses, or other programs have reduced scrap rates.

TURNOVER/ABSENTEEISM

➤ Are there patterns or discernable causes? By age? Sex?
➤ How do these records compare with those of other employers?
➤ Determine differences before and after programs aimed at lowering turnover or absenteeism.

PRETEST/POSTTEST SCORES

➤ Determine if orientation or training programs improve test scores or job performance.
➤ How well do test scores relate to job performance?

INTERNAL PLACEMENT RECORDS

➤ What percentage of jobs are filled internally?
➤ How well do internally promoted candidates perform?
➤ Do replacement charts/summaries indicate sufficient promotable talent?

SELECTION RECORDS

➤ Is the performance of recruits better according to the source from which they were recruited?
➤ Are recruitment and selection costs comparable with other firms?

Figure 19-8

(continued)

EMPLOYEE FILES
➤ Are employee files in order, properly completed?
➤ Do records contain accurate information for making employee decisions?
➤ Is this employee making reasonable career progress?
➤ Is this employee a source of discipline or interpersonal problems?

SPECIAL PROGRAMMING REPORTS
➤ Are special programs achieving the desired results?
➤ Is the firm in compliance with COBRA for medical coverage to former employees and dependents?
➤ Is the firm in compliance with citizenship requirements under immigration reform?

based trends suggests whether specific challenges are becoming more or less important to those surveyed.

Historical Analysis

Not all the issues of interest to a human resource audit are revealed through interviews or surveys. Sometimes insight can be obtained by an analysis of historical records. These reviews are done to ensure compliance with company procedures and laws. The records normally reviewed by an audit team are listed in Figure 19-8.[26]

Safety and health

Safety and health audits. An analysis of safety and health records may reveal violations of the Occupational Safety and Health Act. Under the recordkeeping requirements of OSHA, the audit team should find detailed records of all safety and health violations. Patterns of accidents by job classifications, location, supervisor, employee seniority, age, sex, and type of violation may uncover targets for additional safety training or equipment. Insurance companies or private consultants may assist the audit team in analyzing these statistics.

Grievance audits. The audit team also may be able to uncover a pattern in employee grievances addressed through the company's in-house complaint process (discussed in Chapter 17) or through the union-management grievance procedure (discussed in Chapter 18). Patterns may emerge by job classification, supervisor, union representative, age group, or contract provision. If patterns are detected, human resource specialists seek the causes of grievances. If union officials participate in finding such patterns, they may support management's suggested changes, which usually involve training or the rewording of the union-management agreement.

Compensation audits. Audit teams carefully review the department's compensation practices. Primarily, they study the level of wages, incentives, benefits, and services that are provided. If jobs have been priced properly through job evaluations and salary surveys, pay levels are fair. Benefits and services also are studied to learn if they are competitive with those of other employers and in compliance with government regulations.

Affirmative Action

Affirmative action audits. The audit team also reviews the firm's compliance with equal opportunity laws. Although most large employers have a compliance officer to monitor the affirmative action program, the audit team serves as a further check. It usually focuses on hiring, placement, and compensation practices as applied to protected groups. Of particular concern is the progress being made by the company compared with the goals in its affirmative action plan. If discrimination exists, the team informs management of the need for corrective action.[27]

Program and policy audits. Besides safety, grievance, compensation, and affirmative action programs, audits evaluate many other programs and policies to determine if they are doing what was intended.

Seafood Canners

Two years after Seafood Canners, Inc., adopted a "promotion-from-within" policy, most supervisors still were recruited from outside the firm. Few workers applied for supervisory openings, even though these jobs were posted throughout the plant and employees were encouraged to apply. The audit team learned that during peak seasons, production workers earned more money than supervisors because of overtime pay and the incentive system. Many employees viewed supervisory jobs as more responsibility with less pay. To remedy the problem, supervisors were given a percentage of their department's production bonus. A year later, 90 percent of the supervisory openings were filled internally.

As the Seafood Canners example illustrates, policies (promote from within) may conflict with other programs (the incentive system). And legal requirements (overtime pay) may conflict with the department's goals. Virtually every policy or program affects others. Thus, a thorough audit needs to include all the major human resource policies and programs and a study of how they relate to one another.

19. ASSESSING PERFORMANCE AND PROSPECTS

External Information

Checking the environment

Another tool of the audit team is external information.[28] Outside comparisons give the audit team a perspective against which their firm's activities can be judged. Some needed information is readily available, while other data may be difficult to find. Perhaps the most significant source of external information is the federal government. Through the Department of Labor, numerous statistics and reports are compiled. The Department regularly publishes information about future employment opportunities, employee turnover rates, work force projections, area wage and salary surveys, severity and frequency rates of accidents, and other data that can serve as benchmarks for comparing internal information.

State unemployment offices and industrial development commissions often provide additional information that can be used for comparative purposes. Work force demographics—age, sex, education, and racial composition—are commonly available from state agencies and are useful for evaluating affirmative action programs.

Industry associations usually make specialized data available to members. Of most use to audit teams are statistics on industry norms—such as turnover, absenteeism, standard wage, growth and accident rates, standardized job descriptions, fringe benefit costs, and sample union-management agreements.

Professional associations often provide similar information to members of the profession. Studies conducted by the association may include salary and benefit surveys, demographic profiles, and other data that can serve as standards against which the department's efforts are measured. Consultants and university research bureaus may be able to provide information as well.

Human Resource Research

Field experiments

Another tool available to human resource departments and audit teams is the research experiment, particularly the *field experiment* that compares an experimental and a control group under realistic conditions. Experimentation is used to research issues of absenteeism, turnover, job satisfaction, compensation, safety, and other activities. For example, the department may implement a safety training program for half of the supervisors. This half is the experimental group. The control group is composed of the supervisors who are not given training. The safety records of both groups are compared several months after the program is completed. If the experimental group has a significantly lower accident rate, then there is evidence that the safety training program was effective. A *cost-benefit analysis* can then be conducted by comparing the *costs* of the training with the *benefits* to the company to determine if the training is cost-effective.

Cost-benefit analysis

Experimentation does have some drawbacks. Many managers are reluctant to experiment with workers because of morale problems and potential dissatisfaction among those who are not selected. Employees involved in the experimental group may feel manipulated. The experiment may also be confounded by changes in the work environment or simply by the two groups talking to each other about the experiment.

International Audits

Human resource audits are more complex and more important when international organizations are involved. The complexity of auditing human resource activities across foreign borders is compounded by differences in laws, languages, cultures, traditional practices, and expectations. Audit teams from the home country have a tendency to use home-country experiences and standards as benchmarks against which the evaluation is conducted. The problem this tendency introduces is that variations may seem wrong merely because they are variations from the experiences of the auditors. For example, discrimination by sex, race, tribal grouping, social status, religion, caste, or some other non-meritorious criteria may violate company policies but may also be an expected, even necessary practice in some foreign countries.

The great difficulty for the audit team is to identify areas of variation from company practices that are not justified by the foreign context. On the one hand, the human resource function seeks uniformity in practices and procedures across all operations to ensure compliance with company policies and to ensure a uniform corporate culture. On the other hand, competition, laws, culture, and employee satisfaction may demand variations from company policies, practices, and procedures. Variations should be noted so that policy makers can decide whether such differences should be allowed to continue. Inquiries about the purpose of the variations may reveal appropriate justification or poor management practices. Of particular importance are variations that violate home-country laws even though the variation is an accepted practice in the foreign country. For example, bribes to government officials are a common practice in some countries but when done by U.S. firms are in violation of the *Foreign Corrupt Practices Act*.

Foreign Corrupt Practices Act

Audits are of particular importance precisely because of the wide variability in a global operation. Differences in education, experience, culture, and other factors may lead to different human resource practices that are, at best, inefficient, and, at worse, ineffective. Unless business necessity justifies differences, the goal should be uniformity in policies, practices, and procedures throughout the organization. This is not uniformity for its own sake. Instead, uniformity facilitates ease of administration and smoother reassignment of personnel and makes the use of research into intracompany comparisons easier and more accurate.

THE AUDIT REPORT

Performance feedback

Research approaches and tools are used to develop a picture of the organization's human resource activities. For this information to be useful, it is compiled into an audit report. The *audit report* is a comprehensive description of human resource activities that includes both commendations for effective practices and recommendations for improving practices that are less effective. A recognition of both good and bad practices provides a balanced assessment and encourages acceptance of the report.

Audit reports often contain several sections. One part is for line managers, another is for managers of specific human resource functions, and the final part is for the human resource manager. For line managers, the report summarizes their human resource objectives, responsibilities, and duties. Examples of duties include interviewing applicants, training employees, evaluating performance, motivating workers, and satisfying employee needs. The report also identifies people problems. Violations of policies and employee relations laws are highlighted. Poor management practices are revealed in the report along with recommendations.

The specialists who handle employment, training, compensation, and other activities also need feedback. The audit report that they receive isolates areas of good and poor performance within their functions. For example, one audit team observed that many jobs did not have qualified replacements. This information was given to the manager of training and development along with the recommendation for more programs to develop promising supervisors and managers. The report also may provide other feedback, such as attitudes of operating managers about the specialists' efforts. Sometimes external data is provided to show what other companies are doing and to establish other standards for comparison.[29]

The human resource manager's report contains all the information given to both operating managers and staff specialists. In addition, the manager gets feedback about:

HR manager's report

➤ Attitudes of operating managers and employees about the department's benefits and services

➤ A review of the department's objectives and its plans to achieve them

➤ Human resource problems and their implications

➤ Recommendations for needed changes and priorities for their implementation.

With the information contained in the audit report, the human resource manager can take a broad view of the human resource function. Instead of solving problems in a random manner, the manager now can focus on those that have the greatest potential for improving the department's contribution to the firm. Perhaps most important, the audit serves as a map to future efforts and as a reference point for future audits. With knowledge of the department's present performance, the manager can make long-range plans to upgrade crucial activities. These plans identify new goals for the department, which serve as standards for future audit teams.

HUMAN RESOURCE PROSPECTS FOR THE FUTURE

Audits are necessary but backward-looking. They only uncover the results of past decisions. Although past performance should be evaluated, human resource departments also should look to the future. Without a future orientation, the department becomes reactive, not proactive, and reactive approaches allow minor problems to become major ones. Challenges that are likely to impact human resource management are briefly discussed here to increase awareness of their potential importance. The major categories of concern include:

Future challenges

➤ Globalization, diversity, and the environmental context

➤ Employee rights

➤ Employee performance and productivity

➤ The challenging role of human resource management.

Globalization, Diversity, and the Environmental Context

Profound changes are altering the competitive environment. The United States and Canada are virtually eliminating all barriers to free trade between them. Strong efforts are underway to add Mexico to create a North American trade bloc. At the same time, the European Economic Community is becoming more closely integrated, creating still another zone of free trade. Brazil, Argentina, Uruguay, and Paraguay are working steadily toward the creation of yet another trade bloc. And East Asia, led by Japan, contains some of the world's leading exporters. At the same time, the deregulation of transportation, airlines, and financial institutions within the United States has increased the intensity of competition in these industries. Governments at the federal, state, and local levels are under considerable budgetary pressures to perform in the face of limited resources. The combination of these and other trends has placed growing pressures on organizations to perform better in terms of productivity, quality, time, and service.

Although technology, capital, materials, and energy are vital inputs to any organization, improved performance ultimately rests with the people who use these resources. But, just as the demands on human resources are increasing, personnel experts and managers in the United States, Canada, and many European countries are confronted by a rapidly diversifying work force. Consider these U.S. trends and their potential impact on human resource management:

➤ By the year 2000, 63 percent of all women over age 16 will be in the work force, up from 57 percent in 1990.[30]

➤ The black work force is projected to increase twice as fast and the Hispanic labor force is expected to increase four times faster than the white work force.[31]

➤ Annual immigration into the United States will average 600,000 a year during the 1990s.[32]

➤ "Non-Caucasians, women, and immigrants are projected to make up more than five-sixths, or 83 percent, of the new additions to the work force between now and the next century. . . ."[33]

➤ More than 85 percent of those who will be working in 2001 are already in the work force today, and most will need training and retraining.[34]

➤ Half the children under the age of one live in families where both parents work.[35]

➤ The work force in the United States will grow at a rate of only 1.2 percent a year during the 1990s, down from 2.9 percent as recently as the 1970s.[36]

➤ The number of people employed by temporary-help firms has increased 400 percent.[37]

➤ Part-time workers represent 17.4 percent of the U.S. work force and 20 percent of the work force in Denmark, Norway, Sweden, and the Netherlands.[38]

➤ Mandatory retirement ages have been abolished.[39]

➤ The number of AIDS cases is growing rapidly. More workers are likely to die from AIDS in the 1990s than from automobile accidents.[40]

➤ The United States has posted the slowest productivity growth among all major industrialized nations.

The implications of increased competition and work force diversity are countless. Some obvious ones are that human resource departments will be pressured for additional employment flexibility and for additional child-care *and* eldercare assistance from their workers. This flexibility likely will be achieved through flexible benefits, flextime schedules, part-timers, temporary workers, and telecommuting. Rapid rises in health-care costs (fueled, in part, by AIDS) and low productivity growth rates will put *downward* pressure on *real* (inflation and tax-adjusted) wage increases, causing compensation almost certainly to be more closely tied to performance.[41]

Employee Rights

Beginning in 1842, when the Supreme Court of the Commonwealth of Massachusetts ruled that merely joining a union was not a criminal conspiracy, judicial opinions and legislation have expanded employee rights. The employer's right to lay off workers has been limited by the *Worker Adjustment and Retraining Act* (WARN).[42] Likewise, employee terminations have been constrained by the EEOC, OSHA, NLRB, and court rulings that limit the "employment-at-will" doctrine. And experience suggests that further legislative and judicial efforts will expand employment-related rights even further.[43] Although no one argues against protecting workers in a society of wage earners, the result of these growing limitations is increased responsibility and complexity for human resource managers.

And the list of present and future challenges continues to grow. The rights of smokers and nonsmokers provide an example that is part of a larger concern about workplace safety and health. Included here are concerns about radiation exposure from video display terminals and radon gas in the office to chemicals and solvents in the factory. Human resource professionals also are involved with fearful employees and AIDS-infected coworkers.[44] Another long-simmering issue is comparable worth.[45] Should comparable work be paid equally? Or should "market rates," based on supply and demand considerations, prevail? Explosive medical costs are likely to put additional demands on employers beyond the extended coverage requirements of COBRA. And concerns over employee privacy—which have already caused many employee assistance programs to use outside counselors—are likely to grow as employee records become more readily accessible electronically.[46]

Employee Performance and Productivity

Real wages cannot go up faster than productivity. The wealth and well-being of society depends on the productivity of its work force. No major industrial nation has had *worse* productivity improvement than the United States during the last two decades. None. Not Great Britain. Not Italy. Not France. And certainly not Japan or Germany. Although the United States remains the worldwide productivity leader (in both total and per capita productivity), the effects of losing that leadership in such industries as automobiles, shipbuilding, steel, consumer electronics, and others have led to serious economic dislocations for employers and employees. These dislocations will spread unless productivity improves relative to our trading partners.

The competitive advantage increasingly is to be found in the creativity of employees. Tapping that wellspring may be the best hope for both emerging and mature industries. Improved productivity through people is ultimately the fountainhead of all human progress. And human resource professionals are key players in improving people productivity. Through pay and incentive systems geared to increased productivity, the department can help align labor costs with performance. Pay-for-performance, however, assumes measurable performance.

Improved appraisal systems are likely to be demanded by cost-conscious executives seeking to identify and reward top performers. In turn, those top performers will need sophisticated career planning assistance, training, flexible working hours, and flexible compensation systems—systems that proactive professionals are already designing and testing.

The Challenging Role of Human Resource Management

Competitive pressures are forcing many organizations to down-size in an attempt to become smaller and more efficient at the same time that the work force is becoming more diverse.[47] The inevitable result will be more challenges and a more important role for human resource managers. This additional importance will also mean additional responsibilities. The traditional duties of obtaining, maintaining, and retaining a qualified work force will be expanded by additional challenges that will demand even greater professionalism from the department leader and support staff.

Strategic contribution

Increasingly, human resource managers are expected to contribute to the organization's strategic thinking. Marketing, production, and financial strategies depend upon the abilities of the firm's human resources to execute these plans. To assist with the "people side" of implementation, human resource directors will be forced to uncover, through audits and research, the causes and solutions to people-related problems. Their diagnostic abilities to assess present and potential human issues will be needed as they and their staffs increasingly serve as internal consultants to others who are facing human resource-related challenges. They then will be called on to facilitate changes in the organization that maximize the human contribution. In short, the traditional administrative skills associated with human resource management must grow to accommodate diagnostic, assessment, consultant, and facilitative skills.[48]

At the same time, human resource processionals must continue to address societal, organizational, functional, and personal objectives that challenge the organization.

Societal challenges. Modern societies prosper or decline through the productive contribution of their organizations. It is, therefore, not surprising that society takes an active interest in these engines of wealth. Legislative and judicial trends increasingly put individual rights above those of organizations. The success of this trend during the last 60 years has led to employers becoming vehicles of social policy. Equal employment laws and the affirmative action plans they spawned, for example, have allowed organizations to achieve more racial equality in one generation than did a civil war and a century of "separate but equal" policies. More needs to be done, but social planners, legislators, and judges have learned to use modern organizations as instruments of social policy. The trend is likely to continue.

Organizational and functional challenges. The human resource function exists to further organizational effectiveness. Sometimes organizational effectiveness means pursuing societal objectives because the consequences of doing otherwise may be deceptive or illegal. This organizational challenge also means that the department's goals—goals of efficiency or professionalism, for example—must be balanced against the organization's strategy and objectives. The human resource department is a service department. When its members forget that, they cease serving the objectives of the organization.

Personal challenges. People have personal goals that human resource professionals help them attain, at least insofar as these goals enhance the individual's contribution to the organization. Human resource professionals often go further, helping people attain goals that have little relationship to their job. They create employee assistance programs, for example, because, as a former vice president of personnel at State Farm Insurance companies observes: ". . . we look at the employee as a *whole* person, not just a worker."[49]

State Farm Insurance

The humanistic view often means becoming an advocate for employees. This is not an advocacy intended to conflict with the organization, but an advocacy that realizes people are the ultimate resource of any organization. By advocating employee needs, operating managers and human resource professionals help our organizations—those most inventive developments of the twentieth century. By undertaking the challenge of making our organizations more productive and satisfying places, the wealth and well-being of society prospers—now and into the twenty-first century.

SUMMARY

A HUMAN RESOURCE audit evaluates the human resource activities used in an organization. Its purpose is to ensure that operating managers and human resource specialists are following policies and maintaining an effective work force.

The scope of the audit involves human resource specialists, operating managers, employees, and the external environment. Inputs are sought from all four sources because each has a unique perspective. And to be truly effective, human resource activities must do more than meet the wishes of experts. They must meet the needs of employees and operating managers as well as challenges from the environment and the company's strategic plans.

The audit team uses a variety of research approaches and tools. Along with internal comparisons, the team compares the firm's efforts against those of other companies or against standards developed by external authorities and internal statistics. It may also evaluate compliance with laws or objectives set by management.

Research tools include interviews, questionnaires, surveys, internal records, external sources or experimentation, and international audits. Through these tools, the audit team is able to compile an audit report. The audit report gives feedback to top management, operating managers, human resource professionals, and the human resource manager. Armed with this information, the manager can then develop plans to ensure that human resource activities make an effective contribution to the organization. If human resource management is to be responsible, it needs to review its past performance through audits and research. At the same time, it needs a future orientation to anticipate upcoming challenges. Finally, a proactive view encourages human resource professionals to contribute to both employee and company goals.

With all of the challenges facing human resource professionals, their role is sure to grow in scope and importance. The key to this growth is how well human resource professionals can help employees make better contributions to their organizations. It is through their contributions that organizations prosper. And it is through these life-giving and life-sustaining organizations that we prosper as individuals and as a society.

Terms for Review

Human resource audit
Audit teams
Applied research
Management by objectives (MBO) approach

Exit interviews
Field experiment
Audit report

Review and Discussion Questions

1. Since government agencies, union leaders, and employees are likely to point out mistakes in policies, practices, and procedures, why conduct a human resource audit?

2. What research approach do you think should be followed for each of these areas of concern to the audit team: (*a*) the evaluation of a new company-sponsored drug rehabilitation program, (*b*) an analysis of employee tardiness patterns, (*c*) the appropriateness of present recruiting costs?

3. What are exit interviews and why are they used?

4. If someone who worked for you suggested a new idea to control absenteeism and you considered it feasible, how would you test the idea?

5. If you were assigned to audit an overseas operation's human resource function, what considerations would you want to discuss with your boss before you left for the assignment? What types of issues would you emphasize upon your return?

6. What types of information should be put in an audit report for the: (a) employment manager, (b) assistant plant manager, and (c) human resource director?

7. In the last two decades, many cultural values have changed, some rather drastically. Briefly describe how human resource management might be affected by these changes: (a) the trend toward smaller families, (b) increased participation of women in the work force, (c) the aging of the work force and the general population.

8. Identify and discuss the major forces impacting human resource management during the 1990s. In your answer, address how these changes are likely to impact the practice of human resource management.

INCIDENT 19-1
Employee Challenges Fish Camps, Inc.

Fish Camps, Inc. sells and rents fishing and camping gear. Much of its business depends on the summer fishing season in the Pacific Northwest of the United States and southwestern Canada. Although year round sales justify staying open through the winter, Fish Camps' main business is the summer tourists. As a result, employment is seasonal, peaking at nearly 80 employees in seven locations in the summer.

The jobs of chief bookkeeper and personnel director are held by the same person, Janice Rae. After attending a six-week course about human resource management, she decided to use a mixture of phone and face-to-face interviews, a year's worth of written exit interviews, and a homemade attitude survey to assess employee attitudes and job satisfaction. The survey was distributed to all employees in early August, when employment levels in the company were at their highest.

From the interviews and attitude surveys, the Janice made the following observations:

➤ Nearly two-thirds of the employees felt little loyalty to the firm because they considered their jobs temporary.

➤ Many employees applied for work at Fish Camps, Inc. because they needed summer jobs, which were rare in the rural areas of the fishing camps.

➤ Although the firm gave few benefits, many workers commented that sales discounts and reduced rental rates on equipment were an important "extra."

➤ Every supervisor mentioned that the most important selection criterion was whether an applicant knew about fly fishing.

➤ Employee turnover was very low. But many employees indicated that they would quit if they could find a better-paying job.

➤ Several employees who had worked for the firm in previous years thought it was unfair that they received the same hourly wage as new employees.

1. If you were the consultant, what recommendations would you make to the owner about (*a*) the high number of employees who would quit if other work was available, (*b*) the types of people recruited, and (*c*) the treatment of employees who have worked for the firm in previous seasons?

2. Should the company treat year-around employees differently than those who just work for the summer? If so, what differences in treatment do you recommend?

References

1. Paul J. Champagne and R. Bruce McAfee, "Auditing Sexual Harassment," *Personnel Journal* (June 1989), p. 139.

2. Raymond E. Miles and Charles C. Snow, "Designing Strategic Human Resources Systems," *Organizational Dynamics* (Summer 1984), p. 36.

3. *Positioning Corporate Staff for the 1990s* (New York: Towers, Perrin, Forster & Crosby, Inc., 1986), p. 9.

4. Miles and Snow, op. cit., pp. 36–52; Karen A. Golden and Uasudevan Ramanujam, "Between a Dream and a Nightmare: On the Integration of Human Resource Management and Strategic Business Planning Process," *Human Resource Management* (Winter 1985), pp. 429–452. See also John Hoerr, "Human Resources Managers Aren't Corporate Nobodies Anymore," *Business Week* (Dec. 2, 1985), pp. 58–59.

5. Brian D. Steffy and Steven D. Maurer, "Conceptualizing and Measuring the Economic Effectiveness of Human Resource Activities," *Academy of Management Review*, vol. 13, no. 2 (1988), pp. 271–286. See also Bruce R. Ellig, "Improving Effectiveness Through an HR Review," *Personnel* (June 1989), pp. 56–63.

6. Warren D. Gross, "Pump Up HR Productivity!" *Personnel* (August 1989), pp. 51–53.

7. George E. Biles and Randall S. Schuler, *Audit Handbook of Human Resource Practices: Auditing the Effectiveness of the Human Resource Function* (Alexandria, Va.: The American Society for Personnel Administration, 1986). See also Walter R. Mahler, "Auditing PAIR," in Dale Yoder and Herbert G. Heneman, Jr., eds., *Planning and*

Auditing PAIR (Washington, D.C.: Bureau of National Affairs, Inc., 1976), pp. 2–92.

8. Miles and Snow, op. cit., pp. 36–52. See also Golden and Ramanujam, op. cit.

9. "Becoming a Business Partner First," *Personnel Administrator* (Dec. 1986), pp. 61–65, 118.

10. Thomas J. Peters and Robert H. Waterman, Jr., *In Search of Excellence: Lessons from America's Best-Run Companies* (New York: Harper & Row Publishers, Inc., 1982).

11. John A. Hooper, Ralph F. Catalanello, and Patrick L. Murray, "Showing Up the Weakest Link," *Personnel Administrator* (April 1987), p. 53.

12. Alfred H. Lievertz, "Developing Your Functional Fingerprint," *Personnel Administrator* (Jan. 1987), pp. 61–65.

13. Dean F. Berry, *The Politics of Personnel Research* (Ann Arbor: Bureau of Industrial Relations, Graduate School of Business Administration, University of Michigan, 1967).

14. Robert L. Mathis and Gary Cameron, "Auditing Personnel Practices in Smaller-sized Organizations: A Realistic Approach," *Personnel Administrator* (April 1981), pp. 45–50.

15. Robert O. Hansson, Nancy D. Smith, and Pamela S. Mancinelli, "Monitoring the HR Job Function," *HRMagazine* (Feb. 1990), pp. 76–78.

16. Harry Levinson, "You Won't Recognize Me: Predictions about Changes in Top-Management Characteristics," *Academy of Management Executive*, vol. II, no. 2 (1987), pp. 119–125.

17. Champagne and McAfee, op. cit.

18. Victoria Kaminski, "There's a Better Way to Conduct Attitude Surveys," *Personnel Administrator* (July 1983), pp. 62–63.

19. Dow Scott, Diana Deadrick, and Stephen Taylor, "The Evolution of Personnel Research," *Personnel Journal* (August 1983), pp. 624–629.

20. Barbara Whitaker Shimko, "All Managers Are HR Managers," *HRMagazine* (Jan. 1990), pp. 67–68, 70.

21. Anne S. Tsui, "Defining the Activities and Effectiveness of the Human Resource Department: A Multiple Constituency Approach," *Human Resource Management* (Spring 1987), pp. 35–69.

22. Lievertz, op. cit.

23. Donald A. Drost, Fabius P. O'Brien, and Steve Marsh, "Exit Interviews: Master the Possibilities," *Personnel Administrator* (Feb. 1987), pp. 104–110.

24. Walter Kiechel III, "The Art of the Exit Interview," *Fortune* (August 13, 1990), pp. 114–115.

25. Kaminski, op. cit.

26. Hooper, Catalanello, and Murray, op. cit.

27. Joel Dreyfuss, "Get Ready for the New Work Force," *Fortune* (April 23, 1990), pp. 165–181.

28. Anne S. Tsui, "Personnel Department Effectiveness: A Tripartite Approach," *Industrial Relations* (Spring 1984), pp. 184–196.

29. Biles and Schuler, op. cit.

30. Diane Crispell, "Workers in 2000," *American Demographics* (March 1990), p. 36.

31. Ibid., p. 38.

32. Robert W. Goddard, "Work Force 2000," *Personnel Journal* (Feb. 1989), p. 68.

33. Ibid.

34. "Pace of Change Is Challenge for HRM, Analyst Says," *Resource* (Oct. 1986), p. 4.

35. Ibid.

36. Goddard, op. cit.

37. "New BNA Report Details Changes in Work Patterns," *Resource* (Dec. 1986), p. 3.

38. John Naisbitt and Patricia Aburdene, *Megatrends 2000* (New York: William Morrow and Company, Inc., 1990), p. 534.

39. The 1986 amendments to the Age Discrimination in Employment Act extend coverage to those over 70 (the act applied previously only to those between 40 and 70). Excluded from coverage are executives, and until 1994, university professors, police, and firefighters are not covered.

40. Marilyn Chase, "In Lives and Dollars the Epidemic's Toll Is Growing Inexorably," *The Wall Street Journal* (May 18, 1987), pp. 1, 17.

41. Dreyfuss, op. cit, p. 165.

42. Betty Southard, Wayne E. Barlow, and D. Diane Hatch, "Employers Must Notify Employees of Plant Closure," *Personnel Journal* (Oct. 1988), p. 22.

43. James Fraze and Martha I. Finney, "Employee Rights Between Our Shores," *Personnel Administrator* (March 1988), pp. 50–54.

44. Phyllis Schiller Myers and Donald W. Myers, "AIDS: Tackling a Tough Problem through Policy," *Personnel Administrator* (April 1987), pp. 95–108, 143. See also *Ideas and Trends* (Chicago: Commerce Clearing House, 1986), p. 108.

45. U.S. Comp. Worth Bill Draws Fire in Hearing," *Resource* (May 1987), pp. 1, 9.

46. Joe Pasqualetto, "Staffing, Privacy and Security Measures," *Personnel Journal* (Sept. 1988), pp. 84–89. See also Morton E. Grossman and Margaret Magnus, "The Growing Dependence on HRIS," *Personnel Journal* (Sept. 1988), pp. 53–59.

47. Jay R. Galbraith and Robert K. Kazanjian, "Organizing to Implement Strategies of Diversity and Globalization: The Role of Matrix Design," *Human Resource Management* (Spring 1986), pp. 37–54.

48. James W. Walker, "Human Resource Roles for the '90s," *Human Resource Planning*, vol. 12, no. 1 (1989), pp. 55–61.

49. State Farm Insurance Companies, *Operation Understanding* (April–May 1983), p. 1.

GLOSSARY

Absentees   Absentees are employees who are scheduled to be at work but are not present.

Accident and sickness policies   Accident and sickness policies usually provide a minimum-care stipend for several weeks up to six months to help employees defray the loss of income while they are sick or recovering from an accident.

Accreditation   Accreditation is a process of certifying the competence of a person in an area of capability. The American Society for Personnel Administration operates an accreditation program for personnel professionals.

Active listening   Active listening requires the listener to stop talking, to remove distractions, to be patient, and to empathize with the talker.

Adverse selection   Adverse selection occurs when an insurance company has a disproportionately high percentage of insureds who will make claims in the future. Adverse selection often results when people are given a chance to buy insurance without prescreening, which often means that a higher than normal proportion have a condition that is likely to cause them to be frequent claimants.

Advisory authority   See Staff authority.

Affirmative action programs   Affirmative action programs are detailed plans developed by employers to undo the results of past employment discrimination, or to ensure equal opportunity in the future.

Age Discrimination in Employment Act of 1967 (as amended)   This act prohibits discrimination in employment because of age against those who are 40 years old or older.

American Federation of Labor and Congress of Industrial Organization (AFL-CIO)   The AFL-CIO is a federation of most national unions. It exists to provide a unified focal point for the labor movement, to assist national unions, and to influence government policies that affect members and working people.

American Society for Personnel Administration (ASPA)   ASPA is the major association for professional personnel specialists and administrators.

Americans with Disabilities Act   The Americans with Disabilities Act makes it unlawful to discriminate against the qualified handicapped. Employers are expect to make reasonable accommodations to enable the person to do the job.

Applied research   Applied research is a study of practical problems, the solutions of which will lead to improved performance.

Arbitration   Arbitration is the submission of a dispute to a neutral third party.

Assessment centers   Assessment centers are a standardized form of employee appraisal that relies on multiple types of evaluation and multiple raters.

Associate membership   Associate membership in a labor organization allows people who are not employed under a union contract to affiliate with a union by paying fees and dues in return for union-supported benefits.

624   GLOSSARY

Attitude surveys Attitude surveys are systematic methods of determining what employees think about their organization. The surveys are usually done through questionnaires. Attitude survey feedback results when the information collected is reported back to the participants. This process then is usually followed by action planning to identify and resolve specific areas of employee concern.

Attrition Attrition is the loss of employees who leave the organization's employment.

Audit report The audit report is a comprehensive description of personnel activities. It includes both commendation for effective practices and recommendations for improving practices that are ineffective.

Audit team An audit team consists of those people who are responsible for evaluating the performance of the personnel department.

Authorization cards Authorization cards are forms that prospective union members sign. The cards indicate their wish to have an election to determine whether a labor organization will represent the workers in their dealings with management.

Autonomous work groups Autonomous work groups are teams of workers, without a formal company-appointed leader, who decide among themselves most decisions traditionally handled by supervisors.

Autonomy Autonomy is having control over one's work.

Bargaining book A bargaining book is a compilation of the negotiation team's plans for collective bargaining with labor or management. Increasingly, the bargaining book is being replaced by information stored in a company or union computer.

Bargaining committee The union bargaining committee consists of union officials and stewards who negotiate with management's representatives to determine the wages, hours, and working conditions to be embodied in the labor agreement.

Barriers to change Barriers to change are factors that interfere with employee acceptance and implementation of change.

Barriers to communication Barriers to communication are interferences that may limit the receiver's understanding.

Behavior modeling Behavior modeling relies on the initiation or emulation of a desired behavior. A repetition of behavior modeling helps to develop appropriate responses in specified situations.

Behaviorally anchored rating scales (BARS) BARS rate employees on a scale that has specific behavioral examples on it to guide the rater.

Behavior modification Behavior modification states that behavior depends on its consequences.

Blind ads Blind ads are want ads that do not identify the employer.

GLOSSARY 625

Bona fide occupational qualifications (BFOQ) A BFOQ occurs when an employer has a justified business reason for discriminating against a member of a protected class. The burden of proving a BFOQ generally falls on the employer.

Bottom-line test The bottom-line test is applied by the Equal Employment Opportunity Commission to determine if a firm's overall selection process is having an adverse impact on protected groups. Even though individual steps in the selection process might exhibit an adverse impact on a protected group, the firm will be considered in compliance if the overall process does not have an adverse effect.

Boulwarism Boulwarism is a negotiation strategy developed by General Electric. Using this approach the company made its "best" offer to the union at the beginning of negotiations, then remained firm unless the union could find where management had erred in the calculations used to arrive at the offer. This strategy was ruled as an unfair labor practice by the National Labor Relations Board and by the federal courts.

Brainstorming Brainstorming is a process by which participants provide their ideas on a stated problem during a freewheeling group session.

Buddy system The "buddy system" of orientation exists when an experienced employee is asked to show a new worker around the job site, conduct introductions, and answer the newcomer's questions.

Burnout Burnout is a condition of mental, emotional, and sometimes physical exhaustion that results from substantial and prolonged stress.

Business agent A business agent is a full-time employee of a local (usually craft) union. The business agent helps employees resolve their problems with management.

Business unionism Business unionism describes unions that seek to improve the wages, hours, and working conditions of their members in a businesslike manner. (See *Social unionism.*)

Buy-back Buy-backs occur when an employee who attempts to resign is convinced to stay in the employment of the organization. Normally the person is "bought back" with an offer of increased wages or salary.

Cafeteria benefit programs Cafeteria benefit programs allow employees to select the fringe benefits and services that answer their individual needs.

Career A career is all the jobs that are held during one's working life.

Career counseling Career counseling assists employees in finding appropriate career goals and paths.

Career development Career development consists of those experiences and personal improvements that one undertakes to achieve a career plan.

Career goals Career goals are the future positions that one strives to reach. These goals serve as benchmarks along one's career path.

Career path   A career path is the sequential pattern of jobs that form one's career.

Career planning   Career planning is the process by which one selects career goals and paths to those goals.

Career plateau   A career plateau occurs when an employee is in a position that he or she does well enough not to be demoted or fired but not well enough to be promoted.

Cause-and-effect diagrams   Cause-and-effect or fishbone diagrams begin with a known effect such as a defective part. From that effect, an individual or group attempts to brainstorm the various possible contributing factors—usually people, machines, materials, and methods. Then each element that could be contributing toward this effect undergoes further scrutiny.

Change agents   Change agents are people who have the role of stimulating and coordinating change within a group.

Checkoff   A checkoff provision in a union-management labor agreement requires the employer to deduct union dues from employee paychecks and to remit those monies to the union.

Civil Rights Act of 1964   This act was passed to make various forms of discrimination illegal.

Closed shop   A closed shop is a workplace where all employees are required to be members of the union before they are hired. These arrangements are illegal under the National Labor Relations Act.

Codetermination   Codetermination is a form of industrial democracy first popularized in West Germany. It gives workers the right to have representatives vote on management decisions.

Cognitive dissonance   Cognitive dissonance results from a gap between what one expects and what one experiences.

Cognitive models of motivation   Cognitive models of motivation depend on the thinking or feeling (that is, cognition) within each individual.

Coinsurance clause   A coinsurance clause is a provision in an insurance policy that requires the employee to pay a percentage of the insured's expenses.

Communication   Communication is the transfer of information and understanding from one person to another.

Communication overload   A communication overload occurs when employees receive more communication inputs than they can process or more than they need.

Communication process   A communication process is the method by which a sender reaches a receiver. It requires that an idea be developed, encoded, transmitted, received, decoded, and used.

GLOSSARY   627

Communication system A communication system provides formal and informal methods for moving information throughout an organization so that appropriate decisions are made.

Comparable worth Comparable worth is the idea that a job should be evaluated as to its value to the organization and then paid accordingly. Thus jobs of comparable worth would be paid equally. For example, two people with widely different jobs would both receive the same pay if the two jobs were of equal value to the employer.

Comparative evaluation approaches Comparative evaluation approaches are a collection of different methods that compare one person's performance with that of coworkers.

Compensation Compensation is what employees receive in exchange for their work, including pay and benefits.

Comprehensive Employment and Training Act of 1973 (CETA) CETA was a broad-ranging act designed to provide job training, employment, and job-hunting assistance to less advantaged persons. It has since been replaced by the *Job Partnership Training Act*.

Concentration in employment Concentration exists when an employer (or some subdivision such as a department) has a higher proportion of employees from a protected class than is found in the employer's labor market. (*See Underutilization*.)

Concessionary bargaining Concessionary bargaining occurs when labor-management negotiations result in fewer employer-paid fringe benefits or wage concessions, such as a freeze or wage cut.

Conciliation agreement A conciliation agreement is a negotiated settlement agreeable to the EEOC and to all parties involved. Its acceptance closes the case.

Consolidated Omnibus Budget Reconciliation Act of 1986 (COBRA) COBRA requires employers to extend medical-related insurance availability to employees who leave employment and to extend coverage to the employee's dependents when their status changes and they are no longer eligible as dependents. (This change may occur because of divorce, college graduation, or marriage of a child-dependent, for example.)

Constructs Constructs are substitutes for actual performance. For example, a score on a test is a construct for actual learning.

Content theories of motivation Content theories of motivation describe the needs or desires within us that initiate behavior.

Contract labor Contract labor consists of people who are hired (and often trained) by an independent agency that supplies companies with needed human resources for a fee.

Contributory plans Contributory plans are fringe benefits that require both the employer and the employee to contribute to the cost of the insurance, retirement, or other employer benefit.

Coordinated organizing Coordinated organizing occurs when two or more unions pool their resources to organize a targeted employer or group of employees.

GLOSSARY

Corrective discipline Corrective discipline is an action that follows a rule infraction and seeks to discourage further infractions so that future acts are in compliance with standards.

Counseling Counseling is the discussion of an employee problem with the general objective of helping the worker cope with it.

Counseling functions Counseling functions are the activities performed by counselors. They include advice, reassurance, communication, release of emotional tension, clarified thinking, and reorientation.

Craft unions Craft unions are labor organizations that seek to include all workers who have a common skill, such as carpenters or plumbers.

Critical incident method The critical incident method requires the rater to report statements that describe extremely good or extremely bad employee behavior. These statements are called critical incidents, and they are used as examples of good or bad performance in rating the employee.

Decision-making authority *See Line authority.*

Deductible clause A deductible clause is a provision in an insurance policy that requires the insured to pay a specified amount of a claim before the insurer is obligated to pay.

Deep sensing meeting At a deep sensing meeting a manager or personnel specialist uses probing questions to understand the issues on employees' minds.

Deferral jurisdictions Deferral jurisdictions are areas in the United States where the EEOC will refer a case to another (usually a state or local) agency.

Deferred stock incentive systems These incentives award stock that becomes owned by employees gradually over several years.

Delegation Delegation is the process of getting others to share a manager's work. It requires the manager to assign duties, grant authority, and create a sense of responsibility.

Delphi technique The Delphi technique solicits predictions from a panel of experts about some specified future development(s). The collective estimates are then reported back to the panel so that the members may adjust their opinions. This process is repeated until a general agreement on future trends emerges.

Demographics Demographics is the study of population characteristics.

Demotions Demotions occur when an employee is moved from one job to another that is lower in pay, responsibility, and organizational level.

Development Development represents those activities that prepare an employee for future responsibilities.

GLOSSARY

Dictionary of Occupational Titles (DOT) The *Dictionary of Occupational Titles* is a federal government publication that provides detailed job descriptions and job codes for most occupations in government and industry.

Differential validity Differential validity is used to demonstrate that tests or other selection criteria are valid for different subgroups or protected classes.

Directive counseling Directive counseling is the process of listening to an employee's emotional problems, deciding with the employee what should be done, and then telling and motivating the employee to do it. (*See Nondirective counseling.*)

Discipline Discipline is management action to encourage compliance with the organization's standards.

Dismissal Dismissal is the ultimate disciplinary action because it separates the employee from the employer for a cause.

Disparate impact Disparate impact occurs when the results of an employer's actions have a different effect on one or more protected classes.

Disparate treatment Disparate treatment occurs when members of a protected class receive unequal treatment.

Downsizing Downsizing means a scaling back of an organization's employment levels, usually through attrition, early retirement programs, or layoffs.

Downward communication Downward communication is information that begins at some point in the organization and then feeds down the hierarchy to inform or influence others in the firm.

Dual responsibility for human resource management Since both line and staff managers are responsible for employees, production, and quality of work life, a dual responsibility for human resource management exists.

Due process Due process means that established rules and procedures for disciplinary action are followed and that employees have an opportunity to respond to the charges made against them.

Early retirement Early retirement occurs when a worker retires from an organization before the "normal" retirement age.

Employee assistance programs (EAPs) EAPs are company-sponsored programs to help employees overcome their personal problems through direct company assistance, counseling, or outside referral.

Employee handbook The employee handbook explains key benefits, policies, and general information about the employer.

Employee involvement (EI) Employee involvement consists of a variety of systematic methods that enable employees to participate in the decisions that affect them.

GLOSSARY

Employee Retirement Income Security Act (ERISA) ERISA was passed by Congress to ensure that employer pension plans meet minimum participation, vesting, and funding requirements.

Employment freeze An employment freeze occurs when the organization curtails future hiring.

Employment function The employment function is that aspect of personnel responsible for recruiting, selecting, and hiring new workers. This function is usually handled by the employment section or employment manager of a large personnel department.

Employment references Employment references are evaluations of an employee's work performance. They are provided by past employers.

Employment tests Employment tests are devices that assess the probable match between the applicants and the job requirements.

Equal Employment Act of 1972 This act strengthened the role of the Equal Employment Opportunity Commission by amending the Civil Rights Act of 1964. The 1972 law empowered the EEOC to initiate court action against noncomplying organizations.

Equal employment opportunity Equal employment opportunity means giving people a fair chance to succeed without discrimination based on factors unrelated to job performance—such as age, race, or national origin.

Equal Employment Opportunity Commission (EEOC) The EEOC is the federal agency responsible for enforcing Title VII of the Civil Rights Act, as amended.

Equal employment opportunity laws Equal employment opportunity laws are a family of federal and state acts that seek to ensure equal employment opportunities for members of protected groups.

Equal Pay Act of 1963 This act prohibits discrimination in pay because of a person's sex.

Equifinality Equifinality means that there are usually multiple paths to an objective.

Equity theory Equity theory suggests that people are motivated to close the gap between their efforts and the perceived amount and appropriateness of the rewards they receive.

Ergonomics Ergonomics is the study of biotechnical relationships between the physical attributes of workers and the physical demands of the job. The object of the study is to reduce physical and mental strain in order to increase productivity and quality of work life.

Error of central tendency The error of central tendency occurs when a rater evaluates employee performance as neither good nor poor, even when some employees perform exceptionally well or poorly. Instead, the rater rates everyone as average.

GLOSSARY

Evaluation interviews Evaluation interviews are performance review sessions that give employees feedback about their past performance or about their future potential.

Executive orders Executive orders are presidential decrees that normally apply to government contractors or managers in the executive branches of the federal government. By President.

Exit interviews Exit interviews are conversations with departing employees to learn their views of the organization.

Expatriate An expatriate is a person who lives and works in a foreign country.

Expectancy Expectancy is the strength of a person's belief that an act will lead to a particular outcome.

Expectancy theory Expectancy theory states that motivation is the result of the outcome one seeks and one's estimate that action will lead to the desired outcome.

Expedited arbitration Expedited arbitration is an attempt to speed up the arbitration process. It may include an arrangement with the arbitrator for him or her to be available on short notice (one or two days) and to render a quick decision at the conclusion of the hearings (sometimes an oral decision is used in these cases).

Experience rating Experience rating is a practice whereby state unemployment offices determine an employer's unemployment compensation tax rate based on the employer's previous experience in providing stable employment.

Experiential learning Experiential learning means that participants learn by experiencing in the training environment the kinds of problems they face on the job.

Exposure Exposure means becoming known by those who decide on promotions, transfers, and other career opportunities.

Extrapolation Extrapolation involves extending past rates of change into the future.

Facilitator A facilitator is someone who assists quality circles and the quality circle leader in identifying and solving workplace problems.

Factor comparison method The factor comparison method is a form of job evaluation that allocates a part of each job's wage to key factors of the job. The result is a relative evaluation of the organization's jobs.

Fair employment practices Fair employment practices are state and local laws that prohibit employer discrimination in employment against members of protected classes.

Fair Labor Standards Act of 1938 (FLSA) FLSA is a comprehensive federal law affecting compensation management. It sets minimum-wage, overtime pay, equal pay, child labor, and record-keeping requirements.

Federal Mediation and Conciliation Service (FMCS) The FMCS was created by the Labor Management Relations Act of 1947 to help labor and management resolve negotiation impasses peacefully through mediation and conciliation without resort to a strike. The FMCS also is a source of qualified labor arbitrators.

Feedback Feedback is information that helps evaluate the success or failure of an action or system.

Field experiment A field experiment is research that allows the researchers to study employees under realistic conditions to learn how experimental and control subjects react to new programs and to other changes.

Field review method The field review method requires skilled representatives of the personnel department to go into the "field" and assist supervisors with their ratings. Often it is the personnel department's representative that actually fills out the evaluation form after interviewing the supervisor about employee performance.

Flextime Flextime is a scheduling innovation that abolishes rigid starting and ending times for each day's work. Instead, employees are allowed to begin and end the workday at their discretion, usually within a range of hours.

Flexyear Flexyear is a scheduling concept that allows workers to be off the job for part of the year. Employees usually work a normal work year in less than twelve months.

Forced choice method The forced choice method of employee performance evaluation requires the rater to choose the most descriptive statement in each pair of statements about the employee being rated.

Foreign Corrupt Practices Act The Foreign Corrupt Practices Act outlaws the use of bribes or bribe-like payments in dealing overseas under a variety of conditions.

Foreign national A foreign national is a person who is a citizen of one country living and working in another country.

Four-fifths rule The four-fifths rule is a test used by the EEOC. When the selection ratio of protected-class applicants is less than 80 percent (or four-fifths) of the selection ratio for majority applicants, adverse impact is assumed.

Fully insured workers Fully insured workers are employees who have contributed forty quarters (ten years) to social security.

Functional authority Functional authority allows staff experts to make decisions in specified circumstances that are normally reserved for line managers.

Funded plan Funded plans require an employer to accumulate monies in advance so that the organization's contribution plus interest will cover its obligation.

Funded retirement plans A funded retirement plan is one in which the employer sets aside sufficient money to meet the future payout requirements.

GLOSSARY

Gainsharing   Gainsharing matches an improvement (gain) in company performance to some distribution (sharing) of the benefits with employees.

Glass ceiling   Glass ceiling refers to the idea that people can see higher-level positions but are blocked from attaining higher-level positions by a real, but unseen barrier, such as discrimination. The term is most often applied to the careers of women who are often blocked from achieving the senior most positions in a company. It also applies to foreign nationals who may be blocked from the senior most positions in a company based in another country.

Golden parachutes   Golden parachutes are agreements by the company to compensate executives with bonuses and benefits if they should be displaced by a merger or acquisition.

Grapevine communication   Grapevine communication is an informal system that arises spontaneously from the social interaction of people in the organization.

Grievance procedure   A grievance procedure is a multistep process that the employer and union jointly use to resolve disputes that arise under the terms of the labor agreement.

Griggs v. Duke Power Company   The U.S. Supreme Court case held that when an employment criterion disproportionately discriminates against a protected class, the employer is required to show how the criterion is job-related.

Guaranteed annual wage   A guaranteed annual wage assures workers of receiving a minimum amount of work or pay during the course of a year.

Guest workers   Guest workers are foreign nationals allowed to work in another nation, generally to alleviate a labor shortage or provide a desired skill, knowledge, or ability.

Halo effect   The halo effect is a bias that occurs when a rater allows some information to disproportionately prejudice the final evaluation.

Harassment   Harassment occurs when a member of an organization treats an employee in a disparate manner because of the worker's sex, race, religion, age, or other protected classification.

Hazard communication   A hazard communication, required under Occupational Safety and Health Act rules and regulations, is issued by an employer to inform employees about the nature of hazardous materials being used at work.

Health maintenance organizations (HMOs)   HMOs are a form of health insurance whereby the insurer provides the professional staff and facilities needed to treat their insured policyholders for a predetermined monthly fee.

Hot-stove rule   The hot-stove rule states that disciplinary action should have the same characteristics as the penalty a person receives from touching a hot stove. That is, the discipline should be with warning, immediate, consistent, and impersonal.

House organs A house organ is any regularly published organizational magazine, newspaper, or bulletin directed to employees.

Human resource audit A human resource audit evaluates the personnel activities used in an organization.

Human resource forecasts Human resource forecasts predict the organization's future demand for employees.

Human resource planning Human resource planning systematically forecasts an organization's future supply of, and demand for, employees.

Human resources Human resources are the people who are ready, willing, and able to contribute to organizational goals.

Imminent danger An imminent danger is a situation that is likely to lead to death or serious injury if allowed to continue.

Improshare plans Improshare plans are a form of gainsharing that focuses on reducing the labor hours used to produce a given level of output, with part of the savings shared with the employees.

Incentive systems Incentive systems link compensation and performance by paying employees for actual results, not for seniority or hours worked.

Indexation Indexation is a method of estimating future employment needs by matching employment growth with some index, such as sales growth.

Industrial democracy Industrial democracy refers to giving employees a larger voice in making the work-related decisions that affect them.

Industrial unions Industrial unions are labor organizations that seek to include all of an employer's eligible workers regardless of whether they are skilled, semiskilled, or unskilled.

In-house complaint procedures In-house complaint procedures are organizationally developed methods for employees to register their complaints about various aspects of the organization.

Job analysis Job analysis systematically collects, evaluates, and organizes information about jobs.

Job analysis schedules Job analysis schedules are checklists or questionnaires that seek to collect information about jobs in a uniform manner. (They are also called job analysis questionnaires.)

Job banks Job banks exist in state employment security offices. They are used to match applicants with job openings.

GLOSSARY

Job code   A job code uses numbers, letters, or both to provide a quick summary of the job and its content.

Job description   A job description is a written statement that explains the duties, working conditions, and other aspects of a specified job.

Job enlargement   Job enlargement means adding more tasks to a job in order to increase the job cycle.

Job enrichment   Job enrichment means adding more responsibilities, autonomy, and control to a job.

Job evaluations   Job evaluations are systematic procedures to determine the relative worth of jobs.

Job families   Job families are groups of different jobs that require similar skills.

Job-flo   Job-flo is a monthly report of frequently listed openings from job banks throughout the country.

Job grading   Job grading is a form of job evaluation that assigns jobs to predetermined classifications according to the job's relative worth to the organization. This technique is also called the job classification method.

Jobholder reports   Jobholder reports are reports to employees about the firm's economic performance.

Job information service   The job information service is a feature of state employment security agencies that enables job seekers to review job bank listings in their efforts to find employment.

Job instruction training   Job instruction training is training received directly on the job. It is also called "on-the-job training."

Job performance standards   Job performance standards are the work requirements that are expected from an employee on a particular job.

Job posting program   Job posting informs employees of unfilled job openings and the qualifications for these jobs.

Job progression ladder   A job progression ladder is a particular career path where some jobs have prerequisites.

Job ranking   Job ranking is one form of job evaluation that subjectively ranks jobs according to their overall worth to the organization.

Job rotation   Job rotation is the process of moving employees from one job to another in order to allow them more variety in their jobs and the opportunity to learn new skills.

Job satisfaction   Job satisfaction is the favorableness or unfavorableness with which employees view their work.

GLOSSARY

Job sharing Job sharing is a scheduling innovation that allows two or more workers to share the same job, usually by each working part-time.

Job specifications A job specification describes what a job demands of employees who do it and the human skills that are required.

Job Training Partnership Act of 1983 This act provides federal funds to authorized training contractors, often city or state government agencies. These monies are used to train people in new, employable skills. (It replaces the Comprehensive Education and Training Act of 1973.)

Joint study committees Joint study committees include representatives from management and the union who meet away from the bargaining table to study some topic of mutual interest in the hope of finding a solution that is mutually satisfactory.

Juniority Juniority provisions require that layoffs be offered first to senior workers who may accept or refuse them. If sufficient senior workers do not accept the layoffs, then management is free to lay off the least senior workers.

Key jobs Key jobs are those that are common in the organization and in its labor market.

Key subordinates Key subordinates are those employees who are crucial to a manager's success in a particular job.

Labor agreement A labor agreement, which is also called a labor contract, is a legal document that is negotiated between the union and the employer. It states the terms and conditions of employment.

Laboratory training Laboratory training is a form of group training primarily used to enhance interpersonal skills.

Labor Management Relations Act of 1947 (LMRA) The LMRA, also known as the Taft-Hartley Act, amended the National Labor Relations Act of 1935 by designating specific union actions that were considered to be unfair labor practices. The act also created the Federal Mediation and Conciliation Service and enabled the President of the United States to call for injunctions in national emergency strikes.

Labor-Management Reporting and Disclosure Act of 1959 (LMRDA) The LMRDA, also called the Landrum Griffin Act, amended the National Labor Relations Act. It created the union members' "bill of rights" by giving union members certain rights in dealing with their union. The law also established detailed reporting requirements for those who handle union funds.

Labor market The labor market is the area in which the employer recruits.

Labor market analysis Labor market analysis is the study of the employer's labor market to evaluate the present or future availability of workers.

GLOSSARY

Labor shortages   Labor shortages are a scarcity of people to fill job openings.

Landrum-Griffin Act   See Labor-Management Reporting and Disclosure Act of 1959.

Law of effect   The law of effect states that people learn to repeat behaviors that have favorable consequences, and they learn to avoid behaviors that have unfavorable consequences.

Layoffs   Layoffs are the separation of employees from the organization for economic or business reasons.

Learning curve   A learning curve is a visual representation of the rate at which one learns given material through time.

Learning curve for change   The learning curve for change is a charted representation of the period of adjustment and adaptation to change required by an organization.

Learning principles   Learning principles are guidelines to the ways in which people learn most effectively.

Legal insurance   Legal insurance is usually a group insurance plan provided by the employer that reimburses the insureds when they have specified legal expenses or provides the insureds with access to legal assistance at predetermined (and usually low) rates.

Leniency bias   A leniency bias occurs when employees are rated higher than their performance justifies.

Leveraging   Leveraging refers to resigning in order to further one's career with another employer.

Life plan   A life plan is that often ill-defined series of hopes, dreams, and personal goals that each person carries through life.

Lifetime employment   Lifetime employment refers to employer guarantees, stated or implied, that assure the employee employment for his or her lifetime.

Line authority   Line authority allows managers to direct others and to make decisions about the organization's operations.

Listening   Listening is a receiver's positive effort to understand a message transmitted by sound.

Local unions   Local unions are the smallest organizational unit of a union. They are responsible for representing the members at the worksite.

Long-term disability insurance   Long-term disability insurance provides a proportion of a disabled employee's wage or salary. These policies typically have long waiting periods and seldom allow the employee to attain the same income level that existed before the disability.

Lost-time accidents These are severe job-related accidents that cause the employee to lose time from his or her job.

Maintenance factors Maintenance factors are those elements in the work setting that lead to employee dissatisfaction when they are not adequately provided. These factors are also called hygiene factors or dissatisfiers. They include working conditions and fringe benefits.

"Make-whole" remedies When an individual is mistreated in violation of employment laws, the wrongdoer usually is required to make up the losses that were suffered by the employee because of the wrongdoing.

Management by objectives (MBO) MBO requires an employee and superior to jointly establish performance goals for the future. Employees are subsequently evaluated on how well they have obtained these agreed-upon objectives.

Management inventories Management inventories summarize the skills and abilities of management personnel. (*See Skills inventories*, which are used for nonmanagement employees.)

Management rights Management rights are the rights and freedoms that an employer needs to manage the enterprise effectively. These areas of discretion usually are reserved by management in the labor agreement.

Maturity curves Maturity curves are used to compensate workers based on their seniority and performance. Normally, these compensation plans are limited to professional and technical workers.

Mentor A mentor is someone who offers informal career advice.

Merit-based promotions Merit-based promotions occur when an employee is promoted because of superior performance in the present job.

Merit raises Merit raises are pay increases given to individual workers according to an evaluation of their performance.

Motivation Motivation is a person's drive to take action because that person wants to do so.

Motivational factors Motivational factors are those elements in the work environment that motivate the individual. They are sometimes called motivators and satisfiers.

National Institute of Occupational Safety and Health (NIOSH) NIOSH was created by the Occupational Safety and Health Act to conduct research and to develop additional safety and health standards.

GLOSSARY 639

National Labor Relations Act of 1935 (NLRA) The NLRA, also known as the Wagner Act, was passed by Congress to ensure that covered employees could join (or refrain from joining) unions for the purpose of their own mutual aid and protection and for negotiating with employers. The act also created the National Labor Relations Board.

National Labor Relations Board (NLRB) The NLRB was created by the National Labor Relations Act to prevent unfair labor practices and to conduct union representation elections.

National unions National unions are the parent bodies that helps organize, charter, guide, and assist their affiliated local unions.

Needs assessment Needs assessment diagnoses present problems and future challenges that can be met through training and development.

Net benefit Net benefit means that there will be a surplus of benefits after all costs are included.

Nominal group techniques (NGT) NGT is a group method of drawing out ideas from people on a specified topic. It requires participants to list their ideas and then share them in round-robin fashion with the group and a facilitator. Once all the ideas of the group are vented, duplicate ideas are eliminated and clarification follows. Then the members of the group vote on what they believe to be the best or the most important items they uncovered through the NGT process.

Noncontributory benefit plans Noncontributory benefit plans are fringe benefits that are paid entirely by the employer. (See Contributory plans.)

Nondeferral jurisdictions Nondeferral jurisdictions are areas where the EEOC finds no qualified agency to which it may defer cases.

Nondirective counseling Nondirective, or client-centered, counseling is the process of skillfully listening to an employee and encouraging him or her to explain bothersome problems, to understand them, and to determine appropriate solutions.

Nonmonetary incentives Nonmonetary incentives, such as recognition, reward employees for desired performance without the use of money.

Nonverbal communication Nonverbal communication is action that communicates without spoken words.

Obsolescence Obsolescence results when an employee no longer possesses the knowledge or ability to perform successfully.

Occupational Outlook Handbook The *Occupational Outlook Handbook* is published by the U.S. Department of Labor. It indicates the future need for certain jobs.

Occupational Safety and Health Act of 1970 (OSHA) OSHA is a broad-ranging law that requires employers to provide a work environment that is free of recognized safety and health hazards.

GLOSSARY

Occupational Safety and Health Administration The Occupational Safety and Health Administration is located in the U.S. Department of Labor and is responsible for enforcing the Occupational Safety and Health Act.

Occupational Safety and Health Review Commission The Occupational Safety and Health Review Commission is the federal agency that reviews on appeal the fines given to employers by the Occupational Safety and Health Administration for safety and health violations.

Open communication Open communication exists when people feel free to communicate all relevant messages.

Open-door policy An open-door policy encourages employees to go to their manager or even to higher management with any problem that concerns them.

Open system *See System.*

Operating authority *See Line authority*

Organization culture An organization's culture is the product of all the organization's features—such as its people, objectives, technology, size, age, unions, policies, successes, and failures. It is the organization's "personality."

Organization development (OD) OD is an intervention strategy that uses group processes to focus on the whole organization in order to bring about planned changes.

Organization development process The OD process is complex and difficult to implement. It consists of seven steps: initial diagnosis, data collection, data feedback and confrontation, action planning and problem solving, team building, intergroup development and evaluation, and follow-up.

Organizational climate Organizational climate is the favorableness or unfavorableness of the environment for people in the organization.

Organizing committee An organizing committee consists of employees who guide the efforts needed to organize their fellow workers into a labor organization.

Orientation programs Orientation programs familiarize primarily new employees with their roles, the organization, its policies, and other employees.

Outplacement Outplacement occurs when an organization assists its present employees in finding jobs with other employers.

Pareto analysis Pareto analysis is a means of collecting data about the types or causes of production problems in descending order of frequency.

Participation rates Participation rates are the percentages of working-age men and women in the work force.

GLOSSARY 641

Participative counseling   Participative counseling seeks to find a balance between directive and nondirective counseling techniques, with the counselor and the counselee participating in the discussion and solution of the problem.

Part-time layoffs   Part-time layoffs occur when an employer lays off workers without pay for a part of each week, such as each Friday.

Paternalism   Paternalism exists when management assumes that it alone is the best judge of employee needs and therefore does not seek or act upon employee suggestions.

Pattern bargaining   Pattern bargaining occurs when the same or essentially the same contract is used for several firms, often in the same industry.

Patterns and practices   When discrimination is found to exist against a large number of individuals who are in a protected class, a pattern and practice case exists.

Pay-for-knowledge compensation systems   These systems provide employees higher pay as an incentive for each new skill or job they learn.

Payout standards   Payout standards are the benchmarks or triggers that determine whether an incentive or gainsharing award is earned.

Performance appraisal   Performance appraisal is the process by which organizations evaluate employee performance.

Performance measures   Performance measures are the ratings used to evaluate employee performance.

Performance standards   Performance standards are the benchmarks against which performance is measured.

Perks   Perks stands for prerequisites that are associated with the fringe benefits of a given job. The term "perks" is often used as shorthand or human resource slang for fringe benefits.

Personnel barriers   Personnel barriers are communication interferences that arise from human emotions, values, and limitations.

Personal leave days   Personal leave days are normal workdays that an employee is entitled to take off. (In some firms personal leave days are used instead of sick days.)

Personnel management   Personnel management is the study of how employers obtain, develop, utilize, evaluate, maintain, and retain the right numbers and types of workers. Its purpose is to provide organizations with an effective work force.

Peter Principle   The Peter Principle states that in a hierarchy, people tend to rise to their level of incompetence.

Piecework   Piecework is a type of incentive system that compensates workers for each unit of output.

GLOSSARY

Placement Placement is the assignment of an employee to a new or different job.

Point system The point system is a form of job evaluation that assesses the relative importance of the job's key factors in order to arrive at the relative worth of jobs.

Political grievances Political grievances are filed or supported because of their political implications, not their merits.

Portability clauses Portability clauses allow workers to transfer accumulated pension rights to their subsequent employer when they change jobs.

Position analysis questionnaire (PAQ) The PAQ is a standardized, preprinted form that collects specific information about jobs.

Precedent A precedent is a new standard that arises from past practices of either the company or the union.

Preferential quota systems Preferential quota systems exist when a proportion of the job openings, promotions, or other employment opportunities is reserved for members of a protected class who have been previously discriminated against.

Pregnancy Discrimination Act of 1978 This act prevents discrimination in employment against women who are pregnant and able to perform their jobs. The law amends the Civil Rights Act of 1964.

Prevailing wage rates Prevailing wage rates are the rates most commonly paid for a given job in a specific geographical area. They are determined by a wage and salary survey.

Preventive discipline Preventive discipline is action taken to encourage employees to follow standards and rules so that infractions are prevented.

Private placement agencies Private placement agencies are for-profit organizations that help job seekers find employment.

Proactive human resource management Proactive human resource management exists when decision makers anticipate problems and take affirmative steps to minimize those problems rather than wait until after a problem occurs before taking action.

Problem-solving interviews These types of interviews rely on questions that are limited to hypothetical situations or problems. The applicant is evaluated on how well the problems are solved.

Production bonuses Production bonuses are a type of incentive system that provides employees with additional compensation when they surpass stated production goals.

Production sharing plans Production sharing plans are gainsharing approaches that reward employees for exceeding predetermined production levels.

Productivity Productivity is the ratio of a firm's output (goods and services) divided by its input (people, capital, materials, energy).

GLOSSARY   643

Professional associations   Professional associations are groups of workers who voluntarily join together to further their profession and their professional development. When these associations undertake to negotiate for their members, they are also labor organizations.

Profit sharing   Profit sharing exists when an organization shares a proportion of its profits with the workers, usually on an annual basis.

Profit-sharing plans   Profit-sharing plans enable eligible employees to receive a proportion of the organization's profits.

Progressive discipline   Progressive discipline requires strong penalties for repeated offenses.

Promotion   A promotion occurs when an employee is moved from one job to another that is higher in pay, responsibility, and/or organizational level.

Protected groups   Protected groups are classes of people who are protected from discrimination under one or more laws.

Psychic costs   Psychic costs are the stresses, strains, and anxieties that affect a person's inner self during a period of change.

Pygmalion effect   The Pygmalion effect occurs when people live up to the highest expectations others hold of them.

Qualifiable worker   A qualifiable worker is one who does not currently possess all the requirements, knowledge, skills, or abilities to do the job, but who will become qualified through additional training and experience.

Qualified handicapped   The qualified handicapped are those mentally or physically handicapped individuals who, with reasonable accommodations, can perform successfully.

Quality circles   Quality circles are small groups of employees who meet regularly with a common leader to identity and solve work-related problems.

Quality of work life   Quality of work life means having good supervision, good working conditions, good pay and benefits, and an interesting, challenging, and rewarding job.

Quality of work life efforts   Quality of work life efforts are systematic attempts by an organization to give workers a greater opportunity to affect their jobs and their contributions to the organization's overall effectiveness.

Rap sessions   Rap sessions are meetings between managers and groups of employees to discuss complaints, suggestions, opinions, or questions.

Rate ranges Rate ranges are pay ranges for each job class.

Rating scale A rating scale requires the rater to provide a subjective evaluation of an individual's performance along a scale from low to high.

Rational validity Rational validity exists when tests include reasonable samples of the skills needed to perform successfully or where there is an obvious relationship between performance and other characteristics that are assumed to be necessary for successful job performance.

Reactive human resource management Reactive human resource management exists when decision makers respond to problems instead of anticipating problems before they occur. (*See Proactive management.*)

Realistic job preview (RJP) An RJP allows the job applicant to see the type of work, equipment, and working conditions involved in the job before the hiring decision is finalized.

Recency effect The recency effect is a rater bias that occurs when a rater allows recent employee performance to sway the overall evaluation.

Recruitment Recruitment is the process of finding and attracting capable applicants for employment.

Red-circle rates Red-circle rates are wages or salaries that are inappropriate for a given job according to the job evaluation plan.

Regulations Regulations are legally enforceable rules developed by government agencies to ensure compliance with laws that the agency interprets and administers.

Rehabilitation Act of 1973 This act prohibits discrimination against those who are handicapped but qualified to perform work. It applies to employees who receive federal monies and to federal agencies. (*See the Americans with Disabilities Act*)

Reinforcement schedules Reinforcement schedules are the different ways that behavior reinforcement can be given.

Relations by objectives Relations by objectives is a program created by the Federal Mediation and Conciliation Service to improve labor-management cooperation between participating parties.

Reliability Reliability means that a selection device (usually a test) yields consistent results each time an individual takes it.

Relocation policies Relocation policies are the company guidelines used to determine the benefits and other assistance that will be provided employees who must move domestically or internationally in connection with their jobs.

Relocation programs Relocation programs are company-sponsored fringe benefits and assistance that aid employees who must move in connection with their jobs.

GLOSSARY

Repatriation programs   Repatriation programs are company sponsored efforts to relocate an employee back to his or her home country.

Repetition   Repetition facilitates learning through repeated review of the material to be learned.

Repetitive strain injury   A repetitive strain injury occurs when a worker's job requires constant repetition of movement that leads to some form of strain on the body. For example, "tennis elbow" occurs for some people who play tennis; typist and word processor operators are sometimes afflicted with carpal tunnel syndrome, which is an inflammation of the nerves in the wrist.

Replacement charts   Replacement charts are visual presentations of who will replace whom in the organization when a job opening occurs.

Resistance to change   Resistance to change arises from employee opposition to change.

Résumé   A résumé is a brief listing of an applicant's work experience, education, personal data, and other information relevant to the applicant's employment qualifications.

Reverse discrimination   Reverse discrimination occurs when an employer seeks to hire or to promote a member of a protected class over an equally (or better) qualified candidate who is not a member of a protected class.

Reward-performance model   The reward-performance model combines the strengths of other motivational approaches. It argues that properly reinforced behavior enhances an individual's self-image and, therefore, the individual's self-expectations. These self-expectations lead to greater effort, and the rewards for this effort continue to reinforce the behavior.

Role ambiguity   Role ambiguity results when people are uncertain of what is expected of them in a given job.

Role playing   Role playing is a training technique that requires the trainee to assume different identities in order to learn how others feel under different circumstances.

Rucker plan   Rucker plans are cost-reduction gainsharing approaches used to reduce labor and material costs by sharing a proportion of the savings with employees.

Sandwich model of discipline   The sandwich model suggests that a corrective comment should be sandwiched between two positive comments in order to make the corrective comment more acceptable.

Scanlon plan   The Scanlon Plan is an incentive program that compensates eligible employees for improvements in labor costs that are better than the previously established company norms.

Search firms   Search firms are private for-profit organizations that exist to help employers locate hard-to-find applicants.

Selection interviews   Selection interviews are a step in the selection process whereby the applicant and the employer's representative have a face-to-face meeting.

Selection process   The selection process is a series of specific steps used to decide which recruits should be hired.

Selection ratio   The selection ratio is the ratio of the number of applicants hired to the total number of applicants.

Self-actualization   See *Self-fulfillment needs*.

Self-fulfillment needs   Self-fulfillment needs are the needs people have that make them feel they are becoming all that they are capable of becoming. This need also is called self-actualization.

Self-funding   Self-funding occurs when an organization agrees to meet its insurance obligations out of its own resources.

Seniority   Seniority means the length of a worker's employment in relation to other employees.

Seniority-based promotions   Seniority-based promotions result when the most senior employee is promoted into a new position.

Severance pay   Severance pay is a payment made to workers when they are dismissed from the company. Employees who are terminated because of their poor performance or behavior are usually not eligible.

Shelf-sitters   "Shelf-sitters" is a slang term for upwardly immobile managers who block promotion channels.

Shorter workweeks   Shorter workweeks are employee scheduling variations that allow full-time workers to complete their week's work in less than the traditional five days. One variation is forty hours work in four days.

Skills inventories   Skills inventories are summaries of each employee's skills and abilities. (Skills inventories usually refer to nonmanagement workers. See *Management inventories*.)

Socialization   Socialization is the ongoing process by which an employee adapts to an organization by understanding and accepting the values, norms, and beliefs held by others in the firm. Orientation programs—which familiarize primarily new employees with their role, the organization, its policies, and other employees—speed up the socialization process.

Social Security Act of 1935   This act established the social security program of the federal government, which taxes workers and employers in order to create a fund from which Medicare, retirement, disability, and death payments are made to covered workers and their survivors.

GLOSSARY

647

Social unionism   Social unionism describes unions that seek to further their members' interests by influencing the social, economic, and legal policies of government at all levels—city, county, state, and federal. (*See Business unionism.*)

Sociotechnical systems   Sociotechnical systems are interventions in the work situation that restructure the work, the work groups, and the relationship between the workers and the technology they use to do their jobs.

Specialization   Specialization occurs when a very limited number of tasks are grouped into one job.

Sponsor   A sponsor is a person in an organization who can create career development opportunities for others.

Staff authority   Staff authority is the authority to advise, not direct, others.

Staffing table   A staffing table lists anticipated employment openings for each type of job.

State employment security agency   A state employment security agency (or unemployment office) matches job seekers with employers who have job openings.

Steering committee   The steering committee is part of a quality circle or other employee involvement effort and usually includes the top manager of the worksite (such as a plant manager) and his or her direct staff.

Steward   A union steward is elected by workers (or appointed by local union leaders) to help covered employees present their problems to management.

Stock options   Stock options are fringe benefits that give the holder the right to purchase the company's stock at a predetermined price.

Strategic plan   A strategic plan identifies a firm's long-range objectives and proposals for achieving those objectives.

Stress   Stress is a condition of strain that affects one's emotions, thought processes, and physical condition.

Stress interviews   Stress interviews rely on a series of harsh, rapid-fire questions that are intended to upset the applicant and show how the applicant handles stress.

Stressors   Stressors are conditions that tend to cause stress.

Stress-performance model   The stress-performance model shows the relationship between stress and job performance.

Stress threshold   A stress threshold is the level of stress that a person can tolerate before feelings of distress begin.

Strictness bias   A strictness bias occurs when employees are rated lower than their performance justifies.

Structural unemployment Structural unemployment occurs when people are ready, willing, and able to work, but their skills do not match the jobs available.

Structured interviews Structured interviews use a predetermined checklist of questions that usually are asked of all applicants.

Suggestion system Suggestion systems are a formal method for generating, evaluating, and implementing useful employee ideas.

Suitable employment Suitable employment means employment for which the person is suited as a result of education, training, or experience.

Supplemental unemployment benefits (SUB) SUB is an employer-provided fringe benefit that supplements state unemployment insurance when an employee is laid off.

System A system is two or more parts (or subsystems) working together as an organized whole with identifiable boundaries. An open system is one that is affected by the environment.

Taft-Hartley Act See Labor-Management Relations Act of 1947.

Taft-Hartley injunctions Taft-Hartley injunctions allow the President of the United States to seek a court order to delay a labor-management strike for eighty days. During this cooling-off period, the government investigates the facts surrounding the dispute.

Task identity Task identity means doing an identifiable piece of work, thus enabling the worker to have a sense of responsibility and pride.

Task significance Task significance means knowing that the work one does is important to others in the organization and outside of it.

Time studies Time studies are measurements of how long a job takes to perform.

Title VII Title VII refers to the part of the Civil Rights Act of 1964 that requires equal employment opportunities without regard to race, color, religion, sex, pregnancy, or national origin.

Training Training represents activities that teach employees how to perform their present jobs.

Transference Transference refers to how applicable the training is to actual job situations, as evaluated by how readily the trainee transfers the learning to his or her job.

Transfers Transfers occur when an employee is moved from one job to another that is relatively equal in pay, responsibility, and organizational level.

Turnover Turnover is the loss of employees by the organization. It represents those employees who depart for a variety of reasons.

GLOSSARY 649

Two-tiered wage rate   A pay structure that occurs when one group of employees (usually new hires) receives a different wage rate than other employees. The employer achieves lower labor costs by paying new workers less while previously hired union members usually are able to retain their existing wage rates.

Two-tiered orientation program   A two-tiered orientation program exists when both the personnel department and the immediate supervisor provide an orientation for new employees.

Two-way communication   Two-way communication means that a sender and a receiver are exchanging messages so that a regular flow of communication is maintained.

Underutilization   Underutilization occurs when a department or an entire organization has a smaller proportion of members of a protected class than is found in the firm's labor market. (See Concentration in employment.)

Unemployment compensation   Unemployment compensation is payment to those who lose their jobs, are unemployed, are seeking new employment, and are willing and able to work.

Unfair labor practices (ULPs)   ULPs are violations of the National Labor Relations Act, as amended. These unfair practices are specific activities that employers and labor organizations are prohibited from doing.

Union-management agreement   See Labor Agreement.

Union members' bill of rights   The union members' bill of rights refers to Title I of the Labor-Management Reporting and Disclosure Act of 1959, which established the specific rights of union members in dealing with their unions.

Union organizers   Union organizers are people who assist employees in forming a local union.

Union shop   A union shop is a workplace where all employees are required to join the local union as a condition of employment. New employees are usually given thirty, sixty, or ninety days in which to join.

Unstructured interview   An unstructured interview uses few, if any, planned questions to enable the interviewer to pursue, in depth, the applicant's responses.

Upward communication   Upward communication is communication that begins at some point in the organization and then proceeds up the hierarchy to inform or influence others.

Validity   Validity means that the selection device (usually a test) is related significantly to job performances or to some other relevant criterion.

Variety Variety in jobs means being able to use different skills and abilities.

Vertical staffing meetings Vertical staffing meetings occur when managers meet with two or more levels of subordinates to learn of their concerns.

Vestibule training Vestibule training occurs off the job on equipment or methods that are highly similar to those used on the job. This technique minimizes the disruption of operations caused by training activities.

Vesting Vesting is a provision in retirement plans that gives workers rights to retirement benefits after a specified number of years of service, even if the employee quits before retirement.

Vietnam Era Veterans Readjustment Act of 1974 This act prohibits certain government contractors from discriminating in employment against Vietnam era veterans.

Wage and salary surveys Wage and salary surveys are studies made by an organization to discover what other employers in the same labor market are paying for specific key jobs.

Wage compression Wage compression occurs when the difference between higher- and lower-paying jobs is reduced. This compression usually results from giving larger pay increases to lower-paying jobs.

Wagner Act *See* National Labor Relations Act of 1935.

Walk-ins Walk-ins are job seekers who arrive at the personnel department in search of a job without any prior referrals and not in response to a specific ad or request.

Want ads Want ads describe the job and its benefits, identify the employer, (or employment agency), and tell those who are interested how to apply.

Weighted checklist A weighted checklist requires the rater to select statements or words to describe an employee's performance or characteristics. After those selections are made, different responses are given different values or weights in order to determine a quantified total score.

Weighted incentive systems These systems reward executives on the basis of improvements in multiple areas of business performance. Depending on the weights used, part of the incentive bonus can be tied to improvements in market share, profit margins, return on assets, cash flow, or other indexes.

Welfare secretary The welfare secretary was a forerunner of the modern personnel specialist. Welfare secretaries existed to help workers meet their personal needs and to minimize any tendency of workers to join unions.

Well pay Well pay is a fringe benefit, provided by some employers, that pays employees for unused sick leave.

GLOSSARY

Wildcat strikes   Wildcat strikes are spontaneous work stoppages that take place in violation of the labor contract and are officially against the wishes of the union leaders.

Workers' compensation   Workers' compensation is payment made to employees for work-related injuries or to their families in the event of the workers' job-caused death.

Work flow   Work flow is the sequence of jobs in an organization needed to produce the firm's goods or service.

Work measurement techniques   Work measurement techniques are methods for evaluating what a job's performance standards should be.

Work practices   Work practices are the set ways of performing work in an organization.

Work sampling   Work sampling means using a variety of observations on a particular job to measure the length of time devoted to certain aspects of the job.

Work simplification   Work simplification means simplifying jobs by eliminating unnecessary tasks or reducing the number of tasks by combining them.

Write-ins   Write-ins are those people who send in a written inquiry, often seeking a job application.

652   GLOSSARY

NAME INDEX

Abramson, Herbert, 525
Abramson, Leonard, 491
Aburdene, Patricia, 620
Adams, Faneuil, Jr., 191
Adams, John D., 526
Agarwala-Rogers, Rekha, 555
Aggarwal, Sudhir, 460, 461
Aggarwal, Sumer C., 460, 461
Aldrich, Mark, 117
Alexander, Ralph W., 262
Alliger, George M., 335
Anderson, Richard C., 405
Angle, Harold L., 191
Arnold, William, 556
Asherman, Ira G., 557
Ashworth, D. Neil, 493
Austin, Keith, 290
Ayers, Nancy, 301

Baal, Trudy, 301
Bacarach, Samuel B., 190
Bailey, Roy, 406
Baird, Lloyd, 34
Baker, Nancy Croft, 304
Baldwin, Timothy T., 334
Bamberger, Peter, 190
Banas, Paul, 308
Banks, Christina G., 369
Bannister, Brendan D., 371
Barber, Alison E., 224, 261
Barlow, Wayne E., 116, 525, 620
Barrett, Gerald V., 117, 437
Bartlett, C.J., 370
Baxter, Neale, 226
Beason, George M., 266
Beatty, Richard W., 373
Beck, Bob, 404
Becker, Gary S., 333
Beck, Melinda, 62
Belt, John A., 266
Bennett, Rita, 83
Berger, Susan, 300
Bernstein, Aaron, 32, 333, 492
Berry, Dean F., 619
Berstein, Irving, 589
Biles, George E., 618
Binning, John F., 265
Biondi, Cynthia G., 405
Birch, William J., 373
Black, Robert F., 439

Blanchard, Kenneth, 369
Blencoe, Allyn G., 162
Blocklyn, Paul L., 82, 263, 335, 405
Blodgett, Douglas, 116
Bohlander, George W., 405, 589, 590
Bond, Floyd A., 302
Boroski, John W., 166, 191
Boskin, Michael J., 524
Boyacigiller, Nakiye, 83
Bracker, Jeffrey S., 193, 335
Brandt, Ellen, 84
Brandt, Richard, 63, 405, 437
Brannen, Dalton E., 261
Bratkovich, Jerold R., 405
Bray, Douglas W., 372
Breakiron, Larry P., 342
Bremmer, Brian, 224
Brenenstuhl, Daniel, 302
Brennan, E. James, 437
Brenner, Otto, 590
Brett, Jeanne M., 494
Briscoe, Dennis R., 32
Brittain, William P., 304
Brooks, Brian J., 461
Broszeit, Richard K., 404
Broussard, Richard D., 261
Brown, Barbara K., 264
Bryant, Don, 192
Buchele, Robert, 117
Buford, James A., 369
Bujan, Ronald, 491
Bulkeley, William M., 192, 407
Buller, Paul F., 373
Bunning, Richard L., 460
Burkhalter, Bettye B., 369
Butler, Owen B., 225
Byrne, John, 264
Byrne, John A., 265, 406

Cairo, Peter C., 405
Caldwell, Philip, 590
Caldwell, Sharon A., 265
Calkins, Laurel B., 525
Camden, Carl, 227
Cameron, Gary, 619
Campbell, Donald J., 372
Campbell, Mary Ellen, 556
Campion, Michael A., 161, 264
Caprino, Mariann, 227
Cardy, Robert, 370

Carroll, Stephen J., Jr., 162, 524
Carson, Teresa, 406
Carulli, Lorraine M., 403
Catalanello, Ralph F., 619
Cederholm, Lars, 85
Champagne, Paul J., 618
Chapman, Fern Schumer, 263
Chase, Marilyn, 620
Chauran, Tim, 261
Chen, Chris, 225
Clegg, Chris W., 555
Clement, Ronald W., 302, 369
Cluff, Larry F., 493
Cochran, Daniel S., 493
Cogger, John W., 265
Cohen, Yinon, 192
Cohn, Bob, 495
Cole, Albert, Jr., 495
Cole, Kenneth J., 226
Collins, Eliza G. C., 116
Collyer, Rosemary M., 266
Commons, John R., 589
Conley, Patrick R., 161
Conway, Michael A., 437
Cook, Dan, 32
Cooke, Janet, 252
Cook, Suzanne H., 261
Coombs, Michael W., 303
Cooper, Elizabeth A., 117
Cooper, William H., 303
Copenhaver, Lisa, 554
Cornelius, Edwin T., III, 161, 162
Cosin, Elizabeth M., 263
Cote, Andre, 404
Crandall, Lin P., 461
Crandall, Rebecca, 526
Crandall, Robert, 31
Crano, William D., 263
Crispell, Diane, 63, 620
Crocker, Olga L., 63
Crystal, Graef S., 438
Cunningham, J. Barton, 163
Curington, William P., 460
Cutcher-Gershenfeld, Joel, 332, 589, 591
Cuthrell, Stephen, 304
Cutler, Blayne, 261

Dalton, Dan R., 301
Dantico, John A., 437

Davis, Keith, 32
Dawson, Christopher M., 335
Deadrick, Diana, 263, 619
Debats, Karen E., 32
de Bernardo, Mark A., 191
Decker, Patrick G., 370
Deets, Norman R., 369
DeLaps, Judith A., 161
Delbecq, A.L., 192
Denisi, Angelo S., 162, 266, 371
Denton, D. Keith, 494
Dertien, Marvin G., 407
Dessler, Gary, 117
Deutsch, Claudia H., 83, 406
Dibble, Sandra, 64
Dickey, John D., 332
DiMattia, Dominic J., 333
Dole, Elizabeth, 558, 560
Doverspike, Dennis, 437
Dowling, Peter J., 82
Doyel, Hoyt, 459
Drasgow, Fritz, 262
Dreher, George F., 301
Dreyfuss, Joel, 63
Dricall, Lisa, 405
Driscoll, Lesa, 557
Driscoll, Lisa, 437
Drost, Donald A., 619
Drucker, Peter F., 62
Duffy, Elaine M., 304
Dugoni, Bernard L., 267
Dumaine, Briane, 555
Duncan, Susan J., 491
Dunkin, Amy, 459
Dunlop, John T., 558
Dunn, J.D., 161
du Pont, Pierre Samuel, 498
Durling, Bette Bardeen, 117
Dwyer, Paula, 524
Dyer, Lee, 190, 191

Eberle, Ted, 163
Edwards, Cathy, 226
Eichel, Larry, 163, 493
Ellis, James E., 63
Engardio, Pete, 32
Evans, Val M., 225
Ewing, David W., 303, 557
Eyres, Patricia S., 370

Faley, Robert H., 115
Farish, Phil, 192, 404, 589
Farley, John A., 267
Farris, G.E., 163
Feinstein, Selwyn, 224, 525
Ferman, Louis A., 332
Ferrara, Peter J., 524
Festinger, L., 301
Fierman, Jaclyn, 406
Finney, Martha I., 404, 620

Fiorito, Jack, 192
Fisher, Anne B., 554
Fisicaro, Sebastiano A., 370
Fitz-enz, Jac, 33
Flanagan, John C., 371
Flughum, Judy B., 438
Foegen, J. H., 491
Fogel, Daniel S., 405
Foley, Patrick, 545
Ford, J. Kevin, 333, 334
Ford, Robert C., 556
Ford, Robert N., 163
Foxman, Loretta D., 162, 404, 406
Fox, Marilyn L., 460
Fox, William M., 334, 369
Fraser, Jill Andresky, 224
Fraze, James, 620
Frederick, William C., 32
Freedman, Alex M., 493
French, Wendell, 64
Friedman, Lee, 161
Friedman, Martin G., 370
Frierson, James G., 115
Frisch, Michael H., 265
Fulmer, William E., 32

Gaertner, Karen N., 300, 403
Galbraith, Jay R., 621
Galen, Michele, 116, 557
Gallagher, Richard E., 526
Gallo, Frank, 332
Ganger, Ralph E., 335
Garcia, Mario F., 265
Garland, Susan B., 524, 526
Garson, Barbara, 162
Gatewood, Wallace, 116
Gehrman, Douglas B., 192
Geisinger, Kurt F., 267
Gelfond, Susan, 439
George-Perry, Sharon, 492
Gerevas, Ronald E., 405
Gideon, Thomas F., 590
Gilley, Jerry W., 404
Gleckman, Howard, 115, 524
Glicken, Morley D., 335
Glickstein, Gloria, 226
Goddard, Robert W., 63, 620
Gold, David, 115, 438
Goldmacher, Edward S., 161
Goldstein, Mel A., 265
Golesorkhi, Banu, 84
Gomersall, Earl G., 301
Gompers, Samuel, 558, 562, 563
Goodale, James G., 34
Goodell, Richard R., 372
Gould, Carole, 227, 302
Graham, Harry, 589
Granger, Barbara B., 371
Grant, Philip C., 160
Graves, J. Peter, 372
Graves, Laura M., 224

Greenberger, Robert S., 406
Green, David, 334
Greenlaw, Paul S., 115
Greenman, Russell L., 524
Greenwell, Duff A., 33
Gricar, Barbara Gray, 526
Grossman, Morton E., 161
Gross, Warren D., 618
Grubbs, Lisa L., 303
Guelker, Richard, 63
Gupta, Anil K., 191
Gupta, Nina, 460
Gustafson, D.H., 192
Guzda, Hank, 162

Hackman, J.R., 163
Hakel, Milton D., 161
Halcrow, Allan, 225
Hall, Douglas T., 34, 405
Hallett, Jeff, 62, 225
Hamilton, Joan O'C., 116
Hammer, Edson G., 265
Hammonds, Keith H., 116
Hansson, Robert O., 619
Harper, Douglas C., 492
Harris, Marilyn A., 303
Harris, Michael M., 372
Harrison, Edward L., 303
Harvey, Barron H., 493
Harvey, Michael C., 84, 302
Harvey, Robert J., 161
Hatch, D. Diane, 116, 525, 620
Hauck, Warren C., 459
Hayes, Mary, 526
Hedge, Jerry W., 370
Heider, Dorothy, 404
Henemen, Herbert, 191
Henning, Dale, 64
Herren, Laura M., 33
Herzberg, Frederick, 163
Heshizer, Brian, 589
Hickerson, Karl A., 405
Hilgert, Raymond L., 304
Hill, David, 556
Hills, Frederick S., 437, 460
Hixon, Allen L., 191
Hoerr, John, 33, 161, 191, 332, 555
Hoffman, Carl C., 438
Hoffman, Kathleen P., 438
Hollandsworth, James G., Jr., 264
Hollmann, Robert W., 556
Hom, Peter, 371
Hong, Adrian Teo Kim, 333
Hooper, John A., 619
Hoover, David H., 407
Hoover, John J., 526
Hopkins, H. Donald, 526
Hoshiai, Yuriko, 224
Hough, Susan, 302
Howard, Cecil G., 302
Howe, Irene Chew Keng, 333

Howe, Nancy, 161
Hoyman, Michele, 332
Huchendorf, Karen, 300
Hudson, Joseph, 373
Hughes, Gary L., 263, 373
Hull, Raymond, 302
Hunsaker, Philip L., 303
Hunsicker, J. Freedly, Jr., 117
Hurlock, Jim, 591
Hutchins, Dexter, 557
Hutton, Thomas J., 33
Hyatt, James C., 62
Hyatt, Joshua, 224
Hymowitz, Carol, 303, 494, 556

Ilgen, Daniel R., 267
Ingram, Earl, II, 460
Inwald, Robin, 263
Irvin, John S., Jr., 589

Jablin, F.M., 264
Jackson, Pauly R., 555
Jacobs, Grover T., 369
Janak, Elizabeth A., 335
Jeanneret, P.R., 161
Jenkins, G. Douglas, Jr., 460
Jenkins, John, 163
Jennings, Eugene E., 406, 407
Jerdee, Thomas H., 405, 493
Johns, Horace E., 85
Johnson, Charles D., 263
Johnson, Harold E., 226
Johnson, Spencer, 369
Johnson, Terry R., 333
Johnston, William B., 85

Kaminski, Victoria, 619
Kanter, Rosabeth Ross, 435, 555
Kantrowitz, Barbara, 526
Kantz, E. Theodore, 224
Kaplan, Philip, 525
Kapstein, Jonathan, 494, 555
Karren, Ronald J., 264
Kautz, E. Theodore, 85
Kavanagh, Michael J., 370
Kaye, Beverly, 407
Kazanjian, Robert K., 621
Keating, Richard C., 524
Keller, Jack, 404
Kelly, Helen J., 509
Kelly, Joan L., 117
Kelly, Kevin M., 267
Kemp, Nigel J., 555
Kenney, Roberta M., 227
Kerwin, Kathleen, 459
Kiechel, Walter, III, 264, 373, 620
Kinicki, Angelo J., 371
Kirkland, Richard I., Jr., 461
Kirk, William Q., 84

Kirnan, Jean Powell, 267
Kirrane, Diane E., 332
Kleiman, Lawrence S., 265
Klein, Alfred, 492
Kleiner, Brian H., 554
Klotchman, Janis, 303
Kochan, Thomas A., 591
Koepp, Stephen, 370
Kohl, John P., 115, 302
Konovsky, Mary A., 436
Konrad, Alison M., 435
Kopecky, Robert J., 225
Koretz, Gene, 525, 588
Kramon, Glenn, 491
Kravetz, Dennis J., 33
Krebs, Valdis E., 143, 161, 162
Kroll, Mark J., 437
Krzystofiak, Frank, 370
Kuchta, William J., 403
Kuttner, Robert, 461

Landen, Dutch, 555
Latham, Gary P., 333, 369, 371
Laurent, Andre, 83
Lawler, Edward E., III, 61, 163, 435, 436, 437, 554
Lawler, Kathy A., 492
Lawrence, Stephanie, 304
Lawrie, John W., 333, 373
Leach, John J., 404
Leana, Carrie R., 303
Ledford, Gerald E., Jr., 554
Ledvinka, James, 262, 263
Lee, Cynthia, 371, 372
Lees-Haley, Paul R., 525
Leibman, Michael S., 191, 192, 333
Leonard, Bill, 32
Leonard, Jonathan S., 261
Levine, Cindy, 403
Levine, Jonathan B., 333
Levinson, Harry, 619
Levitan, Sar A., 332, 462
Levy, Martin, 371
Lievertz, Alfred H., 619
Lindroth, Joan, 62, 193
Litteret, Joseph A., 33
Livingston, J. Sterling, 555
Locher, Alan H., 304, 369
Locklear, Toni S., 371
Loenko, Thomas A., 262
Long, Richard C., 265
Lopez, Bruno, 224
Loretto, Vincent, 262
Lotito, Michael J., 263
Louis, Arthur M., 435
Luthans, Fred, 460, 491
Lutz, J. Gary, 589
Lyons, Paul V., 494

MacAdam, Maureen, 162

McAdams, Jerry, 459
McAfee, R. Bruce, 618
McClelland, Valorie A., 556
McClure, Lynne, 32, 556
McElwain, James E., 83
McEvoy, Glenn M., 373
McFillen, James M., 370
McGarrah, Harry A., 509
McGee, Lynne F., 460
Machalaba, Daniel, 369
McIntosh, Lehmann Phyllis, 591
McKersie, Robert B., 589, 590
McLaughlin, Frank S., 556
McLaughlin, Steven D., 333
McManis, Gerald L., 191, 192, 333
MacMillan, Ian C., 32
McMillan, John D., 405
McMurray, Robert N., 264
McQuigg-Martinez, Beverly, 335
McShane, Steven L., 301
Maddox, Robert C., 84
Madigan, Beth, 438
Madigan, Robert M., 263, 407, 437, 460
Magnus, Margaret, 161, 226
Mahoney, Thomas A., 117, 190
Maier, R.F., 373
Main, Jeremy, 524
Mancinelli, Pamela S., 619
Manegold, C.S., 224
Manz, Charles C., 191, 334
Markham, Steven E., 437, 459, 460
Markowitz, Jerrold, 161
Marsh, Steve, 619
Marsick, Victoria J., 85
Martin, Christopher L., 264
Martin, James E., 438, 439
Massengill, Douglas, 116
Mathis, Robert L., 619
Maurer, Steven D., 618
Mausner, Bernard, 163
May, Bruce D., 526
Mayo, Elton, 62
Meglino, Bruce M., 266
Meier, Thomas K., 302
Meisinger, Susan, 63, 161
Melcher, Richard A., 494
Mello, Craig, 301
Mellor, Earl F., 494
Merey, Pearl, 460
Merwin, John, 303
Merzer, Martin, 116
Meshoulam, Ilan, 34
Messe, Lawrence A., 263
Messmer, Max, 297
Miles, Gregory L., 32
Miles, Raymond E., 191, 618
Milkovich, George T., 190
Miller, Donald B., 332
Miller, James Grier, 33
Miller, Jessie Louise, 33
Mills, Ted, 554
Miner, John B., 162, 369, 370

Miner, Mary Green, 162, 370
Minken, Suzanne L., 439
Mirides, Ellryn, 404
Mitchell, Brooks, 264
Mitchell, Daniel J. B., 63, 436, 439, 491, 588
Mitchell, Russell, 63
Mobley, William H., 301
Moffat, Susan, 82
Monat, Jonathan S., 335
Montana, Patrick J., 33, 524
Mooney, Thomas B., 303
Moorhead, Gregory, 191
Moravec, Milan, 301, 372, 407
Morgan, Brian S., 556
Moser, H. Ronald, 85
Mullins, Terry W., 265
Murino, Catherine, 495
Murphy, Betty Southard, 116, 525
Murphy, Kevin R., 369
Murray, Alan, 459
Murray, Patrick L., 619
Myers, Donald W., 335, 621
Myers, M. Scott, 301
Myers, Phyllis Schiller, 621

Nagao, Dennis H., 264
Naisbitt, John, 31, 620
Nash, Allan N., 162, 524
Nash, Deborah F., 33
Nathan, Barry R., 262
Neale, Margaret A., 495
Neff, Robert, 224, 266
Nehrbass, Richard G., 265
Neider, Linda L., 303
Nelson, Reed E., 303
Newman, Jerry, 370
Newman, Lewis, 403
Newsom, Walter B., 493
Newstrom, John W., 334
Nichols, Leland C., 373
Niehoff, Mariless S., 333
Nkomo, Stella M., 264
Noe, Raymond A., 333, 406
Noroian, Cheryl L., 403
Northcraft, Gregory B., 495
Nota, Bruna, 301

O'Brien, Fabius P., 619
O'Brien, Richard M., 304
O'Dell, Carla, 459, 461
Odiorne, George S., 192, 193
O'Donnell, Kevin J., 492
Oldfield, Kenneth, 301
Olian, Judy D., 263
O'Reilly, Brian, 84, 227
Otten, Alan L., 193
Overman, Stephanie, 492
Owens, Thomas, 461

Panaro, Gerard P., 266
Pasqualetto, Joe, 193, 621
Pati, Gopal C., 263
Paulson, Morton C., 117
Pawlik, Vicki, 554
Pearson, John N., 193, 335
Peres, Richard, 225, 261
Perlman, Selig, 558
Persons, W.R. "Buck," 559
Peter, Laurence J., 302
Petersen, Donald J., 116
Petersen, Peter B., 62
Peterson, Melanie M., 438, 439
Peterson, Richard B., 590
Peters, Thomas J., 619
Pfeffer, Jeffrey, 192, 435
Phelps, Mark I., 438, 461
Pingpank, Jeffrey C., 303
Piotrowski, Chris, 404
Pollock, Michael A., 161
Polsky, Walter L., 162, 404, 406
Poole, Jeanne C., 85, 224
Popovich, Paula, 267
Porter, Lyman W., 266, 554
Posner, B., 224
Post, James E., 32
Powell, Bill, 224
Powell, Gary N., 224, 226
Prien, Erich P., 263, 373
Pursell, Elliot D., 264

Rachel, Frank M., 161
Raelin, Joseph A., 406
Ramer, C.Z., 226
Recio, Maria E., 224, 266
Reed, David, 557
Reed, Paul R., 437
Reilly, Anne H., 494
Reinhardt, Claudia, 301
Reynolds, Calvin, 82, 83
Rice, Faye, 116
Richardson, Reed C., 589
Richman, Louis S., 62, 83, 524
Richter, Judith, 405
Riemer, Blanca, 494
Riles, Thomas, 459
Rinella, Sal D., 225
Ritzer, George, 64
Roberts, Irene (Rennie) C., 13
Robertson, Thomas M., 405
Robinson, James D., III, 12-13
Rodgers, Raymond, 302
Rodgers, Waymond, 84
Rogers, Everett M., 555
Roghaar, Steven R., 373
Rollins, Thomas, 405
Romans, M. Jay, 333
Ronen, Simcha, 83
Rosen, Benson, 118, 405, 493
Rosen, Hjalmar, 590

Rosenstein, Lyn, 195-196
Rosinger, George, 371
Ross, Joel E., 404
Ross, Joyce D., 32
Ross, Patrick C., 226
Ross, Timothy L., 459, 460
Rothenbach, William F., 404
Rothfeder, Jeffrey, 557
Rout, Lawrence, 261, 556
Rowan, Roy, 406
Rowe, Mary P., 116
Rowe, P.M., 265
Rowland, Kendrith M., 193
Ruch, William A., 32, 554
Russell, Nancy, 492
Ryan, Ann Marie, 372
Rynes, Sara L., 224, 261

Saari, Lise M., 333
Sabo, Richard, 443
Sackett, Paul R., 161, 372
Sahl, Robert J., 436
St. John, Walter D., 556, 591
Saltzman, Amy, 302, 405
Salzman, Marian L., 334
Santora, Joyce E., 459
Saporito, Bill, 556
Savich, Richard S., 84, 302
Sayles, Leonard, 589
Scattaregia, Julie H., 265
Schappe, Robert H., 163
Schaubroeck, John, 372
Schein, Lawrence, 17
Schein, Virginia E., 266
Schiemann, William A., 556
Schiller, Zachary, 63, 116
Schippmann, Jeffrey S., 373
Schmertz, Eric J., 524
Schnitzer, Robert J., 493
Schoenfeldt, Lyle F., 263
Schreier, James W., 225
Schuler, Randall S., 32, 82, 526, 618
Schulhop, Robert J., 461
Schultz, Richard, 524
Scott, Dow, 619
Scott, K. Dow, 263, 437, 460
Scott, R. Craig, 261
Scwartz, John, 62
Seamonds, Jack A., 439, 461
Sedel, Rae, 83
Seibert, Eugene H., 191, 493
Seibert, Joanne, 191, 493
Seltzer, G., 191
Sewell, Carole, 266
Sewell, John, 78
Sharon, Amiel T., 405
Shaw, Gaylord, 556
Shaw, James B., 303
Sheahan, Robert H., 117
Sheibar, Paul, 162, 261, 556
Shenkar, Oded, 83

Sherwood, John J., 163
Shimko, Barbara Whitaker, 33, 619
Shore, Richard, 591
Simon, Sidney H., 525
Sims, Henry P., Jr., 334
Siwolop, Sana, 555
Smith, Eddie C., 190, 436
Smith, Nancy D., 619
Smith, Roger B., 328, 336
Smith, Ronald E., 301
Smith, Shirley J., 493
Smith, William, 226
Snow, Charles C., 191, 618
Snyderman, Barbara, 163
Solomon, Charlene Marmer, 264
Solomon, Jolie, 84
Southard, Betty, 620
Sprig, John E., 162
Springen, Karen, 62
Stagner, Ross, 590
Stalcup, R.J., 193
Stanton, Erwin S., 266
Starcevich, Matt M., 335
Staudohar, Paul D., 303
Steele, Bernadette, 405
Steers, Richard, 266
Steffy, Brian D., 618
Stephens, David B., 302
Stepp, John R., 591
Stevens, George E., 302, 304, 369, 557
Stier, Dave, 33
Stonebraker, Peter W., 460, 491
Stone, Dianna L., 265
Stone, Eugene F., 265
Stone, Thomas H., 192
Stout, Hilary, 491
Strauss, George, 589
Strob, Linda K., 494
Strom, Stephanie, 224
Stubblefield, Guy, 263
Summers, Scott L., 193
Susser, Peter A., 526
Sutton, Edward E., 335
Swinyard, Alfred W., 302
Sykes, J. Arnold, 335

Tannenbaum, Frank, 558
Tasini, Jonathan, 589, 591
Taylor, Frederick, 39, 42, 147

Taylor, M. Susan, 262
Taylor, Stephen, 619
Teel, Kenneth S., 369
Teets, Patricia, 34
Thaler, Ruth E., 64
Thiederman, Sondra, 265
Thomas, Roosevelt I.R., Jr., 114
Thornburg, Linda, 83
Thurow, Lester, 459
Ticer, Scott, 333
Todor, William D., 301
Tolchin, Martin, 492
Tomkiewicz, Joseph, 590
Torres, Carol, 25-26, 27
Townsend, Patrick, 226
Trautman, Gerald H., 92, 115
Trost, Cathy, 494, 556
Trotter, Richard, 116
Tseng, Anthony Tsai-pen, 333
Tsiantar, Dody, 62
Tsui, Anne S., 619, 620
Tucker, D.H., 265
Tullar, William L., 265
Tully, Shawn, 224, 262
Tung, Rosalie L., 84, 191, 302
Turner, Ernie, 85
Turnquist, Philip H., 493
Twomey, David P., 115
Tyler, D. Timothy, 369

Unger, Beth, 115
Unwalla, Darab, 404

Vance, Sandra Lee, 557
Van de Ven, Andres H., 191, 192
Vanner, Bruce S., 525
Veres, John G., III, 371
Verespej, Michael A., 524
Verlander, Edward G., 405
Voluck, Philip R., 525
Von Glinow, Mary Ann, 225, 435
Von Kampen, Joe, 579-580

Waldersee, Robert, 491
Walker, Alfred J., 63
Walker, James W., 62, 64, 190, 192, 621
Wallace, Bill, 227

Wallrapp, Gary G., 302
Walls, James D., 262
Wall, Toby D., 555
Walton, Richard E., 556, 590
Wanous, John P., 267, 300
Warmke, Dennis L., 264
Waterman, Robert H., Jr., 619
Weaver, Craig S., 524
Weaver, Kristen R., 589
Weber, Joseph, 405, 437
Wehrenberg, Stephen B., 334
Weinberg, Edgar, 591
Wendt, George R., 162
Wernke, Diane, 461
Werther, William B., Jr., 32, 63, 163, 227, 336, 372, 406, 554, 555, 589, 590
Weston, Devid J., 264
Wexley, Kenneth N., 333, 334, 369
Wheeler, Kevin, 301
Wherry, Robert J., Sr., 370
White, Harold C., 32, 64, 590
Whiteside, David E., 161
Wiersma, Uco, 371
Williams, Kevin J., 266
Wilson, Marie, 495
Winston, Judith A., 115
Withers, Claudia A., 115
Withey, Michael J., 303
Witkin, Elliot, 261
Wolfe, Michael N., 64, 162
Wolf, William B., 63
Woodman, Richard W., 163
Woodruff, David, 558
Woolman, C. E., 8
Work, Clemens P., 439, 461
Wright, Robert Granford, 31
Wright, Wayne L., 437
Wroten, Steven P., 334

Yeager, Raymond J., 333
Youngblood, Stuart A., 266
Yu, Winifred, 266

Zacur, Susan Rawson, 116
Zeidner, Moshe, 262
Zirkel, Perry A., 589
Zwerdling, Daniel, 555

SUBJECT INDEX

The following abbreviations are used in this index: (Human Resources), HRD (Human Resources Department), HRIS (Human resource information system), HRM (Human Resources Management), HRP (Human Resource Planning), and QWL (Quality of work life).
Organizations, government institutions and laws are listed by their titles, initials, or acronyms.
Personal names are listed in the NAME INDEX.

Absenteeism, 479, 601, 605
Abuse, verbal, 553, 581
Accidents:
  catastrophes and fatal, 513
  lost-time, 498, 506, 509, 510-511, 574
  prevention of, 497-498, 508, 512-513
  and sickness policies, 471-472
Accreditation, 54-55
Across-the-board pay raise, 427
Adjustment, wage and salary, 431
Adverse selection, 233-234, 466
Advertising, recruitment and, 200, 206-208, 286-287
Advisable discrimination, 91
Advisory arbitration, 577
Advisory authority. See Staff Authority
Advocacy roles, HRM, 582, 599, 615
Affirmative action programs, 87-88, 176, 212, 597, 607
  development and, 327-328
  EEO laws and, 100, 106-110, 117, 199-120
  Executive Order 11246 and, 105
  major steps in, 108-110, 605
AFL-CIO, 564, 566
Age Discrimination in Employment Act (1967 and 1986), 42, 91, 101, 168, 186, 288, 294, 414, 493, 620
Age groups, work force, 46-47, 601
  See also Retirement
Agencies:
  credential verification, 251
  employment, 209-210
  temporary help, 212-213
Aging of the work force, 46, 601
Agreements, labor, 14, 51-52, 573-575, 579
AIDS and HIV diseases, 100, 170, 240, 468, 550, 612

Albemarle Paper Company v. Moody, 93, 236, 238, 262
Alcoholism, 236, 484, 548
Aliens. See Illegal aliens; Immigration
Alternative delivery systems (ADS), 470
American Bankers Insurance Group, 203, 241
American Federation of Labor and Congress of Industrial Organization (AFL-CIO), 564, 566
American Guard Agency, 595-596
American Society for Personnel Administration. See Society for Human Research Management
American Society for Training and Development (ASTD), 308
Americans with Disabilities Act (ADA, 1990), 43, 100, 201-202, 216, 240, 253-254
  training about the, 310
American Telephone and Telegraph Company. See AT&T
Analysts, job and compensation, 126, 127-135
Anheuser-Busch, 386
Anti-discrimination laws. See Equal employment opportunity (EEO) laws
Apple computers, 143
Applicants, job. See Candidates, job
Application forms, job, 216-221
Applied research. See Human resource management audits
Apportionment of wages for key jobs, 418-419
Appraisal. See Performance appraisal
Apprenticeship programs, 316, 318
Aptitudes, work, 387, 389
Arab cultures. See Moslem cultures
Arbitration, types of, 577-579
Artificial intelligence, 47
Assembly-line work, 148
Assessment centers, 360-362, 368
Assessment, employee, 25, 76-77
Asset, employees as an, 308
Assumptions, cultural, 67-68, 79, 150, 236, 396
AT&T (American Telephone and Telegraph Company), 327, 328
  EEO case at, 87-88, 99-100, 106
Athletic teams, company, 507-508
Attitudes about work, 45, 53, 564
  See also Quality of work life efforts

(QWL)
Attitude surveys, 546-547, 604-606
Attitude tests, 239-240
Attorneys, labor, 568-569, 572
Attrition, work force, 186, 288-289, 300
"At will" statements, 220
Audits, business, 451, 596
Audits, HR research, 176-179, 366
  reports, 609-610
  scope of, 169-170, 595-599
  tools of, 602-609
Audit team, 598
Authority, HRD, 20-22, 57-58
Automation, 48
Autonomous work groups, 145-146, 156-157, 540-541
Autonomy, worker, 151

Baby boom generation, the, 44, 46, 185, 502
Background, applicant, 251-253
Back pay, court-ordered, 88, 102, 429
Bank of America (B of A), 288
Banks, sick leave, 479
Bargaining committee, 565
Bargaining, union-management, 565, 570, 572-574
  See also Unions, labor
Base pay, 432-433
Bechtel Company, 359
Behavioral interviews, 243-244
Behavioral studies, 40-41, 150-151, 541
Behavior expectation scales (BES), 352-353
Behavior, job, 340-341
  job design and, 146, 148, 150-154
  See also Performance appraisal
Behavior modeling, 319-320
Behavior modification, 323-324
Behavior observation scales (BOS), 352-353, 354
Bell-shaped curve distribution, 356
Benchmarks:
  external job comparison, 423-425
  HR audit, 600, 609
  internal job comparison, 416-423
  sex-linked job evaluation, 430-431
  See also Performance standards
Bendix Company, 547
Benefits, employee, 25, 612
  administration of, 486-488

658 INDEX

costs of, 464, 467-469, 497, 503-504, 523
eligibility for, 212-213, 256, 482, 500-501, 504-506, 511-513
foreign assignment, 73, 75, 396
history of, 42-43, 505-506
legally mandated, 498-499
nonretirement social security, 500-501
recruitment and, 203-204, 279, 465-466
and services, 482-486, 615
social security, 499-502
union-negotiated, 575
See also Compensation, employee
Benefits, fringe, 432, 433, 449, 450, 486-487
types of, 464-465
See also Services, employee
B.F. Goodrich, 386
Biases, 284, 448
selection interviewing and, 241-251
and subjectivity of performance measures, 344-345, 348, 359
types of rater, 345-347
Bill of rights, union members,' 569-570
Binding arbitration, 577
Bio-medical Instrumentation, Inc. (BMI), 81-82
Birth rates, U.S., 44, 185, 189-190
Blacklisting, 520, 566
Blind ads, 206
Body language, 247-250, 281
Boeing Corporation, 509, 537
Bona fide occupational qualification (BFOQ), 95, 246
Bonding, employee, 252-253
Bonuses:
compensation, 432, 439, 442, 444, 473
production, 446, 454-456
referral, 205
Bottlenecks, production, 149
Bottom-line test (EEOC), 233-234
Bottom-up communication, 543-547
Brazil, labor in, 159-160
Breaks, on-the-job, 478
Brevard General Hospital questionnaire, 128-132
Buddy system, 280, 282-283
Budgets, organization, 169, 172, 203, 274
See also Costs
Bumping rights, 286
Burger King, 70, 203
Burnout, employee, 391
Business agent, union, 564
Business unionism, 563
Buy-back, employee, 214

Cafeteria benefit programs, 487-488
Candidates, job:
application forms for, 216-221
benefits sought by, 204
channels for recruiting, 204-215, 235
errors by, 250-251

external supply of, 184-186, 232-233
four-fifths rule for, 233-234
internal supply of, 176-183, 232, 377-381
selection ratio of, 232-233
testing, 235-241
See also Recruitment of employees
Career counseling, 387-390
Career development, 176, 184, 329, 377, 597
HRD supported, 382-391, 397-400
individual, 391-397
overseas performance and, 74-76, 395-397
programs, 198, 361, 377-378
See also Development; Training
Career goals, 376-377
Career path, 377
Career planning, 376-381, 388-389
benefits of, 383-384
HRD and, 382-391, 397-400
Career plateau, 325-326, 390-391
Career positions, human resource department, 18-19
Casefile, Inc., 403
Case law on employment, 109, 577
Albemarle Paper Company v. Moody, 93, 236, 238, 262
Boureslan vs. Aramco Co., 69
Connecticut v. Teal, 93, 234
Diaz v. Pan American World Airways, Inc., 95
and EEO at AT&T, 87-88, 99-100, 106
Garcia v. San Antonio Transit Authority, 437
General Electric v. Gilbert, 93
Griggs v. Duke Power Company, 93, 144, 236, 262
International Brotherhood of Teamsters v. United States, 96
Meritor Savings Bank v. Vinson, 95
Rowe V. General Motors, 345
United States v. Georgia Power Company, 199, 205
United Steelworkers of America and Kaiser Aluminum & Chemical Corporation v. Weber, 96, 106, 206, 207, 328
U.S. Supreme Court, 69, 93
Wards Cove v. Antonio, 93
worker's compensation, 509
Case study, 320-321
Cash bonuses, 450
Casinos Unlimited, 113-114
Caste systems, host-country, 69, 173
Caterpillar Tractor Company, 469, 538
CEOs (Corporate executive officers), 180
Certification, professional HRM, 54-55
Challenger space-shuttle disaster, 543-544
Challenges to unemployment claims, 503-504
Change-in-control contracts, 64

Channels:
communication, 542-547
for recruitment, 204-215
Characteristics of jobs, human, 130-131
Charts:
employee replacement, 181-182, 361
organization, 16, 17, 380, 564-565
Checklist:
orientation, 279
performance appraisal, 348-350
postinterview, 248-249
Checkoff, union dues, 575
Chevron Corporation, 543
Child care issues, 246, 480, 482
and services, 46, 484-485
Children, benefits for, 505
Chrysler Corporation, 300, 519
Citibank, 232
Civil Rights Act (1964), 42, 90-100, 310, 414
See also Title VII (CRA of 1964)
Civil Rights Act (1991), 43, 94, 96, 99
Civil rights legislation, history of, 42-43, 168
Civil Service Reform Act (1978), 341
Claims:
unemployment, 503-504
worker's compensation, 507-510
Classifications, job, 145-146, 417, 426-428, 433
Clearance, security, 253
Coaching, job, 316, 318
COBRA. See Consolidated Omnibus Budget Reconciliation Act
Codes:
appraisal method, 348-350
job classification, 136, 138, 145
Codetermination of decision-making, 452-453, 539-540
in Europe, 69
Cognitive dissonance, 273
Coinsurance clause, 468
Colgate-Palmolive, 71-72, 326
Collective bargaining. See Bargaining; Unions, labor
Colleges. See Educational institutions
Commissions, 447
Commissions, employment practices, 103-104
Commitment, employee, 30-31
Communication, internal, 541-547, 576, 579
Communications, hazard, 514-515
Community service activities:
encouragement of, 413, 479, 485-486
individual, 392, 395
jury duty, 291-292, 480
Companies, QWL, 537
Comparable worth:
job comparisons and, 416-425
jobs of, 102-103, 613
Comparative approach, HR research, 600

INDEX   **659**

Comparative evaluation of employees, 355-357, 358
Comparisons, job. See Job evaluation
Compensation, employee, 14, 25
  apportionment of for key jobs, 418-419
  automatic adjustments of, 431
  bonus, 432, 439, 442, 444, 473
  comparable pay and, 430-431
  employee performance and, 413
  equal jobs and equal pay, 51, 101-102
  experience, 202
  guaranteed, 473
  international, 75-76, 396, 424, 431-432
  pay levels, 425-426, 509-510, 561
  pay raises, 101, 427, 429, 447-448
  pay ranges, 198, 426-427
  policies, 198, 202, 340, 430-431, 443-446, 509-510, 605, 607
  severance pay, 292, 472
  structure, 426-427, 430-431
  surveys of wage and salary, 424-426
  wage compression and, 429
  for work-related injuries, 497
  See also Benefits, employee; Gainsharing
Compensation management, 412-413, 597
  major phases of, 415-425
  objectives of, 414-415
  See also Incentives; Job analysis information
Competition:
  by business competitors, 169, 613-614
  gainsharing and, 452-456
  for HR, 196, 200-201, 215
Complaints, employee, 293, 325, 513, 520-521, 567-568, 599, 606-607
  grievance procedures and, 325, 564, 574-577, 575-576, 587-588, 605, 606-607
  submission of, 544-545
  See also Unions, labor
Compliance approach, HR research, 600-601, 605-606
Compliance, legal, 25, 41, 344-345
  auditing, 598-599
  EEO enforcement and, 97-99, 105
  employee compensation and, 414-415
  placement and, 293-294
  and required services to employees, 14, 15
  under OSHA, 511-521
  voluntary, 96, 101, 106, 512-513
  See also Case law on employment; Laws, labor
Comprehensive Employment and Training Act (CETA, 1973), 42
Comprehensive Omnibus Budget Reconciliation Act (COBRA, 1986), 42, 293
Compulsory laws, 506
Computerization:
  effects of, 48, 328

HR department, 52, 143-145
  of human resource inventories, 178-179, 181, 187-188, 231
  of interviews, 241
  performance measurement and, 343-344
  training and, 321-322, 328
  See also Human resource information system (HRIS)
Concentration (over-representation), 108, 109
Conciliation agreements, EEOC negotiation and, 87-88, 98-100
Concurrent validity of testing, 237
Conditions, working. See Working conditions
Conferences, employee, 74
Connecticut v. Teal, 93, 234
Consent decrees, EEO, 88, 106
Consolidated Edison Company, 287
Consolidated Omnibus Budget Reconciliation Act (COBRA, 1986), 504-505
Constructs, job, 343
Construct validity (testing), 237
Content validity (testing), 237
Contract labor, 49, 198, 212-213, 223, 289, 476, 523
Contractors, federal government, 104-105
Contracts, union, 572-574, 575, 579, 583
Contributory plans (retirement), 474
Control Data Corporation, 295-296, 504, 548
Control group, 608
Control systems, job, 142-143, 597
Conversation, job-related. See Interviews
Cooling-off period, 570
Cooperation, union-management, 559-560, 574, 578-584
Core benefits, 487
Core hours, 480
Corning Glass Works, 306-308, 451
Corrective discipline, 549
Cost-benefit analysis, 608
Cost-of-living index (COLA), 431, 438, 575
Costs:
  appraisal, 353, 354, 360-361
  arbitration decision, 577-578
  budgets and, 169, 172, 203, 274
  employee benefit, 464, 467-469, 497, 503-504, 523
  employee turnover, 273-274
  fringe benefit, 464
  health insurance, 467-469
  international employment, 214-215
  new employee, 256
  productivity and labor, 432-433, 454-456
  recruitment, 203
  supplemental non-wage, 497
  training, 155, 274, 308
  unemployment compensation, 503-504, 523

Counseling:
  retirement, 288-289, 477-478, 501
  services, 483-485, 509, 547-548
  See also Career planning
Courtesy interviews, 235
Coverage. See Benefits, employee; Protected groups (EEO)
Craft unions, 564, 565
Credit unions, 483
Criminal acts by employees, 230
Critical incident method, 350-352, 549-550
Cross-training, 155, 156-157, 317-318
CT-General Hospital, 331-332
Cultural diversity, 44-47
  of assumptions, 53, 67-68, 79, 150, 236, 396
  cross-cultural bias and, 346
  international operations and, 47, 72-75, 77-80, 173, 214-215, 283, 550
Culture, organization, 52-53, 74, 275-283, 535, 609
Cycles, business, 49

Day-care programs, 203
Dayton Power and Light, 574, 583
Death of employees, 506, 513, 519
Decentralization, HRM, 68-69
Decision-making:
  by employees, 452-453, 532, 534-536
  dispute arbitration, 577-579
  See also Managers
Deductible clause, insurance, 468
Deductions, social security, 500
Deep sensing meeting, 545
Deferral jurisdictions (EEO), 97-98
Deferred stock incentive systems, 451
Defined benefit plan, 475
Defined contribution plan, 475
Delegation of responsibility, 15, 306
Delphi technique, 171-172
Delta Air Lines, 8, 19, 30-31
Demand for human resources, 168-175
  causes of, 168-170
  estimates of, 174-175
  forecasting, 171-173, 611-612
  See also Labor market
Democracy, industrial, 456, 536, 539-540
Demographics, 44, 46-47, 608
  trends in, 78-79, 184-186, 477, 611-612
Demotions, employee, 286, 302
Dental insurance, 470-471
Departing employees, hiring, 213-214
Department, Labor. See under U.S.
Deregulation of business, 327
Development, 597
  affirmative action and, 327-328
  importance of, 306-310
  long-term HR, 324-329
  of present employees, 14, 21
  See also Career Development; Training
Diaz v. Pan American World Airways, Inc.,

660 INDEX

95
Dictionary of Occupational Titles (DOT), 136, 138, 145, 424
Differential validity of testing, 237-238
Differently abled persons, 100, 201-202, 240
Digital Equipment Corp., 45-46
Direct compensation, 413, 465, 497
Direct performance observation, 343, 345
Disability plans, 432-433, 464-465, 471-472
Disabled employees, 100, 240, 508-509
Discharge. See Separation, employee
Disciplining employees, 320, 520, 548-550, 553, 575, 578
Discount plan, employee, 483
Discrimination:
  laws against, 42-43, 104, 201, 520-521
  overseas laws and, 69
  patterns of, 87-88, 99-100, 294, 345-347
  pregnancy, 42, 93-94, 471-472, 480
  racial, 94-95
  role playing and, 319
  sex-based, 68, 93-95, 101-103, 108-109, 429-430
  union activities and, 566-567
  See also Case law on employment
Dismissal, employee, 503-504
Disparate impact, 92-94, 233-234
Disparate treatment, 92
Displaced workers, 211
Dispute resolution, union-management, 570-578
Diverse, Inc., 402
Diversity, work force, 43-47, 179, 611-612
Divorced employees, 478, 505
Documentation. See Information systems; Records
DOT (Dictionary of Occupational Titles), 136, 138, 145, 424
Dow Chemical Corporation, 66-67, 72, 73, 74
Dow Jones & Company, Inc., 377-378
Down-sizing, organization, 169, 290, 300, 382, 426, 477, 559-560, 583, 614
Downward communication, 542-543
Drop-ins, job applicant, 205, 235
Drug-Free Workplace Act (1990), 43
Drug testing, employee, 45, 236, 239-240, 254, 484
"Druthers Program" (career), 377-378
Dual-career families, 214, 286, 481-482, 485, 612
Dual responsibility for HRM. See under Human resources management (HRM)
Due process, 549
Dues, union, 566, 575
Duke Power Company, 93, 144
Du Pont, 477, 484-485, 497-498
Duties, job, 129-130, 133

Early retirement, 46, 186, 288-289, 477
Easter Bunny job, 102
Eastman Kodak, 166
Economic environments:
  challenges of, 49-50, 539-540, 612
  measures of, 200-202
Education:
  applicant, 217, 219
  assistance programs, 203-204, 311, 325-326, 482
  career information, 384-385
  improvement of, 196, 211-212
  job success and, 202, 379
  remedial, 308, 326
Educational institutions, 308
  recruitment from, 199-200, 204, 205, 210, 244, 245
  See also Training
EEO. See Equal employment opportunity (EEO) laws
Efficiency and job design, 147-149, 152-154
Elder care, 485
Election, union, 568
Elective laws, 506-507
ELEVEN-C, OSHA section, 520-521
Eligibility. See Benefits, employee; Names of laws
Emerson Electric Company, 559
Empirical validation of testing, 237-238
Employee assistance programs (EAPs), 483, 548
Employee handbooks, 278-279
Employee involvement (EI), 534-536, 571, 582
  in participative management, 36-37, 535-536, 540-541
Employee ownership, 452-453
Employee relations, 14, 25
Employee Retirement Income Security Act (ERISA, 1974), 42, 475-476
Employees:
  advocacy and concern for, 582, 599, 615
  benefits sought by, 466-467, 486-488
  career concerns of, 381-382
  career development by, 391-397
  complaints by, 293, 513, 520-521, 567-568, 599, 606-607
  counseling for, 288-289, 477-478, 483-485, 501, 509, 547-548
  gainsharing by, 452-456
  involvement of, 534-436, 571, 582
  job sharing by, 296-297, 481-482
  knowledge-based pay for, 448-449
  OSHA rights of, 520-521
  overtime and exempt, 429
  participative management by, 36-37, 535-536, 540-541
  placement of, 283-287
  ratio measures of, 17, 172, 233-234
  rights of, 69-70, 291-292, 509-510, 520-521, 569-570, 613, 614
  self-appraisals by, 358-359
  separation of, 287-292
  skills inventories, 170, 176-179
  socialization of, 277-278
  stock ownership by, 450, 452-453, 483
  testing, 235-241
  union contract understanding by, 579-580, 582
  See also Human resources; Performance appraisal; Productivity
Employee stock option plans (ESOPs), 452-453, 483
Employee unions. See Unions, labor
Employer retaliation, 97, 520
Employment-at-will doctrine, 291, 293, 549-550, 613
Employment freeze, 186, 189-190, 288, 289
Employment function, 230
  See also Human resource departments (HRDs)
Employment hours, guaranteed, 441-442
Employment income security, 472-474
Employment references, 220, 252
Employment tests, 93, 235-241, 323, 343
  validity of, 236-238
Empowerment, employee, 535-536
Enforcement:
  of EEO laws and orders, 97-99, 105, 110
  safety inspections and, 513-514, 518-519
  See also Compliance, legal
Entry-level jobs, 44, 184, 204
Environmental challenges to HRM, 35-59, 611-612
  community attitudes as, 185
  recruitment and, 200-202
  steps in dealing with, 41, 43, 608
Environments:
  hazardous work, 25, 514
  job design and work, 148, 149-150, 327-328, 538-539
  nonunion, 50, 51, 429, 466, 568-569, 570-571, 584
  training, 315-322
  See also External environment
Equal Employment Opportunity Act (1972), 42, 97
Equal Employment Opportunity Commission (EEOC), 97-99
  Uniform Guidelines on Employee Selection, 233-234
Equal employment opportunity (EEO) laws:
  affirmative action programs and, 106-110, 117, 327-328
  employment tests and, 236-238
  enforcement of, 97-99, 105, 110
  exceptions to, 95-97, 100, 101, 550
  executive orders and, 104-105
  federal, 90-103, 216
  overviews of, 87-90, 110-112, 117

state and local, 103-104, 209, 216
  for women, 79-80, 93-95, 101-103, 430-431
Equal Pay Act (1963), 42, 91, 101-102, 414, 429-430
Equifinality of objectives, 52-53
Equity, job:
  external, 423-425
  internal, 416-423
Equity ownership, 451
Ergonomics, 149, 539
Error of central tendency, 346
ESOPs. See Employee stock option plans
Estimates of demand for HR, 174-175
Ethics:
  business, 283, 293
  job applicant, 251-252
  selection process, 220, 251, 256
  SHRM code of, 56
  See also Honesty
European Institute of Business Administration (INSEAD), 68
Europe, Western, 186, 550, 611
  cultural assumptions in, 68, 69-70
  guest workers in, 45
  work practices in, 157, 290, 473, 482, 501, 536, 539-540, 561-562
Evaluation:
  interviews, 364-366
  of overseas performance, 74-75
  of training, 322-324
Executive orders and EEO laws, 104-105
Executives:
  career paths of, 378-381, 392-393, 398-399
  HRM leadership by, 498, 533, 544-545, 593-594
  incentives for, 449-451
  international jobs for, 66, 197, 431-432
  perks for, 432, 450
  recruitment of, 180-181, 209-210
  reduction of, 290
  testing, 235-236
  training, 317-318
  See also Managers
Exempt employees, 429
Exit interviews, 603-604, 617-618
Expatriates. See Foreign assignments; Immigration, work force
Expedited arbitration, 578
Experience, candidate, 202, 210, 217-220
Experience rating, employer, 503
Experimental Negotiations Agreement, 580-581
Expert forecasts of HR needs, 171-172
Exposure, career, 392
External environment:
  economic, 49-50, 200-202, 539-540, 612
  HR supply in the, 184-186, 423-425
  influences of the, 41, 43-50, 168-169, 200-202, 326, 596
  See also Environments

External equity of jobs, 423-425
Extrapolation forecasting, 172
Exxon Corporation, 180, 201, 282

FAA and PATCO, 571-572
Facilities, employee benefit, 295, 484-485
Factor comparison method, 417-421, 431
Fair employment practices (state and local laws), 89-90, 97-98, 103-104
Fair Labor Standards Act (FLSA, 1938)), 201, 293, 414-415, 429
Fairness of pay structures, 430-431
Falsification of records, 516, 519
Families:
  benefits for, 471, 472, 476, 485-486, 504-505, 548
  concerns of, 73, 203, 214
  spouse benefits for, 476, 477-478, 485
  two-career, 214, 286, 481-482, 485
Fast trackers, 398-399
Federal agencies, 325-326, 341, 417, 429, 481, 583-584
  employee strikes and, 571-572
  executive orders governing, 89-90, 104-105
  See also U.S.
Federal Aviation Administration (FAA), 571-572
Federal equal employment laws, 42-43, 90-103
  Age Discrimination in Employment Act (1967), 91, 101
  Americans with Disabilities Act (ADA, 1990), 100
  and comparable worth, 102-103
  enforcement of, 97-99, 105
  Equal Pay Act (1963), 91, 101-102
  lists of, 42-43
  overviews of, 88-90, 91
  Pregnancy Discrimination Act (1978), 42, 93-94, 471-472, 480
  Title VII (1964), 90-100
  Vietnam Era Veterans Readjustment Act (1974), 91, 103
Federal Labor Relations Authority, 572
Federal Mediation and Conciliation Service (FMCS), 570
Feedback:
  attitude survey, 546-547
  career development, 399-400
  employee motivation and, 152, 364
  for evaluation, 25, 142-143, 312, 338, 351-352
  grapevine, 544-545
  to HRD, 366, 534, 545
  orientation program, 272-273, 281-282
  to raters, 347
  selection process, 256-257
  training, 315, 320
  See also Performance appraisal
Fee-paid position placement, 209-210

Female-dominated occupations, 430-431
Fiduciary standards, 475-476
Field experiments, 608
Field review method, 353-354
Files. See Records, employee
Film Recovery Systems, Inc., 514
Financial protection for workers, 499-510
  social security, 499-502
  sources of, 498-499
Financial services, 483
"Find the best" fallacy, 202
Fines, OSHA, 514-516, 519
Firing. See Separation, employee
Fish Camps, Inc., 617-618
Flat rates of pay, 426
Flexible benefit programs, 487-488
Flextime, 46, 480-481
Florida Power and Light, 355
Follow-up:
  inspections, 514
  orientation program, 281-282
  training, 322-324
Forced choice method of rating, 349-350
Forced distributions, 356
Ford Motor Company, 532, 535-536, 539
Forecasting techniques, HR demand, 171-173
Forecasts, human resources, 171-173, 611-612
Foreign assignments:
  benefits of, 180-181, 395-397, 431-432, 450, 485
  challenges of, 66-67, 70-73, 74-76, 198, 214-215, 326-327
Foreign Corrupt Practices Act, 283, 609
Foreign nationals:
  assessment of, 76-77, 236, 248-250, 346
  expectations by, 150
  as illegal aliens, 96-97, 253
  laws dealing with, 96-97, 253, 283, 294, 396, 473
  recruitment of, 72-73, 78-79, 198-199, 201, 210, 214-215, 248-250, 283, 326
  See also Immigration; Names of countries
Forms:
  audits of, 601
  exit interview, 603
  job analysis questionnaire, 139-142
  job application, 216-221
  job description, 137
  postinterview checklist, 248-249
  rating, 346
  replacement summary, 183
  skills inventory, 177-178
  See also Manuals; Questionnaires
Fort Worth Cab and Baggage Company, 230
Four-fifths rule (EEOC), 233-234
Freedom on the job, 151
Freeze, employment, 186, 189-190, 288, 289

662 INDEX

Frigidaire, 12
Fringe benefits, 432, 433, 449, 450, 464-465, 486-487
Full-service human resource departments, 13-14, 17, 18-19
Fully insured workers, 501
Functional authority, 20
Functional objectives, 11, 15
Funded pension plans, 474
Future-oriented appraisals, 357-362, 610-615

Gaines Pet Food, 540, 541
Gainsharing:
  administration, 445-446
  cost reduction and, 454-456
  eligibility and coverage, 444-445
  employee ownership, 452-453
  Improshare plans, 455-456
  payout standards, 445
  production-sharing plans, 453-454
  profit-sharing plans, 454
  purpose of, 443-444
  Rucker plan, 455-456
  See also Incentives
G. D. Searle & Co., 214
General Dynamics, 71
General Electric (GE), 157, 178, 325, 399, 469
General Electric v. Gilbert, 93
General Motors (GM), 7, 145-146, 328, 345, 399, 532
  unions and, 559
Genetic testing, 239-240
Geography and employment, 201, 204, 206, 208, 211
Germany, 539
Glass ceiling, 72, 395, 396
Glendale Federal Savings and Loan, 363
Global Banking, 368
Global economy, 6
Global organizations, 560-561
  compensation adjustments in, 431-432
  HRM in, 66-69, 299, 403, 611-612
  incentive systems, 451-452
  international employee relations in, 76-80, 179, 282-283
  planning and staffing, 70-76, 79-80, 179, 180-181, 196-197, 198-199, 299, 326-327, 395-397
  See also Internationalization of business
Godfather roles, 74
Golden parachutes, 292, 473
Good-faith attempt at employment, 502-503
Good faith bargaining, 567, 569
Government agencies:
  employment service, 208-209
  HRM in, 104-105, 167, 174, 177-178, 182
  training programs, 211-212

Government intervention:
  compensation management and, 429-430
  health insurance and, 467
  history of, 42-43, 87, 499, 502, 613
  HRM and, 37, 40, 50, 61
  in labor relations, 561-562, 566-571, 584, 613
  worker safety and, 510-512
  See also Names of specific laws and court cases
Grapevine communication, 544-545
Graphic response tests, 239-240
Graphs, scattergram, 425-426
Greyhound Corporation, 92
Grievance committee, 564
Grievance procedure and resolution, 325, 564, 574-577, 575-576, 587-588, 605, 606-607
  See also Unions, labor
Griggs v. Duke Power Company, 93, 144, 236, 262
Groups:
  audit team, 598
  autonomous work, 145-146, 156-157, 540-541
  coded occupational, 136, 138
  insurance for, 466
  interviewing in, 242
  job analysis panel, 134
  participative management, 36-37, 535-536, 537, 540-541
  professional associations and, 54-56, 210-211, 220, 395, 424, 608
  quality circle, 537-538
  rap session, 545
  union-management problem-solving, 536, 538
  See also Networks
Grumman Corporation, 475
Guaranteed annual wage (GAW), 473
Guaranteed employment hours, 441-442
Guest workers, 45, 184

Halo effect, 248, 250, 345-346
Handicapped workers, 100, 201-202
Hanes Group, 382
Harassment, prohibited, 94-95, 520
Harris Mini-Computers, Inc., 21
Hawthorne studies, 40
Hay Plan (job evaluation), 423
Hazard communication ruling, 514-515
Hazardous work environments, 514
Hazards, occupational, 25, 514
Hazing of newcomers, 275-276
Headhunters, 210
Health facilities, 295
Health insurance, employee, 253, 294, 466-471, 486-487, 490, 502
Health maintenance organizations (HMOs), 469-470

Hearings, arbitration, 579
Herman Miller, Inc., 292, 473
Hewlett-Packard, 74
High-hazard industries, 513
High school degree requirement, 93
High schools. See Educational institutions
Hiring decision, 96-97, 253, 255-256
  See also Selection process
History:
  applicant work, 217-218, 219
  of labor laws, 42-43, 91, 201, 497, 499, 503, 504, 505-506
  of personnel management, 38-43, 91, 381, 441, 536, 537-538, 562-563
  records analysis for organization, 605-607
  of unions, 42-43, 562-564, 566, 568, 584
HMOs, 469-470
Hobbies, candidate, 220
Holidays, paid, 479
Home-office workers, 60-61
Honesty:
  of HRD members, 256
  job applicant, 220, 251
  tests, 239-240
  See also Ethics
Honeywell, Inc., 103
Horizontal loading, 155-156
House organs, 543
HRIS. See Human resource information system
Human characteristics of jobs, 130-131, 133, 140-141
Human interfaces, 149
Human resource audits. See Human resource management audits
Human Resource Certification Institute (HRCI), 54-55
Human resource departments (HRDs):
  appraisal and feedback to, 365-366, 366
  authority of, 20-22, 57-58
  career planning and, 382-391, 397-400
  centralization or decentralization of, 68-69
  components of, 17-18
  employee relations practices of, 540-550
  feedback to, 366, 534, 545
  full-service, 13-14
  future challenges for, 610-615
  hierarchy of jobs in, 17, 19
  influence on QWL, 532-534
  information systems, 51-52, 143-145, 542-543
  key roles in, 17, 18-19, 57-58, 353-354, 501-502
  legally required benefits and services and, 498-499, 584-585
  the organization of, 16-22, 68-69
  policy statements by, 95
  QWL efforts by, 532-534
  selection interviewing by, 245-250
  size of, 17, 21

INDEX **663**

unnoticed functions of, 540
Human resource information system (HRIS), 24, 124-125, 126-127, 187-188, 386-387, 597, 598
　organization and legal issues, 143-145, 505
　OSHA case recordability and, 518-519
　See also Computerization; Records
Human resource management audits, 176-179, 366, 594
　reports, 602, 609-610
　research approaches to, 600-601
　scope of, 169-170, 595-599, 602
　tools of, 602-609
　See also Job analysis information
Human resource managers:
　authority of, 57-58, 533
　ethics of, 56
　knowledge areas of, 88, 124, 585, 614
　professionalism of, 53-57
　responsibilities of, 88, 610
　role perceptions of, 57
Human resource planning (HRP), 22, 30-31, 165-167, 597
　advantages of, 166-167, 179, 180, 195, 199, 383-384
　forecasting techniques, 171-173
　future-oriented performance appraisal and, 357-362
　implementation of, 170, 186-188, 503-504
　stages of complexity in, 173, 288
Human resource research. See Human resource management audits
Human resources (HR):
　demand for, 168-175, 186-188
　the supply of, 175-187, 287-292, 294-297
Human resources management (HRM):
　activities, 12-15, 111-112, 127, 195-196
　challenges facing, 24, 550, 584-585
　dual responsibility for, 20-22, 107-108, 110-111, 541, 594
　future aspects of, 610-615
　the history of, 42-43
　importance of, 7-8, 57-58, 593-594
　innovations, 292, 536-540
　input-output data, 25-27
　model of, 22-26
　objectives of, 11-12, 601
　primary functions of, 57, 229-230
　proactive vs. reactive, 27, 28
　purpose of, 10-11
　reports, 609-610
　responsibility for, 14-15, 18-19, 20-22, 57-58
　subsystems, 24-25
　unions and, 562-563, 584-585
　viewpoints of, 28
　See also Management
Hyatt Hotels Corporation, 545
Hypothetical scenario interviews, 244

IBM (International Business Machines), 155, 165-166, 274, 289-290, 308, 325, 399, 542, 543, 544-545
Ideas, employee. See Information systems
Illegal aliens, hiring, 96-97, 253
Illiteracy, 308, 322
Imagined grievances, 576
Immigration Reform and Control Act (1986), 42, 96-97, 201-202
Immigration, work force, 45-46, 77-78, 96-97, 150, 186, 236, 550, 612
　See also Foreign nationals
Imminent danger, 513, 516
Impact, disparate, 92-94, 233-234
Improshare plans, 455-456
Incentives:
　administration of, 445-446
　compensation, 413, 441-442, 468
　eligibility and coverage, 444-445
　executive, 449-451
　international, 451-452
　nonmonetary, 449
　payout standards, 445
　purpose of, 443-444, 607
　recruitment, 203-204
　safety, 517-518
　See also Benefits, employee; Gainsharing
Incentive systems, 441-443
　commission, 447
　maturity curves, 447
　pay-for-knowledge compensation, 448-449
　piecework, 446-452
　production bonus, 446
Income security, employment, 472-474
Incompetence, employee, 297
Indemnity plans, medical, 469-470
Indexation of employment patterns, 172, 431
Indirect compensation, 413, 464-467
　See also Benefits, fringe
Indirect performance observation, 343, 345
Industrial democracy, 456, 536, 539-540
Industrial engineering, 147-148
Industrialization, 48
Industrial relations departments, 585
Industrial unions, 564, 565
Inflation protection, 467
Information:
　labor force, 185-186
　right-to-know laws (OSHA), 514-515
Information systems:
　computerized, 52, 143-145
　employee, 541-547
　human resource department, 51-52, 143-145, 542-543
　internal and informal, 541-547
　See also Human resource information system (HRIS)
Information, wage and salary survey, 424
In-house complaint procedures, 544-545
Injunctions, strike delay, 570
Injury, worker. See Accidents
INSEAD, 68
Inspections, safety, 497-498, 512, 513-514
Insurance:
　benefits, 464, 487, 510
　disability, 432-433, 509-510
　health-related, 253, 294, 466-471, 486-487, 490, 502
　pension, 475-476
　See also Social security
Insured pension plan, 475
Intel Corporation, 464-465, 470-471, 479
Intermedics, Inc., 485
Internal environment. See Organizations
Internal equity of jobs, 416-423
Internal supply of HR, 175-183
International Association of Machinists Union, 509
International Brotherhood of Teamsters v. United States, 96
International Harvester (Navistar), 472-473
Internationalization of business:
　audit team, 609
　employee relations and the, 76-80, 150, 198, 346, 395-397, 431-432
　HRM and the, 37, 76, 97, 135, 166, 180-181, 199, 282-283, 299, 368, 403, 539-540
　incentive systems and, 450, 451-452
　overview of, 66-70
　recruitment and, 71-72, 173, 196-197, 214-215, 223
　See also Global organizations
International Warehousing, Inc., 299-300
Interstate commerce regulation, 566
Intervention, legal. See Government intervention
Interviewees:
　errors by, 250-251
　roles of, 247-250
Interviewers, roles of, 245-250
Interviews:
　audit and exit, 603-604
　complaint, 544-545
　courtesy, 235
　employee evaluation, 364-366
　job analysis, 133-134
　problem-solving, 364, 366
　selection process, 241-251
　supervisory, 254
Inventories:
　management and skills, 170, 176-179
　self-assessment, 388-389
Involuntary separation, 502
"Islands, work," 539

Japan, 45, 243
  labor shortage in, 79, 186, 197
  work practices in, 68, 72, 215, 290, 393, 444, 450, 473, 501
Job analysis information, 143-145, 157-158, 597
  applications of, 135-142, 341-344, 353-354, 448
  collection of, 127-135
  common factors in, 417-421
  legal aspects of, 144, 293-294
  overview of, 126-127, 416
  questionnaires for, 128-133
  See also Human resource information system
Job analysis schedules, 417
Job analysts, roles of, 127-135
Job application forms, 216-221
Job banks, 208-209
Job classifications, 145-146, 417, 426-428, 433
Job codes, 136, 138, 145
Job control systems, 142-143, 597
Job cycles, 148
Job descriptions, 108-109, 135-140, 202
  methods for comparing, 416-423
  union, 564
  See also Performance measures
Job design and redesign:
  behavioral elements, 146, 148, 150-154
  environmental elements, 148, 149-150, 327-328, 538-539
  organizational elements, 147-149, 170
  overviews, 145-147
  techniques of, 154-157
  tradeoffs in, 152-154, 294, 449
Job Element Inventory, 128
Job enlargement, 155
Job enrichment, 155-156
Job evaluation, 142-143, 416-423
  comparable pay and, 430-431
  factor comparison for, 417-421
  point system, 421-423, 430
Job families, 145, 386, 388
Job-flo report, national, 208-209
Job grading, 138, 417, 426-427, 447
Job-hopping, 392-393
Job identification, 127, 129
Job information service, 208-209
Job instruction training, 316-317
Job logbook, employee, 134
Job Match selection system, 232
Job performance standards, 133, 140-143, 341-342, 352-354, 446
Job-posting programs, 286-287
Job preview, realistic (RJP), 254-255
Job progression ladder, 386-387, 523
Job ranking, 416, 423, 447
Job requirements, 110, 126-127
  education-based, 93
  sex-linked, 95, 108-109
Job rotation, 74, 316, 326-327, 390, 539

cross-training and, 155, 156-157, 317-318
Job satisfaction. See Satisfaction, employee
Job sharing, 296-297, 481-482
Job specifications, 140-141
Job Training Partnership Act (JTPA, 1983), 42, 212
John Deere Harvester Works, 384-385, 387, 389-390, 397, 398
John Hancock Financial Services, 195-196
Johnson Wax Company, 331, 361-362
Joint study committees, 582-583
Juniority. See Seniority
Jurisdictions of employment-related laws, 89-90, 515-516
Jury service, 291-292, 480

Kaiser Aluminum & Chemical Corporation, 96, 106, 328
Karma Records, 458
K & D Company, 523
Kentucky Fried Chicken (KFC), 197
Key jobs, 418-419, 425-426
Key managers, 533
Key subordinates, 394
Kimberly-Clark, 482, 547-548
Knowledge-based pay, 448-449
Knowledge tests, 238-240
Kuder Preference Record, 387

Labor agreements, 14, 51-52, 573-575, 579, 583
  See also Bargaining
Laboratory training, 322
Labor costs, 432-433, 454-456
Labor Department. See under U.S.
Labor laws. See Laws, labor
Labor-Management Relations Act (LMRA, 1947), 42, 568-571
Labor-Management Reporting and Disclosure Act (LMRDA, 1959), 570, 571
Labor-management systems, 561-571
Labor market:
  analysis, 171-175, 611-612
  challenges and compensation, 428-433
  diversity of the, 43-47, 179, 611-612
  expectations, 150, 155
  skills availability in the, 150, 165, 184-186
  supply and demand, 150, 184-188, 196-197, 204, 428
  wage and salary surveys, 423-425
  wage rates, 102-103, 428
Labor unions. See Unions, labor
Ladder, job, 386-387, 523
Landrum-Griffin Act. See Labor Management Reporting and Disclosure Act (LMRDA, 1959)
Landrum-Griffin Act, 1959

Language skills:
  English, 202, 236, 326
  work force, 45-46, 135, 179, 308, 322, 396, 543
Last-offer arbitration, 577
Latin America, 72, 78, 215
Laws, labor, 201
  history of, 42-43, 91, 201, 497, 499, 503, 504, 505-506
  sources and jurisdictions of, 69, 89-90, 506-507, 568-569
  union-management relations and, 566-571, 577
  See also Case law on employment; Names of specific laws and cases
Layoffs, 109, 212-213, 289-291, 295-297, 300, 472-474, 503-504, 577-578
  policies for avoiding, 443, 503
Leading economic indicators, 200
Leading questions, 250
Learning curve, 313-314
Learning principles, 313-316
Leasing of employees, 213
Least squares method, 426
Leave, employee:
  educational, 326
  for pregnancy, 93-94
  social service, 485-486
  timing of, 186, 479
Lectures, training, 316, 318
Legal insurance, group, 472
Legislation, employee-related, 50, 201
  history of, 40-43, 499
  importance of to HRD, 498-499
  See also Case law on employment
Legitimate grievances, 576
Leniency bias, 346
Leveraging, career, 392-393
Liability, legal, 230
  See also Compliance, legal
Lie detector tests, 239-240
Life insurance, 471
  jobs, 195-196
Life plan, 388-389
Lifetime employment. See Japan
Lincoln Electric Company, 441-442, 443
Line (or operating) managers, 230-231, 610
  authority of, 20-22, 57-58, 111, 279-280, 284
  interviews by, 254
  placement decisions by, 284-286, 311
  training by, 318, 331
  training of, 107-108, 282, 317-318, 320, 325-326, 331, 386
  See also Managers
Literacy tests, 236
LMRA, 42, 568-571
LMRDA, 570, 571
Loading, job, 155-156
Local employment:
  labor pool, 184-185, 199, 208-209

INDEX   **665**

laws, 89-90, 103-104
  training programs, 211-212
Local unions, 69, 564-565
Lockheed Engineering & Management Service Company, 476
Logbook, employee job, 134
Long-term disability insurance (LTD), 471
Long-term incentives, 449-450
Lost-time accidents, 498, 506, 509, 510-511, 574
Low-hazard industries, 512-513, 523-524
Lump-sum bonuses, 432-433

McDonnell Douglas Corporation, 317-318
McGraw-Hill, 399
Mail-in assessments, 362
Mailing lists, 211
"Make-whole" remedies, 99-100
Malingering, employee, 507
Management:
  inventories, 176-179
  participative, 36-37, 535-536, 540-541, 571
  rights, 577
  ULPs by, 566-567
  unions and, 559-560, 561-571, 577-584
  See also Human resources management (HRM)
Management by objectives (MBO), 52-53, 359-360, 448
  HR research, 600-601
Management by walking around, 542, 545
Managers, 184
  auditing compliance of, 598-599
  cultural assumptions held by, 68
  HRM responsibilities of, 14-15, 171-172, 398-399, 533, 542
  key subordinates and, 394
  See also Executives; Line (or operating) managers
Manning tables, 174-175
Manuals, 238
  job point system, 422-423
  labor agreement, 574
  orientation, 279, 282, 483, 487
  programmed learning, 321-322
  See also Forms
Marine Midland Bank, 413
Market, labor. See Labor market
Market wage rates, 428
Marriott Corporation, 601
Massachusetts Mutual Life Insurance Company, 487
Matsuhita Electric, 294
Maturity curves, 447
Maytag Company, 155
MBO. See Management by objectives
Measurement systems. See Performance measures
Mechanistic job design, 148
Media:
  advertising, 206-208
  internal communication, 103, 542-547
Mediation, federal, 570
Medical evaluation, 253-254
Medical insurance, 468-469, 486-487, 504-505
Medical tests, 239-240
Mental demands of a job, 138, 140-141, 151, 509
Mental health insurance, 471
Mentorship programs, 66-67, 71, 326, 393
Merck & Company, 347, 356
Mergers and acquisitions, 292, 473
  HR needs during, 169-170, 291
Merit-based promotions, 284-285
Merit pay, 101, 429
  bonuses, 442
  raises, 427, 447-448
Merrill Lynch, 229
Metropolitan Life, 272-273, 274
Mexico, working in, 72, 215
Migration, work force, 45-46, 77-78
Military experience (applicant), 42, 91, 103, 211, 218, 219
Minimum-wage, 429
Minorities, recruitment of, 88
  See also Protected groups (EEO)
Mixed format interviews, 243-244
Mixed unions, 564
Mobil Chemical Company, 512-513
Mobility, job, 392-393
Model, HR. See Systems model
Models, computer forecasting, 172-173
Monitoring, performance, 343-344
Moonlighting, skills from, 179
Morale. See Quality of work life efforts (QWL)
Moslem cultures, 68, 69, 79, 199, 346
Motivation, employee, 30-31, 155-156, 359-360, 532-534, 538, 552
  See also Incentives; Satisfaction, employee
Motorola, 36-37, 41, 45, 49-50, 308
Mountain Bell Telephone Company, 478
Multinational corporations. See Global organizations
Multiunion associations, 566

National Aeronautics and Space Administration (NASA), 543-544
National Center of Employee Ownership, 453
National Commission for Manpower Policy, 185
National Food Brokers, 259-260
National Football League Players Association, 567
National Institute of Occupational Safety and Health (NIOSH), 514
National Labor Relations Act (NLRA, 1935), 201, 293, 566-568
National Labor Relations Board (NLRB), 567-568
National Steel Corporation, 453
National unions, 96, 509, 559, 560, 565-566, 580-581
  See also Names of individual unions
Needs assessment, training, 310-312
Negotiations, union-management, 570-578
  do's and don'ts, 574
Nelson Radar Company, 210
Networks:
  computer, 143-144
  informal, 74, 280, 286, 395, 478, 536
  mentorship, 66-67, 71, 326, 393
New-hire costs, 203
Newsletters, company, 103, 543, 599
New United Motor Manufacturing, Inc. (NUMMI), 7
New ventures, HR planning for, 169-170, 172
New York Telephone, 329
NFL players strike, 567
NIOSH. See National Institute of Occupational Safety and Health
NLRB, 567-568
Nominal group techniques (NGT), 171
Noncontributory benefit plans, 474
Nondeferral jurisdictions (EEO), 97-98
Nonmonetary incentives, 449
Nonpay benefits, 432
Nonprofit organizations, 485-486
Nontraditional pay plans, 441-442
Nonunion environments, 50, 51, 429, 466, 568-569, 570-571, 584
Nonverbal communication, 247-250, 281
Notice of layoffs, advance, 43, 168-169, 290, 613
Notification of unsuccessful applicants, 255
Nucor Corporation, 453-454

Objectives, 594
  employee, 338-340
  functional, 11, 15
  HRM, 10-11, 66, 614-615
  management by (MBO), 52-53, 359-360, 448, 600-601
  organizational, 11, 15, 169-170, 465-466, 615
  personal, 11-12, 15, 615
  relations by (RBO), 583
  societal, 11, 12, 13, 15, 50, 465, 614
  union, 562, 563, 580-581
Objectivity of performance measures, 343-345
Observation, job analysis, 135
Obsolescence, employee, 324-326
Occupational Safety and Health Act (OSHA, 1970), 42, 499, 510-521
  Employee rights under, 520-521
  inspections, 512, 513-514
  objectives of, 512

records, 518, 606
violations and penalties under, 516
Occupational Safety and Health Administration (OSHA), 512, 519
Oceaneering International, 510
Offers, union and management, 574
Office of Federal Contract Compliance Programs (OFCCP), 105
Office of Personnel Management (U.S.), 105, 341
Ogilvy & Mather International, 321
Ohio Bell Telephone Company, 156, 533
Old-boy networks, 395
Older workers, 46, 601
Older Workers Benefit Protection Act (1990), 43
Open-door policies, 542, 545
Open houses, 214
Openings, job:
 planning for, 180-186, 195
 See also Recruitment of employees
Open systems, 20-21, 28, 562-563, 585
 See also Systems model
Opinions, personal, 345-347
Oregon Logging Company, 579-580
Organizational objectives and HRM, 11, 15, 169-170, 465-466, 615
Organization charts, 380
 employee replacement, 181-182, 361
 HRDs in, 16, 17
 union, 564-565
Organization culture, 52-53, 74, 535, 609
 orientation programs, 275-283
Organization development. See Development
Organizations:
 career planning benefits to, 383-384
 challenges to improvement of, 8-10
 down-sizing of, 169, 290, 300, 382, 426, 477, 559-560, 583, 614
 employee training benefits to, 309, 324-329
 external challenges to, 41, 43-50
 history and records of, 605-607
 importance of, 6-8
 internal challenges within, 50-57, 108, 198-199, 230-231
 names of QWL-concerned, 537
 policies and recruitment, 198-199
 QWL and EI interventions by, 536-540
 supply of HR within, 175-183, 198, 283-287, 381, 398-400, 523, 581
Organizing. See Unions, labor
Orientation programs, 597
 benefits of, 280-281
 content and responsibility for, 278-279
 follow-up, 281-282
 international, 73, 282-283
 opportunities and pitfalls of, 279-280
 purposes of, 272-274, 275-277
 socialization and, 277-278
OSHA. See Occupational Safety and Health Act
Outplacement assistance, 186, 292, 473
Outside authority approach, HR research, 600
Overseas jobs. See Foreign assignments; Global organizations
Overspecialization, job, 155-157
Overtime hours and pay, 223, 429, 437, 439, 442, 607

Paired comparisons, 357, 358
Pan American World Airways, 95
Panels, job analysis, 134
Paperwork. See Forms; Records, employee
Parachutes, golden or silver, 292, 473
Participation, learner, 314
Participation rates by age of workers, 46-47, 601
Participative management program (PMP), 36-37, 535-536, 540-541
Part-time employment, 198, 212-214, 289, 295-296, 501, 612, 617
PATCO strike, the, 571-572
Paternalism, 40
Paternity leave, 480
Pay. See Compensation, employee
Paychecks, extra income and, 445-446
Pay-for-knowledge compensation, 448-449
Pay-for-performance plans, 443-446
Payouts, productivity, 443-444, 454-456
Payout standards, 445
Peer pressure, 156-157, 275-276
 productivity and, 445, 446, 478
Penalties, employee, 549-550
Penalties, employer:
 EEO violation, 99-100
 OSHA violation, 514-516, 519
Pensions, employee, 432-433, 474-478, 575
 See also Social security
Pepsi Cola Company, 321, 450
Performance appraisal, 14, 24, 139, 597
 comparative methods of, 355-357, 358
 employment testing and, 236-241, 354-355
 future-oriented, 357-362, 399-400, 613-614
 implications of, 362-366
 key elements of, 340-344
 legal constraints and, 344-345
 overviews of, 338-340, 355
 past-oriented, 347-357
 rater bias and, 345-347, 595-596
 for replacement openings, 181-183, 399-400
 uses of, 339
Performance-based compensation, 441-442
Performance measures, 341-342, 343-344, 600-601
computer-assisted, 343-344
 executive incentives and, 450-451
 See also Audits, HR research
Performance standards, 133, 140-143, 341-342, 352-354, 446
Performance tests and observations, 239-240, 354-355
Permissible discrimination, 91
Personal data, applicant, 216-217
Personal leave days, 479
Personal objectives, HRM and, 11-12, 15, 615
Personnel. See Employees; Human resources
Personnel departments, evolution of, 38-43, 230, 585
Personnel records. See Privacy; Records, employee
Peter Principle, the, 284-285
Phillips Petroleum Company, 326
Physical demands of work, 140-141
 ergonomics and, 149, 539
 repetitive strain and, 516, 523-524
Physical protection for workers, 498-499, 510-521, 550
 OSHA and, 510-521
 sources of, 498-499
Picketing, union, 569
Piecework incentive systems, 445, 446-452
Pizza Hut, 202
Placement:
 activities, 14, 180-181
 advertising, 206-208
 assistance, 208-209, 210
 effectiveness, 292-293
 employee, 283-287, 399-400
 legal compliance and, 293-294
 tests, 40
 See also Separation
Planning, HR. See Human resource planning (HRP)
PMP program, 36-37, 45
Point allocation method, 357
Point system, job evaluation, 421-423, 430
Policies, insurance. See Insurance
Political grievances, 576-577
Polygraph Protection Act (1988), 43
Polygraph tests, 43, 239-240
Pool of applicants, 195, 397
Portability, pension plan, 474, 475-476
Position analysis questionnaire (PAQ), 128, 145
Postinterview checklists, 248-249
Postretirement counseling, 478
PQ Corporation of Valley Forge, 110
Praise program, OSHA, 513
Precedents, arbitration, 578, 579
 See also Case law on employment
Predictive validity of testing, 237-238
Preferential quota systems, 96
Preferred-provider organizations (PPOs), 470

Pregnancy Discrimination Act (1978), 42, 93-94, 471-472, 480
Premiums, collection of, 505
Prerequisite jobs, 386-387, 523
Presidential orders, U.S. See Executive orders
Pretraining assessment, 323
Prevailing wage rates, 428
Prevention of claims against employers, 508
Preventive discipline, 548-549
Preview, realistic job (RJP), 254-255
Pricing jobs, 425-427
Prior consultation, 581
Prison penalties, 514, 570
Privacy:
   for complaints, 544-545
   employee or applicant, 52, 240, 484, 548, 613
   See also Records, employee
Private placement agencies, 209-210
Proactive HRM, 27, 28, 195-196, 201-202, 325, 497-498, 578-580
Probation, employee, 256
Problem-solving:
   groups, 536, 538
   interviews, 364, 366
Production bonuses, 446
Production-sharing plans, 453-454
Productivity:
   as a ratio, 9-10
   committees, 582-583
   decline of U.S., 613-614
   examples of, 30-31
   job design and, 146, 153, 276-277, 532
   nontraditional compensation and, 443-444, 453-454
   peer pressure and, 445, 446
   standards, 169, 448
Professional Air Traffic Controllers' Organization (PATCO), 571-572
Professional associations, 54-56, 210-211, 220, 395, 424, 608
Professional in Human Resources (PHR), 54-55
Professionalism in human resource management, 53-55, 69-70
Profit-sharing plans, 444-445, 449
Programmed learning, 321-322
Progressive discipline, 549-550
Projections, HR demand, 172-175
Promote-from-within policies, 198, 283-286, 398-399, 399-400, 523, 581
Promotion, employee, 180-181, 361-362
   policies on internal, 198, 232, 283-286, 399-400, 581, 607
Protected groups (EEO), 90-96, 107-108, 216, 236, 346, 397
   four-fifths ratio rule, 233-234
   interviewing members of, 245-246
   over- and under-representation of, 108, 199-200, 238, 471-472

training of, 212, 327-328
Protection of employees, 25
   international, 75-76, 497
   legally required, 497-499
Protection of employers, under worker's compensation laws, 508
"Prudent man" rule, 475-476
Psychological tests, 238-239, 360
Publications:
   external information, 185-186
   internal communication, 103, 543, 599
Publicity for employee benefits, 487
Public Law 97-221, 481
Public service. See Community service activities
Purposes of HRM. See Objectives
Pygmalion effect, 536

Quaker Oats, 468-469
Qualifiable workers, 107
Qualified domestic relations orders (QDRO), 478
Qualified handicapped, 100, 201-202
Quality circles, 537-538
"Quality from the Start" program, 272-273, 274
Quality of work life efforts (QWL):
   employee communication and, 541-547, 552-553, 571-572
   and employee involvement (EI), 534-540
   HRD roles in, 532-534, 541-542
   intervention approaches, 536-540
Quasar company, 294
Questionnaires:
   attitude survey, 546-547, 604-606
   interview questions and, 243-250, 603
   job analysis, 128-133
   job application, 216-221
   See also Forms
Quotas. See Preferential quota systems; Protected groups (EEO)
QWL. See Quality of work life efforts
Qyx, Inc., 201

Racial discrimination, 94-95
Raiding:
   corporate, 453
   of employees, 210, 215, 292, 473
Raises, pay. See Compensation, employee
Ralph Parsons Company, 287
Ranking method of appraisal, 355
Rapport in interviews, 246-247
Rap sessions, 545
Rate ranges, job class, 426-427
Rating, performance:
   methods, 347-357
   scales, 339, 348, 349
Rational validity of testing, 237-238
Raytheon Corporation, 509

Reactive approach to HRM, 27, 28
Reading tests, 236
Realistic job preview (RJP), 254-255
Recency effect, 347, 351
Recertification, PHR, 55
Records, company:
   grievance, 577
   QWL documentation, 533
   types of, 602-606
   See also Forms; Human resource information system (HRIS)
Records, employee, 52, 255-256, 283, 598, 600-601, 606
   critical incident, 350-352, 549-550
   OSHA, 512, 518-519
Recruiters, 195, 200
Recruitment of employees, 24, 195-197, 597
   benefits and, 203-204, 279, 465-466
   channels of, 204-215
   constraints on, 197-204
   international, 71-72, 173, 196-197, 214-215, 223
   job application forms for, 216-221
   overviews of, 195-197
   timing of, 174-175
   See also Selection process, the
Red-circle rates (wage), 428
Redesign, job, 154-157
References, job-related, 220, 251-253
Referrals, employee, 205, 214
Rehabilitation Act (1973), 42
Rehiring employees, 213-214
Relations by objectives (RBO), 583
Relative worth of jobs. See Comparable worth
Relevance, training, 314
Reliability, test, 238
Religious beliefs and attitudes, 68, 69, 79, 173, 199, 346
Religious organizations as employers, 97, 189-190, 505
Relocation policies, 485
   international, 75-76, 199, 395-397, 431-432
Remedial education, 308
Remedies, legal, 97-100
   See also Compliance, legal
Renting employees, 213
Repatriation programs, 75-76
Repetition, learner, 314
Repetitive strain syndrome, 516, 523-524, 539
Replacement, employee, 318
   charts, 181-182, 361
   summaries, 181-183
   See also Succession planning
Representatives, union, 564
Research. See Human resource management audits
Resignations, employee, 294-295, 392-393, 399, 402

Responsibilities, job, 130, 133, 146-147, 155-156
   cost reduction plans and, 454-456
   evaluation and comparison of, 416-423
Resumes, applicant, 206, 251
Retirement:
   benefits, 288, 474-478, 502
   early, 46, 186, 288-289, 477
   mandatory, 170
   and temporary employment, 213, 289, 295
Retirement Equity Act (REA, 1984), 42, 478
Retraining programs, 211-212, 509, 539
Returning employees (from abroad), 66-67
Reverse discrimination, 106, 107, 328, 550
Reward systems, non-traditional, 441-442
Rights, management, 577
Rights of workers. See Employees, rights of
Right-to-know laws, OSHA, 514-515
Right-to-sue letter, EEOC, 98-99
Right-to-work laws, 569
Rings of defense, 295-296, 504
Robert Hall International, 297
Robotics, 48
Role-playing, 319, 363, 547
Rotation, job, 74, 155, 316, 317-318, 326-327, 390, 539
Roy Rogers Restaurants, 601
Rucker plan, 455-456

Sabbatical, paid, 466, 479
Safety, employee, 550
   OSHA and, 510-521, 605
   policies, 497-498, 517-518, 606
   training, 323-324
Salary surveys, 423-425
   See also Compensation, employee
Sales levels, 169, 200
Sanctions on employers, 201
"Sandwich" generation, 485
Santa Claus job, 102
Sara Lee Corporation, 180
Satisfaction, employee:
   auditing, 599, 602-606
   benefits and, 486-487
   career development and, 381
   cognitive dissonance and, 273
   job design and, 146, 151-154, 155-156
   low pay and, 412-413
   QWL efforts and, 532-534
   unions and, 564
   See also Benefits, employee; Motivation, employee
Saturn Corporation, 145-146, 156
Saudi Arabia, 199
Savings account, educational, 482
Scanlon plan, 454-456
Scattergram, 425-426
Schedules (work), 480-482

   flexible, 46, 480-481
Schools. See Educational institutions
Scientific management movement, the, 39-40
Scores, training, 328
Scrap rates, 605
Seafood Canners, Inc., 607
Search firms, professional, 209-210, 274
Search, unemployed worker job, 502-503
Security, employee. See Placement
Selection interviews, 241-251
   steps in, 245-248
   types of, 242-245
Selection process, the, 13, 24, 110, 597
   8 step, 233, 235-256
   employment tests and, 235-241
   feedback, 256-257, 605
   hiring decisions and, 255-256, 283-284
   inputs and challenges to, 230-231
   medical evaluation and, 253-254
   outcomes of, 256-257, 605
   overviews, 229-230, 231-235, 256-258, 384-385
   preliminary reception and, 235
   realistic job previews (RJP) and, 254-255
   references and background checking, 251-253
   supervisory interviews and, 254
   training and, 313
   uniform guidelines, 233-235
   See also Recruitment of employees
Selection ratio, 232-233
Self-appraisals, 358-359
Self-assessment, career, 388-389
Self-audits, 598
Self-inspection, workplace, 517-518
Self-nominations:
   for development, 311, 394-395
   for jobs, 286-287
Self-study, 321-322
Seminars, career information, 384-385
Seniority, 51, 101, 559-560, 575
   promotions based on, 285, 581
   rights and EEO, 88, 95-96, 429-430
Senior management candidates, 180-181, 360, 398-399
Senior Professional in Human Resources (SPHR), 54-55
Sensitivity training, 322
Sentry Insurance Company, 295
Separation, employee, 213-214, 287-292, 472-473, 502-504
   prevention of, 294-297, 503
   union activities and, 566-567, 571-572
   See also Placement
Services, employee, 482-486, 615
   administration of, 486-488
   legally required, 14, 15
7-Eleven company, 181-182, 398
Severance pay, 292, 472
Sex-based discrimination issues, 68, 93-95, 101-103, 429-430

   job stereotypes and, 108-109
Sexual harassment discrimination, 94-95
Sharing, job, 296-297, 481-482
Shenandoah Life Insurance, 124, 126, 146-147
Shortages, manpower, 184-187
Shorter workweeks, 480
Short-term incentives, 449-450
SHRM, 54-57, 109, 235, 286, 424
Shutdown, employer, 479
Sick days and well pay, 468-469, 478-479
Siemens Company, 539
Signature, applicant, 218, 220
Silver parachutes, 292, 473
Simulation, job, 229, 254-255, 315, 320-321, 354-355, 360
Skill-based pay, 448-449
Skills:
   inventories, 170, 176-179
   job specification of, 140, 217, 219, 417-421
   for job success, 202, 360-362, 447-449
"Slave labor act," 569
Small business, 505, 506, 568-569
Smoking in the workplace, 53, 516
Social expectations, 150
Socialization, employee, 277-278
Social security, 498, 499-502
Social Security Act (1935), 500-502
Social services for employees, 483-486
Social unionism, 563, 566
Societal objectives, HR and, 11, 12, 13, 15, 50, 465, 614
Society for Human Research Management (SHRM), 54-57, 109, 235, 286, 424
Sociotechnical systems, 538-539
Solar Turbines International, 538
Southern California Edison, 469
"Southern strategy," 559
Southland Corporation, 181-182, 398
Southmore Hospital, 435
"Speak Ups!," 544-545
Specialization, job, 148, 152-154
Sponsor, career, 393
Spouses of workers, 73, 476, 477-478, 485
Staff authority, 20-22, 57-58
Staffing, 597
   internal, 198, 283-286, 398-399, 399-400, 523, 581
   overseas, 70-73, 173
   table, 174-175
   work scheduling and, 480-482
Stalled careers, 390-391
Standards:
   appraisal system, 341-342
   interviewing, 241-242
   job performance, 133, 140-143, 341-342, 352-354, 446
   uniform employee, 92-93, 128-133, 150, 609
Star program, OSHA, 512-513
State employment-related laws, 89-90,

103-104, 430, 515-516
State employment security agencies, 208-209, 424, 502, 608
State Farm Insurance Companies, 180, 598
State Mutual Life Assurance Company, 203
Statistics, 172
  AIDS epidemic, 170
  applicant information checking, 251
  HR audit research, 600-601, 605-607, 608
  immigration, 77-79
  job pricing with, 425-427
  on gainsharing, 452
  on performance appraisal uses, 338
  on resignation reasons, 294-295
  on termination reasons, 297
  recruitment cost, 203
  union membership, 560-561
  worker injury, 510-511, 516
  work force, 46, 611-612
Status, employment:
  desired, 217, 219
  permanent or temporary, 198, 212-213
Steelcase, Inc., 490-491
Steward, union, 564
Stock options, employee, 450, 452-453, 483
Strategic plans, HRM and, 169-170, 596, 614
Strategy-environmental fit, 596
Stress, 391, 508-509
Stress interviews, 229, 243-245
Strictness bias, 346
Strikes, union, 457, 503, 570, 580
Strong Vocational Interest Blank, 387
Structural unemployment, 211-212
Structured interviews, 243-244
Students, recruitment of, 72, 199-200
Subfactor points, job, 422-423
Subjectivity of performance measures, 344-345, 348, 359
Substance abuse, 484
Success criteria, job, 140-142
Succession planning, 180, 232, 382
  international, 70-71, 180-181
  See also Promotion, employee
Suggestion systems, 546
"Suitable employment," 502-503
Supervisors, job:
  appraisal and ratings by, 339-340, 342-344, 347-357
  attitudes about, 604
  evaluation of, 362
  HRD consultation with, 134, 139, 171-172, 311, 353-354
  interviews by, 254
  orientation by, 278-280
  training by, 318
  training of, 320
Supplemental unemployment benefits

(SUB), 473-474
Suppliers, contract, 295-296
Surpluses, HR, 186
Survey techniques:
  HR demand forecasting, 171-172
  wage and salary, 424-425
Survivorship options, 476, 477-478
Sweden, 157
Systems model, human resource management, 22-26, 28, 593
  application of the, 25-26
  input-output data, 25-27, 147
  subsystem roles in the, 24-25

Taft-Hartley Act. See Labor-Management Relations Act (LMRA, 1947)
Taft-Hartley injunctions, 570
Takeovers, company, 292, 473, 475
Talent inventories, 176-179
Task identity, 151, 152, 311-312
Task significance, 152
Tax breaks, 465, 502
Taxes:
  insurance and, 466-467
  lowering unemployment, 503-504, 523
  overseas work and, 396, 432
Tax Reform Act (1986), 475
Teamwork. See Groups
Technology:
  displacement, 169
  impacts of changes in, 47-48, 150, 327, 328
Temporary and contract workers, 198, 212-213, 223, 289, 295, 476, 523
Termination, employee, 213-214, 291-292, 503-504
Tests:
  employment, 93, 235-241, 323, 343
  professional SHRM, 54-55
  vocational, 387
Texas Instruments (TI), 275-277, 281
Third parties, 583
3M (Minnesota Mining and Manufacturing), 386
"Tiger teams", Boeing, 537
Time-off benefits, 478-480
Timing:
  of employee leave, 186, 479
  of employee testing, 241, 363
  of reward payouts, 445-446, 455
  selection process, 230-231
  work scheduling and, 480-482
Title VII (CRA of 1964), 42, 90-100, 107, 414
  amendments, 94
  enforcement of, 97-99
  exceptions to, 95-97, 100
  Section 703(a) and (d), 90-92
  Section 703(h), 95-96
Title IX (Social Security), 499
Top-down communication, 542-543

Towers, Perrin, Forster & Crosby, 385
Toyota, 7, 232
Tradeoffs in job design, 152-154
Tradespeople. See Unions, labor
Tradition and work practices, 149
Training, employee, 21, 100, 597
  affirmative action and, 327-328
  approaches and tradeoffs, 306-307, 315-322, 324-329
  benefits of, 307-310, 509
  costs, 155, 274, 308
  cross-training, 155, 156-157, 317-318
  evaluation of, 322-324, 610
  importance of, 306-310, 392, 399, 599
  international, 74
  job design and, 148, 153-154
  levels of, 306-308
  of line managers, 107-108, 310
  objectives, 312-313, 517
  on union contracts, 579-580, 582
  program development, 310-315
  of qualifiable candidates, 196, 287
  for quality circles, 538
  of raters and evaluators, 362-364
  state employment, 208-209
  See also Development; Educational institutions
Training programs, education and, 211-212, 513
Transference, training, 314, 323-324
Transfers, employee, 285-286, 289, 290, 317-318, 426
  career development and, 378-381, 390, 394-395
  international, 72-73, 299, 395-397
Trends:
  demographic, 44, 78-79, 184-186, 477, 611-612
  projection of, 172
"Trolling for open doors," 542, 545
Troubleshooting in global organizations, 77
Trusted pension plan, 475
Trust, union-management, 574, 581-584
TRW, HRIS at, 143, 204
Try program, OSHA, 513
Tuition assistance, 203-204, 311, 325-326, 482
Tuition refund programs, 482
Turnover, employee, 140, 154, 170, 255, 259-260, 277, 294-295, 319, 485, 601, 605
  career development and, 392-393
  of newcomers, 273-276, 435
  training and, 328-329, 399
Two-tiered orientation program, 278
Two-tiered wage structure, 51, 432
Two-way communication, 542, 545, 582

ULPs, 566-567
Underspecialization, job, 152-155
Understudy jobs, 318

Underutilization (under-representation), 108, 109
Undocumented aliens, 201
Unemployment, 502-504
    funds, 474
    rates, 184-185
    structural, 211-212
Unemployment compensation, 157, 482, 502-504
Unemployment insurance, 290
Unemployment offices. See State employment security agencies
Unfair labor practices (ULPs), 566-567, 568-569
Unfunded pension plans, 474
Uniformity, 609
    of employee benefits, 486, 503, 506
    of job analysis, 128-133, 150
Uniform selection guidelines. See under Equal Employment Opportunity Commission (EEOC)
Unionization, resistance to, 559
Union-management agreement. See Labor agreements
Union-management relations, 14, 139, 540, 559-560, 580
    cooperative, 559-560, 574, 578-584
    problem-solving groups and, 536
Union shop, 575
Unions, labor, 40, 50-51, 201, 211, 285, 286, 429, 445, 466, 472, 482
    bill of rights, 569-570
    complaints about, 570
    cooperation with management, 559-560, 578-584
    dispute resolution, 570-578
    history of, 42-43, 562-564, 566, 568, 584
    HRM and, 562-563, 584-585, 597
    international competition and, 560-561
    labor-management systems and, 561-571
    membership statistics, 560-561
    seniority and, 88, 95-96
    strikes by, 457, 503, 570, 580
    structure and functions, 563-566
    two-tiered wage structure for, 51, 432
United Automobile Workers, 559, 560, 565, 582
United Parcel Service (UPS), 342
United States:
    military services, 178, 204, 211, 319
    productivity improvement, 613-614
    See also Federal agencies; U.S.
United Steelworkers of America and Kaiser Aluminum & Chemical Corporation v. Weber, 96, 106, 206, 207, 328
United Steelworkers Union, 580-581
University of Michigan Center for Ergonomics, 539
Unpaid leaves, 480
Unsolicited job recruits, 205

Unstructured interviews, 243
Upward communication systems, 543-547
U.S. Attorney General, 98-99
U.S. Bureau of Labor Statistics, 516
U.S. Department of Commerce, 200
U.S. Department of Health and Human Services, 501
U.S. Department of Labor, 105, 185, 208-209, 424, 429, 475, 512, 519, 570, 608
U.S. Employment Service, 208-209, 502
U.S. Supreme Court. See Case law on employment
U.S. Veterans Administration (VA), 25-26, 27

Vacancies, job, planning for, 180-186
Vacations, paid, 466, 473, 479
Validation, test, 236-238
Variety and boredom, job, 151-152, 155
Vendors, outside, 295-296
Verbal abuse, 553, 581
Vertical loading, 155-156
Vertical staffing meetings, 545
Vestibule training, 319
Vesting, pension, 474, 475, 476
Veterans Administration (VA), 25-26, 27
Veterans, employment for, 42, 91, 103, 211, 218, 219
Video display terminals (VDTs), 508-509, 516
Videos, training, 316, 318, 321, 347, 363
Vietnam Era Veterans Readjustment Act (1974), 42, 91, 103
Violations, OSHA, 514-516
Violence against customers, 230
Vision insurance, 470
Vocational schools. See Educational institutions
Vocational tests, 387
Volume of business, 200
Voluntary compensation. See Benefits, fringe
Voluntary group membership, 538
Voluntary resignations, 294-295
Voluntary worker protection program, 512-513
Volunteerism. See Community service activities
Volvo Motor Company, 540, 541

Wage surveys, 423-426
    See also Compensation, employee
Wagner Act. See National Labor Relations Act (NLRA, 1935)
Walk-ins, job applicant, 205, 235
Wall Street Journal, The, 386-387
Want ads, 200, 206
Weighted checklist, 348-350
Weirton Steel Corporation, 453
Welfare programs. See State employment

    security agencies
Welfare secretaries, 39
Well care, 469-470
Well pay, 478-479
Western Electric, 40, 325
Westinghouse, 448-449
Wheaton Glass Company, 102
Whistle-blowers, 293
Wildcat strikes, 580
Witnesses, arbitration hearing, 579
Women workers, 46
    comparable pay and, 430-431
    cultural diversity and, 79-80, 173, 199, 326, 346
    disproportionate representations of, 108, 327
    equal employment opportunity for, 79-80, 93-95, 101-103, 430-431
    equal pay and, 101-102, 430-431
    motherhood and, 203, 484-485
    networking by, 395
    pregnancy of, 42, 93-94, 471-472, 480
    and sex-based discrimination, 68, 93-95, 101-103, 108-109, 429-430
    sexual harassment of, 94-95
    See also Protected groups (EEO)
Word-of-mouth recruitment, 205
Worker Adjustment and Retraining Notification Act (WARN, 1988), 43, 168-169, 290, 613
Worker organizations, 40
Workers' compensation. See Compensation, employee
Worker's compensation laws, 497, 505-510, 519
Worker unions. See Unions, labor
Work flow, 148-149
Work force. See Labor market
Working conditions, 25, 131-132, 139, 140-142, 255, 418, 514, 516
    See also Safety, employee
Work measurement. See Performance measures
Work permits for non-citizens, 96
Work practices, 149
Work simplification, 148, 154-155
Workweeks, 480-482, 504
Write-ins, job applicants, 205
Writing job advertisements, 206-208

Xerox Corporation, 308, 311, 338-340, 359-360, 483-484, 485-486

"Yellow dog" contracts, 566

LMRA created
1) Federal Mediation + Conciliation Service
2) authorized Taft Hartley injunction.